# Dictionary of Literary Biography

## Dictionary of Literary Biography Documentary Series

# Dictionary of Literary Biography Yearbooks

1980 edited by Karen L. Rood, Jean W. Ross, and Richard Ziegfeld (1981)

1981 edited by Karen L. Rood, Jean W. Ross, and Richard Ziegfeld (1982)

1982 edited by Richard Ziegfeld; associate editors: Jean W. Ross and Lynne C. Zeigler (1983)

1983 edited by Mary Bruccoli and Jean W. Ross; associate editor Richard Ziegfeld (1984)

1984 edited by Jean W. Ross (1985)

1985 edited by Jean W. Ross (1986)

1986 edited by J. M. Brook (1987)

1987 edited by J. M. Brook (1988)

1988 edited by J. M. Brook (1989)

1989 edited by J. M. Brook (1990)

1990 edited by James W. Hipp (1991)

1991 edited by James W. Hipp (1992)

1992 edited by James W. Hipp (1993)

1993 edited by James W. Hipp, contributing editor George Garrett (1994)

1994 edited by James W. Hipp, contributing editor George Garrett (1995)

1995 edited by James W. Hipp, contributing editor George Garrett (1996)

1996 edited by Samuel W. Bruce and L. Kay Webster, contributing editor George Garrett (1997)

1997 edited by Matthew J. Bruccoli and George Garrett, with the assistance of L. Kay Webster (1998)

1998 edited by Matthew J. Bruccoli, contributing editor George Garrett, with the assistance of D. W. Thomas (1999)

1999 edited by Matthew J. Bruccoli, contributing editor George Garrett, with the assistance of D. W. Thomas (2000)

2000 edited by Matthew J. Bruccoli, contributing editor George Garrett, with the assistance of George Parker Anderson (2001)

2001 edited by Matthew J. Bruccoli, contributing editor George Garrett, with the assistance of George Parker Anderson (2002)

# Concise Series

**Concise Dictionary of American Literary Biography**, 7 volumes (1988–1999): *The New Consciousness, 1941–1968; Colonization to the American Renaissance, 1640–1865; Realism, Naturalism, and Local Color, 1865–1917; The Twenties, 1917–1929; The Age of Maturity, 1929–1941; Broadening Views, 1968–1988; Supplement: Modern Writers, 1900–1998.*

**Concise Dictionary of British Literary Biography**, 8 volumes (1991–1992): *Writers of the Middle Ages and Renaissance Before 1660; Writers of the Restoration and Eighteenth Century, 1660–1789; Writers of the Romantic Period, 1789–1832; Victorian Writers, 1832–1890; Late-Victorian and Edwardian Writers, 1890–1914; Modern Writers, 1914–1945; Writers After World War II, 1945–1960; Contemporary Writers, 1960 to Present.*

**Concise Dictionary of World Literary Biography**, 10 volumes projected (1999–    ): *Ancient Greek and Roman Writers; German Writers; African, Caribbean, and Latin American Writers; South Slavic and Eastern European Writers.*

Dictionary of Literary Biography® • Volume Two Hundred Seventy-Four

# John Dos Passos's *U.S.A.:*
## A Documentary Volume

Dictionary of Literary Biography® • Volume Two Hundred Seventy-Four

# John Dos Passos's *U.S.A.*:
## A Documentary Volume

Edited by
Donald Pizer
*Tulane University*

A Bruccoli Clark Layman Book

GALE®

THOMSON
★
GALE

Detroit • New York • San Diego • San Francisco • Cleveland • New Haven, Conn. • Waterville, Maine • London • Munich

**THOMSON**

**GALE**

**Dictionary of Literary Biography**
**Volume 274: John Dos Passos's**
*USA:* A Documentary Volume
Donald Pizer

**Advisory Board**
John Baker
William Cagle
Patrick O'Connor
George Garrett
Trudier Harris
Alvin Kernan
Kenny J. Williams

**Editorial Directors**
Matthew J. Bruccoli and Richard Layman

**LIBRARY OF CONGRESS CATALOGING-IN-PUBLICATION DATA**

John Dos Passos's USA : a documentary volume / edited by Donald Pizer.
    p. cm. — (Dictionary of literary biography ; v. 274)
"A Bruccoli Clark Layman book."
Includes bibliographical references and index.
    ISBN 0-7876-6018-3
    1. Dos Passos, John, 1896–1970. U.S.A.
    2. Dos Passos, John, 1896–1970—Knowledge—United States.
    3. Literature and society—United States—History—20th century.
    4. National characteristics, American, in literature.
    5. United States—In literature.
    I. Pizer, Donald.
    II. Series.

PS3507.0743U535 2003
813'.52—dc21
    2002155621

Printed in the United States of America
10 9 8 7 6 5 4 3 2 1

*To the late Elizabeth Dos Passos and to Lucy Dos Passos Coggin in appreciation for their generous support of Dos Passos scholarship.*

# Contents

# Plan of the Series

The advisory board, the editors, and the publisher of the *Dictionary of Literary Biography* are joined in endorsing Mark Twain's declaration. The literature of a nation provides an inexhaustible resource of permanent worth. Our purpose is to make literature and its creators better understood and more accessible to students and the reading public, while satisfying the needs of teachers and researchers.

To meet these requirements, *literary biography* has been construed in terms of the author's achievement. The most important thing about a writer is his writing. Accordingly, the entries in *DLB* are career biographies, tracing the development of the author's canon and the evolution of his reputation.

The purpose of *DLB* is not only to provide reliable information in a usable format but also to place the figures in the larger perspective of literary history and to offer appraisals of their accomplishments by qualified scholars.

The publication plan for *DLB* resulted from two years of preparation. The project was proposed to Bruccoli Clark by Frederick G. Ruffner, president of the Gale Research Company, in November 1975. After specimen entries were prepared and typeset, an advisory board was formed to refine the entry format and develop the series rationale. In meetings held during 1976, the publisher, series editors, and advisory board approved the scheme for a comprehensive biographical dictionary of persons who contributed to literature. Editorial work on the first volume began in January 1977, and it was published in 1978. In order to make *DLB* more than a dictionary and to compile volumes that individually have claim to status as literary history, it was decided to organize volumes by topic, period, or

genre. Each of these freestanding volumes provides a biographical-bibliographical guide and overview for a particular area of literature. We are convinced that this organization—as opposed to a single alphabet method—constitutes a valuable innovation in the presentation of reference material. The volume plan necessarily requires many decisions for the placement and treatment of authors. Certain figures will be included in separate volumes, but with different entries emphasizing the aspect of his career appropriate to each volume. Ernest Hemingway, for example, is represented in *American Writers in Paris, 1920–1939* by an entry focusing on his expatriate apprenticeship; he is also in *American Novelists, 1910–1945* with an entry surveying his entire career, as well as in *American Short-Story Writers, 1910–1945, Second Series* with an entry concentrating on his short fiction. Each volume includes a cumulative index of the subject authors and articles.

Since 1981 the series has been further augmented by the *DLB Yearbooks*, which update published entries, add new entries to keep the *DLB* current with contemporary activity, and provide articles on literary history. There have also been nineteen *DLB Documentary Series* volumes, which provide illustrations, facsimiles, and biographical and critical source materials for figures, works, or groups judged to have particular interest for students. In 1999 the *Documentary Series* was incorporated into the *DLB* volume numbering system beginning with *DLB 210: Ernest Hemingway*.

We define literature as the *intellectual commerce of a nation:* not merely as belles lettres but as that ample and complex process by which ideas are generated, shaped, and transmitted. *DLB* entries are not limited to "creative writers" but extend to other figures who in their time and in their way influenced the mind of a people. Thus the series encompasses historians, journalists, publishers, book collectors, and screenwriters. By this means readers of *DLB* may be aided to perceive literature not as cult scripture in the keeping of intellectual high priests but firmly positioned at the center of a nation's life.

*DLB* includes the major writers appropriate to each volume and those standing in the ranks behind them. Scholarly and critical counsel has been sought in deciding which minor figures to include and how full their entries should be. Wherever possible, useful references are made to figures who do not warrant separate entries.

Each *DLB* volume has an expert volume editor responsible for planning the volume, selecting the figures for inclusion, and assigning the entries. Volume editors are also responsible for preparing, where appropriate, appendices surveying the major periodicals and literary and intellectual movements for their volumes, as well as lists of further readings. Work on the series as a whole is coordinated at the Bruccoli Clark Layman editorial center in Columbia, South Carolina, where the editorial staff is responsible for accuracy and utility of the published volumes.

One feature that distinguishes *DLB* is the illustration policy—its concern with the iconography of literature. Just as an author is influenced by his surroundings, so is the reader's understanding of the author enhanced by a knowledge of his environment. Therefore *DLB* volumes include not only drawings, paintings, and photographs of authors, often depicting them at various stages in their careers, but also illustrations of their families and places where they lived. Title pages are regularly reproduced in facsimile along with dust jackets for modern authors. The dust jackets are a special feature of *DLB* because they often document better than anything else the way in which an author's work was perceived in its own time. Specimens of the writers' manuscripts and letters are included when feasible.

Samuel Johnson rightly decreed that "The chief glory of every people arises from its authors." The purpose of the *Dictionary of Literary Biography* is to compile literary history in the surest way available to us—by accurate and comprehensive treatment of the lives and work of those who contributed to it.

The *DLB* Advisory Board

# Introduction

In August 1938 Jean-Paul Sartre, later famous as a principal voice in French existentialism, declared that John Dos Passos was "the greatest writer of our time." This comment occurs at the conclusion of a discussion of Dos Passos's *Nineteen-Nineteen* (1932), the second of the three novels of *U.S.A.* (1938), and is the product of Sartre's examination of the fictional strategy and themes of the trilogy as a whole as they appear in more particular form in that work. The first novel in the series, *The 42nd Parallel,* had been published in 1930; Dos Passos completed the trilogy in 1936 with the publication of *The Big Money* (an event greeted by his appearance on the cover of the 10 August issue of *Time* magazine that year), and in January 1938 he collected the three novels into one work, *U.S.A.* When Sartre made his evaluation, Dos Passos was, indeed, one of the most well-known and highly regarded American novelists, both at home and abroad, with *U.S.A.* generally recognized as one of the most significant works of modern American literature.

The reasons for the decline in Dos Passos's reputation after this high point until his death on 28 September 1970—as well as for a falling off, many commentators would argue, in the quality of his work—have been pursued by several critics and biographers, most notably by Townsend Ludington in his *John Dos Passos: A Twentieth Century Odyssey* (1980). Now, more than sixty years after the appearance of the trilogy and more than thirty since Dos Passos's death, at least two conclusions can be made about the relationship between his career as a whole and *U.S.A.* in particular: that the decline in Dos Passos's general reputation—a condition that owed much to his political views after 1937—adversely affected for many years the recognition of the centrality and importance of *U.S.A.;* and that, over the last several decades, this pattern has been reversed as renewed acceptance of the greatness of the trilogy has revived interest in Dos Passos's work and career as a whole.

The revitalized appreciation of *U.S.A.* has occurred along several fronts. The intense interest in the nature of modernism as a body of ideas and literary methods has led many readers to one of the major instances in early-twentieth-century American fiction of modernist experimentation. The rise as well in recent years in the belief that literary expression is above all a form of cultural expression has encouraged a fresh engagement with the vast display of social behavior, material culture, and popular belief in the trilogy. Finally, new generations of readers have rediscovered the fictional strength of *U.S.A.*–a strength that makes fresh and compelling Dos Passos's attempt in the work to come to grips with the nature of modern American civilization. As though to signify the return of *U.S.A.* to its place as a work equal in stature to any in American expression, the three novels were republished in 1996 by the Library of America in a one-volume hardback edition as part of its effort to make American classics available to a general audience. In 2000 Houghton Mifflin republished the trilogy in an attractive paperback edition intended for college students.

The purpose of the present volume is to make *U.S.A.* more accessible to readers of all kinds by offering a body of documentary material bearing on various areas of importance and interest in the trilogy. These are: the relationship between Dos Passos's life and the intent, meaning, and form of *U.S.A.;* the origin and nature of the experimental forms in the trilogy; the principal sources and background for the many aspects of American life between 1900 and 1930 depicted in the novels; and the publication history, initial critical reception, and later critical estimation of *U.S.A.* Choosing material to include has been no easy task given the vast range of early-twentieth-century American intellectual, social, political, and artistic life represented in the trilogy. In addition, the John Dos Passos Collection at the University of Virginia Library contains a great deal of manuscript material bearing on the origin and composition of *U.S.A.,* and since publication the trilogy has attracted much significant research and critical commentary. But though some areas of interest may not be given all the space and documentation they deserve, it is hoped that the volume will provide useful insights both into the nature and quality of *U.S.A.* and into its relationship to Dos Passos's life and times.

Omissions in excerpted material are indicated by a line of periods in the text. All passages from *U.S.A.* are from the 1996 Library of America edition.

Although the second volume of *U.S.A.* was originally published in 1932 as *1919,* Dos Passos changed the title to *Nineteen-Nineteen* for the first edition of *U.S.A.* in 1938, and it remained *Nineteen-Nineteen* in all subsequent editions of the trilogy published during his lifetime. The novel is therefore referred to as *Nineteen-Nineteen* throughout this book.

*—Donald Pizer*

## Acknowledgments

This book was made possible by the large collection of authorial materials in the John Dos Passos Papers at the University of Virginia Library, which Dos Passos donated to the library toward the end of his life.

This book was produced by Bruccoli Clark Layman, Inc. Karen L. Rood is senior editor. Bland Lawson was the in-house editor.

Production manager is Philip B. Dematteis.

Administrative support was provided by Ann M. Cheschi and Carol A. Cheschi.

Accountant is Ann-Marie Holland.

Copyediting supervisor is Sally R. Evans. The copyediting staff includes Phyllis A. Avant, Caryl Brown, Melissa D. Hinton, Philip I. Jones, Rebecca Mayo, Nancy E. Smith, and Elizabeth Jo Ann Sumner.

Editorial associates are Amelia B. Lacey, Michael S. Martin, Catherine M. Polit, and William Mathes Straney.

In-house prevetting is by Nicole A. La Rocque.

Permissions editor and database manager is Amber L. Coker.

Layout and graphics supervisor is Janet E. Hill. The graphics staff includes Zoe R. Cook and Sydney E. Hammock.

Office manager is Kathy Lawler Merlette.

Photography supervisor is Paul Talbot. Photography editor is Scott Nemzek.

Digital photographic copy work was performed by Joseph M. Bruccoli and Zoe R. Cook.

Systems manager is Marie L. Parker.

Typesetting supervisor is Kathleen M. Flanagan. The typesetting staff includes Patricia Marie Flanagan, Mark J. McEwan, and Pamela D. Norton. Freelance typesetters are Wanda Adams and Rebecca Mayo.

Walter W. Ross did library research. He was assisted by Jo Cottingham and the following other librarians at the Thomas Cooper Library of the University of South Carolina: circulation department head Tucker Taylor; reference department head Virginia W. Weathers; reference department staff Brette Barron, Marilee Birchfield, Paul Cammarata, Gary Geer, Michael Macan, Tom Marcil, Rose Marshall, and Sharon Verba; interlibrary loan department head John Brunswick; and interlibrary loan staff Robert Arndt, Hayden Battle, Alex Byrne, Bill Fetty, Marna Hostetler, and Nelson Rivera.

# Permissions and Sources

Albert and Shirley Small Special Collections Library, University of Virginia, for unpublished letters from John Dos Passos to Charles Bernardin (3 January 1942, 17 March 1950).

Arcade Publishing for selection from Arlen J. Hansen, *Gentlemen Volunteers: The Story of the American Ambulance Drivers in the Great War, August 1914–September 1918* (1996).

*The Atlantic Monthly* for Theodore Spencer, "Novelists Who Explore" (October 1936).

Cambridge University Press for selection from Thomas F. Strychacz, *Modernism, Mass Culture, and Professionalism* (1993). © 1993 by Cambridge University Press. Reprinted with the permission of Cambridge University Press.

Virginia Spencer Carr for selection from her *Dos Passos: A Life* (Garden City, N.Y.: Doubleday, 1984).

*Clio* for Barry Maine, "Representative Men in Dos Passos' *The 42nd Parallel*" (Fall 1982).

Lucy Dos Passos Coggin for selections from John Dos Passos, *U.S.A.* (New York: Harcourt, Brace, 1938; reprint, New York: Library of America, 1996); *One Man's Initiation–1917* (New York: Doran, 1920); Newsreel I, *The 42nd Parallel* (New York: Harper, 1930); introduction to *The 42nd Parallel* (New York: Modern Library, 1937); *The Best Times: An Informal Memoir* (New York: New American Library, 1966); "The Writer as Technician" (*American Writers' Congress,* 1935); and "Contemporary Chronicles" (*Carleton Miscellany,* 1961). Reprinted by permission of Lucy Dos Passos Coggin.

The Continuum International Publishing Group for selection from Claude Edmonde Magny, *The Age of the American Novel: The Film Aesthetic of the Fiction Between the Two Wars,* translated by Eleanor Hochman (New York: Ungar, 1972). Reprinted by permission of The Continuum International Publishing Group.

Lewis Coser for selection from Irving Howe and Coser, *The American Communist Party: A Critical History, 1919–1957* (Boston: Beacon, 1957).

John Patrick Diggins for his "Dos Passos and Veblen's Villains," *Antioch Review,* 23 (Winter 1963).

D. Gene England for his "The Newsreels of John Dos Passos' *The 42nd Parallel,*" dissertation, Austin: University of Texas, 1970.

Samuel French, Inc., for Paul Shyre, "Production Notes for 'U.S.A.,'" in Shyre and John Dos Passos, *U.S.A.: A Dramatic Revue* (1960 [c. 1963]).

The Gale Group for selection from John H. Wrenn, *John Dos Passos* (New York: Twayne, 1961). © 1961 The Gale Group. Reprinted by permission of The Gale Group.

Harcourt for selection from Alfred Kazin, *On Native Grounds: An Interpretation of Modern American Prose and Literature.* Copyright 1942 and renewed 1970 by Alfred Kazin, reprinted by permission of Harcourt, Inc.

The Harvard Common Press for selections from *The Fourteenth Chronicle: Letters and Diaries of John Dos Passos,* edited by Townsend Ludington (Boston: Gambit, 1973). Copyright © 1973, reprinted with permission from The Harvard Common Press, Boston, MA.

Harvard University Press for selections from David Bordwell, *The Cinema of Eisenstein* (1993); and Donald Fleming, "Harvard's Golden Age," in Bernard Bailyn and others, *Glimpses of the Harvard Past* (1986). Reprinted by permission of the publisher from *The Cinema of Eisenstein* by David Bordwell, pp. 120–123, Cambridge, Mass.: Harvard University Press. Copyright © 1993 by the Presidents and Fellows of Harvard College. Reprinted by permission of the publisher from *Glimpses of the Harvard Past* by Bernard Bailyn and others, pp. 83–84, 88–90, Cambridge, Mass.: Harvard University Press. Copyright © 1986 by the Presidents and Fellows of Harvard College.

South Atlantic Modern Language Association for Barry Maine, "*U.S.A.*: Dos Passos and the Rhetoric of History," *South Atlantic Review,* 50 (January 1985).

Southern Illinois University Press for selection from Donald Pizer, *Twentieth-Century American Literary Naturalism: An Interpretation* (1982). © 1982 by Southern Illinois University Press, reprinted by permission of the publisher.

Dana L. Thomas for selection from his *Lords of the Land: The Triumphs and Scandals of America's Real Estate Barons, from Early Times to the Present* (New York: Putnam, 1977).

*TLS: The Times Literary Supplement* for unsigned review of *The 42nd Parallel* (4 September 1930).

*Twentieth Century Literature* for Janet G. Casey, "Historicizing the Female in *U.S.A.*" (Fall 1995); and David L. Vanderwerken, "Dos Passos and His 'Old Words'" (May 1977).

University of Illinois Press for Melvyn Dubofsky, "Disorder and Decline, 1918–24," "Employers Strike Back," and "From 'Pure and Simple Unionism' to Revolutionary Radicalism," in *We Shall Be All: A History of the Industrial Workers of the World,* edited by Joseph A. McCartin (1988). Copyright 2000 by Board of Trustees of the University of Illinois. Used with the permission of the University of Illinois Press.

University of Massachusetts Press for selection from Laura Browder, *Rousing the Nation: Radical Culture in Depression America* (1998). © 1998 by the University of Massachusetts Press.

University of Texas Press for George Knox, "Voice in the *U.S.A.* Biographies," *Texas Studies in Literature and Language,* 4 (Spring 1962). © 1962 by the University of Texas Press.

University Press of Colorado for selections from Melvin Landsberg, *Dos Passos' Path to U.S.A.: A Political Biography, 1912–1936* (1972).

University Press of Virginia for selections from Donald Pizer, *Dos Passos' U.S.A.: A Critical Study* (1988).

*Works and Days* for Clara Juncker, "Romancing the Revolution: Dos Passos' Radical Heroines" (Spring 1990).

# Illustrations

Albert and Shirley Small Special Collections Library, University of Virginia, for facsimiles of John Dos Passos's Harvard compositions, manuscript and typescript pages from *U.S.A.,* 3 November 1944 letter to Robert Hillyer, Red Cross letter of introduction, Verdun citation, and New York Public Library call slips.

Allen and Unwin, Ltd., for photograph of Sergei Eisenstein during the filming of *Old and New.*

American Society of Mechanical Engineers for photograph of Frederick W. Taylor.

AP/Wide World Photos for photographs of Dos Passos in his Provincetown, Massachusetts, home; William Faulkner, Malcolm Cowley, and Dos Passos; and Theodore Dreiser, Samuel Ornitz, and Dos Passos in Harlan County, Kentucky.

Bettman/Corbis for photographs of Emma Goldman and street rioting at the 16 February 1934 Socialist Party meeting at Madison Square Garden. © Bettman/Corbis.

Billy Rose Theater Collection, New York Public Library for the Performing Arts, Astor, Lenox and Tilden Foundation, for photograph of John Howard Lawson.

Citadel Press for photograph of Gary Cooper and Marlene Dietrich.

Lucy Dos Passos Coggin for photographs of Dos Passos; his parents, John Randolph and Lucy Madison Dos Passos; his first wife, Katy Smith Dos Passos; and his second wife, Betty Holdridge Dos Passos; and lithograph caricature of John Randolph Dos Passos.

Columbia University Press for photograph of Thorstein Veblen.

Comunità Pedemontana dal Piave al Brenta for photograph of American Red Cross ambulance in Italy.

Columbia University Rare Book and Manuscript Library for photograph of Randolph Bourne.

Doubleday & Co. for photographs of William Jennings Bryan and Jean Harlow.

Dutton/Penguin Putnam, Inc., for photograph of Josef von Sternberg and Marlene Dietrich.

Florida State Archives for photographs of Miami real estate office and land auction.

Fogg Art Museum, Harvard University, for painting by Robert Hallowell of John Reed and photograph of Louise Bryant.

William L. Foley Collection for poster advertising *Our American Boys in the European War*.

Samuel French, Inc., for facsimile of cast list and credits from Paul Shyre and Dos Passos, *U.S.A.: A Dramatic Revue* (1960 [c. 1963]).

Gambit for photographs of Dos Passos in Ambulance Corps uniform; Edmund Wilson; and Christopher Holdridge, John Dos Passos, Lucy Dos Passos, Rumsey Marvin, and Betty Holdridge Dos Passos.

George Arents Library, Syracuse University, for photograph of Robert Hillyer.

George Eastman House International Museum of Photography and Film for photograph of Rudolf Valentino's funeral procession.

Hall of History Foundation, Schenectady, New York, for photograph of Charles Proteus Steinmetz at Camp Mohawk.

Harper for photograph by Purdy of Le Baron Russell Briggs.

Harvard University Press for photographs of Matthews Hall and the Harvard Union on the Harvard campus.

Hastings House for photograph of William Randolph Hearst estate at San Simeon, California.

Henry Holt and Co. for photographs of George and Clara St. John and drawing of Choate School campus.

Houghton Mifflin for Reginald Marsh illustrations from Dos Passos, *U.S.A.* (Boston: Houghton Mifflin, 1946). © 1946 by Houghton Mifflin Co. © renewed

by Houghton Mifflin Co. Reprinted by permission of Houghton Mifflin Co.

Indiana University Press for photograph of Vera Buch Weisbord, Ellen Dawson, Albert Weisbord, and Fred Beal.

Library of Congress, Prints and Photographs Division, Historic American Buildings Survey, for photograph of Robie House, Chicago. Reproduction no. HABS, ILL, 16-CHIG, 33-2.

Lion Collection, New York Public Library, for photograph of Walt Whitman.

Lost Coast Press for photograph of Carl G. Fisher.

Luther Burbank Museum, Santa Rosa, California, for photograph of Thomas Edison, Luther Burbank, and Henry Ford.

Museum of Modern Art, New York, for photograph of J. P. Morgan and stills from the movie *The Passaic Textile Strikes*.

National Archives for Woodrow Wilson political cartoon from *New Masses*.

National Portrait Gallery for photograph of Theodore Roosevelt.

New York Public Library for the Performing Arts for photograph by Jacob Schloss of Isadora Duncan.

W. W. Norton and Co. for photographs of Big Bill Haywood and of Wright brothers' first flight at Kitty Hawk, N.C.

Octagon Books for photograph of Bartolomeo Vanzetti and Nicola Sacco.

Oxford University Press for photograph of Andrew Carnegie.

Princeton Book Co. for Kees van Dongen poster of Isadora Duncan.

Scribners for photograph of David Lloyd George, Vittorio Orlando, Georges Clemenceau, and Woodrow Wilson at Versailles.

Syracuse University Press for photographs of Eugene Debs and Bernarr Macfadden.

Time, Inc., for cover of *Time* (10 August 1936).

Times Books for the backdrop of the 1923 Paris ballet *Within the Quota*.

United Press International for photographs of Dos Passos picketing the Boston State House; Evarts, Kentucky, citizens; and striking textile workers in Passaic, New Jersey.

University of California, Berkeley, for photograph of William Randolph Hearst.

University of Chicago Press for photograph of Samuel Insull.

University of Illinois Press for photograph of "Aunt" Molly Jackson and Theodore Dreiser.

University of New Mexico Press for photograph by Aurelio Castro Carazo of Minor Cooper Keith.

University of Utah Press for photograph of Joe Hill.

University of Washington Libraries for photograph of Wesley Everest.

University Press of Colorado for photograph of Norton-Harjes Ambulance Service vehicles in France.

Vought Aircraft Industries for photographs of airplane assembly and testing at Chance Vought factory in Long Island City, New York.

Washington State Historical Society for photographs of Wesley Everest's burial and grave marker and facsimile of the police report on the examination of Everest's corpse.

Weidenfeld & Nicolson/Avant-Scene Cinema for still from Sergei Eisenstein movie *The Strike*.

John Wiley & Sons for political cartoon and front cover of *New Masses*.

Dictionary of Literary Biography® • Volume Two Hundred Seventy-Four

# John Dos Passos's *U.S.A.:*
## A Documentary Volume

# Dictionary of Literary Biography

# A Brief Life of John Dos Passos

## By Donald Pizer

John Roderigo Dos Passos was born in Chicago on 14 January 1896, the son of John Randolph Dos Passos, a wealthy Wall Street lawyer of Portuguese ancestry, and Lucy Madison, from an old Virginia family. His parents were both entangled in unsuccessful marriages, and though they lived together intermittently from the early 1890s, they were unable to marry until 1910, after the deaths of both of their spouses. For the first fifteen years of his life their son lived with his mother, largely in Europe, and was known as John Madison. Only in 1911 did he assume the last name of his father.

Dos Passos did not hide this aspect of his background from close friends, but it became widely known only with the publication of his autobiography, *The Best Times: An Informal Memoir,* in 1966. There is little doubt that his background played a major role in his life and writing. Although his father's wealth provided him with an upper-class youth–tutors, private schools, and foreign travel–Dos Passos, from almost his earliest expression, viewed the world around him, that is, his condition as an American, from the perspective of an outsider. Both his Portuguese ancestry and his "irregular" birth encouraged him–indeed, perhaps forced him–to view the American experience with a freedom and insight not always granted those fully in its mainstream. Throughout his life Dos Passos was therefore able to bring a sympathetic understanding to the aspirations and values of the nation while maintaining a sharp eye for the distinction between these beliefs and the actuality before him.

After years of travel with his mother ("a hotel childhood," he later called it), Dos Passos attended Choate, an exclusive Connecticut boys' school, and then entered Harvard University in 1912. He fully embraced the lively undergraduate literary scene, writing poems, sketches, essays, and even most of a novel, contributing to *The Harvard Monthly,* and making many friends among the literary set, including E. E. Cummings and Robert Hillyer. Upon graduation in 1916 Dos Passos was persuaded by his father to study in Spain for a year, despite his interest in participating in war relief. His father's death in January 1917 (his mother had died in 1915) freed him to pursue a more independent existence. He returned to America, settled for a period in Greenwich Village (then already in full swing as the center of American bohemianism), and in the spring of 1917 volunteered for the Norton-Harjes Ambulance Corps, an elite group of Harvard graduates serving as ambulance drivers on the western front. Dos Passos's service as an ambulance driver–first at Verdun in August 1917 and then in northern Italy (with the American Red Cross) in fall of that year through spring 1918–was one of the catalytic experiences of his life. Like many young Americans now seeing World War I at first hand (Cummings and Ernest Hemingway, for example), he was struck by the difference between the traditional rhetoric of the noble, heroic, and self-sacrificing that had been applied to the war and the mechanized carnage of combat itself. He was also confirmed in his belief that war aided in the perpetuation of class hatred, social bias, and the abuse of power. America, Dos Passos was now ready to believe, had been betrayed by those who manipulated language and restricted individual freedom in order to achieve the prerogatives of a modern industrialized society.

After being forced out of the Red Cross because of the antiwar sentiments expressed in his correspondence, Dos Passos returned to America in mid 1918. He then enlisted in the Army Medical Corps, was sent back to Europe in November 1918, just as the war was drawing to a close, and served a dreary eight months

3

until his discharge in France. While awaiting calls to duty at Verdun in the summer of 1917, Dos Passos had begun a novel, in collaboration with his fellow ambulance driver Hillyer, on the progress of an American youth from the innocence of a middle-class upbringing to the bitter enlightenment provided by the war. When Hillyer and he went their separate ways after a brief period of common effort, Dos Passos continued work on the novel himself, and now, discharged from the army, he sought to publish the final portion, dealing with the protagonist's experiences at Verdun. It was accepted by an English firm and was published in October 1920 as *One Man's Initiation–1917*.

The openly expressed antiwar beliefs of *One Man's Initiation–1917*, however, did not relieve Dos Passos of the immense accumulation of anger occasioned by his experiences as an ambulance driver viewing the immediate consequences of combat and as an enlisted man undergoing the humiliations and oppressions of the military power structure. The product of this outrage was the novel *Three Soldiers*, written largely in Spain during 1919–1920 and published in New York in September 1921. The novel, which details the psychical disintegration of three American enlisted men serving in France, was the first work by an American author that depicted less than enthusiastically America's participation in the war. (Hemingway's *The Sun Also Rises* [1926] and *A Farewell to Arms* [1929] and Cummings's *The Enormous Room* [1922] were still to come.) At the age of twenty-five Dos Passos therefore found his career launched in a storm of controversy, and for the next two decades he was to be identified by the general public as a prominent member of a group of American writers alienated from the nation and its culture.

In Dos Passos's case the condition of alienation was indeed literally played out by his frequent and lengthy stays abroad in the period between the wars. During the 1920s he often joined Hemingway, F. Scott and Zelda Fitzgerald, and Gerald and Sara Murphy in Paris and Antibes. There were also journeys to Spain, the Near East, and North Africa. Amazingly, Dos Passos was able to remain productive despite this constant movement, having acquired early in his life the ability to write wherever he was. But there were also periods, especially when he was seeking to complete a major work, when he settled down–initially in New York and later in Provincetown, Massachusetts, where he acquired his first permanent residence through his marriage in August 1929 to Katy Smith, who owned a home there.

Aside from *Three Soldiers*, Dos Passos's major work of the 1920s was the experimental novel *Manhattan Transfer*, written during 1923–1925 and published by Harper's in November 1925. Influenced by new cur-

rents in both fiction and painting that sought to redefine the nature of these art forms, Dos Passos created in *Manhattan Transfer* not a conventional novel of plot and character but rather a fictional panorama of early-twentieth-century New York life expressed through brief, fragmented, and often entirely disconnected moments and scenes. New York is a multitude, he appeared to be saying, and here is that multitude in the form best expressive of its nature. While hailed as a significant breakthrough in fiction by many writers (Sinclair Lewis wrote a notable positive review), the novel was also widely attacked. Whatever its reception, however, Dos Passos, as can now be seen from the perspective of his career as a whole, had found, in planning and writing the novel, both his métier and his method for future major work. His subject was to be the ethos of a cultural place and moment, and he was to chronicle them (he later identified his fiction as "chronicles") through devices that sought to represent their fullness and complexity while rendering as well their underlying ethos.

As the 1920s advanced, many young American artists and writers were increasingly critical of the failings of their nation's capitalistic system (the lack of social justice and an inhospitality to the life of the mind and spirit were major complaints) and drawn to the alternative provided by the Soviet Union during its pre-Stalin years. Dos Passos also moved in this direction. He helped in the founding of the Marxist journal the *New Masses* in early 1925, became a member of the left-leaning New Playwrights Theatre in 1926 (his friend, John Howard Lawson, an acknowledged Communist, was a fellow member), and made the almost obligatory trip to Russia in 1928. No doubt the most significant event of this phase of Dos Passos's career, however, was his participation during 1926 and 1927 in the efforts to prove the innocence and save the lives of Nicola Sacco and Bartolomeo Vanzetti.

Although Sacco and Vanzetti had been convicted in 1921 for robbery and murder, efforts by the American intelligentsia to save the two Italian-born anarchists did not intensify until it became clear, in 1926, that they were not to receive a new trial and would indeed be executed. In June of that year Dos Passos interviewed Sacco and Vanzetti, reviewed the case, and became convinced that they had committed no crimes but were rather being railroaded to their deaths because of their beliefs. Between June 1926 and their execution in August 1927, he wrote and campaigned on their behalf; shortly before the execution he was arrested in Boston, along with many notable literary figures of the day, for illegally demonstrating. Not long after the deaths of Sacco and Vanzetti, in the fall of 1927, Dos Passos began *The 42nd Parallel* (1930), the first volume of what was to become *U.S.A.* (1938).

Dos Passos shifted, as did many writers and intellectuals in his generation, from an endorsement during the 1920s of leftish and often specifically communist beliefs and activities to a gradual disengagement as the 1930s proceeded and finally to a full withdrawal and rejection of the Communist Party and its goals by the close of the decade. In the early 1930s he was still sufficiently in tune with the Left to play a significant role in the party-dominated investigation of the Harlan County, Kentucky, miners' strike and to vote for the Communist Party candidate for president. In 1934, however, Dos Passos publicly criticized the party's strong-arm tactics in breaking up a Socialist Party meeting, and in 1935 he read a paper at the American Writers' Congress attacking the official party line on literary expression. His letters of the period to such friends as Hemingway, the critic Edmund Wilson, and Lawson reveal the basis of these actions. The Communist Party in America, Dos Passos now believed, had become, in its role as a vehicle of Soviet policy, unresponsive to the history and character of the American experience and was indeed, in its fascistic tendencies, increasingly a threat to American democracy. These beliefs, which find their way into *The Big Money* (1936), the third volume of the *U.S.A.* trilogy, received their fullest and sharpest confirmation in Dos Passos's interpretation of the Spanish Civil War.

As reflected in his early collection of travel sketches, *Rosinante to the Road Again* (1922), Dos Passos was powerfully drawn to what he held to be the intense, almost anarchistic independence of the Spanish mind and spirit. In 1936, when Spain became embroiled in a civil war in which the legitimate government of the Left, whose members ranged from Communists to liberal democrats, was threatened by a reactionary armed revolt, he strongly supported the loyalist side. As the war proceeded, however, and especially after his trip to Spain in the spring of 1937, Dos Passos became convinced that the loyalist cause was being betrayed by its communist component, which was attempting to use the war to prepare for a seizure of power in Spain. His essay "Farewell to Europe" (1937), which he published on his return, and his 1939 novel *Adventures of a Young Man,* both of which featured sustained attacks on leftish ideology and practices, were in effect farewells to this earlier phase of his career.

Dos Passos's literary production during the 1930s was dominated by the separate publication of the three volumes of *U.S.A.* in 1930, 1932, and 1936 and then the publication of the trilogy as a whole in 1938. Soon after his death in 1970 a widespread belief took hold—and persists to this day—that the 1920s (marked by the publication of *Three Soldiers* and *Manhattan Transfer*) and the 1930s (the decade of *U.S.A.*) constitute the high point of Dos Passos's literary career and that the last three decades of his career were distinguished by the thin efforts of a crabbed reactionary, earning him a well-deserved obscurity. This belief owes much to mid-twentieth-century American literary politics. Dos Passos's break with the Left in the late 1930s angered an entire generation of the New York literary establishment, a resentment cemented by his later often strident support of right-wing positions and leaders. Much of his work after 1937, whatever its nature or quality, was therefore frequently reviewed in the context of his later politics. Dos Passos's declining reputation was also in part the product of the inevitable sense, in estimating the quality of his later work, of a falling off from his earlier fiction, an impression created by the realization that in *U.S.A.* he had produced one of the masterpieces of American and world literature. Whatever the quality of this later work, in other words, it appears lackluster in comparison with *U.S.A.*

This view of the last three decades of Dos Passos's life, though true in part—he had shifted to the right, and his writing was no longer up to the level of *U.S.A.*—does not do justice to the fullness and integrity of his later career. After a good deal of war-related reportage in America, the Far East, and Europe, Dos Passos devoted much energy over the next twenty-five years to a series of works on early American political history in order to document in the country's past his intense belief, one that runs through all his prior fiction, that the preservation of individual freedom was the nation's greatest and most significant contribution to world history. This effort began with *The Ground We Stand On* in 1941, but its linchpin was a biography of Thomas Jefferson, begun in 1944 and published in 1954 as *The Head and Heart of Thomas Jefferson.* It also included *The Men Who Made the Nation* (1957), *Prospects of a Golden Age* (1959), and *The Shackles of Power: Three Jeffersonian Decades* (1966). Much of Dos Passos's fiction of this period is related to this Edenic conception of American history in that it depicts various ways in which contemporary American life constituted a betrayal of the golden age of the founding fathers' faith in the ideal of personal liberty. Perhaps the most ambitious work along these lines is *Midcentury* (1961), a caustic account, relying on the same devices as those used in *U.S.A.,* of the Franklin D. Roosevelt and Harry Truman years.

Dos Passos's personal life achieved a stability during this period that differed remarkably from his earlier, extraordinarily peripatetic existence. Katy Dos Passos died in an automobile accident in 1947; in

*Dos Passos in his Provincetown, Massachusetts, living room in the early 1940s (AP/Wide World Photos)*

1949 Dos Passos married Betty Holdridge, a young widow, and settled with her in a restored colonial house on a portion of his father's former property in rural northern Virginia. A child, Lucy, was born in 1950, and so Dos Passos found himself, during the last two decades of his life, a landed squire and a family man. Honors also came during these final years, principally election to the American Academy of Arts and Letters in 1947, the Gold Medal in fiction of the National Institute of Arts and Letters in 1957, and the valuable Antonio Feltrinelli Prize in fiction from the Accademia Nazionale dei Lincei in 1967. As always, however, Dos Passos's activist politics made him a controversial figure, as, for example, his support of Senator Joseph McCarthy's communist witch-hunts and his attack on the power of labor unions. To those who considered these positions antithetical to his earlier leftish activities, Dos Passos replied that the central thread linking his beliefs and actions throughout his life was his attack on any condition or idea which threatened individual liberty. John Dos Passos died on 28 September 1970.

# A *U.S.A.* Chronology

**November 1925**  *Manhattan Transfer,* Dos Passos's experimental novel in which he uses some of the same devices he is to develop further in *U.S.A.* (such as multiple plots, popular songs, and newspaper excerpts), is published by Harper and Brothers.

**December 1925**  Dos Passos accepts an invitation to become a member of the executive committee of *New Masses,* a left-wing magazine.

**May 1926**  *New Masses* publishes Dos Passos's "300 N.Y. Agitators Reach Passaic," a satirical sketch dealing with a strike by textile workers in Passaic, New Jersey.

**June 1926**  Dos Passos journeys to Boston and Plymouth to interview Nicola Sacco and Bartolomeo Vanzetti, two immigrant anarchists accused of a payroll robbery and murder. The August *New Masses* publishes Dos Passos's report on the case, in which he maintains their innocence.

**Spring 1927**  The Sacco-Vanzetti Defense Committee publishes Dos Passos's *Facing the Chair: Story of the Americanization of Two Foreignborn Workmen,* a 128-page attack on the prosecution of the two figures.

**21 August 1927**  Dos Passos is arrested in Boston for participating in a demonstration on behalf of Sacco and Vanzetti as their execution nears.

**October 1927**  *New Masses* publishes Dos Passos's poem "They Are Dead Now," portions of which are later used in *The Big Money* (1936).

**Fall 1927**  Dos Passos begins work on *The 42nd Parallel.*

**Summer–Fall 1928**  Dos Passos visits the Soviet Union, where he meets many artists and writers, including the experimental movie director Sergei Eisenstein.

**19 February 1930**  *The 42nd Parallel* is published by Harper and Brothers.

**Fall 1931**  Dos Passos completes *1919* (1932), but Harper's is reluctant to publish the novel because it includes a negative portrayal of the financier J. P. Morgan, who aided the firm during a financial difficulty years earlier.

**5–10 November 1931**  Dos Passos travels to Harlan County, Kentucky, with a group led by Theodore Dreiser and sponsored by the Communist-based National Committee for the Defense of Political Prisoners, to investigate repressive conditions during a strike by local coal miners.

**March 1932**  *Harlan Miners Speak: Report on Terrorism in the Kentucky Coal Fields,* with contributions by Dos Passos, is published by Harcourt, Brace.

**10 March 1932**  *1919* is published by Harcourt, Brace. The novel appears with this version of the title in this edition only; for its republication in the completed *U.S.A.* trilogy in 1938, Dos Passos titles it *Nineteen-Nineteen,* the form used in all subsequent editions.

| | |
|---|---|
| **Spring–Summer 1932** | Dos Passos suffers from rheumatic fever; recurrences of the disease over the next several years slow his work on the third volume of *U.S.A.* |
| **November 1932** | Dos Passos votes for William Z. Foster, the Communist Party candidate for president. |
| **March 1934** | Dos Passos is one of the signers of "An Open Letter to the Communist Party," published in *New Masses,* protesting the party's disruption of a Madison Square Garden meeting of the Socialist Party. There is increasing criticism of the Communist Party in his letters and writing during this period. |
| **July–October 1934** | Dos Passos is in Hollywood working for Paramount Pictures as a screenwriter for a movie directed by Josef von Sternberg and starring Marlene Dietrich. |
| **1 August 1936** | *The Big Money* is published by Harcourt, Brace. |
| **10 August 1936** | Dos Passos is on the cover of *Time* magazine. |
| **November 1937** | *The 42nd Parallel,* slightly revised and with a new preface by Dos Passos, is published in the Modern Library series. |
| **27 January 1938** | *U.S.A.,* with a new general introduction to the trilogy ("U.S.A."), is published by Harcourt, Brace. |
| **1939** | *U.S.A.* appears in the Modern Library series and for several generations is widely read in this form. |
| **1946** | *U.S.A.* is republished by Houghton, Mifflin in a limited edition, with illustrations by Reginald Marsh. |
| **October 1959** | A "dramatic revue" version of *U.S.A.,* adapted by Paul Shyre, opens Off-Broadway in New York and runs for almost a year. |

# CHAPTER 1:

# THE EDUCATION OF THE CAMERA EYE

*The fifty-one Camera Eye passages interspersed throughout the three volumes of* U.S.A. *provide a suggestive introduction to the ways in which a young man from a privileged background became one of the principal radical literary voices of the late 1920s and early 1930s. Using fragments of Dos Passos's inner life from his childhood until late 1931, the Camera Eye records the various stages in this development. After his protected youth and education at Choate and Harvard, Dos Passos's first major encounter with the world at large was as an ambulance driver on the Verdun front in the summer of 1917. From the end of World War I to the mid 1920s, his principal effort was to establish himself as a writer. In the late 1920s Dos Passos, like many in his generation, moved increasingly toward the Left, stimulated by a belief in the inherent social inequities of American capitalism, as symbolized by the execution of Nicola Sacco and Bartolomeo Vanzetti and the oppression of the working class during the Harlan County, Kentucky, coal strikes. By the early 1930s, when Dos Passos was engaged in writing* The Big Money, *however, he was becoming increasingly disillusioned with the Left and was beginning his long passage toward the conservatism of his final years.*

*After an introductory essay on the coherence and meaning of the Camera Eye as a whole, this chapter presents documentary material, juxtaposed with Camera Eye sections, for each of these stages in Dos Passos's development toward the composition of* U.S.A.

*John Dos Passos (Collection of Lucy Dos Passos Coggin)*

## The Coherence of the Camera Eye
Donald Pizer

*The seemingly miscellaneous and discontinuous fragments of Dos Passos's personal life depicted in the Camera Eye also form a coherent narrative of a young man's maturation into adult masculine sexuality and social responsibility.*

Most general readers of John Dos Passos' *U.S.A.* have been troubled by the Camera Eye portion of the trilogy. The subject matter of these brief stream of consciousness fragments from Dos Passos'

life is of course necessarily obscure. Even for close readers of the trilogy the events of the Camera Eye were difficult to identify until the appearance of Dos Passos' autobiography *The Best Times* in 1966 and Townsend Ludington's edition of *The Fourteenth Chronicle: Letters and Diaries of John Dos Passos* in 1973.[1] In addition, the comparative brevity of each of the often widely dispersed 51 Camera Eye passages in an extremely long work (almost 1500 pages in the Modern Library edition) makes it difficult to maintain a sense of thematic continuity from one

*Left: Dos Passos's father, John Randolph Dos Passos, who came from an immigrant family and achieved great success as a Wall Street lawyer; right: Dos Passos's mother, Lucy Sprigg Madison Dos Passos, as a vivacious and fashionable young woman (Collection of Lucy Dos Passos Coggin)*

Camera Eye to the next. Thus, the Camera Eye in *U.S.A.* has usually either been read casually–almost as an awkward interruption–or for its occasional reference to events present as well in other portions of the trilogy.

Recently, however, a number of critics of Dos Passos' work have begun to examine the Camera Eye more closely. In particular, it has become not uncommon to discuss the entire Camera Eye sequence in *U.S.A.* as a kind of development novel in which Dos Passos presents the reader with a valuable and suggestive account of his maturation as an artist.[2] This critical effort runs counter to the thrust of Dos Passos' own late and repeated comment that his principal intent in the Camera Eye was to "drain off the subjective."[3] By this remark Dos Passos meant that he included the Camera Eye largely for the negative purpose of restricting his subjective experience to that portion of *U.S.A.* and thereby supposedly increasing the objectivity of the remainder of the trilogy. Most critics of *U.S.A.*, however, now believe that the Camera Eye not only dramatizes the development of an artist's credo but also is intimately related in its themes to those of the trilogy as a whole. I would like to contribute to this growing sense of the significance and centrality of

the Camera Eye in *U.S.A.* by offering an interpretation of this stream of consciousness novel within a novel which stresses the importance of the sexual motif both in it and in the entire trilogy.

It is of value in this regard to recall that *U.S.A.* is a work both of the 1920s and the 1930s–that, though begun in 1927, it was largely written in the post-crash years. The Camera Eye is indebted in its themes and techniques to some of the principal literary preoccupations conventionally attributed to these decades. The Camera Eye is Joycean both in its specific kind of stream of consciousness–that in which the consciousness moves freely through time yet is also responsive to a particular social and physical "present"–and in its motifs of the search by an artist for a home and a father.[4] As a work of the 1930s, the Camera Eye presents the successful completion of this search as an acceptance by the artist of his committed role within the class struggle. As a work of the 1920s, the Camera Eye, now more covertly and often principally through image and symbol, identifies specific social values, attitudes, and activities with specific sexual values, attitudes, and activities. While Dos Passos was not seeking to render his inner life in Freudian terms, he nevertheless does so in the sense that his recollection of his

*Left, Dos Passos at about age three, probably in Brusssels; right, Dos Passos at about age ten in London,*
*where he attended the Peterborough Lodge School (Collection of Lucy Dos Passos Coggin)*

life through stream of consciousness is closely related to psychoanalytic self-revelation in which there is a constant intertwining of the sexual and almost every other phase of one's experience. Thus, in the Camera Eye Dos Passos depicts his maturation into literary radicalism both as a sexual development into a proper masculinity and as a discovery of a literary creed which is symbolically a father and a home.

This is not to say that each of the 51 segments of the Camera Eye contributes equally and clearly to this theme. There is perhaps more variation in content and tone in the Camera Eye than in any other portion of the trilogy. Nevertheless, the Camera Eye as a whole has a pervasive and discernible direction, a direction which also has a distinctive cast in each of the three novels of the trilogy. The Camera Eye in *The 42nd Parallel* deals with Dos Passos' life from his early childhood to his departure for Europe in 1917 and dramatizes principally his gradual recognition that there are "two nations," those of "topdog" and "underdog," and that these have sexual significance for him. In *Nineteen-Nineteen* the Camera Eye depicts Dos Passos' experiences in Europe between 1917 and 1919 and both his discovery of a need and desire to play an active, masculine role in literary and social affairs and his failure to find a proper

means for doing so. And, finally, the Camera Eye in *The Big Money* describes Dos Passos' ineffectual search during the 1920s for a fully masculine literary identity and his discovery at last of that identity through his participation in the Sacco-Vanzetti case and the Harlan County miners' strike. At the close of the Camera Eye, Dos Passos stands revealed as a modern approximation of Walt Whitman.[5] He is ready to tell the truth about American life with his father's masculine honesty and vigor and will thereby aid in the restoration of the underlying purpose and ideals of America.

I

The general texture of Dos Passos' early life as depicted by the Camera Eye in *The 42nd Parallel* is of constant physical movement within the social world of the upper middle class. In carriages and on trains and boats, in Holland and England and in Massachusetts, Connecticut, Washington, D.C., Philadelphia, and Virginia, we encounter Dos Passos in a world of servants, boarding schools and Harvard, luxurious travel, country estates, yachting, and edifying visits. Within this world, Dos Passos' mother and father (the "He" and "She" of the Camera Eye consciousness) play conventional parental roles.

*Political cartoon satirizing John Randolph Dos Passos for his support of monopoly capitalism. Strewn behind him are his books on trusts and investment law. In his pocket is a scroll titled "Dan'l Sully's Interests." Sully was a broker who attempted to corner the cotton market in 1904 and went bankrupt (Collection of Lucy Dos Passos Coggin).*

The mother is a figure who initially expresses accepted class attitudes ("Workingmen and people like that laborers travailleurs greasers")[6] and a feminine aversion to violence and conflict (as in the first Camera Eye, when she and Dos Passos take refuge under a shop counter) and who later fades into a debilitating illness ("He was very gay and She was feeling well for once") (*42P,* p. 173). The father, the "strong athletic man . . . immensely energetic," described by Ludington,[7] is powerfully masculine in thought and action. Willing to state and act on unpopular opinions ("What would you do Lucy if I were to invite one of them [a Negro] to my table?" and "Why Lucy if it were necessary for the cause of humanity I would walk out and be shot any day") (*42P,* p. 13), he is also a man who carries his flask

wherever he goes, recites *Othello* in cabs, and enjoys swimming and yachting.

Early in the Camera Eye, Dos Passos begins to associate his upper class experience with his mother's feminine conventionality and lack of strength and the lower class world, which he occasionally encounters, with his father's masculinity, both because of the greater vigor of this world and because of its more openly expressed sexuality. This pattern of association is probably indebted to Dos Passos' awareness of his father's Portuguese immigrant background and his mother's roots in a socially prominent Maryland family. But it is also, and more fully, a product of the sexual conventions of Dos Passos' youth, in which a Victorian gentility still masked the expression of sex in upper middle class life, while working class experience was assumed to be more openly and aggressively sexual. Initially, this association is communicated largely by images and brief incidents in which the boyish Dos Passos is fearful during moments when a masculine sexuality is linked to his father or to the working class. Traveling by train at night with his mother through an industrial landscape, he peeks "out of the window into the black rumbling dark suddenly ranked with squat chimneys and you're scared of the black smoke and the puffs of flame that flare and fade out of the squat chimneys" (*42P,* p. 25). And when challenged at school about his political opinions (opinions which are also his father's), he can only reply "all trembly" (*42P,* p. 58).

Camera Eye (7), which describes Dos Passos on an ice skating pond during the period he was attending Choate, brings to the surface his permanent association of class and sexual roles. The section is important and brief enough to quote in its entirety:

> skating on the pond next the silver company's mill where there was a funny fuzzy smell from the dump whaleoil soap somebody said it was that they used in cleaning the silver knives and spoons and forks putting shine on them for sale  there was shine on the ice early black ice that rang like a sawblade just scratched white by the first skaters  I couldn't learn to skate and kept falling down look out for the muckers everybody said bohunk and polack kids put stones in their snowballs write dirty words up on walls do dirty things up alleys their folks work in the mills
>
> we clean young American Rover Boys handy with tools Deerslayers played hockey Boy Scouts and cut figure eights on the ice Achilles Ajax Agamemnon I couldn't learn to skate and kept falling down (*42P,* p. 81)

*John Randolph Dos Passos, right, in a photograph believed to have been taken in Madeira at his wedding to Lucy Madison in the summer of 1911 (Collection of Lucy Dos Passos Coggin)*

The immigrant background "muckers" play roughly and unfairly and revel in an unclean sexuality; the Rover Boys lead clean American lives of ritualized activities, codes, and roles. Dos Passos at this point identifies with and aspires to the Rover Boys ("*we* clean young American Rover Boys"), a group which includes hockey and figure skating among its activities. But "I couldn't learn to skate and kept falling down." His ineptness signifies that he is between two worlds. As his father's son his true identity is with the outsider "muckers," but as his mother's son he condemns their overt sexuality and endorses the conventional and derivative upper class roles of the Rover Boys. Dos Passos' illegitimacy probably strengthened his sense of not belonging to the world he aspired to and thus his ineptness in its skills. (Metaphorically speaking, his father and mother had also done "dirty things up alleys.") He, therefore, carries with him throughout his upper middle class boyhood and early youth a sense of displacement. He responds deeply to the story of the man without a country (*42P*, pp. 147–148) and considers himself without either a home ("I wished I was home but I hadn't any home" [*42P*, p. 224]) or a religion (*42P*, pp. 206–207). But as a "displaced person," Dos Passos' life also increasingly takes on the shape of a search for a home and a father–that is, for a creed and a course of action which will embody in compelling symbolic form the values he attributes to his father.

In other Camera Eye passages in *The 42nd Parallel,* Dos Passos' overt condemnation yet underlying desire for the greater sexual vitality and experience of lower class life emerges clearly. Near his parents' Virginia farm he meets at a freight crossing a youth who "couldn't have been much older 'n me . . . he had curly hair and wisps of hay in it and through his open shirt you could see his body was burned brown to the waist I guess he wasn't much account" (*42P*, pp. 92–93). Dos Passos' early encounters with girls also bring into the open his association of a desirable sexual freedom with lower class life and of a cold formality with upper class experience. In juxtaposed Camera Eye sequences, he sits in a well-to-do suburban Pennsylvania church listening to girls singing "chilly shrill soprano" in the choir and watching them in their "best hats and pretty pink green blue yellow dresses" (*42P*, p. 108). Then, in the Camera Eye which follows, he has his first sexual experience, as Jeanne, the young family maid from the Jura, takes him into her bed one night, "and afterwards you knew what girls were made like" (*42P*, p. 130).

As Dos Passos moves into adolescence, he discovers in specific single instances confirmation of his linking of sexual attitudes and values with class. At a summer resort he meets a Methodist minister's wife.

a tall thin woman who sang little songs at the piano in a spindly lost voice who'd heard you liked books and grew flowers and vegetables and was so interested because she'd once been an Episcopalian and loved beautiful things and had had stories she had written published in a magazine . . . and she wore thin white dresses and used perfume and talked in a bell-like voice about how things were lovely as a lily (*42P*, p. 238)

With this woman, with her thin aestheticism and suppressed sexuality, Dos Passos "felt you ought to put your arm round her and kiss her only you didn't want to" (*42P*, p. 238). Rather, you "wished you had the nerve to hug and kiss Martha the colored girl they said was half Indian." And though he does not have the nerve, "but Oh God not lilies" (*42P*, p. 239).

Parallel to this scene is Dos Passos' visit to "historic Quebec" with a group of students in the care of several older men. One of these guides, a singer, takes a homosexual interest in Dos Passos:

it's raining in historic Quebec and walking down the street alone with the baritone he kept saying about how there were bad girls in a town like this and boys shouldn't go with bad girls and the Acropolis and the bel canto and the Parthenon and voice culture and the beautiful statutes of Greek boys and the Winged Victory and the beautiful statues

but I finally shook him and went out on the cars to see the falls of Montmorency famous in song and story and a church full of crutches left by the sick in St. Anne de Beaupré

and the gray rainy streets full of girls (*42P*, pp. 284–285)[8]

Dos Passos' identification of effeminacy and homosexuality with the upper class and of masculine sexuality with the lower continues in the Harvard portions of the Camera Eye in *The 42nd Parallel*. As in his Quebec visit, experience now presents Dos Passos with clear choices. There is the world of Jeanne, the colored servant, and the Quebec girls, and there is the world of shrill sopranoes, the minister's wife, and the baritone. But the Harvard Camera Eye passages add an important new element to this distinction. Now the upper class becomes associated in Dos Passos' mind not only with sexual inadequacy but with a destructive social blindness. In a bitterly ironic Camera Eye section dealing with the Lawrence strikes of 1912, the Rover Boys of Choate reappear as young Harvard men who become scabs on a street car line:

what the hell they were a lot of wops anyway bohunks hunkies that didn't wash their necks ate garlic with

squalling brats and fat oily wives the damn dagoes they put up a notice for volunteers good clean young

to man the streetcars and show the foreign agitators this was still a white man's (*42P*, p. 245)

Two men from "Matthews" answer the call, and while they are horseplaying on a car, one accidentally kills the other, and "now the fellow's got to face his roommate's folks" (*42P*, p. 246).

Yet despite Dos Passos' restlessness ("can't sleep") because of his realization of the social blindness of his world, he doesn't have

the nerve to break out of the bellglass

four years under the ethercone breathe deep gently now that's the way be a good boy one two three four five six get A's in some courses but don't be a grind be interested in literature but remain a gentleman don't be seen with Jews or socialists (*42P*, pp. 301–302)

The Harvard bellglass is that of a sexless or effeminate aestheticism—"grow cold with culture like a cup of tea forgotten between an incense-burner and a volume of Oscar Wilde cold and not strong like a claret lemonade drunk at a Pop Concert in Symphony Hall" (*42P*, p. 302). Opposed to it is an "outside" of raucous activity and striving in the "real" world of industrial America—"the streetcarwheels screech grinding in a rattle of loose trucks round Harvard Square and the trains crying across the saltmarshes and the rumbling siren of a steamboat leaving dock and the blue peter flying and millworkers marching with a red brass band through the streets of Lawrence Massachusetts" (*42P*, p. 302). But, Dos Passos concludes, "I hadn't the nerve" (*42P*, p. 302).

Dos Passos' occasional efforts to break out of the bellglass end not in action or commitment but in a seemingly inevitable return to his class. He and a friend attend some radical meetings in New York, and afterwards "we had several drinks and welsh rabbits and paid our bill and went home and opened the door with a latchkey and put on pajamas and went to bed and it was comfortable in bed" (*42P*, p. 350). The concluding Camera Eye of *The 42nd Parallel* finds Dos Passos on his way to Europe during wartime. Perhaps, it is implied, he will discover in the upheaval of war an answer to his dilemma of how to identify and commit himself to the home and father which he senses are somewhere in the world of radical struggle.

II

The initial Camera Eye in *Nineteen-Nineteen* sets the tone for all the passages in this portion of the tril-

*Early view of the Choate campus (from George St. John, Forty Years at School, 1959)*

ogy. It begins with a coalescing of the news of the deaths of Dos Passos' parents–his mother in May, 1915, his father in January, 1917. With their deaths, the "bellglass" is "shattered" (*1919*, p. 11). Gone is the protective shield they provided (a shield which included Choate and Harvard), and gone, too, therefore, is the barrier between himself and experience which their protectiveness included. Both they and Dos Passos' earlier life are now dead:

> we
>
> who had heard Copey's beautiful reading voice and read the handsomely bound books and breathed deep . . . of the waxwork lilies and the artificial parmaviolet

scent under the ethercone and sat breakfasting in the library where the bust was of Octavius
> were now dead at the cableoffice (*1919*, p. 11)

The Camera Eye continues by juxtaposing this rejected effete world ("*I'm so tired of violets/Take them all away*") (*1919*, p. 10) and the experience of men at war, an experience ranging from ordinary tasks ("washing those windows/K.P./cleaning the sparkplugs with a pocketknife") to whores, bombardment, and death (*1919*, pp. 11–12). Now that the barriers are down, the war can provide Dos Passos with the kind of experience which might lead to the full discovery of his true identity and role. The initial Camera Eye in *Nineteen-Nineteen* thus ends:

*George St. John, who became headmaster of Choate in 1908 (while Dos Passos was a student there), and his wife, Clara (from St. John, Forty Years at School, 1959)*

CHARLES TOWNSEND COPELAND,
A.B.
Assistant Professor of English

*Photograph from the 1916 Harvard yearbook of Dos Passos's
English professor, known to the students as "Copey"
(The Lilly Library, Indiana University)*

"tomorrow I hoped would be the first day of the first month of the first year" (*1919*, p. 12).

In the Camera Eye sections which follow, the experience which represents to Dos Passos a powerfully attractive combination of masculinity and of integrity of feeling and expression has a distinctively Hemingway cast. It is while threatened by death or when engaged in drinking, eating, whoring, and adventure with his comrades that Dos Passos communicates a sense of a new life. Under bombardment at the Marne, with the shells "pounding the thought of death into our ears" (*1919*, p. 71), his response to the stimulation of that thought is both sexual and intoxicating: "the winey thought of death stings in the spring blood that throbs in the sunburned neck up and down the belly under the tight belt hurries like cognac in the tips of my toes and the lobes of my ears" (*1919*, pp. 71–72). And the Camera Eye which describes Dos Passos' trip to Italy with his ambulance section—a passage which begins and ends with the refrain "11,000 registered harlots said the Red Cross Publicity Man infest the streets of Marseilles" (*1919*, p. 148)—combines the lush richness of the French landscape with the camaraderie of men eating and drinking while on the loose.

War as a "real" masculine experience—the experience of both death and life—supplies the matrix for the emergence of the motif which is to dominate the Cam-

era Eye from this point on, the motif of the distinction between life as Dos Passos now understands it and the language conventionally used to disguise the true nature of experience.[9] Thus, in a Camera Eye passage which is filled with the horrors of war—

> remembering the grey crooked fingers the thick drip of blood off the canvas the bubbling when the lungcages try to breathe the muddy scraps of flesh you put in the ambulance alive and haul out dead (*1919*, p. 101)—

the physical images of man's destructiveness are combined with the heroic language of patriotism and, in particular, with Patrick Henry's "Give me liberty or give me death" (*1919*, pp. 102–103). Such language is corrupt, it is implied, both because it drives men into the horror of war and because it then disguises that horror. During their trip to Italy, the ambulance section is accompanied by a living example of a failure in truth-telling about this horror, a "Successful Story Writer [who] it turned out he was not writing what he felt he wanted to be writing What can you tell them at home about the war?" (*1919*, p. 150).

Dos Passos has now reached a felt though still not clearly articulated understanding of the basic relationship between art and life. Life is experience in its masculine cast of the complete range of human feelings and activities, and art is the effort to render this kind of experience with virile honesty and full attention to the frequent ugliness and injustice of experience. Apparently believing, however, that he is still deficient in experience, Dos Passos enters the army as an enlisted man and is exposed to the drudgery, squalor, mindlessness, and destructiveness of life on its lowest level. But the army, though it contributes to Dos Passos' "education," is itself a prison of the spirit. Dos Passos' discharge at Tours in the spring of 1919 is thus like a second rebirth as he once again escapes a repressive world for one of a new freedom. In Paris after his discharge, he feels the richness of life with a masculine sexual energy and excitement and with an imagery of rebirth which echoes almost precisely the imagery of his earlier escape from the bellglass:

> Paris comes into the room in the servantgirl's eyes the warm bulge of her breasts under the grey smock the smell of chicory in coffee scalded milk and the shine that crunches on the crescent rolls stuck with little dabs of very sweet unsalted butter. . . .

> Today is the sunny morning of the first day of spring    We gulp our coffee splash water on us jump into our clothes run downstairs step out wideawake into the first morning of the first day of the first year (*1919*, pp. 343, 344)

First Love *(his tale by any other name would sing as sweet)*

"The thoughts of youth are long long thoughts" to quote our favorite poet & platitudinarian

The schoolroom was intolerably hot that June afternoon. The long low room, the rows of backs in front of him seemed numbingly oppressive to the dark haired boy whose seat was in the far corner. With a book open on the scarred desk before him, he ~~sat~~ stared through the open window at a patch of blue sky that contrasted dazzlingly with the dull brown shadow of the schoolroom. Outside trees waved in the faint breeze, while crickets and june-bugs kept up a merry humming din. The branch of a creeper that

*Manuscript page of a story by Dos Passos, with Professor Copeland's comments at the top, that was published in the October 1915 issue of* The Harvard Monthly *(Albert and Shirley Small Special Collections Library, University of Virginia)*

But France offers no means for the expression of Dos Passos' emerging sense of his identity as an artist. In the 1919 May Day riots, he is the outsider who takes refuge in the back room of a café where he drinks "grog americain" (*1919*, p. 401). And the French radical movement itself lacks energy and direction, as is suggested by its degeneration into an Anarchist picnic where Dos Passos meets a girl who "wanted liberty fraternity equality and a young man to take her out" (*1919*, p. 420). Like the girl in a New York taxicab in an important *Big Money* Camera Eye passage, the French girl does not provide Dos Passos a means for the expression of a radical masculinity despite the sexuality of their encounter. Beneath her revolutionary activities she is really a girl in search of a good time—"she wanted l'Amérique la vie le theatre le feev o'clock le smoking le foxtrot" (*1919*, p. 420)—and thus offers the radical artist principally an opportunity for the betrayal of his goals.

The final Camera Eye in *Nineteen-Nineteen* is chronologically out of order in that it returns Dos Passos to his period as an enlisted man in France. Nevertheless, it sums up his development by the close of the second novel of the trilogy. He is an army casual loading scrap iron on to railcars in the morning and unloading it in the afternoon while his discharge is delayed because his service record—that is, his identity—has been lost. Thus, the two "rebirths" of *Nineteen-Nineteen* are in truth false dawns. Although Dos Passos has escaped from the prison of both Harvard and the army, neither his full identity nor his role as an artist has been fully discovered, and he is still engaged in the meaningless tasks which life presents him.

### III

In *The Big Money* the Camera Eye passages are dominated by the related motifs of traveling and of trying on literary roles—of search as both physical and artistic restlessness. The theme of search begins with the initial Camera Eye of *The Big Money* with Dos Passos' reaction to post-war America on his return from France. The harbor scenes evoke memories of place and season, but once he is fully in touch with America the images shift to those of a 1920s world of crushing normalcy on the one hand and social oppression on the other:

the crunch of whitecorn muffins and coffee with cream gulped in a hurry before traintime and apartmenthouse mornings stifling with newspapers and the smooth powdery feel of new greenbacks and the whack of a

cop's billy cracking a citizen's skull and the faces blurred with newsprint of men in jail (*BM*, p. 27)

Escape into art appears to be the only response to these conditions, but escape into the roles either of "artist as world traveler" or of "artist as successful novelist" brings no relief. In each instance, Dos Passos must adopt a false identity appropriate to the role, as is suggested by the dress suit he is forced to wear both in Beirut and New York. In Beirut, after crossing the desert by camel, "scarcelybathed he finds himself cast for a role provided with a white tie carefully tied by the vice-consul stuffed into a boiled shirt a tailcoat too small a pair of dress-trousers too large" (*BM*, p. 30). And on his return to New York—after the great success of *Three Soldiers*—he "finds waiting again the forsomebodyelsetailored dress suit" (*BM*, p. 31) of a literary personage expected to read poetry to attentive audiences. These, Dos Passos concludes, are not "any of the positions for which he made application at the employment-agency" (*BM*, p. 31).

The 1920s Greenwich Village cocktail party world also does not provide a context for self-discovery. In the Camera Eye passage devoted to such a party, the imagery of effeminate artiness and of role-playing clearly relates the falsity of this world to that of Eliot's Prufrock setting. At the party, "the narrow yellow room teems with talk" (*BM*, p. 125), and the hostess finds

every man his pigeonhole
the personality must be kept carefully adjusted over the
        face
to facilitate recognition she pins on each of us a badge
        (*BM*, p. 125)

To escape being pinned, Dos Passos must

walk the streets and walk the streets inquiring of Coca Cola signs Lucky Strike ads pricetags in storewindows scraps of overheard conversations stray tatters of newsprint yesterday's headlines sticking out of ashcans

for a set of figures a formula of action an address you don't quite know (*BM*, p. 149)

In this search, "a formula for action" now has special appeal—"to do to make there are more lives than walking desperate the streets hurry underdog do make" (*BM*, p. 149)—and he briefly adopts the role of social agitator, of "a speech urging action in the crowded hall" (*BM*, p. 149). But he finds himself merely sloganizing in his reaching out for approval, and disappointedly returns home

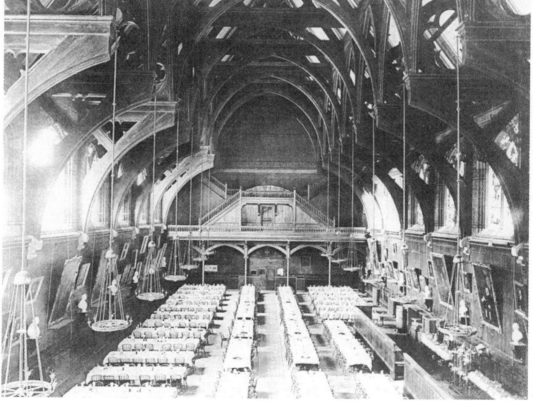

*Top: Matthews Hall in the Harvard Yard, where Dos Passos lived as a freshman (1912–1913); bottom: interior of the nearby Harvard Union, where he dined (Albert and Shirley Small Special Collections Library, University of Virginia)*

after a drink and a hot meal and read (with some difficulty in the Loeb Library trot) the epigrams of Martial and ponder the course of history and what leverage might pry the owners loose from power and bring back (I too Walt Whitman) our storybook democracy (*BM*, p. 150)

New York in the early 1920s thus provides Dos Passos with the opportunity to choose between two opposing literary roles, neither of which is satisfactory. He can be the class conscious radical who is ineffectually seeking a way to contribute to the restoration of "our storybook democracy." Or he can be the successful artist who finds excitement in the intimate connection between sex and money:

money in New York (lipstick kissed off the lips of a girl fashionablydressed fragrant at five o'clock in a taxicab careening down Park Avenue when at the end of each crosstown street the west is flaming with gold and white smoke billows from the smokestacks of steamboats leaving port and the sky is lined with greenbacks . . .

dollars are silky in her hair soft in her dress sprout in the elaborately contrived rosepetals that you kiss become pungent and crunchy in the speakeasy dinner sting shrill in the drinks (*BM*, pp. 150–151)

But this kind of sexual excitement is not an adequate conclusion to his search. "If not why not?" he asks; and from "somebody in [his] head" comes the answer, "liar" (*BM*, p. 151). The sexuality of the Big Money–as Charley Anderson and Richard Savage are discovering in the narratives of this portion of *U.S.A.*–betrays rather than affirms and supports a masculinity of strength and purpose.

So Dos Passos must still search while "peeling the speculative onion of doubt" (*BM*, p. 151)–doubt imaged in the following Camera Eye section as a harbor fog which hinders his efforts to begin his true journey:

tonight start out ship somewhere join up sign on the dotted line enlist become one of
hock the old raincoat of uncertitude . . .
to rebuild yesterday (*BM*, p. 196)

But he again wanders the streets in "aimless walks,"

an unidentified stranger
destination unknown
hat pulled down over the has he any? face (*BM*, p. 197)

Dos Passos' search for a fully expressive masculine literary identity and role ends in the related settings of the Plymouth of the Sacco-Vanzetti case and the Harlan County of the miners' strike. In these examples of the organized oppression of freedom and democracy by the very institutions established to safeguard them, Dos Passos discovers his theme and his function as a writer. He is to tell the truth about America, and particularly about the corruption and subversion of the "old words" of freedom and justice by those in power, and thus play an active part in the struggle to return us to "our storybook democracy." As he walks through Plymouth,

pencil scrawls in my notebook the scraps of recollection the broken halfphrases the effort to intersect word with word to dovetail clause with clause to rebuild out of mangled memories unshakably (Oh Pontius Pilate) the truth (*BM*, p. 436)

Returning to Boston, he asks,

how can I make them feel how our fathers our uncles haters of oppression came to this coast    how say Don't let them scare you    how make them feel who are your oppressors America
    rebuild the ruined words worn slimy in the mouths of lawyers districtattorneys collegepresidents judges without the old words the immigrants haters of oppression brought to Plymouth how can you know who are your betrayers America (*BM*, p. 437)

With the deaths of Sacco and Vanzetti, the struggle appears to be lost–"there is nothing to do we are beaten . . . our work is over" (*BM*, p. 462). But, in fact,

the old words of the immigrants are being renewed in blood and agony tonight do they know that the old American speech of the haters of oppression is new tonight . . . the language of the old beaten nation is not forgotten in our ears tonight
    the men in the deathhouse made the old words new before they died (*BM*, p. 463)

"We stand defeated America," the Camera Eye ends. "We stand defeated," however, only in the sense of the failure to save Sacco and Vanzetti. The "old words" were made new again in the strength and courage of Sacco and Vanzetti and in the beauty and power of Vanzetti's language of freedom and hope in his letters. And in this lesson the writer can find his true task. So in Harlan County, which in the crushing of the striking miners by corporate and state power represents in microcosm the betrayal of American ideals, Dos Passos can end the Camera Eye in *U.S.A.* with the defiant and challenging charge to himself, "we have only words against" (*BM*, p. 525).

MONTHLY BOARD (1916)

P. C. Rodgers     J. S. Watson, Jr.     C. G. Paulding     W. H. Shattuck     Robert Littell
Thacher Nelson     C. A. Trafford, Jr.     R. S. Mitchell     J. R. Dos Passos, Jr.     Robert Hillyer

*Dos Passos with other members of the* Harvard Monthly *board, 1916 (The Lilly Library, Indiana University)*

### IV

The Camera Eye in *U.S.A.* is a story of maturation. The young Dos Passos who falsely identified himself with the "topdog" ("we . . . Rover Boys") at last realizes that he too is oppressed within the American system ("we stand defeated"). The writer who sought in travel, success, bohemianism, and "greenback" sex an identity for himself as an artist at last finds it in his role as one who can help revive the "old words" through his art. And the boy who hid under the counter with his mother during a moment of social upheaval is capable at last of his father's aggressive expression in both word and action of rebellious values.

When we read *U.S.A.* we are encountering, somewhat as in a familiar kind of romantic poem ("Out of the Cradle Endlessly Rocking," for example), both an account of the growth of an artist's imagination and the product of that growth, that is, the poem itself. *U.S.A.*, of course, differs from this kind of romantic poem in that it sharply bifurcates

the history of artistic development and the product of that development. The Camera Eye presents us with a stream of consciousness account of the growth of the artist's imagination up to the point of the composition of the work we are reading. The remainder of the trilogy presents us with an interpretation of American social life which is the result of the act of composition by the mature artist. Yet this bifurcation should not disguise the intimate connection between the Camera Eye and the rest of the trilogy. When Dos Passos reveals to us in the Camera Eye that he has made his literary sensibility whole and insightful by maturing into the identity of his father, and that this identity involves above all a masculine honesty and vigor of thought and expression, he is also revealing to us one of the principal reasons for the failure of American life as depicted elsewhere in the trilogy. For in each of the other modes of *U.S.A.*—in its newsreels, biographies, and above all in its major narratives, from Mac and Moorehouse to Charley Anderson and Richard Savage—a feminization or inadequacy of male sexuality

21

is closely related to a failure in intellectual honesty and strength and thus a failure to contribute to the preservation of the "old words."[10] Although Dos Passos felt that he himself had struggled through to a return to his home and father, America as a whole had failed to do so. And he made this theme one of the principal themes of his trilogy.

Dos Passos does not "drain off" his subjective experience in the Camera Eye and thereby assure a greater objectivity in the remainder of the trilogy. He rather depicts openly in the Camera Eye deeply personal preoccupations which underlie many of the central themes of *U.S.A.* as a whole. The belief that *U.S.A.* is principally a novel of social documentation arises out of its cultural role in the 1930s and the fictional mode of its narratives. It is, in fact, a work in which Dos Passos' sense of himself is a major contribution to the thematic complexity and energy which we are increasingly realizing are the sources of its permanence.

*—Modern Fiction Studies,*
26 (Autumn 1980): 417–430

### Notes

1. John Dos Passos, *The Best Times: An Informal Memoir* (New York: New American Library, 1966) and *The Fourteenth Chronicle: Letters and Diaries of John Dos Passos*, edited by Townsend Ludington (Boston: Gambit, 1973). Melvin Landsberg also contributes to an understanding of the autobiographical foundation of the Camera Eye in his *Dos Passos' Path to U.S.A.: A Political Biography, 1912–1936* (Boulder: Colorado Associated University Press, 1972), as does James N. Westerhoven in his "Autobiographical Elements in the Camera Eye," *American Literature*, 48 (November 1976): 340–364.

2. The best and fullest of these discussions occurs in David L. Venderwerken's "*U.S.A.*: Dos Passos and the 'Old Words,'" *Twentieth Century Literature*, 23 (February 1977): 195–228; see especially pp. 206–215. See also Townsend Ludington, "The Ordering of the Camera Eye in *U.S.A.*," *American Literature*, 49 (November 1977): 443–446; and Iain Colley, *Dos Passos and the Fiction of Despair* (Totowa, N.J.: Rowman & Littlefield, 1978), pp. 66–119 passim.

3. See the interviews by David Sanders in *Writers at Work: The Paris Review Interviews, Fourth Series*, edited by George Plimpton (New York: Viking, 1976), p. 81; and Frank Gado in *First Person: Conversations on Writers and Writing*, edited by Gado (Schenectady, N.Y.: Union College Press, 1973), p. 52. Both interviews occurred in 1968.

4. See John Wrenn (*John Dos Passos* [New York: Twayne, 1961]) for frequent allusions to this theme in Dos Passos' work from *Rosinante to the Road Again* (1922) to *U.S.A.*

5. See in this connection Lois Hughson, "In Search of the True America: Dos Passos' Debt to Whitman in *U.S.A.*," *Modern Fiction Studies*, 19 (Summer 1973): 179–192.

6. *U.S.A.: The 42nd Parallel* (New York: Modern Library, 1938), p. 25. Citations will hereafter appear in the text. Since the three novels of *U.S.A.* are paginated separately in this edition, I will cite both the novel and the page number, using the following abbreviations: *42P–The 42nd Parallel; 1919–Nineteen-Nineteen;* and *BM–The Big Money.*

7. Ludington, ed., *The Fourteenth Chronicle*, p. 3.

8. It is perhaps worth noting that whereas in the ice skating scene Greek masculine role models are an accepted staple of upper middle class education ("Achilles Ajax Agamemnon"), they are here found suspect because of their implied homosexuality.

9. The theme of the "old words" in *U.S.A.* is best discussed by Vanderwerken, "*U.S.A.*: Dos Passos and the 'Old Words'"; and by John Lydenberg, "Don Passos' *U.S.A.*: The Words of the Hollow Men," in *Essays on Determinism in American Literature*, edited by Sidney J. Krause (Kent, Ohio: Kent State University Press, 1964), pp. 97–107, reprinted in *Dos Passos, the Critics, and the Writer's Intention*, edited by Allen Belkind (Carbondale: Southern Illinois University Press, 1971), pp. 93–105.

10. A parallel theme—one which I cannot explore here—exists in Dos Passos' treatment of female sexuality in *U.S.A.* Most of the major women figures in the trilogy either exploit their sex or are exploited sexually—in both instances principally because they have accepted conventional sexual identities and roles—in ways which contribute to the decay of the "old words."

## CHILDHOOD AND EDUCATION

*In recalling his parents, Dos Passos often stressed, as in Camera Eye (4), his father's strength of will and body and his mother's passivity. Although John Randolph Dos Passos (1844–1917) was the son of an immigrant Portuguese cobbler, he became a successful and wealthy Wall Street lawyer. Lucy Sprigg Madison Dos Passos (1854–1915) was from a prominent Virginia family. Dos Passos himself, because his interests were bookish rather than athletic, was unhappy at Choate, a Connecticut prep school based on English models.*

### The Camera Eye (4)

*Two suggestive images of John Randolph Dos Passos's projection of male strength are presented in the fourth Camera Eye: as the outsider Othello capable of winning the patrician Desdemona, and as a powerful athlete.*

riding backwards through the rain in the rumbly cab looking at their two faces in the jiggly light of the four-wheeled cab and Her big trunks thumping on the roof and He reciting Othello in his lawyer's voice

*Her father loved me, oft invited me*
*Still questioned me the story of my life*

*From year to year, the battles, sieges, fortunes*
*That I have past.*
*I ran it through, even from my boyish days,*
*To th' very moment that he bade me tell it*

*Wherein I spoke of the most disastrous chances*
*Of moving accidents by flood and field*
*Of hairbreadth 'scapes i' th' imminent deadly breach*

why that's the Schuylkill    the horse's hoofs rattle sharp on smooth wet asphalt after cobbles    through the gray streaks of rain the river shimmers ruddy with winter mud    When I was your age Jack I dove off this bridge through the rail of the bridge we can look way down into the cold rainyshimmery water    Did you have any clothes on?    Just my shirt

*– The 42nd Parallel, pp. 32–33*

## Dos Passos to Charles W. Bernardin, 17 March 1950

*Bernardin, a professor at Villanova University, was preparing a biography of Dos Passos and often queried him about specific phases of his life. Here Dos Passos recalls his "misfit" years at Choate.*

Westmoreland, Va.
March 17, 1950

Dear Bernardin,

Your letter gave me gooseflesh. Unless memory is singularly deceptive I hated boarding school. The only thing I remember with pleasure is canoeing on the Quinnipiac. Choate when I was there was a very different place from the present gloss-coated academy. It was still run by three old ladies, the Misses Choate. One of them encouraged me to paint in watercolor. The St. Johns, who made the school a success, arrived about the middle of my stay. They were always very nice to me and I had a real fondness for Mrs. St. John who was the daughter of a Yale Greek professor and well grounded in the classics, as people used to say. When I first went there, Choate had only thirty or forty pupils. I still can't visit a boy's school without having a queasy chill feeling in the midriff. In low moments I can still cheer myself up by telling myself that no matter how bad things are at least I'm not at boarding school. That's no criticism of the school which I imagine was distinctly above the average. Having been to school in England where they really made you study, having a trace of a French accent and extremely bad eyesight I was very much of a misfit there.

. . . . . . . . . .

Yrs,
JDP

* * *

*Le Baron Russell Briggs, Harvard English professor who was dean of the faculty of arts and sciences while Dos Passos was a student (Photo by Purdy)*

## Harvard

*Dos Passos was at Harvard from 1912 to 1916, a period that falls within Donald Fleming's account of Harvard's Golden Age. Fleming intends by this designation to indicate the presence of instructors of wit and brilliance and of students drawn from families accustomed to national leadership. Dos Passos, however, though he made many friends among his fellow classmates interested in writing, felt stifled by the intellectual posturing and thin aestheticism cultivated by students and faculty alike, as is suggested in the twenty-fifth Camera Eye ("grow cold with culture like a cup of tea forgotten between an incense burner and a volume of Oscar Wilde"). He wrote reviews, sketches, and poems for* The Harvard Monthly, *but his stories in particular often expressed themes of escape from an oppressive atmosphere similar to that of the Harvard "bellglass."*

*It was uncommon during this period for Harvard undergraduates to engage in social activism, and when they did, it was usually on the side of their own class. Although Dos Passos, especially on his frequent trips to New York, sought to learn more about the burgeoning radical movements of his day, he remained the outsider who, at the close of the political rally, came home to a comfortable bed.*

## Harvard's Golden Age
Donald Fleming

*In this prose tapestry of figures and events in the Harvard of roughly 1890–1920, Fleming attempts to re-create some of the larger-than-life professors and their students, some of whom went on to become famous. Particularly notable is Professor Charles Townsend "Copey" Copeland; Dos Passos profited from his writing course but was later to reject his aestheticism.*

. . . . . . . . . .

The important thing about Copey and the other members of the dwindling band of professors-in-the-Yard is the opportunity they give you to meet distinguished older men whom you admire, on highly informal terms. There are some magical places right in the Yard where your dreams of hearing interesting people talk about interesting things can actually come true. Copey's "Wednesday evenings after ten," when he holds open house, are the Harvard undergraduates' salon. He may invite you to meet Minnie Maddern Fiske, though probably not, but he will certainly see that you get to meet glamourous upperclassmen like Jack Reed from Oregon or Walter Lippmann. When these favorites are present, there is a good deal of chaffing between them and Copey, which is an eye-opener to you, and he does not seem to mind that Jack Reed has written a rather double-edged poetic tribute to him in the *Lampoon:*

> Don't your acolytes distress you,
>     In their circle Johnsonese?
> Vying which shall cry "God bless you!"
>     When you sneeze?

Some of your more severely intellectual classmates look down on Copey's Wednesdays as miscellaneous and undiscriminating. They hope to be invited home by Professor George Herbert Palmer of the Philosophy Department, whose wife Alice Freeman Palmer is as famous as he is and a former president of Wellesley. But the ultimate accolade is to be invited, as Van Wyck Brooks and his sidekick Max Perkins are, to one of the legendary Dante readings that Charles Eliot Norton, though retired, still gives at Shady Hill for selected undergraduates, who are almost stunned at impinging upon the consciousness of a man who had known Thackeray and Ruskin. Even if you do not aim as high as that, you can probably point out within a radius of six blocks from Harvard Square, in the "good" section of Cambridge, the houses of many of your professors, and though few work as hard at it as Copey or the Palmers, your chances of being entertained by some of them in the course of your college days are good.

You need some relaxation after these high-keyed social evenings with the faculty. You can play billiards at Leavitt and Peirce's—billiards is a gentleman's game, though you certainly ought not to be hanging around pool parlors. You can participate in dramatic performances in the new Harvard Stadium, including a pageant about Joan of Arc, with mammoth choruses to sop up all interested undergraduates. You can sing in the Glee Club. You *can* go to the Fogg Museum, which has been around since the mid-1890s, but the holdings are rather thin unless your heart leaps up at the sight of plaster casts. You can go out for the *Crimson* (briefly known as the *Magenta!*), or the *Lampoon,* or the *Advocate,* which is work but also fun—in fact, it is much to be feared that in every generation the contributors to the *Lampoon* get more laughs out of it than the readers. It was long before your time, but in view of what has become of him since, people are still talking about how William Randolph Hearst came to Harvard in the 80s and fitted out a sumptuous editorial sanctum for the *Lampoon* at his father's expense; but to show they could not be bought, the editors would not use it—then.

. . . . . . . . . .

Your other great favorites are probably in literature. The elegantly dressed and disdainful Barrett Wendell, one of the Boston Wendells, with a high-pitched English accent that he brought back from an early trip abroad, teaches English and even American literature, though he says of the latter that it is "of little lasting potence." He boasts that his greatest service to America has been in combating coeducation at Harvard. You are not present, though he probably wouldn't care, when he has a memorable exchange with the young historian Roger Merriman.

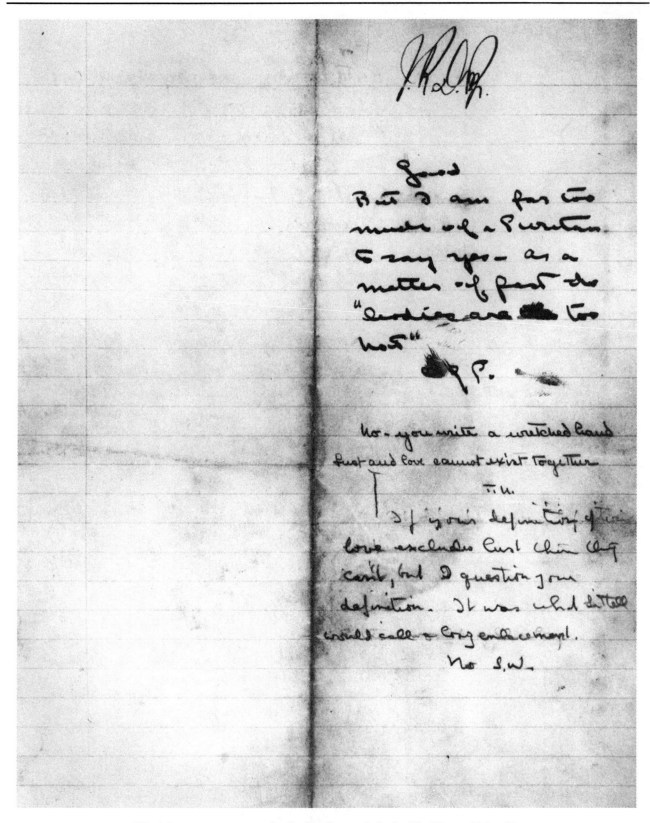

*Editorial comments on a manuscript that Dos Passos submitted to* The Harvard Monthly
*(Albert and Shirley Small Special Collections Library, University of Virginia)*

MATTHEWS HALL          MASSACHUSETTS HALL                    HOLLIS HALL

THE YARD IN 1916

*The Harvard Yard as it appeared the year of Dos Passos's graduation (The Lilly Library, Indiana University)*

### JOHN RODERIGO DOS PASSOS, Jr.

Born January 14, 1896, at Chicago, Illinois. Home address, 1201 19th Street, Washington, District of Columbia. Prepared at Choate School. In college four years as undergraduate. *Monthly*, Cercle Français. Secretary *Monthly* 1915-1916.

*Dos Passos's senior-class photograph from the 1916 Harvard yearbook (The Lilly Library, Indiana University)*

"In all the 25 years you have known me, Roger, have you ever heard me utter one liberal sentiment?"

"Not one, sir."

"Thank God."

When the eager undergraduate congratulated Wendell on his appointment as visiting professor at the Sorbonne and asked if Mrs. Wendell would be accompanying him to Paris, Wendell is supposed to have replied, "Young man, would you take a ham sandwich to a banquet?" Wendell's colleague, George Lyman Kittredge, the Shakespeare expert, is relished for his gigantic ego and impromptu wit, classically wrapped up together when he fell off the dais and said, "At last, I find myself on the level of my audience." The other great "character" on the Harvard faculty in your time is not particularly popular, though the consecrated few who take his courses think it is a matter of caviar to the general. Irving Babbitt, trained in Sanskrit, ostensibly teaches French, described in his own words as a "cheap and nasty substitute for Latin." In reality, Babbitt pursues his vendetta against Rousseau and permissiveness.

By no means all of the highly popular courses are soft options—Kittredge's certainly isn't—but cheer up, in times of peril, "the Widow Nolen" will take a motherly interest in your problems—William W. Nolen ('84), who runs the most famous of numerous cramming schools in the Square. For any of the big courses where the market is strong enough, he offers printed lecture notes, digests of the required reading, and forced feeding just before the examination. If you can pay the Widow's fees, you can escape from Harvard almost totally uneducated. Many do.

Among your classmates who take at least some of their work seriously, a high proportion feel that Harvard's main justification is to be "the college for writers." The teachers who arouse really passionate feelings, pro and con, are the ones that slave over your compositions or crack the whip over those that do—Dean Briggs in English 5, Copey in English 12, the otherwise forgotten Lewis E. Gates (briefly assisted by William Vaughn Moody) in English 22, George Pierce Baker in English 47, the unique Drama Workshop where you write, produce, and act your own plays. Some of these courses have severely limited enrollments, and you despair of getting in, but somebody has to win the draw. Copey, an assiduous self-publicizer, is better known in the outside world than Briggs, but the best Harvard writers prefer Briggs by a landslide (with a scatter-ing of votes for Gates—Gertrude Stein took English 22, with Moody grading her themes, and so did Frank Norris, who conceived the germ of three of his novels as daily exercises for this course and dedicated *McTeague* to Gates). Those who either don't take Copey's course, or don't take to it, include Van Wyck Brooks, T. S. Eliot, Conrad Aiken, John Dos Passos, and John P. Marquand. It is really only the budding journalists that admire Copey—but Walter Lippmann and John Reed are among them. It doesn't matter. If you amount to anything as a writer, nothing will persuade Copey that you didn't take his course and didn't like him. George Pierce Baker's 47 Workshop attracts all the aspiring playwrights, but as luck would have it, only two are going to be remembered in the history of the drama—T. S. Eliot and Eugene O'Neill (special student 1914–1915).

This, then, was Harvard in what is traditionally regarded as its golden age. Was there any prevalent tone or animus in the instruction in Eliot's time marking it off from other phases in Harvard's history? With the caution that no university is ever of a single piece, there was a remarkably candid embrace of advocacy on the part of many leading professors—in fact, the ones who were most popular. They were trying, more or less blatantly, to make converts to their own view of the world, seen as an instrumentality for giving direction to a student's entire life and defining his relationship to society. No doubt it was partly for this reason, as well as to allay any public apprehensions about the nakedness of their advocacy, that there was a surprising amount of recourse to adversary proceedings in the curriculum. The Democrat Henry Adams tried to create a foil for himself in the Republican Henry Cabot Lodge, and in later years Albert Bushnell Hart and Edward Channing were perceived, more subtly, as foils. The antithetical twins of the Philosophy Department, James and Royce, deliberately traded courses. Palmer filled in for Royce on the mutually acceptable understanding that he would do his best to root up "Royce's tender seedlings." But the point of these tremendously liberal proceedings was to legitimize advocacy. In Santayana's graphic metaphor, his colleagues in the Philosophy Department were glad to stock all kinds of shoes in their common shop window; but the object was to fit your own customer with the right shoes, all the better for letting him satisfy himself that the others wouldn't do.

..........

—Bernard Bailyn and others, *Glimpses of the Harvard Past* (Cambridge: Harvard University Press, 1986), pp. 83–84, 88–90

## The Camera Eye (20)

*A cautionary tale derived from the Lawrence, Massachusetts, textile strike of 1912, when the streetcar workers struck in sympathy with the mill workers. A Harvard student, playing at strikebreaking, participates in the high-stakes "game" of class conflict and loses.*

when the streetcarmen went out on strike in Lawrence in sympathy with what the hell they were a lot of wops anyway bohunks hunkies that didn't wash their necks ate garlic with squalling brats and fat oily wives the damn dagoes they put up a notice for volunteers good clean young

to man the streetcars and show the foreign agitators this was still a white man's

well this fellow lived in Matthews and he'd always wanted to be a streetcar conductor     they said Mr. Grover had been a streetcar conductor in Albany and drank and was seen on the street with floosies

well this fellow lived in Matthews and he went over to Lawrence with his roommate and they reported in Lawrence and people yelled at them Blacklegs Scabs but those that weren't wops were muckers a low element they liked each other a lot this fellow did and his roommate and he got up on the platform and twirled the bright brass handle and clanged the bell

it was in the carbarn     his roommate was fiddling with something between the bumpers and this fellow twirled the shiny brass handle and the car started and he ran down his roommate and his head was mashed just like that between the bumpers and killed him dead just like that right there in the carbarn and now the fellow's got to face his roommate's folks

*—The 42nd Parallel,* pp. 214–215

### The Camera Eye (25)

*The two worlds of Harvard are depicted: inside, the life of high culture, proper behavior, and valuable contacts; outside, that of "the streetcarwheels screech," a world of ugliness and violence but nevertheless the desirable "real" world.*

those spring nights the streetcarwheels screech grinding in a rattle of loose trucks round the curved tracks of Harvard Square dust hangs in the powdery arclight glare allnight till dawn can't sleep

haven't got the nerve to break out of the bell-glass

four years under the ethercone breathe deep gently now that's the way be a good boy one two three four five six get A's in some courses but don't

be a grind be interested in literature but remain a gentleman don't be seen with Jews or socialists

and all the pleasant contacts will be useful in Later Life say hello pleasantly to everybody crossing the yard

sit looking out into the twilight of the pleasantest four years of your life

grow cold with culture like a cup of tea forgotten between an incenseburner and a volume of Oscar Wilde cold and not strong like a claret lemonade drunk at a Pop Concert in Symphony Hall

four years I didn't know you could do what you Michaelangelo wanted to say

Marx

to all

the professors with a small Swift break all the Greenoughs in the shooting gallery

but tossed with eyes smarting all the spring night reading *The Tragical History of Doctor Faustus* and went mad listening to the streetcarwheels screech grinding in a rattle of loose trucks round Harvard Square and the trains crying across the saltmarshes and the rumbling siren of a steamboat leaving dock and the blue peter flying and millworkers marching with a red brass band through the streets of Lawrence Massachusetts

it was like the Magdeburg spheres the pressure outside sustained the vacuum within

and I hadn't the nerve

to jump up and walk out of doors and tell them all to go to take a flying

Rimbaud

at the moon

*—The 42nd Parallel,* pp. 262–263

### The Camera Eye (26)

*Dos Passos portrays the volatile world of New York radical political activism in early 1917.*

the garden was crowded and outside Madison Square was full of cops that made everybody move on and the bombsquad all turned out

we couldn't get a seat so we ran up the stairs to the top gallery and looked down through the blue air at the faces thick as gravel and above them on the speakers' stand tiny black figures and a man was speaking and whenever he said war there were hisses and whenever he said Russia there was clapping on account of the revolution I didn't know who was speaking somebody said Max Eastman and somebody said another guy but we clapped and yelled for the revolution and hissed for Morgan and

*Emma Goldman (1869–1940), the anarchist writer and lecturer, addressing an outdoor meeting. Arrested more than one hundred times between 1908 and 1911, Goldman was deported from the United States in 1919 (Bettman Archive).*

the capitalist war and there was a dick looking into our faces as if he was trying to remember them

then we went to hear Emma Goldman at the Bronx Casino but the meeting was forbidden and the streets around were very crowded and there were moving vans moving through the crowd and they said the moving vans were full of cops with machineguns and there were little policedepartment Fords with searchlights and they charged the crowds with the Fords and the searchlights every-body talked machineguns revolution civil liberty freedom of speech but occasionally somebody got into the way of a cop and was beaten up and shoved into a patrol wagon and the cops were scared and they said they were calling out the fire department to disperse the crowd and everybody said it was an

outrage and what about Washington and Jefferson and Patrick Henry?

afterwards we went to the Brevoort it was much nicer everybody who was anybody was there and there was Emma Goldman eating frankfurters and sauerkraut and everybody looked at Emma Goldman and at everybody else that was anybody and everybody was for peace and the coöperative commonwealth and the Russian revolution and we talked about red flags and barricades and suitable posts for machineguns

and we had several drinks and welsh rabbits and paid our bill and went home, and opened the door with a latchkey and put on pajamas and went to bed and it was comfortable in bed

*–The 42nd Parallel,* pp. 301–302

# WORLD WAR I

*Dos Passos experienced the war in three phases: as a member of the Norton-Harjes volunteer ambulance corps at Verdun during August 1917; in Italy, on the northern front, as a member of an American Red Cross ambulance unit from November 1917 to June 1918; and as an enlisted man in the United States Army from August 1918 to July 1919, with service in France from late November 1918 (after the end of the war). All three of these phases find their way into various portions of U.S.A., but Dos Passos's consciousness was most intensely seared by his initial personal experience of modern mechanized slaughter at Verdun. The impact of this experience is reflected in his bitter and angry letters of the period, in the Camera Eye passages devoted to it, and in the repetitive presence of several of its most poignant moments in his later work. Most of all, Dos Passos's experience of Verdun constituted his loss of innocence; society, he now fully realized, could organize itself into an efficient device for killing the powerless individual.*

## The Ambulance Corps
Arlen J. Hansen

*Volunteer service in the French ambulance corps attracted many young men in the period before America's entrance into the war. Often, as with Dos Passos, joining the ambulance service provided an opportunity to see the war without compromising one's pacifist beliefs.*

When the German army invaded Belgium on August 4, 1914, the ambulance corps of the French army consisted of horse-drawn wagons designed for the Franco-Prussian War of 1870–1871. At the time, the French had only two sections of motorized ambulances, with twenty cars in each section, although the superiority of motorized ambulances was self-evident. From the very beginning, the French army faced two problems regarding their ambulance service: getting their hands on cars (automobile production was, understandably, a low priority in Europe) and finding qualified drivers (able-bodied men were needed in the trenches).

A potential resolution of this dilemma lay in the United States. American manufacturers, who were already turning out Packards, Cadillacs, and Fords at an impressive rate, were always on the lookout for new markets. Moreover, hundreds, if not thousands, of American boys had been caught up in the automobile craze and loved to get behind a steering wheel and drive—anything, anywhere. With the Allies' blessing, young Americans eagerly began volunteering for ambulance duty in Europe almost immediately after war broke out. They even offered to bring their own cars.

*Vehicles of the Norton-Harjes Ambulance Service in France (Harvard University Library)*

*Poster for a 1916 propaganda movie (courtesy of the William L. Foley Collection)*

Initially, the majority of the volunteers came from Ivy League universities and Eastern prep schools. According to the American Field Service *Bulletin* of 8 December 1917, 348 volunteers had joined the American Field Service from Harvard; 202 from Yale; 187 from Princeton; 122 from Cornell; 70 from California; and 58 from Stanford. Columbia, MIT, and Penn provided the American Field Service over 40 volunteers; Chicago, Amherst, Michigan, Williams, Syracuse, Wisconsin, Washington (St. Louis), and Illinois sent more than 30. In addition, four of the very first drivers came from St. Paul's School in Concord, New Hampshire; and Phillips Academy, Andover, sent an entire section. There were also several hundred young men with similar backgrounds who drove for the Norton-Harjes sections (such as John Dos Passos and E. E. Cummings) or for the American Red Cross in Italy in 1918 (Julien Green and Ernest Hemingway). In addition to succumbing to the romantic dream of driving a motorized ambulance in glorious battle, many of these young men had been to Europe on personal grand tours, some had friends or relatives living there, and nearly all feared that the very Anglo-Franco culture they venerated was in jeopardy. For many of them, the act of volunteering tended to be a conservative gesture, a manifestation of their desire to serve and protect the established sociopolitical systems of Republican France and Imperial England. As the war progressed and the press and the public turned against Germany, the volunteer fervor spread from Tory, Ivy League classrooms to white-collar offices and middle-class living rooms throughout the United States.

## AMERICAN RED CROSS

### (SECTIONS SANITAIRES AUX ARMÉES)

H. H. HARJES, Délégué Officiel et Chef des Sections
Sanitaires.

RICHARD NORTON, Administrateur et Directeur
du Service aux Armées.

A. T. KEMP, Administrateur et Directeur du Service
Intérieur.

Téléphone : Passy 43-80.

Bankers : MORGAN, HARJES & Cie.,
31, Boulevard Haussmann.

Accountants : MARWICK, MITCHELL & Co.,
5, Rue Daunou.

7, Rue François Iᵉʳ.

PARIS, le

THE SECRETARY OF STATE

WASHINGTON

June 15, 1917.

To the
Diplomatic and Consular Officers
of the United States of America,
in Great Britain and France.

Gentlemen:

At the instance of the Honorable
James Brown Scott, a former Solicitor of the
Department of State and now Major and Judge
Advocate, U.S.A., it gives me pleasure to in-
troduce to you Mr. John R. Dos Passos, Jr. of
New York City, who is about to proceed to
France for service with the American Motor
Ambulance Corps.

I commend Mr. Dos Passos to your
attention and will appreciate any courtesies
which you may be able to extend to him, consistently with your official duties.

I am, Gentlemen,

Your obedient servant,

Robert Lansing.

The original of this
letter is in the files
of the American Red Cross
5 Rue François Premier, Paris.

*Dos Passos's American Red Cross letter of introduction, which was arranged by James Brown Scott, a friend of his aunt Mary Lamar Gordon, and which he carried with him when he arrived in France in late June 1917 (Albert and Shirley Small Special Collections Library, University of Virginia)*

Ambulance work evolved into two general categories. One was a sort of jitney duty that took place well behind the front lines, and concerned the transfer of wounded soldiers (*blessés*) from one hospital to another, from sanitary trains to urban hospitals, or, in the coastal sectors, to and from hospital ships. Jitney duty normally involved a daily routine with regular hours, seldom taking the drivers closer to the front than the outlying hospitals in small or mid-size cities like Montdidier or Amiens. The various civilian and military hospitals in Paris, and other major medical centers such as Bordeaux or London, had their own ambulances pick up and distribute the *blessés* who arrived on daily sanitary trains. For the first six months of the war, rear-line jitney duty was the only type of work American volunteers were allowed.

The second type of ambulance duty took the drivers as close to the trenches as the roads allowed. Ambulances working the front lines brought wounded men from the advanced dressing stations (*postes de secours*) back to evacuation hospitals, which could usually be reached by car in about forty-five minutes. Typically, a wounded soldier was taken by his comrades directly to a first-aid station set up in the trenches. From there he would be carried by stretcher-bearers (*brancardiers*) through a communication trench leading back to the nearest *poste de secours*. Ideally, the *postes* would be located less than a mile from the first-line trenches in some type of bombproof structure, such as a specially timbered cave or a reinforced farmhouse cellar.

At the *postes de secours,* on-duty physicians cleaned and dressed the wounds, immobilized fractures, or, in the most severe cases, performed emergency amputations. At the beginning of the war, *blessés* were kept at the *postes* until an ambulance could get there, but the American ambulanciers introduced a different practice, one greatly appreciated by the wounded soldiers. "Before the coming of the American cars, ambulances came up to the *postes de secours* only when called," one driver noted, pointing to the change the Americans made. "The American Section established a service on the spot," he said, "so that the waiting was done by the driver of the ambulance and not by the wounded." From the *postes de secours,* the driver took his *blessés* back to a triage hospital (triage is the act of dividing the wounded into three types: those requiring immediate treatment, those that could be sent straight to a rear-line hospital, and those destined for the moribund ward), if there was one, and then on to an evacuation hospital safely beyond the range of enemy guns. There, the injured men were carefully examined, and treated if necessary, before being sent further back by train to a fully equipped urban hospital. As much as historians or military administrators would like to classify, standard-

*Dos Passos in his American Red Cross Ambulance Corps uniform ( from Townsend Ludington, ed.,* The Fourteenth Chronicle, *1973)*

ize, or otherwise sort out the various types of hospitals into evacuation—as opposed to, say, triage—hospitals, the fact is that each medical unit pretty much defined its own function, depending on staff, proximity to the battlefield, and available equipment. For example, the evacuation hospitals particularly close to the front often performed triage, whereas others seldom did.

The great majority of American drivers served in one of three major volunteer groups. The first corps in the field was the Harjes Formation, a small contingent consisting of five Packards. Established by H. Herman Harjes, the senior partner of the Morgan-Harjes Bank in Paris, this ambulance unit was sometimes called the Morgan-Harjes Section. Richard Norton's Anglo-American Volunteer Motor-Ambulance Corps was initially sponsored by the British Red Cross and supported by the London-based St. John Ambulance Association. In 1916, Norton and Harjes combined their efforts under the auspices of the American Red Cross, after which the units became known as the Norton-Harjes, or Red Cross, Sections. The third volunteer group evolved from a field service sent out by the American Military Hospital in Paris (Neuilly). A.

Piatt Andrew organized this scattered assortment of ambulances originally intended to relieve the overworked hospitals north and west of Paris, into an autonomous corps called the American Ambulance Field Service. The AAFS (later abbreviated to simply AFS) eventually became the most complete volunteer operation in France. In addition to overseeing several ambulance and camion (truck) sections, Andrew's organization ran its own repair park, training camp, and stateside recruiting and fund-raising network.

As the war progressed, the American volunteer units grew steadily. Richard Norton's Anglo-American Volunteer Motor-Ambulance Corps consisted of twenty-five ambulances in operation in June of 1915. By November, a month before he and Harjes merged their sections, Norton had sixty cars in the field. By Christmas of 1915, Harjes had expanded his formation to forty ambulances; in addition, he had established a ski team of fifty Norwegian and American volunteers to serve in the Vosges. When the United States declared war on Germany on April 6, 1917, the combined Norton-Harjes operations numbered thirteen sections, with well over one hundred ambulances and two hundred men. Andrew's American Field Service had increased even more dramatically, with thirty complete sections in the field in April.

By the time the U.S. Army took over these organizations in October of 1917, over 3,500 Americans had served as drivers. The story of these gentlemen volunteers—a chronicle of heroics and horrors, manners amid madness—has never been fully told.

—*Gentlemen Volunteers: The Story of the American Ambulance Drivers in the Great War, August 1914 –September 1918* (New York: Arcade, 1996), pp. xiv–xvii

### Dos Passos to Rumsey Marvin, 23 August 1917

*Dos Passos met Rumsey Marvin, who was to be a lifelong friend, in 1915. His letters to Marvin render the horror, bitterness, and anger, combined with an exhilarating excitement, that constituted his response to the killing fields of Verdun.*

[Near Verdun]
*Aug 23 [1917]*

Dear Rummy

I've been meaning to write you again & again—but I've been so vastly bitter that I can produce nothing but gall and wormwood

The war is utter damn nonsense—a vast cancer fed by lies and self seeking malignity on the part of those who don't do the fighting.

Of all the things in this world a government is the thing least worth fighting for.

None of the poor devils whose mangled dirty bodies I take to the hospital in my ambulance really give a damn about any of the aims of this ridiculous affair—They fight because they are too cowardly & too unimaginative not to see which way they ought to turn their guns—

For God's sake, Rummy boy, put this in your pipe and smoke it—everything said & written & thought in America about the war is lies—God! They choke one like poison gas—

I am sitting, my gas mask over my shoulder, my tin helmet on my head—in a poste de secours—(down underground) near a battery of 220s which hit one over the head with their infernal barking as I write.

Apart from the utter bitterness I feel about the whole thing, I've been enjoying my work immensely—We've been for a week in what they say is the hottest sector an ambulance ever worked—All the time—ever since our section of twenty Fiat cars climbed down the long hill into the shot-to-hell valley back of this wood that most of our work is in, we've been under intermittent bombardment.

My first night of work I spent five hours in a poste de secours under poison gas—Of course we had our masks—but I can't imagine a more hellish experience. Every night we get gassed in this sector—which is right behind the two points where the great advance of the 21st of August was made—look it up & you'll see that we were kept busy—we evacuated from between the two *big hills*.

It's remarkable how many shells can explode round you without hitting you.

Our ambulance however is simply peppered with *holes*—how the old bus holds together is more than I can make out—

Do send news of yourself—and think about the war—and don't believe anything people tell you—'ceptin tis me—or anyone else whose really been here.

Incidentally Jane Addams account that the soldiers were fed *rum* & ether before attacks is true. No human being can stand the performance without constant stimulants—

It's queer how much happier I am here in the midst of it than in America, where the air was stinking with lies & hypocritical patriotic gibber—

The only German atrocity I've heard of was that they sent warning to a certain town three days before they dropped aero bombs on it so that the wounded might be evacuated from the hospitals—

Even French atrocities that you hear more of—slitting the throats of prisoners etc.—sort of fade away in reality—We've carried tons of wounded Germans and have found them very pleasant & grateful & given just as much care as the French. The prisoners & their captors laugh & chat & kid each other along at a great rate.

In fact there is less bitterness about the war—*at the front*—than there is over an ordinary Harvard-Yale baseball game.

It's damned remarkable how universally decent people are if you'll only leave them to themselves—

I could write on for hours, but I'm rather sleepy—so I think I'll take a nap among the friendly fleas—

Love
Jack

—Townsend Ludington, ed., *The Fourteenth Chronicle: Letters and Diaries of John Dos Passos* (Boston: Gambit, 1973), pp. 91–93

---

## *The Camera Eye (29)*

*Dos Passos writes of being at Verdun in a new uniform with recently cropped hair, waiting to go up to the front for the first time.*

the raindrops fall one by one out of the horsechestnut tree over the arbor onto the table in the abandoned beer-garden and the puddly gravel and my clipped skull where my fingers move gently forward and back over the fuzzy knobs and hollows

spring and we've just been swimming in the Marne way off somewhere beyond the fat clouds on the horizon they are hammering on a tin roof    in the rain in the spring after a swim in the Marne with that hammering to the north pounding the thought of death into our ears

the winey thought of death stings in the spring blood that throbs in the sunburned neck    up and down the belly under the tight belt    hurries like cognac into the tips of my toes and the lobes of my ears and my fingers stroking the fuzzy closecropped skull

shyly tingling fingers feel out the limits of the hard immortal skull under the flesh    a deathshead and skeleton sits wearing glasses in the arbor under the lucid occasional raindrops inside the new khaki uniform inside my twentyoneyearold body that's been swimming in the Marne in red and whitestriped trunks in Chalons in the spring

—*Nineteen-Nineteen*, pp. 420–421

## *The Camera Eye (30)*

*A respite in a secluded garden to the rear of the front provides one of the enduring images in Dos Passos's memory of the war.*

remembering the grey crooked fingers the thick drip of blood off the canvas the bubbling when the lungcases try to breathe the muddy scraps of flesh you put in the ambulance alive and haul out dead

three of us sit in the dry cement fountain of the little garden with the pink walls in Récicourt

*No        there must be some way        they taught us Land of the free        conscience        Give me liberty or give me        Well they give us death*

sunny afternoon        through the faint aftersick of mustardgas I smell the box the white roses and the white phlox with a crimson eye        three brownandwhite-striped snails hang with infinite delicacy from a honey-sucklebranch overhead        up in the blue a sausageballoon grazes drowsily like a tethered cow there are drunken wasps clinging to the tooripe pears that fall and squash whenever the near guns spew their heavy shells that go off rumbling through the sky

with a whir that makes you remember walking in the woods and starting a woodcock

welltodo country people carefully built the walls and the little backhouse with the cleanscrubbed seat and the quartermoon in the door like the backhouse of an old farm at home    carefully planted the garden and savored the fruit and the flowers and carefully planned this war

*to hell with 'em        Patrick Henry in Khaki submits to shortarm inspection and puts all his pennies in a Liberty Loan        or give me*

arrivés        shrapnel twanging its harps out of tiny powderpuff clouds invites us delicately to glory        we happy watching the careful movements of the snails in the afternoon sunlight talking in low voices about

*La Libre Belgique        The Junius papers        Areopagitica Milton went blind for freedom of speech        If you hit the words Democracy will understand        even the bankers and the clergy-men        I        you        we        must*

*When three men hold together*
*The kingdoms are less by three*

we are happy talking in low voices in the afternoon sunlight about après la guerre that our fingers our blood our lungs our flesh under the dirty khaki feldgrau bleu horizon might go on sweeten grow until we fall from the tree ripe like the tooripe pears        the arrivés know and singing éclats sizzling gas shells theirs is the power and the glory

*or give me death*

—*Nineteen-Nineteen*, pp. 446–447

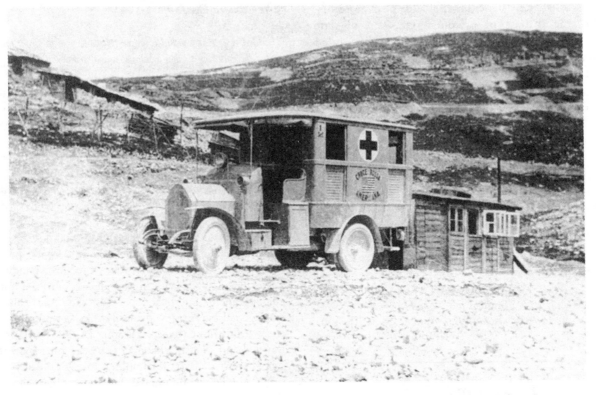

*American Red Cross ambulance in Italy (from Giovanni Cecchin,* Americani Sul Grappa, *1984)*

### The Camera Eye (32)

*The United States has entered the war, and Richard Norton, one of the founders of the Norton-Harjes ambulance unit of "Gentlemen Volunteers," is to hand over its administration to the American Red Cross, whose officers have just arrived overseas. In a moment of farce, a round of German shelling introduces the officers to the war.*

à quatorze heures precisement the Boche diurnally shelled that bridge with their wellknown precision as to time and place     à quatorze heures precisement Dick Norton with his monocle in his eye lined up his section at a little distance from the bridge to turn it over to the American Red Cross

the Red Cross majors looked pudgy and white under their new uniforms in their shined Sam Browne belts in their shined tight leather puttees     so this was overseas

so this was the front     well     well

Dick Norton adjusted his monocle and began to talk about how as gentlemen volunteers he had signed us up and as gentlemen volunteers he bade us farewell     Wham the first arrivé the smell of almonds the

sunday feeling of no traffic on the road not a poilu in sight     Dick Norton adjusted his monocle     the Red Cross majors felt the showering mud     sniffed the lyddite     swift whiff of latrines and of huddled troops

Wham Wham Wham like the Fourth of July the shellfragments sing our ears ring

the bridge is standing and Dick Norton adjusting his monocle is standing talking at length about gentlemen volunteers and ambulance service and la belle France

The empty staffcar is standing

but where are the majors taking over command who were to make a speech in the name of the Red Cross? The slowest and pudgiest and whitest of the majors is still to be seen on his hands and knees with mud all over his puttees crawling into the abris and that's the last we saw of the Red Cross majors

and the last we heard of gentlemen

or volunteers

*—Nineteen-Nineteen, pp. 479–480*

\* \* \*

## Verdun: The Road to the Front

*One of the recurrent images in Dos Passos's memory of the Verdun campaign was that of drunken French soldiers being transported to their near-certain deaths while Dos Passos himself sat drinking wine in the local schoolmaster's garden. The inherent moral absurdity of the moment, of the attempt to maintain conventional human relationships and values in the face of the slaughter of innocents, remained with him for the rest of his life.*

### Dos Passos to Marvin, 29 August 1917

*By the summer of 1917 entire units of French soldiers had mutinied by refusing to advance to the front. One response of their officers was to get the men drunk before an engagement. Dos Passos's awareness of the deep bitterness of the average French soldier toward the war was facilitated by his fluent French.*

*Aug 29th [1917]*

I am sitting in the charming weedgrown garden of a little pink stucco house whose shell only remains & if fortune favors I shall finish this letter. It is a delightful day of little sparkling showers out of thistledown clouds that the autumn-nipped wind speeds at a great rate across the sky. I've not been on duty today–so I've been engaged in washing off to the best of my ability the grime and fleas of two nights in a dugout. Nos amis les boches have been keeping us excessively busy too, dropping large calibre shells into this town; as if the poor little place were not smashed up enough as it was.

We stayed for two weeks with our feet in the mud at Erize la Petite–a puny & ungracious hole–There the only interest was watching the troops, loaded on huge trucks–*camions*–go by towards the front where an attack was prophesied.

For some reason nothing I've seen since has affected me nearly as much as the camion loads of dusty men grinding through the white dust clouds of the road to the front. In the dusk always, in convoys of twenty or more escorted by autos full of officers, they would rumble through the one street of the ruined village.

The first night we were sitting in a tiny garden–the sort of miniature garden that a stroke of a sorcerer's wand would transmute into a Versailles without changing any of its main features–talking to the schoolmaster and his wife; who were feeding us white wine & apologizing for the fact that they had no cake. The garden was just beside the road, and through the railing we began to see them pass. For some reason we were all so excited we could hardly speak– Imagine the tumbrils in the Great Revolution–The men were drunk & desperate, shouting screaming jokes, spilling wine over each other–or else asleep with ghoulish dust-powdered faces. The old schoolmaster kept saying in his precise voice–"Ah, ce n'était pas comme ça en 1916 . . . Il y avait du discipline. Il y avait du discipline."

And his wife–a charming redfaced old lady with a kitten under her arm kept crying out

"Mais que voulez vous? Les pauvres petits, Ils savent qu'ils vont à la mort"–I shall never forget that "ils savent qu'ils vont à la mort"–You see later, after the "victory," we brought them back in our ambulances, or else saw them piled on little two wheeled carts, tangles of bodies with grey crooked fingers and dirty protruding feet, to be trundled to the cemeteries, where they are always busy making their orderly little grey wooden crosses–

Its curious. Do you remember Jane Addams statement that everyone in America jeered at, about the French soldiers–all the soldiers in fact, being doped with rum? Its absolutely true–Of course anyone with imagination could have guessed anyway–(there went a shell–near our cantonment, too) that people couldn't stand the frightful strain of deathly–literally so–dullness without some stimulant–In fact strong tobacco very strong red wine, known to the poilus as Pinard, and a composition of rum & ether–in argot, agnol, are combined with the charming camaraderie you find everywhere–the only things that make life endurable at the front–

Having our headquarters in the much bombarded remnants of a village, we do our business in a fantastic wood, once part of the forests of Argonne–now a "ghoul haunted woodland"; smelling of poison gas, tangled with broken telephone wires, with ripped pieces of camouflage– (the green cheesecloth that everything is swathed in to hide it from aeroplanes), filled in every hollow with guns that crouch and spit like the poisonous toads of the fairytales. In the early dawn after a night's bombardment on both sides it is the weirdest thing imaginable to drive through the woodland roads, with the guns of the batteries tomtomming about you & the whistle of a departing shell & the occasional rattling snort of an arrivée. A great labor it is to get through, too, through the smashed artillery trains, past piles of splintered camions and commissariat wagons. The wood before and since the attack–the victory of August 21st look it up & you'll know where I was–has been one vast battery–a constant succession of ranks of guns hidden in foliage, and dugouts, from which people crawl like gnomes when the firing ceases and to which you scoot when you hear a shell that sounds as if it had your calling card on it–

The thing is that we, on our first service, landed in the hottest sector ambulance ever ambled in. My first night out I was five hours under gas–of course with a mask, or I shouldn't be here to tell the tale–

But the whole performance is such a ridiculous farce. Everyone wants to go home, to get away at any cost from the hell of the front. The French soldiers I talk to all realize the utter uselessness of it all; they know that it is only the greed and stubbornness and sheer stupidity of the allied governments &, if you will, of the German government, that keeps it going at all—Oh but why talk?—its so useless—There is one thing one learns in France today, the resignation of despair—

Still, I'm much happier here, really in it than I've been for an age. People don't hate much at the front; there's no one to hate, except the poor devils across the way, whom they know to be as miserable as themselves. They don't talk hypocritical bosh about the beauty & manliness of war; they feel in their souls that if they weren't cowards they would have ended the thing long ago—by going home, where they want to be. And lastly and best, they don't jabber about atrocities—of course, everyone commits them—though about one story in a million that reaches our blessed Benighted States is true.

But I really must shut up. More later—

Love—

Jack

—Ludington, ed., *The Fourteenth Chronicle*, pp. 96–98

### One Man's Initiation–1917

Dos Passos

*During their period at Verdun, Dos Passos and his Harvard friend Robert Hillyer worked together on a novel called* Seven Times Around the Walls of Jericho. *The novel was to depict the life of a young American, Martin Howe, as he engages the difficulties of the world, culminating in his experience of the war. Hillyer soon dropped out of the project, but Dos Passos continued to work on the novel through his ambulance and army service. In late 1918 he completed the last section, which depicts his autobiographical protagonist at the Verdun front, and this portion was published in London in 1920 as* One Man's Initiation–1917. *The remainder of the novel remains unpublished.*

The schoolmaster's garden was full of late roses and marigolds, all parched and bleached by the thick layer of dust that was over them. Next to the vine-covered trellis that cut the garden off from the road stood a green table and a few cane chairs. The schoolmaster, something charmingly eighteenth-century about the cut of his breeches and the calves of his legs in their thick woolen golf-stockings, led the way, a brown pitcher of wine in his hand. Martin Howe and the black-haired, brown-faced boy from New Orleans who was his car-mate followed him. Then came a grey woman in a pink knitted shawl, carrying a tray with glasses.

"In the Verdunois our wine is not very good," said the schoolmaster, bowing them into chairs. "It is thin and cold like the climate. To your health, gentlemen."

"To France."

"To America."

"And down with the Boches."

In the pale yellow light that came from among the dark clouds that passed over the sky, the wine had the chilly gleam of yellow diamonds.

"Ah, you should have seen that road in 1916," said the schoolmaster, drawing a hand over his watery blue eyes. "That, you know, is the Voie Sacrée, the sacred way that saved Verdun. All day, all day, a double line of camions went up, full of ammunition and ravitaillement and men."

"Oh, the poor boys, we saw so many go up," came the voice, dry as the rustling of the wind in the vine-leaves, of the grey old woman who stood leaning against the schoolmaster's chair, looking out through a gap in the trellis at the rutted road so thick with dust, "and never have we seen one of them come back."

"It was for France."

"But this was a nice village before the war. From Verdun to Bar-le-Duc, the Courrier des Postes used to tell us, there was no such village, so clean and with such fine orchards." The old woman leaned over the schoolmaster's shoulder, joining eagerly in the conversation.

"Even now the fruit is very fine," said Martin.

"But you soldiers, you steal it all," said the old woman, throwing out her arms. "You leave us nothing, nothing."

"We don't begrudge it," said the schoolmaster, "all we have is our country's."

"We shall starve then. . . ."

As she spoke the glasses on the table shook. With a roar of heavy wheels and a grind of gears a camion went by.

"O good God!" The old woman looked out on to the road with terror in her face, blinking her eyes in the thick dust.

Roaring with heavy wheels, grinding with gears, throbbing with motors, camion after camion went by, slowly, stridently. The men packed into the camions had broken through the canvas covers and leaned out, waving their arms and shouting.

"Oh, the poor children," said the old woman, wringing her hands, her voice lost in the roar and the shouting.

"They should not destroy property that way," said the schoolmaster. . . . "Last year it was dreadful. There were mutinies."

Martin sat, his chair tilted back, his hands trembling, staring with compressed lips at the men who jolted by on the strident, throbbing camions. A word formed in his mind: tumbrils.

In some trucks the men were drunk and singing, waving their bidons in the air, shouting at people along the road, crying out all sorts of things: "Get to the front!" "Into the trenches with them!" "Down with the war!" In others they sat quiet, faces corpse-like with dust. Through the gap in the trellis Martin stared at them, noting intelligent faces, beautiful faces, faces brutally gay, miserable faces like those of sobbing drunkards.

At last the convoy passed and the dust settled again on the rutted road.

"Oh, the poor children!" said the old woman. "They know they are going to death."

They tried to hide their agitation. The schoolmaster poured out more wine.

"Yes," said Martin, "There are fine orchards on the hills round here."

"You should be here when the plums are ripe," said the schoolmaster.

A tall bearded man, covered with dust to the eyelashes, in the uniform of a commandant, stepped into the garden.

"My dear friends!" He shook hands with the schoolmaster and the old woman and saluted the two Americans. "I could not pass without stopping a moment. We are going up to an attack. We have the honour to take the lead."

"You will have a glass of wine, won't you?"

"With great pleasure."

"Julie, fetch a bottle, you know which. . . . How is the morale?"

"Perfect."

"I thought they looked a little discontented."

"No. . . . It's always like that. . . . They were yelling at some gendarmes. If they strung up a couple it would serve them right, dirty beasts."

"You soldiers are all one against the gendarmes."

"Yes. We fight the enemy but we hate the gendarmes." The commandant rubbed his hands, drank his wine and laughed.

"Hah! There's the next convoy. I must go."

"Good luck."

The commandant shrugged his shoulders, clicked his heels together at the garden gate, saluted, smiling, and was gone.

Again the village street was full of the grinding roar and throb of camions, full of a frenzy of wheels and drunken shouting.

"Give us a drink, you."

"We're the train de luxe, we are."

"Down with the war!"

And the old grey woman wrung her hands and said:

"Oh, the poor children, they know they are going to death!"

—*One Man's Initiation—1917* (London: Allen & Unwin, 1920), pp. 26–30

## From *The Best Times: An Informal Memoir*
Dos Passos

*In his autobiography Dos Passos recalls the same event as that fictionalized in* One Man's Initiation—1917. *Robert and Van are Robert Hillyer and Frederick Van der Arend, two of his ambulance-corps friends.*

The latrine rumors were confirmed. The Verdun offensive was on. The same letter told of the three of us sitting in a tiny garden back of a buttressed wall that overlooked the through street in a village and seeing the attacking corps go through. This was the *Voie Sacrée.*

We had struck up an acquaintance with the local schoolmaster on a little stream to which Robert and I had retired in a moment of leisure to sail paper boats. I called mine *le bateau ivre:* I was saturated with Rimbaud that week and never went anywhere without a volume of his verse in my pocket. The schoolmaster was quietly fishing for trout. He showed us how to find helgramites under the stones. The incongruity of finding a man troutfishing under shellfire carried us away. We decided he was a natural philosopher, a Jean-Jacques Rousseau *de nos jours.* When he invited us to drink *un verre de vin blanc* with him we eagerly accepted.

The same evening, with our faces freshwashed and our hair plastered down, Van and Robert and I knocked on his door. He ushered us into his small terraced garden that hung over the street. His wife was charming, a pale woman with huge shining black eyes. She had in her arms a winsome little cat, with eyes, oddly enough, of a luminous brown. We sat at a round marble table perched above the street among the roses and balsams.

We had hardly taken our first sip of wine before the truck convoys began rumbling through. Our faces were on a level with the faces of the men joggling through the narrow street. They were piled thick in the gray jolting trucks. Some were drunk and shouting and waving their canteens. Others stood silent and sullen. Many of them shook their fists at the gendarmes in the sentry box at the corner. "*Mort aux vaches,*" they kept yelling. All looked as ghastly as dead men in their shroud of white dust. The convoy seemed endless. Gears grinding, the trucks roared past. They churned up the dust in the narrow street. The dust coated our table and our hair and the flowers in the little garden. We sat there trying to make polite French conversation while anguish clutched at our throats.

Through the metallic clatter and the clamor of drunken voices we could hear our hosts whispering to each other. "It wasn't like that in '16," the schoolmaster would groan. I began to think of him as the schoolmaster of "La Dernière Classe," Daudet's story that brought such patriotic tears to the eyes of generations of French schoolchildren. "Poor little devils," his wife would answer, "they know they are going to their death." Then she would hug

*Dos Passos's Verdun citation, which he received for ambulance duty in the Allied offensive of August 1917 to retake land captured by the Germans in the Battle of Verdun the previous year (Albert and Shirley Small Special Collections Library, University of Virginia)*

*Dos Passos (third from left, wearing eyeglasses) with American Red Cross unit under review, Milan, December 1917*
*(from Giovanni Cecchin,* Americani Sul Grappa, *1984)*

the cat convulsively to her and kiss it all over its face. "It was not like that in '16. There's no discipline any more. Look, they are tearing the canvas covers off the trucks."

They said the same things over and over again. The trucks kept roaring past. There were beardless boys and sturdy youths and middleaged men with mustaches. Faces merged into a blur. All we could see in the dim light was the desperation in their eyes. We tried to say comforting things to the schoolmaster and his wife, but our mouths were stopped with dust. With a "Merci, bonsoir," we slunk away. We felt as if we had been whipped. The memory obsessed me for years.

–*The Best Times: An Informal Memoir* (New York: New American Library, 1966), pp. 52–53

### Dos Passos to José Giner Pantoja

*Dos Passos met José Giner Pantoja, a young Spaniard, in late 1916 while studying architecture in Madrid. This letter to Giner, which fell into the hands of Red Cross authorities, led to Dos Passos's dismissal from the ambulance corps and his return to America.*

[Bassano, Italy, February–March 1918]

My Dear Friend,

Forgive me for another badly and hastily written letter. Again I would rather have written in Spanish, but the idea puts me in a blue funk because I love your beautiful language so much it would be very painful to make it read like Italian. Having been reading and speaking Italian all the time I've been here, I know that if I had written in Spanish I would have succeeded only in producing a miserable mélange.

Here, in this quiet place, where one has so much time, while waiting in the rain, in the yards of hospitals, or in ambulances smelling of carbolic, I think often of you and the lovely plains of Castile. From a distance war must seem a little theoretical, but here, or anywhere at the front, I assure you it is a wholly different matter. It is boredom, slavery to all the military stupidities, the most fascinating misery, the need for warmth, bread, and cleanliness. I assure you there is nothing beautiful about modern war. I have lived in it for a year now, and many illusions have crossed the river Styx. It is nothing but an enormous, tragic digression in the lives of these people.

Rather it is for you people, you who inhabit those countries that are above the battle, to assume the struggle for progress on behalf of this wretched and tormented civilization of ours. For all the things of the mind, for art, and for everything that is needed in the world, war—I mean modern war—is death. And beyond those things, what is there on earth that is worth anything? No, it's up to you, who can make revolutions either quietly or violently, who are trying vainly, perhaps, to evolve a purpose for the life of our times, it is up to you to safeguard all the finest human things, while the rest of us struggle on brutally with suicidal madness. Why? For lies, even for some truths, for greedy nations in a world drunk on commercialism.

I am very much afraid that you Spaniards are a little idealistic about this evil European world and about America, in . . . perhaps, but Great God, to what end? Everywhere it seems to me there is nothing, either for the rich or the poor, but slavery; to industry, to money, to the mammon of business, the great God of our times. And where in all that are the good things to be found? The things that give life an added dimension, that go beyond the struggle to fill the belly, for mere existence.

It seems to me that only in your Spain and in Russia is the conquest not quite complete—it is in part because of that I love Spain so much.

And my own poor country—it seems to me that with the war, with the military service law, liberty there is extinguished for a long time to come, and the day of triumph for plutocracy has arrived.

In this connection, one of my best friends is now in Madrid—Arthur McComb—who, being an unshakable anti-militarist, has had to leave the United States and will stay in Spain, I think, for a long time. He is an intelligent fellow and very likable, and I have taken the liberty of telling him to go to see you, because I knew that there was no one in Spain who could give him as much information as you. Excuse my informality, which you may credit to American rudeness. Besides, I have never been able to get used to convention, even in America.

I would be extremely pleased to get one of your charming letters. My address is care of Consolato Americano, C.R.A. Sezione I. Au revoir, your very good friend.

—Ludington, ed., *The Fourteenth Chronicle*, pp. 152–153

## From Dos Passos's Diary

*The ideas and language of this diary passage—of Western (and American) industrial and militaristic might forming itself into a machine-like organization for the suppression of individual freedom—constitute one of Dos Passos's principal themes in his depiction of the war in his fiction from* One Man's Initiation–1917 *through* Three Soldiers *(1921) to* Nineteen-Nineteen.

[Italy]
*April 20th* [1918]
Last night I had an awfully interesting talk with Charley A. and Rieser and Tom Wharton about the war and pacifism. C. A. it came out is a believer in the individual, put himself down as a conscientious objector on the draft—He's going—he says—to refuse to serve.

Talk with Tom Wharton & Carolt and even Rieser, who although a violent anti German and in favor of the war in every way and in suppressing antiwar opinion during the war—is sincerely down on militarism—for some reason I suddenly became tremendously hopeful—Here were three people—Americans out of totally different environments all absolutely determinedly against the machine that has been crushing us all—Even if we are slaves we are unwilling ones. When you think of these people and our friends—and of Baldwin and that sort of man, who believes but who is carried along in the swirl out of our natural American easygoingness. Oh I cant write straight this morning, but I am anxious to get this down—

God if I could see clearly what to do—

I suppose one should do something conspicuous if possible—I hate conspicuousness—We have so much to do—it will take generations to leaven the great stupid mass of America—we are in the position of the first Russian revolutionists who struggled and died in despair and sordidness—we have no chance of success, but we must struggle—live—I dont know why—I hardly believe in it—yet

The world as it is at present hardening into organization seems to be a worse place for humanity than it has almost ever been before—too—it has possibilities—It is better to be dead than living

Now is the time when the effort has got to come—perhaps out of the great stupid mass of America—from under the crushing weight of industry—there must be so many of us—yet so few—

Perhaps being in France will teach some of the people

—Ludington, ed., *The Fourteenth Chronicle*, pp. 179–180

*Dos Passos in 1924*

## THE RADICAL YEARS

Dos Passos's engagement with the Left—that is, the Communist Party as well as the many social and literary groups it dominated—occurred roughly from the mid 1920s to mid 1930s, the period when he was conceiving and writing U.S.A. More precisely, his participation in the activities of the Left began in May and June 1926, when he became a member of the New Masses editorial board, visited the site of the Passaic, New Jersey, textile strike and wrote a brief essay about it, and went to Boston to interview the jailed Bartolomeo Vanzetti. Dos Passos's political involvement intensified over the next four or five years following the executions of Nicola Sacco and Vanzetti in 1927 and, after 1929, the collapse of the economy into the misery of the Depression.

Dos Passos, however, as commentators have unanimously agreed and he himself claimed, was never a communist. Although he found that the party and its many activities reflected his own effort to achieve greater social justice, he did not accept Marxist dogma, instinctively resisted the party's demand for uniformity of belief, and, as the 1930s advanced, found its Stalinist bullying mentality increasingly repugnant. By early 1934 Dos Passos was becoming more and more openly critical of the Communist Party and its methods, foretelling the complete divorce from the Left that was to come in 1937 with his bitter rejection of the Stalinist presence in the Spanish Civil War.

Given the range and depth of Dos Passos's participation in the social and political turmoil of the late 1920s and early 1930s, it is no wonder that this phase of his life, and indeed that of the nation as a whole, enters fully into U.S.A. Not only are such specific events as the Passaic strike, the Sacco and Vanzetti case, and the Harlan County, Kentucky, miners' strike portrayed in Camera Eye episodes and in several of the narratives, but the entire novel is also in a sense constructed on the foundation of the issues raised by the social crises of the time. What kind of nation has America become, Dos Passos asks in the trilogy, when so many lives are wasted or misspent, and how can Americans return to the effort to fulfill their ideal conception of themselves as a nation?

## The Move toward a Radical Stance

As Camera Eye (45) and (46) suggest, Dos Passos had great difficulty in the mid 1920s defining his role as an American writer. The scintillating Greenwich Village world in which he lived on and off during this period had the attraction of permitting personal freedom but was intellectually and politically shallow. At the same time, an activist political role ("a speech urging action in a crowded hall") filled him with doubts about his own beliefs and the motives of his fellow radicals. He still felt the need, however, to aid in the recovery of "our storybook democracy," and in 1926 Dos Passos made several significant gestures in that direction when he became a member of the executive board of the decidedly left-wing journal the New Masses and reported sympathetically on a strike of textile workers at Passaic, New Jersey. But even these acts took place in the context of self-doubt and uncertainty: Dos Passos is still the peeler of the "speculative onion of doubt" at the close of Camera Eye (46), and his account of the Passaic strike ironically subverts the intellectualized radicalism of "the people who had come from New York."

### The Camera Eye (45)

A Village cocktail party of the early 1920s; some of the images—the teasing woman, the pinned-on identity—appear to be borrowed from T. S. Eliot's "The Love Song of J. Alfred Prufrock" (1920). Edmund Wilson, in his fictional portrait of Dos Passos as Hugo Bamman in the Greenwich Village novel I Thought of Daisy (1929), noted Bamman's habit of leaving his hat near the door at parties to facilitate a swift exit.

the narrow yellow room teems with talk under the low ceiling and crinkling tendrils of cigarette-smoke twine blue and fade round noses behind ears under the rims of women's hats in arch looks changing arrangements of lips the toss of a bang the wise I-know-it wrinkles round the eyes all scrubbed

*In a frequently reproduced 1925 photograph, Dos Passos poses against a blighted industrial landscape, thereby illustrating both his bourgeois radical character and his working-class métier (Collection of Lucy Dos Passos Coggin).*

stroked clipped scraped with the help of lipstick rouge shavingcream razorblades into a certain pattern that implies

this warmvoiced woman who moves back and forth with a throaty laugh head tossed a little back distributing with teasing looks the parts in the fiveoclock drama

every man his pigeonhole

the personality must be kept carefully adjusted over the face

to facilitate recognition she pins on each of us a badge

today entails tomorrow

Thank you but why me? Inhibited? Indeed goodby

the old brown hat flopped faithful on the chair beside the door successfully snatched

outside the clinking cocktail voices fade

even in this elderly brick dwellinghouse made over with green paint orange candles a little tinted calcimine into

Greenwich Village

the stairs go up and down

lead through a hallway ranked with bells names evoking lives tangles unclassified

into the rainy twoway street where cabs slither slushing footsteps plunk slant lights shimmer on the curve of a wet cheek a pair of fresh-colored lips a weatherlined neck a gnarled grimed hand an old man's bloodshot eye

street twoway to the corner of the roaring avenue where in the lilt of the rain and the din the four directions

(the salty in all of us ocean the protoplasm throbbing through cells growing dividing sprouting into the billion diverse not yet labeled not yet named

always they slip through the fingers

the changeable the multitudinous lives)

box dizzingly the compass

—*The Big Money*, pp. 872–873

### The *New Masses* and the 1926 Passaic Strike
Melvin Landsberg

*Although the* New Masses *later became a Communist Party organ, it was founded in 1926 with the support of radicals of various stripes to provide a vehicle of expression not available elsewhere. The Passaic strike became one of its first great causes. Because Passaic was within easy reach of Manhattan and because the issues of the strike seemed to be clear-cut—a group of manufacturers, aided by local authorities, was seeking not only to cut the wages of already underpaid workers but also to deny them their civil rights—the strike attracted the active engagement of an unusually large number of New York writers, artists, and intellectuals.*

The establishment of *New Masses* in 1926 helped to focus Dos Passos' attention upon questions of labor organization and leftist ideology. Besides giving him a convenient vehicle for publishing on these subjects, it probably put him into more intimate contact than he had known before with a large and varied group of radicals. At the end of 1922 the editors of the *Liberator* turned the magazine over to the Workers (Communist) party, thus ending a decade of independence for the *Masses* and the *Liberator*. Two years later the career of the *Liberator* ended, when the periodical was combined with two others to become an official Communist party organ edited by Earl Browder.[1] After the demise of the *Liberator*, Joseph Freeman and Michael Gold discussed establishing a "broad united front" of liberal and radical writers and artists around a new *Masses*. For money, they turned to Scott Nearing and Roger Baldwin, both of whom were influential in the American Fund for Public Service, to which "a Yan-

*Dos Passos's close friends John Howard Lawson and Edmund Wilson, who
were among the contributing editors for* New Masses

kee philosophical anarchist" Charles Garland had given his million dollar inheritance. The Garland fund subsequently gave Freeman $27,000 with which to support the new periodical for three years, on the conditions that *New Masses* be edited by him and not be controlled in any way by the Communist party.[2]

When, after considerable delay, *New Masses* appeared in 1926, it listed as its editors Egmont Arens, Joseph Freeman, Hugo Gellert, Michael Gold, James Rorty, and John Sloan. Dos Passos and Paxton Hibben were among the sixteen members of the executive board. It was perfectly natural, writes Joseph Freeman, for Dos Passos to join in founding the periodical: "He and Edmund Wilson had been in Greenwich Village, they had known the Masses group, they were new writers, they sympathized with labor and radicalism. Dos Passos . . . was sympathetic to the Russian Revolution and to American reform. Besides, we all met socially, we were friends, this was our community. So when we sent out letters for a meeting to found the N. M., Dos got one and showed up."[3]

Dos Passos' close friends Edmund Wilson and John Howard Lawson were among the contributing editors, and some of the others were Sherwood Anderson, Van Wyck Brooks, Stuart Chase, Floyd Dell, Max Eastman, Waldo Frank, Arturo Giovan-

nitti, Susan Glaspell, Lewis Mumford, Eugene O'Neill, Elmer Rice, Carl Sandburg, Upton Sinclair, Genevieve Taggard, Louis Untermeyer, Mary Heaton Vorse, and Art Young.[4]

Freeman says that of the fifty-six writers and artists involved in the venture, only two were members of the Communist party and fewer than a dozen were sympathizers with it.[5] Dos Passos agrees in substance, writing that most of the people concerned "could hardly have been called Marxists." "It's amusing to remember," he commented in 1956, "that in those carefree days a Communist party-member and an anarcho-syndicalist and even some sad dog of a capitalist who believed in laissez faire could sit at the same table and drink beer together and lay their thoughts on the line. It wasn't that you respected the other fellow's opinions exactly, but you admitted his right to remain alive."[6]

At the full editorial meetings, there were sharp political debates. One exchange of opinion, which found its way into print, establishes Dos Passos' views at the time. His attitude toward Bolshevik certainties was as cold as it had been in his "The Caucasus Under the Soviets" (1922). Michael Gold had called him a "bourgeois intellectual," and Dos Passos replied in an article "The New Masses I'd Like." As technology grew in America, he wrote, general ideals increasingly tended to restrict themselves "to Karl Marx, the first chapter of Genesis and the hazy scientific mysticism of the Sunday supplements." He objected to dogma, particularly the type imported from abroad. Since Columbus' time, he wrote, imported systems had been the curse of the continent. If the writers of *New Masses* explored the minds of the working class without preconceptions, they might be able to formulate a theory for action; if they approached the task with Marxist preconceptions, they would suffer the fate of finding exactly what they had been looking for.[7]

*New Masses* came into existence during the Passaic textile workers' strike of 1926, a long, momentous battle which gave the editorial board its first cause. The Communist party was responsible for initiating the strike. One of the party's organizers informed a Communist leader, Benjamin Gitlow, that Botany Mills of Passaic, New Jersey, had announced a ten per cent wage cut, to begin in October 1925, and Gitlow placed Albert Weisbord, a graduate of the City College of New York and Harvard Law School, in charge of organizing a strike. Gitlow estimates that seventeen thousand workers, chiefly foreign-born and unskilled, walked out as the strike spread through Passaic and its environs.[8] Since some of the mills did not shut down completely and many of the skilled workers remained on the job, the strikers undertook mass picketing; in thousands they marched past the mills, crossing the bridges between towns, singing their strike songs.

The United Front Textile Committee, the union in charge of the strike, claiming that the workers were receiving between $10 and $19 a week, demanded higher pay, shorter hours, and recognition of the union. The employers rejected all the union's demands, replying that average pay was between $15 and $23 a week, that business conditions made a wage cut necessary, and that the strike was caused by outside agitators. Asserting that Weisbord was a Communist, the employers refused to see a committee headed by him.

Until March 2, 1926, the strike was fairly peaceful. On that day the Passaic police harassed, and finally dispersed with tear gas and fire hoses, strikers who had emerged from a meeting hall a block from the Botany plant and were straggling peacefully past the mill. The next day small boys throwing stones and ice angered the Clifton police, who thereupon charged the strikers and their sympathizers on the dividing line between Clifton and Passaic, chased newspaper photographers intent on taking pictures of the scene, and beat reporters.

A crisis occurred when Forstmann and Huffmann announced on April 8 that their mill would open in a few days, and the strikers planned a strong picket line. Police and deputy sheriffs subsequently halted pickets in Garfield and ordered them to walk away from the Forstmann and Huffmann mills. "The leaders refused," reported the *New York Times,* "and Sheriff Nimmo [of Bergen County] read the Riot act, a statute adopted after the Civil War, ordering the dispersal of a crowd within an hour." The police did not wait an hour. "In a few minutes half a dozen arrests were made." Justice of the Peace Louis Hargreaves, who had previously fixed pickets' bail at $500, raised it in some instances to $10,000.[9] He refused to allow stenographic notes to be made of the court's proceedings, claiming he was presiding over not a court of law but a court of martial law.

Holding that a reading of the Riot Act imposed martial law, the Garfield police banned all gatherings, even those in private halls and on private grounds. Then the sheriff of Passaic County announced that he was preparing a similar ban. The American Civil Liberties Union and the League for Industrial Democracy denied that the Riot Act established martial law. On April 14 Norman Thomas tested the Riot Act by speaking from a tree stump on ground rented by the League for Industrial Democracy. He was arrested, denied counsel, and arraigned secretly before Judge Hargreaves, who set bail at $10,000. Later Sheriff Nimmo announced that he would not permit the Reverend John Haynes Holmes to speak in the strike area; Holmes, pastor of the Community Church in New York, had planned to speak under the auspices of the American Civil Liberties Union. By mid-April it seemed the strike must collapse, for Weisbord and most of the ostensible leaders were in jail. But the strikers fought with some success in the courts, and the strike continued.[10]

That April Dos Passos journeyed to the strike area with a group of intellectuals and afterward published an account of the event in *New Masses.* With irony he described the visitors' talking of the Bill of Rights as, clad in warm overcoats, they rode in taxicabs and shiny sedans toward "the place where the meeting was going to be forbidden." The deputies politely held the doors of the sedans open, and the visitors retreated past impoverished strikers and back to New York; only one man was arrested.[11]

*—Dos Passos' Path to U. S. A.: A Political Biography, 1912–1936 (Boulder: Colorado Associated University Press, 1972), pp. 125–131*

*Striking Passaic, New Jersey, textile workers, February 1926 (United Press International)*

## Notes

1. Joseph Freeman, *An American Testament* (New York: Farrar & Rinehart, 1936), pp. 308–310; M. L. interview with Joseph Freeman, 5 June 1956; Robert Minor, "Growth," *Liberator*, 7 (October 1924): 6.

2. Freeman, *An American Testament*, pp. 338–339; letter from Freeman to M. L., 17 May 1956.

3. Letter from Freeman to M. L., 17 May 1956. See Cowley, *Exile's Return*, p. 223.

4. *New Masses*, 1 (May 1926): 3.

5. Freeman, *An American Testament*, p. 379.

6. John Dos Passos, *The Theme Is Freedom* (New York: Dodd, Mead, 1956), p. 7.

7. Dos Passos, "The New Masses I'd Like," *New Masses*, 1 (June 1926): 20. The debates at the editorial meetings are referred to in Freeman, *An American Testament*, p. 379.

8. Benjamin Gitlow, *I Confess* (New York: E. P. Dutton, 1940), pp. 363–366.

9. *New York Times*, 18 April 1926, sec. 1, p. 24.

10. Ibid., 1926: 14 April, p. 25; 15 April, p. 1; 18 April, sec. 1, p. 24; 30 April, p. 7; 1 May, p. 19.

11. Dos Passos, "300 N.Y. Agitators Reach Passaic," *New Masses*, 1 (June 1926): 8; Freeman, *An American Testament*, p. 386.

## *The Camera Eye (46)*

*The "onion of doubt": Dos Passos presents New York as the site of political activism on the one hand and personal gratification on the other. Which is he to choose, when in fact both are unsatisfactory?*

walk the streets and walk the streets inquiring of Coca Cola signs Lucky Strike ads pricetags in storewindows scraps of overheard conversations stray tatters of newsprint yesterday's headlines sticking out of ashcans

for a set of figures a formula of action an address you don't quite know you've forgotten the number the street may be in Brooklyn a train leaving for somewhere a steamboat whistle stabbing your ears a job chalked up in front of an agency

to do to make there are more lives than walking desperate the streets hurry underdog do   make

a speech urging action in the crowded hall after handclapping the pats and smiles of others on the platform the scrape of chairs the expectant hush the few coughs during the first stuttering attempt to talk straight tough going the snatch for a slogan they are listening and then the easy climb slogan by slogan to applause (if somebody in your head didn't say liar to you and on Union Square that time you leant from a soapbox over faces    avid young opinionated old the middleaged numb with overwork eyes bleared with newspaperreading    trying to tell them the straight dope    make them laugh tell them what they want to hear wave a flag whispers the internal agitator crazy to succeed)

you suddenly falter ashamed flush red break out in sweat    why not tell these men stamping in the wind that we stand on a quicksand?    that doubt is the whetstone of understanding is too hard hurts instead of urging    picket John D. Rockefeller the bastard if the cops knock your blocks off it's all for the advancement of the human race while I go home after a drink and a hot meal and read (with some difficulty in the Loeb Library trot) the epigrams of Martial and ponder the course of history and what leverage might pry the owners loose from power and bring back (I too Walt Whitman) our storybook democracy

and all the time in my pocket that letter from that collegeboy asking me to explain why being right which he admits    the radicals are in their private lives such shits

lie abed underdog (peeling the onion of doubt) with the book unread in your hand and swing on the seesaw maybe after all maybe topdog    make

money    you understood what he meant the old party with the white beard beside the crystal inkpot at the cleared varnished desk in the walnut office in whose voice boomed all the clergymen of childhood and shrilled the hosannahs of the offkey female choirs    All you say is very true but there's such a thing as sales    and I have daughters I'm sure you too will end by thinking differently    make

money in New York (lipstick kissed off the lips of a girl fashionablydressed fragrant at five o'clock in a taxicab careening down Park Avenue when at the end of each crosstown street the west is flaming with gold and white smoke billows from the smokestacks of steamboats leaving port and the sky is lined with greenbacks

the riveters are quiet the trucks of the producers are shoved off into the marginal avenues

winnings sing from every streetcorner

crackle in the ignitions of the cars swish smooth in ballbearings sparkle in the lights going on in the showwindows croak in the klaxons tootle in the horns of imported millionaire shining towncars

dollars are silky in her hair soft in her dress sprout in the elaborately contrived rosepetals that you kiss become pungent and crunchy in the speakeasy dinner sting shrill in the drinks

make loud the girlandmusic show set off the laughing jag in the cabaret swing in the shufflingshuffling orchestra click sharp in the hatcheck girl's goodnight)

if not why not? walking the streets rolling on your bed eyes sting from peeling the speculative onion of doubt if somebody in your head    topdog?    underdog?    didn't (and on Union Square) say liar to you

—*The Big Money*, pp. 892–894

## 300 N.Y. Agitators Reach Passaic
Dos Passos

*The ineffectuality of the "people who had come from New York" in the face of both the physical power of the authorities and the need of the striking workers renders one basis for Dos Passos's doubt in an activist role.*

The people who had come from New York roamed in a desultory group along the broad pavement. We were talking of outrages and the Bill of Rights. The people who had come from New York wore warm overcoats in the sweeping wind, bits of mufflers, and fluffiness of women's blouses fluttered silky in the cold April wind. The people who had come from New York filled up a row of taxicabs, shiny sedans of various makes, nicely upholstered, the shiny sedans started off in a procession towards the place where the meeting was going to be forbidden. Inside we talked in a desultory way of outrages and the Bill of Rights, we, descendants of the Pilgrim Fathers, the Bunker Hill Monument, Gettysburg, the Boston Teaparty.... Know all men by these presents.... On the corners groups of yellowish grey people standing still, square people standing still as chunks of stone, looking nowhere, saying nothing.

At the same place where the meeting was going to be forbidden the people from New York got out of the shiny sedans of various makes. The sheriff was a fat man with a badge like a star off a Christmas tree, the little eyes of a suspicious landlady in a sallow face. The cops were waving their clubs about, limbering up their arms. The cops were redfaced, full of food, the cops felt fine. The special deputies had restless eyes, they were stocky young men crammed with pop and ideals, overgrown boy-scouts; they were on the right side and they knew it. Still the shiny new double-barrelled riot guns made them nervous. They didn't know which shoulder to keep their guns on. The people who had come from New York stood first on one foot then on the other.

Don't shoot till you see the whites of their eyes....

All right move 'em along, said the sheriff. The cops advanced, the special deputies politely held open the doors of the shiny sedans. The people who had come from New York climbed back into the shiny sedans of various makes and drove away except for one man who got picked up. The procession of taxis started back the way it had come, down empty streets protected by deputies with shiny new riot guns, past endless facades of deserted mills, past brick tenements with ill-painted stoops, past groups of squat square women with yellow grey faces, groups of men and boys standing still, saying nothing, looking nowhere, square hands hanging at their sides, people square and still, chunks of yellowgrey stone at the edge of a quarry, idle, waiting, on strike.

—*New Masses*, 1 ( June 1926): 8

\*\*\*

*Bartolomeo Vanzetti and Nicola Sacco after three years of imprisonment ( from Marion Denman Frankfurter and Gardner Jackson, eds.,* The Letters of Sacco and Vanzetti, *1928)*

## Sacco and Vanzetti

*Dos Passos's powerful and resonant response to both the Sacco and Vanzetti case and the Harlan miners' strike arose from his belief that the two Italian-born anarchists and the Kentucky miners were being deprived of their fundamental right of equality before the law because of their beliefs or their poverty. Undoubtedly, this violation of a basic American civil right–of a right infused with an almost religious sanctity–so affronted Dos Passos that the Sacco-Vanzetti case propelled him into a fully committed personal and literary activism, a role later confirmed by the Harlan strike.*

*The following material documenting Dos Passos's engagement in the Sacco and Vanzetti case falls into several categories: an overview of the case and of Dos Passos's involvement in it provided by scholars and by Dos Passos's own later recollections; Dos Passos's efforts, following his visit to Vanzetti in June 1926, to convince others that the trial of the two men had been a miscarriage of justice; his increasing anger as the date of the executions drew near, culminating in his personal participation in the demonstrations of August 1927 protesting that impending action; and his bitter recognition, following the executions, that it was the function of the writer to engage his audience in the meaning of their deaths for the nature and future of American democracy.*

### Dos Passos and the Sacco-Vanzetti Case
Melvin Landsberg

*Landsberg, the principal historian of Dos Passos's political beliefs and activities, provides an overview of the Sacco-Vanzetti case and of Dos Passos's involvement in it.*

In Bridgewater, Massachusetts, on December 24, 1919, two armed men attacked a truck which was carrying the payroll of the L. Q. White Shoe Company. They exchanged gunfire with the guards and fled. The attempt at robbery was unsuccessful, and nobody was shot.

A successful payroll robbery occurred less than four months later, on April 15, 1920, in South Braintree, Massachusetts. Two men killed a paymaster and a guard who were taking a $16,000 payroll from one building of the Slater and Morrill shoe factory to another. The assailants, with a third man who may have participated in the shooting, got into a car containing two others. Several persons observed the fleeing robbers, and a stolen car used in the flight was found two days later.[1]

Sacco and Vanzetti, two radical aliens who had been moderately active in strikes before the war and had fled to Mexico to evade the draft in 1917, were arrested on May 5, 1920, not long after the height of the red scare. The prosecution later claimed that the police had simply been looking for Italians who might be trying to get the use of a car, especially if their manner seemed surreptitious. (State witnesses spoke of the murderers as being Italian-looking.) Both Sacco and Vanzetti were carrying guns. When they were questioned, they gave answers that were incorrect or deliberately false. On June 22, at the Plymouth court, District Attorney Katzmann brought Vanzetti to trial, before Judge Webster Thayer, for the Bridgewater holdup. The prosecution's case was weak, but the defense's must have appeared weaker, for Vanzetti did not testify. He was found guilty and on August 16 was sentenced to from twelve to fifteen years for assault with intent to rob.

On May 31, 1921, Sacco and Vanzetti were placed on trial for the South Braintree holdup and murder. Thayer again presided and Katzmann again prosecuted. At this second trial, in Dedham, the state offered eyewitness testimony to the defendants' guilt, claimed that a bullet found in the body of the murdered guard had been fired from Sacco's revolver, and alleged that the actions of the defendants at the time of the arrest showed consciousness of guilt. The state also tried to show that a cap found at the scene of the crime had belonged to Sacco and that the revolver Vanzetti had been carrying was one taken from the murdered guard.

The eyewitness testimony against the defendants appears to have been notoriously weak; it was frequently discredited and more than offset by that of the eyewitnesses for the defense. The cap was of common size and color, and the state's theory regarding Vanzetti's revolver was mere speculation; Vanzetti established a different line of ownership. On the question of whether the fatal bullet had come from Sacco's gun, two experts testified for the state. One said he was "inclined to believe" that the bullet had come from Sacco's pistol, and the other said the bullet was "consistent" with being fired from that pistol. Two experts for the defense said that in their opinion the bullet had not been fired from Sacco's gun. District Attorney Katzmann misrepresented the strength of his experts' testimony, but the lawyers for the defense did not expose its defects, and they presented their own ballistic evidence poorly. The judge failed to describe the testimony of the state experts adequately in his charge to the jury, and he probably gave a wrong impression of its strength.

In Judge Thayer's charge to the jury, he emphasized the issue of consciousness of guilt. Why had Sacco and Vanzetti been carrying revolvers and why had they lied to the police? Vanzetti claimed that he carried a revolver to protect money he used in his business as a fish peddler. Sacco said he had been planning to shoot some of his cartridges in a deserted place before leaving on an imminent

trip to Italy. Both men said that, anticipating government raids, they had been seeking an automobile to remove radical literature from the homes of their friends. They claimed they had believed they were being arrested as radicals (the district attorney had not informed the two that they were suspected of murder) and said they had lied to the police to protect their friends.

Katzmann succeeded in making the defendants' radicalism a chief issue. His lengthy and sarcastic examination seemed so successful in appealing to antislacker and antiradical sentiment that the defense found it necessary to insist that one might be guilty of radicalism without being guilty of murder. The defense made a feeble effort to show by detailed chronological references to past events how the defendants' minds had been disturbed by fear not only of prosecution, but also of illegal violence and even of murder by government agents. Thayer blocked this argument, and he did not allow counsel for the defense to probe the motives of a state witness who had himself recently pleaded guilty to larceny. In his charge to the jury Thayer spoke of the jurors' service as a patriotic duty and reminded them of the heroic dead of the World War. On July 14, 1921, the jury returned a verdict of guilty.

Sacco's and Vanzetti's Italian friends came to their aid immediately after the arrests. By May 1920 these friends had organized the Sacco-Vanzetti Defense Committee, which worked singlemindedly in behalf of the defendants until the very end. For the Dedham trial the committee engaged attorney Fred H. Moore, who had defended Ettor and Giovannitti in 1912 and had done other defense work for the I.W.W. Since Sacco and Vanzetti were radicals and labor agitators, Moore used his familiar labor channels of publicity, and the case became another labor defense case. The New England Civil Liberties Committee and the liberal League for Democratic Control became apprehensive about the likelihood of an unfair trial and helped the defendants.

Between the end of the Dedham trial and November 1923 the defense presented five motions for a new trial on grounds of newly discovered evidence. The first charged that the foreman of the jury had exhibited revolver cartridges in the jury room, and this complaint was later supplemented with an affidavit that before the trial the future foreman had said, "Damn them, they ought to hang them anyway." The second motion was based in part on the discovery of an eyewitness previously known to the police but overlooked by the defense. From the seat in the getaway car where the prosecution placed Sacco, a robber had shot at this witness from a distance of a few feet, and the witness was sure that Sacco had not been that assailant. The third and fourth motions, as well as parts of the second, attempted to discredit witnesses; there were retractions and consequent re-retractions of testimony. The fifth motion offered additional ballistic evidence and an affidavit from one of the state's experts saying that he and the prosecution

## The Official Bulletin of the
# SACCO-VANZETTI DEFENSE COMMITTEE
## of Boston, Massachusetts

256 HANOVER STREET            Rooms 17-18            TEL. RICHMOND 4665

VOL I — No. 7        Mail Address: P. O. BOX 93, HANOVER STREET STATION — BOSTON, MASS.        DECEMBER 1926

the purpose of the aforementioned organizations, or an accurate account of funds received and disbursed by them. We have been given to understand by the International Labor Defense that there are a number of Sacco-Vanzetti Conferences throughout the country from which we have never received any report. This was the reason why the Committee has repeatedly advised friends of the Sacco-Vanzetti case to communicate directly with this office.

## TWO INTERVIEWS
By JOHN DOS PASSOS

### With Vanzetti

The Charlestown House of Correction is built like a church in the shape of a cross. Visitors wait in the chancel and are ushered into the crossing where the high altar would be in a Catholic church. There, facing a warden at a desk, is a semicircle of benches. On all the benches are couples of people talking a little breathlessly.

Of each of these couples one is a convict, the other is a friend, a brother, a wife. The visitors from the outside sit uneasily; they feel ashamed of the freshness of their cheeks, of the smell of freedom on their clothes; like visitors in a hospital they wish they were out again and feel ashamed of themselves for wishing it. The prisoners have only one wish; they keep glancing to the right and left over their shoulders. It is for fear of something that they keep glancing over their shoulders as they talk to the people from the outside.

Vanzetti sits on the bench, thickchested and calm. If you didn't know him you could tell that he was different. He has a look of broadbrowed calm about him. His lips don't tremble when he smiles under his thick moustache. But it is the calm of a man with his back to the wall. He too glances from time to time over his shoulder as if to make sure that there is nobody creeping up behind him.

"Well what do you think?" we ask each other. The Case is something separate, far away, like a prizefight heard over the radio. "Pretty bad," says Vanzetti. "I have to work hard, very hard now. There are many things I want to write and maybe I have not much time." He has about three hours a day to read papers and write letters and articles. The rest of the time he works in the shop making automobile license plates. "But it is so difficult to write in jail. Before I could work hard nine hours, eleven hours a day, and then sit down and write. It poured out, straight from the heart. Often I would not have made a single correction in an article. But now, word by word. It is so difficult to write in a cell."

Somehow we got talking about the clergy. Both the Catholic priest and the Protestant chaplain had written articles and made public statements against him. It was demoralizing to the other prisoners to have a convicted murderer escape the Chair year after year like this. "They hate me because I am atheist," said Vanzetti. "If I went to them and made myself humble and said 'Father I am sorry, please give me absolution,' they would help me." They feel as bitterly towards him as doctors toward a sickman who won't buy their medicine.

"At last I ask to see Father Murphy. He trembled like a leaf. I ask to see him to say to him, 'What have I done to him to plot against me that way,' He trembled like a leaf and said nothing, only smooth words. If I would be a criminal he would want to save my soul. Maybe, even the cardinal would intercede for me. They hate me because I am not a criminal." In jail once you're caught in the trapnet of the law, the worst crime of all is to be innocent.

Time was getting short. The hour would soon be up. And what about a compromise?

What if as a result of the change of front of many respectable people in Boston, of the Boston Herald's advocacy of an impartial investigation of the case, he should be offered a commuted sentence or a pardon? Since the Mooney case it's getting fashionable to imprison a man for life if you can't fasten any crime on him except that of being a radical.

"Tell them," said Vanzetti quietly, without a quiver in his voice, "that I shall refuse to apply for pardon or commutation or anything. Why should I when I am innocent?"

* * * * *

### With Sacco

It was mealtime when I went to see Sacco. The other prisoners filed by us as we sat on the bench talking; young men mostly, walking heavily with their hands in their armpits. Through the bars you can see trees and the sky and clouds.

Sacco has been six and half years in Dedham jail, six and a half years of walking in a file with his hands in his armpits. A prisoner awaiting sentence is given no work to do. The only break was when he was sent to the State hospital for the insane, when he collapsed after a thirty one day huger strike. "I don't care how it ends, if it would only end," he says.

They had told me that Sacco was broken by the ordeal; but not at all. There is still an occasional flush of color in his waxy prison cheeks. We talked about how amazing was the amount of agony a man could stand. A dog under the same conditions would have been dead long ago. But he didn't say much about the Case. He was sick of talking about the Case, of thinking about the Case. He told me about when he'd been a kid in a little town in southern Italy before he'd come to America. His life before he had fallen into the ghastly trap in Brockton that May evening six and a half years ago had been pretty happy on the whole. He liked to talk about it.

His father was a wine and oil merchant. Sacco worked for him when he was little in the vineyards and the dry sunny olive orchards. But better than school or work in the fields he liked machinery. When he was fifteen he got a job stoking the donkey engine that ran the big thresher that threshed all the wheat in the region. It was about that time that he began to dream of coming to America, the land of machinery. When he was seventeen he came to America with his brother. His first job was as waterboy with a road gang. When they let him work on the steamroller he was absolutely happy. He loved the land machinery. When winter came he got a job in the Hopedale Mills, and eventually finding that an unskilled laborer was everybody's doormat, learnt to run an edging machine in a shoe factory.

From then on he was pretty prosperous. He was married and had a son. He was making good money. He began to think about the people who weren't so well off as he was. He had been brought up in an atmosphere of political talk. His father, back in Torremaggiore, had been a republican; his brother, later mayor of the town, a Socialist. When Sacco lived in Milford he went to socialist meetings. But he found more intelligent men among the anarchists. They were more awake, more anxious to improve themselves, he said.

So little by little he found himself allied with the local Italian anarchist groups, meeting Sundays and evenings at the Circolo di Studi Sociali. He was active in the Hopedale strike, was arrested for making a speech during the agitation in sympathy with the Minnesota strike in 1916. So it was inevitable that he should have been one of the first to agitate for a protest against the arrest of Salsedo and Elia in the red raids of 1920.

of protest against Salsedo's murder when he was arrested with Vanzetti that May night in a Brockton street car.

Since then. . . . six and a half years of jail. Twenty-three hours a day alone in a cell.

"I don't care how it all ends, if it only ends," he says.

Commutation? Pardon? I didn't dare mention then to him.

"If we had been convicted of radicalism it would have been all right," he said. "But why convict us of murder?"

*Issue of the monthly bulletin providing news sympathetic to the Sacco and Vanzetti case that included Dos Passos's interviews with the accused men, conducted eight months before they were executed (Collection of Richard Layman)*

had deliberately misled the jury on the question of whether the fatal bullet had come from Sacco's gun. Judge Thayer denied all five motions on October 1, 1924.

Almost immediately after Thayer's decision, Fred Moore and other defense lawyers withdrew from the case, and William G. Thompson, a conservative Boston lawyer, became chief defense counsel. Attorney Thompson now undertook an appeal to the Supreme Judicial Court, the highest tribunal in Massachusetts. That court could determine whether the defendants had received a trial according to law, but it could not weigh the evidence again. Thompson charged that the trial judge had used his discretionary powers incorrectly or with prejudice. He appealed from Thayer's denial of the defense's plea that the verdict was against the weight of the evidence. He appealed too from the judge's denial of the first motion for a new trial, that part of the second motion dealing with a new eyewitness, and the fifth motion. The attorney had filed all his supporting material by November 10, 1925, and it seemed that his last major task would be to argue the briefs accompanying that material. Suddenly an event occurred which opened an entirely new line of defense.

Celestino Madeiros, like Sacco an inmate of the Dedham jail who had been found guilty of murder, wrote a note confessing his part in the South Braintree murder and exonerating Sacco and Vanzetti. Madeiros would not identify his confederates, but the defense established a hypothesis placing the guilt on the Morelli gang of Providence, Rhode Island. That gang had stolen shipments of shoes from the Slater and Morrill factories in the past; several of its members fitted descriptions given by eyewitnesses to the South Braintree crime; and one member resembled Sacco strongly. On May 26, 1926, two weeks after the Supreme Judicial Court denied Thompson's appeal, the defense submitted the Madeiros confession as grounds for still another appeal for a new trial, and in addition presented affidavits to show that the United States Department of Justice, though believing the two defendants innocent, had improperly helped Katzmann to prepare a case against them. Thayer again denied a new trial on October 23, 1926, saying that he could not find for a fact that Madeiros had told the truth.

The knowledge of Sacco's and Vanzetti's radicalism became more and more widespread between the time of their conviction and May 1926. Even before the trial Eugene Lyons had gone to Europe and interested the Italian press in the case, and Art Shields, another left-wing journalist, had written a pamphlet about it. European leftists demonstrated violently over the verdict. After the conviction civil liberties groups continued to be active in the prisoners' behalf. In spite of the conservative policies of the A.F.L., its conventions asked for a new trial in 1922, and in 1924 called the men "victims of race and national prejudice and class hatred."[2]

Dos Passos first became involved in the work of the Sacco-Vanzetti Defense Committee when an anarchist printer, Aldino Felicani, the man most responsible for organizing the defense, asked him to report a motion for a new trial.[3] There was much about the case to arouse him in favor of the defendants. His own indignation over America's participation in World War I made Sacco's and Vanzetti's unwillingness to enter the army appear creditable. From the start, radicals had linked the case with Attorney General Palmer's unlawful behavior, which had outraged Dos Passos at the beginning of the decade, and now affidavits from former Justice Department agents seemed to confirm their accusations. Dos Passos' Latin origins and his cosmopolitanism helped to make him exceptionally impatient of agitation against Italians.[4] His travels in Spain had given him some understanding of anarchism among Mediterranean peoples, and he was able to see and present the ideologies of the two defendants sympathetically.

In writing on behalf of the defendants, Dos Passos consulted with anarchists and I.W.W. men on the Sacco-Vanzetti Defense Committee. Felicani he describes as one of the "straightest" people he has ever known.[5] Although Dos Passos became more friendly with the committee than with the Communist defense, he did not participate in controversies between the two.[6]

Before Dos Passos published anything on behalf of Sacco and Vanzetti, he spoke to each of them personally. He seems to have been the member of the *New Masses* staff who visited Vanzetti in the Charlestown House of Correction in June 1926 and heard him complain about how poorly the defense's case was being presented to the public.[7] The interviews were decisive in convincing Dos Passos that the defendants were really as well as technically innocent. Thirty years later, in reviewing the case, he commented: "Any man, I suppose, is capable of any crime, but having talked to Sacco and Vanzetti themselves it's impossible for me to believe they could have committed that particular crime."[8]

Dos Passos' comment on the case in the August 1926 issue of *New Masses* bore a title reflecting his emotional reaction to the visits–"The Pit and the Pendulum." The article differed from his pamphlet of the next year mainly in its brevity. He characterized Vanzetti's anarchism as "less a matter of labels than of feeling, of gentle philosophic brooding." Four months later the official bulletin of the Sacco-Vanzetti Defense Committee carried Dos Passos' account of his interviews with the men.[9] Then in 1927 the committee published Dos Passos' 127-page pamphlet *Facing the Chair*.

Why had Sacco and Vanzetti, Dos Passos asked, been indicted for murder? He recalled as background the hatreds stirred up during the World War; the fears to which government officials had succumbed over the unsolved bombings in 1919; the sailing of the *Buford;* and the January raids. He quoted at length from the pamphlet *Illegal Practices of the Department of Justice,* which twelve well-known lawyers, including Roscoe Pound and Felix

Frankfurter, had prepared in May 1920. Public opinion had demanded a solution to the South Braintree murder and robbery, Dos Passos said, and the local authorities had felt that proving reds guilty would please people. The United States Department of Justice had helped frame the two because it had been unable to secure evidence upon which to deport them as radicals.[10]

After the war, Dos Passos said, Vanzetti had gone to New York as a delegate of a group of Italian anarchists, syndicalists, and Socialists. His purpose had been to hire a lawyer and arrange bail for an Italian anarchist printer Andrew Salsedo and Salsedo's friend Elia. In New York Vanzetti had heard rumors that the possession of any literature that might be interpreted as subversive could lead not only to deportation but also to the third degree. On May 3, 1920, Salsedo had jumped or been pushed from the Justice Department's offices on the fourteenth floor of a building where he had been secretly imprisoned for eight weeks and evidently tortured. Two days later Sacco and Vanzetti had set out with other members of their group to hide dangerous literature. When they were arrested, they were carrying the draft of a handbill announcing a meeting to protest Salsedo's death; they were carrying revolvers too, probably out of a feeling of bravado, for they did not intend to let Salsedo's fate befall them.

Where, Dos Passos inquired, did the case stand? On October 23, 1926, Judge Thayer had denied motions for a new trial in a 30,000-word document that read like a personal apologia rather than an impartial decision. Quoting from affidavits as he went along, Dos Passos described the evidence presented at the hearing. The defense could, before Thayer passed sentence, he wrote, appeal to the Supreme Judicial Court on grounds of procedure. Afterward the defense could appeal to the governor for executive clemency, or to the Supreme Court of the United States on the ground that Sacco and Vanzetti had not received due process. In all these recourses, Dos Passos saw little hope. Sacco and Vanzetti, he added, wanted neither a pardon nor a commutation of sentence to life. They were entitled to complete acquittal.

Sacco and Vanzetti were symbols, Dos Passos said, of all the immigrants who had built the country's industries and had received for their work "a helot's position under the bootheels of the Arrow Collar social order"; the two men symbolized the dream of a saner society.[11]

The hardships of immigrant textile workers in Passaic were fresh memories for Dos Passos, but there were older and perhaps more haunting ones; what experiences had led him to contrast, in *Streets of Night*, the vitality of Boston Italians with the frustrated refinement of Cambridge Anglo-Saxons? Drawing force from his discontent with American industrial society, he castigated Sacco's and Vanzetti's accusers.

Although Dos Passos contended that the framing of Sacco and Vanzetti had been conscious and deliberate, he believed that to understand it completely one had to be familiar with "the psychology of frame-ups." There exists an unconscious or subconscious desire, he wrote, to incriminate people whom one dislikes. For half a century, and particularly since the assassination of McKinley, the anarchist had been a "bogey" in America. Dos Passos traced the ideals of Latin anarchists back to the hope of Christ's kingdom on earth. The hope had disappeared after the first millennium, but in modern times many Italians had looked forward to finding an ideal land in America. Those Italian immigrants who had not yielded to the system of "dawg eat dawg" (here we may recall the opportunism of Fuselli, the second-generation Italian American in *Three Soldiers*) had become anarchists.

At the Plymouth trial, Thayer had said that highway robbery was consistent with Vanzetti's ideas. If there were terrorists among the anarchists, Dos Passos asserted, their presence did not make the two terms synonymous; there had been terrorists among oppressed and despised sects since the world began. Of course, employers found it easy to think of an anarchist who organized their employees as a terrorist. Still, Dos Passos mused, there was perhaps a reason deeper than loss of profits for the hatred of Sacco and Vanzetti. "The people of Massachusetts centuries ago suffered and hoped terribly for the City of God. . . . The irrational features of this case of attempted communal murder can only be explained by a bitterness so deep that it has been forgotten by the very people it moves most fervidly."[12]

Dos Passos devoted the final fifty-six pages of his pamphlet to a chronological account of the case, including a detailed analysis of the murder trial based on his perusal of 3,900 pages of official transcript. At Vanzetti's trial for attempted robbery, Dos Passos wrote, his lawyer probably had sacrificed him deliberately. The lawyer had certainly shown criminal negligence in not permitting Vanzetti to take the stand and in not filing a bill of exceptions. Some of the testimony at the first trial was, Dos Passos added, patently incredible; moreover, several state witnesses had changed their original accounts to favor the prosecution. If Vanzetti's witnesses had been Americans instead of Italians, their testimony would have been accepted. At the second trial, Dos Passos wrote, the identification testimony had been overwhelmingly in favor of Sacco and Vanzetti, but the court had made patriotism an issue and had stressed the question of whether the defendants' behavior upon arrest indicated consciousness of guilt. Their behavior had in reality been due to "the consciousness of the dead body of their comrade Salsedo lying smashed in the spring dawn two days before on the pavement of Park Row."[13]

Dos Passos had written in "The Pit and the Pendulum" that defense attorney William G. Thompson wished to continue believing in the honesty of Massachusetts justice and in the fairness and humanity of the typical Harvard-bred Bostonian. As the facts he encountered every day made such belief difficult, Thompson wished he were out of the case. In the pamphlet, Dos Passos wrote more favorably of Thompson. It was largely due, he said, to Thompson's personal influence and his reputation for conservatism and integrity that lawyers, college professors, ministers, and newspaper readers generally were now becoming interested in the Sacco-Vanzetti case. Thayer's last denial of a new trial had helped to awaken some of the "respected" members of the community, people who had not suspected that anything but justice was meted out in the courts. The truth had to be told so that if Sacco and Vanzetti were executed, no one could plead ignorance of the facts. If they died, Dos Passos declared, in words crucial for his own history, "what little faith millions of men have in the chance of Justice in this country will die with them."[14]

The Supreme Judicial Court rejected all further appeals of the defense, and on April 9, 1927, Judge Thayer sentenced Sacco and Vanzetti to death. On June 1 Governor Fuller took the extraordinary step of appointing an advisory committee [the Lowell Committee] to investigate whether the trial had been fairly conducted, whether subsequently discovered evidence justified a new trial, and whether Sacco and Vanzetti seemed guilty beyond a reasonable doubt. This action was an acknowledgment of the steady growth of doubt among lawyers, newspaper editors, and other influential citizens. There was, on the other hand, widespread hostility to a review. The Massachusetts House had on April 14 defeated by a vote of 146 to 6 a resolution calling for a commission to study the case. Probably four in five, perhaps nine in ten, Boston lawyers held that nothing should be permitted to damage the reputation of the state judicial system. A majority of the people of Massachusetts believed that the major need in the Sacco-Vanzetti affair was to protect the American way of life against radicals throughout the world.[15]

The report of the Governor's committee upheld the trial and the verdict. It asserted that Judge Thayer had tried to be scrupulously fair, although he had been indiscreet in conversation with outsiders during the trial. As for District Attorney Katzmann's cross-examination, it had been justified as an attempt to determine whether Sacco's "profession that he and his friends were radicals liable for deportation was true, or was merely assumed for the purpose of the defense."[16] The report dismissed Madeiros' confession as worthless and uncorroborated, and it denied that newly discovered evidence justified a new trial. Sacco and Vanzetti were guilty beyond a reasonable doubt, the report declared, adding that their guilt rested upon a cumulation of factors, none of which was conclusive.

. . . . . . . . . .

Until the very end most of the people with whom Dos Passos was working on the case were confident that Sacco and Vanzetti would obtain a new trial. The report of Governor Fuller's committee and the refusal of Justices Holmes and Brandeis to issue a writ of habeas corpus astonished them. Dos Passos (covering the action for the *Daily Worker*), Edna St. Vincent Millay, Hibben, and Lawson were among those arrested during demonstrations against the executions.[17]

Felix Frankfurter had concluded a book defending Sacco and Vanzetti by asserting that while American criminal procedure had its defects, one would be mistaken to "find in an occasional striking illustration of its fallibilities an attack upon its foundations or lack of loyalty to its purposes."[18] But to Dos Passos, reflecting upon the heavy penalties imposed under the wartime Sedition Act and conscious of current judicial and police abuses, the executions were evidence that opponents of capitalism could not expect justice in the courts. In appealing to Lowell's conservatism, Dos Passos invoked some of his own characteristics and desires; his radicalism was to a great extent conservative in its inspiration, motivated by a desire to safeguard or reclaim historic freedoms and to sustain civilization.

The Sacco-Vanzetti affair was as important in directing his interests as a creative writer as in directing his politics. The affair supplied a new impetus for his studying American society—its leaders, its myths, its ideologies, its source of information.

Gardner Jackson, one of the leaders of the Sacco-Vanzetti Defense Committee, recalled that on the night when the report of the Lowell Committee had been issued, he and Dos Passos went to see the publisher of the *Boston Herald*, Robert Lincoln O'Brien. The *Herald* had that previous year published a highly influential editorial denouncing Judge Thayer's handling of the case. Now O'Brien outraged Jackson by his urbane manner, his refusal to listen, his wisecracks. After the two had departed, Dos Passos said to Jackson, "Don't take it so hard. He's nothing but an old feather duster."[19]

"They Are Dead Now—," Dos Passos' first literary comment on the executions, in October 1927, may appear merely to echo his remark to Jackson (and echo a theme of *The Garbage Man* and *Manhattan Transfer*) as it contrasts the physically dead Sacco and Vanzetti with their spiritually dead executioners. But Dos Passos had greatly altered his view, already a sufficiently troubled one, of the spiritual solvency of most middle-class Americans. He now undertook to study, analyze, and discuss their class and to make explicit judgments upon it. In *Airways, Inc.* (1928) he described the partiality of a middle-class family toward capitalism, but that play was a comparatively minor effort. For Dos Passos, the culmination of the Sacco-Vanzetti affair was *U.S.A.*, a study of the minds, characters, and fates of a dozen Americans during the first third of the twentieth century.

—*Dos Passos' Path to U.S.A.*, pp. 132–140, 142

### Notes

1. For the history of the case, see G. Louis Joughin and Edmund M. Morgan, *The Legacy of Sacco and Vanzetti* (New York: Harcourt, Brace, 1948), passim.

2. Ibid., pp. 221–242.

3. Letter from John Dos Passos to M. L., 26 June 1956.

4. Dos Passos, *The Best Times* (New York: New American Library, 1966), p. 166.

5. Letters from Dos Passos to M. L., 26 June 1956 (for Felicani), and 23 September 1957.

6. Ibid., 1 February 1957. See Joughin and Morgan, *The Legacy of Sacco and Vanzetti*, p. 24.

7. Nicola Sacco and Bartolomeo Vanzetti, *The Letters of Sacco and Vanzetti,* edited by Marion Denman Frankfurter and Gardner Jackson (New York: Viking, 1928), pp. 201–202.

8. Dos Passos, *The Theme Is Freedom* (New York: Dodd, Mead, 1956), p. 11.

9. Dos Passos, "The Pit and the Pendulum," *New Masses,* 1 (August 1926): 30; idem, "Two Interviews," *Official Bulletin of the Sacco-Vanzetti Defense Committee of Boston, Massachusetts,* 1 (December 1926): 3–4.

10. Dos Passos, *Facing the Chair* (Boston: Sacco-Vanzetti Defense Committee, 1927), pp. 19–20.

11. Ibid., p. 45.

12. Ibid., pp. 57–58.

13. Ibid., p. 116.

14. Ibid., p. 127.

15. See Joughin and Morgan, *The Legacy of Sacco and Vanzetti,* pp. 221–271, 299.

16. *New York Times,* 7 August 1927, sec. 1, p. 23. The quotation is from the report.

17. Dos Passos, *The Theme Is Freedom,* p. 39; idem, *The Best Times,* p. 172; *New York Times,* 11 August 1927, p. 1; 12 August, p. 2; 23 August, p. 4; 24 August, p. 2.

18. Felix Frankfurter, *The Case of Sacco and Vanzetti* (Boston: Little, Brown, 1927), p. 108.

19. M. L., interview with Gardner Jackson, 16 October 1957.

### From *The Best Times: An Informal Memoir*
Dos Passos

*Forty years after the events, Dos Passos reviews in his autobiography both his permanent revulsion regarding the miscarriage of justice represented by the Sacco-Vanzetti case and his later realization that the case provided the Communist Party with a golden opportunity to pursue its own aims.*

These were the years when we were trying to revive the *Masses.* The old *Masses,* since its suppression during the Wilson administration's drive to eliminate pacifist sentiment during the first war, had become a kind of labarum to a whole generation of refractory young people. *The New Masses* was organized in an effort to build a pulpit for native American radicalism. We felt that the Marxist Leninist line did not apply to the United States. The Marxist codifiers had long since labeled our heresy American Exceptionalism. Never much of a hand to work with organizations, I justified my connection with *The New Masses* to myself as a means of getting firsthand knowledge of the labor movement. The hardcore dogmatists were already leery of my attitude. Though I hadn't yet read Roger Williams I was already the Seeker in matters political as he was the Seeker in matters religious.

If I remember right Egmont Arends, a broadminded fellow without a theoretical bone in his body, was still editor when I went down to Boston to do an article for *The New Masses* on the Sacco-Vanzetti case. I was interested because the men were anarchists, and I had a good deal of sympathy for their naive convictions, so like the delusions of the early Christians who thought the world would come to an end in the year one thousand, and because they were Italians. In college and out I had personally felt the frustrations that came from being considered a wop or a guinea or a greaser.

It is hard to explain to people who never lived through the early twenties the violence of the revulsion against foreigners and radicals that went through the United States after the first world war. To young men who had come home from Europe convinced that militarism was the enemy of civilization this reaction seemed to embody all the evil passions that militarism fed on. When we took up for Sacco and Vanzetti we were taking up for freedom of speech and for an even-handed judicial system which would give the same treatment to poor men as to rich men, to greasy foreigners as to redblooded Americans.

Aldino Felicani, the Italian printer who dedicated his life to heading up the defense committee, seemed to me to be an honest man from the first time I met him. I felt the same about many of his associates. It was impossible to talk with Bartolomeo Vanzetti when I went to see him at the Charlestown Penitentiary, where he was serving time on his conviction in the Bridgewater case, without being taken with the man's aloofness from egotistical preoccupations. It was hard to imagine the gentle and cogitative fishmonger taking part in a holdup, even in a holdup in what he might consider a good cause. Nobody in his right mind who was planning such a thing would take a man like that along.

When I was getting up a pamphlet for the defense committee I went to North Plymouth and talked to most of Vanzetti's alibi witnesses. I came away convinced that they were telling the truth. Young Brini seemed to me particularly intelligent and trustworthy. To me the story that Vanzetti was selling eels that Christmas Eve morning of 1919 was more credible on the face of it than his "identification" by witnesses who thought he was the foreign-looking man with a shotgun they had seen in the winter twilight a good six months before they gave their testimony in the Plymouth court. Vanzetti's indictment along with Sacco's for the murder of Parmenter and Berardelli in the South Braintree holdup the following April seemed to me to be standard frame-up procedure on the part of the district attorney. If the man you are charging has already been convicted of a crime you have won half your case.

Talking to Nicola Sacco behind the green bars of Dedham jail, I found him very much the good citizen which his character witnesses described. Where Vanzetti was reflective Sacco was a simple outgoing sort of man. It seemed barely possible that he might have convinced himself that seizing money from a capitalist paymaster to be used for the defense of his persecuted comrades was a justifiable act in the class war. The spring of 1920 saw the height of the delirium of arrests and deportation of alleged radicals instigated by Woodrow Wilson's Attorney General. All this was brought close to the Boston anarchists by newspaper headlines reporting that on May 3 their comrade Salsedo had jumped or been thrown to his death from the fourteenth floor of the building on Park Row where he was supposedly being put through the third degree by Department of Justice agents.

Writing about these things forty years after it is hard to reconstruct the frenzy of the Palmer raids. Radicals, foreign and domestic, were being denounced and herded into jails by law officers and such civilian organizations as the American Legion all over the country.

The red baiters had their justification too. The butchery of their opponents on which the revolutionaries in Russia founded the soviet power was fresh in people's minds. Such anarchist exploits as the Wall Street explosion, with its toll of dead and wounded and the bombing of Attorney General Palmer's house in Washington, made a mockery of the plea that anarchists and communists were merely philosophical dissenters.

A. Mitchell Palmer's reign of terror accounted for the fact that Sacco and Vanzetti carried guns when they were arrested on that streetcar in Brockton. They thought they were being arrested for deportation. The agent who arrested them admitted that he was under the impression that he was picking up an associate of theirs named Boda against whom he had evidence to justify deportation proceedings. My hunch was, though I never asked him the direct question, that Vanzetti refused to testify in his own behalf in his first trial at Plymouth for fear he might be trapped into giving information damaging to other members of the anarchist group to which all these men belonged. There are still unexplained mysteries. It is even possible that some

## FACING THE CHAIR

STORY OF THE AMERICANIZATION
OF TWO FOREIGNBORN WORKMEN

*by*

### JOHN DOS PASSOS

PUBLISHED BY
SACCO-VANZETTI DEFENSE COMMITTEE
BOSTON, MASS.
1927

*Title page for Dos Passos's 128-page tract, rushed into print after the sentencing of Sacco and Vanzetti in early April 1927 and before their execution in August, in which he recounts the weakness of the case against the two men (Collection of Donald Pizer)*

of Sacco's and Vanzetti's friends were, as Carl Tresca hinted years later, involved with professional criminals such as the Morelli gang in acts of violence. What stood out clear as day was that Sacco and Vanzetti were not being given a fair trial.

The crux of the Sacco-Vanzetti case, on which all the agitation was based, was this conviction, shared by many people who were not in any way radicals, that the prosecution was a frame-up. Due to an eccentricity, which I understand has been since corrected, in Massachusetts procedure, there was no way of getting a hearing for fresh evidence turned up by the defense after conviction. Judge Thayer refused to admit the Madeiros confession or any other new leads. When the case was argued on appeal before the Massachusetts Supreme Court it could be argued on the record only. There is no question that Judge Thayer and most of the jury thought they were performing a stern civil duty by seeing to it that "the anarchistic bastards" should properly be hanged. The nearest thing to a review of the evidence was by the commission Governor Fuller appointed to advise him on pardon or commutation.

The only one of the three I'd had contact with, President Lowell of Harvard, had seemed to me to be a wellintentioned gentleman of considerable intelligence; I was appalled when he put his name to the report that sent Sacco and Vanzetti to their deaths. Even to this day, when the passions of the hour have cooled, it is hard to understand how a trained historian could have shown so little curiosity about the human background of the case. Like the Supreme Judicial Court, Governor Fuller's three commissioners stuck to the record and the record killed.

From the point of view of twentieth-century history the question of Sacco's and Vanzetti's guilt or innocence is secondary to the fact that the worldwide agitation in their favor proved to be the testing ground of one of the most effective weapons in the war for the destruction of the capitalist order. The Sacco-Vanzetti agitation proved to be the last mighty effort of the loosely organized anarchist movement which grew out of the split between Bukharin and Marx in the First International. The widespread protest that started as a spontaneous expression of anarchist ideals and hatreds ended pretty much under Communist Party control.

In Boston the work of the Defense Committee was hampered by continual patient efforts of the American C. P. to take charge of the agitation. The propaganda schools in Moscow learned an important lesson in international politics from the Sacco-Vanzetti agitation. Griefs and discontents, properly stimulated and directed, were more effective than armies in the world struggle for power.

. . . . . . . . . .

The summer of 1927 saw the last frantic struggle to save the lives of Sacco and Vanzetti. April 9th of that year Judge Thayer finally got around to sentencing them to death. My wisecracking friends from midtown New York had been kidding me about my radical frenzies until it seemed to me I must be about as Marx-struck as Xavier Guerrero. Scott Fitzgerald, with whom I had a long session during some short visit of his to New York at about this time, was particularly funny about it, kidding and serious too. He was on firm ground when he begged me to keep novelwriting and propaganda separate. Even a touch of propaganda would ruin my work if it hadn't ruined it already. I can still remember the scornful look on his pale face. His features seemed particularly carefully delineated, like a sketch by James Montgomery Flagg, that day.

All the same Sacco-Vanzetti was becoming the fashionable cause. Picketing the Boston statehouse was the one a day good deed of the literary radicals that summer. I even managed to get hauled in myself.

The joke was it was all a mistake. True to my conviction that I should stick to the position of observer I did not think it was my business to picket or march. When *The Daily Worker,* of all papers, asked me to report the excitements in Boston, I was perfectly willing to send in a daily article. Though I was thoroughly aware of the tension between the Communists and the anarchist defense committee, my attitude, somewhat naive at the time, was that it didn't matter where you published so long as they printed what you wrote. *Litera scripta manent.*

While I was trotting around getting stories from the picketers one afternoon the cops made one of their periodical raids. They pushed me into the paddywagon with the rest. The cops were quite unmoved when I tried to produce credentials as a reporter for *The Daily Worker.*

Still the police had been told to treat the picketers gently. The ride in the paddywagon was made delightful by the fact that I found myself sitting next to Edna St. Vincent Millay. Outside of being a passable poet Edna Millay was one of the most attractive women who ever put pen to paper. The curious glint in her coppercolored hair intoxicated every man who saw her. Besides having violet eyes and the loveliest hair in the world Edna Millay had a wealthy husband. We had hardly time to choose our places in the cells at the Joy Street station before Eugene Boissevain was bailing us out. The charge was "sauntering and loitering." I was one of the bunch who chose to stand trial and, months later, when everybody was forgetting Sacco and Vanzetti, had the somewhat barren satisfaction of being acquitted.

–*The Best Times: An Informal Memoir* (New York: New American Library, 1966), pp. 166–169, 172

## The Pit and the Pendulum
Dos Passos

*Dos Passos recounts his visit to Sacco and Vanzetti in jail.*

Dedham is the perfect New England town, white shingleroofed houses, polished brass knockers, elmshaded streets. Dedham has money, supports a polo team. Many of the wealthiest and oldest families in Massachusetts have houses there. As the seat of Norfolk County it is the center of politics for the region. Dedham has always stood for the traditions of the Bay State. Dedham was pro-British during the war; even before the Lusitania the people of Eastern Massachusetts were calling the Germans Huns. Dedham has always stood for Anglo-Saxon supremacy, and the white man's burden. Of all white men the whitest are those descendants of Puritan shipowners and brokers and ministers who own the white houses with graceful colonial doorways and the trim lawns and the lilac hedges and the elms and the beeches and the barberry bushes and the broad A and the cultivated gesturelessness of the New English. When the Congregational God made Dedham he looked upon it and saw that it was good.

But with the decline of shipping and farming a three-fold population has grown up in the ring of factory towns round Boston, among which Dedham itself sits primly disdainful like an old maid sitting between two laborers in a trolley car. There is the diminished simonpure New England population, protestant in faith, republican in politics and mostly "professional" in occupation. Alongside of that is the almost equally wealthy Irish Catholic element, Democratic, tending to make a business of politics and of the less severely respectable trades and industries. Under both of these is the population of wops, bohunks, polacks, hunkies, dagoes, some naturalized and speaking English with an accent, others unnaturalized and still speaking their native peasant dialects; they do the work. These three populations hate each other with a bitter hatred, but the upper two manage to patch up their rancor when it becomes a question of "furriners." In industrial disputes they find that they are all hundred per cent Americans. Meanwhile the latest-come immigrants are gradually gaining foothold. The Poles buy up rundown farms and get the tired and stony land back to the point of bearing crops. The Italians start truck gardens in back lots, and by skillful gardening and drudgery bring forth fiftyfold where the American-born couldn't get back the seed they sowed.

The Portuguese work the cranberry bogs and are reviving the shore fisheries. The American-born are seeing their own state eaten up from under their feet. Naturally they hate the newcomers.

The war exalted hatred to a virtue. The anti-Red agitation, the Ku Klux Klan, the activities of the American Security League and the American Legion have been a sort of backwash of hate dammed up by the signing of the peace. It was when that pent-up hatred and suspicion was tumultuously seeking an outlet that Sacco and Vanzetti, wops, aliens, men who spoke broken English, anarchists, believing neither in the Congregationalist or the Catholic God, slackers who had escaped the draft, were arrested, charged with a particularly brutal and impudent murder. Since that moment the right-thinking Puritan-born Americans of Massachusetts have had an object, a focus for the bitterness of their hatred of the new young vigorous unfamiliar forces that are relentlessly sweeping them onto the shelf. The people of Norfolk County, and of all Massachusetts, have decided that they want these men to die.

The faces of men who have been a long time in jail have a peculiar frozen look under the eyes. The face of a man who has been a long time in jail never loses the tightness under the eyes. Sacco has been six years in the county jail, always waiting, waiting for trial, waiting for new evidence, waiting for motions to be argued, waiting for sentence, waiting, waiting, waiting. The Dedham jail is a handsome structure, set among lawns, screened by trees that wave new green leaves against the robbins-egg sky of June. In the warden's office you can see your face in the

*Left: Dos Passos picketing the Boston State House as the 23 August 1927 date of Sacco and Vanzetti's execution approached (the woman behind him may be Dorothy Parker); right: Dos Passos under arrest (United Press International)*

light brown varnish, you could eat eggs off the floor it is so clean. Inside the main reception hall is airy, full of sunlight. The bars are cheerfully painted green, a fresh peagreen. Through the bars you can see the waving trees and the June clouds roaming the sky like cattle in an unfenced pasture. It's a preposterous complicated canary cage. Why aren't the birds singing in this green aviary? The warden politely shows you to a seat and as you wait you notice a smell, not green and airy this smell, a jaded heavy greasy smell of slum, like the smell of army slum, but heavier, more hopeless.

Across the hall an old man is sitting in a chair, a heavy pear-shaped man, his hands hang limp at his sides, his eyes are closed, his sagged face is like a bundle of wet newspapers. The warden and two men in black stand over him, looking down at him helplessly.

At last Sacco has come out of his cell and sits beside me. Two men sitting side by side on a bench in a green bird cage. When he feels like it one of them will get up and walk out, walk out into the sunny June day. The other will go back to his cell to wait. He looks younger than I had expected. His face has a waxy transparency like the face of a man who's been sick in bed for a long time; when he laughs his cheeks flush a little. At length we manage both of us to laugh. It's such a preposterous position for a man to be in, like a man who doesn't know the game trying to play chess blindfolded. The real world has gone. We have no more grasp of our world of rain and streets and trolleycars and cucumbervines and girls and gardenplots. This is a world of phrases, *prosecution, defence, evidence, motion, irrelevant, incompetent and immaterial.* For six years this man has lived in the law, tied tighter and tighter in the sticky filaments of law-words like a fly in a spiderweb. And the wrong set of words means the Chair. All the moves in the game are made for him, all he can do is sit helpless and wait, fastening his hopes on one set of phrases after another. In all these lawbooks, in all this terminology of clerks of the court and counsel for the defence there is one move that will save him, out of a million that will mean death. If only they make the right move, use the right words. But by this time the nagging torment of hope has almost stopped, not even the thought of his wife and children out there in the world, unreachable, can torture him now. He is numb now, can laugh and look quizzically at the ponderous machine that has caught and mangled him. Now it hardly matters to him if they do manage to pull him out from between the cogs, and the wrong set of words means the chair.

Nicola Sacco came to this country when he was eighteen years old. He was born in Puglia in the mountains in the heel of Italy. Since then up to the time of his arrest he has had pretty good luck. He made good money, he was happily married, he had many friends, latterly he had a garden to hoe and rake mornings and evenings and Sundays. He was unusually powerfully built, able to do two men's work. In prison he was able to stand thirty-one days of hunger strike before he broke down and had to be taken to the hospital. In jail he has learned to speak and write English, has read many books, for the first time in his life has been thrown with nativeborn Americans. They worry him, these nativeborn Americans. They are so hard and brittle. They don't fit into the bright clear heartfelt philosophy of Latin anarchism. These are the people who cooly want him to die in the electric chair. He can't understand them. When his head was cool he's never wanted anyone to die. Judge Thayer and the prosecution he thinks of as instruments of a machine.

The warden comes up to take down my name. "I hope your wife's better," says Sacco. "Pretty poorly," says the warden. Sacco shakes his head. "Maybe she'll get better soon, nice weather." I have shaken his hand, my feet have carried me to the door, past the baggy pearshaped man who is still collapsed half deflated in the chair, closed crinkled eyelids twitching. The warden looks into my face with a curious smile, "Leaving us?" he asks. Outside in the neat streets the new green leaves are swaying in the sunlight, birds sing, klaxons grunt, a trolleycar screeches round a corner. Overhead the white June clouds wander in the unfenced sky.

Going to the Charlestown Penitentiary is more like going to Barnum and Baileys. There's a great scurry of guards, groups of people waiting outside; inside a brass band is playing "Home Sweet Home." When at length you get let into the Big Show, you find a great many things happening at once. There are rows of benches where pairs of people sit talking. Each pair is made up of a free man and a convict. In three directions there are grey bars and tiers of cells. The band inside plays bangingly "If Auld Acquaintance Be Forgot." A short broadshouldered man is sitting quiet through all the uproar, smiling a little under his big drooping mustache. He has a domed, pale forehead and black eyes surrounded by many little wrinkles. The serene modeling of his cheek-bones and hollow cheeks makes you forget the prison look under his eyes. This is Vanzetti.

Bartolomeo Vanzetti was born in Villafalletto, in a remote mountain valley in Piedmont. At the age of thirteen his father apprenticed him to a pastry-cook who worked him fifteen hours a day. After six years of grueling work in bakeries and restaurant kitchens he went back home to be nursed through pleurisy by his mother. Soon afterwards his mother died and in despair he set out for America. When after the usual kicking around by the Ellis Island officials he was dumped on the pavement of Battery Park, he had very little money, knew not a word of the language and found that he had arrived in a time of general unemployment. He washed dishes at Mouquins for five dollars a week and at last left for the country for fear he was getting consumption. At length he got work in a brick kiln near Springfield. After that he worked for two years in the stone pits at Meriden, Connecticut. Then he went back to New York and worked for a while as a pastrycook again, and at last settled in Plymouth where he worked in various factories and at odd jobs, ditch-digging, clamdigging, icecutting, snoeshoveling and a few months before his arrest, for the sake of being his own boss, bought a pushcart and peddled fish.

All this time he read a great deal nights sitting under the gasjet when every one else was in bed, thought a great deal as he swung a pick or made caramels or stoked brick kilns, of the workmen he rubbed shoulders with, of their position in their world and his, of their hopes of happiness and of a less struggling animallike existence. As a boy he had been an ardent Catholic. In Turin he fell in with a bunch of socialists under the influence of De Amicis. Once in America he read St. Augustine, Kropotkin, Gorki, Malatesta, Renan and began to go under the label of anarchist-communist. His anarchism, though, is less a matter of labels than of feeling, of gentle philosophic brooding. He shares the hope that has grown up in Latin countries of the Mediterranean basin that somehow men's predatory instincts, incarnate in the capitalist system, can be canalized into other channels, leaving free communities of artisans and farmers and fishermen and cattlebreeders who would work for their livelihood with pleasure, because the work was itself enjoyable in the serene white light of a reasonable world.

Vanzetti has served six years of the fifteen year term. How many more of them will he live to serve? And the wrong set of words means the chair!

William G. Thompson, the Boston lawyer who is conducting the defence, who is making the moves in the law game that mean life or the Chair to these two men, is a very puzzled man. As a man rather than as a lawyer he knows that they did not commit the crimes of which they are accused. The refusal of the Supreme Court of Massachusetts to entertain his motion for a new trial, the attitude of his friends, of the press, of Governor Fuller try him sorely. He wishes he were well out of it. He wants to go on believing in the honesty of Massachusetts justice, in the humanity and fair mindedness of the average educated Harvard-bred Bostonian. The facts he handles daily compel him to think otherwise. He wishes he were well out of it. And the wrong set of words means the chair!

And for the last six years, three hundred and sixty-five days a year, yesterday, today, tomorrow, Sacco and Vanzetti wake up on their prison pallets, eat prison food, have an hour of exercise and conversation a day, sit in their cells puzzling about this technicality and that technicality, pinning their hopes to their alibis, to the expert testimony about the character of the barrel of Sacco's gun, to Madeiros' confession and Weeks'

corroboration, to action before the Supreme Court of the United States, and day by day the props are dashed from under their feet and they feel themselves being inexorably pushed towards the Chair by the blind hatred of thousands of wellmeaning citizens, by the superhuman involved stealthy soulless mechanism of the law.

*—New Masses, 1 (August 1926): 10–11, 30*

### The Camera Eye (49)

*Since Bartolomeo Vanzetti was a fish peddler in North Plymouth, Massachusetts, Dos Passos weaves into his accounts of his visit to the town and his interview with Vanzetti at the Charlestown prison the powerful historical irony of Vanzetti as a persecuted latter-day pilgrim fighting for the same freedoms that the original Pilgrim settlers had fought for.*

walking from Plymouth to North Plymouth through the raw air of Massachusetts Bay at each step a small cold squudge through the sole of one shoe

looking out past the grey framehouses under the robinsegg April sky across the white dories anchored in the bottleclear shallows across the yellow sandbars and the slaty bay ruffling to blue to the eastward

this is where the immigrants landed the roundheads the sackers of castles the kingkillers haters of oppression this is where they stood in a cluster after landing from the crowded ship that stank of bilge    on the beach that belonged to no one    between the ocean that belonged to no one and the enormous forest that belonged to no one that stretched over the hills where the deertracks were up the green rivervalleys where the redskins grew their tall corn in patches forever into the incredible west

for threehundred years the immigrants toiled into the west

and now today

walking from Plymouth to North Plymouth suddenly round a bend in the road beyond a little pond and yellowtwigged willows hazy with green you see the Cordage    huge sheds and buildings companyhouses all the same size all grimed the same color a great square chimney long roofs sharp ranked squares and oblongs cutting off the sea    the Plymouth Cordage    this is where another immigrant worked hater of oppression who wanted a world unfenced    when they fired him from the cordage he peddled fish    the immigrants in the dark framehouses knew him bought his fish listened to his talk following his cart around from door to door    you ask them    What was he like?    why are they scared to talk of Bart scared eyes narrowing black with fright?    a barber the man in the little grocerystore the woman he boarded with    in scared voices they ask Why won't they believe? We knew him

We seen him every day Why won't they believe that day we buy the eels?

only the boy isn't scared

pencil scrawls in my notebook the scraps of recollection the broken halfphrases the effort to intersect word with word to dovetail clause to rebuild out of mangled memories unshakably (Oh Pontius Pilate) the truth

the boy walks shyly browneyed beside me to the station talks about how Bart helped him with his homework wants to get ahead      why should it hurt him to have known Bart? Wants to go to Boston University      we shake hands     don't let them scare you

accustomed the smokingcar     accustomed the jumble of faces rumble cozily homelike towards Boston through the gathering dark     how can I make them feel how our fathers our uncles haters of oppression came to this coast     how say     Don't let them scare you     how make them feel who are your oppressors America

rebuild the ruined words worn slimy in the mouths of lawyers districtattorneys collegepresidents judges     without the old words the immigrants haters of oppression brought to Plymouth how can you know who are your betrayers America

or that this fishpeddler you have in Charlestown Jail is one of your founders Massachusetts?

                                        —*The Big Money*, pp. 1134–1135


## An Open Letter to President Lowell
Dos Passos

*After Sacco and Vanzetti were sentenced to death in April 1927, the governor of Massachusetts named a committee of distinguished citizens, including A. Lawrence Lowell, the president of Harvard, to advise him about how to respond to the sentence. Lowell, who had been president of the university during Dos Passos's time there, was liberal in his political beliefs, and much hope had been placed in his membership on the committee. Hence, Dos Passos's tone of betrayal in his "open letter" after the committee found nothing irregular in the judicial proceedings leading to the conviction and sentencing of the two men.*


To the Editor of The Nation:

Sir: I am asking the courtesy of your columns for the enclosed open letter to President Lowell of Harvard that no publication in Boston seems willing to publish.

                                        John Dos Passos

Boston, August 9

As a graduate of Harvard University I feel that I have the right to protest against the participation of the president of that university in the report on the Sacco-Vanzetti case presented to Governor Fuller by his advisory committee. I feel that you have put your name and indirectly the name of the university you represent to an infamous document. This is no time for mincing words. You have made yourself a party to a judicial murder that will call down on its perpetrators the execration of the civilized world. What it means is that you are allowing a Massachusetts politician to use the name of Harvard to cover his own bias and to whitewash all the dirty business of the arrest of these men at the time of the anarchist raids and their subsequent slow torture by the spiteful and soulless mechanism of the law. They have probably told you that this was a mere local decision on a Boston murder case, but to any man with enough intelligence to read the daily papers it must be clear that somehow it has ceased being a Boston murder case. Sacco and Vanzetti starving in their cells in the death house and the authorities of the State of Massachusetts building the electric chair in which to burn them to death have become huge symbols on the stage of the world. The part into which you have forced Harvard University will make many a man ashamed of being one of its graduates.

Many of us who have watched the case for years felt that your appointment as a member of the committee assured at least a modicum of fair play and of historical perspective in the conduct of the investigation. This hope was pretty well shattered when it was announced that the investigation was to be carried on behind closed doors. If there was nothing to hide, why the secrecy? Since when have star chamber proceedings been part of the American judicial system?

The published report has confirmed our worst forebodings. With inconceivable levity you counsel the electrocution of two men because it "seems" to you that the enormous mass of evidence piled up by the defense in seven years' heartbreaking work should be dismissed, like the rent in the lining of the cap that you wrongly assert fitted Sacco, as so trifling a matter in the evidence of the case that it seems to the committee by no means a ground for a new trial. Did the committee feel that the prosecution's case was so weak that they had to bolster it by fresh deductions and surmises of their own?

The report in its entirety is an apology for the conduct of the trial rather than an impartial investigation. Reading it, the suspicion grows paragraph by paragraph that its aim was not to review but to make respectable the proceedings of Judge Thayer and the District Attorney's office. Not in a single phrase is there an inkling of a sense on your part or on that of your colleagues of the importance of the social and racial backgrounds of the trial. Your loose use of the words "socialistic" and "communistic" prove that you are ignorant or careless of the differences in mentality

---

## Newsreel LXVI

*As the day of Sacco and Vanzetti's execution neared, the U.S. Supreme Court declined to intervene. Dos Passos juxtaposes reports of demonstrations occurring throughout the world with snatches of the Communist Party anthem, "The Internationale." The newsreel ends with a passage from one of Vanzetti's deeply moving prison letters to his family.*

### HOLMES DENIES STAY

*A better world's in birth*

### Tiny Wasps Imported From Korea In Battle To Death With Asiatic Beetle

BOY CARRIED MILE DOWN SEWER; SHOT OUT ALIVE

### CHICAGO BARS MEETINGS

*For justice thunders condemnation*

### Washington Keeps Eye On Radicals

*Arise rejected of the earth*

PARIS BRUSSELS MOSCOW GENEVA ADD THEIR VOICES

*It is the final conflict
Let each stand in his place*

### Geologist Lost In Cave Six Days

*The International Party*

### SACCO AND VANZETTI MUST DIE

*Shall be the human race.*

*Much I thought of you when I was lying in the death house— the singing, the kind tender voices of the children from the playground where there was all the life and the joy of liberty—just one step from the wall that contains the buried agony of three buried souls. It would remind me so often of you and of your sister and I wish I could see you every moment, but I feel better that you will not come to the death house so that you could not see the horrible picture of three living in agony waiting to be electrocuted.*

*— The Big Money, pp. 1155–1156*

---

involved in partisanship in the various schools of revolutionary thought.

This is a matter of life and death, not only for Sacco and Vanzetti but for the civilization that Harvard University is supposed to represent. The Sacco-Vanzetti case has become part of the world struggle between the capitalist class and the working class, between those who have power and those who are struggling to get it. In a man in high office ignorance of the new sprouting forces that are remaking society, whether he is with them or

against them, is little short of criminal. It is inconceivable that intelligent reading men can be ignorant in this day of the outlines of anarchist philosophy. Instead of crying ignorance it would be franker to admit that as anarchists and agitators you hate these men and disapprove of their ideas and methods. But are you going to sacrifice the integrity of the legal system to that feeling? Are you going to prove by a bloody reprisal that the radical contention that a man holding unpopular ideas cannot get a free trial in our courts is true?

I cannot feel that either you or your colleagues have understood the full purport of your decision. If you had you would certainly have made out a more careful case for yourselves, one less full of loopholes and contradictions. It is upon men of your class and position that will rest the inevitable decision as to whether the coming struggle for the reorganization of society shall be bloodless and fertile or inconceivably bloody and destructive. It is high time that you realized the full extent of the responsibility on your shoulders.

As a Harvard man I want to protest most solemnly against you smirching the university of which you are an officer with the foul crime against humanity and civilization to which you have made yourself accessory.

John Dos Passos, '16
—*Nation*, 125 (24 August 1927): 176

### Vanzetti's Statement Upon Receiving Sentence

*Made to a reporter, Vanzetti's statement quickly became a rallying cry for the Left throughout the world.*

"If it had not been for these thing, I might have live out my life talking at street corners to scorning men. I might have die, unmarked, unknown, a failure. Now we are not a failure. This is our career and our triumph. Never in our full life could we hope to do such work for tolerance, for joostice, for man's onderstanding of man as now we do by accident. Our words—our lives—our pains—nothing! The taking of our lives—lives of a good shoemaker and a poor fish-peddler—all! That last moment belongs to us—that agony is our triumph."

—*The Letters of Sacco and Vanzetti*, edited by Marion Denman Frankfurter and Gardner Jackson (New York: Viking, 1928), p. [v]

### The Camera Eye (50)

*Brutally repressed demonstrations occurred throughout America and in many foreign cities on the night of the execution of Sacco and Vanzetti. In the midst of this moment of*

## SCENES FROM THE FUNERAL PROCESSION

THE FUNERAL CORTEGE PASSING TH ROUGH SCOLLAY SQUARE WHERE THE
POLICE TRIED TO SPL IT THE PROCESSION

ALONG TREMONT STREET NEAR ARLINGTON SQUARE. TWO HUNDRED THOUSAND
WATCHERS SAW THE FUNERAL PROCESSION PASS OVER SIX MILES
OF BOSTON STREETS TO FOREST HILLS CEMETERY

*Scenes from Vanzetti's funeral procession published in the bulletin of the Sacco-Vanzetti Defense Committee*
*(Collection of Richard Layman)*

*defeat, however, Dos Passos repeats Vanzetti's statement of belief in the triumph inherent in their martyrdom.*

    they have clubbed us off the streets    they are stronger    they are rich    they hire and fire the politicians the newspapereditors the old judges the small men with reputations the collegepresidents the wardheelers (listen businessmen collegepresidents judges America will not forget her betrayers) they hire the men with guns    the uniforms the policecars the patrolwagons

    all right you have won    you will kill the brave men our friends tonight

    there is nothing left to do    we are beaten    we the beaten crowd together in these old dingy schoolrooms on Salem Street shuffle up and down the gritty creaking stairs sit hunched with bowed heads on benches and hear the old words of the haters of oppression    made new in sweat and agony tonight

    our work is over    the scribbled phrases    the nights typing releases the smell of the printshop the sharp reek of newsprinted leaflets    the rush for Western Union stringing words into wires the search for stinging words to make you feel who are your oppressors America

    America our nation has been beaten by strangers who have turned our language inside out who have taken the clean words our fathers spoke and made them slimy and foul

    their hired men sit on the judge's bench they sit back with their feet on the tables under the dome of the State House they are ignorant of our beliefs they have the dollars the guns the armed forces the powerplants

    they have built the electricchair and hired the executioner to throw the switch

    all right we are two nations

    America our nation has been beaten by strangers who have bought the laws and fenced off the meadows and cut down the woods for pulp and turned our pleasant cities into slums and sweated the wealth out of our people and when they want to they hire the executioner to throw the switch

    but do they know that the old words of the immigrants are being renewed in blood and agony tonight do they know that the old American speech of the haters of oppression is new tonight in the mouth of an old woman from Pittsburgh of a husky boilermaker from Frisco who hopped freights clear from the Coast to come here in the mouth of a Back Bay socialworker in the mouth of an Italian printer of a hobo from Arkansas    the language of the beaten nation is not forgotten in our ears tonight

    the men in the deathhouse made the old words new before they died

*If it had not been for these things, I might have lived out my life talking at streetcorners to scorning men. I might have died unknown, unmarked, a failure. This is our career and our triumph. Never in our full life can we hope to do such work for tolerance, for justice, for man's understanding of man as how we do by an accident*

    now their work is over    the immigrants haters of oppression lie quiet in black suits in the little undertaking parlor in the North end    the city is quiet    the men of the conquering nation are not to be seen on the streets

    they have won why are they scared to be seen on the streets? on the streets you see only the downcast faces of the beaten    the streets belong to the beaten nation    all the way to the cemetery where the bodies of the immigrants are to be burned    we line the curbs in the drizzling rain we crowd the wet sidewalks elbow to elbow silent pale looking with scared eyes at the coffins

    we stand defeated America

    *—The Big Money, pp. 1156–1158*

### Review of Eugene Lyons's *The Life and Death of Sacco and Vanzetti*
Dos Passos

*Dos Passos used his review of Eugene Lyons's* The Life and Death of Sacco and Vanzetti *(1927) to call for a memorial to the two men in the form of writing "fiery and accurate" in its portrayal of the injustices their deaths represented. In a sense,* U.S.A. *was his own response to this demand.*

    The names of Sacco and Vanzetti are fading fast into the cloudland of myth where they are in danger of becoming vague symbols like God, country and Americanism. One of the most extraordinary things about industrial society of the present day is its idiot lack of memory. Tabloids and movies take the place of mental processes, and revolts, crimes, despairs pass off in a dribble of vague words and rubber stamp phrases without leaving a scratch on the mind of the driven instalment-paying, subway-packing mass. It is up to the writers now to see to it that America does not forget Sacco and Vanzetti so soon as it would like to. Czar Will Hays of the moving picture industry has thrown the glove in our faces by ordering all news films dealing with the most dramatic episode in the industrial war of our time to be taken from the vaults and burned.

Eugene Lyons fires the first gun with this rapid and fluent account of the case from its beginning on a Brockton street car to its end the night of August 22, 1927, when the death house in Charlestown jail suddenly swelled to become the whole world. In this excellent pamphlet Lyons has done exactly what he set out to do, which was to write an account of this seven years of agony of the working class that would be immediately available to men of all languages and conditions. I can't imagine how this particular job could have been done better.

But there remain a lot of other jobs to be done. Every detail must be told and retold. Sacco and Vanzetti must not have died in vain. We must have writing so fiery and accurate that it will sear through the pall of numb imbecility that we are again swaddled in after the few moments of sane awakening that followed the shock of the executions. America must not be allowed to forget. All the elements on the public stage who consider themselves alive and who are considered alive, college professors, writers, labor leaders, prominent liberals, protested that they were mighty shocked and that *if* the state of Massachusetts went ahead with the executions. . . . Workers all over the country felt their blood curdle at the thought. Well, it has come to pass. Well, we have protested. Our blood has curdled. What are we going to do now?

*—New Masses,* 3 (November 1927): 25

* * *

# Harlan

*At the onset of the Depression many violent conflicts arose between company owners seeking to minimize labor costs and employees attempting to preserve the advantages in pay and conditions they had gained in the 1920s. The coal-mining industry in particular, with its history of similar struggles going back to the late nineteenth century, experienced several such conflicts; the dispute in Harlan County, Kentucky, during the summer and fall of 1931 received the most national attention. As was true in many such disputes, the mine owners controlled the county both economically and politically, while the miners had as resources only their own desperate resolution and the occasional aid of two competing national mine unions, the Communist-dominated National Miners' Union and the relatively conservative United Mine Workers.*

*By the fall of 1931 the dominant mood of the Harlan miners and their families was that of fear—fear of armed intimidation by the owners and law agencies of the county and fear of starvation for those fired or locked out because of union activity. In this climate the National Committee for the Defense of Political Prisoners, a Communist front organization, decided to send a committee of writers, artists, and party functionaries to Harlan. Ostensibly, their role was to permit the working people of Harlan to tell their story of poverty and oppression to the nation as a whole; covertly, it was to bolster the standing of the National Miners Union in its efforts to organize the county's miners.*

*Dos Passos was attracted to the venture in part because of his respect for the chairman of the committee, Theodore Dreiser. And though by 1931 he had come to recognize the often suspect motives underlying Communist exploitation of specific instances of social injustice in America, he was also strongly drawn by the symbolic significance of an instance in which a group of "native stock" Americans were finding the means for expressing their condition and needs in the "voices" of writers. It is no coincidence, therefore, that Dos Passos concludes the last Camera Eye segment in U.S.A. with the recognition by the autobiographical figure who is to write the trilogy that in opposition to the material strength of those in power "we have only words against."*

## The 1931 Harlan Miners' Strike
John W. Hevener

*Hevener provides an account of the events in Harlan County, including the miners' extreme poverty and the suppression of their efforts to form a union, leading up to Dos Passos's arrival, in early November 1931, as a member of the Dreiser investigating committee.*

In 1931, the National Miners Union organizers arrived in Harlan County exhausted and chastened by their recent experience in leading forty thousand miners of western Pennsylvania, eastern Ohio, and northern West Virginia in the largest strike ever conducted under the auspices of the Communist party. In the Pittsburgh strike, the first large strike the union had conducted alone, the NMU had demonstrated that it knew how to start but not to end a strike; it suffered a stunning defeat, which, in party chairman William Z. Foster's opinion, "dealt the N.M.U. a fatal blow."[1]

The union had little chance for success in Kentucky. It lacked the local cadre of disciplined Communist party leadership that it had enjoyed in the northern coal fields; when the union arrived, there was not a single functioning Communist party unit in the state of Kentucky, and at no time were there more than twenty local or outside trained party members operating in the field. The union's sizable contingent of immigrant leaders, bearing names like Borich, Kemenovich, and Wagenknecht, were at a disadvantage among a native-born, Anglo-Saxon, Protestant population who were suspicious even of WASP labor organizers from Pennsylvania. The Communists' atheist, interracial, collectivist, and pro-Soviet views, once known, directly affronted the Harlan miners' fundamentalist religion, racism, individualism, and patriotism. Because the governor and sheriff had attributed earlier violence to radical activity, antiradical hysteria was

*Dos Passos, Theodore Dreiser, and Samuel Ornitz in Harlan County, Kentucky, 1931, while serving on an
investigative committee sponsored by the Communist Party–controlled National Committee for the Defense
of Political Prisoners (Associated Press/Wide World)*

already building and soon reached fever pitch. The Communists confronted a wave of repression and vigilantism beyond anything the UMW had recently experienced. Reluctant to burn their fingers again on a strike, NMU leaders procrastinated, but impatient local miners ultimately propelled them into the unpromising struggle.[2]

During the UMW strike in Harlan County, from May 26 until late June, 1931, the National Miners Union was preoccupied with its northern strike and took little notice of the Kentucky struggle. Not until May 21, seventeen days after the Battle of Evarts, did the Communist press first mention the Harlan struggle. In mid-June, J. Louis Engdahl, chairman of the Communist relief auxiliary, the International Labor Defense, journeyed to Harlan to offer legal assistance to Jones, Hightower, and other defendants in the Evarts murder case, but the UMW men rejected his offer. In late June, a week after the R. W. Creech Coal Company resumed operation and the UMW strike was definitely lost, the first NMU organizer, Dan Slinger, alias Dan Brooks, and a younger female representative of the ILD, Jessie Wakefield, were sent to Harlan County. They went at the behest of a tiny group of strikers who had been impressed by the militant rhetoric of the *Daily Worker*

and who in early June had asked its editor to send NMU organizers. While the National Guard remained in the county, radical literature–the *Daily Worker, Southern Worker, Labor Unity,* and *New Pioneer*–was widely circulated, and the NMU established seven soup kitchens, a most effective recruiting device for starving miners. By early July, ten NMU local unions had been formed.[3]

On July 15, twenty-seven southeastern Kentucky delegates, led by Dan Brooks, Bill Duncan, Jim Grace, and Jim Garland, attended an NMU convention in Pittsburgh. One of the Harlan delegates assured the group that "nobody has any use for the UMW after seeing how they've done us in Harlan. Everybody is wanting to join the National Miners Union."[4] Jim Grace, a Holiness preacher from Harlan, emotionally depicted the starvation of the Kentucky miners and the Red Cross's and UMW's refusal to assist them. Grace urged the delegates to "take our guns and pistols out of their hiding places, and use them on traitors and gun-men who represent our present form of Government" and brought the delegates to their feet wildly applauding when he described the recent Battle of Evarts, "when several gun-men bit the dust of Kentucky, at the hands of the mining slaves." Frank Borich, the NMU's national secretary, reported that since the

UMW strike had failed and the miners had been disillusioned with the compromising AFL union, the NMU had been actively organizing in Kentucky; he promised relief to Harlan strikers and asserted that a strike would be called at the next convention.[5] On July 22, the NMU issued a charter to the Harlan County miners.[6]

The Harlan coal operators, county officials, and the local press quickly acted to make the union's Communist connections the central issue. Instead of feeding people, alleviating suffering, and attempting to secure employment for blacklisted miners, the Harlan powers chose to suppress ideas, to halt distribution of relief, and to jail or expel from the county both the radical organizers and their followers. Erroneously attributing the earlier violence to radical agitation rather than to starvation and repression, county leaders sought to prevent a second outbreak of violence by using hunger and coercion, the causes of the first. Rationalizing their actions as necessary for social peace and the preservation of their very civilization, the coal operators, the sheriff, the courts, the press, civic groups, veterans' organizations, vigilantes, and the United Mine Workers combined to destroy the radical movement.

The local press helped establish a climate favorable to ruthless suppression. As soon as he learned there was a Communist in the county, editor Alverson asserted that "*an iron heel must be used to stamp out the foul growth.*" And the editor of the *Pineville Sun* urged Bell County officials to crush communism without "too many scruples as to the methods."[7]

At the same time, every effort was made to squelch outside journalistic criticism of either hunger or repression. From across the mountain at Norton, Virginia, *Crawford's Weekly,* edited by Bruce Crawford, a member of the National Committee for the Defense of Political Prisoners, directed a steady barrage of criticism at Harlan operators and county officials. On July 28, when Crawford and a friend visited Harlan to gather news, a hidden assailant shot the editor in the ankle. In mid-August, Boris Israel, a twenty-one-year-old reporter for the Federated Press, a radical labor news service, arrived in Harlan to report the Evarts murder trial. On opening day, three men, one of whom Israel identified as Deputy Sheriff "Two-Gun" Marion Allen, abducted him from the courtroom, drove him to the top of a hill overlooking the county seat, threatened his life, and shot him in the leg as he ran from the hill. After having his wound dressed in Pineville, he fled Kentucky and failed to return to Harlan to press charges.[8] Federated Press replaced Israel with Mrs. Harvey O'Conner. On the day of her arrival, she received a note from "100% Americans and we don't mean maybe," warning her that she had "been here too long already" and to "remember that the other red neck reporter got what

was coming to him, so don't let the sun go down on you here."[9] She did not.

Censorship was not confined to the radical press. The *Knoxville News-Sentinel,* which boasted a county circulation of six thousand compared to the hometown daily's four thousand, favored unionism, UMW or NMU. During the troubled summer of 1931, at least seven large coal companies prohibited circulation or possession of the Tennessee daily. "Uncle Bob" Lawson, superintendent at Cornett-Lewis, barred the paper at his camp because he believed it to be a "Red" or "Bolshevik" journal that published false and "dark pictures" of Harlan County.[10] When the Knoxville paper published a series of particularly critical articles by Benton J. Stong, the Harlan Kiwanis Club and the *Harlan Daily Enterprise* organized a boycott of the *News-Sentinel* and against the wholesale merchants of Knoxville until the newspaper ceased publishing "twisted, distorted, misrepresented and misinterpreted" views of Harlan County.[11]

Utilizing Kentucky's statute on criminal syndicalism, the sheriff attempted to jail or expel radical leaders. Soon after Bill Duncan and Jim Grace returned from the NMU convention, deputies raided their homes in search of radical literature. Duncan was arrested, and warrants issued for Grace's arrest forced him to pursue his activities in some other southeastern Kentucky county and eventually in New York City, where he solicited miners' relief. After having her automobile dynamited on August 6, ILD representative Jessie Wakefield was arrested on a charge of criminal syndicalism, as was Arnold Johnson, a seminary student representing the American Civil Liberties Union. Failing to post a $10,000 bond, the pair were held in the Harlan County jail for five weeks. Given their choice of transferring to an isolated Jackson County jail or leaving the state, on September 12 they departed Kentucky.[12]

The NMU's seven soup kitchens became favorite targets of suppression. Interestingly, the feeding stations posed a special problem for the Communists, who insisted on feeding white and black miners under the same roof and at the same table. Black miners, knowing that it would invite attack by county officials as an affront to community customs, strenuously opposed the practice and insisted on taking their meager allotments home for consumption. On August 11, deputies arrested Finley and Caleb Powers, who operated one of the feeding stations, on charges of banding and confederating; early the same morning, dynamite destroyed the Evarts kitchen. Two weeks later, deputies jailed Debs Moreland, proprietor of the Pansy feeding station. Released a month later, Moreland reopened the kitchen for two weeks. Again, deputies took him into custody, allegedly beat him, and forced him to flee the county.

On Sunday evening, August 30, the Clovertown soup kitchen was the scene of two deaths. Having driven out to inspect the kitchen, Deputy Lee Fleenor focused his car headlights on the building and stepped out into the shadows. Three frightened men, Joe Moore, Julius Baldwin, an NMU local secretary, and his brother, Jeff Baldwin, rushed out into the headlights' glare with guns drawn and fired at Fleenor. Escaping injury, Fleenor killed Moore and Julius Baldwin and seriously wounded Jeff. Tried for murder only after a county political shakeup a year later, Fleenor was acquitted by a jury after a five-minute deliberation.[13]

Florence Reece, a balladeer whose husband joined the NMU, later recalled the repression. "When the thugs were raiding our house off and on, and Sam was run off, I felt like I just had to do something to help. The little children, they'd have little legs and a big stomach. Some men staggered when they walked, they were so hungry. . . . We didn't even have any paper, so when I wanted to write "Which Side Are You On?" I just jerked the calendar off the wall and sat down and wrote the words down on the back."[14] She scribbled a militant strike call:

With pistols and with rifles
They take away our bread
And if you miners hinted it
They'll sock you on the head.

Which side are you on?
Which side are you on?

Gentlemen, can you stand it?
Oh, tell me how you can?
Will you be a gun thug
Or will you be a man?

Which side are you on?
Which side are you on?[15]

This rarely militant folksong, carried east by the visiting organizers, was to become one of America's most popular and enduring labor songs.

By late October. the raids had taken their toll. "Relief cut down to practically nothing," reported a Communist field organizer to New York headquarters. "All the kitchens but one closed in the last few weeks, the one operating is operating on credit."[16] The remaining kitchen was undoubtedly located beyond Harlan's borders. Earlier, the same source had reported: "Everything collapsed for a time; there was no functioning Party, no meetings of miners' locals, nothing in fact except submission to repeated raids upon miners' homes, searches, seizures, shootings, etc."[17]

Before the local movement collapsed, however, Harlan residents feared an outburst of violence when the Harlan County Circuit Court convened on April 17 to try the Evarts murder cases. A week earlier, the same day the Evarts soup kitchen was destroyed, a stink bomb was detonated in the automobile driven by the miners' defense attorneys, Ben Golden of Pineville and United States Congressman John M. Robison. That weekend the ILD called for miners and their families to stage a mass demonstration in front of the Harlan jail and courthouse when court convened. The ILD demanded a jury composed solely of laborers, immediate release of all prisoners of the class war, dismissal of all company-paid mine guards, and freedom for the miners to organize, picket, and strike. Sheriff Blair publicly assured miners that the Evarts defendants would receive a fair trial and banned all public demonstrations for its duration. On Friday and Saturday nights the glare of flaming crosses illuminated the mountains overlooking the county seat, and ominous booms of exploding dynamite echoed across the valley to call attention to the spectacle. Although the local editors seemed puzzled by the exhibition, its meaning could not have been lost on the miners and Communists who watched through the barred windows of the Harlan County jail or who scurried furtively about the county to organize Monday's demonstration. Local citizens nervously awaited the opening of court.[18]

When court convened, Commonwealth's Attorney W. A. Brock requested a change of venue for the eighteen Evarts defendants, and on August 24, Judge D. C. Jones transferred the cases to the distant Bluegrass counties of Montgomery and Clark. This surprise action removed from Harlan County the most obvious rallying point for radical agitation, and NMU support there all but collapsed.

Although the Harlan miners were severely suffering, their mood had grown fatalistic. "It's possible to be bitter hungry most all of the time and still keep alive. That's what most of us do, I guess," a Harlan miner's wife explained. Having suffered one disastrous defeat, most Harlan miners had been rehired and had grown fearful of unions, investigations, and strangers.[19] As a result of the intensity of the antiradical campaign, the transfer of the Evarts murder cases to distant parts, and the unresponsiveness of the Harlan miners, the National Miners Union transferred its base of operations to neighboring Bell County around September 1.[20] In the Straight Creek section of Bell County and the Brush Creek section of Knox County, the NMU enjoyed a far greater response; thereafter, those counties served as the focal point of radical agitation, strikes, demonstrations, and investigations.

To revive waning interest in the NMU's organizing campaign and potential strike, the ILD invited

*Citizens lining a street in the Harlan County town of Evarts, May 1931 (United Press International)*

another new Communist auxiliary, the National Committee for the Defense of Political Prisoners, to investigate and publicize conditions in the Harlan and Bell County coal fields. Angered by the earlier shooting of his NCDPP colleague, Bruce Crawford, and alarmed by the ILD's contention that Harlan operators and county officials were perpetrating a "reign of terror" upon starving miners, the novelist Theodore Dreiser, currently serving as NCDPP chairman, and eleven other left-wing writers conducted a two-day investigation in early November.[21] Involved were Dreiser, author of *Sister Carrie* and *An American Tragedy;* John Dos Passos, author of the *U.S.A.* trilogy; Samuel Ornitz, author of *Haunch, Paunch and Jowl;* Lester Cohen, author of *Sweepings;* Bruce Crawford, editor of *Crawford's Weekly;* Charles Rumford Walker, later author of *American City;* Walker's wife, Adelaide, a former actress; Harry Gannes, *Daily Worker* editor; Melvin P. Levy, NCDPP secretary; George Mauer, ILD representative; Dreiser's secretary, Julia Parker (alias Celia Kuhn); and his friend Marie Pergain.

Governor Sampson's military observer who accompanied the committee on its rounds judged the group as "decidedly radical or communistic. . . . They are certainly anti-capitalistic and believe that the system of the United States Government is wrong, and that one must not be too cautious in bringing about a change."[22] A member of the American Friends Service Committee, which fed Harlan children that winter, thought the writers demonstrated a preference for "changing horses and dumping their rider into the stream."[23] Although a few members of the committee were committed radicals, most were troubled liberals stung by the Depression-induced poverty, the unemployment, and the apparent breakdown of capitalism. Many were wrestling with the whole question of the artist's role in society: should he stand above it, completely committed to art for art's sake, or should he become actively involved in shaping a better civilization? All were seeking an answer, but few had yet found any. Their observations among the Kentucky miners had an important impact on these sensitive individuals. When Dreiser visited Kentucky, he stood at a crossroads of his career. Earlier in the year, at the behest of Communist party boss William Z. Foster, he had investigated the NMU's Pennsylvania coal strike and produced a report condemning the quiescent UMW and praising its aggressive Communist rival, the NMU.[24] For him, the Kentucky investigation and report, *Harlan Miners Speak,* represented a repeat performance that merely confirmed his deeply held prejudices. His most recent biographer believed that when Dreiser reached Kentucky, "he was unrivaled in his violence, his misinformation and his blind hatred for capitalists" whom he had formerly respected as "ruthless but essential" men of action.[25] Malcolm Ross astutely observed that had Dreiser in 1932

> approached Harlan people in the creative mood of *Sister Carrie,* he might have written something to be remembered long after the last load of Harlan coal has been mined. But Dreiser today is a bitter man. He is sickened by observing decades of injustice with the sensitized vision of an artist. When in the coal fields he closed his eyes to everything except the most dire wretchedness his guides could find for him. He snubbed the rather racy individuals who run things in those parts, and consequently they besmirched him with an immorality charge wholly irrelevant to the issue. This confirmed Dreiser's preconceived opinion of them. He was satisfied, for he had come to make war.[26]

In 1931, Dreiser's observations of capitalist failure in Pennsylvania and Kentucky and the apparent Communist economic stability he saw during a winter tour of the Soviet Union convinced him that communism was the solution for the United States' social and economic ills. Thereafter, he abandoned his literary career for that of pamphleteer and agitator. The following year, he began seeking membership in the Communist party; but because of his inability to accept party discipline, he was long denied admission. In 1945, long after most other American literary radicals had grown disenchanted with communism, Dreiser was at last admitted to the CPUSA.[27]

As a result of the Kentucky experience, John Dos Passos veered in the opposite direction. Since the Sacco and Vanzetti executions in 1927 he had moved steadily leftward, but in Kentucky, he watched Communist organizers manipulate the misers' misery to promote the party's cause, abuse the sincere IWW and UMW members, and deny legal assistance to imprisoned miners who refused to join their movement. Convinced that the Communists were using the miners as "pawns" and "making mon-

keys of the warmhearted liberals" like himself, he edged away from them and moved gradually to the political right.[28]

Harry Gannes, George Maurer, and Celia Kuhn were already directly affiliated with one or another organization of the Communist party apparatus; and Sam Ornitz, later a defendant in the Hollywood Ten trial, had already expressed his revolutionary views before reaching Harlan in a strident *New Masses* article entitled "Bleeding Bowels in Kentucky."

At formal hearings in Pineville and Harlan, Mrs. Jim Grace, a local NMU organizer, had carefully preselected friendly witnesses and freely prompted those who faltered in their testimony. Two outside NMU organizers, Ruth Decker and Mrs. Tom Myerscough, conducted the committee on a tour of the left fork of Straight Creek, Bell County, an older coal field where most mines had been exhausted and the camps abandoned. Unemployed and blacklisted miners and their families had occupied the rent-free, deserted dwellings. This area and the adjoining Wallins Creek section of Harlan County, where the closure of two huge Ford Motor Company mines in 1929 and 1931 had left large numbers of miners unemployed, possessed the worst housing and dietary conditions in southeastern Kentucky.[29] John Dos Passos portrayed these miners' houses as Florida shanties, constructed of thin sheathing lined with newspapers to break the wind, roofed with tar paper, and floored with rotten and broken boards. "The first step I took into the cabin," he wrote, "the floor creaked so I put my hand against the wall to steady myself. The rotten boards gave. With several people crowding into it, the crowded cabin looked as if it would crumple up at any minute. The floor of the kitchen had already caved in."[30]

The committee chose not to view Harlan County's newer, more permanent, model coal camps, such as Closplint or Lynch, the latter alone housing twelve thousand persons, equal to one-third the total population of Bell County.

Here on Straight Creek, the committee discovered Aunt Molly Jackson, local midwife, coal miner's wife, minstrel of the Kentucky miners' strike, a woman destined to become one of the more famous folksingers of the radical thirties. Aunt Molly's Scotch-Irish great-grandfather had stolen his bride from a Cherokee chief in Oklahoma and brought her to Eastern Kentucky's Clay County. There in the region's preindustrial era, in Aunt Molly's words, "the good old days [before] the coal operators began to swindle and cheat," her mother's family—the Robinsons—and her father's family—the Garlands—dwelt

*"Aunt" Molly Jackson with Dreiser in Kentucky, November 1931 (from Shelly Romalis,* Pistol Packin' Mama:
Aunt Molly Jackson and the Politics of Folksong, *1999)*

for seven generations. Life dealt harshly with this coal miner's daughter, born Mary Magdalene Garland in 1880. When she was three, her father moved the family to Laurel County to open a store. Because he sold groceries to miners on credit, the store failed after only two years, and he was forced into the coal mines, working six days per week and preaching once on Saturday and twice on Sunday. When Molly was six, her mother died of tuberculosis. Her father remarried and fathered eleven additional children, a total of fifteen. At fourteen, Molly married Jim Stewart and quickly bore two children. After nursing in a Clay County hospital for a decade, in 1908 she moved to Harlan County, where, acting as a midwife, she eventually delivered 884 babies. In 1917, her husband was killed by a slate fall in the mine, and she married another miner, Bill Jackson. Meanwhile, mining accidents blinded her father and a brother and killed another brother and one of her sons.[31]

In only three months during the fall of 1931, thirty-seven Straight Creek children died in the old midwife's arms. Diseases of poverty—tuberculosis, pellagra, and bloody flux—took their lives. "I still hear hungry children cry," she recalled more than twenty

years later. "I saw my own sister's little fourteen-month-old baby girl starve to death for milk while the coal operators was riding around in fine cars with their wives and children all dressed up in diamonds and silks, paid for by the blood and sweat of the coal miners."[32] The old lady, who had sung and put together songs since childhood, set her feelings to verse in "I Am a Union Woman" in 1931. "The bosses ride fine horses / While we walk in the mud," she protested. "Their banner is the dollar sign / While ours is striped with blood."[33]

Her miseries, most of them directly attributable to the dangers and inequities of coal mining, radicalized Aunt Molly. "I've been . . . accused of being a Red," she later complained. "I never heard tell of a Communist until after I left Kentucky [1932]—then I had passed fifty—but they called me a Red. I got all of my progressive ideas from my hard tough struggles, and nowhere else."[34]

Her miner father, who had always preached unionism along with the gospel, had taught her to act on her beliefs. Since age five, she had attended union meetings, picketed, sung, and organized. In 1931 her younger half-brother Jim Garland, convinced that the United Mine Workers had betrayed the miners' cause, sheltered the popular young Communist youth organizer Harry Simms and became district organizer for the NMU; and Aunt Molly joined the radical union. She was jailed in Clay County, and her husband was forced to divorce her to keep his mining job. Impressed with her during their November visit, the Dreiser Committee took her out of the Cumberlands to solicit funds in thirty-eight states for the striking miners. Twenty-one thousand people heard her and Jim Garland perform at New York's Coliseum and contributed $900 to the miners' cause. Badly crippled in a bus accident while touring Ohio and rejected by the left-wing Workers Music League, which at the time saw no use for her militant mountain songs beyond the immediate campaign, she returned to the Cumberlands.[35]

*—Which Side Are You On? The Harlan County Coal Miners, 1931–1939* (Urbana: University of Illinois Press, 1978), pp. 56–67

## Notes

1. Theodore Draper, "Communists and Miners, 1928–1933," *Dissent*, 9 (Spring 1972): 391; William Z. Foster, *Pages from a Worker's Life* (New York: International, 1939), p. 182.

2. Draper, "Communists and Miners," pp. 382–384.

3. Ibid., p. 381; *Conditions in Coal Fields in Harlan and Bell Counties, Kentucky* (Washington, D.C.: U.S. Government Printing Office, 1932), pp. 11, 46–47, 123–125; *Harlan Miners Speak: Report on Terrorism in the Kentucky Coal Fields* (New York: Harcourt, Brace, 1932), pp. 34, 45–47, 239.

4. *Daily Worker*, 17 July 1931, quoted in Draper, "Communists and Miners," p. 381.

5. Anonymous letter, 20 July 1931, NA, RG/280, "Coal Miners (Southeastern Ky.)," Box 294.

6. *Harlan (Ky.) Daily Enterprise*, 11 September 1931.

7. Editorial, ibid., 9 August 1931 (italics are the editor's); editorial, *Pineville (Ky.) Sun*, 13 August 1931.

8. *Harlan Daily Enterprise*, 28 July, 18 August 1931; *Harlan Miners Speak*, pp. 81–82; testimony of Henry M. Lewis, LFCH, pt. 11, p. 4009.

9. *Harlan Daily Enterprise*, 26–27 August 1931.

10. John A. Dotson, "Socio-Economic Background and Changing Education in Harlan County, Kentucky," dissertation, George Peabody College for Teachers, 1943, p. 47; *Knoxville (Tenn.) News-Sentinel*, 17 December 1931.

11. *Harlan Daily Enterprise*, 23 August 1931.

12. Ibid., 6 August, 25 August, 13 September 1931; *Pineville Sun*, 13 August 1931; editorial, ibid., 24 September 1931; *Harlan Miners Speak*, pp. 46, 71–73, 92–96.

13. Draper, "Communists and Miners," pp. 386–387; *Harlan Daily Enterprise*, 11 August, 31 August, 29 September 1931, 29 August 1932; *Harlan Miners Speak*, pp. 47, 97–100, 121.

14. "Which Side Are You On? An Interview with Florence Reece," *Mountain Life & Work*, 48 (March 1972): 23–24.

15. Mrs. Reece confused the year of the NMU campaign; it was 1931, not 1930.

15. Ibid., p. 23.

16. S. Bowen [Clara Holden], 28 October 1931, Harry M. Wicks Papers, quoted in Draper, "Communists and Miners," p. 383.

17. Anonymous [Clara Holden?], 18 September 1931, Wicks Papers, quoted ibid., pp. 382–383.

18. *Harlan Daily Enterprise*, 13–14 August, 16 August 1931; Don Whitehead, "Take It or Leave It," *Harlan Enterprise*, 17 August 1931; U.S. conciliation commissioner to Hugh L. Kerwin, 20 August 1931, NA, RG/280, "Coal Miners (Southeastern Ky.)," Box 294.

19. Quoted by Margaret Lane, "Noted Woman Writer Tells the Story of Terrible Conditions Existing in Harlan County Field," *United Mine Workers Journal*, 15 December 1931, p. 12.

20. Editorial, *Pineville Sun*, 3 September 1931; Malcolm Ross, *Machine Age in the Hills* (New York, 1933), p. 174.

21. Lawrence Grauman Jr., "'That Little Ugly Running Sore': Some Observations on the Participation of American Writers in the Investigations of Conditions in the Harlan and Bell County, Kentucky, Coal Fields, 1931–32," *Filson Club History Quarterly*, 36 (October 1962): 348; *Harlan Miners Speak*, pp. 4, 7.

22. Testimony of Major George M. Chescheir, *Conditions in Coal Fields*, p. 146.

23. Ross, *Machine Age in the Hills*, p. 171.

24. Walter Wilson to Theodore Dreiser, 12 July 1931, Theodore Dreiser Papers, University of Pennsylvania; "President Green Hauls Theodore Dreiser over the Coals for his Vicious Attack on the Union," *United Mine Workers Journal*, 15 July 1931, pp. 8–9; W. A. Swanberg, *Dreiser* (New York, 1965), p. 381.

25. Swanberg, *Dreiser*, p. 391.

26. Ross, *Machine Age in the Hills*, pp. 170–171.

27. Daniel Aaron, *Writers on the Left: Episodes in American Literary Communism* (New York: Harcourt, Brace & World, 1961), p. 178; Swanberg, *Dreiser*, p. 389.

28. John Dos Passos, *The Theme Is Freedom* (New York: Dodd, Mead, 1956), p. 87; Robert H. Footman, "John Dos Passos," *Sewanee Review*, 47 (July–September 1939): 371.

29. Testimony of Chescheir, *Conditions in Coal Fields*, pp. 138–140, 145–146, 149, 151; Herndon J. Evans, "Kentucky Hits Communism," *Kentucky Progress Magazine*, 4 (April 1932): 28.

30. *Harlan Miners Speak*, pp. 278, 286.

31. John Greenway, *American Folksongs of Protest* (Philadelphia: University of Pennsylvania Press, 1953), pp. 252–255, 257–259.

32. Ibid., pp. 258, 274.

33. Ibid., pp. 253–254; "I Am a Union Woman" is quoted by R. Serge Denisoff in *Great Day Coming: Folk Music and the American Left* (Urbana: University of Illinois Press, 1971), p. 25.

34. Greenway, *American Folksongs of Protest*, pp. 261–262.

35. Ibid., pp. 253–254, 258–260, 265, 271; Denisoff, *Great Day Coming*, pp. 46–47.

## Harlan: Working Under the Gun
### Dos Passos

*"Harlan: Working Under the Gun" is Dos Passos's fullest account of his visit to Harlan. Some highlights of his report are the inclusion of Aunt Molly Jackson's lyrics (Jackson was to become famous as a performer at radical rallies); the interview of Sheriff John Henry Blair in his office, which was to serve as the setting of* Camera Eye (51); *and a reference to the infamous "toothpick indictment" of Dreiser for adultery. (The basis for the indictment was that toothpicks placed outside the door of Dreiser's hotel room were found undisturbed the morning after a woman was seen entering his room in the evening.) Much of Dos Passos's article was included in the full report of the committee,* Harlan Miners Speak: Report of Terrorism in the Kentucky Coal Mines *(1932).*

Everybody knows that the coal industry is sick and that the men working at our most dangerous occupation (every sixth man is injured in the course of a year) are badly off, but few Americans outside of the miners themselves understand how badly off, or how completely the "American standard of living" attained in some sections during boom years, with strong unions working under the Jacksonville agreement, has collapsed. The coal operators, who have been unable to organize their industry commercially or financially along modern lines, have taken effective common action in only one direction: in an attack against the unions, the wage scales and the living conditions of the men who dig the coal out for them. Harlan County in eastern Kentucky, which has been brought out into the spotlight this summer by the violence with which the local Coal Operators' Association has carried on this attack, is, as far as I can find out, a pretty good medium exhibit of the entire industry: living conditions are better than in Alabama and perhaps a little worse than in the Pittsburgh district. The fact that the exploited class in Harlan County is of old American pre-Revolutionary stock, that the miners still speak the language of Patrick Henry and Daniel Boone and Andrew Jackson and conserve the pioneer traditions of the Revolutionary War and of the conquest of the West, will perhaps win them more sympathy from the average American than he would waste on the wops and bohunks he is accustomed to see get the dirty end of the stick in labor troubles.

### I: War Zone

I am sad and weary, I've got the
    hongry ragged blues,
Not a penny in my pocket
    to buy one thing I need to use
I was up this mornin
    with the worst blues ever had in my life
Not a bit to cook for breakfast
    or for a coalminer's wife.

The mines in Harlan County are in the forks and creeks of the upper part of the Cumberland River. A comparatively new coal field, first developed on a large scale during the boom in production that went along with the European War, its output is said to be a very high grade of bituminous. The miners were organized 90 percent by the United Mine Workers of America around 1917. In the 1920 boom a union miner was sometimes able, hiring several "chalkeyes" (inexperienced helpers) at $8 a day, to clear two or three hundred dollars a month. Railways pushed into the leafy valleys of the Cumberland range, fairly prosperous towns grew up. The population of Harlan County increased three or fourfold. Local business men who had managed to get hold of coal lands prospered on leases and royalties. Mountaineers who had lived poor and free on their hillside farms came down into the valleys to work in the mines and live in "patches" of temporary houses, put up by the companies. The race for riches went to the heads of the miners. The union turned into a racket and lapsed. Financiers skimmed the cream off the coal companies and left them overcapitalized and bankrupt. In the fat years no one thought of taking any measures of civic organization to help tide them over the lean years that were to follow—a typical American situation. Headlong deflation left the coal operators broke and the miners starving.

Last winter was pretty bad. When spring came along, the miners around Evarts began to think something ought to be done to revive the old locals of the U.M.W. of A. Wages had been steadily slipping. Conditions of safety were getting worse. A few old Wobblies and radicals began to talk class war; some of the youngsters began to wonder about socialism. A meeting was held in Pineville to talk about union organization. Two hundred men lost their jobs and were blacklisted. The coal operators, scared by the flood of anti-Red propaganda fed them through detective agencies and professional labor-baiting organizations, began to hire extra guards. Their position depended on their underselling the coal regions where traces of unionism still remained. Trusting to the terrible unemployment to break any strike that might be pulled, they took the offensive. In April they started evicting active union men from their houses. In the eastern counties of Kentucky every man considers himself entitled to carry a gun and to protect himself with it against insult and aggression. It was not long before a skirmish took place between miners and guards sworn in as deputies. This was followed, on May 5, by an out-and-out battle on the road outside of Evarts.

The townspeople of Evarts explain it this way: The town was full of evicted miners who seem to have had the pretty complete sympathy of the townspeople

*Dust jacket for the 1932 collection that included Dos Passos's "Harlan: Working Under the Gun" (Collection of Richard Layman)*

(the small merchants and storekeepers are against the mine operators because they force the miners to trade at the company commissaries). Feeling was running high. The mine guards made a practice of riding slowly through the town with their cars in second, machine guns and sawed-off shotguns sticking out of the windows, "tantalizing us," as one man put it. The morning of the fight, a rumor went around that the sheriff was going to bring in some carloads of scabs. Miners congregated on the road across the bridge from Evarts. The Coal Operators' Association claims that the miners were lying in ambush, an assertion which the miners deny. A carload of deputies came in from Harlan town. Shooting began, and lasted for thirty minutes. In the course of it three deputies were killed and several wounded; one miner was also killed and others wounded. Deputies then took Evarts by storm and arrested everybody they could lay their hands on. For some time the town had been under the cross-fire of their machine guns. The next morning Judge D. C. Jones—his wife is a member of

the Hall family, which has mining interests in the vicinity—called a grand jury which the miners assert was illegally picked, made them a fiery speech denouncing I.W.W.'s and Reds. This grand jury returned thirty triple-murder indictments and thirty indictments for banding and confederating. Among those indicted were the town clerk and chief of police of Evarts. From then on through the summer the elected town officers of Evarts were superseded by the high sheriff's men, whose salaries are paid by the coal operators. No indictments were returned against mine guards or deputy sheriffs who had taken part in the battle, or against a mine guard who later killed Chasteen, a restaurant owner in Evarts who was on the miners' side.

About that time, so far as I can make out, the communist-affiliated National Miners' Union, which was conducting a strike against the Pittsburgh Terminal Company, sent organizers into eastern Kentucky, and N.M.U. locals began to be formed out of the wreckage of the old U.M.W. of A. In Evarts itself the I.W.W. seems to have had more influence than the Communists. The thing is that the miners felt that they were fighting for their lives and were ready to join any organization that would give them back solidarity and support them in their struggle against intolerable conditions. I talked to men who had joined all three unions.

Meanwhile the Coal Operators' Association was out to crush radicalism in Harlan County. The automobile of the I.L.D. relief worker was mysteriously dynamited. The soup kitchen in Evarts, which was feeding four hundred men, women and children a day, was blown up. In an attack on another soup kitchen at the swimming hole near Wallins Creek, two union men were killed and several wounded. Union organizers were beaten and run out of the county. Bruce Crawford of Crawford's Weekly, who greatly annoyed Sheriff Blair by publishing the miners' side of the story, was mysteriously shot from ambush. Boris Israel, Federated Press correspondent, was seized on the steps of the courthouse at Harlan, taken for a ride in perfect Chicago style, thrown out of the car on a lonely road and shot. Houses were raided, and many union sympathizers (among them Arnold Johnson, a theological student, who was an investigator for the American Civil Liberties Union) were arrested and jailed on the charge of criminal syndicalism. The Knoxville News Sentinel, a Scripps-Howard paper which printed stories about the frightful plight of the miners, was taken out of the newsstands in Harlan and its reporters were so intimidated the editor never dared send the same man up to Harlan twice.

All this time in the adjacent Bell County, where living conditions among the miners are worse if possible than in Harlan, the high sheriff has told the coal operators that if they make any trouble, he will cancel the deputy commissions of the mine guards, with the result that there has been no bloodshed, although there have been successful strikes in small mines along Straight Creek.

## II: Enter the Writers' Committee

When my husband works in the coalmines,
    he loads a car on every trip,
Then he goes to the office that evenin
    an gits denied of scrip—
Jus because it took all he had made that day
    to pay his mine expenses—
Jus because it took all he had made that day
    to pay his mine expenses.
A man that'll jus work for coal light an carbide
    he ain't got a speck of sense.

Breakfast in the station at Cincinnati. After that the train crosses the Ohio River and starts winding through the shallow valleys of the rolling section of central Kentucky. At lunch time to get to the dining car we have to walk through a federal prison car on its way to Atlanta. Change at Corbin onto a local train for Pineville. The Louisville papers say Governor Sampson is sending a detachment of militia into Harlan County. As we got near Pineville the valleys deepen. Steep hills burnished with autumn cut out the sky on either side. There's the feeling of a train getting near the war zone in the old days.

At the station is a group of miners and their wives come to welcome the writers' committee: they stand around a little shyly, dressed in clean ragged clothes. A little coaldust left in men's eyebrows and lashes adds to the pallor of scrubbed faces, makes you think at once what a miserable job it must be keeping clean if you work in coal. At the Hotel Continental Mr. Dreiser is met by newspaper men, by the mayor and town clerk of Pineville, who offer their services "without taking sides." Everybody is very polite. A reporter says that Judge D. C. Jones is in the building. A tall man in his thirties, built like a halfback, strides into the lobby. There's something stiff and set about the eyes and the upper part of his face; a tough customer. When he comes up to you you realize he must stand six-feet-six in his stocking feet. He and Mr. Dreiser meet and talk rather guardedly. Judge Jones says he's willing to answer any questions put to him about the situation in Harlan County. Mr. Dreiser and Judge Jones are photographed together on the steps of the hotel. Mrs. Grace of Wallins Creek, the wife of Jim Grace, a union organizer who was beaten up and run out of the county, comes up and asks Judge Jones why the sheriff's deputies raided her house and ransacked her things and her boarders' rooms. The interview comes abruptly to an end.

When the members of the committee settle down at a long table in a room off the lobby to decide on a plan of procedure, stories start pouring in. Mr. Dreiser, after questioning Mrs. Grace about her husband's former employment—a former miner now working in a store, he was prominent in organizing the N.M.U.—asks her how he was arrested:

A. I was not with him, but he was arrested in Letcher County. Neon. Him and Tom Myerscough were together.

Q. What were they doing?

A. They were trying to get the union organized. They were organizing against starvation. They were establishing a union for better conditions.

Q. What happened to him?

A. After they came to the house looking for him, he went away and stayed at a friend's house and then he and Tom went to Neon, Letcher County. There he was arrested and took to jail in Neon. Then he was turned over to the Jenkins' bunch of gunmen.

Q. Well, what happened then?

A. Him and Myerscough were turned over to the Harlan County bunch and they takes them over to the Big Black Mountains of Virginia. They bust him in the face and broke his cheek bone. They kicked him in the back. He ran into the woods and they fired at him.

Q. How many shots did they fire?

A. About fifty I guess.

Q. Did they hit him?

A. Well he was grazed at the elbow.

Q. What did he do?

A. He went on to Middlesboro and stayed at a friend's house. But I didn't know. When I first got word that Mr. Grace and Tom was held in jail, I didn't know whether he was in Harlan, Jenkins, or Neon. I goes out and went to get somebody to find out. We thought they were killed. I started to get hold of the I.L.D. and I just happened in where Mr. Grace was and I asked the lady whether her husband was there and I found out that Jim was there. His face and eyes was swollen black and blue. He was crazy as a loon.

Then she testified to raids on her house and her boarders' rooms being searched for I.W.W. and Com-MU-nist literature. Then an organizer for the union testified about having his house broken into and his guns seized (the possession of firearms is legal in Kentucky), a vice president of the Kentucky State Federation of Labor turned over some documents to the effect that when the state militia came in after the Evarts battle last spring the operators had promised the U.M.W. of A. that they wouldn't take that opportunity of importing scabs, and in spite of that had imported scabs. A young man brought a mysterious message warning the writers' committee not to attend the meeting called by the National Miners' Union at Wallins Creek on Sunday, as there'd surely be trouble there. Bruce Crawford told the story of his quarrel with Sheriff John Henry Blair: how Blair had gone to see him in Norton and complained of the attitude of his paper, had

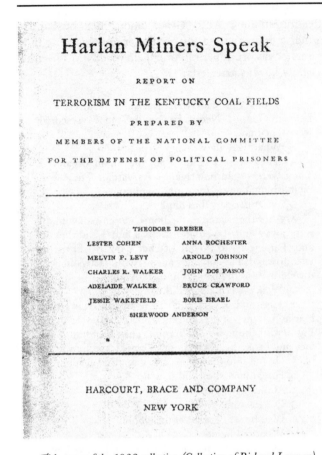

## Harlan Miners Speak

REPORT ON

TERRORISM IN THE KENTUCKY COAL FIELDS

PREPARED BY

MEMBERS OF THE NATIONAL COMMITTEE

FOR THE DEFENSE OF POLITICAL PRISONERS

THEODORE DREISER

LESTER COHEN      ANNA ROCHESTER

MELVIN P. LEVY      ARNOLD JOHNSON

CHARLES R. WALKER      JOHN DOS PASSOS

ADELAIDE WALKER      BRUCE CRAWFORD

JESSIE WAKEFIELD      BORIS ISRAEL

SHERWOOD ANDERSON

HARCOURT, BRACE AND COMPANY

NEW YORK

*Title page of the 1932 collection (Collection of Richard Layman)*

taken a subscription and left, and how the next time Crawford went to Harlan several shots had been fired at him as he crossed the swinging footbridge over the river, one of them nicking him in the ankle. The most moving testimony was that of Jeff Baldwin, whose brother Julius had been killed by deputies at the swimming-hole soup kitchen. His story was that two or more deputies had driven up the dirt road that leads up the hill from the main road to the shack where the soup kitchen was located, had stopped the sedan so that the headlights shone full in the door dazzling the group of miners standing around it, that one deputy, Lee Fleener by name, had first yelled "Put up your hands" and then immediately opened fire. Baldwin's brother and another man had been killed and he himself wounded in the shoulder as he ducked for shelter inside the shack. In spite of the fact that the coroner's jury had named Lee Fleener and other persons unknown as the murderers, no action had been taken by the county prosecutor.

Next day the committee went up to Harlan, a fine ride up the magnificent valley of the Cumberland

River. Harlan is a lively little town; stores and bank buildings attest to the slightly flimsy prosperity of the boom period; the handsome courthouse takes away a little from the gimcrack air of a Southern industrial town.

Meanwhile, in a crowded room in the Llewellyn Hotel, miners and their wives were telling their stories:

Q. For how many years have you been a miner?

A. From twenty to twenty-five years.

Q. Have you done most of your mining here in Harlan County?

A. Since 1917. . . .

Q. When you were in good standing with this union [the United Mine Workers] how much did you make a day?

A. When we had a union here I could make from four dollars to five dollars to six dollars a day.

Q. How much did you make a month?

A. Anywhere maybe along from eighty dollars to one hundred.

Q. How much did you work for after the union broke up?

A. They kept cutting wages down till you hardly couldn't make anything at all. . . .

Q. This thirty dollars that you would get, was it in scrip or in cash?

A. No, sir, you hardly ever drew any money on that. You traded your scrip in at the store, the company store, and part of the time they had you in debt.

Q. Did you buy clothing at the company store or food?

A. Food. I couldn't get enough to buy clothes.

Q. How did you get clothing?

A. I generally sent out to beg and did the best I could.

This miner testified that since he'd been fired he had lived "on the mercy of the people." Being asked what criminal syndicalism, the charge on which he had been arrested and bonded over to keep the peace, meant to him, he said: "The best I can give it is going against your country, but that is something I never did do. I never thought about such a thing. . . . My family always fought for the country and I've always been for it."

Then Mr. Dreiser questioned a woman who refused to give her name, saying she was afraid her husband would lose his job if the boss found out she'd testified. They were living in a company house, where they'd been living for three weeks. In that time the husband had received only scrip.

A. We have just managed to exist. I will tell you that I've had just one dollar in the last three days to live on, my husband and myself and two children.

Q. I wonder how you distribute that money around.

A. We live on beans and bread. We don't get no dinner. . . . There don't none of you know how hard a man works that works in the mines and I'll tell you what I had to put in his bucket this morning for him to eat and work hard all day. There was a little cooked punkin and what you folks call white meat, just fat white bacon, and that's what he took to the mines to eat and work on and he had water gravy for breakfast and black coffee.

Q. And what's water gravy?

A. Water and grease and a little flour in it.

Q. What do you give the children?

A. They had the same breakfast and they don't get no dinner. . . . They're not in a situation to go to school because they have no shoes on their feet and no underwear on them and the few clothes they have, they are through them.

In the afternoon Mr. Dreiser visited Sheriff Blair in his office and asked him some questions. The sheriff said that the National Mine Workers was a communist organization and that the U.M.W. of A. had not been, that he considered The Daily Worker and all other Communist, I.W.W. or Red publications illegal, and explained that most of the deputies he had sworn in were mine guards paid by the coal operators. He didn't know how many deputies he had sworn in. The only money they got from his office were fees for arrests and summonses. He brought the interview to a lively close by serving Bruce Crawford with a $50,000 civil suit for slander.

Next morning County Prosecutor Will Brock was interviewed. He said he approved of unionism, if it was a legal unionism like that of the U.M.W. of A., but that he considered all this I.W.W.-Communist agitation illegal and seditious. As an example of a fellow that he'd thought at first was decent and that had then turned out to be a Communist, he mentioned Arnold Johnson, investigator for the American Civil Liberties Union. The interview was made fairly tense by the interruptions of an attorney named Jones, who shares his office with him, who said he was just waiting to tell the whole damned bunch what he thought of them; on being asked about a deputy named Heywood who was reputed to be a Chicago gunman, he said grimly through his teeth: "All right, if you want to see him so bad, you'll see him." We learned afterward that his brother had been killed in the Evarts fight, and that he himself had taken part in raids on miners' houses.

### III: The Meeting in Straight Creek

All the women in this coalcamp
   are sittin with bowed down heads
All the women in this coalcamp
   are sittin with bowed down heads
Ragged an barefooted an their
   children acryin for bread
No food no clothes for our children
   I'm sure this ain't no lie
No food no clothes for our children

I'm sure this ain't no lie
  If we can't get no more for our labor
   we will starve to death and die.

Straight Creek is the section of Bell County that has been organized fairly solid under the National Miners' Union. Owing, the miners say, to the fair-minded attitude of the sheriff, who has not allowed the mine guards to molest them, there has been no bloodshed, and a three weeks' strike ended the week before we got there with several small independent operators signing agreements with the union at thirty-eight cents a ton and allowing a union checkweighman. They say thirty-eight cents is not a living wage but that it's something to begin on. The committee had been invited to attend a meeting of the N.M.U. local at the Glendon Baptist Church and walked around the miners' houses first. The militia officers who accompanied us were impressed with the utter lack of sanitation and the miserable condition of the houses, tumble-down shacks set up on stilts with the keen mountain wind blowing through the cracks in the floor.

### IV: Last Vestige of Democracy

This minin town I live in
   is a sad an a lonely place,
This minin town I live in
   is a sad an a lonely place,
For pity and starvation
   is pictured on every face,
Everybody hongry and ragged,
   no slippers on their feet,
Everybody hongry and ragged,
   no slippers on their feet,
All goin round from place to place
   bummin for a little food to eat.
Listen my friends and comrades
   please take a friend's advice,
Don't put out no more of your labor
   till you get a livin price.

Evarts is probably one of the few towns in the United States that still has democratic government. In spite of the fact that it's hemmed in on every side by coal-company property, that the chief of police and town clerk were arrested and charged with murder after the battle in May and that the town policing was done all summer by company guards, at the November election they put in a pro-miner town council by something like 200 to 80 votes. Most of the men at present on trial for their lives come from Evarts, and as far as I could find out from talking around, they have the complete sympathy of the local population. It is in Evarts that the union movement started, and there the miners were first accused of being Reds when it was discovered by the Coal Operators' Association that one of the U.M.W. of A. locals had taken out an I.W.W.

charter. The miners on trial were being defended by the General Defense Committee, the old Wobbly defense, that is unwilling to cooperate with the Communist-affiliated I.L.D. defending the criminal syndicalism and banding and confederating cases that have grown out of attempts to suppress the National Miners' Union. So far as I could make out, the county authorities consider members of either organization equally without human rights. Possibly the I.W.W. occupies a slightly better position, owing to its connection with U.M.W. of A. officials who have contacts with state (Democratic) politics, and to its soft pedaling of class-war talk. But the real point is that the situation of the miners is so desperate that they'll join anything that promises them even temporary help. I asked one man if he'd go to work again under the present scale, supposing he could get past the blacklist. He said, "You starve if you work an' you starve if you don't work. A man 'ud rather starve out in the woods than starve workin' under the gun."

The meeting at Wallins Creek took place in the high-school building and passed off without disorder, though you got the impression that the people who attended it were pretty nervous. The local small merchants seemed strong for the N.M.U. and somebody had put up a banner across the main street that read, "Welcome I.L.D., National Miners' Union, Writers' Committee." The next morning the committee packed up its testimony and left for New York, to be followed by the "toothpick indictment" of Mr. Dreiser and a general indictment of all concerned, including the speakers at the miners' meeting, for criminal syndicalism.

The midwife at Straight Creek, Aunt Molly Jackson, who later spoke at the meeting and sang these blues of her own composing that I've been quoting at the heads of the sections, was questioned by Mr. Dreiser:

Q. Can you tell us something about the conditions of the people in this hollow?

A. The people in this country are destitute of anything that is really nourishing to the body. That is the truth. Even the babies have lost their lives and we have buried from four to seven a week during the warm weather . . . on account of cholera, flux, famine, stomach trouble brought on by undernourishment. Their food is very bad, such as beans and harsh foods fried in this lard that is so hard to digest. . . . Families have had to depend on the Red Cross. The Red Cross put out some beans and corn.

Q. Do they give it to everyone that asks?

A. No, they stop it when they know a man belongs to the union.

Q. What did they say about it?

A. The Red Cross is against a man who is trying to better conditions. They are for the operators and they want the mines to be going, so they won't give anything to a man unless he does what the operators want him to. . . . I talked to the Red Cross lady over in Pineville. I said there's a lot of little children in destitution. Their feet are on the ground. They have come so far. They are going to get pneumonia and flu this winter that will kill them children off.

Q. Did she offer to give you any relief?

A. No, because they was members of the National Miner's Union. They said, "We are not responsible for

## Dos Passos Appeals for Aid to Miners' Families

*After returning to New York, the Dreiser Committee set about publicizing the conditions at Harlan and establishing groups to aid the miners. Dos Passos himself spoke at a rally and contributed this letter, which received a wide mailing.*

National Committee to Aid
Striking Miners Fighting
Starvation
New York City
*January, 1932*

Dear Friend:

Having just come back from a trip with the Dreiser Committee around Harlan County, Kentucky, and spoken to the miners and seen how they live, I can assure you that the name of this committee is no exaggeration.

The miners, their wives and children live in crumbling shacks, many of them clapboard, through whose cracks pour the lashing mountain winds, rain and snow. "We're not afraid of the wind", said a mother of five, "it's the loose boards in the walls."

A few crumbs of cornbread usually—a piece of salt pork occasionally—a few pinto beans for the more fortunate—this is their food. "Last summer we ate grass—this winter, I guess we'll eat snow," said another mother.

Wages? Aunt Molly Jackson, wife of a Straight Creek, Kentucky miner, said, "Better starve striking than starve working in the muck of a mine." If the men go on strike against these intolerable conditions, the slight local and Red Cross Relief being offered is entirely cut off and they are evicted from their houses. Then they face the entire armed force of the law, which in Kentucky, means vicious courts, jails, tear-gas-bombs, guns—manned by thugs known to have been "imported" especially for the miners.

Schools? Shoeless children are school-less children. Many lack even underwear. Thru the gray of any morning one can see a group of mourners behind a shack—a gash in the mountain-side, a little pine coffin lowered into the earth, and the earth close around the remains of a child that did not have a chance to live.

Can you give something to help bring food to the mouths of these freezing, starving children?

Gratefully
John Dos Passos
Chairman

—Ludington, ed., *The Fourteenth Chronicle*, p. 401

those men out on strike. They should go back to work and work for any price that they will take them on for."

The meeting in the Baptist Church was conducted by a young fellow who'd been a preacher. Men and women spoke. Two representatives of the I.L.D. made speeches. One of the miners said in his speech that the reason they called them Reds was because the miners were so thin an' poor that if you stood one of 'em up against the sun you'd see red through him. All through the meeting a stout angry woman, who we were told was the bookkeeper at the Carey mine and the Red Cross distributor, stood in the aisle with her arms akimbo glaring at the speakers as if she was going to start trouble of some kind. All she did was occasionally to taunt the chairman with the fact that he owed her ten dollars. The high point of the meeting was Aunt Molly Jackson's singing of her blues:

Please don't go under those mountains
   with the slate ahangin over your head,
Please don't go under those mountains
   with the slate ahangin over your head,
An work for jus coal light an carbide
   an your children acryin for bread;
I pray you take my council
   please take a friend's advice:
Don't load no more, don't put out no more
   till you get a livin price.

         —*New Republic*, 69 (2 December 1931): 62–67

### The Camera Eye (51)

*Three Harlan vignettes—of the miners' shacks at Straight Creek, miners in jail, and the sheriff's office—contribute to Dos Passos's final realization (in the last Camera Eye in the* U.S.A. *trilogy) that to alleviate such misery in the face of the combined power of wealth and the law "we have only words against."*

at the head of the valley in the dark of the hills on the broken floor of a lurchedover cabin a man halfsits halflies propped up by an old woman two wrinkled girls that might be young   chunks of coal flare in the hearth flicker in his face white and sagging as dough   blacken the caved-in mouth the taut throat the belly swelled enormous with the wound he got working on the minetipple

   the barefoot girl brings him a tincup of water   the woman wipes sweat off his streaming face with a dirty denim sleeve   the firelight flares in his eyes stretched big with fever in the women's scared eyes and in the blanched faces of the foreigners

   without help in the valley hemmed by dark strike-silent hills the man will die (my father died we know what it is like to see a man die) the women will lay him out on the rickety cot the miners will bury him

in the jail it's light too hot the steamboat hisses we talk through the greenpainted iron bars to a tall white mustachioed old man some smiling miners in shirtsleeves a boy faces white from mining have already the tallowy look of jailfaces

   foreigners what can we say to the dead?   foreigners what can we say to the jailed?   the representative of the political party talks fast through the bars join up with us and no other union we'll send you tobacco candy solidarity our lawyers will write briefs speakers will shout your names at meetings they'll carry your names on cardboard on picketlines   the men in jail shrug their shoulders smile thinly our eyes look in their eyes through the bars   what can I say?   (in another continent I have seen the faces looking out through the barred basement windows behind the ragged sentry's boots I have seen before day the straggling footsore prisoners herded through the streets limping between bayonets   heard the volley

   I have seen the dead lying out in those distant deeper valleys)   what can we say to the jailed?

in the law's office we stand against the wall the law is a big man with eyes angry in a big pumpkinface who sits and stares at us meddling foreigners through the door the deputies crane with their guns   they stand guard at the mines   they blockade the miners' soupkitchens   they've cut off the road up the valley   the hiredmen with guns stand ready to shoot (they have made us foreigners in the land where we were born they are the conquering army that has filtered into the country unnoticed they have taken the hilltops by stealth they levy toll they stand at the minehead   they stand at the polls   they stand by when the bailiffs carry the furniture of the family evicted from the city tenement out on the sidewalk they are there when the bankers foreclose on a farm they are ambushed and ready to shoot down the strikers marching behind the flag up the switchback road to the mine those that the guns spare they jail)

   the law stares across the desk out of angry eyes his face reddens in splotches like a gobbler's neck with the strut of the power of submachineguns sawedoffshotguns teargas and vomitinggas the power that can feed you or leave you to starve

   sits easy at his back is covered he feels strong behind him he feels the prosecutingattorney the judge an owner himself the political boss the minesuperintendent the board of directors   the president of the utility the manipulator of the holdingcompany

he lifts his hand towards the telephone
the deputies crowd in the door
we have only words against
         —*The Big Money*, pp. 1207–1210

* * *

## The Withdrawal

*The Stalinist purges of the early 1930s and the concomitant absolutist positions and methods of the American Communist Party increasingly alienated Dos Passos from the far Left. There was never a formal break, but an informal one occurred in March 1934 when he, along with several other writers, protested the Communist disruption of a Socialist Party meeting at Madison Square Garden. More revealing are Dos Passos's letters to Edmund Wilson in late 1934 and early 1935, in which he openly expressed his dismay over the seeming dismissal by the party, in both the Soviet Union and the United States, of a commitment to individual freedom of belief and action. His fullest statement of his deepest values in relation to the aims of the writer in America occurs in the address he prepared for the 1935 meeting of the American Writers' Congress, a left-wing organization. In the midst of a group committed to doctrinal orthodoxy, Dos Passos wrote eloquently of the ideal of artistic freedom.*

## AN OPEN LETTER TO THE COMMUNIST PARTY

*Communist Party doctrine held that socialism threatened communism because its efforts to achieve social change through democratic means delayed the onset of the revolutionary change that was indeed the only way radical change could be effected. By 1934 this animosity had been reinforced by the Stalinesque principle of an absolute party discipline that labeled all other leftish parties as "deviationist"; hence, the Communist Party effort to break up the Socialist meeting. Several prominent writers, among them the dramatist Elmer Rice and the critics Lionel Trilling and Edmund Wilson, signed the protest letter, signaling the beginning of the withdrawal of the American intellectual Left from Communist support.*

The undersigned wish to protest against the disruptive action of the Communist Party which led to the breaking up of the meeting called by the Socialist Party in Madison Square Garden of February 16th.

The rising of the Austrian Socialists was an event whose tragic outcome does not lessen its inspiration to a world menaced by Fascist repression. To honor the heroic struggle, and to protest the slaughter of working-class men, women and children, the Socialist Party called a strike and a mass meeting in the Garden.

This meeting ended in shameful disorder. Instead of working-class unity, factional warfare ruled. Speakers were howled down, fists flew, chairs were hurled, scores were injured. And since these riotous events were broadcast over a country-wide radio network, they became a disaster of national scope in the struggle for unity against Fascism.

We do not approve the Socialist leadership in Austria or the United States. In Austria the policy of tol-

erating Fascist advances until Fascism forced the turn doomed the workers to a purely defensive and hopeless, however gallant, struggle. In the United States Socialist leaders have rejected several calls for united working-class protest. In the instance of the Garden meetings, their action in ignoring all militant labor groups, while inviting such reactionaries as Matthew Woll, indicates only too well a policy which we irreconcilably oppose.

All this, however, does not diminish the culpability and shame of the Communists. Their disconcerted booing and yelling was disorderly and provocative in the extreme and belied their cries of "Unity" and "United Front." The result was the disruption of working-class action in support of the Austrian workers.

The Daily Worker of February 16th says: "Anyone who splits the ranks of the workers at this time helps the Fascists, injures the valiant struggle of our heroic brothers in Austria, and is a contemptible enemy of the working class." We who write this letter watch with sympathy the struggles of militant labor and aid such struggles. We agree with the statement of the Daily Worker. And it is with horror that we see the Communist Party play the part against which it itself has warned.

Signed:

| | |
|---|---|
| Louis Berg | Meyer Shapiro |
| Will Gruen | John Dos Passos |
| Elinor Rice | Clifton Fadiman |
| Robert Ford | John McDonald |
| James Rorty | Edmund Wilson |
| Diana Rubin | John Chamberlain |
| Louis Grudin | Margaret de Silver |
| Anita Brenner | George D. Herron |
| Felix Morrow | Meyer A. Girshick |
| Elliot E. Cohen | Gilbert C. Converse |
| George Novack | Samuel Middlebrook |
| Lionel Trilling | Robert Morss Lovett |

John Henry Hammond Jr.
—*New Masses*, 10 (6 March 1934): 8

### Dos Passos to Edmund Wilson, 23 December 1934

*Dos Passos's correspondence with the notable American literary critic Edmund Wilson during late 1934 and 1935 reveals his efforts, now that he has accepted the failure of Stalinesque communism abroad and in America, to discover a more satisfactory base of social and political belief. He does so by affirming the permanent value of those institutions, largely derived from America's Anglo-Saxon heritage, committed to the preservation of individual liberty.*

. . . . . . . . . .

8

NEW MASSES

# To John Dos Passos

DEAR Comrade Dos Passos: We have received for publication a copy of the following letter which bears your signature in company with other names.

### AN OPEN LETTER TO THE COMMUNIST PARTY

The undersigned wish to protest against the disruptive action of the Communist Party which led to the breaking up of the meeting called by the Socialist Party in Madison Square Garden of February 16th.

The rising of the Austrian Socialists was an event whose tragic outcome does not lessen its inspiration to a world menaced by Fascist repression. To honor the heroic struggle, and to protest the slaughter of working-class men, women and children, the Socialist Party called a strike and a mass meeting in the Garden.

This meeting ended in shameful disorder. Instead of working-class unity, factional warfare ruled. Speakers were howled down, fists flew, chairs were hurled, scores were injured. And since these riotous events were broadcast over a country-wide radio network, they became a disaster of national scope in the struggle for unity against Fascism.

We do not approve the Socialist leadership in Austria or the United States. In Austria the policy of tolerating Fascist advances until Fascism forced the turn doomed the workers to a purely defensive and hopeless, however gallant, struggle. In the United States Socialist leaders have rejected several calls for united working-class protest. In the instance of the Garden meetings, their action in ignoring all militant labor groups, while inviting such reactionaries as Matthew Woll, indicates only too well a policy which we irreconcilably oppose.

All this, however, does not diminish the culpability and shame of the Communists. Their disconcerted booing and yelling was disorderly and provocative in the extreme and belied their cries of "Unity" and "United Front." The result was the disruption of working-class action in support of the Austrian workers.

The Daily Worker of February 16th says: "Anyone who splits the ranks of the workers at this time helps the Fascists, injures the valiant struggle of our heroic brothers in Austria, and is a contemptible enemy of the working class." We who write this letter watch with sympathy the struggles of militant labor and aid such struggles. We agree with the statement of the Daily Worker. And it is with horror that we see the Communist Party

play the part against which it itself has warned.

Signed:

Louis Berg
Will Gruen
Elinor Rice
Robert Ford
James Rorty
Diana Rubin
Louis Grudin
Anita Brenner
Felix Morrow
Elliot E. Cohen
George Novack
Lionel Trilling
John Henry Hammond, Jr.

Meyer Schapiro
John Dos Passos
Clifton Fadiman
John McDonald
Edmund Wilson
John Chamberlain
Margaret de Silver
George D. Herron
Meyer A. Girshick
Gilbert C. Converse
Samuel Middlebrook
Robert Morss Lovett

THE NEW MASSES of course does not speak for the Communist Party. In this editorial we are addressing you, one of the best-known contributors to THE NEW MASSES, simply as your co-workers in a revolutionary enterprise.

As regards you, the statement, "We who write this letter watch with sympathy the struggles of militant labor and aid such struggles" holds true, we believe. We have often turned to you for sympathetic co-operation and support. Your books have helped mold a challenging attitude toward capitalism and its concomitant evils. For years you have been a contributor to THE NEW MASSES; the writers in and close to the revolutionary movement have, in many instances, regarded you as their literary guide and inspiration.

In view of this we were sorry to find you disagreeing with the Communist Party and criticizing, in a none too friendly tone, one of its efforts in the extremely difficult task of achieving American working-class unity. We do not want to repeat our editorial "The Lesson of Madison Square Garden" of the Feb. 27 issue. We hope you have read it, but in view of the letter you have signed, we are inclined to believe you have not. No adequate analysis of any situation can be made, unless all the factors involved are known and considered. We wonder to what extent you (who, by the very nature of your work, are not directly engaged in the day to day struggles to forge proletarian unity) are in a position to possess the prerequisite specific information.

Our sole disagreement over the

united front concerns tactics. There are two possible approaches in this matter; the united front from above or the united front from below which forces a united front with the leadership. Let us examine each of these possibilities.

The united front from above. Judging from the affiliations of the signers of the open letter, we believe your criticism of the Communist tactics is based on the Communist Party's failure to effect a united front with the Socialist Party leadership. Yet by signing this very letter you place yourself in a position which would render it impossible for you to form a united front with the Socialist leadership. You commit the deadly sin of criticizing the Socialist leadership! The letter you signed says: "In the instance of the Garden meeting, their action in ignoring all militant labor groups, while inviting such reactionaries as Matthew Woll, indicates only too well a policy which we irreconcilably oppose."

You also indicate that the Socialist leaders in the United States "have rejected several calls for united working-class protest." You agree with us when you state, "In Austria the policy of tolerating Fascist advances until Fascism forced the turn doomed the workers to a purely defensive and hopeless, however gallant, struggle."

Your public disapproval the Socialist leaders will never forgive. Their main reason for refusing a united front with the Communist Party is their objection to criticism of their policies. You know, of course, that the Communist Party does not demand immunity from criticism as a condition for a united front. By the mere publication of this letter you obviate the possibility of your joining in a united front with the Socialist leadership. They would not have you, for the very same reason that they would not have the Communists. Yet would you keep silent concerning their policies? Keep silent about their fatal "lesser evil" theory which step by step led the workers of Germany and Austria into the concentration camps and death chambers of Fascism? Your letter is proof that you cannot and will not be silent, and by silence acquiesce in these major crimes of the Socialist leadership.

What remains to be done then? The

*First page of the* New Masses *editorial (6 March 1934) responding to Dos Passos's*
*"An Open Letter to the Communist Party" (Collection of Richard Layman)*

Have you read [William Henry] Chamberlin's *Russia's Iron Age*? When I was in Moscow he seemed to me to be the straightest and best informed of the foreign newspapermen I met there. The book is damned informative–though of little eventual value, because Chamberlin has no broad basis for his slants only the little chickenshit middle class attitudes of a bright student in a girl's college–But in point of fact–if you can disassociate the fact from the eye of the beholder–I find everything I saw, or heard from Gantt and others–confirms his worst suspicions. This business about Kirov looks very very bad to me. In fact it has completely destroyed my benefit-of-the-doubt attitude towards the Stalinists–It seems to be another convolution of the self destructive tendency that began with the Trotski-Stalin row. From now on events in Russia have no more interest–except as a terrible example–for world socialism–if you take socialism to mean the educative or constructive tendency rather than politics. The thing has gone into its Napoleonic stage and the progressive tendencies in the Soviet Government have definitely gone under before the self-protective tendencies. The horrid law of human affairs by which any government must eventually become involved in power for itself, killing for the pleasure of it, self perpetuation for its own sake, has gone into effect. That doesn't mean that before that happened, enormous things were not accomplished, things that it will take the rest of the world a century to absorb–If that is true, it would be mere mealymouthedness to say I hope it isn't, because I'm pretty well convinced it is true–all the orthodox communists overhere can do is lead their followers up a blind alley and obediently dissolve when the next war begins. I certainly dont think anything can be gained by denouncing them or publicizing the situation in any way–but I think that those who are more interested in getting at realities than being on the right side, should keep the situation pretty thoroughly in mind in elaborating theories or laying down ground work for writings.

Naturally I agreed with Sidney Hook in his plea for democracy in the soviets–but Mr. Hook did not tell us how to get it in the soviets or anywhere else. Surely Mr. Hook doesn't think that the lack of democracy in Russia is due to anybody's wickedness–I suppose you could make out a case for Slavic atavism as Chamberlin does–but that seems to me to be a sort of afterthefact explanation that would be no help to people trying to avoid the same pitfall another time. Meanwhile I think we should be very careful not to damage any latent spores of democracy that there still may be in the local American soil. After all the characteristic institutions of the Anglo Saxon nations survived feudalism and Tudor absolutism (not that they ever completely existed, but they've been and still are in the background of the minds of Englishmen and Americans and Australians) and there's no reason why they shouldn't survive monopoly capitalism–

. . . . . . . . . .

–Ludington, ed., *The Fourteenth Chronicle*, pp. 458–460

## Dos Passos to Wilson, January 1935

. . . . . . . . . .

Whether the Stalinist performances are intellectually justifiable or not, they are alienating the working class movement of the world. What's the use of losing your "chains" if you get a fringe squad instead?– The Sahr vote shows horribly the state of the European popular mind–Some entirely new attack on the problem of human freedom under monopolized industry has got to be worked out–if the coming period of wars and dictatorships gives anybody a chance to work anything out–that's why it seems to me that backing the American communists is like suddenly coming out for the Anabaptists or the abolitionists–I cant see that the Trotskyites are any better–because they've definitely lost the popular pulse–for Muste to join them seems to me to be political suicide. About Russia I should have said not politically useful rather than politically interesting–I suspect that a vast variety of things are going on in Russia under the iron mask of the Kremlin, but I dont think that any of them are of use to us in this country–if our aims are freedom and the minimum of oppression–because they are working out various forms of organization that our great conjunctions are also working out in a very small way. While those forms were headed towards workers' democracy they were enormously interesting but since they seem to have turned away from that (the decline of the Soviets the absence of the secret ballot–disappearance of factory committees and of the Workers and Peasants' Inspection) I personally would prefer the despotism of Henry Ford, the United Fruit and Standard Oil than that of Earl Browder and Amster and Mike Gold and Bob Minor and I think most nonintellectual producers feel the same way. By Anglo Saxon Institutions I mean the almost obliterated traditions of trial by jury common law etc–they dont count for much all the time, but they do constitute a habit more or less implanted in Western Europeans outside of Russians–Just compare our civil war with the Russian civil war–compare the treatment–the runaround if you like, an American citizen gets in Washington, applying for information at the pension office say,

*Protesters at a 16 February 1934 Socialist Party meeting at Madison Square Garden that was disrupted by Communists, who turned the meeting into a riot (© Bettmann/Corbis)*

and the treatment a Soviet citizen gets from a bureau in Moscow where he has to transact some kind of business. After all its by things like that not by the allurements of doctrine that the average American makes his choices in styles of government–granting that he's in a position to make any choices at all. My enthusiastic feelings, personally, about the U.S.S.R. have been on a continual decline since the early days. The steps are the Kronstadt rebellions, the Massacres by Bela Kun in the Crimea, the persecution of the S.R.'s, the N.E.P., the Trotsky expulsion, the abolition of factory committees, and last the liquidating of the Kulaks and the Workers and Peasants Inspection–which leaves the Kremlin absolutely supreme. I dont know why I should blurt all this out except that since I've been laid up I've been clarifying my ideas about what I would be willing to be shot for and frankly I dont find the Kremlin among the items.

. . . . . . . . . .

–Ludington, ed., *The Fourteenth Chronicle,* pp. 461–462

## The Writer as Technician
Dos Passos

*The American Writers' Congress, a meeting of left-wing writers, occurred in early April 1935. Dos Passos was asked to contribute a paper to be read at the meeting, and though it arrived too late for that purpose, it was published in the proceedings of the congress later that year. Dos Passos's eloquent plea in his paper that the writer be permitted the freedom of his imagination was, as he knew, directly contrary to the Communist Party position that the writer's principal commitment should be to the depiction of social reality in relation to the class struggle.*

Anybody who can put the words down on paper is a writer in one sense, but being able to write no more makes a man a professional writer than the fact that he can scratch up the ground and plant seeds in it makes him a farmer, or that he can trail a handline overboard makes him a fisherman. That is fairly obvious. The difficulty begins when you try to work out what really distinguishes professional writing from the average man's letters to his family and friends.

In a time of confusion and rapid change like the present, when terms are continually turning inside out and the names of things hardly keep their meaning from day to day, it's not possible to write two honest paragraphs without stopping to take crossbearings on every one of the abstractions that were so well ranged in ornate marble niches in the minds of our fathers. The whole question of what writing is has become particularly tangled in these years during which the industry of the printed word has reached its high point in profusion and wealth, and, to a certain extent, in power.

Three words that still have meaning, that I think we can apply to all professional writings, are discovery, originality, invention. The professional writer discovers some aspect of the world and invents out of the speech of his time some particularly apt and original way of putting it down on paper. If the product is compelling, and important enough, it molds and influences ways of thinking to the point of changing and rebuilding the language, which is the mind of the group. The process is not very different from that of scientific discovery and invention. The importance of a writer, as of a scientist, depends upon his ability to influence subsequent thought. In his relation to society a professional writer is a technician just as much as an electrical engineer is.

As in industrialized science, we have in writing all the steps between the complete belt conveyer factory system of production and one man handicraft. Newspapers, advertising offices, moving picture studios, politi-

# AMERICAN WRITERS' CONGRESS

### Edited by Henry Hart

INTERNATIONAL PUBLISHERS
NEW YORK

*Title page of the 1935 volume that included Dos Passos's*
The Writer as Technician *(Thomas Cooper Library,*
*University of South Carolina)*

cal propaganda agencies, produce the collective type of writing where individual work is indistinguishable in the industrial effort. Historical and scientific works are mostly turned out by the laboratory method by various coworkers under one man's supervision. Songs and ballads are often the result of the spontaneous feelings of a group working together. At present stories and poems are the commonest output of the isolated technician.

Any writer who has ever worked in any of these collective undertakings knows the difficulties of bucking the routine and the office-worker control that seems to be an inseparable part of large industrial enterprises, whether their aims are to make money or to improve human society. It is a commonplace that business aims, which are to buy cheap and sell dear, are often opposed to the aims of the technician, which are, insofar as he is a technician and not a timeserver, the development of his material and of the technical possibilities of his

work. The main problem in the life of every technician is to secure enough freedom from interference from the managers of the society in which he lives to be able to do his work. As the era of free competition gives way to that of monopoly, with the corresponding growth of office-worker control, inner office intrigue and other stifling diseases of bureaucracy, it becomes increasingly hard for the technician to get that freedom. Even in a country that is organizing to build for socialism, instead of for the growth of the wealth and power of a few bosses, the need for functional hierarchies on an enormous scale and the difficulty of keeping the hierarchies alive through popular control, makes the position of the technician extremely difficult, because, by his very function, he has to give his time to his work instead of to "organizational problems." When you add the fact that the men behind the desks in the offices control the police power, indirectly in this country, but directly in many others, which can at the whim of some group of officials, put a man in jail or deprive him of his life and everything that makes life worth living, you can see that the technician, although the mechanical means in his power are growing every day, is in a position of increasing danger and uncertainty.

The only name you can give a situation in which a technician can do his best work, and be free to give rein to those doubts and unclassified impulses of curiosity that are at the root of invention and discovery and original thinking, is liberty. Liberty in the abstract is meaningless outside of philosophical chessgames. Then too the word has taken on various misleading political colorations. In America it means liberty for the exploiter to cut wages and throw his workers out on the street if they don't like it; in most of the newspapers of the world it means something connected with the privileges of the commercial classes. But, underneath, it still has a meaning that we all know, just as we know that a nickel is a nickel even if the Indian and the buffalo have been rubbed off. A writer, a technician, must never, I feel, no matter how much he is carried away by even the noblest political partisanship in the fight for social justice, allow himself to forget that his real political aim, for himself and his fellows, is liberty.

A man can't discover anything, originate anything, invent anything unless he's at least morally free, without fear or preoccupation insofar as his work goes. Maintaining that position in the face of the conflicting pulls of organized life demands a certain amount of nerve. You can see a miniature of the whole thing whenever a man performs even the smallest technical task, such as cleaning a carburetor, or taking a bead on a target with a rifle. His state of mind is entirely different from that of the owner of the car who wants to get somewhere, or of the man himself a second before he

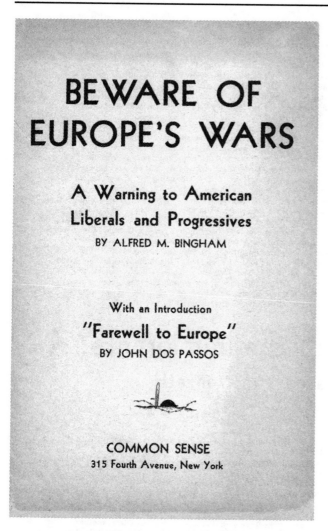

BEWARE OF
EUROPE'S WARS

A Warning to American
Liberals and Progressives
BY ALFRED M. BINGHAM

With an Introduction
"Farewell to Europe"
BY JOHN DOS PASSOS

COMMON SENSE
315 Fourth Avenue, New York

*Cover of the 1937 pamphlet that included Dos Passos's essay
expressing his dismay over Communist efforts to dominate
the Loyalist cause in the Spanish Civil War
(Collection of Richard Layman)*

put his eye to the sight, all of a fluster to win the match or in a panic of fear lest his enemy shoot him first. This state of mind, in which a man is ready to do good work, is a state of selfless relaxation, with no worries or urges except those of the work at hand. There is a kind of happiness about it. It is much nearer the way an ordinary day-laborer feels than it is the way a preacher, propagandist or swivelchair organizer feels. Anybody who has seen war knows the astonishing difference between the attitude of the men at the front, who are killing and dying, and that of the atrocity-haunted citizenry in the rear.

At this particular moment in history, when machinery and institutions have so outgrown the ability of the mind to dominate them, we need bold and original thought more than ever. It is the business of writers to supply that thought, and not to make themselves

figureheads in political conflicts. I don't mean that a writer hasn't an obligation, like any other citizen, to take part if he can in the struggle against oppression, but that his function as a citizen and his function as a technician are different, although the eventual end aimed at may in both cases be the same.

To fight oppression, and to work as best we can for a sane organization of society, we do not have to abandon the state of mind of freedom. If we do that we are letting the same thuggery in by the back door that we are fighting off in front of the house. I don't see how it is possible to organize effectively for liberty and the humane values of life without protecting and demanding during every minute of the fight the liberties of investigation, speech and discussion that are the greatest part of the ends of the struggle. In any organization a man gives up his liberty of action. That is necessary discipline. But if men give up their freedom of thought what follows is boss rule thuggery and administrative stagnation. It is easy to be carried away by the temporary effectiveness of boss rule, but it has always ended, in small things and in great, in leaving its victims stranded bloodless and rotten, with all the problems of a living society of free men unsolved. The dilemma that faces honest technicians all over the world to-day is how to combat the imperial and bureaucratic tendencies of the groups whose aims they believe in, without giving aid and comfort to the enemy. By the nature of his function as a technician, the writer finds himself in the dangerous and uncomfortable front line of this struggle.

In such a position a man is exposed to crossfire and is as likely to be mowed down by his friends as his enemies. The writer has to face that. His only safety lies in the fact that the work of an able technician cannot be replaced. It is of use and pleasure to mankind. If it weren't for that fact, reluctantly recognized, but everywhere and always recognized, the whole tribe of doubters, inventors and discovers would have been so often wiped out that the race would have ceased to produce types with those peculiar traits.

It's an old saying, but a very apt one, that a writer writes not to be saved but to be damned.

I feel that American writers who want to do the most valuable kind of work will find themselves trying to discover the deep currents of historical change under the surface of opinions, orthodoxies, heresies, gossip and the journalistic garbage of the day. They will find that they have to keep their attention fixed on the simple real needs of men and women. A writer can be a propagandist in the most limited sense of the word, or use his abilities for partisan invective or personal vituperation, but the living material out of which his work is built must be what used to be known as the humani-

as its enemies, to get rid of such cases." So the professor closes his argument with the stern pronouncement, and his bankers and business men auditors applaud, and know they are listening to a true progressive!

The professor admits that we have "mass poverty" today. That is the advantage of having a Harvard background and the opportunities of advance information which a great university full of researchers gives to a man. In May, 1935, Professor Carver had learned of the existence of mass poverty in America! And he knew exactly how to cure it, and tells us in his pamphlet. On page 61 I read the following sentence: "The plan outlined on pages 86 and 87 contains the principal items of a comprehensive program for the prevention of mass poverty." Eagerly I turn to pages 86 and 87 for that revelation; and what do you think I found? I found that the pamphlet ended on page 84!

This reminds me of a little campaign pamphlet which somebody got out in California last year. It was labeled on the outside, "What Governor Merriam will do to end poverty in California," and when you turned to the inside, you discovered that all the pages were blank. This was a profound statement of truth as well as a good joke; and the same applies to the typographical error which some printer has perpetrated on the professor.

His remedy is, in brief, that the laboring classes are not to be so numerous. The professor is a little cautious about telling just how this is to be arranged, but I venture to assume that he does not intend to have working-class babies drowned when they are born, but hopes to have them prevented from getting a start in life. I can tell him that when he starts to put that program into action he will have as difficult a time with the authorities of the Catholic Church as I had in my campaign.

In conclusion, I put this little problem up to Harvard's great economist. What if it should be too late, Professor Carver? What if too many members of the working class have already got into existence in America? We now have more than twenty-five million on charity, public and private, and they are going to live quite a while—even though we may continue to cut down their dole. You admit that we have to give them relief; and what if the dole should bankrupt the country before the receivers of the dole die off?

I also have been giving lectures in California, Professor Carver, and telling my hearers about mass poverty. Among the things I told them was this: "The capitalist class of America has built a marvelous machine of production. They have made it perfect in every detail, except for one great oversight—they have not provided any flying machines to take the superfluous workers off to some other planet!"

# Have You Thought of the Immigrants?
## The Triumph of Sacco and Vanzetti

### BY JOHN DOS PASSOS

*The following imaginative sketch, a tribute to the memory of the Italian immigrants Sacco and Vanzetti, electrocuted in the internationally famous labor frame-up in Massachusetts in 1927, is a part of a forthcoming novel by the author of "1919" and "42nd Parallel." The final novel in this great trilogy will be entitled "The Big Money" and before its spring publication another of its "camera eye" sections will appear in "Common Sense." The paragraphs in italics below are direct quotations from the letters of Sacco and Vanzetti written in jail before their death.*

WALKING from Plymouth to North Plymouth through the raw air of Massachusetts Bay, at each step a small cold squudge through the sole of one shoe, looking out past the grey frame houses under the robinsegg April sky across the white dories anchored out in the bottleclear shallows across the yellow sandbars and the slaty bay ruffling to blue to eastward. . . . This is where the immigrants landed, the roundheads, the sackers of castles, the kingkillers, the haters of oppression, this is where they stood clustered on the beach after landing from the crowded ship that stank of bilge and immigrants, immigrants escaped from oppression clustered on the beach that belonged to no one, between the ocean that belonged to no one and the enormous forest that belonged to no one, that stretched over the hills where the deertracks were, up the green river-valleys where the redskins grew their tall corn in patches, forever into the incredible west.

For three hundred years the immigrants streamed into the west. And now . . .

Walking from Plymouth to North Plymouth, suddenly round a bend in the road beyond a little pond and yellow twigged willows hazy with green you see the Cordage; huge sheds and buildings, company houses all the same size, all grimed the same color, a great square chimney, long roofs, sharp ranked squares and oblongs cutting off the sea. The Plymouth Cordage. This is where another immigrant worked who hated oppression. He talked about an unfenced world. When they fired him from the Cordage he peddled fish. The immigrants in the dark frame houses knew him, bought his fish, listened to his talk. Following his cart around from door to door you ask them: What was he like? Why are they scared to talk of Bart, scared because they knew him, scared eyes narrowing black with fright? The barber, the man in the little grocery store, the woman he boarded with. In scared voices they ask: why won't they believe? We know him, we see him every day. Why won't they believe that day we buy the eels? Only the boy isn't scared.

My pencil scrawls in my notebook, the scraps of recollection, the broken half phrases, the effort to intersect word with word, to dovetail phrase with phrase, to rebuild out of mangled memories unshakeably the truth.

The browneyed highschool boy walks shyly beside me to the station; talks about how Bart helped him with his homework, wants to go to Boston University, wants to get ahead. Why should it hurt him to have known Bart? We shake hands. Don't let them get you scared.

The accustomed smoking car, the accustomed jumble of

*Heavily edited excerpt from* The Big Money, *beginning with* Camera Eye (49), *published in* Common Sense
*(Collection of Richard Layman)*

ties: the need for clean truth and sharply whittled exactitudes, men's instincts and compulsions and hungers and thirsts. Even if he's to be killed the next minute a man has to be cool and dispassionate while he's aiming his gun.

There is no escaping the fact that if you are a writer you are dealing with the humanities, with the language of all the men of your speech of your generation, with their traditions of the past and their feelings and perceptions. No matter from how narrow a set of convictions you start, you will find yourself in your effort to probe deeper and deeper into men and events as you find them, less and less able to work with the minute prescriptions of doctrine; and you will find more and more that you are on the side of the men, women and children alive right now against all the contraptions and organizations, however magnificent their aims may be, that bedevil them; and that you are on the side, not with phrases or opinions, but really and truly, of liberty, fraternity, and humanity. The words are old and dusty and hung with the dirty bunting of a thousand crooked orations, but underneath they are still sound. What men once meant by these words needs defenders to-day. And if those who have, in all kinds of direct and devious ways, stood up for them throughout history do not come out for them now to defend them against the thuggery of the bosses and the zeal of the administrators, the world will be an even worse place for men, women and children to live in than it is at present.

–Henry Hart, ed., *American Writers' Congress* (New York: International, 1935), pp. 78–82

## Dos Passos to Charles W. Bernardin, 3 January 1942

*In a letter to Bernardin, who was writing his biography, Dos Passos seeks to clarify his relationship to the various Communist-led or -supported movements in which he was involved from 1919 to the early 1930s.*

571 Commercial Street
Provincetown, Massachusetts
3 January 1942

Dear Mr. Bernadin,

Your suggested thesis is unfortunately based on a misconception which is so current that I am taking a few minutes off to explain it a little. There has been

current a tendency for many years to lump all forms of protest against our ways of doing things in this country (or better against of doing things) in the period 1919–1933 as communism. No description could be further from the truth, though there have been times when liberals and communists have worked together for certain specific aims, which they desired for very different reasons. Probably the only time I accepted, in my own mind, any large part of the communist thesis (i.e. class war, salvation by revolution, the destiny of the working class etc.) was in 1919–21 or thereabouts. The terrific events at Kronstadt woke me up–as they did some other American liberals who were confusing the Russian revolution with the spirit of 1776. From then on until the advent of Stalin to power I had a sympathetic interest in the Soviet Union–where I felt that it was possible that something very useful to the world might be being created. In this country I cooperated with the communists in various enterprises such as the Playwrights' Theatre, their campaign for the coal miners in Kentucky and even once cast a "protest" vote for the communist candidates (1928), but by 1930 or '31 I felt that Marxism was a very dangerous pseudo-religion with a fake scientific base (a little like Mohammedanism say–if you substitute Marx's real historical ability for Mohammed's peculiar statebuilding ability) and that from the point of view of the principles of 1776 the whole business was a dead end.

The Sacco-Vanzetti case is an excellent example. The liberals were trying to protect our historic tradition by demanding a fair trial; the bulk of the agitation was carried on by anarchists or trade-union workers, in the last months before the execution of the two men, the communists horned in on the business and carried off two victims for their martyrology. The peculiar complications of this period, during which the totalitarian parties were developing, are of great historical interest, so if you are writing about it, let me beg of you, not to take any current phraseology for granted and to examine very carefully all preconceptions. . . .

To tell the truth my point of view toward politics has always been that of a reporter more than that of the addict of any particular philosophy, though I have considered it my duty to put in a word wherever I could for the underdog. . . .

Sincerely yours,

John Dos Passos

# CHAPTER 2:

# *U.S.A.*–CONCEPTION AND METHOD

Although each of the three novels of U.S.A. handles different subject matter, the trilogy as a whole deploys the single formal fictional construct of dividing the depiction of the nation into four strikingly distinctive modes of representation. The trilogy also maintains a dominant thematic overview of this material. The nature of Dos Passos's experimental devices and of what he wishes readers to understand about modern American life by means of these devices are, of course, the central concerns of most critical discussions of the trilogy. This section offers an introduction to these subjects through three kinds of material: the conception and function of each of the modes; the major role played by montage—that is, the ordering of the modal segments—in the expression of theme; and the possibility of conceiving of the intent of the trilogy as a whole in Whitmanesque terms. Each of the sections devoted to Dos Passos's four fictional modes in the trilogy—the Camera Eye, the biographies, the narratives, and the Newsreels—features criticism bearing on the technique of that mode and on its relationship to the work as a whole. These sections also offer samples of Dos Passos's creative method in the form of manuscript passages of a modal segment in process juxtaposed with the published version of the passage.

Katy Smith, a longtime friend of Ernest Hemingway. She and Dos Passos met and fell in love at Hemingway's house in
Key West in spring 1928, as Dos Passos was beginning work on The 42nd Parallel
(Collection of Lucy Dos Passos Coggin).

*Katy and John Dos Passos were married in Ellsworth, Maine, on 19 August 1929 and, after a brief stay in Maine, returned to the house in Provincetown that she and her brother Bill owned, where Dos Passos put the finishing touches on* The 42nd Parallel. *He handed over the completed typescript to his editor on 3 October 1929 (Collection of Lucy Dos Passos Coggin).*

*Katy and John Dos Passos's Provincetown, Massachusetts, cottage, where Dos Passos wrote much of* Nineteen-Nineteen *and* The Big Money *(Collection of Lucy Dos Passos Coggin)*

# THE CAMERA EYE

### The Camera Eye as Symbolic Poem
Donald Pizer

*Pizer attempts to unravel the puzzle that is the form of Dos Passos's Camera Eye segments by analyzing two characteristic examples as symbolic poems—that is, as fragments of Dos Passos's outer experience and inner life woven into a complex whole to achieve a single basic effect.*

. . . . . . . . . .

Although Dos Passos never explained the specific meaning of the title "The Camera Eye," it would appear that he intended to imply the dual potential of this image of vision. The camera is a symbol of impersonal and "objective" depiction. But it is also possible to look through the "eye" or lens of the camera to see within the camera itself. Translated into the material of *U.S.A.*, the Camera Eye mode is the consciousness of the author; the remainder of the work is the American world at large that the author has sought to depict as accurately as possible. This interpretation is confirmed by first impressions of the Camera Eye segments, since they indeed seem to be miscellaneous collections of stream-of-consciousness fragments from various moments of Dos Passos' life. Dos Passos himself later tended to support this notion of the Camera Eye as principally unfocused autobiography when he commented that his purpose in including this material was to increase the objectivity of the rest of the trilogy. "That's why I put the Camera Eye things in *U.S.A.*," he noted; "it was a way of draining off the subjective by directly getting in little bits of my own experience."[1] The architectonics of the Camera Eye segments in *U.S.A.* also seem to confirm a largely negative role for this material. The fifty-one brief Camera Eye segments are widely dispersed in an extremely long work (about 1,500 pages in the 1938 edition), which makes it difficult for readers to maintain a sense either of the relationship of one Camera Eye segment to another or of the distinctive form of the mode.

The Camera Eye, however, is a coherent autobiography . . . with a coherent form, and its account of Dos Passos' inner life is not merely a negative "draining off" of the subjective but also plays a major role in the juxtapositional form of the trilogy as a whole. To find the sources of the Camera Eye in Dos Passos' life[2]–a task made easier since the publication of his autobiography in 1966 and of two lengthy biographies in recent years–is thus not to diminish the character of the Camera Eye portion of *U.S.A.* as a created or made object. Dos Passos' choice of which events in his life to depict, and his careful molding of each of these into a contribution to the emerging theme of the search for identity and role by the Camera Eye persona, constitute an artistic recreation of life. Nor are the individual segments of the Camera Eye the product of a free-association stream-of-consciousness memory act. The available manuscript evidence reveals that Dos Passos often did begin the composition of a segment by jotting down several images. (The Camera Eye contains some of the obsessive images found elsewhere in his writing, such as night journeys by train as a child, or the cook's red-haired daughter of his adolescence, or his garden "retreat" at Verdun.) But after this beginning, the segment underwent careful expansion and revision, both in content and form, until it reached its finished state.[3] Both the origin and the nature of the Camera Eye thus suggest that it can be most profitably discussed as a form of autobiographical symbolic poetry. A segment of the Camera Eye does not render dramatically the workings of a consciousness at a specific moment of experience, as in conventional stream-of-consciousness expression. Rather, it renders a frame of mind or attitude from a phase of Dos Passos' psychic life by means of a series of carefully selected and ordered personal images that evocatively express the phrase.

Of course, some Camera Eye segments fulfill this function more fully and directly than others. *The 42nd Parallel,* which has a greater number of Camera Eye segments than the other novels in the trilogy, contains several that serve principally to capture the anecdotal debris of the memory of childhood. But as the trilogy advances and as the consciousness re-creating the past focuses more directly on the crises of his youth and adulthood, each of the Camera Eye segments takes on the character of a unified and complete poem–of a re-creation through image and symbol of a state of mind and feeling–that is also a stage in the larger poem of the coming into maturity and vision of the artist's imagination.

These symbolic poems, which constitute the episodes in the traditional romantic subject of the journey of the artist's spirit, reveal several major influences on their style and form. Joyce obviously contributed some of the conventional "signals" for the representation of the inner life in the superficial discontinuities and unconventional punctuation of the Camera Eye form.[4] But the principal influences on Dos Passos' style in the Camera Eye are undoubtedly Whitman and Eliot.[5] From the first comes an emphasis on grammatical and verbal parallelism as a basic structural device within an unmetrical form, and from the second the organization of each of the Camera Eye segments into a series of brief narrative or dramatic vignettes that themselves rely largely on private image and symbol. A Camera Eye segment is therefore a stylized recreation of feeling rather than an attempt to render immediate feeling, as in stream-of-consciousness writing. I state the difference again because in it lies an explanation not only of the sophisticated obliqueness of the Camera Eye style but also of the carefully wrought relationship of each segment to parallel (though differently expressed) moments in the lives of juxtaposed biographical and narrative figures. To stress that each Camera Eye segment is an individually conceived poem also helps explain the great variety of form and tone among them. Some are largely narrative or anecdotal; some detail only one incident, others combine several; some are comic and farcical, others angry and passionate. Each, to use the inevitable term, is an objective correlative to Dos Passos' state of mind, feeling, or spirit at a specific moment of his development, and each takes a form appropriate to that moment. Dos Passos' Camera Eye style is thus Joycean, not in the adoption of a Joycean form of the interior monologue, but rather in the bravura variations of style used for the expression of the interior self.

Camera Eye (28) is a good example of the form of the Camera Eye. The segment occurs early in *Nineteen-Nineteen* and is devoted to the impact on Dos Passos of his parents' deaths (in May 1915 and January 1917) and of his army service (during 1918–19).

*The Camera Eye* (28)

when the telegram came that she was dying (the streetcarwheels screeched round the bellglass like all the pencils on all the slates in all the schools) walking around Fresh Pond the smell of puddlewater willow-buds in the raw wind shrieking streetcarwheels rattling on loose trucks through the Boston suburbs    grief isnt a uniform and go shock the Booch and drink wine for supper at the Lenox before catching the Federal

*I'm so tired of violets*
*Take them all away*

when the telegram came that she was dying the bell-glass cracked in a screech of slate pencils    (have you ever never been able to sleep for a week in April?) and He met me in the gray trainshed my eyes were stinging with vermillion bronze and chromegreen inks that oozed from the spinning April hills    His moustaches were white the tired droop of an old man's cheeks    She's gone Jack grief isn't a uniform and the in the parlor    the waxen odors of lilies in the parlor (He and I we must bury the uniform of grief)

then the riversmell the shimmering Potomac reaches the little choppysilver waves at Indian Head there were mockingbirds in the graveyard and the roadsides steamed with spring    April enough to shock the world

when the cable came that He was dead I walked through the streets full of fiveoclock Madrid seething with twilight in shivered cubes of aguardiente redwine gaslampgreen sunsetpink tileochre    eyes lip red cheeks    brown pillar of the throat    climbed on the night train at the Notre station without knowing why

*I'm so tired of violets*
*Take them all away*

the shattered iridescent bellglass the carefully copied bust the architectural details the grammar of styles

it was the end of that book and I left the Oxford poets in the little noisy room that smelt of stale oliveoil in the Pension Boston    Ahora    Now    Maintenant    Vita Nuova    but we

who had heard Copey's beautiful reading voice and read the handsomely bound books and breathed deep (breathe deep one two three four) of the wax-work lilies and the artificial parmaviolet scent under the ethercone and sat breakfasting in the library where the bust was of Octavius

were now dead at the cableoffice

on the rumblebumping wooden bench on the train slamming through midnight climbing up from the steerage to get a whiff of Atlantic on the lunging steamship (the ovalfaced Swiss girl and her husband were my friends) she had slightly popeyes and a little gruff way of saying *Zut alors* and throwing us a little smile a fish to a sealion that warmed our darkness    when the immi-

gration officer came for her passport he couldn't send her to Ellis Island la grippe espagnole she was dead

washing those windows
K.P.
cleaning the sparkplugs with a pocketknife
A.W.O.L.
grinding the American Beauty roses to dust in that whore's bed    (the foggy night flamed with proclamations of the League of the Rights of Man)    the almond smell of high explosives sending singing éclats through the sweetish puking grandiloquence of the rotting dead

tomorrow I hoped would be the first day of the first month of the first year

–(*NN*, 9–12)

The theme of Dos Passos' release through his parents' deaths and his military service from a death in life to a potential rebirth is expressed in personal images that are knitted together by a parallel rhetorical form. So the death of the mother–"when the telegram came"–is in the context of restrictive Harvard images (the bellglass above all) and of an April funeral journey to the family's Virginia estate (itself echoing "When Lilacs Last in the Dooryard Bloom'd"), which suggest a possible life out of death as the genteel shackles of family and school begin to loosen. The father's death ("when the cable came") confirms a belief in an emergent freedom as activities associated by Dos Passos with restriction (the architectural studies imposed on him by his father, the ethercone and lilies of Harvard) "were now dead at the cableoffice." (The dense and complex flower imagery of the segment, culminating in the crushing of the American Beauty roses in the whore's bed, is worthy of Eliot at his richest.) The death of the young Swiss girl on the journey home to America appears to stress the need for the young to pursue life before death overtakes them. And then abruptly life itself overtakes Dos Passos in the ironical "freedom" of his army service, in which he is thrust into the stark physicality of empty tasks, raw sexuality, and violent death. Is this the freedom and life he wished to break through to and hold? The poem does not answer the question; rather, it dramatizes the emotional reality of this phase of Dos Passos' life as he is released from the protective cocoon of youth into an ambiguous freedom–"tomorrow I hoped would be the first day of the first month of the first year."

Camera Eye (44), which occurs early in *The Big Money,* deals with Dos Passos' travels in the Near East in the fall of 1921 and with the notoriety he gained both from this adventure and from the publication of *Three Soldiers* while he was abroad.

*The Camera Eye (44)*

the unnamed arrival

(who had hung from the pommel of the unshod white stallion's saddle

a full knapsack

and leaving the embers dying in the hollow of the barren Syrian hills where the Agail had camped when dawn sharpshining cracked night off the ridged desert had ridden toward the dungy villages and the patches of sesame and the apricotgardens)

shaved off his beard in Damascus

and sat drinking hot milk and coffee in front of the hotel in Beirut staring at the white hulk of Lebanon fumbling with letters piled on the table and clipped streamers of newsprint

addressed not to the unspeaker of arabic or the clumsy scramblerup on camelback so sore in the rump from riding

but to someone

who

(but this evening in the soft nightclimate of the Levantine coast the kind officials are contemplating further improvements

scarcelybathed he finds himself cast for a role provided with a white tie carefully tied by the viceconsul stuffed into a boiled shirt a tailcoat too small a pair of dresstrousers too large which the kind wife of the kind official gigglingly fastens in the back with safetypins which immediately burst open when he bows to the High Commissioner's lady    faulty costuming makes the role of eminent explorer impossible to play    and the patent leather pumps painfully squeezing the toes got lost under the table during the champagne and speeches)

who arriving in Manhattan finds waiting again the forsomebodyelsetailored dress suit

the position offered the opportunity presented the collarbutton digging into the adamsapple while a wooden image croaks down a table at two rows of freshlypressed gentlemen who wear fashionably their tailored names

*Katy and John Dos Passos, with her brother Bill (center), who sometimes lived with them, summer 1932.* Nineteen-Nineteen *was published on 14 March, and Dos Passos immediately began work on* The Big Money: *"A lot of characters are climbing out of windows already and I'm barely under weigh on last tome," he wrote Hemingway in May 1932 (Collection of Lucy Dos Passos Coggin).*

stuffed into shirts to caption miles lightyears of clipped streamers of newsprint

    Gentlemen I apologize it was the wrong bell it was due to a misapprehension that I found myself on the stage when the curtain rose the poem I recited in a foreign language was not mine in fact it was somebody else who was speaking it's not me in uniform in the snapshot it's a lamentable error mistaken identity the servicerecord was lost the gentleman occupying the swivelchair wearing the red carnation is somebody else than

    whoever it was who equipped with false whiskers was standing outside in the rainy street and has managed undetected to make himself scarce down a manhole

    the pastyfaced young man wearing somebody else's readymade business opportunity

    is most assuredly not

    the holder of any of the positions for which he made application at the employmentagency (*BM*, 29–31)

The unkempt and inept desert traveler finds himself cast into new and "improved" roles, first of eminent explorer, then in New York of eminent author, both of which are symbolized by ill-fitting borrowed costumes. In his dismay, he recalls a slightly earlier incident (at Tiflis) of mistaken identity that had forced him into an uncomfortable public role ("I found myself on stage"). The need to escape these roles is paramount, and in the counterdisguise of "false whiskers" he "make[s] himself scarce down a manhole." Whatever he wanted out of life, these were not "the positions for which he made application at the employmentagency." As in the previous example, Dos Passos in this Camera Eye was attempting to render a specific phase of his personal life. But the inherently comic and farcical aspects of the reluctant public figure–the roles pressed upon him, the frantic efforts to escape–result in a different kind of Camera Eye. The entire segment is built on the incrementally comic image of the costumes Dos Passos is forced to wear, and the segment concludes with his burlesque adoption of yet another disguise to escape further persecution. In addition, the narrative pace is swifter in this Camera Eye, as befits its lighter tone. The segment, in brief, has its own poetic coherence– that of comic escape–that lends the entire piece its own successful shape and character. It is one of the obvious paradoxes of Dos Passos' literary career that though he wrote and published much poetry throughout his early career, almost all his poems are weakly derivative exercises in an impersonal imagism.[6] It was only when he turned to the deeply personal themes and images of his own life in the seemingly nonpoetic form of the Camera Eye that his poetic voice found its best expression.

    –*Dos Passos' U.S.A.: A Critical Study* (Charlottesville: University Press of Virginia, 1988), pp. 56–63

## Notes

1. Frank Gado, "John Dos Passos," in *First Person: Conversations on Writers and Writing,* edited by Gado (Schenectady, N.Y.: Union College Press, 1973), p. 52. See also David Sanders, "John Dos Passos," in *Writers at Work: The Paris Review Interviews, Fourth Series,* edited by George Plimpton (New York: Viking, 1976), p. 81.

2. See James N. Westerhoven, "Autobiographical Elements in the Camera Eye," *American Literature,* 48 (November 1976): 340–364.

3. Two surviving examples are Dos Passos' careful revision of Camera Eye (25) on his failure to escape the Harvard ethercone (acc. no. 5950, box 14) and his recasting of a single Camera Eye on his life in New York during the early 1920s into the three separate segments of Camera Eye (45) to (47) (Notebook, pp. 59–64, acc. no. 5950, box 4).

4. Linda W. Wagner, "John Dos Passos: Reaching Past Poetry," *Essays in Honor of Russel B. Nye,* edited by Joseph Waldmeir (East Lansing: Michigan State University Press, 1978), p. 240.

5. The continuing influence of Eliot is clearly evident in Dos Passos' poem "Lines to a Lady," in *The American Caravan,* edited by Van Wyck Brooks and others (New York: Macaulay, 1927), pp. 454–460. For Whitman's influence on the form of the Camera Eye, see Robert P. Weeks, "The Novel as Poem: Whitman's Legacy to Dos Passos," *Modern Fiction Studies,* 26 (Autumn 1980): 431–446.

6. See Dos Passos' collection of his early poems, *A Pushcart at the Curb* (New York: Doran, 1922). The Dos Passos Papers also contains many unpublished early poems.

### *The Camera Eye* (49)

    *Comparison of the typescript draft (reproduced on the following pages) with the final version below provides an instance of Dos Passos's revision and further construction of a key Camera Eye. The relatively straightforward verbal refining of the typescript is followed by significant new material, including Dos Passos's initial overt introduction of the vital concept of the desecration of "the old words."*

walking from Plymouth to North Plymouth through the raw air of Massachusetts Bay at each step a small cold squudge through the sole of one shoe

    looking out past the grey framehouses under the robinsegg April sky across the white dories anchored in the bottleclear shallows across the yellow sandbars and the slaty bay ruffling to blue to the eastward

    this is where the immigrants landed the roundheads the sackers of castles the kingkillers haters of oppression this is where they stood in a cluster after landing from the crowded ship that stank of bilge

The Camera Eye

~~walking~~ from Plymouth to North Plymouth

*walking* with a small cold squudge through the sole

of one shoe at each step in the raw air

under the paling afternoon sun the robbnsegg

April sky looking past the grey frame houses across the

dories pointed bright white all at the same angle to the

beach anchored out in the bottleclear shallows across the

yellow ~~####~~ sandbars at the ruffled slatecolored bay

brightening to blue towards the horizon

Milton Commonwealth

thinking ∧immigrants Bradford roundheads

*haters of oppression* ∧

regicides, this is where they landed from the crowded ship

stinking of b~~il~~ge and immigrants on the beach behind

the yellow bars from out of the ocean that belonged to

no one at the edge of the enormous forest that stretched

to the Appalachians that belonged to no one

*the haters of oppression*

to found a government where right should rule

suddenly round the bend in the road the high

palings the little pond fenced in with its bare yellow-

twigged willows the Cordage

∧ company houses all the same size all grimed

the same color the square chimney the long roofs the sharp

ranked squares and oblongs cutting off the sea

                                      *this*

he worked here ~~the~~ immigrant peddled fish here

talked of an unfenced world where right should rule

from the palings of the Cordage to the palings

*They know him here*        *scared*

of the penitentiary ~~these~~ immigrants ~~are~~ ~~afraid~~ to talk

*scared because they know him*

of Bart ∧scared black eyes   the barber the man in the

*he lodged with*

little grocery store the woman, in her stuffy parlor Why

wont they believe ? We know him we see him every day

*Two-page typescript draft of Camera Eye (49) from* The Big Money *(Albert and Shirley Small Special Collections Library, University of Virginia)*

"hy wont they believe that day we buy the eels?

of recollection ~~thr blunt~~ pencil scribbles in my notebook the scraps
futile halfphrases halfsentences the effort to intersect
word with word to dovetale phrase with phrase  to rebuild
out of mangled memories unshakeably the event

the browneyed highschool kid walks shyly beside me
to the station talked about how he wants to go to Boston
University Bart helped him with his schoolwork Dont let
them scare you we shake hands Goodby Dont let them scare
you

of oppression  but how ~~can I~~ to make the oppressors feel why the immigrants haters
came how get through the fences ~~the~~ cops ~~the dicks the~~ detective agencies
company guards  ~~the~~ lawyers ~~the~~ wardens  ~~the~~ judges the
college presidents who make you ashamed to look a
fellowcountryman in the eye  how to make the people
know dont let them scare you who are your betrayers America

The accustomed smoking car the accustomed
cosily homelike
joggle of faces rumbled ~~stuffy~~ through the gathering
dark how to rebuild the ruined words worn away
in the mouths of ~~cowards cops~~ lawyer district attorneys
judges college presidents
haters of oppression  ~~how to strike a spark from the~~ the old woods they
brought to Plymouth ~~that have been~~ now so fouled by
so often
being sold so cheap
without the woods how can you know
who are your ~~betr~~ oppressors America?

on the beach that belonged to no one    between the ocean that belonged to no one and the enormous forest that belonged to no one that stretched over the hills where the deertracks were up the green rivervalleys where the redskins grew their tall corn in patches forever into the incredible west

for threehundred years the immigrants toiled into the west

and now today

walking from Plymouth to North Plymouth suddenly round a bend in the road beyond a little pond and yellowtwigged willows hazy with green you see the Cordage    huge sheds and buildings companyhouses all the same size all grimed the same color a great square chimney long roofs sharp ranked squares and oblongs cutting off the sea    the Plymouth Cordage    this is where another immigrant worked hater of oppression who wanted a world unfenced    when they fired him from the cordage he peddled fish    the immigrants in the dark framehouses knew him bought his fish listened to his talk following his cart around from door to door    you ask them    What was he like?    why are they scared to talk of Bart scared because they knew him scared eyes narrowing black with fright?    a barber the man in the little grocerystore the woman he boarded with in scared voices they ask Why won't they believe? We knew him We seen him every day Why won't they believe that day we buy the eels?

only the boy isn't scared

pencil scrawls in my notebook the scraps of recollection the broken halfphrases the effort to intersect word with word to dovetail clause to rebuild out of mangled memories unshakably (Oh Pontius Pilate) the truth

the boy walks shyly browneyed beside me to the station talks about how Bart helped him with his homework wants to get ahead    why should it hurt him to have known Bart? wants to go to Boston University    we shake hands    don't let them scare you

accustomed the smokingcar    accustomed the jumble of faces rumble cozily homelike towards Boston through the gathering dark    how can I make them feel how our fathers our uncles haters of oppression came to this coast    how say    Don't let them scare you    how make them feel who are your oppressors America

rebuild the ruined words worn slimy in the mouths of lawyers districtattorneys collegepresidents judges    without the old words the immigrants haters of oppression brought to Plymouth how can you know who are your betrayers America

or that this fishpeddler you have in Charlestown Jail is one of your founders Massachusetts?

–*The Big Money*, pp. 1134–1136

## THE BIOGRAPHIES

### Representative Men in Dos Passos's *The 42nd Parallel*
Barry Maine

*In an essay on the nature and purpose of the biographies in U.S.A., Maine examines the biographies in the first volume of the trilogy and argues that they are closely related to the central historical theme of the trilogy as a whole–that Americans are individually responsible for the tragic loss of their heritage of freedom.*

Anyone who has read John Dos Passos's *U.S.A.* trilogy will admit to a fondness for the biographical sketches of famous Americans like Henry Ford, William Randolph Hearst, Woodrow Wilson, Thomas Edison, and Eugene Debs. The "Biographies" in *U.S.A.* stand out as anomalous in American literature, and in the years since they first appeared between eye-catching collages of newspaper copy and popular song lyrics, brief installments of impressionistic autobiography, and large chunks of fictional narrative in *The 42nd Parallel* (1930), *1919* (1932), and *The Big*

*Socialist Party leader and perennial presidential candidate Eugene V. Debs, the subject of the first biography in* The 42nd Parallel, *"Lover of Mankind" (from H. Wayne Morgan,* Eugene V. Debs: Socialist for President, *1962)*

*Money* (1936), they have lost neither their novelty nor their slightly scandalous air of historical revisionism. Actually, Dos Passos's attitude toward these "great men" is very close to our own, despite the fact that he more often than not based his judgments on feeling rather [than] exhaustive research. Often he would read a biography of one of these figures in preparation for a sketch and then use the material to support an entirely different set of conclusions. As a "contemporary chronicler," as he liked to call himself, Dos Passos made his own participation in the life of his times his primary source of historical evidence.

Throughout his long literary career Dos Passos wrote both fiction and history, and it is not always easy to distinguish one from the other. In the *U.S.A.* trilogy historical personages do not enter the fictional narrative as they do in the historical novel (consider, for instance, the Scott novel or even Doctorow's *Ragtime,* which covers the same historical period as the first two volumes of the Dos Passos trilogy); instead, they are, in keeping with Dos Passos's profound respect for history, treated separately as representative men.

Little has been written about the biographies in *U.S.A.* because there has been little disagreement over Dos Passos's attitude toward each of these "great men" in American history. There is no mistaking the undisguised hero worship in some of the sketches, or the bitterness and personal attack in others. With very little modification, the prevailing view of their overall function in the trilogy has remained essentially that of Alfred Kazin's in *On Native Grounds:* in the biographies of famous industrialists, financiers, inventors, entrepreneurs, labor leaders, politicians, and other national celebrities, Dos Passos speaks in the "formal and ironic voice of History" of minds and wills universally subordinate to political, social, and economic forces beyond individual control.[1] Together the biographies spell defeat for the democratic principles upon which the nation was founded, and individually they register Dos Passos's admiration or scorn for each of these "great men" and the role each tried to play in history, only to be swept along with everyone else through the dynamo of historical determinism. They are commemorated or hung in effigy along a chronicle of increasing despair.

Central to nearly every book Dos Passos ever wrote–to the novels, travel essays, political tracts, histories, and biographies alike–is some fundamental relationship between individual men and history. That relationship is remarkably consistent throughout the Dos Passos canon, but we will never recognize it in the *U.S.A.* trilogy so long as we ritualistically invoke historical determinism as the governing thesis of the trilogy, or so long as we forget that there can be no history in *U.S.A.* without the men who made it. For

if individuals are so subject to forces beyond their control, just so much fuel for the dynamo, then why has Dos Passos included among his representative men those who profoundly affected the political course and economic development of America in this century, men like Andrew Carnegie, J. P. Morgan, Henry Ford, Theodore Roosevelt, and Woodrow Wilson, just to name a few? There can be no denying the impact, for better or for worse, that these men have made upon America and the world. Nor does Dos Passos himself deny it. The purpose of many of the biographical sketches would seem to be to draw attention to, not away from, the significance of individual men in history. Few readers fail to notice the conspiratorial view of history which dominates the *U.S.A.* novels, and yet some would have us imagine a conspiracy without conspirators.

Who or what is responsible for the steady decline Dos Passos perceived in economic opportunity, free speech, social justice, personal freedoms, and other commonly held democratic ideals during the first three decades of the twentieth century? Universal laws of history, emergent political, social, and economic forces, or Americans themselves? Surely the sense of betrayal which is expressed ever more vehemently as the chronicle proceeds, culminating in the penultimate "Camera Eye" section recording Dos Passos's outrage over the execution of Sacco and Vanzetti ("listen businessmen collegepresidents judges America will not forget her betrayers"), confirms that men are not wholly absolved of responsibility for their own history. Therefore I cannot agree with those, like historian John P. Diggins, who claim that men are powerless to effect historical change in *U.S.A.*[2] The power to affect, though perhaps not to shape, the course of history does appear to lie within the reach of some men, though nearly always the wrong men, in Dos Passos's *U.S.A.* The greed and hypocrisy and lack of vision among America's industrial and political leaders, along with the intellectual timidity, social prejudices, and spinelessness of the American populace, share the blame equally, in Dos Passos's view, with historical laws and economic forces for the betrayal and eventual defeat of democratic principles in America.

The larger issue at stake, it seems to me, is whether we can say of *U.S.A.* what T. S. Eliot said of *Ulysses,* that it brings order to the "immense panorama of futility and anarchy which is contemporary history."[3] Or must we concur with Diggins that *U.S.A.* "is neither guided by a principle of historical explanation nor inspired by a vision of historical meaning"?[4] Our answer will depend on how we perceive the relationship between individual men and history in the *U.S.A.* novels. A closer look at the "biographies" in *The 42nd*

*Populist political leader William Jennings Bryan, "The Boy Orator of the Platte" in* The 42nd Parallel *(courtesy of the Nebraska State Historical Society)*

*Parallel* alone, where the pattern of individual responsibility in history is immediately established in the trilogy, will show that *U.S.A.* is less a demonstration of historical determinism and the futility of Man's efforts to free himself from a vast social and economic mechanism which controls his destiny, than it is a bitter indictment of a nation's collective failure to make the machine run the way it ought to. This should bring *U.S.A.* more in line with Dos Passos's later work, particularly his treatment of the Founding Fathers as effective agents of positive historical change in *The Ground We Stand On* (1941), *The Men Who Made the Nation* (1957), and in subsequent biographies and historical narratives, and more in line with his faith in politics as well.

Dos Passos was busy collecting materials for *The 42nd Parallel* as early as the spring of 1927. In June of 1926 he had contributed a brief statement of his position regarding the politics of contemporary literature to the second issue of the *New Masses,* a magazine of the radical Left of which he was soon to become an editor. On the back cover of that very issue there is a poster art sketch of Luther Burbank, who had died that year, with a brief eulogy printed underneath: "Old pious ladies railed at him—ministers preached against him—the Ku

Klux Klan threatened him—because he tried to make a heaven on earth." If Luther Burbank of Burbank potato fame seems an unlikely hero of the radical Left, it is probably because we remember him, if at all, as a horticulturist rather than as a symbolic victim of puritan narrowmindedness and American group conformity. But this is how he was eulogized by the *New Masses,* and by Dos Passos himself in *The 42nd Parallel* in his biographical sketch, "The Plant Wizard."

Luther Burbank was actually a cause célèbre during the Progressive era. His successful experiments in cross-fertilization produced new hybrids which were hailed as evidence of everything from Man's supremacy over Nature to America's Manifest Destiny. Burbank himself was courted in the press and by the public as a genius, a wizard, and a national hero. His achievements, though considerable, were so blown up by the press that he became, in the judgment of recent scholarship, a victim of hero worship.[5] His colleagues resented the publicity he received and his work was unfairly discredited or ignored by the scientific community.

But the Burbank of Dos Passos's "The Plant Wizard" is a victim of something other than hero worship. Dos Passos relates how, at an early age, Burbank had ceased to believe in the punishing God of his New England forefathers, and had moved West in body, and in spirit. Soon he made it possible for America to "cash in" on natural selection. But late in his life, only a few months after the highly publicized Scopes trial, Burbank casually referred to himself as an "infidel" in the course of an interview with an ambitious reporter. What he had never denied—his belief in evolution—suddenly became offensive and scandalous, and the story provoked the anger of fundamentalists who then waged a nationwide campaign against him. He died shortly thereafter, a victim, in Dos Passos's view, of the sort of narrowmindedness that breeds conformity and inhibits (in an Emersonian sense) Man's natural gifts.

It might easily be argued that Burbank was more a victim of the public's ravenous appetite for national heroes than a victim of narrow thinking. On the other hand, since Burbank, who lived well into his seventies, spent nearly all of his adult life in contented isolation, aware of the curious and admiring public, but thoroughly and happily involved in his work, it hardly seems appropriate to label him a victim at all.

But Dos Passos knew that America, too, "was hybrid," a nation of immigrants dependent upon religious toleration and progressive thinking. He fashions Luther Burbank into a representative man whose rejection by a fickle and easily manipulated public sounded just one more death knell for progressive thinking in America. Here and throughout the biographies in *U.S.A.* Dos Passos brings historical perspective to his narrative, and a semblance of order to a turbulent and confusing era.

"The Plant Wizard" is the second biographical sketch in *The 42nd Parallel*. The first and third are of labor leaders Eugene Debs and William Haywood. In "Lover of Mankind" Dos Passos expresses his unqualified admiration for Debs and the ideals of organized labor he carried to "railroad workers in their pine-boarded halls . . . to freighthandlers and gandywalkers, to firemen and switchmen and engineers, telling them it wasn't enough to organize the railroadmen, that all workers must be organized . . . for he said: 'While there is a lower class I am of it, while there is a criminal class I am of it, while there is a soul in prison I am not free.'" Eugene Debs is a Dos Passos hero because he led a distinctively American grassroots labor movement. He is the first in a long string of defeated heroes in *U.S.A.* because he was betrayed by the very men whose interests and rights he had championed:

> But where were Gene Debs's brothers in nineteen eighteen when Woodrow Wilson had him locked up in Atlanta for speaking against war . . .
>
> where were the locomotive firemen and engineers when they hustled him off to Atlanta Penitentiary?

Dos Passos saw in the declining fortunes of Eugene Debs at the national polls (running for President four times on the Socialist ticket) a collective betrayal not only of Debs, but of the whole labor movement in America, as a cowardly and intellectually timid populace fell prey to the political rhetoric and false promises of "the flag and prosperity and making the world safe for democracy." Like so many of the biographies in *U.S.A.*, "Lover of Mankind" traces the rise and fall of a Dos Passos hero, with the war marking the abrupt change in fortunes, as the ideals of youth, brotherhood, and solidarity were broken upon the wheels of Wilson's war machine, and then superseded by self-interest in a booming post-war economy.

We find the same rise-and-fall structure repeated in "Big Bill," an elegy in praise of another uniquely American hero, William Haywood, who rose "with" not "from" the ranks of the working classes to become a working class leader and a national spokesman for the I.W.W. His defeat, like Debs's, came in the wave of nationalism and increased social prejudice and oppression at home which accompanied America's entry into the war overseas. Here Dos Passos employs what would become his favorite rhetorical device, the use of the ambiguous pronoun "they" whose antecedent is everyone:

*Minor Cooper Keith, one of the founders of the United Fruit Company and the subject of "Emperor of the Caribbean" in* The 42nd Parallel *(from Watt Stewart,* Keith and Costa Rica: A Biographical Study of Minor Cooper Keith, *1964)*

They went over with the A.E.F. to save the Morgan loans, to save Wilsonian Democracy, they stood at Napoleon's tomb and dreamed empire . . . all over the country at American legion posts and businessmen's luncheons it was worth money to make the eagle scream;

they lynched the pacifists and the proGermans and the wobblies and the reds and the bolsheviks.

Haywood was handed a twenty-year jail sentence for demonstrating in Chicago. He managed to jump bail after two years in Leavenworth and sailed to Russia, where he died in lonely exile.

In "Big Bill," as in "Lover of Mankind," the gathering momentum and early optimism of the American labor movement (fleshed out in the "Mac" narratives) is squelched by increasing nationalism, red scares, new federal laws passed against strikers, increasing prosperity, and by "they," the American people, who lost sight of the principles upon which the nation was founded—equal opportunity, freedom of speech, right to assembly, etc.—and saw only "the flag and prosperity and making the world safe for democracy."

The poisoning of American minds by politicians, the press, public relations men (like J. Ward Moorehouse), and others gradually assumes a major role in the historical process summarized in the biographical sketches and fleshed out in the narrative sections of *U.S.A.* We have already seen Dos Passos point an accusing finger at an American public too easily tricked by political rhetoric and empty promises into betraying men of great talent and vision and integrity. But he holds the politicians and other "strangers who have turned our language inside out who have taken the clean words our fathers spoke and made them slimy and foul" accountable as well. In the fourth biographical sketch of *The 42nd Parallel*, "The Boy Orator of the Platte," Dos Passos passes judgment upon the populist, William Jennings Bryan. His verdict is that Bryan was a great orator with nothing to say. He was a "barn-stormer, exhorter, evangelist," in short, an opportunist with a "silver tongue" who loved to hear the sound of his own voice, who "had to speak, to feel the drawling voices hush, feel the tense approving ears, the gust of handclaps." Dos Passos implied that Bryan spoke up for anything that might sound sweet in the ears of his populist audience. The rhetoric of William Jennings Bryan quoted at length in "The Boy Orator of the Platte" compares unfavorably with the plain talk of orators like Debs and Haywood, and it is finally William Jennings Bryan himself whom Dos Passos condemns in the ironic conclusion to his sketch—not the times, not even what he stood for, but the man himself.

The next two sketches are of industrialists Minor C. Keith and Andrew Carnegie. "Emperor of the Caribbean," the biography of Keith, is as revealing of Dos Passos's conception of history as any single sketch in the novel. And unlike most of the biographical sketches, this one was culled from a single source, Samuel Crowther's *The Romance and Rise of the American Tropics* (1929), a very defensive history of the role of American corporations in the economic development of the Caribbean. Dos Passos's account, though borrowing heavily from the details, organization, and even the wording of Crowther's Horatio Alger story of Keith's rise from necktie salesman to railroad builder (in Central America) to founder of the United Fruit Company, is hardly a defense of the free enterprise system. "Emperor of the Caribbean" is a bitter indictment of American imperialism which was, in Dos Passos's view, fostered by the need to protect the economic interests of a few powerful corporations and the men who owned them.

A few days after Keith died, the *Panama Star Herald* (June 15, 1929) printed an editorial expressing grief for his passing, and praise for the man "who has done more for the development of these countries by appreciation of their potentialities and faith in their development than any other single man." The obituaries for Keith carried by U.S. newspapers were just as laudatory. But Dos Passos saw (or more likely imagined he saw) an "uneasy look under the eyes" in the pictures of Keith carried by the newspapers when he died. In the newspapers and in Crowther's book Keith had been hailed as a great entrepreneur, one of the "Captains of Industry" who had created far more wealth than he had accumulated and had contributed mightily to the material "progress" of Latin American countries. But Dos Passos was justly suspicious and wondered who benefited most from the exploitation of natural resources and cheap labor in underdeveloped countries, and he saw in such exploitation the roots of American imperialism, foreign entanglements, and eventual war:

*Theodore Roosevelt, the "Happy Warrior" of Nineteen-Nineteen (Photograph by Peter A. Juley, National Portrait Gallery, Smithsonian Institution, Washington, D.C.; Gift of Joanna Sturm)*

so they cut down the jungles through Central America to plant bananas,
        and built railroads to haul the bananas,
        and every year more steamboats of the Great White Fleet
        steamed north loaded with bananas,
        and that is the history of the American empire in the Caribbean,
        and the Panama Canal and the future Nicaragua Canal and the marines and the battleships and the bayonets.

One of Dos Passos's principal aims in writing *U.S.A.* was to expose the well-camouflaged economic causes of America's foreign entanglements in Central America, and especially in Europe. He wanted to make very clear what Americans had fought for overseas, and who had benefited most. Therefore he could not resist singling out powerful industrialists like Keith, J. P. Morgan, and Andrew Carnegie for public censure. Though the other narrative devices in *U.S.A.*, and the implications they have for Dos Passos's conception of history, are enough to assure us that he did not share Carlyle's (and Emerson's) belief that history is nothing more than the biographies of "great men," neither should we overlook the very significant role Dos Passos assigns to great men, especially great bad men, in his chronicle—a significance underscored by the harsh satire, bitterness, and outrage which characterizes his biographies of these men.

The next sketch, ironically titled "Prince of Peace," is a tongue-in-cheek parody of the by now familiar Horatio Alger story ("Andrew Carnegie always saved his money / whenever he had a million dollars he invested it"). Though Carnegie's enormous financial success is attributed ostensibly to his faith in America's future economic growth, Dos Passos concludes the sketch on a bitter note by implying that Carnegie was nothing more nor less than a hypocrite, a war profiteer who endowed institutions to "promote universal peace."

By assuming the muckraker's stance, Dos Passos grossly understates Carnegie's entrepreneurial role in the steel industry which, under his control, grew to become the backbone of America's surging industrial economy. Since, in this case, the whole economy got a boost in the arm from such vaguely defined war profiteering, Dos Passos may have felt constrained to impugn the integrity of the man and gloss over the reverberations caused throughout the economy not just by war profits, but by Carnegie's innovations in business management, capital formation, and industrial merger and consolidation. But then Dos Passos neither approved of industrial merger and consolidation, nor hesitated to pass judgment upon popular heroes like Carnegie whom he considered unworthy of emulation.

Thomas Edison gets mixed reviews in "The Electrical Wizard." In order to understand why Edison and other inventors figure so prominently among Dos Passos's representative men, we must go back to a book review Dos Passos wrote for the *New Republic* (December 18, 1929), in which he claimed that Edison was "one of the two or three individuals most responsible for the sort of world we live in today." Dos Passos believed the achievements of Edison, Henry Ford, and Harvey Firestone to be "among the greatest in history" because their inventions and innovations in production produced "a degree of wealth and prosperity absolutely new in history." But he also complained that these men were "like the sorcerer's apprentice who loosed the goblins and the wonder-working broomsticks in his master's shop and then forgot what the formula was to control them by." Consequently, "The Electrical Wizard" is full of praise for Edison's curiosity, practicality, determination, and productivity—the Edison who "grew up with the country." But that praise is finally qualified by Dos Passos's dismay over Edison's lack of foresight—the Edison who never worried about "the social system." Edison is lumped together with Ford and Firestone as men who changed the world without a thought as to the impact their inventions and new modes of production would have upon the organization of labor, the satisfaction derived from work, the social system, human relations, and the quality of life—criticisms deriving, no doubt, from Dos Passos's reading of Thorstein Veblen.

In the aforementioned book review, Dos Passos singled out Charles Proteus Steinmetz, the General Electric mathematician and electrical engineer, as someone who did consider, at all times, the significance of his work in relation to the common everyday individual. Steinmetz was a socialist. But he was also company-owned, and in "Proteus," the next to last biographical sketch in *The 42nd Parallel,* Dos Passos expresses his admiration for Steinmetz and his scorn for General Electric, which used him like "a piece of apparatus . . . until he wore out and died."

Either Dos Passos saw no conflict of interest in Steinmetz's employment, a socialist serving the capitalist free enterprise system, or he preferred to ignore it. Presumably Dos Passos knew that Steinmetz had, in fact, praised large corporations and monopolies, in "America and the New Epoch," as the most capable of managing and organizing men and resources, and most able to subsidize research which might produce no immediate return on investment. He saw no conflict of interest in working for a large corporation as a committed socialist because he believed that such corporations should and eventually would be nationalized. But such a view of socialism, which finds advantages in large corporations over small businesses, and in monopoly over free market competition, would not suit Dos Passos's political purposes, which, no matter how vaguely defined, always involved returning freedom, control, and autonomy to the individual at the expense of the large corporation, and even at the expense of the state. It is not surprising, considering Dos Passos's ideological independence (or confusion), that he chose not to confront the implications of socialism directly in "Proteus." Instead he fashions Steinmetz into another representative man, recognizable as Veblen's "engineer as hireling for the corporation," who, through no fault of his own but rather due to the conditions of his employment, can contribute nothing to the betterment of the social system. And yet Steinmetz receives high marks from Dos Passos for his independence, his willingness to speak out against the capitalist system, and for his integrity. Unlike Edison, Ford, and Firestone, he never "cashed in" personally on his creative talent.

The last representative man in *The 42nd Parallel* is Wisconsin Senator Robert La Follette, "Fighting Bob." La Follette is another of Dos Passos's defeated heroes. In "Fighting Bob" Dos Passos has him bucking one political machine after another in his rise to the United States Senate,

> where he worked all his life making long speeches full of statistics, struggling to save democratic government, to make a farmers' and small businessmen's commonwealth, lonely with his back to the wall, fighting corruption and big business and high finance and trusts and combinations of combinations and the miasmic lethargy of Washington.

Unlike William Jennings Bryan, with whom he begs comparison, La Follette did not always express the popular will. In the final days of the short session of 1917 he led a filibuster which successfully blocked passage, for a short time, of the armed merchant-ship legislation; he also spoke out vehemently against entering the war. Woodrow Wilson labeled him one of "the little group of willful men expressing no opinion but their own." In Dos Passos's account of the standoff,

> the press pumped hatred into its readers against La Follette,
>
> the traitor;
>
> they burned him in effigy in Illinois;
>
> in Wheeling they refused to let him speak.

*Public-utilities financier Samuel Insull, subject of the final biography in* The Big Money, *"Power Superpower" (from Forrest McDonald,* Insull, *1962)*

The conclusion to the sketch, with La Follette standing firm against Wilson and what must have seemed like the entire country in March of 1917, is among the most dramatic and moving passages in the entire trilogy. Though this was a losing struggle, La Follette left behind a "model" state democracy in Wisconsin, and the memory of dramatic and effective protest in the Senate. And he went on to win other political battles for progressive causes in the Senate, though he died, in Dos Passos's view, "an orator haranguing from the capital of a lost republic."

Dos Passos's source for the first half of "Fighting Bob" was La Follette's own *Autobiography* (1913). This is apparent from the details and organization of the sketch. Since La Follette's personal narrative is, for the most part, an account of his political battles with powerful "strong men" like postmaster Boss Keyes, lumber

sized volume—and it would seem that the Legion would not have a minute to spare to make propaganda for gold standard resolutions; to work for increased sales for munitions makers; or to stage "red" hunts for employers.

A few months ago the whole country was shocked to learn that several hundred World War veterans working under practically forced labor conditions on an F.E.R.A. project on the Florida Keys were drowned in a hurricane. Most of them had been in the Bonus Army of 1932. Though the authorities knew that the storm was coming no effort was made to remove the veterans while there was yet time. They were unemployed men; to keep from starving they had been sent to the road-building job on the Keys; a short time before the storm over 500 of them struck against intolerable sanitary conditions in the camps; the National Guard was called out to put them in their places, just as the Regular Army was called out against them in Anacostia Flats in 1932; they were not allowed to leave the Keys in face of the storm. they had no transportation; nothing was done to carry them to safety. How much responsibility had the American Legion's officials in this? None! They were too busy working for the gold standard, for conscription of labor in war-time, for the munitions makers, for the red baiters to waste time on down-and-out ex-soldiers.

Recently at Northport, L. I., 200 veterans in a veterans' hospital were made violently ill from eating rotten meat. Kitchen attendants said that the food was so malodorous that it nauseated them. A part of the meat had been condemned by an inspector of the Department of Agriculture. How long have such conditions existed? What did the American Legion do about it? Were those responsible indicted and put in prison? The only result was that some of those who testified lost their jobs.

And where has the Royal Family been in the struggle for payment of the Bonus? The truth is that most of the Legion's officials have always been *against* the Bonus. While they are in office they pay lip service to it but just as soon as they rate the title of Past National Commander they begin to attack the Legionnaires as "treasury raiders." Among such were Frank D'Olier, Henry D. Lindsley, Frederic Galbraith and others. But since the Bonus Army march of 1932 the leaders have had to make more and more of a pretense of really wanting the Bonus. Hamilton Fish and Col. Knox wanted to take money from relief funds—to penalize the unemployed and not the bankers—to pay off the bonus. It is certain that had the Legion devoted one half as much time to working for the bonus in the past as it did to red hunting it would have been paid long ago.

Most telling criticism of the Royal Family's time wasting and red hunting came, surprisingly enough, from Governor Earle of Pennsylvania. At the 1935 convention of the Pennsylvania Department of the Legion. This Legionnaire said:

> "I warn you that our civilization is in danger if we heed the deceptive cries of special privilege, if we permit our men of great wealth to send us on a wild goose chase after so-called radicals while they continue to plunder the people . . . We are constantly told of the evils of Socialism and Communism. The label is applied to every man, woman and child who dares to say a word which does not have the approval of Wall Street."

Certainly it is high time for the Legion's rank and file to demand that their leaders quit the wild goose chase and attend to the business of the veterans.

# POOR LITTLE RICH BOY

## BY JOHN DOS PASSOS

*Readers of the great series of articles on Hearst by Oliver Carlson and Ernest Sutherland Bates will be interested to see how the same subject is handled by a famous novelist. Like the sketch in the last issue, the following will be a chapter in the author's forthcoming "The Big Money."*

WILLIAM RANDOLPH HEARST was an only son, the only chick in the richlyfeathered nest of George and Phoebe Hearst.

In Eighteen Fifty George Hearst had left his folks and the farm in Franklin County, Missouri and driven a team of oxen out to California. (In Forty Nine the sudden enormous flare of gold had filled the West;

The young men couldn't keep their minds on their plowing on feeding the swill to the pigs on threshing the wheat

when the fires of gold were sweeping the Pacific Slope, cholera followed in the ruts of the oxcarts, they died of cholera round the campfires, in hastilybuilt chinchinfested cabins, they were picked off by hostile Indians, they blew each others' heads off in brawls.)

George Hearst was one of the few who made it;

he developed a knack for placermining;

as a prospector he had an accurate eye for picking a goldbearing vein of quartz;

after seven years in El Dorado County he was a millionaire, Anaconda was beginning, he owned one sixth of the Ophir Mine, he was in on Comstock Lode.

In Sixty One he went back home to Missouri with his pockets full of nuggets and married Phoebe Apperson and took her back out across the plains and the Rockies to San Francisco the new hilly capital of the millionaire miners and built a mansion for her beside the Golden Gate on the huge fogbound coast of the Pacific.

He bought ranches, raised cattle, ran racehorses, prospected in Mexico, employed five thousand men in his mines on his estates, lost and won fortunes in mining deals, played poker at a century a chip, never went out without a bag of clinkers to hand out to old friends down on their uppers,

and died in Washington

a senator,

a rough diamond, a lusty beloved whitebearded old man with the big beak and sparrowhawk eyes of a breaker of trails, the beetling brows under the slouch hat

of an old timer.

*First page of the biography of William Randolph Hearst from* The Big Money *in the March 1936 issue of* Common Sense, *which appeared six months before the novel was published (Collection of Richard Layman)*

king Boss Sawyer, railroad lobbyist Henry C. Payne, and others La Follette numbered among "the handful of men who had destroyed every vestige of democracy" in Wisconsin, he is pitted against those same strong men in "Fighting Bob," and Dos Passos adds Woodrow Wilson to the list. But, as we have seen, the role of powerful individuals is not limited to political history in *U.S.A.*; "Fighting Bob" is just one in a string of biographies in which much of the responsibility for history is attributed to individuals who, for better or for worse, were able to work their wills upon the materials of this earth, or upon the minds of a naive and malleable populace.

To propose or imply that there is no explanation for historical events in *U.S.A.*, or that individuals are but passive objects of social and economic forces beyond their control, is to misread the relationship between individual men and history in the biographies and, I believe it can be shown, in the narrative sections and in the Camera Eye, where Dos Passos records his own gradual awakening to his personal responsibility in history, and his search for a way of fulfilling it through political protest. The pessimism and despair of *U.S.A.* is really an anguished expression of faith in America's potential, tragically unrealized. It is not, as has been thought, an expression of defeat beneath the wheels of a deterministic universe. Everything Dos Passos wrote after *U.S.A.* is testimony against the latter interpretation, and the biographies of representative men in *The 42nd Parallel* should be evidence enough. Individuals acting collectively in a democratic society, or individually in positions of leadership, are held accountable for the direction society moved during the period chronicled. Advances in science, technology, industrialization, capital formation, and the power of the press—all these were determining factors. But Dos Passos holds individuals ultimately responsible for the nation's failure to adapt itself to these advances. Though he is particularly harsh on America's industrial leaders, who in grasping for profits were blind to their responsibility in history, the biographies of the unheeded Debs, Haywood, and La Follette make it plain that the failure to progress as a democratic society was indeed a collective and national one.

This sense of individual responsibility in history is what sustained Dos Passos's interest in the Anglo-Saxon tradition, preserved his faith in democratic government, and eventually provoked his abhorrence of communism, which in his view robbed the individual of his right to assume that responsibility. There were, as Townsend Ludington has suggested in his recent biography of Dos Passos, more personal reasons as well, like the execution of his

friend José Robles by the communists in Spain.[6] But this ideal of responsibility in history, and the opportunities a true democracy afforded for fulfilling it, is what attracted Dos Passos, immediately upon completion of *U.S.A.* and throughout the remainder of his life, to that particular time in American history, the Colonial and Revolutionary period, when a nation's collective participation in history, together with the leadership of great men like Jefferson, Adams, and Tom Paine, produced dramatic results. Though it is true Dos Passos looked back upon America's "storybook" past through less jaundiced eyes, the relationship between individual men and history in *U.S.A.* and in the later histories he wrote of the Colonial period is the same. In *U.S.A.* Dos Passos laments the paucity of truly great men of vision in the present and the shortsightedness of the American people in refusing to follow those few who happened along.

Concerning the role of great men in history, E. H. Carr has made the following observation in *What is History?*:

> What seems to me essential is to recognize in the great man an outstanding individual who is at once a product and an agent of the historical process, at once the representative and the creator of social forces which change the shape of the world and the thoughts of men.[7]

The representative men of Dos Passos's *The 42nd Parallel* are neither greater nor lesser than this. They are not representative men in the Emersonian sense, "lenses through which we read our own minds," because Dos Passos believed with Marx that circumstances make men as much as men make circumstances. But Dos Passos's conception of history differs significantly from the dialectical materialism of Marxist historicism. There is no historical inevitability in *The 42nd Parallel* that can be traced to a clearly defined dialectic. This does not mean that historical events are without cause or direction; it only means that the direction is not written in stone. History is without formula in *The 42nd Parallel*. Dos Passos's conception of history is closest to Veblen's: human societies exist in a state of constant flux, adapting themselves at all times to changing conditions and circumstances. Human nature is the only historical law; hence the focus on individuals in Dos Passos's chronicle. Whether or not he was able to bring the kind of order to "the anarchy which is contemporary history" that T. S. Eliot perceived in *Ulysses* is doubtful. But that is because Joyce wrote fiction, while Dos Passos, more historian than novelist, could not bring more order to anarchy than history, and his conception of it, allowed.

*–Clio,* 12 (Fall 1982): 31–43

## Notes

1. Alfred Kazin, *On Native Grounds: An Interpretation of Modern American Prose Literature* (New York: Harcourt, Brace & World, 1942), pp. 341–359.

2. John P. Diggins, "Visions of Chaos and Visions of Order: Dos Passos as Historian," *American Literature,* 46 (1974): 329–346.

3. T. S. Eliot, "Ulysses, Order, and Myth," *Dial,* 75 (1923): 483.

4. Diggins, p. 334.

5. See Walter Lafayette Howard, "Luther Burbank, a Victim of Hero Worship," *Chronica Botanica,* 9: 299–520; and Peter Dreyer, *A Gardener Touched with Genius: The Life of Luther Burbank* (New York: Coward, McCann & Geoghegen, 1975).

6. Townsend Ludington, *John Dos Passos: A Twentieth Century Odyssey* (New York: Dutton, 1980), p. 463.

7. Edward Hallett Carr, *What is History?* (New York: Random House, 1961), p. 68.

**Voice in the *U.S.A.* Biographies**
George Knox

*Knox describes the various stylistic techniques that make the biographies distinctive as accounts of specific lives.*

. . . . . . . . . .

All of the portraits are built upon conventional third-person narration, although the use to which Dos Passos puts this convention is sometimes peculiar. The broken quality of the narrative is accentuated in the Cummingsesque irregular line length, unconventional punctuation, and lack of capitalization. Sometimes (as in the sketches of Roosevelt and Bryan) the voice of the subject is indicated in italics. In the portraits of Roosevelt and Bryan we hear passages from their speeches. Sometimes the speaker's voice is implied in indirect discourse which is actually the author speaking. In the portrait of Veblen, we hear a "public" voice which often merges with auctorial voice to reinforce the desired feeling of disapproval or approval. Direct dramatic dialogue occurs occasionally, as in "Paul Bunyan," where Everest talks with the mob who attack and kill him. Again, the subject's voice may be used in ballad fashion, as in refrain. "The Body of an American" offers an excellent example of this: "*And there's a hundred million others like me,*" and "Say feller tell me how I can get back to my outfit," or "Say buddy can't you tell me how I can get back to my outfit?" Finally, "Say soldier for chrissake can't you tell me how I can get back to my outfit?" These entries of

*Newspaper publisher William Randolph Hearst, "Poor Little Rich Boy" in* The Big Money *(courtesy of Bancroft Library, University of California, Berkeley)*

subject-voice assume a cumulative force, as in the incremental repetition of lines in the ballad, even though they be separated by one or more paragraphs of other textual material.

Dos Passos uses the incremental repetition technique for several effects. First, he is dealing impressionistically with each person. What is it about that person's life that he wishes to accent? Having selected this factor, he will make it a motif by repeating it. Sometimes such a factor is a statement that person made; or it is the peculiarity of some action. That is, Dos Passos essentializes character through isolating some feature and by repetition making it a "tic." Often we find this in a quoted remark, sometimes in italicized intrusion by the author himself, sometimes in a repeated opinion of the populace. In "Fighting Bob," we find "He was one of 'the little group of willful men expressing no opinion but their own'" repeated crucially at the end:

a stumpy man with a lined face, one leg stuck out in
the aisle and his arms folded and a chewed cigar in the
corner of his mouth
and an undelivered speech on his desk,
a willful man expressing no opinion but his own.

Thus, Dos Passos accents a person's ruling passion, his dominant mood, his prevailing humor, or the consistency of a public reaction.

Dos Passos does not often intrude overt evaluative statements, although his bias is usually obvious enough through innuendo, tonal intensification, and irony. Often, he asks at the end of the selection some question that needs no answer. It contains the answer and a built-in judgment. The portrait of Minor C. Keith, superimposed on the fictional career of J. Ward Moorehouse and amidst the minor swirl of little people struggling in business, ends this way:

Why that uneasy look under the eyes, in the picture of Minor C. Keith the pioneer of the fruittrade, the railroad-builder, in all the pictures the newspapers carried of him when he died?

Endings are particularly important in the portraits. Often the ending is diminuendo, trailing off into anticlimax for ironic effect. Sometimes the whiplash ending achieves its effect through mock concession to opinion hostile to the subject. Again, Dos Passos employs the barbed ending through implied quotation, the echo of a previously repeated direct quotation, from a hostile opponent. A poem-like ending can also embody a final pronouncement, benediction, or malediction. Such is the ending to "The House of Morgan" in *1919:*

(Wars and panics on the stock exchange,
machinegunfire and arson,
bankruptcies, warloans,
starvation, lice, cholera and typhus:
good growing weather for the House of Morgan.)

The distaste for the Morgan financial operations can be contrasted with the neutral-pose which ends "Joe Hill" in *1919:*

They put him in a black suit, put a stiff collar around his neck and a bow tie, shipped him to chicago for a bangup funeral, and photographed his handsome stony mask staring into the future.
The first of May they scattered his ashes to the wind.

Or, the ending is an ironic understatement ("The Body of an American"), the dying-fall, or diminuendo for the trailing-off into futility ("The American Plan" and "Tin Lizzie"). We find also the double-ending, as in the portrait of Thorstein Veblen ("The Bitter Drink"), a last request in italics followed by the author's own tribute. Then, there is the ironic anecdote for ending, as in "Art and Isadora." We also find an example of imitative form in the soaring ending to the portrait of the Wright brothers, an ending of positive force.

Most of the portraits utilize parentheses for varied effects. Usually, the parentheses serve for authorial aside, as Dos Passos takes a position of omniscient observer situated above the drama as narrated. In addition to the parentheses enclosing authorial interpolation, he (as in "The Boy Orator of the Platte") inserts repeated extracts from public statements in order to give the portrait depth and to create an illusion of massive force. Group and "class" opinion is echoed in parentheses, echoes which give the portraits a dialectical dramatism, indicating oppositions between the subject portrayed and the society or segment of society in which the subject acted. He makes use of italicized passages to intensify the dramatic impact. For one thing, he injects extracts from speeches ("Meester Veelson," "The Boy Orator," "The Happy Warrior") for accretive, incremental build-up of tone. Sometimes the public statement is found in lower-case fine print and in upper-case italics ("The Body of an American"). The portrait can end with an italicized statement by the subject, in most cases for irony. He may also interject passages from newspapers ("Adagio Dancer"), and other "documentary" materials, such as telegrams and letters, in italics.

Throughout the trilogy we notice some similarities to Carlylean harangue, as in *The French Revolution,* but more modern stylistic analogues suggest themselves, particularly cinematic techniques. *U.S.A.* as a whole is constructed in the fashion of a panoramic movie, the Hollywood epic, although no derogation of *U.S.A.* is intended in this parallel. The "Newsreel" and "Camera Eye" passages need no detailed explanation to show such correspondence in style. The portraits themselves are perhaps like movie shorts; or, better, documentary film; or "The March of Time" style of exposition. Fluidity of form is primary. Dos Passos tries to establish a sense of background and foreground simultaneously, as when the speeches of Roosevelt, Bryan, Wilson, Wright, *et al,* intrude in the flow of events. We also get the impression of temporally distinct events concurrently.

. . . . . . . . . .

–*Texas Studies in Literature and Language,*
4 (Spring 1962): 111–113

## The Happy Warrior

*Dos Passos carefully reworked the typescript draft of his biography of Theodore Roosevelt in* Nineteen-Nineteen *to achieve the precise ironic effect he wished to convey. Note, for example, the late inclusion of "righteous" in the first sentence.*

The Roosevelts had lived for seven righteous generations on Manhattan Island; they owned a big brick house on 20th Street, an estate up at Dobbs Ferry, lots in the city, a pew in the Dutch Reformed Church, interests, stocks and bonds, they felt Manhattan was theirs, they felt America was theirs. Their son,

Theodore,

was a sickly youngster, suffered from asthma, was very nearsighted; his hands and feet were so small it was hard for him to learn to box; his arms were very short;

his father was something of a humanitarian, gave Christmas dinners to newsboys, deplored conditions, slums, the East Side, Hell's Kitchen.

Young Theodore had ponies, was encouraged to walk in the woods, to go camping, was instructed in boxing and fencing (an American gentleman should know how to defend himself) taught Bible Class, did mission work (an American gentleman should do his best to uplift those not so fortunately situated);

righteousness was his by birth;

he had a passion for nature study, for reading about birds and wild animals, for going hunting; he got to be a good shot in spite of his glasses, a good walker in spite of his tiny feet and short legs, a fair horseman, an aggressive scrapper in spite of his short reach, a crack politician in spite of being the son of one of the owning Dutch families of New York.

In 1876 he went up to Cambridge to study at Harvard, a wealthy talkative erratic young man with sidewhiskers and definite ideas about everything under the sun,

at Harvard he drove around in a dogcart, collected stuffed birds, mounted specimens he'd shot on his trips in the Adirondacks; in spite of not drinking and being somewhat of a christer, having odd ideas about reform and remedying abuses, he made Porcellian and the Dickey and the clubs that were his right as the son of one of the owning Dutch families of New York.

He told his friends he was going to devote his life to social service: *I wish to preach not the doctrine of ignoble ease, but the doctrine of the strenuous life, the life of toil and effort, of labor and strife.*

From the time he was eleven years old he wrote copiously, filled diaries, notebooks, loose leaves with a big impulsive scrawl about everything he did and thought and said;

naturally he studied law.

He married young and went to Switzerland to climb the Matterhorn; his first wife's early death broke him all up. He went out to the badlands of western Dakota to become a rancher on the Little Missouri River;

when he came back to Manhattan he was Teddy, the straight shooter from the west, the elkhunter, the man in the Stetson hat, who'd roped steers, fought a grizzly hand to hand, acted as Deputy Sheriff,

(a Roosevelt has a duty to his country; the duty of a Roosevelt is to uplift those not so fortunately situated, those who have come more recently to our shores)

in the west, Deputy Sheriff Roosevelt felt the white man's burden, helped to arrest malefactors, bad men; service was bully.

All this time he'd been writing, filling the magazines with stories of his hunts and adventures, filling political meetings with his opinions, his denunciations, his pat phrases: Strenuous Life, Realizable Ideals, Just Government, *when men fear work or fear righteous war, when women fear motherhood, they tremble on the brink of doom, and well it is that they should vanish from the earth, where they are fit subjects for the scorn of all men and women who are themselves strong and brave and highminded.*

. . . . . . . . . .

*—Nineteen-Nineteen,* pp. 480–482

12

*righteous*

THE HAPPY WARRIOR  ####          The Roosevelts had lived for seven ,

generations on Manhattan Island; they owned a big

brick house on 20th Street , an estate up at Dobbs

Ferry , ~~a scattering of real estate~~ *lots in the city* , a pew in the

Dutch Reformed Church , ##### interests , stocks and bonds , they

felt Manhattan was theirs , they felt America was theirs. *their son,*

Theodore , was a sickly youngster ,

suffered from asthma , was very nearsighted ; his hands and feet were

so small it was hard for him to learn to box ; his arms were very

short ;

his father was something of a human -

itarian , gave Christmas dinners to newsboys , deplored conditions ,

slums , the East Side , Hell's Kitchen .

Young Theodore had ponies , was

encouraged to ~~be a lot outdoors~~ *walk in the woods, to go camping* , was instructed in boxing and

fencing ( an American gentleman should know how to defend himself)

taught Bible Class , did mission work , (an American gentleman should

do his best to uplift those not so fortunately situated );

*righteousness was his by birth;*

he had a passion for nature study , #

for reading about birds and wild animals , for going ~~out in the woods~~ *hunting*

~~after them~~ *game* ; he ~~was~~ got to be a good shot in #### spite of his glasses ,

a good walker inspite of his tiny feet and short legs, a fair horse-

man , an aggressive scrapper inspite of his short reach , *a ~~smart~~ crack*

*po*litician inspite of ~~being a gentleman~~ *the son of one of the owning Dutch families*

In 1876 he went up to Cambridge to *of New York*

*wealthy* ~~self confident~~ *talkative*

study at Harvard , an erratic young man with sidewhiskers and defin-

ite ideas about everything under ~~heaven~~ *The Sun*

~~There he drove around in a dogcart ,~~

~~collected stuffed birds and mounted the bucks he shot in his trips to~~

*made all the best clubs*

~~the Adirondacks , did and said what he pleased Instite of~~

*Two pages of the typescript draft for the Theodore Roosevelt biography in* Nineteen-Nineteen
*(Albert and Shirley Small Special Collections Library, University of Virginia)*

2                                                    13.

*at Harvard*

~~there~~ he drove around in a dogcart, collected
*mounted*
st~~#~~uffed birds, ~~###~~ *a* specimens he shot ~~on~~ his trips in the Adirondacks;
in spite of not drinking and being somewhat of a prister , having odd
*and the Dickey*
ideas about reform and remedying abuses, he made Porcellian ,and ~~most of #~~
*that were*        *the son*
the ~~best~~ clubs ~~as was~~ his right as ~~a member~~ of one of the ~~oldest~~ owning *Dutch*
families of New York.

He told his friends he was going to devote his life
to social service : <u>I wish to preach not the doctrine of ignoble ease,</u>
<u>but the doctrine of the strenuous life , the life of toil and effort ,of</u>
<u>labor and strife</u> #

*Space*                From the time he was eleven years old he wrote ~~######~~
copiously, ~~#############################~~ filled diaries ,notebooks ,
loose leaves with a big impulsive scrawl about everything he did and thought
and said .

Naturally he studied law .

He married young and went to Switzerland to climb
the Matterhorn ; his first wife's early death broke him all up.He ####
went out to the badlands of western Dakota to become a rancher on the
Little Missouri River;

~~wh~~en he came back to Manhattan he was Teddy , the ###
*from  ,the elkhunter*
straight shooter ~~for~~ the west, the man in the Stetson hat , who'd roped
~~steers fought a grizzly hand to hand. acted as Deputy Sheriff;~~

*a Roosevelt has a duty to this country; the
duty of a Roosevelt is to uplift those not so
fortunately situated, who have come more recently
to our shores;  in the west Deputy Sheriff Roosevelt felt the
white man's burden, helped to arrest malefactors. bad
men ; service was lully*

All this time he'd been writing ~~########~~ , filling the
magazines with stories of his hunts and adventures , filling #### political meetings with his opinions , his denunciations ,his pat phrases:
Strenuous Life , Realizable Ideals, Just Government , <u>when men fear work</u>
<u>or fear righteous war , when women fear motherhood , they tremble on the</u>
<u>brink of doom, and well it is that they should vanish from the earth,</u>
<u>where they are fit subjects for the scorn of all men and women who are</u> ##
<u>themselves strong and brave and highminded</u>

# THE NARRATIVES

## The Form of the Narratives in *U.S.A.*

Donald Pizer

*Pizer makes clear that the flat, often clichéd prose in which the narratives are told constitutes Dos Passos's participation in the technique known as "free indirect discourse," in which the narrative mimics, for satiric purposes, the language, and therefore the mental life, of the characters.*

It was long common in general discussion of twentieth- century American writing to regard the narratives of *U.S.A.* as evidence of Dos Passos' allegiance to the naturalist tradition in American fiction. In flat, colorless prose, the argument goes, Dos Passos in endless detail tells of the external experience of flat, colorless characters who exhibit little or no control over their destinies. There is some truth to this view, in that the total effect of the narratives of *U.S.A.* is of human inadequacy and social coercion. But the means used to achieve this effect are in fact very different from a nonselective accumulation of the externals of life. Like the other modes of *U.S.A.*, though less obviously so, the narrative mode in the trilogy is fully intellectualized and stylized. At its best—which is most of the time—a narrative in *U.S.A.* is at once a dramatic representation of its world and an interpretation of the large-scale designs operative in that world.

It might be expected that Dos Passos would use the opportunity afforded by the need to depict twentieth-century American life through the experience of a sizeable number of fictional characters to select figures who in their totality would constitute a cross section of American life. The narrative figures in *U.S.A.*, however, fail to achieve this kind of representativeness. The group lacks a farmer, factory worker,[1] businessman, or professional (lawyer, doctor, etc.). Almost all the figures are from the Midwest or the East Coast, and there is not a satisfactory (or even a more than miserable) marriage in the lot. This last failure in representativeness—or, more cogently, Dos Passos' impulse toward thematic emphasis through repetition—suggests a possible alternative principle of selection to that of sociological balance, despite the appearance of random sampling and therefore of objectivity in the choice of narrative figures. That is, the division of the "plot" of *U.S.A.* into twelve narrative figures who initially have widely differing backgrounds has something of the same purpose as the use of the documentary in the biographies and Newsreels. In all the modes other than the Camera Eye, Dos Passos wished to create an impression of objective truth, of historical accuracy in fictional form. Hence the use of the documentary in some modes and of a seemingly balanced cross section of American lives in the other. The narrative figures, however, have no special objectivity either in source or in fictional expression. Rather, the narratives of *U.S.A.* are remarkably similar in characterization and plotting to those of conventional novels. The figures usually stem from prototypes in Dos Passos' own experience, and Dos Passos recasts the lives of his prototypes into narratives that approximate specific themes. The narratives of *U.S.A.* are thus stylized, not in constituting a representative sociological spectrum of American life, but rather in suggesting such a representativeness while, in fact, expressing above all Dos Passos' personal vision of American life.

The clearest evidence that Dos Passos sought to rely on some of the traditional thematic devices of fiction in the narratives occurs about halfway through *The 42nd Parallel*, when Eleanor Stoddard and J. Ward Moorehouse, two narrative figures who have already had narrative segments devoted to them, meet in New York.[2] This technique, which I will call interlacing, increases as the trilogy goes forward. It ranges from a casual reappearance of a figure (Moorehouse momentarily drifts into Mac's narrative in Mexico) to the love affairs of Daughter and Richard Savage and of Charley Anderson and Margo. The technique peaks on the several occasions (as in a Paris restaurant at the close of *Nineteen-Nineteen*) when as many as five or six narrative figures are thrown together at a social function. So pervasive is the interlacing of narrative figures in *U.S.A.* that by the close of the trilogy only Mary French has not appeared in the narrative of another figure.

The effect of this device is to bring the narratives of *U.S.A.* close to one aspect of the plotting of a conventional novel. As characters we know fully become involved with other characters we know fully, theme emerges more clearly and powerfully than it would otherwise. An obvious example is the group of narrative figures (Janey, Eleanor, and Savage) who eventually gather around Moorehouse, a clustering that confirms the emptiness of each figure. Another is the love affair between Ben and Mary, in which Mary's abortion and the breakup of their relationship because of their commitment to a radical ideology epitomizes the antihumanism of the far left. These and the many other instances of interlacing in the trilogy appear to work against the logic of the initial and continuing device of separative narratives, the logic that the frequent meeting of such widely dispersed characters would be unlikely. By taking the narratives strongly in the direction of this "unlikelihood," Dos Passos was introducing a self-conscious, and to the reader clearly evident, abstract element as a means of heightening theme. He was, in other words, writing narrative that frequently runs counter to expectation, and he often gained his greatest thematic emphasis at these "points of surprise."

The narratives contain several other conventions that also reflect a stylization of the narrative mode. One such convention is that Dos Passos, though a third-person narrator, does not provide a synopsis or summary of a character's previous experience at the opening of a narrative segment, even though several hundred pages may have elapsed since a narrative segment was last devoted to that character. Another is that the reappearance of a major character in the narrative of a different character does not elicit a sign of recognition from the narrative voice. It is as if the narrator is encountering the figure, whom we as readers are fully acquainted with, for the first time.

Both of these conventions originate in Dos Passos' fidelity to the technique of free indirect discourse as the means of telling the life stories of his narrative figures. Free indirect discourse, or *style indirect libre* as it is commonly called in European literary criticism, is a basic tool of the novelist and can take a variety of complex forms.[3] But to describe it in broad strokes, the author adopting the device writes of a character in the third person but seeks to describe his or her thoughts, feelings, and even actions in an idiom closely associated with that of the character. The extremes in the use of free indirect discourse are the occasional presence of the device for specific moments and figures (as in Dickens) and the complete adoption throughout a novel of the verbal style of the principal characters, in which style becomes part of milieu (as in Zola or in Mailer's *The Executioner's Song*). Dos Passos' use of the technique in the narratives of *U.S.A.* approaches a full commitment to the device. Each narrative has its own verbal style, one seeking to suggest and approximate (rather than to reproduce exactly) the habitual modes of speech and therefore of thought of its narrative figure. In each narrative, Dos Passos is in effect communicating the total personality of the narrative figure by a narrative style that is an expression of that figure. Hence the convention of authorial nonpresence on occasions when a third-person narrator would ordinarily feel free to comment. The illusion that we are confined to the consciousness of the narrative figure through the narrative voice is thus preserved.

Although free indirect discourse has been common in fiction since the origin of the novel, it has had a special fascination for the modernist author since the late nineteenth century. The device permits the combination of two of the major impulses of modern fiction—the desire to depict the commonplace realities of life and the desire to dramatize consciousness. By portraying everyday action and thought in the everyday language habitual to a character, a language that thus powerfully reflects the consciousness of the character, the writer appeared to fulfill both aims simultaneously. Another appeal of the device for the modern novelist is its potential for irony. As most commentators on the technique have noted, it has the capacity to express either the author's sympathetic identification with or his ironic detachment from his central narrative figure. Irony is achieved, of course, by the difference between what a character's mode of expression suggests about his unconscious motives or unexamined values and what we as readers, either from evidence in the narrative or from external bases of judgment, sense are the inadequacies of these motives or values.

Dos Passos' free indirect discourse narrative style in *U.S.A.* exhibits only occasionally the most obvious verbal signs of the device.[4] His third-person narrative contains little vulgarity and few grammatical lapses, and he does not sharply differentiate among regional or ethnic voices. (Opportunities for this kind of distinction were present in the Jewish and Southern backgrounds of Ben Compton and Janey, for example.) He concentrates rather on an effort to render the stereotyped in thought and feeling through stereotypes of language—through the platitudes and clichés, the commonplace evasions and half-truths, the verbal disguises that constitute much discourse. So unobtrusive is the technique that many early (and some later) readers of the trilogy failed to recognize the extent and depth of its ironic intent. Even so ordinarily astute a critic as Edmund Wilson complained to Dos Passos in 1939 that the characters of *U.S.A.* seemed to talk only in clichés.[5] Other critics, however, such as Sartre in 1938 and Claude-Edmonde Magny in 1946, were quick to realize that Dos Passos was attempting to write the narratives in what Sartre called a "public" voice and that this voice constituted both the form and the theme of the narratives.[6]

The impulse behind this vast exercise in free indirect discourse was of course clearly announced by Dos Passos in the trilogy itself, when he concluded the "U.S.A." prologue with the words, "mostly U. S. A. is the speech of the people." As he had also noted in 1935, "language . . . is the mind of the group."[7] To render the language of America is to render the mind of the nation and thus the true nature of the national experience. And since Dos Passos undertook the trilogy with the belief that America had betrayed its "storybook democracy" of equality, freedom, justice, and opportunity and was attempting to disguise and even defend this betrayal by distorting the language of democratic idealism, he was at special pains to render ironically throughout the narratives the vast failure of belief and thus of language that was the twentieth-century American experience.

There is, of course, no single, uniform free-indirect-discourse technique in the narratives of *U.S.A.* Occasionally Dos Passos' own sensibility seems paramount in descriptive or narrative passages that seem to be beyond the verbal ability of the narrative figure. Occasionally, too, a verbal shrillness, suggestive of an authorial editorial voice, enters the narrative, as in the accounts of the suppression of civil rights during the war (*NN*, 173–174).[8] At the other extreme, we are sometimes plunged into the chaotic and fragmented workings of a mind in a manner resembling stream of consciousness. This occurs especially during the closing portions of Charley Anderson's narrative, when he is drunk or seriously ill.[9] Perhaps the clearest and most pervasive indication of the dominance of free indirect discourse as narrative style occurs on the many occasions at the opening of a narrative when the childhood of the narrative figure is described.[10] Here, for example, is the first paragraph of Eveline Hutchins' narrative:

Little Eveline and Arget and Lade and Gogo lived on the top floor of a yellowbrick house on the North Shore Drive. Arget and Lade were little Eveline's sisters. Gogo was her little brother littler than Eveline; he had such nice blue eyes but Miss Mathilda had horrid blue eyes. On the floor below was Dr. Hutchins' study where Yourfather mustn't be disturbed, and Dearmother's room where she stayed all morning painting dressed in a lavender smock. On the groundfloor was the drawingroom and the diningroom, where parishioners came and little children must be seen and not heard, and at dinnertime you could smell good things to eat and hear knives and forks and tinkling companyvoices and Yourfather's booming scary voice. (*NN*, 107)

The irony in this passage is readily apparent but genial as the child's view of her world is gently mocked. More characteristic of the narratives as a whole, however, are the many instances when a narrative figure's thoughts, especially those involving politics or sex and marriage, are rendered in a blatantly clichéd verbal style that clearly reflects the painful inadequacy of his or her stereotyped belief. So, for example, Janey is working at the outbreak of the war as a secretary in a law firm in which one of the partners is of German background. "Mr. Dreyfus was very polite and generous with his employees but Janey kept thinking of the ruthless invasion of Belgium and the horrible atrocities and didn't like to be working for a Hun, so she began looking around for another job" (*FP*, 285). At the other extreme of political awareness, but revealing an equally suspect reliance on the inevitable and hackneyed phrase, is Ben's motive for studying hard and reading Marx. "He was working to be a wellsharpened instrument" (*NN*, 431). As for love, there are J. Ward Moorehouse's aspirations as a young man: "He was twenty and didn't drink or smoke and was keeping himself clean for the lovely girl he was going to marry, a girl in pink organdy with golden curls and a sunshade" (*FP*, 177).

In general, however, the narrative prose of *U.S.A.* is far less blatant in its free-indirect-discourse dramatization of the platitudes and clichés that guide the lives of the characters. Rather, Dos Passos' more common method is to suggest by the jaded and worn language of the narratives the underlying failure of individuality of those who approach life without independent vision and who are therefore strangled by the hold of the conventional upon their lives. Here, for example, is a typical passage of narrative prose, one in which without any bold ironic touches Dos Passos describes Janey's new position in a Washington law office:

Working at Dreyfus and Carroll's was quite different from working at Mrs. Robinson's. There were mostly men in the office. Mr. Dreyfus was a small thinfaced man with a small black moustache and small black twinkly eyes and a touch of accent that gave him a distinguished foreign diplomat manner. He carried yellow wash gloves and a yellow cane and had a great variety of very much tailored overcoats. He was the brains of the firm, Jerry Burnham said. Mr. Carroll was a stout redfaced man who smoked many cigars and cleared his throat a great deal and had a very oldtimey Southern Godblessmysoul way of talking. Jerry Burnham said he was the firm's bay window. Jerry Burnham was a wrinklefaced young man with dissipated eyes who was the firm's adviser in technical and engineering matters. He laughed a great deal, always got into the office late, and for some reason took a fancy to Janey and used to joke about things to her while he was dictating. She liked him, though the dissipated look under his eyes scared her off a little. She'd have liked to have talked to him like a sister, and gotten him to stop burning the candle at both ends. (*FP*, 152)

On the one hand, the passage merely records Janey's impressions of the various members of the firm and thus renders in a mildly ironic manner several of her received opinions: that fine clothes represent distinction, that speech mannerisms signify character, and that there are clear physical stigmata of moral decay—in short, that life is as superficially apparent as she finds it. But the passage also records, with a far deeper and more significant irony, Janey's unconscious absorption in Jerry Burnham and her fear of that absorption, a conflict that she seeks to resolve by adopting the role of "sister" toward him. Janey thus reveals in the seemingly bland prose of this passage her fear of her own emotions and desires, a fear that leads her to erect barriers of conventional and life-denying attitudes between herself and the world.

Each of the narratives of *U.S.A.* demonstrates that its major character is locked in an analogous prison of stereotyped thought and action that is reflected in his language. Of course, Dos Passos' degree of ironic distance varies in his portrayal of the twelve narrative figures, despite the limitations of all the figures. The range extends from Eleanor, whom Dos Passos characterized elsewhere as a "drawing room bitch,"[11] to Margo and Mary, toward whom he felt considerable sympathy. When Margo and Charley become lovers, for example, we are told in Margo's narrative that "Mr. A., as she called him, kept offering to set Margo up in an apartment on Park Avenue, but she always said nothing doing, what did he think she was, a kept woman? She did let him play the stockmarket a little for her, and buy her clothes and jewelry and take her to Atlantic City and Long Beach weekends" (*BM*, 327). The irony in this passage, though clear enough, is also deflected by Dos Passos' identification with Margo's buoyant nature, with her only token and halfhearted self-deception, and thus is more amusing than condemnatory.

This wide variation in the degree and kind of satiric irony in the narratives is significant for its suggestions that the characters differ in their inner natures, that they are not uniformly shallow echoing chambers of the shallowness of their society. Such figures as Eleanor and Moorehouse have indeed found linguistic formulas that at once express an emotional and spiritual aridity and serve as vehicles for social advancement, and Dos Passos' ironic rendering of their formulaic attitudes is usually biting. But for many of the other figures—far more than is usually acknowledged—

MARY FRENCH 1

Poor Daddy never got ~~settled at the dinnertable or~~
*night after supper the way he liked to*
tucked away in bed ᴀ with his reading light over his left shoulder and

his glasses on and the paper in his hand and a fresh cigar in his
*and ring*
mouth but the phone would ring ᴀ or else it would be a knocking at ~~th~~

the back door and Mother would send little Mary to open it and she'd

find a miner standing there whitefaced with his eyelashes and eyebrows

very black from the coaldust saying ~~I wanna see~~ "Doc French pliz ...
       ,,
~~Plz~~ heem coma queek , and Poor Daddy would get up ~~from the table or~~
*in his pyjamas and bathrobe*
out of bed yawning ᴀ and push his untidy grey hair off his forehead
        *Mary  so*
and tell her to ᴀ get his instrument case out of his office for him
*be it tying his necktie as he went*         *Mealtimes it was worse. They never seemed*
and ~~go~~ ᴀ , and half the time he'd been gone all night ᴀ Mother would *to get the*
                                                                *settled at the*
put away the dishes and flounce about the house muttering to herself *table for*
        *that*                                                         *a meal*
~~Mother said~~ if poor Daddy ever took half the trouble with his paying *the*
                                                                       *three*
patients that he did with those miserable foreigners and miners he *of them*
*would*                                                              *without*
ᴀ be a rich man today and she wouldnt be killing herself with housew *That awful*
                                                                     *phone ringing*
work . *Mary hated to hear Mother talk against Daddy like she did.*

Poor Daddy and Mother didn't get along . Mary barely rememb *Daddy*
ered a time  when she was very very small when it had been differen *would*
                        *flowering bushes in the yard.*             *go out*
and they'd lived in Denver in a sunny house with ~~a big garden~~ .That *Mary*
                                                 *that*             *and Mother*
was before Brother ~~died~~ was taken and ~~Daddy~~ lost all ~~his~~ money in *would*
*the*                                                                *sit there*
~~an~~ investment . Whenever anybody said Denver it made her think of *thinking*
sunny . Now they lived in Trinidad where everything was black like *sometime*
       *tall darkening the valley full of rows of dirty shanties,*
coal , the scrawny hills the minetipples the miners the wops and *alone, with*
*hunkies      and the awful saloons and the*  ~~smothers~~ *choky smelter smoke* *the*
greasers and ~~bohunks~~ and the little black trains . In Denver it was *without*
                                                                     *saying*
sunny, and white people lived there ~~and~~ real clean American  childr
*little Mary with her face wrapped round the chairlegs staring at the eyes of two dead*
*wild ducks in the middle of the gingercolored wall paper above* ~~the mantles~~ *Mother's head.*

*Revised typescript of the first narrative section in* U.S.A. *devoted to Mary French, in* The Big Money

the acceptance of formulas and roles causes an intense pain as a sensibility buried within the figure struggles in vain against the life-denying modes of belief and speech that the formulas demand. Such characters as Charley Anderson and Richard Savage approach tragic dimensions in this conflict. A number of other figures, such as Janey or Joe Williams or Ben, though lacking the depth or centrality of Charley or Savage, also exhibit sufficient traces of a repressed emotional nature to engage Dos Passos and us in a complex mix of ironic critique and sympathetic understanding.

–*Dos Passos' U.S.A.: A Critical Study* (Charlottesville: University Press of Virginia, 1988), pp. 63–71

## Notes

1. Dos Passos included a factory worker, Ike Hall, in early drafts of *The Big Money* but cut his narrative at a late stage in the composition of the novel.

2. Even before the meeting, Joe Williams had appeared in Janey's narrative and Eveline in Eleanor's. We do not know at those points, however, that Joe and Eveline will eventually have their own narratives.

3. For my understanding of the device I have relied principally on Roy Pascal's *The Dual Voice: Free Indirect Speech and Its Functioning in the Nineteenth-Century European Novel* (Totowa, N.J.: Rowman & Littlefield, 1977) and Brian McHale's "Free Indirect Discourse: A Survey of Recent Accounts," *PTL,* 3 (1978): 249–287.

4. The fullest account of free indirect discourse in *U.S.A.* is by Brian McHale: "Talking U.S.A.: Interpreting Free Indirect Discourse in Dos Passos' *U.S.A.* Trilogy, Part One," *Degrés* (Brussels), 16 (1978): c1–7; "Part Two," *Degrés,* 17 (1979): d1–20.

5. Edmund Wilson to Dos Passos, 16 July 1939, in Edmund Wilson, *Letters on Literature and Politics,* edited by Elena Wilson (New York: Farrar, Straus & Giroux, 1977), p. 319.

6. Jean-Paul Sartre, "Dos Passos and '1919,'" in Sartre, *Literary and Philosophical Essays,* translated by Annette Michelson (London: Rider, 1955), p. 94; and Claude-Edmonde Magny, *The Age of the American Novel: The Film Aesthetic of Fiction between the Two Wars* (1948; translated by Eleanor Hochman, New York: Ungar, 1972), p. 61.

7. Dos Passos, "The Writer as Technician," in *American Writers' Congress,* edited by Henry Hart (New York: International, 1935), p. 79.

8. Citations to *U.S.A.* here and elsewhere in this essay are to the Modern Library edition (New York, 1939).

9. See *The Big Money,* pp. 233–236, 314–315, 369–377.

10. See Brian McHale, "Speaking as a Child in *U.S.A.:* A Problem in the Mimesis of Speech," *Language and Style,* 17 (Fall 1984): 351–370.

11. Dos Passos to Ernest Hemingway, May 1932, in Townsend Ludington, ed., *The Fourteenth Chronicle: Letters and Diaries of John Dos Passos* (Boston: Gambit, 1973), p. 408.

## Mary French

*Dos Passos revised the opening of the first segment of the Mary French narrative, for instance, changing "died" to "was taken," to reflect Mary's unconscious participation at that stage of her life in the genteel environment her mother sought to establish for the family.*

Poor Daddy never did get tucked away in bed right after supper the way he liked with his readinglight over his left shoulder and his glasses on and the paper in his hand and a fresh cigar in his mouth that the phone didn't ring, or else it would be a knocking at the back door and Mother would send little Mary to open it and she'd find a miner standing there whitefaced with his eyelashes and eyebrows very black from the coaldust saying, "Doc French, pliz . . . heem coma queek," and poor Daddy would get up out of bed yawning in his pyjamas and bathrobe and push his untidy grey hair off his forehead and tell Mary to go get his instrumentcase out of the office for him, and be off tying his necktie as he went, and half the time he'd be gone all night.

Mealtimes it was worse. They never seemed to get settled at the table for a meal, the three of them, without that awful phone ringing. Daddy would go and Mary and Mother would sit there finishing the meal alone, sitting there without saying anything, little Mary with her legs wrapped around the chairlegs staring at the picture of two dead wild ducks in the middle of the gingercolored wallpaper above Mother's trim black head. Then Mother would put away the dishes and clatter around the house muttering to herself that if poor Daddy ever took half the trouble with his paying patients that he did with those miserable foreigners and miners he would be a rich man today and she wouldn't be killing herself with housework. Mary hated to hear Mother talk against Daddy the way she did.

Poor Daddy and Mother didn't get along. Mary barely remembered a time when she was very very small when it had been different and they'd lived in Denver in a sunny house with flowering bushes in the yard. That was before Brother was taken and Daddy lost that money in the investment. Whenever anybody said Denver it made her think of sunny. Now they lived in Trinidad where everything was black like coal, the scrawny hills tall, darkening the valley full of rows of sooty shanties, the minetipples, the miners most of them greasers and hunkies and the awful saloons and the choky smeltersmoke and the little black trains. In Denver it was sunny, and white people lived there, real clean American children like Brother who was taken and Mother said if poor Daddy cared for his own flesh and blood the way he cared for those miserable foreigners and miners Brother's life might have been saved. Mother had made her go into the parlor, she was so scared, but Mother held her hand so tight it hurt terribly but nobody paid any attention, they all thought it was on account of Brother she was crying, and Mother made her look at him in the coffin under the glass.

–*The Big Money,* pp. 856–857

MARGIE DOWLING

When Margie got big enough she used to go #### ###
*with a lantern dark*
across to the station to meet Fred w/inter nights when he ~~was~~
*expected to be getting*
~~got~~ home from the city on the nine fourteen . Fred was
*very little* *Agnes always said* *used to say*
Margie's father . Margie was ~~small~~ for her age, but ~~the~~ her
*broadcloth*
~~little~~ red coat with the fleece collar ~~warm and~~ tickly #u
*all the same* *and left her ~~at~~ chapped*
round her ears was too small for her/, ~~Sometimes there~~
*wrists out* *sleety*
*nights when* ~~stars~~ or the wind ~~full of sleet,~~ whipping roun
the corner of the station , ~~and her hand got ivy holding~~
*old* *and the wire handle cut into her ~~hand~~* *hand.*
~~the lantern~~ ####### ### She hated the old smoky ~~brakeman's~~
*cheery*
lantern ~~and the lamp chimneys that had to be washed and~~ y
the greasy smell of ####### coal oil from when she first
*Still she always wanted to go meet Fred.*
began to remember, Nights when it was moonlight and you *could see*
*tide coming in*
the ~~water~~ all ripply shimmery and the chilly shine on the
*used to* *wanted to go*
flats she didn't take ~~the~~ lantern , but she always ~~went~~ ;
*chill*
always with the same ~~cold dread~~ down her spine ~~making~~ her
*for fear* *and ~~talk~~ in*
hands and feet ~~toy~~ ~~that~~ Fred wouldnt be himself and would
lurch and stum#ble like he sometimes did and be so red#
faced and talk so awful . That was when he was drunk .
*stoop shouldered*
Mr Bemis the ~~hunchback~~ station agent used to kid ####### 
*big ~~ruddment~~* *The* *who was*
about it with Joe Hines ~~who was a~~ section hand and often
*at traintime*
puttering around in the station , and Margie would stand *outside in order not to*
*them*
~~there~~ listening to ~~em~~ saying 'Well here's lettin Fred
*" winter*
Dowling comes in stinkin again tonight . "~~These~~ nights
*about* *It was when*
Fred was the only passenger that ever got off at Broad *he was that*
*way*
Channel . ~~It was when he was drunk that~~ he needed ~~her~~ *Margie* *that*
and the lantern on account of the plank walk over to the
*house being so narrow and slippery.* ~~~~ .

*Revised typescript draft of the first narrative section of* U.S.A. *devoted to Margo Dowling, in* The Big Money
*(Albert and Shirley Small Special Collections Library, University of Virginia)*

# PARTISAN REVIEW

## *A LITERARY MONTHLY*

VOLUME IV, No. 2                                    JANUARY, 1937

*Editors:* F. W. DUPEE, DWIGHT MACDONALD, MARY McCARTHY, GEORGE L. K. MORRIS, WILLIAM PHILLIPS, PHILIP RAHV.

PARTISAN REVIEW *is published monthly at 22 East 17 Street, New York, N. Y. Subscriptions $2.00 yearly; foreign rate $2.50; Canada, $2.25. Manuscripts will not be returned unless accompanied by stamped, self-addressed envelopes. Copyright January, 1938 by* PARTISAN REVIEW. *Entered as second-class matter, November 12, 1937, at the post office at New York, N. Y. under the Act of March 3, 1879.*   357

*Contents page from the magazine issue featuring Dos Passos's narrative of Ike Hall, which had been cut from* The Big Money *(Collection of Richard Layman)*

## Margo Dowling

*For the opening of the first segment of the Margo Dowling narrative, Dos Passos again wished to render a child's voice. He sought through his revisions to simplify even further the diction and syntax of the passage.*

When Margie got big enough she used to go across to the station to meet Fred with a lantern dark winter nights when he was expected to be getting home from the city on the nine fourteen. Margie was very little for her age, Agnes used to say, but her red broadcloth coat with the fleece collar tickly round her ears was too small for her all the same, and left her chapped wrists out nights when the sleety wind whipped round the corner of the station and the wire handle of the heavy lantern cut cold into her hand. Always she went with a chill creeping down her spine and in her hands and feet for fear Fred wouldn't be himself and would lurch and stumble the way he sometimes did and be so red in the face and talk so awful. Mr. Bemis the stoop-shouldered station agent used to kid about it with big Joe Hines the sectionhand who was often puttering around in the station at traintime, and Margie would stand outside in order not to listen to them saying, "Well, here's bettin' Fred Dowlin' comes in stinkin' again tonight." It was when he was that way that he needed Margie and the lantern on account of the plankwalk over to the house being so narrow and slippery. When she was a very little girl she used to think that it was because he was so tired from the terrible hard work in the city that he walked so funny when he got off the train but by the time she was eight or nine Agnes had told her all about how getting drunk was something men did and that they hadn't ought to. So every night she felt the same awful feeling when she saw the lights of the train coming towards her across the long trestle from Ozone Park.

*–The Big Money,* pp. 903–904

# THE NEWSREELS

## The Origin and Intent of the Newsreels
Donald Pizer

*Pizer discusses the source, nature, and purpose of the Newsreels in U.S.A., noting their origin in actual song lyrics and newspaper stories and headlines, their form as a kind of "surreal collage," and their satiric intent.*

Dos Passos did not visit Chicago to take notes for the Newsreel portions of *The 42nd Parallel* until the summer of 1929, when he was well into the composition of the novel. There is little doubt, however, that his general plan for the trilogy included from the beginning the notion of a sardonic documentation of the vacuousness of popular belief and expression in America.[1] As many commentators have noted, there is an attractive symmetry in an epic of American life that ranges in angle of vision from a single consciousness to the mass mind, and the Newsreels were necessary to complete that symmetry. In seeking to document popular expression through the verbatim use of newspaper headlines and stories and of popular song lyrics, Dos Passos was, of course, scarcely breaking new ground. He himself had used newspaper stories, advertising slogans, songs, and jazz in *Manhattan Transfer* and *The Garbage Man,* and there was much comparable reliance on this material of American culture during the 1920s, ranging from Mencken's satiric exhibitions of specimens of American provincial silliness and barbarism to the contrary tendency on the left to sanctify the wisdom and strength of American folk expression.[2]

For *U.S.A.,* Dos Passos narrowed down his interest in the documentation of the popular mind to newspaper writing and the song. The newspaper offered a rich source for the dual effects he wished to achieve in the Newsreels of "the clamor, the sound of daily life" and of "an inkling of the common mind of the epoch."[3] Newspaper stories also provided a series of immediate chronological markers. A good many of the events reported in the headline and story excerpts reprinted by Dos Passos are obscure now and were indeed obscure to a 1930s reader. But many–from presidential elections to the sinking of the *Titanic* and Lindbergh's flight–are part of common historical awareness and thus chronologically site not only a specific Newsreel but also the portion of the novel in which the Newsreel appears. The presence of many items dealing with a particular occasion will also key the reader to the centrality of that event both historically and fictionally, and the initial announcement of a major event in the Newsreels (the Armistice, for example) will prepare him for its full-scale appearance in the other modes. (These obvious functional uses of the Newsreels in relation to major cultural and historical events stressed elsewhere in *U.S.A.* perhaps explain why Dos Passos prepared the Newsreels comparatively late in the composition of each of the novels of the trilogy.) The songs probably appealed to Dos Passos as a further and often comic extension of a prominent feature of newspaper writing in their mindless expression of the platitudinous heart of American feeling and belief.

*Dos Passos's notes for newsreels in* The 42nd Parallel *(Albert and Shirley Small Special Collections Library, University of Virginia)*

Dos Passos' method of preparing each News-reel was to make extensive notes from a single news-paper of items appearing over a period ranging from several days to several months, though occasionally a specific Newsreel will contain material that appeared more than a year apart.[4] He used the Chicago *Tribune* for *The 42nd Parallel* and the New York *World* for *Nineteen- Nineteen* and *The Big Money*. He tended to concentrate on first-page stories—sensational crimes and major international and national news—and he omitted almost entirely material about the arts, theater, books, and society. From his notes, he would compose a Newsreel by careful selection, cutting, rearrangement, repunctuation, and even verbal revision. One curious feature in Dos Passos' preparation of the Newsreels was his habit of leaving blank spaces for the late entry of a song lyric on the otherwise completed typescript of a Newsreel. This practice stemmed, it seems, less from uncertainty about which lyric to include than from doubts about the specific wording of an already chosen lyric. Song lyrics were not available in libraries, and rather than depend on his own memory, Dos Passos had learned to delay their inclusion until he acquired a correct wording.[5] He came to depend especially on his old college friend Ed Massey, who had a reliable and encyclopedic recollection of old popular songs.[6]

There are a number of ways to categorize the Newsreels. Some, as I noted, have a single subject to highlight a major historical event; others have a preponderance of material bearing on an event both because of its historical importance and because the event is prominent elsewhere in the trilogy, as with the Paris peace conference and the Sacco-Vanzetti case. Occasionally, a Newsreel will derive from only one portion of a newspaper in order to stress an aspect of an adjoining modal segment, as when a Newsreel consisting entirely of help-wanted ads is followed by a narrative segment in which seeking a job is prominent. But the great majority of the sixty-eight Newsreels in *U.S.A.* are true miscellanies. Each consists of from roughly ten to twenty items of largely unrelated headlines and news stories, among which brief passages from one or two song lyrics are interspersed. Each is an approximation in verbal form of what its title would imply to readers of the 1930s who were familiar with the movie newsreel—a miscellany of news items mixing the significant (war scenes, for example) and the trivial (a bathing beauty contest).[7]

This pasting up of the miscellaneous "verbal artifacts"[8] of the American popular mind into a kind of surreal collage permitted Dos Passos a number of obvious ironic effects within specific Newsreels. So,

*Singer and actress Ethel Waters, who made a popular 1925 recording of the blues song "Shake That Thing," which is quoted in Newsreel XLVIII (from Donald Bogle,* Toms, Coons, Mulattoes, Mammies, and Bucks, *1997)*

for example, a particular news item or song lyric can stand in clear ironic relationship to the bulk of other items in a Newsreel. In Newsreel XVII various items on the European war are concluded with the stark headline, "BROTHERS FIGHT IN DARK." In Newsreel XIX, the patriotic lyrics of "Over There" are interspersed among a series of news items on increased profits and restrictive social legislation at home. And in Newsreel LXII, items about a devastating Florida hurricane are accompanied by the lyrics of "It Ain't Gonna Rain No More." Far more common, however, is the Newsreel that is a true pastiche in the sense that no dominant ironic device or thread is found. Rather, a number of chords are struck, some with resonance to other chords, others seemingly isolated. Here, for a brief but full example, is Newsreel XLVIII in *The Big Money*:

truly the Steel Corporation stands forth as a corporate colossus both physically and financially.

*Now the folks in Georgia they done gone wild*
*Over that brand new dancin' style*
   Called     Shake     That     Thing

CARBARNS BLAZE

GYPSY ARRESTED FOR TELLING THE TRUTH

Horsewhipping Hastens Wedding

that strength has long since become almost a truism
as steel's expanding career progressed, yet the dimensions thereof need at times to be freshly measured to be
caught in proper perspective

DAZED BY MAINE DEMOCRATS CRY FOR MONEY

*shake that thing*

Woman of Mystery Tries Suicide in Park Lake
*shake that thing*

OLIVE THOMAS DEAD FROM POISON

LETTER SAID GET OUT OF WALL STREET

BOMB WAGON TRACED TO JERSEY

Shake     That     Thing

Writer of Warnings Arrives

BODY FOUND LASHED TO BICYCLE

FIND BOMB CLOCKWORK

*(BM, 46)*

Several items in the Newsreel are linked and thus
comprise a possible ironic theme. The two items on the
strength of the American steel industry, couched in
public-relations prose, are perhaps in ironic juxtaposition to the last five items on a Wall Street bombing.[9]
All is not as secure in American business life as American business life believes it to be. The other items are
far more miscellaneous, though an underlying theme—
one present in many of the Newsreels—is the indiscriminate violence of American life (fire, beatings, suicides).
The lyrics of "Shake That Thing," a popular song of
the early 1920s, seem to be totally unrelated to the
news items except for a possible tenuous link to
"Horsewhipping Hastens Wedding." Newsreel XLVIII
(and many like it) thus has a few suggestive ironic
threads but also much that appears to be a challenge to
a reader's capacity for ingenious overreading. The
effect is therefore much like that of a surreal collage in
which discernible "meaning" is mixed with material
that is present principally to startle or to amuse. One
significant consequence of this effect is that the News-

reels as a whole appear to be a kind of hoax, though a
hoax that is intimately related to the intent of the trilogy. The "history" of our times, as preserved by our
major device for recording events, is a meaningless
"noise" and "clamor" both in the lies purveyed by
sources of public information and in the chaotic mix of
the trivial and the momentous that is the "news." The
Newsreels are carefully constructed to render this
cacophony, to heighten and intensify it to a point at
which we can recognize fully its essential emptiness.
The Newsreels are therefore only seemingly documentary. More significantly, they communicate through
imitative form, through their fragmented meaninglessness, the understanding of American life possessed by
most Americans. It is the task of the other modes of the
trilogy—the Camera Eye, biographies, and narratives—
to make "sense" of the events recorded in the "nonsense" form of the Newsreels.

   –*Dos Passos' U.S.A.: A Critical Study* (Charlottesville:
      University Press of Virginia, 1988), pp. 79–84

### Notes

1. One of Dos Passos' early notebooks for *The 42nd Parallel*
supports this supposition; see Townsend Ludington,
*John Dos Passos: A Twentieth Century Odyssey* (New York:
Dutton, 1980), p. 257.

2. See William Stott, *Documentary Expression and Thirties America* (New York: Oxford University Press, 1973), pp. 120–
122.

3. Frank Gado, "John Dos Passos," in *First Person: Conversations on Writers and Writing,* edited by Gado (Schenectady,
N.Y.: Union College Press, 1973), p. 42; Dos Passos,
"Introductory Note," *The 42nd Parallel* (New York: Modern Library, 1937), p. vii.

4. The account in this paragraph derives from my examination of the notebooks and drafts in the Dos Passos Papers
and from Donald G. England's study, "The Newsreels of
John Dos Passos' *The 42nd Parallel*: Sources and Techniques," Ph.D. dissertation, University of Texas, 1970.

5. See Dos Passos to Dudley Poore, 26 August 1929, Ludington, ed., *The Fourteenth Chronicle: Letters and Diaries of
John Dos Passos* (Boston: Gambit, 1973), p. 394, in which
Dos Passos asks Poore's aid in determining the precise
lyrics for a number of songs.

6. Dos Passos to England, 7 March 1969, cited in England,
"The Newsreels of John Dos Passos' *The 42nd Parallel*,"
pp. 36–37.

7. For the relationship of film newsreels to the contents and
form of Dos Passos' Newsreels, see David Seed, "Media
and Newsreels in Dos Passos' *U.S.A.,*" *Journal of Narrative
Technique,* 14 (Fall 1984): 182–192.

8. The phrase is Charles Marz's in his "Dos Passos's Newsreels: The Noise of History," *Studies in the Novel,* 11 (Summer 1979): 198.

9. The items in Newsreel XLVIII are from the New York
*World* during the month of September 1920.

## Media and Newsreel in Dos Passos' *U.S.A.*
David Seed

*David Seed discusses both the contents and the form of the Newsreels as types of conscious misinformation that illustrate Dos Passos's theme in the trilogy of the dangers inherent in the power of mass media.*

Reporting on the 1932 Republican Convention in Chicago for the *New Republic,* Dos Passos found his attention constantly being diverted from the politicians to the technicians who were working the lights and generally directing the "rumble and chaos" which strongly reminded him of a circus. The experience pointed a moral which was all the more important because the political parties did not seem to have realized it:

> . . . we do not appreciate yet how enormously the whole technique and machinery of politics has been changed by the mechanics of communication. The architecture of stadiums, klieg lights, radio and the imminent danger of fairly perfected television are as important a factor in future political life as committees, votes, resolutions, theories, vested interests.

What starts out as a political report turns into a major comment on political change. Dos Passos' insights were quite consistent with the *New Republic*'s general policy. Earlier in 1932, for instance, Morris B. Cohen had taken James Truslow Adams to task for imagining (in his book *The Epic of America*) that it was possible to divorce the American people from their political and social context. Dos Passos similarly speculates about the "socialization" of the individual's mind which is taking place through the new mass media. Like Cohen he takes as a premise that a man is embedded in his environment and that any change in that environment will have political consequences. The media specifically raise ominous possibilities, as Dos Passos states in a passage unconsciously predicting Dr. Goebbels:

> . . . history, or the mass mind . . . is becoming more and more involved with the apparatus of spotlights, radio, talking pictures, newsprint, so that the image-making faculty, instead of being the concern of the individual mind, is becoming a social business. The control of radio waves is externalizing thought and feeling to a hair-raising degree. A man in his shirt-sleeves handling a battery of spots can give the effect of a great wave of mass emotion in a convention hall. The possibilities of control of the mass are terrifying.[1]

The anxiety which Dos Passos voices here spreads throughout his trilogy *U.S.A.* Those novels cover the first three decades of this century but with the insights of the 1930s. The recurring metaphor of the machine–it is signif-

icant that the first big company to be mentioned deals in *steel*–initially suggests the national war effort but then takes on broader connotations of a more general mechanization of life, even of the processes of thought. Doc Bingham functions primarily as an index of change within this context, appearing initially as an individual confidence-man and then reappearing at the end of the trilogy transformed into a media personality complete with microphones and attendant technicians. Marshall McLuhan has accused Dos Passos of showing the static contemplation of an aesthete, passively noting changes for the worse.[2] It is a particularly ironic charge since, as I shall argue, Dos Passos in fact anticipates some of McLuhan's cultural criticism of the 1950s and 1960s in demonstrating how the media dominate and even shape characters' styles of thought and behavior. *U.S.A.* shows this process at work much more than *Manhattan Transfer* where McLuhan's allegations of a derivative debt to Joyce are more justified. It is anyway very unlikely that the "Aeolus" episode of *Ulysses* could offer a model for the Newsreels of *U.S.A.* because, as Matthew Hodgart has pointed out, the capitalized titles are not so much headlines as captions for imaginary illustrations.[3]

In *Manhattan Transfer* (1925) characters encounter New York's billboards, advertisements and newspaper headlines as part of their general urban environment. New York is defined at one point as "the city of gilt letter signs" but it is primarily Jimmy Herf who pays explicit attention to these aspects of the urban scene and who, as befits an aspiring journalist, toys with imaginary articles.[4] It reflects ironically on his situation that he can only express himself satisfactorily in his imagination, which has been completely penetrated by newspaper idioms. Thus he dramatizes his disenchantment with the urban political system by figuring himself being deported as an undesirable alien and by composing a burlesque civic ritual which derives directly from *Ulysses*. Such a use of media is, however, uncharacteristic in Dos Passos' novel. A cautious montage of song and description at the beginning of Section Three points the way forward to the Newsreels of *U.S.A.* where headlines, fragments of articles read and songs overheard, advertisements, etc. are detached from their narrative contexts and given a separate formal space. In *Manhattan Transfer* they merely join the other environmental details which surround Dos Passos' characters. At the beginning of Section Three the text intercuts between two sequences–a song and a description of ships unloading returning soldiers. One sequence is aural, the other visual, and yet because they both have to be read, the effect is analogous to film montage where, for instance, two parallel sequences temporarily fill the screen. It is difficult to be sure whether Dos Passos knew Eisenstein's theories of montage so early in the 1920s. He did not actually meet the Russian until his visit to that country in 1928.[5] In *Film Form* Eisenstein stresses that orthodox montage depends

118

the government of the United States must insist and
demand that American citizens who may be taken prisoner by one
party or the other as participants in the present ####################
insurrectionary disturbances shall be dealt with          NEWSREEL VIII IX
in accordance with the broad principles of International law

### SOLDIERS GUARD CONVENTION

the Titanic left Southhampton on April 10th on its maiden ~~voy~~

~~age to New York~~ the operation is to be performed against the wishes of

the New York Life according to #Kimmel* Why they know I'm Kimmel in Niles

I'm George to everyone even mother and sister when we meet on the streets

I'm going to Maxim's
Where fun and frolic beams
With all the girls I'll chatter
I'll laugh and kiss and flatter
Lolo , Dodo , Joujou .
Cloclo, Margo ,Froufrou

### TITANIC LARGEST SHIP IN THE WORLD SINKING

                                                      twelve
personally I am not sure that the #### hour day is bad for emp
loyees especially when they insist on working that long in order to
make more money

Still all my song shall be
Nearer My god to thee
Nearer to thee

it was now about one AM,a beautiful starlight night  with no
moon ,The sea was as calm as a pond , just a gentle heave as the boat
dipped up# and down in the swell,an ideal night except for the bitter
cold . In the distance the Titanic looked an enormous length,its great
bulk outlined in black against the starry sky, every porthole and saloon
blazing with light

Mendicant Misses Priviledge of Resting Feet On DiningTable

Ask Methodism To Ougt Trinity

the brides gown is of charmeuse satin with a chiffon veiled lace
waist . The veil is of crepe lisse edged with point de venise a departure
################ from the conventional bridal veil and the bouquet is to
be lilies of the valley and gardenias

Man Who Served Verse with Vernicelli and Puns With Pickles is Gone

Struggle for City of Torreon may Decide Fate of Rebel Forces

sees socilism divorce cause dealer who clung to hoopskirts and #

Civil War stock expires at 77 Federal Grand Jury indicts Armour and Co

for Noninspection of ~~meats~~     machinist drives stolen car filled with his

guests into Calumet River

Lolo, Dodo , Joujou,
Cloclo , Margot , Froufrou
I'm going to Maxim's
And you can go to...

the Titanic slowly tilted straight on end with the stern vertically upward and as it did so the lights in the cabind and saloons which
had not flickered for a moment since we left , died out  ,came on again
for a single flash and finally went out altogether . Meanwhile the machinery rattled through the vessel with ################a rattle and a groan
ing that could be heard for miles . Then with a quiet slanting dive

*Revised typescript for* Newsreel XI *in* The 42nd Parallel, *with Dos Passos's notes to the printer indicating the fonts*
*and typeface sizes he wanted to use (Albert and Shirley Small Special Collections Library, University of Virginia)*

on what he calls a "dominant," i.e. an idea or theme which binds together apparently diverse elements.[6] In the example from *Manhattan Transfer* the common theme–America's role in World War I–is so obvious that there is scarcely any tension between the two sequences. In spite of the Newsreels' title–clearly suggestive of the cinema–they have to be read in a fundamentally different way than the passage described above. In Dos Passos' montage the two juxtaposed sequences are clear in themselves; one temporarily (i.e. for the duration of a paragraph or verse) and *completely* replaces the other; and the two sequences blend together thematically. As we shall see, in the characteristic Newsreel the reader never loses his sense of disparate fragments. The page takes on the qualities of a canvas rather than a movie screen and for that reason Dos Passos' technique now turns to collage.

Dos Passos' title of Newsreel draws the reader's attention to a kind of film which had been in existence at least since 1911 when the first American newsreel began. By the mid-1920s the five major American newsreel companies–Pathé, Fox Movietone, Universal, Hearst International and Paramount–dominated the world market.[7] In April 1927 Fox Movietone News added the first soundtrack which was a subject for complaint by Gilbert Seldes four years later on the grounds that commentaries detracted from their pictorial accuracy.[8] Raymond Fielding has defined the fully-fledged newsreel as ". . . a nine- or ten-minute collection of more-or-less newsworthy footage, comprising eight or nine items, each subject separated abruptly from the others by a title, all of them backed up by a noisy musical score and a highspeed invisible narrator."[9] The most famous single newsreel series was "The March of Time," started in 1935 and therefore too late to influence Dos Passos (*The Big Money* appeared in 1936), which followed previous practice in having a company of actors reenact the week's news items. The series had not been running a year before it was accused of having sold out to the Hearst press in tacitly promoting militarism and reaction.[10]

Considering that the two criticisms of newsreels mentioned above were made in the very journal (the *New Republic*) where Dos Passos tried out sections of *U.S.A.,* we may fairly assume that he too was alerted to possible signs of bias or partiality. We shall see in a moment some examples from the novel's Newsreels which demonstrate sensationalism, but first it is important to note that the inclusion of snatches of song in the very first newsreel suggests the presence of a soundtrack. Although the content of Newsreel 1 refers us to the war with Spain of 1898 over her colonies, the fictional means of "reporting" on these events implies a technology which did not exist before 1927 and which is really typical of the 1930s. Perhaps Dos Passos was

trying to correct the time-lag he noted in his 1932 article between media taking on importance and that importance being recognized.

In spite of the song-fragments being aural, they take their place within texts which have to be *read* not seen. And in spite of Dos Passos' title, the Newsreels scarcely ever allow any individual item to take on the volume it would need to assemble an item in a newsreel which, however briefly, temporarily fills the whole screen. During his discussion of the poetics of the lyric Jonathan Culler takes an article from a French newspaper and reprints it laid out like a modernist poem. Because there is nothing intrinsically poetical about language, Culler argues that the new context and arrangement demand a new way of reading: "To write this as a poem brings into play a new set of expectations, a set of conventions determining how the sequence is to be read and what kind of interpretations may be derived from it."[11] Culler's example and conclusion seem to fit Dos Passos' strategies exactly because the Newsreels have apparently transposed non-literary materials into a literary context. The sheer bulk of the realistic narratives suggests that the Newsreels illustrate them, rather than the narratives the Newsreels. Let us now see if a literary rather than informational reading can bear fruit, taking Newsreel 38 as a typical example.

The opening verse sets the keynote of the whole Newsreel. The song (the "Internationale") embodies the collective voice of aspiring labor, but proves to be just as vulnerable as earlier patriotic hymns (the national anthem in Newsreel 29, the flag-waving songs in Newsreels 19 and 23) to the competing items within the same Newsreel. A headline continues the language of battle but ambiguously relocates it "in the diet." The second headline takes up the second aspect of the "Internationale"–the fact that it is a struggle of *workers*–divorces it from politics by making them members of the Y.M.C.A. and then introduces the topic of theft. The next "paragraph" runs together four typographically distinct items, thereby increasing our impression of sequence. The first two items are identified as public rhetoric by the omitted verb-subjects and relate stylistically to the impersonal verb-constructions used elsewhere in the Newsreel–"the opinion prevails," "it is declared," etc. The first item lays its main emphasis on the phrase "wisdom of people alone" which suggests "*the* people," but could also contain the very opposite meaning: that "people alone" should lead. This possibility is only hinted at before we are confronted with a capitalized boost for the U.S.A. ("SAYS U.S. MUST HAVE WORLD'S GREATEST FLEET") which returns the reader to warfare. A brief but authentically individual account follows of a meeting with wounded Italian soldiers presenting a petition while *German* soldiers rebel in the concluding fragment. In fact a motif of unrest runs right through the Newsreel ("rebel," "riot," "mutiny") but the notion of a clearly defined and final conflict (through the "Internationale") is confused and fragmented. American troops might be sent to "establish order" in Mexico. There are hints of strikes in New York, Lille, China, and Sacramento. It is impossible to attach any clear political hope to these details because, if anything, they suggest a general breakdown in order—with one exception. The headline "GAINS RUN HIGH IN WALL STREET" hints at a point of economic stability within the prevailing disorder. Again and again Dos Passos shows that American finance was the true victor of World War I.

The closer this and the other newsreels are read, the richer they become in meaning. "Diet" in item two is half-repeated at the end of item five ("ORDERED TO ALLOW ALL GREEKS TO DIE") and linked with its rhyming word "riot" in the next item. Subliminal associations are thus built up between rebellion, genocide, and food. The latter is taken up by a French voice questioning the price of butter (profiteering?) in a line which, though askew, fits rhythmically into the "Internationale," and brings its grand rhetoric down to [a] more urgent mundane level. A second but now collective French voice rallies opposition to Bolshevism, a call partly echoed later in the Newsreel by a headline–quotation from a general: "BOLSHEVISM READY TO COLLAPSE." These fragments build up voices in opposition to the "Internationale" quoted throughout the Newsreel. On the one hand the repeated announcements that Bolshevism will collapse are discredited by their sources (generals, industrialists, financiers) and by the reader's consciousness that the Soviet régime has survived; on the other the lyrical hope of one final battle is mocked by the sheer dispersal of issues. Ultimately we are faced here with two rival propagandas. Partly we identify these effects through differences, partly through similarities. The "Internationale" calls for the poor and downtrodden to arise but the only rise that takes place is in the stock market prices. Similarly in Newsreel 36 examples of post-war unrest are counterpointed against quotations from "Mademoiselle from Armentières." Juxtaposition inevitably asks whether the items are related and the song–dealing with rape–offers a metaphorical comment on political events. In the same way Newsreel 61 uses a song about flight to reflect the promotion of real-estate.

In the discussion of Newsreel 38 we have identified a considerable number of traditional literary devices—juxtaposition, contrast, rhyme, and so on. This is exactly the new kind of reading which Culler's (and Dos Passos') rearrangement invites.

And yet does that mean that the new text is autotelic, that the poem is "complete in itself"?[12] The one item in Culler's example which conspicuously does not receive any literary comment is a name. The profusion of names in the Newsreels constantly refers us to individual historical entities, whether people, places or, in the case of Newsreel 38, songs. A second crucial factor prevents us from getting a sense of wholeness in the Newsreels and that is their sheer variety. The multiplicity of topics and the fragmentary nature of most individual items demonstrate that, as Charles Marz has stated, "*U.S.A.* is a continent and a composition ruled by crisis and collision."[13] The collisions take place during the process of reading as the eye's movements are constantly interrupted by gaps in the text, incomplete sentences and shifts in type. It is impossible to read the Newsreels in a simple linear fashion because discontinuities force the eye back to retrace its steps and bridge those gaps. In other words the eye ranges over the Newsreels as spatial areas where the white sections of the page suggest hidden information. Because many sentences are left incomplete and because headlines always imply more information than they can contain within themselves, Dos Passos constantly gives the impression that more is going on off the page. The very style of the Newsreels points towards public events which can only be glimpsed within the novel. They thus represent a border area where the fictional events within the trilogy shade into the passage of history. It is also crucial to the Newsreels' effect that a margin of confusion should be present in the reader's mind. We are led towards making sense of the different items but ultimately prevented from doing so. Dos Passos here draws attention to the ways in which the media bombard the consumer with more information than he can digest. At the same time, however, particular and apparently trivial details might be taken up by later Newsreels and developed so that the reader is both perplexed and left with the uneasy sense that no detail is actually meaningless.

The Newsreels' very fragmentation draws our attention to a stylistic feature which occurs again and again. Newsreel 7, for instance, begins with a headline offering a quotation ("SAYS THIS IS CENTURY . . .") where the omission of the verb's subject pushes the statement towards anonymity. These media voices repeatedly threaten to obliterate individual discourse. As Charles Marz declares, "the Newsreels chronicle the voices of the public sphere; they are the most banal, most impersonal, most mechanical registration of persons and events in the trilogy."[14] The impersonality of the individual items grows out of the omitted subjects, so that we receive some kind of utterance but do not know its source, and from the substitution of non-human subjects for human activities ("COMING YEAR PROMISES REBIRTH . . . ," "BONDS BUY BULLETS," etc.). Newsreel 22, which contains these two headlines, is thus typical in containing an item referring to individuals which is swamped by the rival voices within the same Newsreel. It is not simply a matter of "two men out of the Transvaal district" expressing inconvenient anti-war sentiments, but rather that the surrounding kinds of rhetoric smother their words. The strident headlines, the patriotic song, the quotation from a speech (speeches have been discredited in Newsreel 1 as vehicles for nationalistic propaganda), and the combined item on food and German soldiers with its idiosyncrasy of compound words ("timehonored," "clothesbrush," etc.) exemplify media styles which through sheer noise leave no room for quiet individual statement.

The bizarre collisions between individual items within the Newsreels complicates and reduces their informational value, and defamiliarizes headlines, articles, etc. so much that the reader becomes aware of the news-items' *style* rather than content. Juxtaposition, for instance, and the use of identical capitalization implies that statements take on the same status as actual events. Both become equally news-items. There is a further, deeper implication in this process and one which Dos Passos touches on in his 1932 article: that the public's main access to events is through the media. Hence the comments on news agencies in Newsreels 32 and 44. But the media do not simply channel information; they also screen, select and censor. In *The 42nd Parallel* Dos Passos tends to view the absurdities of media news-coverage with impassive irony. It is only towards the end of that novel and in *Nineteen Nineteen* that his indignation begins to focus on the First World War and specifically on its disastrous consequences for free speech. The man who Mac sees chained to a lamp-post in San Francisco reciting the Declaration of Independence while two policemen try to arrest him stands as a satirical summary of this theme, and relates directly to Dos Passos' ironic framing of his biography of Randolph Bourne, the anti-war journalist, with two Newsreels (22 and 23) full of patriotic items. In 23 a song-quotation replaces a headline to establish a key-note of strident patriotism which characterizes the longest single item in the Newsreel—a passage predicting a war rally in Newark. The collective entities ("patriotic Essex county," "Uncle Sammy," etc.) have not simply replaced individual sentiment, but the future tenses of the article suggest rehearsal and even coercion. The penultimate biography of the trilogy

confirms the possibility that the news can be stage-managed by citing examples of Hearst's behavior in the war of 1898. Stylistic features of the Newsreels thus point to a form of control and manipulation which is clearly political. References to wartime censorship offer obvious examples as does the cautious press-release in Newsreel 37 about the "near mutiny" of American troops in Archangel. In cases such as these information is being filtered in the name of government expediency. In Newsreel 29 an even more bizarre event takes place. Dos Passos assembles fragments reflecting the surge of joy at the news of the armistice, but then towards the end of the new Newsreel a brief item makes it clear that the news is premature—or "unconfirmed" in the official jargon. This Newsreel strikingly demonstrates the public's vulnerability towards the media which here are not only leading but *mis*leading popular sentiment.

. . . . . . . . . .

–*Journal of Narrative Technique*, 14 (Fall 1984): 182–188

## Notes

1. John Dos Passos, "Washington and Chicago II: Spotlights and Microphones," *New Republic* (29 June 1932): 179. Cohen's review ("America: Dream, Epic and Reality") appeared in the issue for 20 January 1932 (p. 274B).

2. Marshall McLuhan, "John Dos Passos: Technique vs. Sensibility," in *The Interior Landscape: The Literary Criticism of Marshall McLuhan*, edited by Eugene McNamara (New York: McGraw-Hill, 1969), p. 50.

3. Clive Hart and David Hayman, eds., *James Joyce's Ulysses: Critical Essays* (Berkeley: University of California Press, 1974), p. 129.

4. John Dos Passos, *Manhattan Transfer* (Boston: Houghton Mifflin, 1953), p. 351.

5. Melvin Landsberg, *Dos Passos' Path to U.S.A.* (Boulder, Colo.: Associated University Press, 1972), p. 156.

6. Sergei Eisenstein, *Film Form and The Film Sense* (Cleveland & New York: Meridian Books, 1957), pp. 64–65.

7. Raymond Fielding, *The March of Time, 1935–1956* (New York: Oxford University Press, 1978), pp. 3–4.

8. Arthur Knight, *The Liveliest Art* (New York: Mentor Books, 1957), pp. 146–147. "Newsreels and Pictures," *New Republic* (11 March 1931): 96.

9. *The March of Time*, p. 3.

10. Selden C. Menefee, "The Movies Join Hearst," *New Republic* (9 October 1935): 241–242.

11. Jonathan Culler, *Structuralist Poetics* (London: Routledge & Kegan Paul, 1975), p. 161.

12. *Structuralist Poetics*, p. 162.

13. Charles Marz, "*U.S.A.*: Chronicle and Performance," *Modern Fiction Studies*, 26, no. 3 (1980): 399.

14. Marz, p. 403.

## Dos Passos to Donald G. England, 9 April 1967

*Preparing for his dissertation on the Newsreels in* U.S.A., *Donald G. England wrote Dos Passos inquiring about the purpose and origin of the Newsreels.*

You are quite right about the Newsreels. I had been in the habit, beginning with my first notes for *Manhatten [sic] Transfer,* of jotting down headlines and bits of news stories that seemed to give a taste of the times and places against which my characters' lives were evolving. When I was working on *42nd Parallel,* these notes began to seem to have an intrinsic value and I began putting them in bodily. I've been doing the same thing in various forms ever since. For the latest development of the style see *Midcentury.*

Some of the notes are put down from memory, others cut out bodily from newspapers, others paraphrased and some may have been made up out of whole cloth.

–Donald G. England, "The Newsreels of John Dos Passos' *The 42nd Parallel:* Sources and Techniques," dissertation, University of Texas, 1970, p. 4

## Newsreel I (1930 version)

*It was that emancipated race*
*That was charging up the hill*
*Up to where them insurrectos*
*Was afightin fit to kill*

black bear at large in Hyde Park Streets news of explorer Peary ASKS LABOR TO CALL HALT Death of Oscar Wilde once famous author dies in poverty in Paris Fierce Fight With Thugs

### CAPITAL CITY'S CENTURY CLOSED

General Miles with his gaudy uniform and spirited charger was the center for all eyes especially as his steed was extremely restless. Just as the band passed the Commanding General his horse stood upon his hind legs and was almost erect. General Miles instantly reined in the frightened animal and dug in his spurs in an endeavor to control the horse which to the horror of the spectators fell over backwards and landed squarely on the Commanding General. Much to the gratification of the people General Miles was not injured but considerable skin was scraped off the flank of the horse. Almost every inch of General Miles's overcoat was covered with the dust of the street and between the shoulders a hole about an inch in diameter was punctured. Without waiting for anyone to brush the dust from his garments General Miles remounted his horse and reviewed the parade as if it were an everyday occurrence.

The incident naturally attracted the attention of the crowd and this brought to notice the fact that the Commanding General never permits a flag to be carried past him without uncovering and remaining so until the colors have past

*And the Captain bold of Company B*
*Was afightin in the lead*
*Just like a trueborn soldier he*
*Of them bullets took no heed*

### OFFICIALS KNOW NOTHING OF VICE

Sanitary trustees turn water of Chicago river into drainage canal LAKE MICHIGAN SHAKES HANDS WITH THE FATHER OF THE WATERS German zuchterverein singing contest for canary-birds opens the fight for bimetallism at the ratio of 16 to 1 has not been lost says Bryan BRITISH BEATEN AT MAFEKING

*For there's many a man been murdered in Luzon*

CLAIMS ISLANDS FOR ALL TIME

Hamilton Club Listens To Oratory By Ex-Congressman Posey of Indiana

NOISE GREETS NEW CENTURY

LABOR GREETS NEW CENTURY

### CHURCHES GREET NEW CENTURY

Mr McKinley is hard at work in his office when the new year begins.

NATION GREETS CENTURY'S DAWN

responding to a toast Hail Columbia! at the Columbia Club banquet in Indianapolis Ind. expresident Benjamin Harrison said in part: I have no argument to make here or anywhere against territorial expansion; but I do not, as some do, look upon territorial expansion as the safest and most attractive avenue of national development. By the advantages of abundant and cheap coal and iron, of an enormous overproduction of food products and of invention and economy in production we are now leading by the nose the original and the greatest of the colonizing nations Society Girls Shocked: Danced with Detectives

*For there's many a man been murdered in Luzon*
*and Mindanao*

### GAITY [sic] GIRLS MOBBED IN NEW JERSEY

one of the lithographs of the leading lady represented her in less than Atlantic City bathing costume, sitting on a redhot stove, in one hand she held a brimming glass of wine in the other ribbons drawn over a pair of rampant lobsters

*For there's many a man been murdered in Luzon*
*and Mindanao*
*and in Samar*

in responding to the toast The Twentieth Century, Senator Albert J. Beveridge said in part: The twentieth century will be American. American thought will dominate it. American progress will give it color and direction. American deeds will make it illustrious.

Civilization will never lose its hold on Shanghai. Civilization will never depart from Hongkong. The gates of Peking will never again be closed to the methods of modern man. The regeneration of the world, physical as well as moral, has begun and revolutions never move backwards

*There's been many a good man murdered in the Philippines*
*Lies sleeping in some lonesome grave.*
                    –*The 42nd Parallel* (New York: Harper, 1930), pp. 1–3

### The Specific Sources of Newsreel I, *The 42nd Parallel*
Donald G. England

*England annotates Newsreel I as it appears in the 1930 edition of* The 42nd Parallel. *Asterisks following item numbers in the Newsreel indicate items omitted in the 1937 second edition of the novel and thus in the 1938 and all subsequent editions of* U.S.A. *as well.*

I–1

These lyrics are from the song "The Emancipated Race." This anonymous song grew out of an incident involving a Negro regiment of the U.S. Army fighting in the Philippines in 1901 and 1902. It is interesting to note the irony in the fact that members of the "emancipated race" were helping put down the Filipinoes' struggle for freedom from American occupation of the islands.

For the complete history and lyrics of the song see Edward Arthur Dolph, *"Sound Off!" Soldier Songs from the Revolution to World War II* (New York, 1942), pp. 207–209.

I–2*

November 26, 1900; *Chicago Tribune*; p. 1; (Headline–"Black Bear At Large In Hyde Park Streets A Terror To Residents")

"An untamed bear roaming about the streets of Chicago is one of the risks to be considered in addition to the numerous robberies. The bear was seen at Forty-sixth street and Indiana avenue yesterday morning by

Policeman John Dunning of the Fiftieth Street Station, and all day complaints from various citizens that a live bear was loose in the streets kept the police busy."

I–3*

November 26, 1900; *Chicago Tribune*; p. 5; (Headline–"Hears News of Explorer Peary")

"Herbert L. Bridgeman, secretary of the Peary Arctic club, tonight gave out extracts from letters received by Mrs. Peary from her husband, Lieutenant Peary, the arctic explorer."

The letters, dated March 12 and 31, 1900, were the first word from Peary since August 28, 1899. The extracts described his winter quarters in Greenland and disclosed plans to continue his expedition to the north pole in the spring.

I–4*

November 29, 1900; *Chicago Tribune;* p. 1; (Exact headline)

The firm of Hibbard, Spencer, Bartlett, and Co. announced that it would build a store and warehouse with non-union labor unless union members changed their present leadership. The firm accused present leadership of being visionaries and malcontents and of using hired thugs to attack non-union workers.

This is Dos Passos' first use of a Newsreel item related to a theme of labor unrest.

I–5*

December 1, 1900; *Chicago Tribune*; p. 1; (Exact headline)
Paris, November 30

"Oscar Wilde died this afternoon of meningitis at a small hotel in the Latin Quarter. For some time he had been living in the Rue des Beaux Arts, where he was known by the name of Monmouth."

The article summarizes his controversial career through his release from prison in March, 1897, and then describes his subsequent life in poverty and obscurity in Paris.

I–6*

December 13, 1900; *Chicago Tribune*; p. 1; (Exact headline)

Alfred Bibble, a traveling salesman, was attacked by two thugs after leaving a Chicago saloon where he had gotten change for a large bill. He put up a fierce fight but yielded when exhausted. Both thieves made their escape.

I–7

December 13, 1900; *Chicago Tribune*; p. 1; (Exact headline)

The article describes the centennial celebration of the establishment of the national capital.

**I–8**
December 13, 1900; *Chicago Tribune;* p. 1; (Quoted from an article)
(see I–7)
   The article describes the centennial celebration of the establishment of the national capital. During the celebration a parade was held. Lieutenant General Miles, mentioned in the quotation, was chief marshal of the parade.
   This entry, together with I–7, marks the close of the 19th century. The ceremony described symbolizes a way of life that soon will vanish. Later items in the Newsreel welcome the 20th century–a century of progress in which people like General Miles will be out of place.

**I–9**
(song–"The Emancipated Race")
(see I–1)

**I–10**
December 28, 1900; *Chicago Tribune;* p. 1; (Exact headline)
   Chicago's Mayor, Chief of Police, and Inspectors professed amazing ignorance of violations of mid-

night closing laws and gambling during the Grand Jury investigations.

**I–11**
January 3, 1900; *Chicago Tribune;* p. 1; ("Summary of The Daily Tribune"–"Sanitary Trustees Turned Water of Chicago River Into Drainage Canal, Opening Sluiceway at Kedzie Avenue.")
(article on p. 9)
   "The opening of the greatest ship canal ever constructed in America and the informal completion of one of the engineering feats in the world's history was accomplished without ceremony."
   "The consummation of the project, on which the people of Chicago have expended upwards of $33,000,000, was free from the formalities which marked 'shovel day' when the work was inaugurated on Sept. 3, 1892."
   The canal connected Lake Michigan with the Mississippi River by way of the Chicago River, the canal, the Des Plaines River, and the Illinois River.

**I–12**
January 19, 1900; *Chicago Tribune;* p. 2; (Cartoon)
(see I–11)
   The cartoon shows two figures shaking hands. One, representing the Mississippi River[,] is introducing himself as "The Father of the Waters" to another figure, labeled "Lake Michigan."

**I–13**
January 1, 1900; *Chicago Tribune;* p. 4; (Paraphrased from an article)
   The illustrated article described the Chicago German community's annual singing contest for canaries, where gold medals are given to the birds with the best singing voices. The züchterverein is made up of about twenty breeders of canaries, and 114 birds are honorary members. Judging and rules are described in the article.

**I–14**
January 7, 1900; *Chicago Tribune;* p. 1; (Paraphrased from an article)
   At a speech before the W. J. Bryan league, it was reported that Bryan declared the currency bill in Congress most objectionable and said he hoped for the free coinage of silver at 16 to 1.
   By the placement of this item immediately after I–13 with no punctuation to separate the two, Dos Passos suggests that Bryan's fight for bimetallism is like the singing of a canary-bird. Later in his biography of Bryan, "The Boy Orator of the Platte," Dos Passos refers to him as the "silver tongue of the plain people." (p. 176) Dos Passos makes the sarcasm of the phrase

TWO OLD RIVALS SHAKE HANDS.

"How do you do; I'm the Father of Waters."
"Glad to meet you; I'm the seventh son of the seventh son of the unsalted sea."

*Cartoon from the 19 January 1900 issue of the* Chicago Tribune *that is described in Newsreel I in* The 42nd Parallel *(Thomas Cooper Library, University of South Carolina)*

unavoidable by amending it to "a silver tongue in a big mouth." (p. 177)

I–15
January 6, 1900; *Chicago Tribune;* p. 1; (Exact headline) Mafeking, December 26, 1899

"At dawn this morning Colonel Baden-Powell organized an unsuccessful attack upon a strong position of the enemy at Game Tree Fort, two miles from Mafeking, from which the Boers had maintained an annoying shell and rifle fire for some weeks."

This reference to the Boer war should be recalled by readers when reading of the same war in Camera Eye (1).

I–16
(song–"The Emancipated Race") (see I–1)

I–17
January 10, 1900; *Chicago Tribune;* p. 1; (Exact headline)

In a speech before the U.S. Senate Senator Beveridge claimed permanent U.S. possession of the Philippines necessary because natives were incapable of selfgovernment [*sic*]. The senate was debating a resolution to make the Philippines, won from Spain in the Spanish-American War, a U.S. territory.

I–18
January 12, 1900; *Chicago Tribune;* p. 1; ("Summary of The Daily Tribune"–"Hamilton Club Celebrated Anniversary of Alexander Hamilton and Listened to an Oration by Ex-Congressman Posey of Indiana") (article on p. 5)

On the occasion of the celebration of Alexander Hamilton's birthday, the Hamilton Club heard Ex-Congressman Posey advocate more territorial expansion for the United States.

I–19
January 1, 1901; *Chicago Tribune;* p. 1; ("Important News and Features"–"Noise Ushers in New Century") (article on p. 2)

"From Van Buren street to the river and from the lake to South Branch, in restaurants, cafes, saloons, in the streets and alleyways, pandemonium greeted the new century."

"Men and women walked the streets with horns to their mouths. Revolvers popped and alleyways were full of snapping firecrackers."

"Cannons were exploded in greeting throughout the city, and in manufacturing districts the shop whistles joined the celebration."

I–20
January 1, 1901; *Chicago Tribune;* p. 1; ("Important News and Features"–Exact headline)

*Cover of the 1918 war-song collection given to soldiers by the YMCA in Paris that included several of the songs referred to in the Newsreels (Collection of Richard Layman)*

(article on p. 2)
New York, January 1, 1901

"'What will the new century do for labor?' was the principal topic at the labor celebration in Arlington Hall.

["]The gathering was under the auspices of the Committee of One Hundred of the Civic federation, and was called Labor's Greeting to the Twentieth Century."

I–21
The source of this item has not been conclusively identified. The entry does not appear in the notes for the Newsreels of *The 42nd Parallel*. At the time he was organizing this Newsreel Dos Passos may have recalled an article from p. 2 of the *Chicago Tribune* for January 1, 1901, headlined "New Year in the Churches." The wording of this entry was obviously intended to parallel that of I–19 and I–20.

I–22
January 1, 1901; *Chicago Tribune;* p. 2; (Exact headline)

On December 31, 1900 President McKinley worked in his office until midnight. "Thus he literally saw the old year and old century out; and the new year and the new century in, surrounded by the cares of office and engaged in the drudgery of actual work."

I–23

January 1, 1901; *Chicago Tribune;* p. 2; (Exact headline)

The article contains a description of celebrations in New York, Boston, Detroit, Philadelphia, and other major cities to greet the new century.

I–24

January 1, 1901; *Chicago Tribune;* p. 3; (Paraphrased from an article)

"The Columbia club opened its new home tonight with a banquet, the chief feature of which was an address by former President Benjamin Harrison."

The remarks by former president Harrison are quoted accurately from the article. Dos Passos' paraphrasing is in the introduction of the quotation.

I–25

January 4, 1901; *Chicago Tribune;* p. 1; (Exact headline)
Cleveland, January 3

"Cleveland society, the feminine part of it, is aghast at the knowledge that many of its members danced with detectives at Ruth Hanna's coming out party in the Chamber of Commerce Building on New Years night. It has been learned that in addition to half a dozen city detectives who attended the party fifty private detectives in dress suits were in the crowd."

Several of the girls thought it fun to introduce the men to young society women at the party and later to make fun of those who had unwittingly danced with the detectives.

I–26

(song–"The Emancipated Race") (see I–1)

I–27

January 15, 1900; *Chicago Tribune;* p. 1; (Headline–"Gaiety Girls Mobbed in New Jersey")

Burton's Carmen Gaiety Girls closed a week's engagement in New Brunswick, N.J. The leading ladies were mobbed at the stage door by admirers after the closing performance.

I–28

January 15, 1900; *Chicago Tribune;* p. 1; (Quoted from an article)

(see I–27)

The leading lady described in this quotation was one of Burton's Gaiety Girls.

I–29

(song–"The Emancipated Race")
(see I–1)

I–30

January 1, 1901; *Chicago Tribune;* p. 3; (Quoted from an article)
(see I–24)

Senator Beveridge's speech was made at the same Columbia Club Banquet addressed by ex-president Benjamin Harrison. The subject of Beveridge's speech was similar to that made by him on January 10, 1900. (see I–17)

I–31

(song–"The Emancipated Race")
(see I–1))
–Donald G. England, "The Newsreels of John Dos Passos's *The 42nd Parallel:* Sources and Techniques," dissertation, University of Texas, 1970, pp. 106, 108, 110, 112, 114, 116, 118.

*Music for the war song quoted in Newsreel XXI in Nineteen-Nineteen, from Popular Songs of the A. E. F.*
*(Collection of Richard Layman)*

*Music for the war song quoted in* Newsreel XXI *in* Nineteen-Nineteen, *from* Popular Songs of the A.E.F.
*(Collection of Richard Layman)*

**Newsreel XXI**

*Dos Passos included the World War I song "Good Morning, Mr. Zip-Zip-Zip!" in Newsreel XXI.*

Goodby Broadway
Hello France
We're ten million strong

## 8 YEAR OLD BOY SHOT BY LAD WITH RIFLE

the police have already notified us that any entertainment in Paris must be brief and quietly conducted and not in public view and that we have already had more dances than we ought

capitalization grown 104% while business expands 520%

### HAWAIIAN SUGAR CONTROL LOST BY GERMANS

efforts of the Bolshevik Government to discuss the withdrawal of the U.S. and allied forces from Russia through negotiations for an armistice are attracting no serious attention

### BRITISH AIRMAN FIGHTS SIXTY FOES

SERBIANS ADVANCE 10 MILES; TAKE 10 TOWNS;
MENACE PRILEP

Good morning
Mr. Zip Zip Zip
You're surely looking fine
Good morning
Mr. Zip Zip Zip
With your hair cut just as short as
With your hair cut just as short as
With your hair cut just as short as mine

## LENINE REPORTED ALIVE

AUDIENCE AT HIPPODROME TESTIMONIALS MOVED TO
CHEERS AND TEARS

several different stories have come to me well authenticated concerning the depth of Hindenburg's brutality; the details are too horrible for print. They relate to outraged womanhood and girlhood, suicide and blood of the innocent that wet the feet of Hindenburg

## WAR DECREASES MARRIAGES AND BIRTHS

*Oh ashes to ashes*
*And dust to dust*
*If the shrapnel dont get you*
*Then the eightyeights must*
*—Nineteen-Nineteen,* pp. 421–422

### Newsreel XI

*In the draft of Newsreel XI Dos Passos included careful instructions to the printer on the various type fonts and sizes for specific sections of the newsreel. When* The 42nd Parallel *was reprinted in 1937, the fonts and sizes in the Newsreels were regularized to conform with those in the last two volumes of the trilogy. This revised format was used for all three novels in the 1938 and all later editions of* U.S.A.

the government of the United States must insist and demand that American citizens who may be taken prisoner whether by one party or the other as participants in the present insurrectionary disturbances shall be dealt with in accordance with the broad principles of international law

### SOLDIERS GUARD CONVENTION

the *Titanic* left Southampton on April 10th on its maiden operation is to be performed against the wishes of the New York Life according to "Kimmel" Why they know I'm Kimmel in Niles I'm George to everyone even mother and sister when we meet on the streets

*I'm going to Maxim's*
*Where fun and frolic beams*
*With all the girls I'll chatter*
*I'll laugh and kiss and flatter*
*Lolo, Dodo, Joujou.*
*Cloclo, Margot, Froufrou*

## *TITANIC* LARGEST SHIP IN THE WORLD SINKING

personally I am not sure that the twelvehour day is bad for employees especially when they insist on working that long in order to make more money

*Still all my song shall be*
*Nearer My God to thee*
*Nearer to thee*

it was now about one AM, a beautiful starlight night with no moon. The sea was as calm as a pond, just a gentle heave as the boat dipped up and down in the swell, an ideal night except for the bitter cold. In the distance the *Titanic* looked an enormous length, its great hulk outlined in black against the starry sky, every porthole and saloon blazing with light

ASK METHODISM TO OUST TRINITY

*the bride's gown is of charmeuse satin with a chiffon veiled lace waist. The veil is of crepe lisse edged with point de venise a departure from the conventional bridal veil and the bouquet is to be lilies of the valley and gardenias*

*Lolo, Dodo, Joujou,*
*Cloclo, Margot, Froufrou*
*I'm going to Maxim's*
*And you can go to . . .*

the *Titanic* slowly tilted straight on end with the stern vertically upward and as it did so the lights in the cabins and saloons which had not flickered for a moment since we left, died out, came on again for a single flash and finally went out altogether. Meanwhile the machinery rattled through the vessel with a rattle and a groaning that could be heard for miles. Then with a quiet slanting dive
*—The 42nd Parallel,* pp. 134–135.

### Newsreel LVI

*Note the late inclusion of the song lyrics. Dos Passos appears to have wished to include "In Carolina" when he was preparing the newsreel and typed in the title as a reminder; he then entered the lyrics by hand when they became available.*

his first move was to board a fast train for Miami to see whether the builders engaged in construction financed by his corporation were speeding up the work as much as they might and to take a look at things in general

Gerald Murphy's backdrop (suggestive of the newsreels in U.S.A.) for his and Cole Porter's 1923 Paris ballet,
Within the Quota, *a production that Dos Passos discussed at length with Murphy*
*(Estate of Honoria Murphy Donnelly)*

*Pearly early in the mornin'*

LUTHERANS DROP HELL FOR HADES

*Oh joy*
*Feel that boat arockin'*
*Oh boy*
*See those darkies flockin'*
*What's that whistle sayin'*
*All aboard toot toot*

AIR REJECTION BLAMED FOR WARSHIP DISASTER

*You're in Ken-tucky just as sure as you're born*
LINER AFIRE

POSSE CLOSING IN ON AIRMAIL BANDITS

*Down beside the summer sea*
*Along the Miami Shore*

*Some one waits alone for me*
*Along Miami Shore*

SINCE THIS TIME YESTERDAY NEARLY TWO THOUSAND
MEN HAVE CHANGED TO CHESTERFIELDS
PEACHES FLED WITH FEW CLOTHES

*Saw a rosebud in a store*
*So I'm goin' where there's more*
*Good-bye blues*

the three whites he has with him appear to be of
primitive Nordic stock. Physically they are splendid creatures. They have fine flaxen hair, blue-green eyes and
white skins. The males are covered with a downlike hair

*Let me lay me down to sleep in Carolina*
*With a peaceful pillow 'neath my weary head*
*For a rolling stone like me there's nothing finer*
*Oh Lordy what a thrill*
*To hear that whip-poor-will*
*In Carolina*

–*The Big Money*, pp. 965–966

280

NEWSREEL ~~####~~ LVI

Pearly early in the mornin'

      His first move was to board a fast train
for Miami to see whether the builders engaged in
construction work financed by his corporation were
speeding up the work as much as they might and to take a
look at things in general.

    LUTHERANS DROP HELL FOR HADES
        Oh joy
     Feel that boat a rockin
        Oh boy
     See those darkies flockin
       What's that whistle sayin
          All aboard toot toot


AIREJECTION BLAMED FOR WARSHIP DISASTER

    You're in Ken-tucky just as sure as you're born

    LINER AFIRE     *— large caps*

*Down beside the Summer sea*
*along Miami shore*    POSSE CLOSING IN ON AIRMAIL BANDITS
*Someone waits alone forme*   SINCE THIS TIME YESTERDAY NEARLY TWO THOUSAND MEN    *Extra large ital caps*
*Along Miami shore*
    HAVE CHANGED TO CHESTERFIELDS    *large caps*

  PEACHES FLED WITH FEW CLOTHES

      Saw a rosebud in a store ~~#####~~
        So I'm goin where there's more
         Goodbye blues

    the three whites he has with him appear to be of
primitive Nordic stock . Physically they are splendid
creatures . They have fine flaxen hair , bluegreen eyes
and white skins . The males are covered with a downlike
hair .

*Let me lay us down to sleep in Carolina*
*With a peaceful pillow beneath my weary head*
*For a rolling stone like me there's nothing finer*
*Oh loody what a thrill*
*To hear the whippoorwill*

                  *In Carolina*

*Revised typescript for Newsreel LVI in* The Big Money, *on which Dos Passos later added the words from the choruses of two 1926 songs, "Along Miami Shore" and "Lay Me Down to Sleep in Carolina" (Albert and Shirley Small Special Collections Library, University of Virginia)*

# THE SHAPING OF THE WHOLE:
# WALT WHITMAN AND MONTAGE

*Dos Passos's pivotal decision to divide his depiction of early-twentieth-century American life into four strikingly varied modal forms resulted in a seemingly fractured narrative without a central focus or meaning. He overcame this difficulty by adopting two related overarching approaches to his material. First, he cast the whole as a Whitmanesque search for the meaning of America by introducing the theme of the search at key moments in the trilogy, as well as throughout the Camera Eye sections, an approach that included the use of many of the poetic devices adopted by Walt Whitman to express this theme. Second, Dos Passos made the fragmentation and discontinuity inherent in his experimental form work for him through the cinematic technique of montage, in which each disparate modal segment of the trilogy comments indirectly on a running theme in the portion of the novel in which it appears, as well as on thematic threads throughout the work as a whole.*

## *U.S.A.:* Language and Form
Donald Pizer

*After noting that* U.S.A. *is in many ways about "the relation of language in America to the American experience," Pizer discusses the thematic and structural importance in the work as a whole of the Whitmanesque figure who seeks to discover America through its language.*

*U.S.A.* is an extraordinarily rich and complex work of fiction. Any effort to reduce the work to a single overarching theme will thus inevitably produce a distorted oversimplification. Yet, if the depth and quality of the trilogy are to be adequately appreciated, some of its larger dimensions require recognition at the outset of any critical discussion. What follows is an attempt to use a key passage from *U.S.A.* as a means of bringing to the fore some important aspects of the work as a whole. The ideas thus introduced will serve as the basis for the more detailed analysis of the full trilogy that is to come.

The passage, one remarked upon by a number of recent critics of *U.S.A.*,[1] occurs at the close of Camera Eye (51) in *The Big Money.* Camera Eye (51), which is the final Camera Eye in the trilogy, stems from Dos Passos' participation in the visit of a committee of left-wing writers, led by Theodore Dreiser, to Harlan County, Kentucky, to investigate conditions arising out of a miners' strike. The miners epitomize working-class life in early 1930s America in that they are poor, exploited, and oppressed. They are kept in this condition not only by the mine operators but by the manipulators of language—the law and the press—who are in the pay of the operators. The committee visits a group of jailed strikers and encounters the red-faced, armed sheriff sitting at his desk, the sheriff who, in the final words of this Camera Eye, feels behind him

the prosecutingattorney the judge an owner himself the political boss the minesuperintendent the board of

directors      the president of the utility the manipulator of the holdingcompany
    he lifts his hands toward the telephone
    the deputies crowd in the door
    we have only words against (*BM,* 524–525)

The unendstopped "we have only words against" is followed on the same page (about three-quarters of an inch of white space) by the words POWER SUPERPOWER, the title of the biography of Samuel Insull. This juxtaposition of the final words of the Camera Eye persona and the title of the biography of a utility holding company magnate is a crystallization of theme and form in the work as a whole. The startling thrust of meaning across the modal barrier between the final Camera Eye and the final biography raises and extends the level of abstraction of the entire moment. Words are all we have against power, and power extends through the economic and political system from a county sheriff to an Insull. But the anger communicated by the Harlan County segment and the satiric irony of the Insull biography illustrate that POWER SUPERPOWER is vulnerable to attack through literary art. We have only words against power in every aspect of American life, and in that uneven conflict lies our despair and our hope.

One way of approaching *U.S.A.* is to recognize that the trilogy is in large part about the relation of language in America to the American experience.[2] The one continuous "story" in the trilogy as a whole is that of the Camera Eye persona. The artist in this story, after many misdirections and uncertainties, comes at last to a realization that the ideals on which the country had been founded, the "old words" of freedom and justice and equality, have been perverted during his own lifetime, and that his duty as a writer is to seek their radical revitalization through a portrayal of their distortion. This warping of the "old words" is dramatized in two major ways in *U.S.A.* The three strategically placed "impersonal" biographies that structure the trilogy—the opening "U.S.A.," "The Body of an American" (which occurs at the close of *Nineteen-Nineteen*), and the final "Vag"—are a concise symbolic dramatization of a failure within American life to find meaning in language. And the other modes of the trilogy—the narratives, biographies, and Newsreels—constitute a massive representation of the corruption of American values as revealed by a corruption of language.

Dos Passos' belief that language was the principal means both for understanding national character and for bringing about social change is revealed in a number of his comments during the years he was preparing *U.S.A.* In the Introduction to a new edition of *Three Soldiers* in 1932 he wrote: "The mind of a generation is its speech. A writer makes aspects of that speech enduring by putting them in print. He whittles at the words and phrases of today and makes them forms to set the mind of tomorrow's generation. That's history. A writer who writes straight is the architect of history."[3] This notion of the writer as a bridge between generations is made even more explicit in one of the most revealing statements ever made by Dos Passos about his intent in *U.S.A.* In "The Writer as Technician," a speech he prepared for delivery at the 1935 American Writers' Congress, Dos Passos wrote that "The professional writer discovers some aspect of his world and invents out of the speech of his time some particularly apt and original way of putting it down on paper." If he is good enough, he "molds and influences ways of thinking to the point of changing and rebuilding the language, which is the mind of the group. . . . There is no escaping the fact," Dos Passos continued, "that if you are a writer you are dealing with the humanities, with the language of all the men of your speech of your generation, with their traditions of a past and their feelings and perceptions." And if you probe deeply enough, you find yourself on the side of "liberty, fraternity, and humanity. The words are old and dusty and hung with the dirty bunting of a thousand crooked orations, but underneath they are still sound. What man once meant by these words needs defenders to-day."[4]

A kind of historical/linguistic/artistic vocation underlies these statements and *U.S.A.* itself. The "old words" are an Edenic past; at one time they were believed in and practiced with full honesty and commitment. But now they have been corrupted and are used falsely, just as the nation itself has been diverted from a practice of their intent and meaning. The function of the artist is to depict this postlapsarian decay of both life and language and thereby to aid in the possible restoration of Eden.

The most schematic dramatization of this conception of a national language and character occurs in the "U.S.A.," "The Body of an American," and "Vag" journey narratives of archetypal Americans. As has often been noted, the "young man" of "U.S.A." is a Whitmanesque seeker.[5] He is attempting to find communion and meaning as he restlessly wanders the cities and regions of America and as he undertakes various occupations. But his search is unsuccessful, and he remains isolated until he realizes that "Only the ears busy to catch the speech are not alone." The idea is pursued:

> It was not in the long walks through jostling crowds at night that he was less alone, . . .
> but in his mother's words telling about longago, in his father's telling about when I was a boy, . . .
> it was the speech that clung to the ears, the link that tingled in the blood; U.S.A.

U.S.A., the vignette concludes, is many things, "But mostly U.S.A. is the speech of the people." The implications of this "prologue" to *U.S.A.* for the work as a whole are clear. Language as used by the people is the means toward recognizing and representing the essential nature of a society, and the writer must seek out this source of meaning in every corner and every activity of the country. The trilogy will itself replicate this quest both in its representation of the great variety of life in America and in its depiction of the artist's search for his own role in relation to the meaning of

America. His own self-reflexive presence, in other words, as a wanderer in search of meaning will authenticate what he eventually discovers in the world at large, and which is depicted in the remainder of the novel. In brief compass and in archetypal form, "the young man" of "U.S.A." is thus the Camera Eye persona of the trilogy as a whole.

This identification of Dos Passos with the Whitmanesque seeker of an American national identity is even more apparent in a portion cut from a draft version of the "U.S.A." vignette. In this passage, "the young man" is for a moment specifically a writer attempting to understand what he has found during his wandering:

> (From the lighted window the writer looks down into the empty street, sees the figures tiny among the dark oblongs of buildings that rise against the city's golden haze, reads carefully sentence[s] men wrote with quill pens a century and a half ago, feels in his nose the dusty smell of old newspapers in the Public Library
> eyes smart with blurred newsprint, head aches to remember the hopes the wants the walks, the half-caught turn of a phrase the line of talk, the speech)
> Before I can do I must know the country the speech.[6]

Although this passage was probably best excised, it nevertheless usefully illustrates the extent to which Dos Passos identified himself with a historical/linguistic vocation. Realizing what the men with quill pens have written, he will seek out what remains of the belief underlying their language in the speech of today–in the newspapers in the library and in the turn of phrase of the street–and out of this twofold awareness he will seek to "do": to depict in *U.S.A.* what he knows.

"The Body of an American" is a summation of what the seeker has discovered about American life and language in the first two decades of the century, a period that climaxes with America's participation in the war and in the peace conference. John Doe, the unknown soldier, is the Whitmanesque wanderer transformed with biting irony into the archetypal American victim of the falsification of belief and language of the period. He is an average commonplace American, his life devoid of any noble purpose or ideals, his mind full of the verbal debris of his time. ("Now is the time for all good men knocks but once at a young man's door, It's a great life if Ish gebibbel"–[*NN*, 471]). He becomes separated from his unit during combat and wants only to return to it, but a stray shell kills him. His death symbolizes the immense chasm that has developed between reality and language. Dos Passos' account of the vacuity of his motives and the emptiness of his "sacrifice" ("the brains oozed out of the cracked skull and were licked up by the trenchrats, the belly swelled and raised a generation of bluebottle flies"–[*NN*, 472]) is ironically interwoven with the "dirty bunting" of resolutions, oratory, and newspaper reports that stress the honor and glory of his death and that parade him as an example of the "justice of his country's cause" (*NN*, 470). "The Body of an Ameri-

*Manuscript page of working notes for* The 42nd Parallel *(Albert and Shirley Small Special Collections Library, University of Virginia)*

can" epitomizes a central theme in the first two novels of the trilogy in that its emphasis on the corruption of the language of belief that the war occasioned expresses in symbolic form a principal cause of the failure of the "old words" in twentieth-century American life.

"Vag" begins with the same phrase that opens "U.S.A."–"The young man." But whereas in "U.S.A." the verb following is "walks," in "Vag" it is "waits." The seeker has now experienced the America of the 1920s and early 1930s; he has been in transient camps and in jails and has been beaten up by cops and driven out of towns. Exhausted and hungry, he waits by the side of the road for a lift while overhead a transcontinental plane flashes by with its well-to-do passengers, signifying the "two nations" (*BM*, 462) that America has become under the impact of the quest for the big money. For the young man, however, the quest is over; what remains are the false promises of American life: "went to school, books said opportunity, ads promised speed, own your home, shine bigger than your neighbor, the radiocrooner whispered girls, ghosts of platinum girls coaxed from the screen, millions in winnings were chalked up on the boards in the offices, paychecks were for hands willing to work, the cleared desk of an executive with three telephones on it" (*BM*, 561). The buoyancy of the seeker in "U.S.A." as he set out to discover the link between a national language and national ideals has met with two powerful shocks. The war revealed the discrepancy between a language of honor and the reality of war itself, and the postwar period revealed the distinction between a language of opportunity and freedom and the reality of a business society. The journey comes to an end as the archetypal American, his mind still filled with the language of possibility and accomplishment, waits "with swimming head, needs knot the belly, idle hands numb, beside the speeding traffic" (*BM*, 561).

–*Dos Passos' U.S.A.: A Critical Study* (Charlottesville: University Press of Virginia, 1988), pp. 35–40

## Notes

1. See, for example, Iain Colley, *Dos Passos and the Fiction of Despair* (Totawa, N.J.: Rowman & Littlefield, 1978), p. 116; Barbara Foley, "The Treatment of Time in *The Big Money:* An Examination of Ideology and Literary Form," *Modern Fiction Studies,* 26 (Autumn 1980): 466; and Jonathan Morse, "Dos Passos' *U.S.A.* and the Illusions of Memory," *Modern Fiction Studies,* 23 (Winter 1977–1978): 554.

2. Earlier discussions of the theme occur in John Lydenberg, "Dos Passos's *U.S.A.:* The Words of the Hollow Men," in *Essays on Determinism in American Literature,* edited by Sydney J. Krause (Kent, Ohio: Kent State University Press, 1964), pp. 97–107; David L. Vanderwerken, "*U.S.A.*: Dos Passos and the 'Old Words,'" *Twentieth Century Literature,* 23 (May 1977): 195–228; and "Dos Passos' Civil Religion," *Research Studies,* 48 (December 1980): 218–228.

3. Dos Passos, "Introduction," *Three Soldiers* (New York: Modern Library, 1932), pp. vii–viii.

4. Dos Passos, "The Writer as Technician," in *American Writers' Congress,* edited by Henry Hart (New York: International, 1935), pp. 79–82.

5. See Lois Hughson, "In Search of the True America: Dos Passos' Debt to Whitman in *U.S.A.,*" *Modern Fiction Studies,* 19 (Summer 1973): 179–192.

6. John Dos Passos Collection, University of Virginia.

## U.S.A.
### Dos Passos

*"U.S.A." is the prologue to the entire trilogy that Dos Passos prepared for the 1938 first edition. Here he makes explicit that the search for the meaning of the nation is above all a search for the meaning of "the speech of the people."*

The young man walks fast by himself through the crowd that thins into the night streets; feet are tired from hours of walking; eyes greedy for warm curve of faces, answering flicker of eyes, the set of a head, the lift of a shoulder, the way hands spread and clench; blood tingles with wants; mind is a beehive of hopes buzzing and stinging; muscles ache for the knowledge of jobs, for the roadmender's pick and shovel work, the fisherman's knack with a hook when he hauls on the slithery net from the rail of the lurching trawler, the swing of the bridgeman's arm as he slings down the whitehot rivet, the engineer's slow grip wise on the throttle, the dirtfarmer's use of his whole body when, whoaing the mules, he yanks the plow from the furrow. The young man walks by himself searching through the crowd with greedy eyes, greedy ears taut to hear, by himself, alone.

The streets are empty. People have packed into subways, climbed into streetcars and buses; in the stations they've scampered for suburban trains; they've filtered into lodgings and tenements, gone up in elevators into apartmenthouses. In a showwindow two sallow windowdressers in their shirtsleeves are bringing out a dummy girl in a red evening dress, at a corner welders in masks lean into sheets of blue flame repairing a cartrack, a few drunk bums shamble along, a sad streetwalker fidgets under an arclight. From the river comes the deep rumbling whistle of a steamboat leaving dock. A tug hoots far away.

The young man walks by himself, fast but not fast enough, far but not far enough (faces slide out of sight, talk trails into tattered scraps, footsteps tap fainter in alleys); he must catch the last subway, the streetcar, the bus, run up the gangplanks of all the steamboats, register at all the hotels, work in the cities, answer the wantads, learn the trades, take up the jobs, live in all the boardinghouses, sleep in all the beds. One bed is not enough, one job is not enough, one life is not enough. At night, head swimming with wants, he walks by himself alone.

No job, no woman, no house, no city.

Only the ears busy to catch the speech are not alone; the ears are caught tight, linked tight by the tendrils of phrased words, the turn of a joke, the singsong fade of a story, the gruff fall of a sentence; linking tendrils of speech twine through the city blocks, spread over pavements, grow out along broad parked avenues, speed with the trucks leaving on their long night runs over roaring highways, whisper down sandy byroads past wornout farms, joining up cities and fillingstations, roundhouses, steamboats, planes groping along airways; words call out on mountain pastures, drift slow down rivers widening to the sea and the hushed beaches.

It was not in the long walks through jostling crowds at night that he was less alone, or in the training camp at Allentown, or in the day on the docks at Seattle, or in the empty reek of Washington City hot boyhood summer nights, or in the meal on Market Street, or in the swim off the red rocks at San Diego, or in the bed full of fleas in New Orleans, or in the cold razorwind off the lake, or in the gray faces trembling in the grind of gears in the street under Michigan Avenue, or in the smokers of limited expresstrains, or walking across country, or riding up the dry mountain canyons, or the night without a sleepingbag among frozen beartracks in the Yellowstone, or canoeing Sundays on the Quinnipiac;

but in his mother's words telling about longago, in his father's telling about when I was a boy, in the kidding stories of uncles, in the lies the kids told at school, the hired man's yarns, the tall tales the doughboys told after taps;

it was speech that clung to the ears, the link that tingled in the blood; U.S.A.

U.S.A. is the slice of a continent. U.S.A. is a group of holding companies, some aggregations of trade unions, a set of laws bound in calf, a radio network, a chain of moving picture theatres, a column of stockquotations rubbed out and written in by a Western Union boy on a blackboard, a publiclibrary full of old newspapers and dogeared historybooks with protests scrawled on the margins in pencil. U.S.A. is the world's greatest rivervalley fringed with mountains and hills, U.S.A. is a set of bigmouthed officials with too many bankaccounts. U.S.A. is a lot of men buried in their uniforms in Arlington Cemetery. U.S.A. is the letters at the end of an address when you are away from home. But mostly U.S.A. is the speech of the people.

*–U.S.A.,* pp. 1–3

\* \* \*

## The Novel as Poem: Whitman's Legacy to Dos Passos
Robert P. Weeks

*Weeks extends the impact of Whitman on* U.S.A. *to include Dos Passos's conscious effort to adapt several of Whit-* *man's most distinctive poetic devices to his own needs in the Camera Eye, Newsreel, and biography portions of the work.*

### I

. . . . . . . . . .

The ambitious title of the trilogy, *U.S.A.,* and the titles of the individual novels, *The 42nd Parallel, 1919,* and *The Big Money,* tell us much about Dos Passos' end and his means. His end is to take the measure of American experience from coast to coast, from the bottom to the top of the social structure during the first three decades of the twentieth century. As the titles of the first two novels suggest, his means are, at least on the surface, aseptically objective, and to the extent that there is bias, its target, as the title of the last novel indicates, is finance capitalism. Probably no other American novel covers a range of American experience as wide and as various as that in *U.S.A.* Dos Passos' ambition is large: to encompass his huge subject he essays not only to write creditable fiction, biography, autobiography, and history but to fuse them into a single narrative structure that possesses unity yet manages to communicate the discontinuity of American experience, in particular the isolation of the lives of individual Americans. The fiction, which constitutes the largest element in the trilogy, consists of the stories of his twelve principal characters who range from Mac, an itinerant typesetter and radical trade unionist, and Joe Williams, a feckless sailor, to J. Ward Moorehouse, a windy public relations tycoon, and Margo Dowling, an ambitious movie star. Interspersed among these fictional narratives is a series of brilliantly concise and evocative biographical sketches of Americans prominent during the period: Edison, Hearst, the Wright Brothers, and twenty-three others.

Throughout the trilogy, there are virtually no clearly identified intersections of the narrative segments and the biographies. In the sixty-eight "Newsreels," Dos Passos fabricates out of headlines, snatches of popular tunes, advertising slogans, and news stories "a verbal collage, a folkpoem for industrial society,"[1] as Arthur Mizener has described it. Pieces of this collage are inserted at intervals through the novel, placing the fiction and biography within the flux of current events.

To these, Dos Passos adds two other elements. There are fifty-one brief, autobiographical passages called Camera Eyes. Most of them, until the end of the novel, make few easily recognizable cross-references to the other elements. Like the Newsreels, the Camera Eyes appear seemingly at random and thus in part serve to emphasize the discontinuity of American life. The last element added by Dos Passos is the prologue and epilogue written to frame the trilogy.

To measure the success with which Dos Passos has orchestrated these varied elements into a purposeful whole, we have available to us several quite different standards. I have mentioned briefly the standard of the well-made Jamesian novel. There is also the naturalistic novel. And more promising than either, there is what Blanche H. Gelfant calls the "synoptic novel." It dramatizes social change by presenting details abstracted from their total context, thereby revealing the essential, if not the total, features of a society.[2] Gelfant's model provides a useful way of rebutting the objections of those who criticize Dos Passos' collectivist novels for failing to give full representation to all aspects of American life. But like the other models, the synoptic novel does not satisfactorily accommodate the varied elements and techniques that Dos Passos pours into *U.S.A.* There is also the possibility of looking outside the novel and seeing the structure of *U.S.A.* as having more in common with a long poem than a novel. *U.S.A.* derives its unity less from an idea than from a vision; therefore, the piling up of odd-sized chunks, fragments, and blocks is no less antithetical to artistic unity in *U.S.A.* than it is, say, in *The Waste Land,* Pound's *Cantos,* or *Leaves of Grass.* And even more than Eliot or Pound, Whitman uses a variety of genres to express his vision: "small imagist poems, versified short stories, realistic urban and rural genre paintings, inventories, homilies, philosophizings, farcical episodes, confessions, and lyrical musings"–to borrow Richard Chase's catalog.[3] Chase calls it a collection unique in American literature, but is *U.S.A.* any less diverse?

To see a three-volume novel as belonging perhaps more nearly to the poetic than the novelistic tradition seems at first not merely arbitrary but far-fetched. But a number of critics have commented on the prevalence of poetic techniques in *U.S.A.,* and one has referred to the novel as a whole in these terms. (Malcolm Cowley called *U.S.A.* a "furious and sombre poem.")[4] If such an approach gives us a fresh glimpse into the sources of the power of *U.S.A.,* then all the taxonomists can be ignored. Perhaps after looking at *U.S.A.* in this way, when we reconsider it as a novel it will be with new respect.

The most fruitful way of approaching the poetic dimension of *U.S.A.* is through the unmistakable impact on it of Whitman. Some of the most brilliant writing in *U.S.A.,* notably the biographies and those Camera Eyes toward the end of the trilogy, makes extensive use of a wide range of such Whitmanesque poetic devices as parallelism, catalogs, the envelope, and parentheses. Moreover, these devices are not used singly but, as they are in Whitman, as integrated elements of the whole work. Finally, if the presence of Whitman's influence on Dos Passos deserves our attention, we might expect to find not only the tributes to the earlier writer, the extensive borrowings and adaptations of his technique, but a common metaphysic. Specifically, we might expect to find some similarity in their view of the situation of the individual in America. And, indeed, we do, for Dos Passos adopts

Whitman's final position that, as Richard Chase puts it, "self and en-masse are in dialectic opposition."[5]

## II

Whitman's unmistakable stamp appears on the first page of *U.S.A.* The prologue begins:

> The young man walks fast by himself through the crowd that thins into the night streets, feet are tired from hours of walking; eyes greedy for warm curve of faces, answering flicker of eyes, the set of a head, the lift of a shoulder, the way hands spread and clench; blood tingles with wants; mind is a beehive of hopes buzzing and stinging; muscles ache for the knowledge of jobs, for the roadmender's pick and shovel work, the fisherman's knack with a hook when he hauls on the slithery net from the rail of the lurching trawler, the swing of the bridgeman's arm as he slings down the whitehot rivet, the engineer's slow grip wise on the throttle, the dirtfarmer's use of his whole body when, whoaing the mules, he yanks the plow from the furrow. The young man walks by himself searching through the crowd with greedy eyes, greedy ears taut to hear, by himself, alone.[6]

*Walt Whitman in 1872. In "Against American Literature" (1916), his first professional magazine publication, Dos Passos wrote, "Here our only poet found his true greatness. Walt Whitman abandoned the vague genteelness that had characterized American writing, . . . and, . . . shouted genially, fervidly his challenge to the future" (Oscar Lion Collection, New York Public Library).*

One is first struck by the reliance on parallelism: "feet . . . eyes . . . blood . . . mind . . . muscles." Then by that most Whitmanesque of catalogs, a catalog of skills and occupations: of the roadmender, fisherman, bridgeman, engineer, dirtfarmer. Each of these devices appears repeatedly throughout the novel. But in terms of giving this huge novel a shape and a focus, what is most significant in this prologue is Dos Passos' use of the solitary young man searching through the crowd, part of it, yet alone. Whitman uses this as the organizing principle of "The Sleepers" (I wander all night in my vision, / Stepping with light feet, swiftly and noiselessly stepping and stopping / Bending with open eyes . . .)[7] and in "Song of the Open Road" but most extensively and brilliantly in "Song of Myself":

Apart from the pulling and hauling stands what I am,

Stands amused, complacent, compassionating, idle, unitary,

Looks down, is erect, or bends an arm on an impalpable certain rest,

Looking with side-curved head, curious what will come next,

Both in and out of the game and watching and wondering at it. (p. 13)

In the last paragraph of Dos Passos' prologue, another debt to Whitman is made clear:

U.S.A. is the slice of a continent. U.S.A. is a group of holding companies, some aggregations of trade unions, a set of laws bound in calf, a radio network, a chain of moving picture theatres, a column of stock-quotations rubbed out and written in by a Western Union boy on a blackboard, a public library full of old newspapers and dogeared history books with protests scrawled on the margins in pencil. U.S.A. is the world's greatest river-valley fringed with mountains and hills. U.S.A. is a set of big-mouthed officials with too many bank accounts. U.S.A. is a lot of men buried in their uniforms in Arlington Cemetery. U.S.A. is the letters at the end of an address when you are away from home. But mostly U.S.A. is the speech of the people. (p. 6)

Until Whitman, no American writer had perceived the United States with its geographical reach and rich diversity as a suitable subject for a single work of literature. In the 1855 Preface to *Leaves of Grass* he wrote, "The United States themselves are essentially the greatest poem" (p. 709), and gave testimony to it in his book. Dos Passos is clearly writing in the same tradition, if one can describe a two-man effort as a tradition, and no one else has ever approached Dos Passos' success in encompassing a significant range of American experience in a single work.

The same nameless, rootless young man reappears in the final chapter or epilogue of *U.S.A.* He is still on the move, hitch-hiking across the U.S.:

The young man waits on the side of the road; the plane has gone; thumb moves in a small arc when a car tears hissing past. Eyes seek the driver's eyes. A hundred miles down the road. Head swims, belly tightens, wants crawl over his skin like ants . . . waits with swimming head, needs knot the belly, idle hands numb, beside the speeding traffic. A hundred miles down the road. (III, p. 494)

Like the center-of-consciousness in "The Sleepers," "Song of the Open Road," and "Song of Myself," Dos Passos' young man tramps a perpetual journey. This fact serves several purposes in *U.S.A.* It expresses American rootlessness, dramatizes the horizontal movement that is the basic rhythmical pattern of *U.S.A.*, and, along with the prologue, places a frame around the three novels in the trilogy. Since the prologue and epilogue were obviously afterthoughts, conceived eight years after publication of the first novel, it is a mistake to claim too much for them. But they do emphasize Dos Passos' debt to Whitman by acknowledging it in the two most conspicuous parts of the novel. To grasp the extent to which Dos Passos uses Whitman's legacy to order, enliven, and unify *U.S.A.*, it is necessary to look more closely at the way in which the narrative structure is fashioned in the longest, best constructed, and climactic novel of the trilogy, *The Big Money*. A major formal characteristic of that novel is its pervasive parallelism.

"Whitman is more coordinate and parallel than anybody,"[8] wrote Randall Jarrell. Whitman's reliance on parallelism resulted from his search for a grammatical and rhetorical structure that would be horizontal in movement, ordering images, occupations, events, names, activities, places—and the words for them—in endless parallel lines, never judging, never ranking, never making logical deductions. Parallelism is both close to the surface in everything Whitman wrote and at rock bottom, for his aesthetic is an expression of his democratic metaphysic with its emphasis on equality and individuality.

My purpose here is to suggest that this technique, so prevalent in Whitman's poetry and so fundamental to his thought, is the most conspicuous element of Dos Passos' style—in the sentence, the paragraph, the chapter, even in the three parallel novels of the trilogy. In their crudest, most insistent form, Dos Passos uses parallels to batter the reader with the pervasiveness of some feature of American life. In *The Big Money* in the same Camera Eye (p. 46) in which he interjects, "(I too Walt Whitman)," Dos Passos uses parallels to emphasize the way the texture of life in New York City in the 1920s is made of money. I have re-cast the lines in Whitmanesque form to emphasize the parallels:

> Winnings sing from every streetcorner:
> Crackle in the ignitions of the cars
> Swish smooth in ballbearings
> Sparkle in the lights going on in the showwindows
> Croak in the klaxons
> Tootle in the horns of imported millionaire towncars
> Dollars are silky in her hair soft in her dress
> Sprout in the elaborately contrived rosepetals that you kiss
> Become pungent and crunchy in the speakeasy dinner
> Sting shrill in the drinks
> Make loud the girlandmusic show
> Set off the laughing jag in the cabaret
> Swing in the shufflingshuffling orchestra
> Click sharp in the hatcheck girl's goodnight.[9]

One must acknowledge it sounds like Whitman–bad Whitman. On the other hand, when Dos Passos uses parallelism not merely as a mechanical formula but as a way of ordering ideas, for example, as a way of communicating the inexorable power of the state, as he does in the following passage from *The Big Money,* he can be very good, indeed. Again, I have re-cast the lines to emphasize the use of parallel structure and punctuated them as Whitman might have:

> America, our nation, has been beaten by strangers
> Who have turned our language inside out,
> Who have taken the clean words our fathers spoke,
> And made them slimy and foul.
> Their hired men sit on the judge's bench,
> They sit back with their feet on the tables under the
>     dome of the State House;
> They are ignorant of our beliefs,
> They have the dollars, the guns, the armed forces, the
>     powerplants;
> They have built the electricchair and hired the execu-
>     tioner to throw the switch.
> All right, we are two nations.[10]

Grim parallels like, "Who have turned our language inside out, / Who have taken the clean words our fathers spoke," have an undeniable rhapsodic power much like an incantation or curse. And the series of parallel assertions beginning "They . . ." dramatizes the direct, lineal, ineluctable evil consequences of great and concentrated power. In form, the passage resembles an envelope–the Biblical prosodists' name for this device. It opens with an idea or proposition, follows it with a series of parallel thoughts, then closes with a concluding thought. One is reminded of the controlled, elevated pronouncements of an Old Testament prophet. Or, more immediately, one is reminded of Whitman, for he uses the envelope often and well.

Through skillful use of parallelism, Dos Passos communicates inexorability; through mastery of the envelope, dignity, calm, and elegance. Most American writers have written of the betrayal of the American dream, but few so eloquently.

Also like Whitman, Dos Passos works variations on the envelope:

> (Wars and panics on the stock exchange,
> machinegunfire and arson,
> bankruptcies, warloans,
> starvation, lice, cholera and typhus:
> good growing weather for the House of Morgan.)
> (II, pp. 293–294)

The first statement is omitted, but the basic strategy is the same: a series of powerful parallel elements capped by an ironic comment.

Sometimes Dos Passos uses the envelope to enclose a man's life:

> Andrew Carnegie started out buying Adams Express
> and Pullman stock when they were in a slump;
>     he had confidence in railroads,
>     he had confidence in communications,
>     he had confidence in transportation,
>     he believed in iron.
>     Andrew Carnegie believed in iron, built bridges
> Bessemer plants blast furnaces rolling mills;
>     Andrew Carnegie believed in oil;
>     Andrew Carnegie believed in steel;
>     always saved his money
>     whenever he had a million dollars he invested it.
>     Andrew Carnegie became the richest man in the
> world
>                         and died. (I, p. 238)

It is a neat parable of a man who devotes himself wholly, even piously, to acquisitiveness, and in the end it avails him nothing. Like the typical Dos Passos envelope, this one is sealed with a bitterly ironic comment.

Envelopes come, of course, in various sizes. The envelope can be almost endlessly expanded through the piling up of parallel elements. It is not far-fetched to see all of *U.S.A.* as an envelope. It opens with the solitary young man walking in search of America; it ends with the search still underway, the young man's hands idle and belly empty–a bitter comment on the American dream. And in between an immense array of parallel happenings: probably never in the history of fiction was a narrative of this length written with so few intersections. The right angle of coincidence is practically never found. For example, the trajectories of the twenty-four historical figures describe parallel lines across the first thirty years of this century. Dos

Passos has, of course, selected men whose lives had a powerful, unidirectional thrust: Ford, Morgan, Debs, Veblen; and in presenting each historical figure he focuses on him alone, practically ignoring both those who acted on him and those he influenced. This gives us a stripped down–and oversimplified–history, but since almost all Dos Passos' public figures are what Riesman would call "inner-directed," to depict them as tracing solitary, parallel paths across the face of America effectively underscores what Dos Passos sees as their most essential trait: their rugged–and in some cases, monomaniacal–individualism. In many of the individual instances it is immensely effective; when all of them are taken together, they powerfully evoke the loneliness of American life.

If one continues the notion of the entire novel as an envelope with various parallel elements laid side by side, the Newsreels confirm beautifully, for not only are they interlarded in the novel like slices of cheese in a sandwich, but each Newsreel itself consists of thinly sliced items–headlines, snatches from popular songs, advertisements–stacked in an absurd array of disconnected parallels. This is also true of the narratives of the twelve fictional characters whose separateness is part of the form of the novel, for each of them, without exception, lives his individual life without any significant interaction with any of the other eleven characters. A lonely crowd. Their loneliness is underscored by their hollowness, for to an extraordinary degree, Dos Passos' fictional characters lack inner lives. Georg Lukács points out that the environment surrounding Dos Passos' characters is rendered with remarkable solidity of specification. "We see the steaming Italian restaurant with the spots of tomato sauce on the tablecloth, the tricolored remains of melted ice-cream on a plate and the like. The individual tones of the various speakers are well described. But what they say is perfect banality. . . ." The shallow, two-dimensional characters who appear against this solid, three-dimensional background lack what Lukács calls "intellectual physiognomies."[11]

His comment is perceptive, but it is too sweeping. For it must be pointed out that the twenty-four historical figures–Veblen, Morgan, Debs, etc.–have intellectual physiognomies, that their ideas and beliefs give their lives direction. The same is true of the narrator of the Camera Eyes. In contrast, the fictional characters–Mac, Mary French, Charlie Anderson, etc.–are guided not from within but from without, moving smoothly, almost brainlessly, parallel to the major resultant forces in their environment. For example, Margo Dowling, the empty, attractive, would-be movie star, moves to Hollywood with little

more self-awareness or volition than an iron filing drawn into a magnetic field.

So we can conclude that parallelism rules *U.S.A.*, aligning its elements from the sub-sentence level to the three novels that compose the trilogy. The title of the first novel–*The 42nd Parallel*–establishes the presiding geometrical principle of the trilogy. Each of the four major components of the novel consists of numerous parallel segments. They are all presented in approximately chronological order, the early biographies, Theodore Roosevelt, William Jennings Bryan, preceding the later ones, William Randolph Hearst and Samuel Insull. The Newsreels, Camera Eyes, and fictional narratives likewise follow rough chronological order. The shifts from a biography, to a segment of Newsreel, to a segment of narrative, to a segment of Camera Eye gives the impression of rapid exposure to successive stretches of parallel lines. There is discontinuity in our glimpses of this world, but the fictive world itself is dominated by inexorable forces that continuously drive the characters their separate ways.

This forbidding atmosphere, however, is repeatedly interrupted and relieved by a wide variety of diverting elements, some of the most effective of which appear to derive from Whitman. For example, as Richard Chase points out, "Song of Myself" is enlivened by colorful invasions by "the normative self, the comic poet and ironic realist,"[12] frequently in the form of odd, witty, quirky questions: "Who goes there? hankering, gross, mystical, nude . . . Where are you off to, lady? . . . The friendly and flowing savage, who is he? . . . Is he some Southwesterner rais'd outdoors? is he Canadian?" (pp. 20, 38, 47, 73).

Allen Ginsberg's witty adaptation of this technique, for example, in "A Supermarket in California," is well known:

I saw you Walt Whitman, childless, lonely old grubber, poking among the meats in the refrigerator and eyeing the grocery boys.

I heard you asking questions of each: Who killed the pork chops? What price bananas? Are you my Angel?[13]

Dos Passos has made similarly effective use of the same technique. For example, in Camera Eye (47) in *The Big Money:*

first a stroll uptown downtown along the wharves under the el peering into faces in taxicabs at the drivers of trucks at old men chewing in lunchrooms at drunk bums drooling puke in alleys what's the newsvender reading? what did the elderly wop selling chestnuts whisper to the fat woman behind the pickle-jars? where is she going the plain girl in the red hat running up the subway steps and the cop joking the other cop across the street? (III, p. 174)

Such questions are but tiny points of color offsetting the long, grey parallels of the narratives, but it would be difficult to overstate their value—and that of similar devices—in brightening up Dos Passos' fictive world, giving it novelty, inwardness, and a sense of freedom.

The Newsreels also brighten the world of *U.S.A.* The tendency has been to see the Newsreel either as "a folk poem," shards of cultural data for some future anthropologist, or as scraps from the screen of disaster and scandal that the kept press erects to mask the serious business of the world: getting power and making money. The following Newsreel can be said to perform both of these functions as it documents the national scene at the time of Harding's death:

Newsreel LII

assembled to a service for the dear departed, the last half hour of devotion and remembrance of deeds done and work undone; the remembrance of friendship and love; of what was and what could have been. Why not use well that last half hour, why not make that last service as beautiful as Frank E. Campbell can make it at the funeral church (nonsectarian)

BODY TIED IN BAG IS FOUND FLOATING

Chinatown my Chinatown where the lights are low
    Hearts that know no other land
        Drifting to and fro

APOPLEXY BRINGS END WHILE WIFE READS
TO HIM

Mrs. Harding was reading to him in a low soothing voice. It had been hoped that he would go to sleep under that influence

DAUGHERTY IN CHARGE

All alone
By the telephone
Waiting for a ring

TWO WOMEN'S BODIES IN SLAYER'S BAGGAGE

WORKERS MARCH ON REICHSTAG CITY
IN DARKNESS

RACE IN TAXI TO PREVENT SUICIDE ENDS
IN FAILURE AT THE BELMONT

PERSHING DANCES TANGO IN THE
ARGENTINE

HARDING TRAIN CRAWLS FIFTY MILES
THROUGH MASSED CHICAGO CROWDS

GIRL OUT OF WORK DIES FROM POISON

MANY SEE COOLIDGE BUT FEW HEAR
HIM

If you knew Susie
Like I know Susie
Oh oh oh what a girl (III, pp. 134–135)

But to characterize a Newsreel like this one as a stockpile of cultural data or a documentation of the process by which the press masks and trivializes American experience is somewhat solemn, academic, and more than a little wrong-headed. The most distinctive quality of the Newsreel is that it's comic; it presents us, as comedy does, not with experience but with spectacle. We tend to forget that *U.S.A.* was conceived in the twenties, that the Newsreel is a product of the Mencken era. It is not merely a collection of clippings; it's a witty collage documenting the absurd spectacle of what Mencken called *boobus Americanus*. Moreover, it reflects in its oblique way the personality of the artist who assembled it as surely as the Camera Eye does. And in keeping with that fact, as the Sacco-Vanzetti case approaches its tragic end, the Newsreels reflect Dos Passos' own despair, but this does not alter the fact that their genius is comic.

Like the Newsreel, the Camera Eye also alters somewhat in the course of the novel. In the first two volumes of *U.S.A.*, its lens is purposely blurred, its pictures somewhat arty. But throughout the trilogy its fundamental nature is unaltered: it is a sensitive and often impressionistic recorder of the experiences of an unnamed "center of consciousness." Like Whitman, who said of *Leaves of Grass,* "everything is literally photographed," Dos Passos, especially in his Camera Eye sections, strives for a photographic impressionism.

Camera Eye (1) begins: "when you walk along the street you have to step carefully always on the cobbles so as not to step on the bright anxious grassblades easier if you hold Mother's hand and hang on it that way you can kick up your toes." By the end of *U.S.A.*, those wispy snapshots of the author's youth have been radically transformed. The parallelism that runs through the clean verse of the biographies has been adapted to the Camera Eyes. Instead of wistful reminiscence we have controlled anger, the terse parallel elements marshalled into envelopes where the powerful emotion is held in balance:

they have clubbed us off the streets they are stronger they are rich they hire and fire the politicians the newspapereditors the old judges the small men with reputations the collegepresidents the wardheelers (listen businessmen collegepresidents judges

America will not forget her betrayers) they hire the men with guns the uniforms the policecars the patrol-wagons

all right you have won you will kill the brave men our friends tonight (III, p. 413)

In an earlier Camera Eye in this final novel, Dos Passos interjected, "I too Walt Whitman." It is a comment he could easily have made at the end of this Whitmanesque passage. Two features should be noted: the restrained but effective use of the catalog (politicians, newspaper editors, etc.) and the parenthetical comment. Could anything be more characteristic of Whitman than that parenthetical aside to the "businessmen collegepresidents judges?" Whitman often uses parentheses to indicate a change of voice or gesture, almost like stage directions for an orator. Obviously, there's an oratorical strain in Dos Passos, too. It joins with the comic elements, the questions, the atmosphere of spectacle and other tokens of the author's presence, all of which work within and around the parallel elements of the novel. They never subdue the geometry, but they relieve it here and there. The end product is a world like the one Mondrian gives us in "Trafalgar Square" and his other map-like diagrams of cities: stark, grim, and inflexible in outline. But Dos Passos, like Mondrian, refuses to be crushed by this world: he discovers bits of color; he highlights incongruities.[14] The result is a work of art dominated by cold geometry but by no means devoid of human wit, warmth, and individuality.

### III

I have described the world of *U.S.A.* as grimly geometrical, and I have suggested that the characters who inhabit this world move across it in lonely parallel columns driven by forces they neither understand nor oppose. This would seem to be much more the world of the naturalistic novel than the world of the realistic novel. Georg Lukács conceives of the realistic novel as an account of the struggle between a superior person and a society he must master.[15] The hero's superiority consists in his awareness of the social forces acting on himself and his determination to oppose them. It is not surprising that Lukács has placed Dos Passos' work outside the realist tradition, as he defines it, for one cannot conceive of any of the dozen fictional characters in *U.S.A.* standing shoulder to shoulder with characters from Balzac or Tolstoy in opposition to the social order. But if dynamic opposition of the human spirit to a given social order is a fruitful way to define realism, and it would seem to be, we should not be too quick in finding *U.S.A.* does not qualify as realism.

Lukács is justified in excluding Dos Passos' fictional characters. But more than practically any novel, *U.S.A.* transcends its characters. They are drab, humorless, unaware, like almost all the faceless victims who straggle through naturalistic novels, but their world is only part of *U.S.A.* Taken as a whole, the novel has about it a sense of surprise and of novelty that reminds us of "Song of Myself." Instead of being a dreary bookkeeping of existence, it gives us a multi-genre show that flashes from biography, to autobiography, to fiction, to journalism; moreover, it extensively and skillfully adapts to the service of the novel various poetic devices. The inventiveness, wit, and audacity given play in the writing of this unconventional novel create in it an atmosphere of freedom.

As we read the novel, we are not unaware of the grimness of the world it pictures, but we are exhilarated by the author's defiance of convention in depicting that world. Alfred Kazin has sensitively described this feeling, saying that as we begin *U.S.A.* we are "surprised, delighted, and provoked by the 'scheme,' by Dos Passos' shifting 'strategy.'" He says further that the book "becomes a book about writing *The 42nd Parallel*. That is the tradition of the romantic poet," he writes, "and reading him we are on every side surrounded by Dos Passos himself: 'his idea.'"[16] These comments apply with even greater force to *The Big Money* because in it the "implied author," to use Wayne Booth's apt term for the author's "second self," takes a much firmer command, focusing the narrative, the Newsreel, and the Camera Eye on the Sacco-Vanzetti case. Moreover, the Camera Eyes lose their sense-bound turbidity and project the sharply focused image of the narrator in his controlled rage at the sell-out of the American dream of equality and justice. So, perhaps the greatest character in *U.S.A.* is, as Kazin has suggested, the book itself. Or what makes better sense to me, the implied author, for it is *his* wit and ingenuity and growing indignation that constantly surprise and delight us. And it is he who adopts the stance of Lukács' hero, fully conscious of the social forces that overwhelm his fictional characters and determined himself to oppose those forces.

Like Walt Whitman, he "Stands amused, complacent, compassionating, idle, unitary, / . . . / Both in and out of the game and watching and wondering at it."

–*Modern Fiction Studies*, 26 (Autumn 1980): 434–446

### Notes

1. Arthur Mizener, "*The Big Money*," in *Twelve Great American Novels* (New York: New American Library, 1967), p. 93.

2. Blanche H. Gelfant, "John Dos Passos: The Synoptic Novel," reprinted in *Dos Passos: A Collection of Critical Essays*,

edited by Andrew Hood (Englewood Cliffs, N.J.: Prentice-Hall, 1974), p. 44.

3. Richard Chase, *Walt Whitman Reconsidered* (New York: William Sloane, 1955), p. 63.

4. Quoted by Mizener in "*The Big Money.*" When *The Big Money* appeared in 1936, according to Mizener, Cowley likened it to *The Waste Land*, a comparison also pursued in E. D. Lowry, "*Manhattan Transfer:* Dos Passos' Waste Land," *University Review,* 30 (Autumn 1963): 49–52.

5. Chase, p. 65.

6. Dos Passos, *U.S.A.* (Boston: Houghton Mifflin, 1960), p. v.

7. Walt Whitman, *Leaves of Grass,* Comprehensive Reader's Edition (New York: W. W. Norton, 1968), p. 424.

8. Randall Jarrell, *Poetry and the Age* (New York: Alfred A. Knopf, 1953), p. 131.

9. The original form of the passage is:

   winnings sing from every streetcorner

   crackle in the ignitions of cars swish smooth in ballbearings sparkle in the lights going on in the showwindows croak in the klaxons tootle in the horns of imported millionaire shining towncars

   dollars are silky in her hair soft in her dress sprout in the elaborately contrived rosepetals that you kiss become pungent and crunchy in the speakeasy dinner sting shrill in the drinks

   Make loud the girlandmusic show set off the laughing jag in the cabaret swing in the shuffling shuffling orchestra click sharp in the hatcheck girl's goodnight

10. The original form of the passage is:

    America our nation has been beaten by strangers who have turned our language inside out who have taken the clean words our fathers spoke and made them slimy and foul

    their hired men sit on the judge's bench they sit back with their feet on the tables under the dome of the State House they are ignorant of our beliefs they have the dollars the guns the armed forces the powerplants

    they have built the electricchair and hired the executioner to throw the switch

    All right we are two nations

11. Quoted by Delmore Schwartz in "John Dos Passos and the Whole Truth," in *Critiques and Essays on Modern Fiction,* edited by John Aldridge (New York: Ronald Press, 1952), p. 184.

12. Chase, p. 59.

13. Allen Ginsberg, *Howl and Other Poems* (San Francisco: City Lights, 1967), p. 23.

14. For a discussion of Dos Passos's use of painterly techniques and effects, see George Knox, "Dos Passos and Painting," *Texas Studies in Literature and Language,* 6 (1964): 22–38.

15. Alfred Kazin, Introduction, Georg Lukács, *Studies In European Realism* (New York: Grosset & Dunlap, 1964), p. xi.

16. Kazin, Introduction, *The 42nd Parallel* (New York: New American Library, 1969), p. xi.

*  *  *

## Montage and *U.S.A.*

Donald Pizer

*Relying on Dos Passos's extant notes and manuscripts, Pizer reconstructs the nature and purpose of Dos Passos's montage technique of discontinuity and juxtaposition in his arrangement of the modal sequences of the trilogy. The illustrations are drawn from manuscripts in the Dos Passos Collection of the University of Virginia Library.*

Each of the modes of *U.S.A.* is a distinctive literary form. Put oversimply, the Camera Eye is prose-poem bildungsroman; the biographies are ironic impressionistic pen portraits; the Newsreels, surreal collages; and the narratives, free-indirect-discourse renderings of archetypal lives. Each mode is also characteristic of a major tendency in the literary expression of the 1920s and is thus not strikingly original to Dos Passos. Although Dos Passos was extending the range and the level of execution of these experimental forms, he did not discover them. What is unique in *U.S.A.* is thus not the modal devices themselves but their combination in a single work that seeks to exploit the special quality of each to achieve an effect that is at once complex and unified.

Dos Passos himself always stressed in accounts of the genesis of *U.S.A.* that his principal creative act in the writing of the trilogy was the placing of the modal segments in relation to each other. His meeting with Sergei Eisenstein in Russia in 1928 confirmed, he later recalled, his belief in "the importance of montage" in expressing theme in all serial art.[1] "By that time I was really taken with the idea of montage," he remarked elsewhere.[2] As he explained to an interviewer, "I always had an interest in contrast, in the sort of montage Griffith and Eisenstein used in film. I was trying to put across a complex state of mind, an atmosphere, and I brought in these things [the Newsreels and biographies] partly for contrast and partly for getting a different dimension."[3]

Several commentators early in the critical history of *U.S.A.* remarked that the trilogy seemed to have been prepared in a manner similar to a film that relies heavily on montage. Delmore Schwartz noted in 1938, for example, that Dos Passos seems to have "put the book together as a motion-picture director composed his film, by a procedure of cutting, arranging, and interposing parts."[4] But in fact *U.S.A.* is far more complex in origin and nature than a film, in that the units that are being cut, arranged, and interposed are strikingly different from each other, while in a film the visual image is the single mode. In other words, by relying on montage in a work that already had a mix of four different literary modes, Dos Pas-

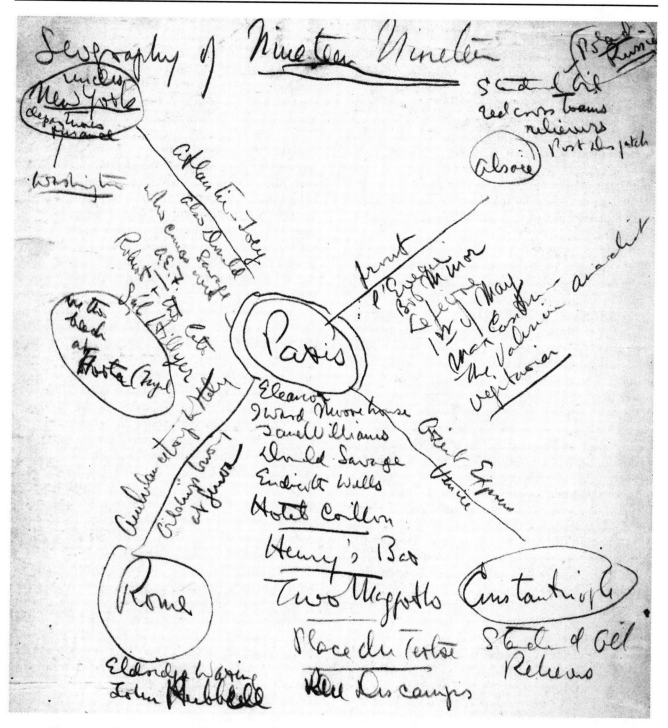

*Figure 1: Dos Passos's notes for the "geography" of* Nineteen-Nineteen, *in which he spatially represented the ways in which place and character would intertwine in the work, with all centering on Paris (Albert and Shirley Small Special Collections Library, University of Virginia)*

sos was raising the stakes, so to speak, beyond those present either in most films or in the fiction of other modernists (Faulkner, for example) who depended on montage. Now a reader would not only be asked to find connections and an ultimate spatial unity in juxtaposed scenes that derive from different plot lines, points of view, and chronologies. He would also be asked to perform the same task in response to modes of expression that were very different from each other both in substance and in manner. And since, as in most writing, the reader's task is also the author's, it is no wonder that Dos Passos recalled his intense preoccupation with this phase of his preparation of the trilogy.

It is possible, with the aid of Dos Passos' surviving notes and manuscripts, to trace with some confidence the way in which he wrote *U.S.A.* Although *The 42nd Parallel* and *Nineteen-Nineteen* are available only in incomplete notes and drafts, *The Big Money* is extant in an almost cradle-to-grave genealogy, from early notes to final printer's copy typescript (only proof is lacking). And since the three novels are essentially similar in form, it is reasonable to extrapolate from *The Big Money* (with confirming details from the manuscripts of the other two novels) to the trilogy as a whole.

Dos Passos began the preparation of each novel in the trilogy by drawing up lists of the characters he wished to include and of the focus of their activities. An early plan for *Nineteen-Nineteen,* entitled "Geography of *Nineteen Nineteen*" (see fig. 1) reveals his method.[5] We know that this is an early sketch, drawn to help Dos Passos scheme out the basic plan of the novel, because Richard Savage is here "Donald Savage" (a name not used in any of the surviving manuscript drafts) and because Alsace and Constantinople are not centers of action in the completed work. Another hint as to Dos Passos' method of construction is present in his early notes for *The Big Money.* Here, a group of notes that includes a list of "Characters for last volume" (some of whom do not appear in the novel) also contains both a list of biographical figures for possible inclusion (fig. 2) and a page in which the two kinds of figures appear together. That Dos Passos' method was to begin each novel by thinking principally of the narrative and biographical figures (and thus of their relationship) is fully confirmed by the initial three draft tables of contents for *The Big Money* (see figs. 3–5), which are (except for the first Camera Eye and the first two newsreels) limited to these two modes. These plans also precede full composition of the novel, since several of the biographies cited (Norris of Nebraska, Oil King, Kingfish the First) do not appear in *The Big Money* and seem never to have been written.

We know from other manuscript evidence that Dos Passos wrote each of the modes independently of the others. That is, for each unit of modal expression–a biography or Newsreel or Camera Eye or complete narrative–there exists a separate and distinctive body of notes, drafts, and final typescript. Thus, the first full typescript of *The 42nd Parallel* (before a missing clean printer's copy was prepared) and the final printer's copy of *The Big Money* have crossed out pagination sequences that reveal that each modal unit had an independent pagination before its inclusion in the full typescript of the novel.[6] (An analogy with assembly-line production, in which independently manufactured components are at last brought together, inevitably comes to mind.) But the separate composition of each mode did not mean that Dos Passos suddenly plunged into the montage process at the completion of the writing of the modes. The evidence of his early lists, charts, and tables of contents is that he was thinking from the beginning both of the relationship of narrative figures to each other, including interlacings (as asides to himself in his notes reveal),[7] and of the relationship of narrative to biographical figures. That Dos Passos began the montage process in this fashion is not surprising. The two modes that allowed him the greatest latitude and thus required the greatest initial planning were the narratives and the biographies. For the Camera Eye and the Newsreel he had in a sense both substance and sequence in hand before composition. The events of his own life supplied a core subject matter and a chronology for the Camera Eye, and the major events of each period served a similar purpose for the Newsreels.

Relying both on manuscript evidence and on hypotheses drawn from the nature of the modes, it is possible to sketch a theory of the composition of the novels of *U.S.A.* that has considerable significance for the quality of the completed work. A general belief about an era leads Dos Passos to the choice of narrative and biographical figures who exemplify the belief, with these figures conceived of from the first in juxtapositional relationships (an Eleanor and a Moorehouse together in Paris, a Hearst implicitly compared to a Moorehouse). The composition of each of the modes now commences, with each written independently of the others and with the Newsreels probably the last undertaken. The composition process as it proceeds has a twofold character. As Dos Passos wrote a narrative or a Camera Eye, he was composing with confidence and authority within the conventions he had established for that mode. But as he wrote he was also both consciously and unconsciously exploring the juxtapositional possibili-

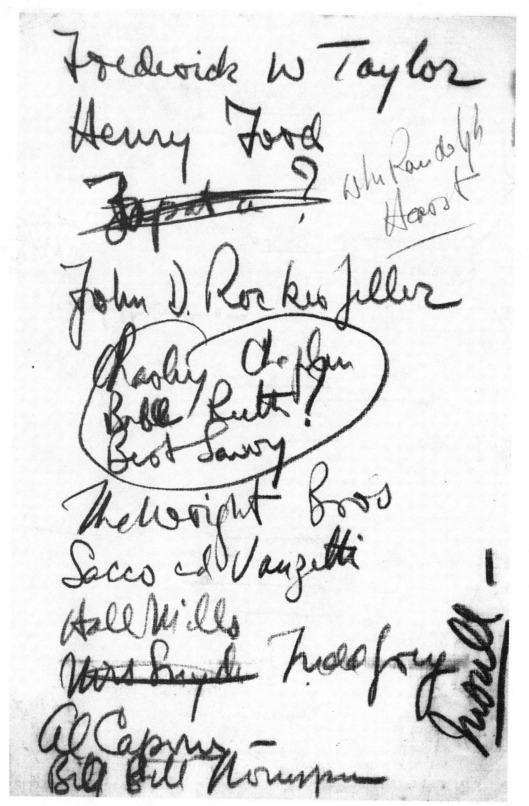

*Figure 2: List of possible subjects for the biographies in* The Big Money *(some of which were not included in the novel), suggesting the range of activities Dos Passos was considering for representation, from industry and invention to popular culture and crime (Albert and Shirley Small Special Collections Library, University of Virginia)*

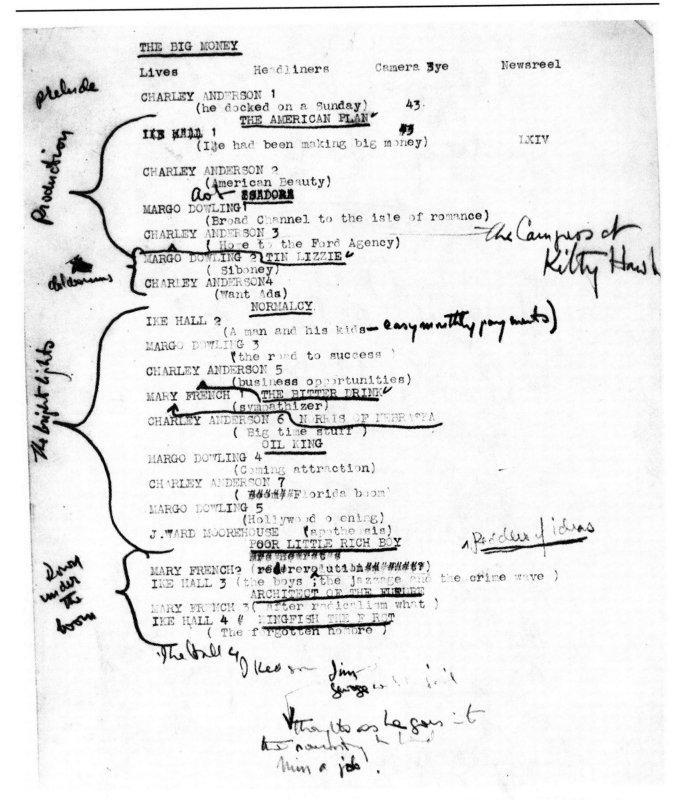

*Figure 3: Probably the earliest trial table of contents for* The Big Money, *in which only the initial Camera Eye and Newsreel segments are indicated, and Ike Hall (an itinerant workingman), John D. Rockefeller ("Oil King"), and Huey Long ("Kingfish the First") are among the narrative and biographical figures; these were later omitted (Albert and Shirley Small Special Collections Library, University of Virginia).*

```
THE BIG MONEY


              CHARLEY ANDERSON
                    The American Plan
              IKE HALL
                    Kitty Hawk
              CHARLEY ANDERSON 2
              MARGO DOWLING
                    Art and Isidora
              CHARLEY ANDERSON 3
                    TIM LIZZIE
              MARGO DOWLING
                    The Sheak
              CHARLEY ANDERSON
                    Normancy
              IKE HALL
              CHARLEY ANDERSON
                    The Bitter Drink
              MARY FRENCH
              CHARLEY ANDERSON 6
                    The Old Prospector
              MARGO DOWLING 4
              CHARLEY ANDERSON 7
              MARGO DOWLING 5
                    Poor Little Rich Boy
              J.WARD MOOREHOUSE
                    Mere Peddler of Tracts
              MARY FRENCH
                    Architect
              MARY FRENCH
                    Kingfish the First
              IKE HALL
```

Figure 4: *Trial table of contents for* The Big Money, *perhaps prepared at roughly the same time as that in figure 3 and suggesting that Dos Passos's initial efforts in creating a juxtapositional structure centered on the relation of narratives to biographies (Albert and Shirley Small Special Collections Library, University of Virginia)*

ties of each modal segment, for he was of course aware that a final and overt act of juxtapositional composition would be required when the modal segments were in fact dispersed throughout the novel. Much of the strength of *U.S.A.* arises out of this combination of a "purity" of expression within a particular mode–pure in the sense of the observance of firm and consistent modal conventions–and the far more indirect suggestiveness of the modal mix.

The effort and care that Dos Passos brought to the writing of each of the modes are revealed by the extant drafts of the narratives of *The Big Money*. For each narrative figure, Dos Passos initially sketched, in broad terms and in only a few pages, the major events of the character's life, with these divided into narrative segments. His next step was to block out in far greater detail the action of a single segment. The final segment of Dick Savage's narrative, for example, is outlined in fifteen numbered incidents (see fig. 11).[8] There would then follow a first holograph draft of the entire narrative. (Dos Passos' letters reveal that he conceived of and wrote each narrative as a single "story," and that he gave all his energy to this narrative until it was completed.[9]) From this holograph a typescript would be prepared, which Dos Passos cut and revised heavily. A second typescript, itself revised, provided the text for integration into the full text of the novel. The seemingly unshaped and artless flow of the narratives, though strikingly different from the mannered symbolism of the Camera Eye, underwent a stone-by-stone preparation similar to that of the prose poems. And what was true of the narratives was also true of the biographies and Newsreels.

Even before he had completed the writing of the individual modes, Dos Passos was engaged in elaborate planning of the juxtapositional order of the modal segments in the book as a whole. His early division of each narrative into segments, and his attachment of specific biographical figures to specific narrative figures (Taylor to Ike Hall, for example), no doubt supplied him with a rough arrangement for this portion of the novel almost from the beginning of the compositional process.[10] But given the complexity and indeterminacy of the task, he was also led to prepare, at various stages in the composition of the novel, draft tables of contents both to record his ideas and to serve as a basis for revision of these ideas. Between approximately early 1935 and early 1936, he prepared at least seven (that is, seven have survived) draft tables of contents of *The Big Money* (see figs. 3–10). The tables are not numbered or dated, but their sequence can be determined by internal evidence.[11] The tables reveal:

1. Although the narratives supplied the base subject matter and structure for the novel, significant changes in narrative content and order did occur in the course of the novel's preparation. Charley, Margo, and Mary are present in the first table (fig. 3) in the number of segments for each narrative as in the published work, except for the minor change of an increase in Mary's segments from three to four. The major changes that occur as the novel goes forward are: the complete cutting of the narrative of Ike Hall (an automobile worker who had appeared as a minor figure in Mac's narrative in *The 42nd Parallel*); the substitution of a Richard Savage for a J. Ward Moorehouse segment at the close of the novel; and a shift in the order of the narrative segments to achieve an even greater early emphasis on Charley Anderson and a later one on Margo and Mary. The Hall material was no doubt cut at a late stage (see figs. 7–8) to shorten the novel (even without it *The Big Money* is still the longest novel in the trilogy), though Dos Passos had completed most or all of the narrative. (He later published several of its segments separately.[12]) Its loss means that the novel lacks a "pure" working-class figure parallel to Mac in *The 42nd Parallel* and Joe Williams in *Nineteen-Nineteen* and in contrast to the middle-class or upward-striving figures in *The Big Money*. The change from Moorehouse to Savage is not so much a change in subject matter–the stress is still on New York advertising and "artistic" life–as in angle of vision through which to depict this world. And the shift in emphasis in the placing of narrative segments appears to follow from Dos Passos' recognition that Charley's New York and Detroit experiences epitomize the early stages of the 1920s boom, while Margo and Mary's movie and radical activities more fully reflect a later phase.

2. Although the biographies were also a key element in the early planning of the strategy of *The Big Money,* they reveal a greater volatility than the narratives. Six of the nine biographies in the completed novel were planned from the beginning (Taylor, Duncan, Ford, Veblen, Hearst, and Frank Lloyd Wright), but in attempting to choose the other three Dos Passos eliminated at various stages George W. Norris, John D. Rockefeller, Huey Long, Coolidge, and Vanzetti before finally selecting the Wright brothers, Valentino, and Insull. Dos Passos' "raw" juxtapositional planning was in terms of the relationship of narrative to biographical figures, as is indicated by the first three draft tables of contents. So, even in the first table, Taylor (the inventor of industrial engineering) is juxtaposed against Anderson and Ike Hall (a user and a victim of the assembly line), Margo is juxtaposed against Duncan, Charley against

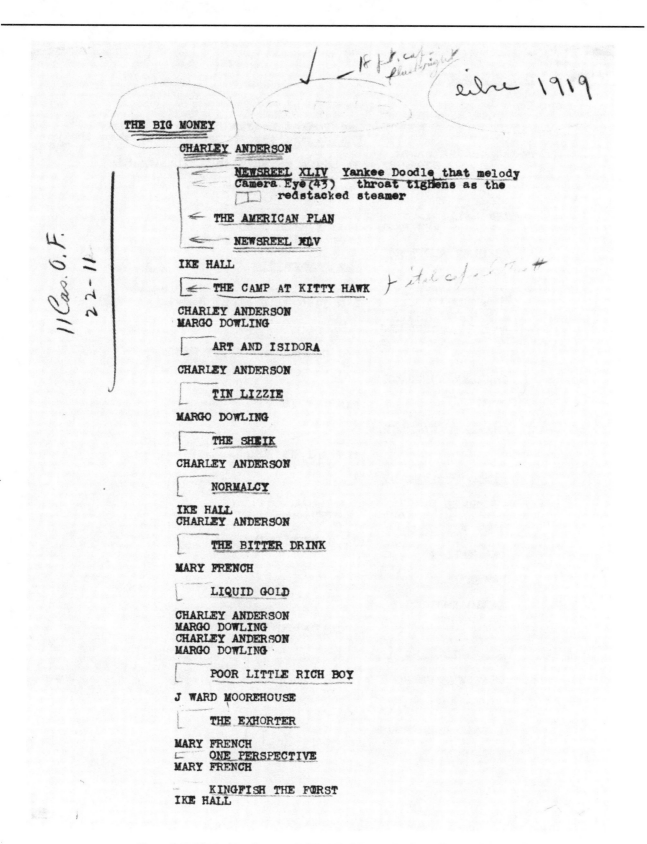

*Figures 5–7: Trial tables of contents for* The Big Money *showing a further refinement of the plan for the biographies and narratives in the volume (Albert and Shirley Small Special Collections Library, University of Virginia)*

THE BIG MONEY

CHARLEY ANDERSON 1
    NEWSREEL Them Yankee Doodle Blues
              the camera eye throat tighens when the
redstacked steamer
    NEWSREEL   ST Louis woman with a Diamond Ring

THE AMERICAN PLAN

IKE HALL 1
    NEWSREEL   Second Hand Rose
               Love will find a way
CHARLEY ANDERSON 2
              the camera eye

    NEWSREFL Three O'clock in the Morning
             I'm just Wild about Haree
MARGO DOWLING 1
    NEWSREEL

              THE CAMPERS AT KITTY HAWK

CHARLEY ANDERSON 3

              TIN LIZZIE

CHARLEY ANDERSON 4

              ART AND ISIDORA

MARGO DOWLING 2

NEWSREEL

MARY FRENCH          THE BITTER DRINK

IKE HALL 2

NEWSREEL

MARGO DOWLING 3

              ADAGIO DANCER

MARGO DOWLING 4

CHARLEY ANDERSON 7

MARGO DOWLING 5

J.WARD MOOREHOUSE

*Figure 6*

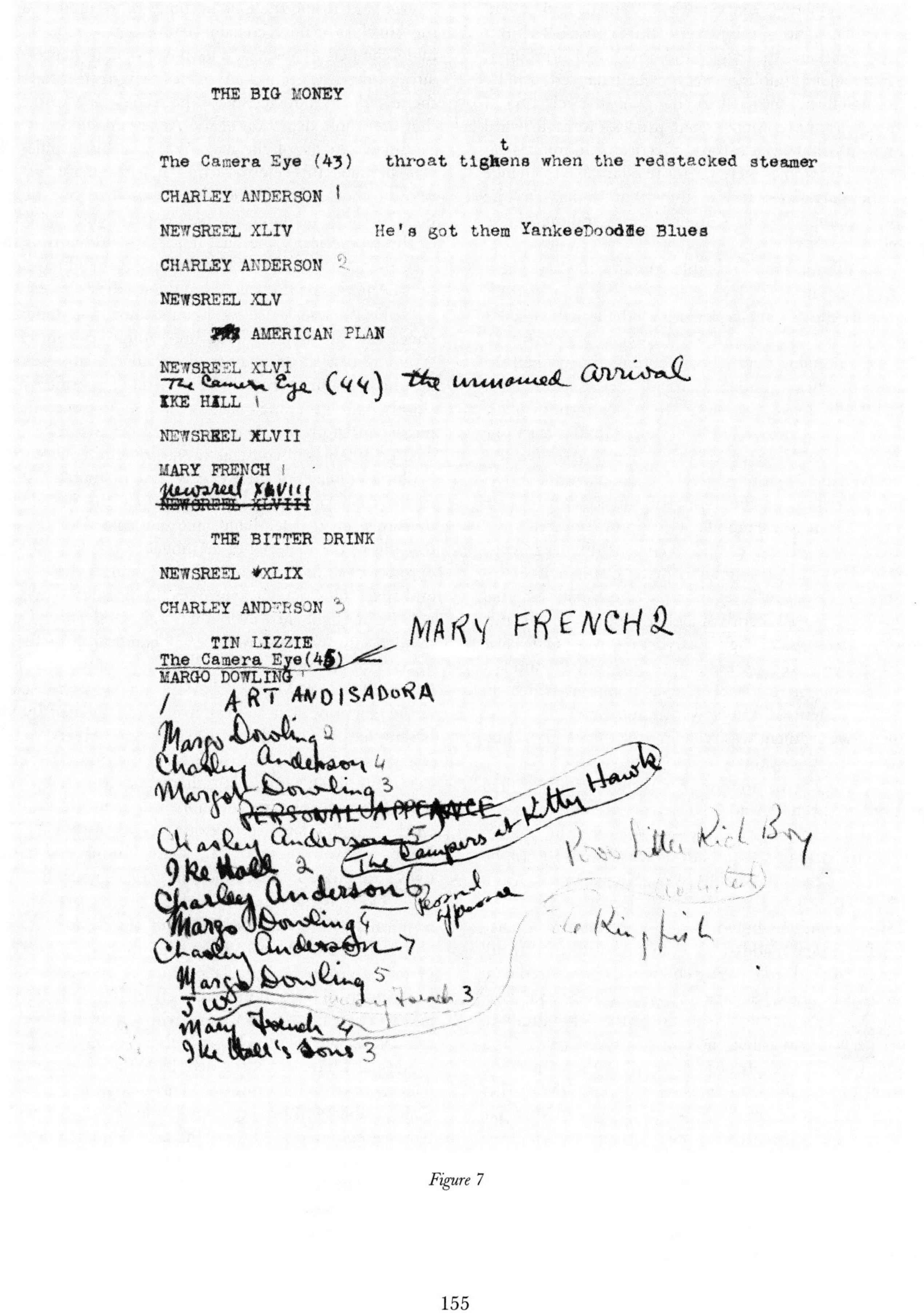

THE BIG MONEY

The Camera Eye (43)     throat tig*t*hens when the redstacked steamer

CHARLEY ANDERSON 1

NEWSREEL XLIV       He's got them YankeeDoodle Blues

CHARLEY ANDERSON 2

NEWSREEL XLV

AMERICAN PLAN

NEWSREEL XLVI
The Camera Eye (44) *the unnamed arrival*
IKE HALL 1

NEWSREEL XLVII

MARY FRENCH 1
~~Newsreel XLVIII~~

THE BITTER DRINK

NEWSREEL XLIX

CHARLEY ANDERSON 3

TIN LIZZIE     MARY FRENCH 2
The Camera Eye (45)
MARGO DOWLING 1

ART AND ISADORA

Margo Dowling 2
Charley Anderson 4
Margo Dowling 3
PERSONAL APPEARANCE   The Campers at Kitty Hawk
Charley Anderson 5
Ike Hall 2
Charley Anderson 6   Poor Little Rich Boy
Margo Dowling 4   Personal Appearance    (concluded)
Charley Anderson 7   The Kingfish
Margo Dowling 5
J. W.
Mary French 3
Mary French 4
Ike Hall's Sons 3

*Figure 7*

155

Ford and Coolidge, Mary against Veblen, and so on. The flexible spine of the novel is thus constructed. But the organizational strategy of the novel, which required that fictional and public archetypes be balanced, usually for ironic effect, lent itself to change in the selection of examples as the compositional process went forward and new possibilities for ironic effect came to mind. And since the biographies were far more adaptable to change than the narratives, it was they that underwent the greatest change in the course of preparation of the novel.

3. Although the first table contains the first Camera Eye and the first Newsreel, the splicing in of these two modes did not in fact begin until the fourth table for the Newsreels and the fifth for the Camera Eye (fig. 7). Three overlapping internal conventions determined the placing of these modal segments. First, and most mechanically, Dos Passos used them as a form of punctuation in the structure of the novel, in that at least one Camera Eye or Newsreel occurs between narrative segments. When a lengthier "pause" in the narrative movement is desired, at the point of introducing a new narrative figure, for example, a group of Newsreels and Camera Eyes will appear between narrative segments. Second, Dos Passos sought to place Camera Eye segments and Newsreels at points where the external events depicted in them coincided roughly, and sometimes precisely (as in the abortive 1919 May Day Paris uprising), with events present in the narratives. And last . . . , he sought to place them at points at which an underlying theme of the Newsreel and especially of the Camera Eye segment was relevant to a theme in the juxtaposed narrative segment or biography.

4. Dos Passos undertook a reshaping of the final portion of the novel at a late stage of revision, as is revealed by the major differences between the conclusions of the next-to-last and last tables (figs. 8–10). In the first of these two, the ending was: Mary French, Camera Eye, Huey Long, and Ike Hall. Dos Passos cut the Ike Hall narrative, shifted Savage's segment to a place just before Mary's, added a Newsreel, substituted Insull for Long, and added the Vag epilogue. The revised conclusion was thus: Savage, Newsreel, Camera Eye, Insull, Mary, and Vag. Aside from the Vag addition, which served primarily as an epilogue to the trilogy as a whole, Dos Passos' purpose in revising the conclusion appears to have been to sharpen its irony. The earlier ending was more emphatically downbeat in that Ike Hall and Mary French–a down-and-out workingman and a worn radical dispirited by ideological disputes– were expressions of the mood of the 1930s. A biography of Huey Long, a potential American dictator of the early 1930s, would have contributed further to this mood. With the omission of Hall and the addition of Savage and Insull, the tone becomes more mixed, since the conclusion now contains figures who have seemingly climbed to success. The more openly depression aura of the first ending now gives way to material and themes more characteristic of the trilogy as a whole, in that the ironic depiction of the American success story dominates many of the narratives and biographies. It was perhaps the reintroduction of this theme in the revised conclusion that led Dos Passos to one of his final revisions (as indicated by the penciled-in addition to the typescript of the final table), the addition of the Vag epilogue. For Vag is in archetypal form a final story of an American who believed in the myth of success.

Dos Passos' use of juxtaposition for thematic effect can be divided into three rough categories: a grouping of a large number of varied modal segments around a major theme or event; a more specific, more closely knit grouping, usually limited to several segments; and a precise thematic link across two segments. The draft tables of contents reveal something about the evolution of each of these effects. The first table (fig. 3), for example, indicates, as is shown by the penciled-in divisions in the left-hand margin, that Dos Passos thought of the material of the novel in relation to large chronological/thematic units, even though these units and their titles do not appear in the finished work. (It will be recalled, however, that *The 42nd Parallel* was divided into five parts in the 1930 edition.) "The bright lights," for example, deals with the apex of the mid- and late-1920s boom. Margo, Charley, and Moorehouse are at the height of their success, a success validated by the biographies of Coolidge, Rockefeller, and Hearst, while Mary, Norris, and Veblen represent the unheeded critical voices of the period. This theme, stated here grossly, will of course resonate far more subtly in the finished work. But this later complexity has its origins in Dos Passos' early grouping of a substantial number of narratives and biographies around a large-scale general idea.

Dos Passos' search for tighter, more specific juxtapositional effects (the second and third kinds noted above) is also evident from the beginning in his juggling of narrative/biography relationships to refine thematic implication. This simultaneous effort both to sharpen and to deepen reached a peak with the blending in of the Newsreels and Camera Eye segments. These modes, as I have already noted, have their own internal coherence–the reflection, in chronological order, of major public and private events–and thus were probably written independently of the planning and composition of the narratives and biographies, as is suggested by their absence from the first three draft tables of contents. But once stated, this notion of "independence" must be qualified by the fact that the same creative mind, compartmentalized only to a degree, wrote all the modes. A

```
          the Camera Eye (43)  throat tightens when the redstacked
               steamer

CHARLEY ANDERSON
NEWSREEL XLIV   COLONEL HOUSE ARRIVES FROM EUROPE
CHARLEY ANDERSON 2
NEWSREEL XLV                                                      hair
          AMERICAN PLAN
NEWSREEL XLVI   Dont bring                         Broadway
the Camera Eye (44)  the unnamed arrival

IKE HALL    1
NEWSREEL XLVII   HELP WANTED ADVANCEMENT

MARY FRENCH 1
NEWSREEL XLVIII That old gang of mine
          THE BITTER DRINK                            girl
CHARLEY ANDERSON 3      newsreel XLIX  the time the place the
          TIN LIZZIE
the Camera Eye (45) from the room full of demanding faces
NEWSREEL L       Truly the Steel Corporation
MARY FRENCH 2
the Camera Eye46fiveoclock taxicab
NEWSREEL LI Tea for Two

MARGO DOWLING 1
          ART AND ISADORA
NEWSREEL LII The Wedding of the painted Doll
MARGO DOWLING 2
NEWSREEL LIII there was nothing significant about the
          morning's trading
          ADAGIO DANCER
NEWSREEL LIV  Just a toy to enjoy for an hour
CHARLEY ANDERSON 4
NEWSREEL LV
CHARLEY ANDERSON 5
NEWSREEL LVI Valencia oh Valencia
MARGO DOWLING 3
the Camera Eye 47  the upside down image on the retina
          THE CAMPERS AT KITTY HAWK
CHARLEY ANDERSON 6
NEWSREEL LVII
IKE HALL AND HIS BOYS
NEWSREEL LVIII  For the sixth week freightcar loadings
MARGO DOWLING 4                    have passed the million #
NEWSREEL LIX his first move was to board a        mark
                    fast train for Miami
CHARLEY ANDERSON 7
MARGO DOWLING 5
NEWSREEL LX
          GRAND OLD MAN
RICHARD ELLSWORTH SAVAGE        Poor Little Rich Boy
NEWSREEL LXI Storm Ties Up Subway
the Camera Eye 48  walking from Plymouth to North Plymouth
MARY FRENCH 3
NEWSREEL LXII Holmes Denies Stay
the Camera Eye 49  they have clubbed up off the streets
NEWSREEL LXIII If it had not been for these things
MARY FRENCH 4
the Camera Eye 50
IKE HALL'S Boys
```

*Figure 8: Trial table of contents for* The Big Money *that shows Dos Passos moving toward the final version, although Hall and Long are still present (Albert and Shirley Small Special Collections Library, University of Virginia)*

THE BIG MONEY
$$$$$$$$$$$$$$

CHARLEY ANDERSON

NEWSREEL XLIV  Yankee Doodle that melodee

                    Twarnt                    CHARLEY ANDERSON
NEWSREEL XLV    ~~$$$$$$$$~~for powder an for storebought hair

        THE AMERICAN PLAN

NEWSREEL XLVI  these are the men for whom the rabid
                                                    steamer
        THE  Camera Eye (43) throat tightens when the redstacked

NEWSREEL XLVII  boy seeking future offered

        The Camera Eye  (44) the unnamed arrival

                                        CHARLEY ANDERSON

NEWSREEL XLVIII truly the steel corporation

        TIN LIZZIE

NEWSREEL XLIX  Jack o diamonds Jack  o diamonds

                                        CHARLEY ANDERSON

NEWSREEL L  Dont blame it all on Broadway

        THE BITTER DRINK

NEWSREEL LI  The sunshine drifted from our alley

                                        MARY FRENCH

T       The Camera Eye (45)  the narrow yellow room teems with talk

                                        MARY FRENCH

        The Camera Eye (46)  walk the streets and walk the streets

NEWSREEL LII assembled to a service for the dear departed

        ART AND ISADORA
NEWSREEL LIII Bye bye blackbird
                                    MARGO DOWLING                 ing
NEWSREEL LIV there was nothing significant about the morning's trad-

        ADAGIO DANCER

NEWSREEL LV  THRONGS IN STREETS

The Camera Eye       (47) sirens bloom in the fog over the harbor

*Figures 9–10: The final version of the table of contents for* The Big Money *(Albert and Shirley Small Special Collections Library, University of Virginia)*

the big money            contents 2

                                   CHARLEY ANDERSON ✓

NEWSREEL LVI   his first move was to board a fast train for Miami ✓

     The Camera Eye ( 48) westbound to Havana Puerto-Mexico Gal- ✓
                                   veston

                                   MARGO DOWLING ✓

NEWSREEL LVII  the psychic removed all clothing

                                  MARGO DOWLING

NEWSREEL LVIII <u>In my deams it always seems</u> ✓

           THE CAMPERS AT KITTY HAWK ✓

NEWSREEL LIX   the stranger first coming to Detroit ✓

                                CHARLEY ANDERSON ✓

NEWSREEL LX   Was Celine to blame ? ✓

                            MARGO DOWLING ✓

NEWSREEL LXI   <u>High high high up in the hills</u> ✓

                         CHARLEY ANDERSON ✓

NEWSREEL LXII   STARS PORTEND EVIL ✓                    C

                       MARGO DOWLING ✓

NEWSREEL LXIII *but a few minutes later this false land disappeared* ✓
ARCHITECT ✓
~~GRAND OLD MAN~~

NEWSREEL LXIV   *WIERO FISH DRAWN FROM SARBASSO SEA* ✓
   The Camera Eye (49)   walking from Plymouth to North Plymouth ✓

NEWSREEL LXV   STORM TIES UP SUBWAY; FLOODS AND LIGHTNING DARKEN CITY C

                      MARY FRENCH ✓

NEWSREEL LXVI   HOLMES DENIES STAY ✓

   The Camera Eye (50)  they have clubbed us off the streets ✓

NEWSREEL LXVII *when things are upset there's always chaos* ✓

     POOR LITTLE RICH BOY ✓

NEWSREEL LXVIII   *WALL STREET STUNNED* ✓

  ~~xxxxxxxxxxxx~~        RICHARD ELLSWORTH SAVAGE ✓
 The Camera Eye (51)
        *POWER SUPERPOWER*
      ~~IMMIGRANT BOY MAKES GOOD~~ ✓

             MARY FRENCH

       *VAG*

*Figure 10*

159

good many Newsreel segments were therefore no doubt "composed" because of Dos Passos' realization that their events would also be present in the narratives, as with the Florida land boom. And Dos Passos' choice of specific instances of the Camera Eye persona's experience in New York as a radical writer was also no doubt influenced by his awareness of the relationship of these activities to the lives of Charley, Savage, and Mary in the city and to Margo's career as an artist.

The first draft table of contents reveals an obvious example of a planned and specific juxtapositional effect when Charley's arrival in New York to face an uncertain future after heroic war service is followed by the parallel arrival of the Camera Eye persona (Camera Eye 43) and by a Newsreel (XLIV) that also deals with a number of returns from Europe to an unquiet America. Much more often, however, the Camera Eye and Newsreel segments are truly "spliced in," in the sense that their relationship to their adjacent biography and narrative segments is neither planned in advance nor precise. Rather, as in the creation of certain kinds of surreal and abstract paintings, Dos Passos was hoping for an inner resonance that might or might not follow from the mixing of modal segments only loosely connected in external character. In order to gain this effect, however, he needed to experiment, to try out relationships. Hence the seven tables of contents, as Dos Passos sifted the mix that constituted this potential, both to express more cogently already planned juxtapositional themes and to bring to the surface unforeseen juxtapositional inference.

The general nature of Dos Passos' experiments in the creation of thematic implication between modal segments can usefully be illustrated by a return to the "only words against / POWER SUPERPOWER" passage that I discussed earlier in connection with the theme and form of the trilogy as a whole. The process of juxtapositional experimentation that produced the passage is as follows. First, Dos Passos decided to substitute Insull for Huey Long as a final biography in the trilogy. (He had listed Insull as a possible biographical figure in early notes but had not included him in the first six draft contents.) In making this change, he was perhaps attracted by the link between a reference to "the manipulator of the holding company" at the close of the Harlan County Camera Eye and Insull, an infamous holding-company magnate of the 1920s. A second step was the revision of the characteristically ironic title of the Insull biography, "Immigrant Boy Makes Good," to a title that links the Camera Eye and the biography even more tightly, in that "power" is doubly present in both segments. The coal miners produce the raw material of power, but power in the sense of economic and political strength belongs to the owners. And Insull's career, as a

director of electricity and gas companies, also illustrates the double meaning of the term. Hence the new title, POWER SUPERPOWER. The third and final step occurred even later in the writing process and requires an explanation in detail.

The setting-copy typescript of Camera Eye (51) (fig. 12) reveals that in this version Dos Passos was thinking of the "we have only words against" passage entirely in relation to its relevance within the Camera Eye. Even his cutting of the last two lines of the segment still leaves "their guns" as the object of "words against." The setting copy of Camera Eye (51) and the opening of the Insull biography in the setting copy (fig. 13) have two additional important characteristics. First, because Dos Passos' method of composition had been to write in independent modal units, he maintained even in the setting copy, for ease of further rearrangement of these units, their separate physical identities. So Camera Eye (51), though paginated now as part of the setting copy (pp. 616–618), has a body of white space at its conclusion, and the following biography of Insull begins at the top of a fresh page with its title. Thus there is still no immediate visual connection between the concluding line of Camera Eye (51) and the title of the biography.

In addition, the setting copy of Camera Eye (51) and the Insull biography reveal that galley proof would, for the first time, have brought the conclusion of the Camera Eye and the title of the biography into inescapable visual juxtaposition. The presence of galley mark 162 on page 616 and of 163 on page 620 indicates that the segments would have been set in close proximity on galley 162. Not only would Dos Passos have seen this physical juxtaposition at this stage—we know that he carefully read and revised proof for *The Big Money*[13]–but he would also have realized that the juxtaposition would be maintained in the printed book, since each new segment did not begin on a new printed page, but was run-on from the preceding segment. It was thus while reading galley that Dos Passos must have seen for the first time the possible relationship between the close of Camera Eye (51) and the title of the Insull biography, realized that that relationship would be preserved in the printed book, and took the leap into a precise but immensely suggestive juxtapositional theme by cutting "their guns."

The process by which Dos Passos reached this explicit crossing of modal barriers is characteristic of analogous but less dramatic and less specifically verbal instances throughout the trilogy. Dos Passos' desire to have the conclusion of *The Big Money* express a theme close to a major theme in the trilogy as a whole had led him to recast the ending of the novel, including the introduction of a new biography with a stronger rela-

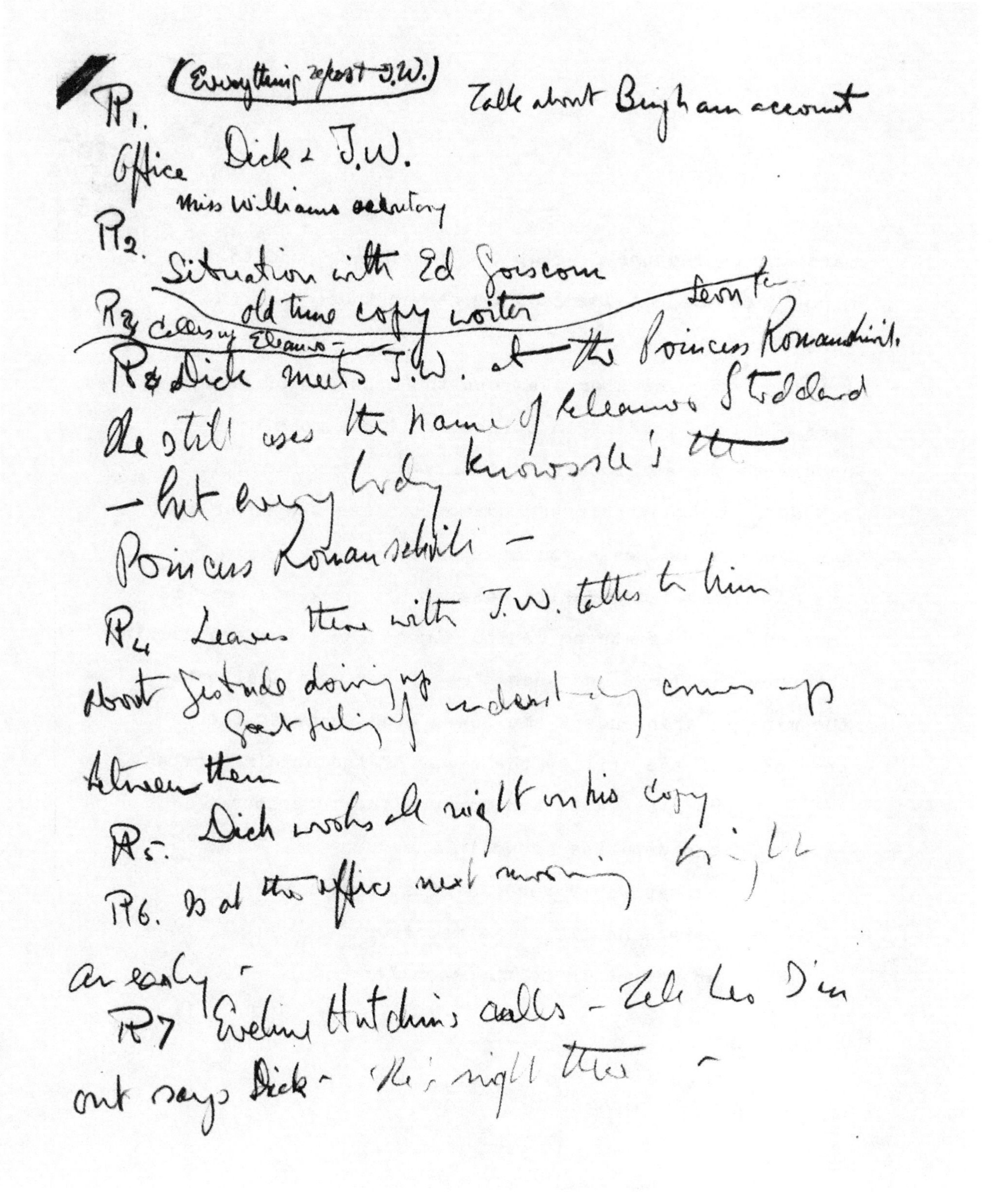

(Everything except J.W.)

R1. Talk about Bingham account

Office Dick & J.W.

Miss Williams secretary

R2. Situation with Ed Griscom

~~R3 old time copy writer~~

R4 Dick meets J.W. at the Princess Romanchiski

She still uses the name of Eleanor Stoddard

— but everybody knows she's the

Princess Romanschiski —

R4 Leaves there with J.W. talks to him

about Gertrude doing up

great feeling of understanding comes up

between them

R5. Dick works all night on his copy

R6. Is at the office next morning bright an early

R7 Evelyn Hutchins calls — Tell her I'm

out says Dick — She's right there —

*Figure 11: Outline for a segment of the Richard Savage narrative in* The Big Money *(Albert and Shirley Small Special Collections Library, University of Virginia)*

marching behind the flag up the switchback road to the

mine ~~they shoot down our brave men~~ those that the

guns spare they jail)

⊏⊐        the law stares across the desk out of angry

eyes his face reddens in splotches like a gobbler's

neck with the strut of the power ~~that~~ submachineguns

sawedoff shotguns teargas and vomitinggas the power that

can feed you or leave you to starve

              ~~the sheriff~~ sits easy at his desk his back is

covered he feels strong behind him he feels the prosecuting

attorney the judge an owner himself the political boss

the mine superintendent the board of directors  the

president of the utility the ~~owner~~ manipulator of the holding company

              he lifts his hand towards the telephone

              the deputies crowd in the door

              we have only words against their guns

              ~~before he lifts the receiver~~

              ~~we must talk to the sheriff~~

*Figures 12–13: Two pages from the setting copy for* The Big Money *showing the end of Camera Eye (51) and the beginning of the Samuel Insull biography (Albert and Shirley Small Special Collections Library, University of Virginia)*

619

POWER    SUPERPOWER————————————— ^ 18 caps

In eighteen eighty when Thomas Edison's agent
was hooking up the first telephone in London, he put an
an ad in the paper for a secretary and stenographer.  The
eager young cockney with sprouting muttonchop whiskers
who answered it

    had recently lost his job as office boy.  In his
spare time he had been learning shorthand and bookkeeping
and taking dictation from the editor of the English
<u>Vanity</u> <u>Fair</u> at night and jotting down the speeches in Par-
liament for the papers.  He came of temperance smallshopkeeper
stock; ~~He was eager to make money, ambitious for power;~~
already he was butting his bullethead against the harsh
structure of cast that doomed boys of his class to a life
alpaca jackets, penmanship, subordination.  To get a job
with an American firm was to put a foot on the rung of a
ladder that led up into the blue.

    He did his best to make himself indispensable;
they let him operate the switchboard for the first half
hour when the telephone service was opened.  Edison noticed
his weekly reports on the electrical situation in England
    and sent for him to be his personal secretary.

    Samuel Insull landed in America on a raw March
day in eightyone.  Immediately he was taken out to Menlo Park,
shown about the little group of laboratories, saw the

*Figure 13*

tionship to its immediately preceding Camera Eye. Once present, this relationship was further tightened and sharpened by a revision of the title of the biography and a final strategic cutting. In approximate form, this was Dos Passos' method throughout, though the degree of interpenetration between specific adjoining modal units, even after their mutual reflection had been increased by shifting, revision, and cutting, differs considerably from instance to instance. In some sections, a large idea planned from the beginning controls the broad statement of theme in a large number of modal segments. In others, at the opposite extreme, a precise event, symbol, or verbal motif connects two segments. Or there is some mix of these extremes. In addition, the degree of planning versus serendipity differs greatly. In this instance, both are present. The shift to Insull and the change in title were the result of conscious efforts to restructure and to sharpen; the discovery of the "words against / POWER SUPERPOWER" passage was the fortuitous product of the earlier experimental industry. Dos Passos, in short, had no uniform way of producing juxtapositional theme, and he produced juxtapositional theme that varied greatly in openness, depth, and intensity. He had realized that the nature of his enterprise required a combination of planning and of seizing upon opportunities that arose when potentially mutually reflective units were already in place. He took advantage of both methods to produce the immense variety and density of juxtapositional implication that is *U.S.A.*

–*Dos Passos' U.S.A.: A Critical Study* (Charlottesville: University Press of Virginia, 1988), pp. 86–95

## Notes

1. John Dos Passos, *The Best Times: An Informal Memoir* (New York: New American Library, 1966), p. 180.

2. David Sanders, "John Dos Passos," in *Writers at Work: The Paris Review Interviews, Fourth Series,* edited by George Plimpton (New York: Viking, 1976), pp. 81–82.

3. Frank Gado, "John Dos Passos," in *First Person: Conversations on Writers and Writing,* edited by Gado (Schenectady, N.Y.: Union College Press, 1973), p. 42.

4. Delmore Schwartz, "John Dos Passos and the Whole Truth," *Southern Review,* 4 (October 1938): 361.

5. All manuscript material cited is in the John Dos Passos Collection, University of Virginia Library. A similar though less elaborate plan exists for *The Big Money.*

6. Probably because of their brevity, neither the Newsreels nor the Camera Eye segments were paginated until their inclusion in the complete typescript of the novel. The narratives of *The Big Money* also have a somewhat more complicated pagination history than the above summary indicates. Since Dos Passos blocked out each narrative in segments before he began writing, the first typescript of the narrative as a whole had separate pagination sequences for each segment. In the preparation of a second typescript of the entire narrative, however, the narrative was paginated in one sequence, and it was this pagination that was then repaginated when the segments of the sequence were placed in the complete typescript of the novel. The large number of crossed-out page numbers on any page of narrative in the final typescript of *The Big Money* (often five or six) thus stems both from the initial single pagination of the narrative as a whole before its inclusion in the final typescript and from changes in the order of material in the final typescript itself. It should also be noted that Dos Passos limited his composition of each narrative figure to the novel he was then writing. That is, though Charley Anderson and Richard Savage appear in earlier novels of the trilogy, their narratives in *The Big Money* were written independently of their narratives in the earlier volumes.

7. Among Dos Passos's notes for Charley Anderson, for example, is the reminder "Dick Savage and Moorehouse come in here somewhere." His notes also contain detailed preliminary plans for the interlacing of Anderson and Margo and for Eveline's various appearances in other narratives.

8. I reproduce as figure 11 only the first page of the four-and-a-half page sequence. That this was Dos Passos' method from the beginning of the trilogy is confirmed by the survival of full preliminary notes for the entire Mac narrative.

9. For example, in an undated letter to Brandt and Brandt, which the firm received on March 30, 1935, Dos Passos noted that he expected to complete the Charley Anderson narrative in a few weeks and that it would be about 150 pages. The final typescript was in fact 187 pages.

10. That Dos Passos' preliminary division of the narratives into segments encouraged juxtapositional planning is suggested by his early note to himself that the first segment of Margo's narrative should come "between Charley Anderson 2 & 3" and the second "between Charley Anderson 4 & 5."

11. Briefly and roughly, the evidence is: the evolution of the initial narrative segments until they reach their final form of four consecutive Charley Anderson segments; the refinement of the subjects, titles, and order of the biographies; and the gradual filling in and ordering of the Newsreel and Camera Eye segments.

12. See "Tin Can Tourist," *Direction,* 1 (December 1937): 10–12, and "Migratory Worker," *Partisan Review,* 4 (January 1938): 16–20. Dos Passos' general conception of Hall was that he had an "extremely limited life."

13. It is clear from Townsend Ludington's account in *John Dos Passos: A Twentieth Century Odyssey* (New York: Dutton, 1980), p. 351, and from Dos Passos' letter to Hemingway of May 31, 1936 (*The Fourteenth Chronicle: Letters and Diaries of John Dos Passos* [Boston: Gambit, 1973], p. 484), that Dos Passos read galley proof in Havana and Miami in late April and early May and page proof in Providence in late May and early June. Although I am assuming that "their guns" was cut in galley proof, it would not affect the argument if it were in fact cut in page proof.

## Contemporary Chronicles
Dos Passos

*Dos Passos describes the various literary and visual art influences that fed into his effort to create a montage novel.*

For something like forty years I've been getting various sorts of narratives off my chest without being able to hit upon a classification for them. There's something dreary to me about the publisher's arbitrary division of every word written for publication into fiction and nonfiction. My writing has a most irritating way of being difficult to classify in either category. At times I would find it hard to tell you whether the stuff is prose or verse. Gradually I've come up with the tag; contemporary chronicle.

The sort of novel I started to try to write in the antediluvian days of the first World War was intended to be very much a chronicle of the present. It was a chronicle of protest. Dreiser and Norris had accustomed us to a dark picture of American society. Greedy capitalists were getting in the way of attainment of the Jeffersonian dream every American had hidden away somewhere in his head.

*Three Soldiers* my first long novel was an attempt to chronicle the feelings and frustrations of the natural-born civilian who found himself in the army. We were all natural-born civilians in the early years of this century. Now we are very much more regimented. It is hard to explain to young people born into today's regimented world how automatically their fathers and grandfathers resented the sort of forcible organization that has become the basis of today's social structure.

*Manhattan Transfer* which followed *Three Soldiers* was an attempt to chronicle the life of a city. It was about a lot of different kinds of people. In a great city there is more going on than you can cram into one man's career.

I wanted to find some way of making the narrative carry a very large load.

The period immediately before and after World War I had been a period of experimentation both in Europe and America. The Europeans have a sense of order and hierarchy that makes them love labels as much as the typical American tends to distrust them. Maybe trying to escape classification is one of our national vices. It certainly is mine. They called the sort of thing I wanted to do futurism or expressionism. I wasn't much interested in the labels on these various literary packages but I was excited by what I found inside.

In a war you spend a lot of time waiting around. While I was in the ambulance service in France and Italy I had managed to find time to read a certain amount of French and Spanish and Italian, poetry mostly.

The Italian futurists, the Frenchmen of the school of Rimbaud, the poets who went along with cubism in painting were trying to produce something that stood up off the page. Simultaneity, some of them called it. That excited me.

Why not write a simultaneous chronicle? A novel full of snapshots of life like a documentary film. I had been very much affected by the sort of novel that Stendhal originated in French with his *Chartreuse De Parme* and Thackeray in English with *Vanity Fair*. I remember reading *Vanity Fair* for the tenth time rather early in my life; after that I lost count. You might call these chronicle novels. *War and Peace* is another example.

In this sort of novel the story is really the skeleton on which some slice of history the novelist has seen enacted before his own eyes is brought back to life. Personal adventures illustrate the development of a society. Historical forces take the place of the Olympians of ancient Greek drama.

I had read James Joyce's *Ulysses* on my way home from Europe laid up with a bad case of flu in a tiny inside cabin down in the third class of a Cunarder. It's a marvelous way to read a book. *Ulysses* got linked in my mind with Sterne's *Tristram Shandy*. They are both subjective novels. My interests were the opposite: I wanted to write objectively. I had been pretty well steeped in the eighteenth century from early youth. Sterne too had tried to make his narrative carry a very large load. In college I had been taken with the crystal literalness of Defoe's narratives and by Fielding's and Smollett's rollicking satire. Fielding and Smollett came easy to me because I'd been prepared for them by Captain Marryat's sea stories of life in the Royal Navy which gave me infinite pleasure when I was a small boy. I read enough Spanish to be interested in Pio Baroja's modern revival of the Spanish picaresque style.

I dreamed of using whatever I'd learned from all these methods to produce a satirical chronicle of the world I knew. I felt that everything should go in: popular songs, political aspirations and prejudices, ideals, hopes, delusions, crackpot notions, clippings out of the daily newspapers.

The basic raw material is everything you've seen and heard and felt, it's your childhood and your education and serving in the army, and travelling in odd places, and finding yourself in odd situations. It is those rare moments of suffering and delight when a man's private sensations are amplified and illuminated by a flash of insight that gives him the certainty that what he is seeing and feeling is what millions of his fellowmen see and feel in the same situation only heightened. Seen a little sharper perhaps.

This sort of universal experience made concrete by the individual's shaping of it, is the raw material of all the imaginative arts. These flashes of insight when strong emotions key all the perceptions up to their highest point are the nuggets of pure gold.

They are rare even in the lives of the greatest poets.

The journeymen of the arts have to eke them out with lower quality ore. A novelist has to use all the stories people tell him about themselves, all the little dramas in other people's lives he gets glimpses of without knowing just what went before or just what will come after, the fragments of talk he overhears in the subway or on a streetcar, the letter he picks up on the street addressed by one unknown character to another, the words on a scrap of paper found in a trashbasket, the occasional vistas of reality he can pick out of the mechanical diction of a newspaper report.

It was this sort of impulse that came to a head in the three U.S.A. novels. Somewhere along the line I had been impressed by Eisenstein's documentary films like the Cruiser Potemkin. Eisenstein used to say that his master in montage was Griffith of the *Birth of a Nation* fame. Montage was the word used in those days to describe the juxtaposition of constrasting scenes in motion pictures. I took to montage to try to make the narrative stand up off the page.

. . . . . . . . . .

–*Carleton Miscellany, 2* (Spring 1961): 25–29

### The Montage of Film Attractions (1924)
Sergei Eisenstein

*The Soviet movie director Sergei Eisenstein describes his montage technique in his early silent movie* The Strike *(1924). (The thirty-eight different shots he notes last only a few minutes on the screen.) As Dos Passos often noted, he was much taken by Eisenstein's striking experimental motion-picture technique.*

The method of the montage of attractions is the comparison of subjects for thematic effect. I shall refer to the original version of the montage resolution in the finale of my film *The Strike:* the mass shooting where I employed the associational comparison with a slaughterhouse. I did this, on the one hand, to avoid overacting among the extras from the labour exchange "in the business of dying" but mainly to excise from such a serious scene the falseness that the screen will not tolerate but that is unavoidable in even the most brilliant death scene and, on the other hand, to extract the max-

*Director Sergei Eisenstein during the filming of his 1929 movie* Old and New (*from Norman Swallow,* Eisenstein: A Documentary Portrait, *1976*)

imum effect of bloody horror. The shooting is shown only in "establishing" long and medium shots of 1,800 workers falling over a precipice, the crowd fleeing, gunfire, etc., and all the close-ups are provided by a demonstration of the real horrors of the slaughterhouse where cattle are slaughtered and skinned. One version of the montage was composed roughly as follows:

1. The head of a bull. The butcher's knife takes aim and moves upwards beyond the frame.

2. Close-up. The hand holding the knife strikes downwards below the frame.

3. Long shot: 1,500 people roll down a slope. (Profile shot.)

4. Fifty people get up off the ground, their arms outstretched.

5. The face of a soldier taking aim.

6. Medium shot. Gunfire.

7. The bull's body (the head is outside the frame) jerks and rolls over.

8. Close-up. The bull's legs convulse. A hoof beats in a pool of blood.

*Assembly of workers voting for a strike in a scene from Eisenstein's 1924 movie* The Strike *(Avant-Scene Cinema)*

9. Close-up. The bolts of the rifles.

10. The bull's head is tied with rope to a bench.

11. A thousand people rush past.

12. A line of soldiers emerges from behind a clump of bushes.

13. Close-up. The bull's head as it dies beneath unseen blows (the eyes glaze over).

14. Gunfire, in longer shot, seen from behind the soldiers' backs.

15. Medium shot. The bull's legs are bound together "according to Jewish custom" (the method of slaughtering cattle lying down).

16. Closer shot. People falling over a precipice.

17. The bull's throat is cut. Blood gushes out.

18. Medium close-up. People rise into the frame with their arms outstretched.

19. The butcher advances towards the (panning) camera holding the blood-stained rope.

20. The crowd rushes to a fence, breaks it down but is met by an ambush (two or three shots).

21. Arms fall into the frame.

22. The head of the bull is severed from the trunk.

23. Gunfire.

24. The crowd rolls down the precipice into the water.

25. Gunfire.

26. Close-up. Teeth are knocked out by the shooting.

27. The soldiers' feet move away.

28. Blood flows into the water, colouring it.

29. Close-up. Blood gushes from the bull's throat.

30. Hands pour blood from a basin into a bucket.

31. Dissolve from a platform with buckets of blood on it . . . in motion towards a processing plant.

32. The dead bull's tongue is pulled through the slit throat (one of the devices used in a slaughterhouse, probably so that the teeth will not do any damage during the convulsions).

33. The soldiers' feet move away. (Longer shot.)

34. The head is skinned.

35. One thousand eight hundred dead bodies at the foot of the precipice.

36. Two dead skinned bull's heads.

37. A human hand in a pool of blood.

38. Close-up. Filling the whole screen. The dead bull's eye.

Final title.

–*S. M. Eisenstein: Selected Works,* edited and translated by Richard Taylor, volume 1: *Writings, 1922–34* (London: BFI / Bloomington: Indiana University Press, 1988), pp. 43–44

## Montage in Theatre and Film
David Bordwell

*Much of Bordwell's explanation of Eisenstein's concept and practice of montage could also apply to Dos Passos and U.S.A.*

Eisenstein is commonly thought of as a "formalist" theorist. But this does not mean that he emphasizes "form" over "content." This distinction does not have much force for him, since he sees both factors as part of a broader process. Like most of those working in the Soviet *technē*-centered trend, he refuses the standard concept of form as a vessel holding "contents." Instead, he conceives form as a transformation of material in accordance with the art work's social tasks. Form also represents the perceptible dimension of the work and thus serves as the basis for the spectator's engagement. Form, as a dynamic process of construction, will therefore trigger the work's effects.

Early on, Eisenstein conceives of the spectator as his material, with the techniques of theatre furnishing the tools for working on it. The particular theatrical production will be built out of attractions–theatrical techniques selected for their power to stimulate strong perceptual and emotional reactions. The attractions will in turn be arranged in a certain pattern. The idea of *montage* represents Eisenstein's most basic and persistent conception of the ways in which formal units may be combined.

The Russian *montazh,* taken from the French *montage,* retains many of its original meanings. One is "machine assembly," in the sense of "mounting" a motor. This sense came to be metaphorically applied to artistic work in the Constructivist era. Photomontage, *litmontazh* ("literature-montage"), and other terms described the construction that resulted from the labors of the artist-engineer. "One does not create a work," writes Eisenstein in his diary in 1919; "one constructs it with finished parts, like a machine. *Montage* is a beautiful word: it describes the process of constructing with prepared fragments."[1]

To the machine-based sense of montage the Constructivist ethos linked a second one: assembling materials in a way that generates a degree of friction among them. In this way, the concept of montage constituted the Constructivists' recasting of the Cubists' practice of collage. The notion of montage as a tension-based assembly is also central to Eisenstein's earliest usage. His productions of Tretyakov's plays became famous for their "montage" of attractions–a dissonant juxtaposition of fragments.

In the theatre, montage was thus a macrostructural principle, a way of governing the overall form of the production. Tretyakov pointed out that theatrical montage could be conceived in two ways, depending on its relation to the plot of the piece. In *The Wiseman,* Ostrovsky's plot provided a minimal continuity for a string of circus and variety attractions. Eisenstein celebrates this aspect in his 1923 manifesto: *The Wiseman* offers "a free montage with arbitrarily chosen independent . . . effects (attractions)."[2] In contrast, in *Do You Hear, Moscow?* Tretyakov indicated that the montage of attractions entered into a dynamic interplay with the plot; the attractions, both naturalistic and stylized, intensified or commented upon the action. The tension-based side of montage remained, less in the friction among separate attractions than in the clash between a relatively coherent plot and moments of amplified, emotionally arousing spectacle. It is this form of construction, the accentuation of a large-scale plot through diverting attractions, that Eisenstein uses in his silent films.

Upon coming to cinema, however, Eisenstein was confronted with a more microstructural conception of montage. In both French and Russian, *montage* also denotes film editing. Although the concept has implications for macrostructure, most writers restrict it to matters involving what we might call the stylistic texture of the film: the ways in which shots A and B could be joined to create a particular impression.

Again it was Kuleshov who gave the concept particular significance. As early as 1917 he argued that cinema is distinguished from other arts by virtue of the fact that montage organizes "separately filmed fragments, disordered and disjointed, into a more advantageous, integral and rhythmical sequence."[3] For Kuleshov, montage was the essential factor differentiating cinema from the other arts and forming the basis of the specific impact that film can make. In a series of informal experiments, he showed that editing could create emotions and ideas not present in either of the single shots. A man and woman look offscreen; cut to a building. We will assume that they are looking at the building, even if the first shot was made in Moscow and the second in New York. A man with a neutral expression looks off; cut to a shot of a banquet table; cut back to him, and now he will look hungry. Kuleshov's doctrine treated montage as the director's principal tool in shaping the exact response desired.

Kuleshov's account was almost wholly craft-bound; he offered no explanation for these phenomena. His student Pudovkin went only a little further, suggesting that certain editing devices are transpositions of ordinary perceptual acts, such as the focusing of attention on a detail or the shifting of attention across a scene.[4] On the whole, however, he too simply recommended certain editing options as most effective in achieving the preferred results. Along similar lines, in 1926 Timoshenko published a detailed typology of montage devices ("concentration" cuts, "expansion" cuts, rhythmic editing, point-of-view editing, and so on). His comprehensive inventory of editing techniques indicates the extent to which Soviet filmmakers sought to put film craft on a systematic basis.

Kuleshov and his followers drew only oblique comparisons between film editing and the Constructivist conception of montage. Dziga Vertov was more forthright. Like Kuleshov, he celebrated the power of editing to create a whole out of details–to assemble a man "more perfect than Adam."[5] But he took the machine analogy much further. For him, the very analysis of movement was an act of montage. So, indeed, was the entire filmmaking process. Selecting and researching a subject, filming it, and assembling the results were to be understood as montage in the broadest sense (72). Film production became like factory production, the assembly of a whole out of pieces trimmed to fit. This analogy between filmmaking and manufacturing forms a major theme of Vertov's *Man with a Movie Camera* (1929).

Immersed in filmmaking, neither Vertov nor the Kuleshovians had the inclination or the leisure to elaborate a broad theory of cinematic montage. The most systematic attempt was made by the Formalist literary theorists, who sketched a poetics of cinema parallel to the one they proposed for literature. Approaching a film as a system of interrelated components, the Formalists studied how formal devices transformed material and accomplished particular functions.

Two important accounts of montage were offered in the 1927 Formalist collection, *The Poetics of Cinema.* Boris Eikhenbaum suggested thinking of montage as purely a stylistic system, distinct from plot construction. He proposed that it was analogous to syntax in language, and he traced levels of articulation: the frame, the "cine-phrase" (a string of shots grouped around an accentual nucleus such as a close-up), and the "cine-period" (a larger unit based on spatiotemporal unity).[6]

By contrast, Yury Tynyanov compared montage to prosody. He argued that editing does not so much group shots as force them into a system of rhythmic equivalences. When shot B replaces shot A, there is a jump like that occurring between lines in verse. The result, according to Tynyanov, is a shift in semantic energy: the break-up into shots or verse lines, by creating equivalent rhythmic units, invites the reader to compare meanings across units. Citing *The Battleship Potemkin* as an example, Tynyanov declared that a plot cannot be easily divorced from its stylistic patterning, and concluded that "the study of plot in cinema in the future will depend on the study of its style and, in particular, of its material."[7]

In the second half on the 1920s Eisenstein draws on all these ideas. Like Kuleshov, he considers that the relation of shot to shot forms "the essence of cinema,"[8] and he uses a pun to stress that a new quality emerges out of the conjuncture. "The conditions of cinema create an 'image' [*obraz*] from the juxtaposition of these 'cuts' [*obrez*]" (80). Like Vertov, he suggests that the montage principle goes beyond the technique of editing. And like the Formalists, he will examine in detail the concrete effects of montage juxtaposition.

He therefore highlights certain features of montage. Editing, coordinating with sharp changes in camera angle, can intensify a sequence's "accuracy and force of impact."[9] Montage can provoke and prolong those associations that distinguish cinematic response from theatrical response. Montage enables the director to dwell on salient material long enough to enable "the thorough inculcation of the associations" (41). Whereas Kuleshov considered montage to be a storytelling technique, Eisenstein sees no reason for it to be bound by plot requirements. As cinema's chief tool for creating perceptual and affective impact, montage can freely deviate from the story's demands, just as the assembly of attractions did in his theatrical productions.

In such ways, Eisenstein follows the Constructivist tradition of treating montage as a strategy for forming material in any medium. One consequence of this decision is an idea that will dominate his career: cinema is not opposed to theatre by virtue of some specific essence, but rather represents the stage beyond theatre in the evolution of art. Eisenstein will soon apply the concept of montage far more broadly than any Constructivist would, finding it in Kabuki, Zola, and *Ulysses.* Denoting both a powerful film technique and a pervasive principle of *poiēsis,* the concept of montage becomes obsessively interrogated and reworked throughout his career.

–*The Cinema of Eisenstein* (Cambridge: Harvard University Press, 1993), pp. 120–123

### Notes

1. Jacques Aumont, *Montage Eisenstein,* translated by Lee Hildreth and others (Bloomington: Indiana University Press, 1987), p. 150.

2. Sergei Eisenstein, "The Montage of Attractions," in *S. M. Eisenstein: Selected Works,* edited and translated by Richard Taylor, volume 1: *Writings, 1922–34* (London: BFI / Bloomington: Indiana University Press, 1988), p. 35.

3. Lev Kuleshov, "The Tasks of the Artist in Cinema," in *The Film Factory: Russian and Soviet Cinema in Documents, 1896–1939,* edited by Taylor and Ian Christie (Cambridge, Mass.: Harvard University Press, 1988), p. 41.

4. V. I. Pudovkin, *Film Technique,* translated by Ivor Montague (London: Vision Press, 1958), pp. 67–73.

5. Dziga Vertov, *Kino Eye: The Writings of Dziga Vertov,* edited by Annette Michelson (Berkeley: University of California Press, 1984), p. 17.

6. Boris Eikhenbaum, "Problems of Cine-Stylistics" (1927), *Russian Poetics in Translation,* 9 (1981): 21–25.

7. Yuri Tynyanov, "The Fundamentals of Cinema" (1927), *Russian Poetics in Translation,* 9 (1981): 52.

8. Eisenstein, "Bela Forgot the Scissors," in *Writings, 1922–34,* p. 79.

9. Eisenstein, "The Montage of Film Attractions," in *Writings, 1922–34,* p. 46.

## *U.S.A.:* Dos Passos and the Rhetoric of History
Barry Maine

*Maine offers one of the fullest readings of the nature of Dos Passos's montage technique in each of the modes as well in the interaction of the modes, all leading to an interpretation of Dos Passos's view of the relationship of the individual to historical process.*

Apart from *The Education of Henry Adams,* there may be no greater anomaly in American historical literature than John Dos Passos's *U.S.A.* trilogy. Dos Passos himself chose the historiographic term "chronicle" for the genre in which he combined fact and fiction in order to bring, as he put it, "some slice of history" back to life ("Novelist" 31).[1]

We have since come to regard *U.S.A.* as a work that stands somewhere between history and fiction, just as Henry Adams's *Education* stands between history and autobiography. Since the contents of *U.S.A.* are partly factual—newspaper clippings and popular song lyrics in the Newsreels, the lives of well-known public figures in the Biographies, autobiographical incidents in the Camera Eye, and even some of the characters in the fictional narratives based on actual people Dos Passos had met during his extensive travels—and since three out of the four narrative devices fall within commonly accepted modes of historical writing—reportage, biography, and autobiography—we are likely to make claims for its historical basis which we are more reluctant to make for the historical novel. Nevertheless, owing to Dos Passos's expressionistic (in the Newsreels) and impressionistic (in the Camera Eye) use of the raw materials of history, and owing also to the fictional mode of the narratives which take up the lion's share of the twelve hundred page plus chronicle, we have been unwilling to call *U.S.A.* history outright. The scholarship on *U.S.A.* has been preoccupied, though not exclusively, with the various ways in which Dos Passos made use of historical materials to write fiction.[2] This is as true of Alfred

Kazin's groundbreaking commentary on *U.S.A.* in *On Native Grounds* (1942) as it is for the most recent book-length studies of Dos Passos's work by Iain Colley, Linda Wagner, and Robert Rosen.

*U.S.A.* holds virtually no place at all in American historiography (despite the fact that it is based on historical research), not only because of its blending of fact and fiction, but because it appears to lack what we expect most from history—historical explanation. Apart from a few isolated passages in the Biographies and Camera Eye, there is no historical commentary to speak of in *U.S.A.* But to argue that historical explanation is absent from *U.S.A.* because there is no historical commentary is to rule out narrative assertions of causality which are made in forms other than explanatory statements using the word "because." The logic of historical causality is only rarely made explicit in *U.S.A.;* more often it is communicated through "montage": for Dos Passos deliberately exploited the language, structure, and rhythm of the cinema to write his own experimental history of America from the turn of the century to the Great Crash.

That Dos Passos borrowed heavily from the narrative techniques of the cinema is not a thesis that needs defending, as Dos Passos himself has confirmed the influence.[3] The titles for two of the four narrative sequences Dos Passos invented to write his history—"Newsreels" and "Camera Eye"—are obvious borrowings from the language of motion pictures. Neither is the narrative function of montage a new subject; it is paid lip service in virtually every critical study. But no one has demonstrated to my satisfaction either the degree to which montage operates as a structuring device in the narrative or, most importantly, the extent to which historical causality in the narrative, and the very view of history that emerges from it, are determined by this structuring device.

To French filmmakers, who first coined the term, "montage" simply meant editing—the joining together of scenes or "shots." But to D. W. Griffith and Sergei Eisenstein montage came to mean a style of editing by which statements could be made indirectly through the careful juxtaposition of shots depicting similar or contrasting situations. In Eisenstein's *Strike* (1925), for example, shots of striking workmen being machine-gunned are intercut with images of oxen being slaughtered.

The narrative of *U.S.A.* is so visibly fragmented that each white space in the text between the conclusion of one narrative sequence (a Newsreel, for instance) and the beginning of another (such as a Biography or Camera Eye) is analogous to the "cut" from one shot to another in an Eisenstein film. Sometimes the experience described in one narrative

INTRODUCTORY NOTE

The 42nd Parallel is the first volume of U.S.A.
~~COURSE OF EMPIRE~~ , a long narrative which deals with the
more or less tangled ~~together~~ lives of a number of
Americans during the first three decades of the present
century . The volumes that follow are called Nineteen Nineteen
and The Big Money . *take in as much as possible the broad*

In an effort to ~~broaden the~~ field of ~~the narrative as~~ the
~~our~~ lives of these lives       Separate
~~much as possible~~ , three ~~extraneous~~ sequences have been threaded
in and out among the stories ~~of the men~~ and women ~~lives~~ .
Of these The Camera Eye aims to indicate the position of the
observer and NEWSREEL to give an inkling of the common mind
                 epoch        Portraits of a number of
of the ~~time~~ . ################################# real people
are
~~interlarded~~ ~~were set in~~ pauses in the narrative because their lives seemed
                 So well        quality
to embody the ###################### of the soil in which Americans
of these generations grew.

This method was used with the idea of coping with the
particular job in hand rather than from any generalized theory
about novelwriting . In fact I dont think any ~~other~~ *such* theory holds
water except that the shape of a piece of work should be imposed,
and in a good piece of work always is imposed, by the matter .
That's more or less of a commonplace of a considerable body of
literary criticism . The difficulty comes when you try to put
                        several people
into words how this occurs . If ~~a number of men are asked to~~
                a man and a woman
describe the same scene , say ###### sitting at a table in
                    are often ours to be        Among
a room and talking , the results ~~will be~~ very different . ~~Out of~~
                                                            Through

*First page of a revised typescript of the introductory note to the 1937 Modern Library edition of* The 42nd Parallel,
*in which Dos Passos sought to explain his modernistic techniques in the novel (Albert and Shirley Small
Special Collections Library, University of Virginia)*

sequence is confirmed or validated, so to speak, by the experience described in the narrative sequence, or "shot," which immediately follows it, such as when Dos Passos's own awkward and confusing transition from military to civilian life in Camera Eye (38) of *1919* is immediately followed by evidence collected in Newsreel XXXIII of a difficult time of adjustment for all returning veterans facing prohibition and unstable labor conditions at home (248–252). Descriptions of similar individual and collective responses to historical events are mutually reinforcing. Or we may find montage operating in the text as a structuring device designed to contrast one response to the historical moment with another, as when the political idealism of Woodrow Wilson depicted in the biographical sketch, "Meester Veelson," is exposed and exploded by the satiric lyrics of a popular song in Newsreel XXX which immediately follows: "You'll get pie / In the sky / When you die" (*1919*) 214–216).

But just as often there is no immediately apparent thematic connection between one narrative sequence and the next. When this occurs, the reader is left with an unsettling sense of disconnectedness in history. As the narrative is to the reader, so is history to Dos Passos's characters: disconnected, chaotic, out of control. On the other hand, the reader of *U.S.A.* enjoys a perspective denied to the characters. Historical causality is, in fact, embedded in the narrative, and the reader may actually be unaware of the degree to which he is being manipulated by it. Ironic counterpointing and thematic juxtaposition occur far more frequently within narrative sequences than between them, and with greater rhetorical effectiveness because the meanings generated by the montage are compressed and concentrated on the page.

Montage within a narrative sequence is most visibly obvious in the Newsreels. Newsreel III, for example, reproduced here in its entirety, evokes an atmosphere of worldwide political violence amidst American indifference and complacency:

"IT TAKES NERVE TO LIVE IN THIS WORLD" LAST WORDS OF GEORGE SMITH HANGED WITH HIS BROTHER BY MOB IN KANSAS MARQUIS OF QUEENSBERRY DEAD FLAMES WRECK SPICE PLANT COURT SETS ZOLA FREE

a few years ago the anarchists of New Jersey, wearing the McKinley button and the red badge of anarchy on their coats and supplied with beer by the Republicans, plotted the death of one of the crowned heads of Europe and it is likely that the plan to assassinate the President was hatched at the same time or soon afterward.

"It's moonlight fair tonight upon the Wabash
From the fields there comes the breath of newmown hay
Through the sycamores the candlelight is gleaming
On the banks of the Wabash far away"

OUT FOR BULLY GOOD TIME

Six Thousand Workmen at Smolensk Parade with Placards Saying Death to Czar Assassin
Riots and Streetblockades Mark Opening of Teamsters Strike

WORLD'S GREATEST SEA BATTLE NEAR

Madrid Police Clash with Five Thousand Workmen Carrying Black Flag
Spectators Become Dizzy While Dancer Eats Orange Breaking Record that Made Man Insane (*Parallel* 47)

The calm at the center of the storm is expressed in the lyrics of Paul Dresser's (Theodore Dreiser's brother) popular hit, "Down Upon the Wabash." It comes as a nostalgic harkening back to a simpler time, a wishful extrication of the machine from the garden.[4] But the lyrics also point up how complacently indifferent most Americans were to the political violence (and its underlying causes–colonialism and economic inequality– exposed by way of montage in Newsreels I and II respectively) springing up all over the globe. The last item in Newsreel III exposes something of the absurd and meaningless spectacle which attracted attention in America, while a far more pressing and serious spectacle of revolt raged within and without her borders.

Although the montage may be less visibly obvious in the other three narrative sequences, it is nonetheless the principal structuring device in each. Each Biography amounts to a series of carefully selected incidents so arranged as to add up to a self-evident historical exemplum. For example, observe how Dos Passos uses imagistic juxtaposition and ironic counterpointing in this excerpt from "Meester Veelson" to portray Wilson's rise to power as nearly incidental, and to expose the hollow ring to his political rhetoric:

Wilson became the state (war is the health of the state), Washington his Versailles, manned the socialized government with dollar-a-year men out of the great corporations and ran the big parade
of men munitions groceries mules and trucks to France. Five million men stood at attention outside of their tarpaper barracks every sundown while they played "The Star-Spangled Banner."
War brought the eighthour day, women's votes, prohibition, compulsory arbitration, high wages, high

rates of interest, cost plus contracts, and the luxury of being a Gold Star Mother.

If you objected to making the world safe for cost plus democracy you went to jail with Debs.

Almost too soon the show was over, Prince Max of Baden was pleading for the Fourteen Points, Foch was occupying the bridgeheads on the Rhine, and the Kaiser, out of breath, ran for the train down the platform at Potsdam wearing a silk hat and some say false whiskers.

With the help of "Almighty God," "Right," "Truth," "Justice," "Freedom," "Democracy," "the Self-determination of Nations," "No indemnities no annexations,"

and Cuban sugar and Caucasian manganese and Northwestern wheat and Dixie cotton, the British blockade, General Pershing, the taxicabs of Paris and the seventyfive gun,

we won the war.

On December 4, 1918, Woodrow Wilson, the first President to leave the territory of the United States during his presidency, sailed for France on board the "George Washington,"

the most powerful man in the world. (*1919* 211–212)

Wilson had risen to power astride historical forces he little understood and hence over which he could exert little control. The "most powerful man in the world" was powerless to arbitrate a just and lasting peace at Versailles. Montage delivers the historical explanation.

Where the fictional narratives are concerned, there is no American writer less Jamesian than Dos Passos. Character motivation is never analyzed by the author and only very rarely by the characters themselves. The absence of introspective characters in the fictional narratives is the book's great shortcoming when it is judged as a novel,[5] but reading *U.S.A.* as an experiment in historical writing, I see an advantage in Dos Passos developing the characters from the outside through the juxtaposition of scenes that show how each of the characters responds (albeit rather compulsively) to the circumstances of the historical moment. For example, when Fainy McCreary (Mac) resolves to make a pile of money out on the road so he can afford to marry the girl he loves, there is no narrator to tell us that neither Mac nor anyone else living in America before the rise of Organized Labor could make any money by the sweat of his brow. Dos Passos prefers montage to authorial comment: we leave Mac resolved to make a pile of money, and pick him up again smashing crates in a dried fruit warehouse in Sacramento (*Parallel* 77). When "cuts" like this one occur throughout a narrative sequence, as in Charley Anderson's gradual capitulation to the pursuit of "The Big Money," an inevitability asserts itself in such a way as to point to another historical exemplum (in this case, the fly in the

ointment of the American Dream: the materialism at its core) rather than an individual dilemma. Fainy McCreary and Charley Anderson are more "representative" and the plots in which they are involved more "descriptive" of a historical process by virtue of the narrative technique Dos Passos borrowed from the cinema.

In the Camera Eye, montage is again the principal structuring device and means of historical commentary, as this excerpt from Camera Eye (20) dramatically illustrates:

> when the streetcarmen went out on strike in Lawrence in sympathy with what the hell they were a lot of wops anyway bohunks hunkies that didn't wash their necks ate garlic with squalling brats and fat oily wives the damn dagoes they put up a notice for volunteers good clean young
>
> to man the streetcars and show the foreign agitators this was still a white man's. . . . (*Parallel* 220)

Ironic counterpointing generated by montage persuades the reader to accept the unspoken premise that bigotry and prejudice accounted for the American public's resistance to the labor movement. Montage of this variety, here and throughout each narrative sequence of *U.S.A.*, manipulates the reader just as powerfully and as irresistibly as the viewer of, for example, Eisenstein's *Potemkin* is manipulated by the juxtaposition of images on the screen.

The collision of voices in Camera Eye (20) is analogous to the fragments of history, real and imagined, which intersect in the composite text of *U.S.A.*, and with the same result: the reader is asked to accept premises that are never explicitly stated. For example, one premise of *The 42nd Parallel*, if it were explicitly stated, would read something like this: public opinion, fed by exaggerated press reports, idealistic political rhetoric, and propaganda spread by wealthy financiers and industrialists through public relations experts, made Wilson's decision to declare war on Germany as inevitable as the public's angry reaction against those who opposed it. Dos Passos never has to defend that thesis because it is never stated: it is developed through montage.

Film theorist Seymour Chatman has argued in a recent study that the dominant mode of narration in film is "presentational, not assertive." "A film," he continues, "doesn't say 'This *is* the state of affairs'; it merely *shows* you that state of affairs," without the necessity of affirming it (128). Historicism is simply plot: whatever happens appears to be the only logical outcome of what preceded it, the only thing that *could* have happened. Causality is present without being asserted. The mode of narration in *U.S.A.* is likewise presentational, not assertive. Aside from the direct historical narration in the Biographies (in which the bulk of historical commentary is still communicated by way of montage rather than direct explanation), and excepting a few direct assertions in some of the late Camera Eye sections, there is no narrator to assert anything. Consequently, there are few assertions for the reader to resist or the author to defend. Instead we are moved to accept an interpretation of recent American history based on premises which are formulated, developed, and defended, not by the logic of analysis and commentary, but by the power of suggestion controlled by montage.

We are moved, in part, by the power of the image to persuade. The photographic image is obviously realistic, but it is also symbolic by virtue of the intense selectivity of the camera lens. Every photograph, whether it be a Matthew Brady, a Walker Evans, or a family-album snapshot, is inherently symbolic of a larger reality only because we assume it to be representative of that larger reality (i.e., the Civil War, the Depression South, a family history). That assumption is based on our faith in the truth expressed by the photographic image ("seeing is believing," "pictures don't lie," etc.) and on our strong desire to understand the past, to make it cohere. The symbolic realism of still and moving pictures is more a product of the viewer's desire to make them symbolic than the result of any symbolism expressed in the images themselves. D. W. Griffith exploited his audience's faith in the photographic image and their desire to understand the past in *Birth of a Nation* (1915), an enormously popular film that Dos Passos had seen and admired. Most film historians agree that *Birth of a Nation,* an emotionally powerful but terribly distorted history of the Civil War and Reconstruction in the South, defined, in effect, the role of the film director for successive generations of moviemakers. "Griffith," writes Everett Carter, "made the ordering and interpretation—the art, in brief—one of the location, the angle, the movement of the camera, and of the juxtaposition of the images the camera records by means of cutting and arranging these images to bring out their significance" (354).

Still and moving photography provided a way of perceiving reality, and a way of ordering and interpreting history, which obviously suited Dos Passos's purposes in *U.S.A.* "The artist," he wrote, "must record the fleeting world the way the motion picture film recorded it. By contrast, juxtaposition, montage, he could build drama into his narrative" ("Novelist" 31). In the Newsreels he exploited the suggestive quality of cultural artifacts (snatches of popular songs and clippings from the newspapers) that, like photographs, possess a symbolic realism and a historical significance for the reader

beyond what their content can account for. The same could be said for the autobiographical significance of each Camera Eye, or the historical significance of each biographical sketch or fictional narrative. The fragmentation in the narrative of *U.S.A.* makes each fragment all that much more historically symbolic because the reader has only fragments, or "images" if you will, of history to satisfy his desire for coherence in the text and his desire to understand the past. During the reading process they become the same desire.[6]

Because the narrative is so fragmented, and the historical argument so embedded in its very structure, no single fragment of historical narration in the text—no single Biography, Newsreel, Camera Eye, or section of fictional narrative—can be read as a link in a chain of historical argument. And yet *U.S.A.* is full of historical arguments which are, paradoxically, never asserted. As a result, we are persuaded not by commentary and analysis, or by statements of cause and effect, or even by a narration of events occurring in sequence, but instead by fragments of newsprint removed from their original context, fictional narratives that tell the histories of characters in "representative" occupations, biographical sketches of public figures, experimental footage in the Camera Eye, and by the montage that results from their ordering in the text, to accept explanations for historical events. Despite the enormous size of the canvas, the collectivism of Dos Passos's chronicle is as illusory as its objectivity, for the entire chronicle is as infused with the historian's personal vision as a film by its director's. In short, Dos Passos's powerfully moving epic is a triumph of editing.

One could argue, I suppose, that Francis Parkman's *France and England in North America* (1865–1892), Page Smith's continuing *A People's History of the United States* (1976– ), and other so-called "narrative histories" are equally the products of editing. But there is a difference in kind between motion picture editing that, barring a narrative voiceover, carries the burden of narration itself (as editing does in *U.S.A.*), and the editing that narrative historians employ in the name of selectivity. Francis Parkman's narration and analysis of the conflict between Montcalm and Wolfe, and the respective forces in America they represented, are right there on the page for readers and scholars to accept or take issue with. Causality in motion pictures, on the other hand, is a hidden agenda.

Hayden White, who has ventured into poststructuralist theories of historical narrative, has gone so far as to assert that historical commentary itself is little more than a formalized projection of qualities assigned to the subject in the historian's original figuration of it. However much this may be true, there is still a difference in kind between the rhetoric of narrative figuration and the rhetoric of commentary: one tells a story while the other explains why it is true. The point I wish to make concerning *U.S.A.* is that Dos Passos employs the rhetoric of neither. American history from 1900 to 1929 is not narrated in *U.S.A.* even though that is its subject. Biography and autobiography are given narrative figuration in the work, but never history. The reader only encounters history between the lines of the text.

So what kind of history has Dos Passos given us in *U.S.A.* and of what value is it? I do not agree with historian John P. Diggins who says that what Dos Passos has given us is only "a vision of chaos" (329 *et passim*). Dos Passos was never a Marxist historian, but the absence of a clear Marxist dialectic working itself out in his history does not mean that he failed to find order in history. On the contrary, the failure of Americans to accept the responsibilities of freedom, to respect and uphold the principles of equal opportunity and freedom of speech upon which their nation was founded, or to see beyond their own selfish material interests, is a collective *moral failure* (for Dos Passos, like Gibbon in the eighteenth century, and like Parkman and the other American Progressive historians writing in the nineteenth century, was a moral historian) that operates as a principle of causality in every narrative sequence. That is why history seems so deterministic in *U.S.A.*, not because individuals are powerless to resist social and economic forces that remove human agency from history, but for the very opposite reason: moral failures carry, in Dos Passos's view, inevitable consequences. I could demonstrate this if I had more space, but surely the sense of betrayal that Dos Passos expresses so vehemently in the penultimate Camera Eye ("listen businessmen collegepresidents judges America will not forget her betrayers") is evidence enough that Dos Passos does not absolve individuals of responsibility for their nation's history.[7] If history seems chaotic in Dos Passos's rendering of it, it has less to do with the supposed absence of causality than the form in which he chose to reveal it.

Dos Passos would probably have agreed with Carlyle that "it is not in acted as it is in written History; actual events are nowise so simply related to each other as parent and offspring are; every single event is the offspring, not of one, but of all other events, prior or contemporaneous and will in turn combine with all others to give birth to new" (551). Robert Scholes has observed that it is now possible to say of narrative what Marx said of religion, that it is an opiate that provides a false sense of coherence, or an illusion of sequence. *U.S.A.* offers no "illusion of sequence," and Dos Passos may in fact have invented his radical form of historical narrative so as to make written history read more like

history as we live it: with no *apparent* control over its direction, ignorant of its ultimate meaning, and yet not blind to the multivarious patterns of causality that suggest themselves at each new turn of events. But *U.S.A.* does much more than mirror back to us our state of confusion over the ultimate direction of history. If we are to adequately assess the value of *U.S.A.* as history, we must first acknowledge the fact that history conceived as a social science has, in our century, pushed into the back seat history conceived as a rhetorical art expressing a national will and purpose. We forget that history was classically a rhetorical enterprise. The editors of *The Harvard Guide to American History* have not forgotten; they enter a plea on behalf of the rhetorical purposes of historical writing so that our histories might once again possess the power to move us from contemplation to action, the power "to make a young man want to fight for his country in war or live to make it a better country in peace" (4). There can be no denying the power of *U.S.A.* to make us hate the many injustices it exposes, such as growing economic inequality, special privilege, bigotry, oppression, and intolerance, and to make us want to work for their amelioration. The purpose of history in the hands of Dos Passos is once again a rhetorical one: to train the good citizen. That is why Dos Passos stresses individual responsibility in history, in the Camera Eye where he traces his gradual awakening to his own, and in the Newsreels, Biographies, and fictional narratives where the satire exposes individual and collective moral failures. In writing *U.S.A.* Dos Passos borrowed his rhetorical devices from the cinema, for he must have sensed in films such as *Potemkin* and *Birth of a Nation* the medium's extraordinary power to arouse and sway an audience. We need only recall the narrative assertions of America's manifest destiny in *Stagecoach, Patton,* and Frank Capra's *Why We Fight* series, or the failure of it in *The Deer Hunter* and *Apocalypse Now,* to realize that, in this century, the movies have appropriated the rhetorical enterprise of history—but not before Dos Passos appropriated the rhetoric of cinematic narrative for the writing of a history whose rhetorical aim would be to urge upon us the need to recover our national ideals.

—*South Atlantic Review,* 50 (January 1985): 75–86

### Notes

1. It has been suggested by John P. Diggins, in the most ambitious study to date of *U.S.A.* as historical literature ("Visions"), that because Dos Passos arranged a "panorama" of historical data "the total meaning of which he did not pretend to comprehend," the historiographic term "chronicle" is an appropriate one, especially if we accept Benedetto Croce's definition of chronicle as "dead history"—dead because the chronicler, unlike the historian,

makes no attempt to understand the ultimate significance of what he records. I think it is a mistake to confuse the sort of chronicle Dos Passos wrote with what Croce condemned. The arrangement of history in *U.S.A.* is not so "random" as Diggins contends, and Dos Passos's quest for historical understanding implicit in that arrangement would probably have pleased Croce more than the ideological conviction that Diggins recommends as a prerequisite to the writing of history.

2. Some recent notable exceptions include the article by Diggins cited above, and articles by Foley, Hughson, and Marz.

3. "Somewhere along the way I had been impressed by Eisenstein's motion pictures, by his version of old D. W. Griffith's technique. Montage was his key word" ("Novelist" 31).

4. For an application of this thesis to the whole of *U.S.A.*, see Ward, 38–61.

5. This criticism was first voiced by Whipple.

6. For this analysis of the reader's response to history I am indebted to Hernadi.

7. For a fuller demonstration of this thesis, see my "Representative Men."

### Works Cited

Carlyle, Thomas. "On History." *The Works of Thomas Carlyle*. New York: Collier Edition, 1897. 14: 546–557.

Carter, Everett. "Cultural History Written with Lightning: The Significance of *Birth of a Nation*." *American Quarterly*, 12 (1960): 347–357.

Chatman, Seymour. "What Novels Can Do That Films Can't (and Vice Versa)." *Critical Inquiry*, 7 (1980): 121–140.

Colley, Iain. *Dos Passos and the Fiction of Despair*. Totowa, N.J.: Rowman & Littlefield, 1978.

Diggins, John P. "Visions of Chaos and Visions of Order: Dos Passos as Historian." *American Literature*, 46 (1974): 329–346.

Dos Passos, John. *The Big Money* (1936).

Dos Passos. "What Makes a Novelist." *National Review* (16 January 1968): 29–32.

Foley, Barbara. "History, Fiction, and Satiric Form: The Example of Dos Passos's *1919*." *Genre*, 12 (1979): 357–378.

Freidel, Frank, and Showman, Richard K., eds. *The Harvard Guide to American History*. Cambridge, Mass.: Harvard University Press, 1974.

Hernadi, Paul. "The Erotics of Retrospection: History-telling, Audience Response, and the Strategies of Desire." *New Literary History*, 12 (1981): 243–252.

Hughson, Lois. "Dos Passos's World War: Narrative Technique and History." *Studies in the Novel*, 12 (1980): 46–61.

Maine, Barry. "Representative Men in Dos Passos's *The 42nd Parallel*." *Clio*, 12 (1982): 31–43.

Marz, Charles. "*U.S.A.*: Chronicle and Performance." *Modern Fiction Studies*, 26 (1980): 398–416.

Rosen, Robert C. *John Dos Passos: Politics and the Writer*. Lincoln: University of Nebraska Press, 1981.

Scholes, Robert. "Language, Narrative, and Anti-Narrative." *Critical Inquiry*, 7 (1980): 204–212.

Wagner, Linda. *Dos Passos: Artist as American*. Austin: University of Texas Press, 1979.

Ward, John William. *Red, White, and Blue: Men, Books, and Ideas in American Culture*. New York: Oxford University Press, 1969.

Whipple, T. K. Review of *U.S.A.*, by John Dos Passos. *Nation* (19 February 1938): 210–212.

White, Hayden. "Fictions of Factual Representation." *The Literature of Fact: Selected Papers from the English Institute*, edited by Angus Fletcher. New York: Columbia University Press, 1976.

# CHAPTER 3:

# BACKGROUNDS AND SOURCES: AMERICAN SOCIETY, 1900–1931

## RADICALISM

*Dos Passos presented in particular three strains in American radicalism from the beginning of the twentieth century to the onset of the Depression: the prominence of the Industrial Workers of the World (IWW) from its founding in 1905 until America entered World War I; the rise of an intellectual Left around 1910 and continuing thereafter; and the increasing role of the Communist Party within the Left during the 1920s.*

## The IWW

*Dos Passos's frequent depiction in the narratives and biographies of* The 42nd Parallel *and* Nineteen-Nineteen *of significant IWW events and personalities constitutes a capsule history of the movement. The IWW had its roots and strongest support in the mining and lumber camps of the Far West (its charismatic leader, Big Bill Haywood, emerged from this setting) and later sought to engage eastern industrial workers. It was ruthlessly suppressed wherever it attempted to play a role in the many labor disputes of the period and thereby produced several martyrs. As with the Socialists and their leader, Eugene Debs, the IWW's opposition to America's entrance into World War I caused it to lose prominence after 1918.*

*In* U.S.A., *Fenian "Mac" McCreary seeks to aid the IWW during the strike of 1906–1907 in Goldfield, Nevada, where Haywood makes a speech. Anne Elizabeth "Daughter" Trent and Ben Compton walk on the picket line in the IWW-led Paterson, New Jersey, textile strike of 1913, which inspired contemporary artists and writers to produce the famous Madison Square Garden pageant depicting the strike. Ben attempts to assert the IWW's right to free speech and assembly during a 1916 demonstration in Everett, Washington, at which several union members were killed. Dos Passos complements these narrative events with biographies of Haywood and the two IWW martyrs Joe Hill and Wesley Everest.*

*Dos Passos sympathetically depicts the pull of the IWW's social ideals but is also at pains, especially in the Mac narrative, to suggest a significant basis for the demise of the movement in the*

*equally powerful pull on the working class of "bourgeois" attractions. (Dos Passos had initially planned to include another IWW narrative figure, Ike Hall. When he decided to omit this narrative from* U.S.A., *he published several completed excerpts from it.)*

### The Origin of the IWW
Melvyn Dubofsky

*Dubofsky presents a brief account of the origin and basic principles of the Industrial Workers of the World.*

For three days [in January 1905] this motley assortment of radicals thrashed out their differences, at last agreeing upon eleven principles for reforming the labor movement. Of these the following were the most significant: (1) creation of a general industrial union embracing all industries; (2) the new organization to be founded on recognition of the class struggle and administered on the basis of an irrepressible conflict between capital and labor; (3) all power to reside in the collective membership; (4) universal free transfer of union cards; and (5) a call for a general convention to form a national labor organization in accordance with the conference's basic principles.[1]

Considerable confusion remained hidden within the eleven principles. The proposed organization ostensibly devoted to industrial unionism, for example, was also dedicated in advance to: "craft autonomy locally; industrial autonomy internationally; working class unity, generally." Just how the conferees expected to retain craft autonomy and industrial unionism, industrial autonomy and working-class solidarity, went unexplained. Apparently, some strange labor metaphysics made some working-class concerns peculiar to certain industries, crafts, or localities, in which case autonomy would prevail. Nor did the conferees reach a consensus about the proper political role for their proposed organization. Socialists saw it essentially as a branch of the party (the SLP, if they were DeLeonites); yet the Westerners, while claiming to be socialists, remained suspicions of politics, politicians, and the state. Representing the Western influence predominant at the January sessions, Hagerty pushed through the following resolution: "That this Union be established as the economic organization of the working class without affiliation with any political party."[2] Hardly a position to excite Socialist party politicians!

But uncertainties and conflicts dissolved in the euphoric atmosphere of the Chicago conference, which, at its end, adopted the famous and widely quoted Industrial Union Manifesto. This manifesto reflected a Marxist view of the evolution of society, a view which Trautmann, Algie Simons, and Hagerty had derived from books, and which Western workers had derived from experience. It also distilled into a few terse paragraphs the signatories' scorn for AFL-type craft unionism. The manifesto, which might be considered the IWW's Old Testament, merits extended quotation.

> The worker wholly separated from the land and the tools with his skill or craftsmanship rendered useless is sunk in the uniform mass of wage slaves. He sees his power of resistance broken by craft divisions, perpetuated from outgrown industrial stages. His wages constantly grow less as his hours grow longer and monopolized prices go higher. Shifted hither and thither by the demands of the profit takers, the laborer's home no longer exists. In his helpless condition, he is forced to accept whatever humiliating conditions his master may impose. . . . Laborers are no longer classified by differences in trade skill, but the employer assorts them according to the machines to which they are attached. These divisions, far from representing differences in skill, or interests among laborers, are imposed by the employers that workers may be pitted against one another . . . and that all resistance to capitalist tyranny may be weakened by artificial, fratricidal distinctions.
>
> . . . [Craft unionism] offers only a perpetual struggle for slight relief within wage slavery. It is blind to the possibility of establishing an industrial democracy wherein there shall be no wage slavery, but where the workers will own the tools which they operate and the products of which they alone will enjoy.[3]

To change this obnoxious craft-union system, the manifesto asked all true believers in industrial unionism to meet in Chicago on June 27, 1905, to establish a new national labor organization based upon the Marxist concept of the class struggle and committed to the construction of the cooperative commonwealth. This invitation was sent to American radicals and trade unionists, and to European labor organizations, among whom it engendered especially acute interest and heated debate. Max Hayes continued to criticize these proposals and to deny that

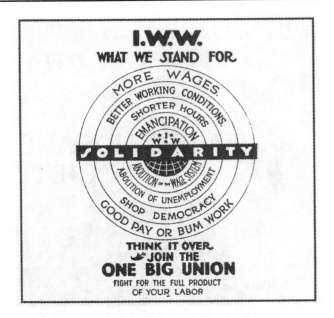

*Poster stating the basic demands of the Industrial Workers of the World for the improvement of working conditions along with the Marxist notion of working class "solidarity" in "one big union" (from Stewart Bird et al.,* Solidarity Forever, *1985)*

Socialists had formulated them. (On the last point he was more than half right.) Even Samuel Gompers joined the debate, devoting three issues of the *American Federationist* to an attack upon the so-called industrial unionists, whom he labeled "union smashers."[4] Algie Simons and Frank Bohn, both participants in the January conference, debated the significance of the manifesto in the *International Socialist Review*. Conceding the importance of the approaching industrial union convention, as well as the failure of the AFL to adjust to contemporary economic life, Simons yet wondered: ". . . Is the present the proper time for such a change to come? If it is not, then this organization will be a thing born out of due time, a cause of disorder, confusion, and injury." For a time, Simons surmounted his doubts and favored the new challenge to the AFL. His reservations nevertheless illustrate just how tenuous indeed was the connection between the Socialist party's anti-AFL faction and the birth of the IWW; only two years after the IWW's birth, Simons' skepticism regarding the new industrial union movement, combined with his reluctance to fight the established unions, led him to desert the Wobblies. Frank Bohn, then a Socialist Labor party member, answered Simons' questions, and in so doing demonstrated why his party, rather than the Socialist party, linked itself tightly to the IWW. Denying the possibility of capturing the old unions by boring from within, Bohn considered the occasion ripe for industrial unionism. Hence he called upon his friends within the SLP and also within the craft unions to enter the proposed new labor organization, scuttle trade unionism, and adopt class-conscious industrial unionism.[5]

*–We Shall Be All: A History of the Industrial Workers of the World* (Urbana: University of Illinois Press, 1988), pp. 78–80

## Notes

1. *Proceedings of the First Convention of the Industrial Workers of the World* (New York, 1905), p. 88.

2. Ibid., p. 86.

3. Ibid., pp. 86–89.

4. Max Hayes, *International Socialist Review*, 5 (February 1905): 500–501; Gompers to Max Morris, 2 February 1905, Gompers Letterbooks, volume 96, AFL-CIO Headquarters, Washington, D.C.; *American Federationist*, 12 (March 1905): 139–141; (April 1905): 214–217; (June 1905): 354–361.

5. Algie M. Simons, *International Socialist Review*, 5 (February 1905): 496–499; Bohn, "Concerning the Chicago Manifesto," *International Socialist Review*, 5 (March 1905): 585–589.

## Solidarity Forever [The IWW "Anthem"]
Ralph Chaplin

*The IWW movement produced an exceptional number of powerful songs, of which "Solidarity Forever" is perhaps the best known.*

[Sung to the tune of *John Brown's Body*]

When the Union's inspiration through the workers
    blood shall run,
There can be no power greater anywhere beneath the
    sun.
Yet what force on earth is weaker than the feeble
    strength of one?
But the Union makes us strong.

*Solidarity forever!*
*Solidarity forever!*
*Solidarity forever!*
*For the Union makes us strong.*

Is there aught we hold in common with the greedy par-
    asite
Who would lash us into serfdom and would crush us
    with his might?
Is there anything left to us but to organize and fight?
For the Union makes us strong. *[chorus]*

It is we who plowed the prairies; built the cities where
    they trade;

Dug the mines and built the workshops; endless miles
    of railroad laid.
Now we stand outcast and starving, 'midst the wonders
    we have made;
But the Union makes us strong. *[chorus]*

All the world that's owned by idle drones is ours and
    ours alone.
We have laid the wide foundations; built it skyward
    stone by stone.
It is ours, not to slave in, but to master and to own,
While the Union makes us strong. *[chorus]*

They have taken untold millions that they never toiled
    to earn,
But without our brain and muscle not a single wheel
    can turn.
We can break their haughty power; gain our freedom
    when we learn
That the Union makes us strong. *[chorus]*

In our hands is placed a power greater than their
    hoarded gold;
Greater than the might of armies, magnified a
    thousand-fold.
We can bring to birth a new world from the ashes of
    the old.
For the Union makes us strong. *[chorus]*

*–Stewart Bird, Dan Georgakas, and Deborah Shaffer, eds., Solidarity Forever: An Oral History of the IWW* (Chicago: Lake View Press, 1985)

## *Big Bill*
Dos Passos

*In this biography and that of Eugene Debs, Dos Passos notes how the vibrant early American radical movement was crushed because of its opposition to American participation in World War I.*

Big Bill Haywood was born in sixty nine in a boarding-house in Salt Lake City.

He was raised in Utah, got his schooling in Ophir a mining camp with shooting scrapes, faro Saturday nights, whisky spilled on pokertables piled with new silver dollars.

When he was eleven his mother bound him out to a farmer, he ran away because the farmer lashed him with a whip. That was his first strike.

He lost an eye whittling a slingshot out of scruboak.

He worked for storekeepers, ran a fruitstand, ushered in the Salt Lake Theatre, was a messengerboy, bellhop at the Continental Hotel.

When he was fifteen

he went out to the mines in Humboldt County, Nevada,

his outfit was overalls, a jumper, a blue shirt, mining boots, two pair of blankets, a set of chessmen, boxinggloves and a big lunch of plum pudding his mother fixed for him.

When he married he went to live in Fort McDermitt built in the old days against the Indians, abandoned now that there was no more frontier;

there his wife bore their first baby without doctor or midwife. Bill cut the navelstring, Bill buried the afterbirth;

the child lived. Bill earned money as he could surveying, haying in Paradise Valley, breaking colts, riding a wide rangy country.

One night at Thompson's Mill, he was one of five men who met by chance and stopped the night in the abandoned ranch. Each of them had lost an eye, they were the only one-eyed men in the county.

They lost the homestead, things went to pieces, his wife was sick, he had children to support. He went to work as a miner at Silver City.

At Silver City, Idaho, he joined the W.F.M., there he held his first union office; he was delegate of the Silver City miners to the convention of the Western Federation of Miners held in Salt Lake City in '98.

From then on he was an organizer, a speaker, an exhorter, the wants of all the miners were his wants; he fought Coeur D'Alenes, Telluride, Cripple Creek,

joined the Socialist Party, wrote and spoke through Idaho, Utah, Nevada, Montana, Colorado to miners striking for an eight hour day, better living, a share of the wealth they hacked out of the hills.

In Chicago in January 1905 a conference was called that met at the same hall in Lake Street where the Chicago anarchists had addressed meetings twenty years before.

William D. Haywood was permanent chairman. It was this conference that wrote the manifesto that brought into being the I.W.W.

When he got back to Denver he was kidnapped to Idaho and tried with Moyer and Pettibone for the murder of the sheepherder Steuenberg, exgovernor of Idaho, blown up by a bomb in his own home.

When they were acquitted at Boise (Darrow was their lawyer) Big Bill Haywood was known as a workingclass leader from coast to coast.

Now the wants of all the workers were his wants, he was the spokesman of the West, of the cowboys and the lumberjacks and the harvesthands and the miners.

*IWW leader Big Bill Haywood, the subject of "Big Bill" in* The 42nd Parallel, *who had the capacity, in his oratory, physical size, and demeanor, to project a sense of raw power (Culver Pictures, Inc.)*

(The steamdrill had thrown thousands of miners out of work; the steamdrill had thrown a scare into all the miners of the West.)

The W.F.M. was going conservative. Haywood worked with the I.W.W. *building a new society in the shell of the old,* campaigned for Debs for President in 1908 on the Red Special. He was in on all the big strikes in the East where revolutionary spirit was growing, Lawrence, Paterson, the strike of the Minnesota ironworkers.

They went over with the A.E.F. to save the Morgan loans, to save Wilsonian Democracy, they stood at Napoleon's tomb and dreamed empire, they had champagne cocktails at the Ritz bar and slept with Russian countesses in Montmartre and dreamed empire, all over the country at American legion posts and business men's luncheons it was worth money to make the eagle scream;

they lynched the pacifists and the proGermans and the wobblies and the reds and the bolsheviks.

Bill Haywood stood trial with the hundred and one
at Chicago where judge Landis the baseball czar

with the lack of formality of a traffic court

handed out his twenty year sentences and thirty-
thousand dollar fines.

After two years in Leavenworth they let them bail
out Big Bill (he was fifty years old a heavy broken man),
the war was over but they'd learned empire in the Hall of
the Mirrors at Versailles;

the courts refused a new trial.

It was up to Haywood to jump his bail or to go back
to prison for twenty years.

He was sick with diabetes, he had had a rough life,
prison had broken down his health. Russia was a workers'
republic; he went to Russia and was in Moscow a couple
of years but he wasn't happy there, that world was too
strange for him. He died there and they burned his big
broken hulk of a body and buried the ashes under the
Kremlin wall.

*—The 42nd Parallel, pp. 87–89*

## The Source of Mac
Townsend Ludington

*Dos Passos met Gladwin Bland, the source of Mac in*
U.S.A., *during a visit to Mexico in the winter of 1926–1927.*

An American whose tales particularly amused
[Dos Passos] was Gladwin Bland, a tall, well-built person somewhat older than he, who for years had been
a member of the revolutionary union, Industrial
Workers of the World (I.W.W.), and an itinerant
worker. But that life had been hard, he told Dos Passos, and he had eventually settled in Mexico, married
a Mexican woman, and was now selling used furniture, among other business enterprises. He was full of
stories about the left-wing movement, Dos Passos
recalled, telling them with a satiric skepticism that
appealed to Dos Passos's own sense of irony. When
he began writing *The 42nd Parallel* a year or so later,
Bland's tales loomed large in Dos Passos's mind, and
the retired Wobbly (as I.W.W. members were nick-
named) became the model for Fenian McCreary, the
most nearly central character in the first volume of the
*U.S.A.* trilogy. Mac's story paralleled Bland's so
closely that, after his wife had read *The 42nd Parallel,*
Bland wrote Dos Passos in mock indignation, declaring, "I can well forgive you for having given me a
dose of clapp but for the incident of the cat [a cat nursing its kittens on the family bed of a woman Mac
sleeps with], never. 'Mi vida del doctor Jekyll y Mister
Hyde' in Mexico was about laid bare in the book."

*—John Dos Passos: A Twentieth Century Odyssey*
(New York: Dutton, 1980), p. 251

## Mac
Dos Passos

*Mac, a printer, has gone to help out the union during the*
*1907 IWW strike at Goldfield, Nevada. Despite learning that*
*his girlfriend, Maisie, is pregnant, he is inspired by Haywood's*
*speech to the miners and, for the moment, decides to remain in*
*Goldfield.*

Mac had hardly gotten off the train at Goldfield
when a lanky man in khaki shirt and breeches, wearing
canvas army leggins, went up to him. "If you don't
mind, what's your business in this town, brother?" "I'm
travelin' in books." "What kinda books?" "School-
books and the like, for Truthseeker, Inc. of Chicago."
Mac rattled it off very fast, and the man seemed
impressed. "I guess you're all right," he said. "Going up
to the Eagle?" Mac nodded. "Plug'll take ye up, the
feller with the team . . . You see we're looking out for
these goddam agitators, the I Won't Work outfit."

Outside the Golden Eagle Hotel there were two
soldiers on guard, toughlooking sawedoff men with their
hats over their eyes. When Mac went in everybody at
the bar turned and looked at him. He said "Good
evening, gents," as snappily as possible and went up to
the proprietor to ask for a room. All the while he was
wondering who the hell he dared ask where the office of
the *Nevada Workman* was. "I guess I can fix you up with a
bed. Travelin' man?" "Yes," said Mac. "In books."
Down at the end a big man with walrus whiskers was
standing at the bar talking fast in a drunken whining
voice, "If they'd only give me my head I'd run the bastards outa town soon enough. Too goddam many lawyers mixed up in this. Run the sonsobitches out. If they
resists shoot 'em, that's what I says to the Governor, but
they're all these sonsobitches a lawyers fussin' everythin'
up all the time with warrants and habeas corpus and
longwinded rigmarole. My ass to habeas corpus." "All
right, Joe, you tell 'em," said the proprietor soothingly.
Mac bought a cigar and sauntered out. As the door
closed behind him the big man was yelling out again, "I
said, My ass to habeas corpus."

It was nearly dark. An icy wind blew through the
ramshackle clapboard streets. His feet stumbling in the
mud of the deep ruts, Mac walked round several blocks
looking up at dark windows. He walked all over the
town but no sign of a newspaper office. When he found
himself passing the same Chink hashjoint for the third
time, he slackened his steps and stood irresolutely on
the curb. At the end of the street the great jagged shank
of a hill hung over the town. Across the street a young
man, his head and ears huddled into the collar of a
mackinaw, was loafing against the dark window of a

hardware store. Mac decided he was a squarelooking stiff and went over to speak to him.

"Say, bo, where's the office of the *Nevada Workman?*" "What the hell d'you wanter know for?" Mac and the other man looked at each other. "I want to see Fred Hoff . . . I came on from San Fran to help in the printin'." "Got a red card?" Mac pulled out his I.W.W. membership card. "I've got my union card, too, if you want to see that."

"Hell, no . . . I guess you're all right, but, as the feller said, suppose I'd been a dick, you'd be in the bullpen now, bo."

"I told 'em I was a friggin' bookagent to get into the damn town. Spent my last quarter on a cigar to keep up the burjwa look."

The other man laughed. "All right, fellowworker. I'll take you round."

"What they got here, martial law?" asked Mac as he followed the man down an alley between two overgrown shanties.

"Every sonofabitchin' yellerleg in the State of Nevada right here in town . . . Lucky if you don't get run outa town with a bayonet in yer crotch, as the feller said."

At the end of the alley was a small house like a shoebox with brightly lit windows. Young fellows in miners' clothes or overalls filled up the end of the alley and sat three deep on the rickety steps. "What's this, a poolroom?" asked Mac. "This is the *Nevada Workman* . . . Say, my name's Ben Evans; I'll introjuce you to the gang . . . Say, yous guys, this is fellowworker McCreary . . . he's come on from Frisco to set up type." "Put it there, Mac," said a sixfooter who looked like a Swede lumberman, and gave Mac's hand a wrench that made the bones crack.

Fred Hoff had on a green eyeshade and sat behind a desk piled with galleys. He got up and shook hands. "Oh, boy, you're just in time. There's hell to pay. They got the printer in the bullpen and we've got to get this sheet out." Mac took off his coat and went back to look over the press. He was leaning over the typesetter's "stone" when Fred Hoff came back and beckoned him into a corner.

"Say, Mac, I want to explain the layout here . . . It's kind of a funny situation . . . The W.F.M.'s goin' yellow on us . . . It's a hell of a scrap. The Saint was here the other day and that bastard Mullany shot him through both arms and he's in hospital now . . . They're sore as a boil because we're instillin' ideas of revolutionary solidarity, see? We got the restaurant workers out and we got some of the minin' stiffs. Now the A.F. of L.'s gettin' wise and they've got a bonehead scab organizer in hobnobbin' with the mineowners at the Montezuma Club."

"Hey, Fred, let me take this on gradually," said Mac.

"Then there was a little shootin' the other day out in front of a restaurant down the line an' the stiff that owned the joint got plugged an' now they've got a couple of the boys in jail for that." "The hell you say." "And Big Bill Haywood's comin' to speak next week . . . That's about the way the situation is, Mac. I've got to tear off an article . . . You're boss printer an' we'll pay you seventeen fifty like we all get. Ever written any?"

"No."

"It's a time like this a feller regrets he didn't work harder in school. Gosh, I wish I could write decent."

"I'll take a swing at an article if I get a chance."

"Big Bill'll write us some stuff. He writes swell."

They set up a cot for Mac back of the press. It was a week before he could get time to go round to the Eagle to get his suitcase. Over the office and the presses was a long attic, with a stove in it, where most of the boys slept. Those that had blankets rolled up in their blankets, those that hadn't put their jackets over their heads, those that didn't have jackets slept as best they could. At the end of the room was a long sheet of paper where someone had printed out the Preamble in shaded block letters. On the plaster wall of the office someone had drawn a cartoon of a workingstiff labelled "I.W.W." giving a fat man in a stovepipe hat labelled "mineowner" a kick in the seat of the pants, Above it they had started to letter "solidarity" but had only gotten as far as "S O L I D A ."

One November night Big Bill Haywood spoke at the miners' union. Mac and Fred Hoff went to report the speech for the paper. The town looked lonely as an old trashdump in the huge valley full of shrill wind and driving snow. The hall was hot and steamy with the steam of big bodies and plug tobacco and thick mountaineer clothes that gave off the shanty smell of oil lamps and charred firewood and greasy fryingpans and raw whisky. At the beginning of the meeting men moved round uneasily, shuffling their feet and clearing the phlegm out of their throats. Mac was uncomfortable himself. In his pocket was a letter from Maisie. He knew it by heart:

DEAREST FAINY:

Everything has happened just as I was afraid of. You know what I mean, dearest little husband. It's two months already and I'm so frightened and there's nobody I can tell. Darling, you must come right back. I'll die if you don't. Honestly I'll die and I'm so lonely for you anyways and so afraid somebody'll notice. As it is we'll have to go away somewheres when we're married and not come back until plenty of time has elapsed. If I thought I could get work there I'd come to you to Goldfield. I think it would be nice if we went to San Diego. I have friends there and they say it's lovely and there we could tell people we'd been married a long time. Please come sweetest little husband. I'm so lonely for you and it's so terrible to stand this all alone. The crosses are kisses. Your loving wife,

MAISIE

XXXXXXXXXXXXXXXX

Big Bill talked about solidarity and sticking together in the face of the masterclass and Mac kept wondering what Big Bill would do if he'd got a girl in trouble like that. Big Bill was saying the day had come to start building a new society in the shell of the old and for the workers to get ready to assume control of the industries they'd created out of their sweat and blood. When he said, "We stand for the one big union," there was a burst of cheering and clapping from all the wobblies in the hall. Fred Hoff nudged Mac as he clapped. "Let's raise the roof, Mac." The exploiting classes would be helpless against the solidarity of the whole working class. The militia and the yellowlegs were workingstiffs too. Once they realized the historic mission of solidarity the masterclass couldn't use them to shoot down their brothers anymore. The workers must realize that every small fight, for higher wages, for freespeech, for decent living conditions, was only significant as part of the big fight for the revolution and the coöperative commonwealth. Mac forgot about Maisie. By the time Big Bill had finished speaking his mind had run ahead of the speech so that he'd forgotten just what he said, but Mac was in a glow all over and was cheering to beat hell. He and Fred Hoff were cheering and the stocky Bohemian miner that smelt so bad next them was clapping and the oneeyed Pole on the other side was clapping and the bunch of Wops were clapping and the little Jap who was waiter at the Montezuma Club was clapping and the sixfoot ranchman who'd come in in hopes of seeing a fight was clapping. "Ain't the sonofabitch some orator," he was saying again and again. "I tellyer, Utah's the state for mansized men. I'm from Ogden myself."

–The 42nd Parallel, pp. 91–95

## Daughter and Ben Compton: The Paterson Textile Strike, 1913

Dos Passos

*Daughter, born and bred on a Texas ranch, is introduced to the world of working-class struggle by Webb, a fellow Columbia University journalism student. In Paterson they*

*Haywood (tall figure on left) leading a parade of textile workers during a January 1913 strike in Paterson, New Jersey, the first significant test of the IWW to organize workers in the East (from Stewart Bird et al.,* Solidarity Forever, *1985)*

*encounter Ben Compton, a New York Jew, who is to become a Communist labor leader.*

After Christmas Webb got all wrapped up in a strike of textile workers that was going on in a town over in New Jersey. One Sunday they went over to see what it was like. They got off the train at a grimy brick station in the middle of the empty business section, a few people standing around in front of lunchcounters, empty stores closed for Sunday; there seemed nothing special about the town until they walked out to the long low square brick buildings of the mills. There were knots of policemen in blue standing about in the wide muddy roadway outside and inside the wiremesh gates huskylooking young men in khaki. "Those are special deputies, the sons of bitches," muttered Webb between his teeth. They went to Strike Headquarters to see a girl Webb knew who was doing publicity for them. At the head of a grimy stairway crowded with greyfaced foreign men and women in faded greylooking clothes, they found an office noisy with talk and click of typewriters. The hallway was piled with stacks of handbills that a tiredlooking young man was giving out in packages to boys in ragged sweaters. Webb found Sylvia Dalhart, a longnosed girl with glasses who was typing madly at a desk piled with newspapers and clippings. She waved a hand and said, "Webb, wait for me outside. I'm going to show some newspaper guys around and you'd better come."

Out in the hall they ran into a fellow Webb knew, Ben Compton, a tall young man with a long thin nose and red-rimmed eyes, who said he was going to speak at the meeting and asked Webb if he wouldn't speak. "Jeez, what could I say to those fellers? I'm just a bum of a college stoodjent, like you, Ben." "Tell 'em the workers have got to win the world, tell 'em this fight is part of a great historic battle. Talking's the easiest part of the movement. The truth's simple enough." He had an explosive way of talking with a pause between each sentence, as if the sentence took sometime to come up from someplace way down inside. Daughter sized up that he was attractive, even though he was probably a Jew. "Well, I'll try to stammer out something about democracy in industry," said Webb.

Sylvia Dalhart was already pushing them down the stairs. She had with her a pale young man in a raincoat and black felt hat who was chewing the end of a half of a cigar that had gone out. "Fellowworkers, this is Joe Biglow from the *Globe*," she had a western burr in her voice that made Daughter feel at home. "We're going to show him around."

They went all over town, to strikers' houses where tired-looking women in sweaters out at the elbows were cooking up lean Sunday dinners of corned beef and cabbage or stewed meat and potatoes, or in some houses they just had cabbage and bread or just potatoes. Then they went to a lunchroom near the station and ate some lunch. Daughter paid the check as nobody seemed to have any money, and it was time to go to the meeting.

The trolleycar was crowded with strikers and their wives and children. The meeting was to be held in the next town because in that town the Mills owned everything and there was no way of hiring a hall. It had started to sleet, and they got their feet wet wading through the slush to the mean frame building where the meeting was going to be held. When they got to the door there were mounted police out in front. "Hall full," a cop told them at the streetcorner, "no more allowed inside."

They stood around in the sleet waiting for somebody with authority. There were thousands of strikers, men and women and boys and girls, the older people talking among themselves in low voices in foreign languages. Webb kept saying, "Jesus, this is outrageous. Somebody ought to do something." Daughter's feet were cold and she wanted to go home.

Then Ben Compton came around from the back of the building. People began to gather around him, "There's Ben . . . there's Compton, good boy, Benny," she heard people saying. Young men moved around through the crowd whispering, "Overflow meeting . . . stand your ground, folks."

He began to speak hanging by one arm from a lamppost. "Comrades, this is another insult flung in the face of the working class. There are not more than forty people in the hall and they close the doors and tell us it's full . . ." The crowd began swaying back and forth, hats, umbrellas bobbing in the sleety rain. Then she saw the two cops were dragging Compton off and heard the jangle of the patrolwagon. "Shame, shame," people yelled. They began to back off from the cops; the flow was away from the hall. People were moving quietly and dejectedly down the street toward the trolley tracks with the cordon of mounted police pressing them on. Suddenly Webb whispered in her ear, "Let me lean on your shoulder," and jumped on a hydrant.

"This is outrageous," he shouted, "you people had a permit to use the hall and had hired it and no power on earth has a right to keep you out of it. To hell with the cossacks."

Two mounted police were loping towards him, opening a lane through the crowd as they came. Webb was off the hydrant and had grabbed Daughter's hand, "Let's run like hell," he whispered and was off doubling back and forth among the scurrying people. She followed him laughing and out of breath. A trolley car was coming down the main street. Webb caught it on the move but she couldn't make it and had to wait for the next car. Meanwhile the cops were riding slowly back and forth among the crowd breaking it up.

. . . . . . . . . .

She didn't see him for several days, then one evening he called and asked her if she wanted to go out on the picket line next morning. It was still dark when she met him at the ferry station. They were both cold and sleepy and didn't say much going out on the train. From the train they had to run through the slippery streets to get to the mills in time to join the picket line. Faces looked cold and pinched in the blue early light. Women had shawls over their heads, few of the men or boys had overcoats. The young girls were all shivering in their cheap fancy topcoats that had no warmth to them. The cops had already begun to break up the head of the line. Some of the strikers were singing *Solidarity Forever*, others were yelling Scabs, Scabs and making funny long jeering hoots. Daughter was confused and excited.

Suddenly everybody around her broke and ran and left her in a stretch of empty street in front of the wire fencing of the mills. Ten feet in front of her a young woman slipped and fell. Daughter caught the scared look in her eyes that were round and black. Daughter stepped forward to help her up but two policemen were ahead of her swinging their night-sticks. Daughter thought they were going to help the girl up. She stood still for a second, frozen in her tracks when she saw one of the policemen's feet shoot out. He'd kicked the girl full in the face. Daughter never remembered what happened except that she was wanting a gun and punching into the policeman's big red face and against the buttons and the thick heavy cloth of his overcoat. Something crashed down on her head from behind; dizzy and sick she was being pushed into the policewagon. In front of her was the girl's face all caved in and bleeding. In the darkness inside were other men and women cursing and laughing. But Daughter and the woman opposite looked at each other dazedly and said nothing. Then the door closed behind them and they were in the dark.

When they were committed she was charged with rioting, felonious assault, obstructing an officer and inciting to sedition. It wasn't so bad in the county jail. The women's section was crowded with strikers, all the cells were full of girls laughing and talking, singing songs and telling each other how they'd been arrested, how long they'd been in, how they were going to win the strike. In Daughter's cell the girls all clustered around her and wanted to know how she'd gotten there. She began to feel she was quite a hero. Towards evening her name was called and she found Webb and Ada and a lawyer clustered around the policesergeant's desk. Ada was mad, "Read that, young woman, and see how that'll sound back home," she said, poking an afternoon paper under her nose.

TEXAS BELLE ASSAULTS COP said one headline. Then followed an account of her knocking down a policeman with a left on the jaw. She was released on a thousand dollars bail; outside the jail, Ben Compton broke away from the group of reporters around him and rushed up to her. "Congratulations, Miss Trent," he said, "that was a darn nervy thing to do . . . made a very good impression in the press." Sylvia Dalhart was with him. She threw her arms around her and kissed her: "That was a mighty spunky thing to do. Say, we're sending a delegation to Washington to see President Wilson and present a petition and we want you on it. The President will refuse to see the delegation and you'll have a chance to picket the White House and get arrested again."

–*Nineteen-Nineteen*, pp. 589–591, 594–595

## I Dreamed I Saw Joe Hill Last Night
Alfred Hayes

*As Dos Passos's biography "Joe Hill" in* Nineteen-Nineteen *recounts, Hill, an IWW agitator, was executed in Utah for a crime he probably did not commit. "I Dreamed I Saw Joe Hill Last Night" became one of the staples of left-wing ballad singers, especially during the 1930s.*

In 1925, a young poet, Alfred Hayes, wrote "I Dreamed I Saw Joe Hill Last Night." Several years later Earl Robinson set the words to music and the song became one of the major factors in the perpetuation of Hill's story. When Paul Robeson sang it before a group of unemployed Welsh miners in London in the 1930's, a listener remembers that the audience was ". . . thunderstruck by the power and beauty of Robeson's rendition of the song." There are other notable accounts of the ballad's impact on people who learned of Hill for the first time through these words:

> I dreamed I saw Joe Hill last night,
> Alive as you and me.
> Says I, "But Joe you're ten years dead,"
> "I never died," says he,
> "I never died," says he.

*Labor activist Joe Hill, the subject of a biography in* Nineteen-Nineteen, *shortly after his arrest in January 1914 ( from Gibbs M. Smith,* Labor Martyr: Joe Hill, *1969)*

"In Salt Lake, Joe," says I to him,
Him standing by my bed,
"They framed you on a murder charge,"
Says Joe, "But I ain't dead,"
Says Joe, "But I ain't dead."

"The copper bosses killed you, Joe,
They shot you, Joe," says I.
"Takes more than guns to kill a man,"
Says Joe, "I didn't die,"
Says Joe, "I didn't die."

And standing there as big as life
And smiling with his eyes,
Joe says, "What they forgot to kill
Went on to organize,
Went on to organize."

"Joe Hill ain't dead," he says to me,
"Joe Hill ain't never died.
Where workingmen are out on strike
Joe Hill is at their side,
Joe Hill is at their side."

"From San Diego up to Maine,
In every mine and mill,
Where workers strike and organize,"
Says he, "You'll find Joe Hill,"
Says he, "You'll find Joe Hill."

I dreamed I saw Joe Hill last night,
Alive as you or me.
Says I, "But Joe, you're ten years dead,"
"I never died," says he,
"I never died," says he.

–Gibbs M. Smith, *Labor Martyr: Joe Hill* (New York:
Grosset & Dunlap, 1969), pp. 194–195

## *Joe Hill*
Dos Passos

A young Swede named Hillstrom went to sea, got himself calloused hands on sailingships and tramps, learned English in the focastle of the steamers that make the run from Stockholm to Hull, dreamed the Swede's dream of the west;

when he got to America they gave him a job polishing cuspidors in a Bowery saloon.

He moved west to Chicago and worked in a machineshop.

He moved west and followed the harvest, hung around employment agencies, paid out many a dollar for a job in a construction camp, walked out many a mile when the grub was too bum, or the boss too tough, or too many bugs in the bunkhouse;

read Marx and the I.W.W. Preamble and dreamed about forming the structure of the new society within the shell of the old.

He was in California for the S.P. strike (*Casey Jones, two locomotives, Casey Jones*), used to play the concertina outside the bunkhouse door, after supper, evenings (*Long-haired preachers come out every night*), had a knack for setting rebel words to tunes (*And the union makes us strong*).

Along the coast in cookshacks flophouses jungles wobblies hoboes bindlestiffs began singing Joe Hill's songs. They sang 'em in the county jails of the State of Washington, Oregon, California, Nevada, Idaho, in the bullpens in Montana and Arizona, sang 'em in Walla Walla, San Quentin and Leavenworth,

forming the structure of the new society within the jails of the old.

At Bingham, Utah, Joe Hill organized the workers of the Utah Construction Company in the One Big Union, won a new wagescale, shorter hours, better grub. (The angel Moroni didn't like labororganizers any better than the Southern Pacific did.)

The angel Moroni moved the hearts of the Mormons to decide it was Joe Hill shot a grocer named Morrison. The Swedish consul and President Wilson tried to get him a new trial but the angel Moroni moved the hearts of the supreme court of the State of Utah to sustain the verdict of guilty. He was in jail a year, went on making up songs. In November 1915 he was stood up against the wall in the jail yard in Salt Lake City.

"Don't mourn for me organize," was the last word he sent out to the workingstiffs of the I.W.W. Joe Hill stood up against the wall of the jail yard, looked into the muzzles of the guns and gave the word to fire.

They put him in a black suit, put a stiff collar around his neck and a bow tie, shipped him to Chicago for a bangup funeral, and photographed his handsome stony mask staring into the future.

The first of May they scattered his ashes to the wind.

–*Nineteen-Nineteen*, pp. 717–718

## The 1916 Everett Massacre
Melvyn Dubofsky

*A pitched battle between IWW members and vigilantes supported by local manufacturers took place in Everett, Washington, in May 1916. The incident received much attention because it raised fundamental free-speech and assembly issues.*

The 1916 employers' open-shop drive had not bypassed Everett; it simply took a different form

*IWW badge commemorating Wobblies slain or injured after they traveled to Everett, Washington, by boat and were confronted at the dock by vigilantes (from Stewart Bird et al.,* Solidarity Forever, *1985)*

there: brutal, violent, and ultimately fatal. On May Day, 1916, the city's unionized shingle weavers (affiliated with the AFL, not the IWW) walked out to protest their employers' refusal to increase wages, which had been cut eighteen months earlier during the recession. Easily identifiable by the fingers they had lost to mill saws, Everett's shingle weavers demanded a share of the lumber industry's new prosperity. Although during earlier labor struggles in Everett the city's employers had been internally divided and unaligned with management interests outside the city, now, in 1916, Everett's mill owners presented a united front and drew upon support from both the state employers' association and the lumbermen's association. This new alignment of forces encouraged Everett's employers to smash the union and to establish the open shop in the city. Resolute mill owners thus hired armed professional strikebreakers to assist them in reopening the mills, and as smokestacks once again darkened the city's sky, resistance among the strikers ebbed. By mid-summer many shingle weavers had returned to work without their union. Those who held out—the most bitter, militant, and sometimes violent of the men—engaged in desultory battles with strikebreakers, who usually got the better of these fights. By mid-August the shingle weavers' strike was a shambles (tile AFL during this time had done almost nothing to save the life of a weak affili-

ate), and one more Northwest labor front had succumbed before the open-shop drive.[1]

With the AFL shingle weavers beaten, the IWW intervened to see what it could salvage from the wreckage. Already well known and widely feared by Everett's employers and citizens, Wobblies for several years had maintained a small local headquarters which provided the city with soapboxers and radical literature. Haywood himself had addressed a large Everett audience in 1913, and Seattle, an IWW hotbed, was just down the Sound from Everett. In the summer of 1916, Seattle came to Everett in the person of James H. Rowan and other IWW agitators. When city officials arrested the agitators, the IWW threatened Everett with "a drastic dose of direct action."[2]

Already triumphant in their conflict with the AFL shingle weavers, Everett employers were not about to open their industry to the IWW. They thus decided to test San Diego's anti-IWW tactics in the Northwest. The local Commercial Club, dominated by the mill owners, organized a vigilante group, which, when denied city cooperation, called upon Donald McRae, the county sheriff, who promised to deputize five hundred volunteers to protect Everett against invasion by outside agitators. Under McRae's leadership, the city's soldier citizens—junior executives, white-collar workers, petty bureaucrats—harassed the Wobblies, breaking up street meetings, pulling Wobs off trains and trolleys, beating them and deporting them.[3]

The battle between Wobblies and vigilantes continued at varying intensity through late August and early September. For a time the IWW thought it had won another triumph for free speech, but then the vigilantes resumed the struggle with a vengeance. As more and more Wobblies came north to Everett, the Commercial Club and Sheriff McRae resorted to San Diego–style measures. On October 30 forty Wobblies arrived on a boat from Seattle prepared to talk their way into Everett's jail. They never even had a chance to begin: McRae and his armed deputies met the Wobs at the boat dock, clubbed them, and escorted them directly to the city jail. That night deputies removed the prisoners from jail and took them to Beverly Park, a local forest preserve, where they stripped their captives and made the Wobblies run a gauntlet of several hundred vigilantes, who delighted in beating the naked prisoners with guns, clubs, and whips.[4] To Wobblies the events of October 30 soon became known as the Everett Massacre. But the "massacre" would pale into insignificance compared to events of the following week.

As reports of the Beverly Park incident trickled back to IWW headquarters in Seattle, Wobbly leaders there decided to stage a mass invasion of Everett in order to confront the vigilantes with the power of numbers. Taking its call for action into isolated logging camps, skid-row hotels, and radical clubs, the IWW pleaded for invaders. Before long, several hundred loggers, itinerants, unemployed workers, radicals, and even a few young students had volunteered to fight in Everett for free speech and for the right to organize unions. Sunday, November 5, was set aside as the day to challenge Everett.

As Sunday approached Wobblies made their way to Everett, the main body, about 250 strong, chartering a small steamer, the *Verona,* to carry them up Puget Sound. On the morning of November 5, a boisterous, happy bunch of workers, who might well have been out on a Sunday pleasure cruise, sang merrily as their boat glided up the Sound.[5]

Everett's employers and vigilantes meanwhile had decided to accept the IWW's challenge and to meet force with force. Informed by private detectives of all the IWW's plans, the Commercial Club knew in advance about the voyage of the *Verona.* Down to Everett's docks marched the vigilantes, deputized by McRae, and armed with rifles, shotguns, and pistols. Fortified with whiskey and motivated by self-righteous notions of civic pride

and respect for the law, McRae's deputies concealed themselves in a warehouse and in several small tugboats, forming a semi-circle around the dock where the *Verona* was expected to land. Soon the concealed deputies, as well as a large crowd which had gathered high on a hilltop above the harbor, heard the strains of song drift across the harbor. "Hold the fort for we are coming, Union men, be strong," the Wobblies sang. As the *Verona* slipped into its dock and sailors made fast the ship's lines, McRae and two other deputies exchanged heated words with the "invaders." Suddenly a shot rang out, and then the sound of gunfire burst out in all directions. Caught in a deadly crossfire, the men aboard the *Verona* panicked, almost capsizing the boat, some of the Wobblies indeed falling overboard and probably drowning. With the men on the tightly snubbed boat providing helpless and inviting targets, deputies rushed out from cover to draw better beads on their intended victims. McRae's men ran around the dock, shooting every which way, never really knowing at whom they were firing. McRae, shot in the leg, fell victim to an unidentified assailant. Behind him other deputies fell, possibly victims of their undisciplined fellows. Finally, at least one Wobbly aboard the ship had the good sense to order the

*The* Verona, *the vessel on which IWW members voyaged from Seattle to Everett, Washington, on 5 November 1916 after an earlier delegation of Wobblies had been beaten and rounded up for arrest by local citizens (from Stewart Bird et al.,* Solidarity Forever, *1985)*

boat's lines cast loose and its engines reversed. Still under constant fire, the *Verona* steamed out into the bay, and as it glided away from Everett, four men lay dead on its decks, one man was dying, and thirty-one others were wounded. An unknown number of passengers had also fallen into the water, their bodies washed away, unknown, unidentified, and unmourned. On the dock, one deputy lay dead, another lay dying, and twenty were wounded. Thus ended Everett's "Bloody Sunday."

To this day no one knows with any certainty who fired the first shot. Nor does anyone know whether the wounded deputies were shot by Wobblies who had come armed, or by their own allies. One lumberman even suspected that members of McRae's army sympathized with the IWW, and that the sheriff "expected trouble from the rear as well as from dead ahead. . . ."[6]

Who fired the first shot is really unimportant. What is significant is that public authorities and private citizens had attempted to deny Wobblies their constitutional right to land at a public dock and to speak in Everett. Even more significant, Everett's leaders decided to deny those rights through the use of force, even at the cost of violence, bloodshed, and death. Of further significance was the refusal of federal authorities, despite appeals from Haywood, the AFL, and influential West Coast citizens and reformers, to intervene on behalf of the rights of American citizens, who happened to be powerless workingmen.[7] The federal government's refusal to intervene on the IWW's behalf in 1916 would take on added import only a year later, when, at the instigation of businessmen and politicians, federal officials would actively repress the IWW.

The only sane note in a chorus of public insanity was struck by Seattle's Mayor Robert S. Gill, who accused Everett's officials of the worst of all crimes: acting illegally in the name of the law. Yet Seattle's press, area businessmen, and scores of political enemies publicly condemned and slandered the Mayor. Not even Gill could save the Wobblies who had returned to Seattle on the *Verona* from being arrested and imprisoned on murder indictments issued by Everett authorities.

–*We Shall Be All: A History of the Industrial Workers of the World* (Urbana: University of Illinois Press, 1988), pp. 338–341

### Notes

1. Norman H. Clark, "Everett, 1916," *Pacific Northwest Quarterly,* 57 (April 1966): 57–64, is the best study of the origins and the implications of the Everett affair.

2. *Industrial Worker,* 5 August 1916, p. 4.

3. Clark, "Everett, 1916," p. 58; *Industrial Worker,* 26 August 1916, p. 1; 12 September 1916, p. 1; 19 September 1916, p. 1; 30 September 1916, p. 1.

4. *Industrial Worker,* 4 November 1916, p. 1; *Solidarity,* 14 October 1916, p. 2; 4 November 1916, p. 1.

5. This account of the Everett Massacre is based upon Clark, "Everett, 1916"; David C. Botting Jr., "Bloody Sunday," *Pacific Northwest Quarterly,* 49 (October 1958): 162–172; Robert L. Tyler, "The Everett Free Speech Fight," *Pacific Historical Review,* 23 (February 1954): 19–30; Anna Louise Strong, "Everett's Bloody Sunday," *Survey,* 37 (27 January 1917): 475–476; for the IWW's official version, see Walker C. Smith, *The Everett Massacre* (Chicago, 1918); *Solidarity,* 11 November 1916, pp. 1, 4; *Industrial Worker,* 11 November 1916, pp. 1–4; 18 November 1916, p. 1.

6. E. G. Ames to Fred Talbot, 10 November 1916, Puget Mill Company Papers.

7. R. H. Mills and others to Woodrow Wilson, 5 November 1916, File 150139-60; Haywood to Wilson, 7 November 1916, File 150139-49; Attorney Thomas W. Gregory to Haywood, and also to Herbert Mahler, 15 November 1916, File 150139-50; Clay Allen to Gregory, 17 November 1916, File 150139-51, all in Department of Justice, Record Group 60, National Archives.

### Ben Compton: The Everett Massacre
Dos Passos

*Ben Compton participates in the IWW effort to test the right of free speech at Everett.*

Bram knew all the ropes. Walking, riding blind baggage or on empty gondolas, hopping rides on delivery wagons and trucks, they got to Buffalo. In a flophouse there Bram found a guy he knew who got them signed on as deckhands on a whaleback going back light to Duluth. In Duluth they joined a gang being shipped up to harvest wheat for an outfit in Saskatchewan. At first the work was very heavy for Ben and Bram was scared he'd cave in, but the fourteen hour days out in the sun and the dust, the copious grub, the dead sleep in the lofts of the big barns began to toughen him up. Lying flat on the straw in his sweaty clothes he'd still feel through his sleep the tingle of the sun on his face and neck, the strain in his muscles, the whir of the reapers and binders along the horizon, the roar of the thresher, the grind of gears of the trucks carrying the red wheat to the elevators. He began to talk like a harvest stiff. After the harvest they worked in a fruitcannery on the Columbia River, a lousy steamy job full of the sour stench of rotting fruitpeelings. There they read in *Solidarity* about the shingleweavers' strike and the free speech fight in Everett, and decided they'd go down and see what they could do to help out. The last day they worked there Bram lost the forefinger of his right hand repairing the slicing and peeling machinery. The company doctor said he couldn't get any compensation because he'd already given notice, and, besides, not being a Canadian . . . A little shyster lawyer came around, to the boarding house where Bram was lying on the bed in a fever, with his hand in a big wad of bandage, and tried to get him to sue, but Bram yelled at the lawyer to get the hell out. Ben said he was wrong, the working class ought to have its lawyers too.

When the hand had healed a little they went down on the boat from Vancouver to Seattle. I.W.W. headquarters there was like a picnic ground, crowded with young men coming in from every part of the U.S. and Canada. One day a big bunch went down to Everett on the boat to try to hold a meeting at the corner of Wetmore and Hewitt Avenues. The dock was full of deputies with rifles, and revolvers. "The Commercial Club boys are waiting for us," some guy's voice tittered nervously. The deputies had white handkerchiefs around their necks. "There's Sheriff McRae," said somebody. Bram edged up to Ben. "We better stick together. . . . Looks to me like we was goin' to get tamped up some." The wobblies were arrested as fast as they stepped off the boat and herded down to the end of the dock. The deputies were drunk most of them, Ben could smell the whiskey on the breath of the redfaced guy who grabbed him by the arm. "Get a move on there, you son of a bitch . . . " He got a blow from a riflebutt in the small of the back. He could hear the crack of saps on men's skulls. Anybody who resisted had his face beaten to a jelly with a club. The wobblies were made to climb up into a truck. With the dusk a cold drizzle had come on. "Boys, we got to show 'em we got guts," a redhaired boy said. A deputy who was holding on to the back of the truck aimed a blow at him with his sap but lost his balance and fell off. The wobblies laughed. The deputy climbed on again, purple in the face. "You'll be laughin' outa the other side of your dirty mugs when we get through with you," he yelled.

Out in the woods where the county road crossed the railroad track they were made to get out of the trucks. The deputies stood around them with their guns leveled while the sheriff who was reeling drunk, and two welldressed middleaged men talked over what they'd do. Ben heard the word gauntlet. "Look here, sheriff," somebody said, "we're not here to make any kind of disturbance. All we want's our constitutional rights of free speech." The sheriff turned towards them waving the butt of his revolver, "Oh, you do, do you, you c—-s. Well, this is Snohomish county and you ain't goin' to forget it . . . if you come here again some of you fellers is goin' to die, that's all there is about it. . . . All right, boys, let's go."

The deputies made two lines down towards the railroad track. They grabbed the wobblies one by one and beat them up. Three of them grabbed Ben. "You a wobbly?" "Sure I am, you dirty yellow . . ." he began. The sheriff came up and hauled off to hit him. "Look out, he's got glasses on." A big hand pulled the glasses

off. "We'll fix that." Then the sheriff punched him in the nose with his fist. "Say you ain't." Ben's mouth was full of blood. He set his jaw. "He's a kike, hit him again for me." "Say, you ain't a wobbly." Somebody whacked a riflebarrel against his shins and he fell forward. "Run for it," they were yelling. Blows with clubs and riflebutts were splitting his ears.

He tried to walk forward without running. He tripped on a rail and fell, cutting his arm on something sharp. There was so much blood in his eyes he couldn't see. A heavy boot was kicking him again and again in the side. He was passing out. Somehow he staggered forward. Somebody was holding him up under the arms and was dragging him free of the cattle-guard on the track. Another fellow began to wipe his face off with a handkerchief. He heard Bram's voice way off somewhere, "We're over the county line, boys." What with losing his glasses and the rain and the night and the shooting pain all up and down his back Ben couldn't see anything. He heard shots behind them and yells from where other guys were running the gauntlet. He was the center of a little straggling group of wobblies making their way down the railroad track. "Fellow workers," Bram was saying in his deep quiet voice, "we must never forget this night."

–*Nineteen-Nineteen*, pp. 728–730

## Centralia and Wesley Everest
Melvyn Dubofsky

*The jingoistic patriotism engendered by World War I increased the intensity and range of anti-IWW feeling in the far Northwest. What became known as the Centralia Conspiracy— the incident on Armistice Day, 1919, at Centralia, Washington, that led to the lynching of Wesley Everest and the subsequent imprisonment of several union members—was a notable instance of the volatile conditions in which the IWW sought to exist.*

Before the year [1919] ended, Wobblies engaged in armed conflict. Centralia, Washington, was a lumber town in a region with a long history of IWW activity. Like most towns in the area, it had a small IWW hall downtown where Wobblies congregated to chat about old times, read radical literature, and discuss when the revolution would come. That particular hall soon became famous. Centralia's American Legionnaires planned to celebrate Armistice Day, 1919, with a parade; a parade, however, that included an unusual touch of patriotic fervor: destruction of the local IWW hall. Knowing what was coming and acting upon legal advice, the Wobblies prepared to defend their hall against attack. When the Legionnaires' line of march approached IWW headquarters, its participants met an

*Wesley Everest, subject of the biography "Paul Bunyan" in Nineteen-Nineteen, a lumberman, war veteran, and IWW member who was lynched following a clash between American Legionnaires and Wobblies on Armistice Day, 1919, in Centralia, Washington (Special Collections Division, University of Washington Libraries)*

ers slain during the attack on the hall, and then tried, convicted, and sentenced to long prison terms.)[1]
— *We Shall Be All: A History of the Industrial Workers of the World* (Urbana: University of Illinois Press, 1988), p. 455

### Note

1. John Dos Passos, *1919* (New York, 1932), pp. 456–461; Ralph Chaplin, *The Centralia Conspiracy* (Seattle, 1920); Walker C. Smith, *Centralia: Was It Murder?* (n.p., 1925); Robert L. Tyler, "Violence at Centralia, 1919," *Pacific Northwest Quarterly*, 45 (October 1954): 116–124; John M. McClelland, Jr., "Terror on Tower Avenue," *Pacific Northwest Quarterly*, 57 (April 1966): 65–72.

### The Lynching of Wesley Everest
Ralph Chaplin

*Chaplin's widely circulated IWW-sponsored pamphlet on the events at Centralia, Washington, served as the source for Dos Passos's recounting of them in* Paul Bunyan. *Note Dos Passos's almost verbatim use of several of Chaplin's reports of statements by Everest.*

November 11th was a raw, gray day; the cold sunlight barely penetrating the mist that hung over the city and the distant tree-cald [*sic*] hills. The "parade" assembled at the City Park. Lieutenant Cormier was marshal. Warren Grimm was commander of the Centralia division. In a very short time he had the various bodies arranged to his satisfaction. At the head of the procession was the "two-fisted" Centralia bunch. This was followed by one from Chehalis, the county seat, and where the parade would logically have been held had its purpose been an honest one. Then came a few sailors and marines and a large body of well dressed gentlemen from the Elks. The school children who were to have marched did not appear. At the very end were a couple of dozen boy scouts and an automobile carrying pretty girls dressed in Red Cross uniforms. Evidently this parade, unlike the one of 1918, did not, like a scorpion, carry its sting in the rear. But wait until you read how cleverly this part of it had been arranged!

The marchers were unduly silent and those who knew nothing of the lawless plan of the secret committee felt somehow that something must be wrong. City Postmaster McCleary and a wicked-faced old man named Thompson were seen carrying coils of rope. Thompson is a veteran of the Civil War and a minister of God. On the witness stand he afterwards swore he picked up the rope from the street and was carrying it "as a joke." It turned out that the "joke" was on Wesley Everest.

unexpected welcome, for inside, as well as on adjoining rooftops, armed Wobblies prepared to fire upon them. A brief and bloody gunfight followed, during which the more numerous Legionnaires stormed the hall and drove the Wobblies into flight. Bloodied and enraged, the Legionnaires pursued the fleeing Wobblies, cornering one of them on the town's outskirts. Wesley Everest, the trapped Wobbly and a distinguished war veteran, attempted to hold off his pursuers in a gun battle that John Dos Passos was later to describe in his novel *1919*. Outnumbered and encircled, Everest had no choice but to surrender to the Legionnaires, who promptly and unceremoniously castrated and then lynched him. (Another group of local Wobblies was later arrested, charged with the murder of two march-

## TERROR IN THE NIGHT

POLICE DEPARTMENT, TACOMA, WASHINGTON     MALE

NAME  Everest ( Man lynched at Centralia)     No.     CLASS  1 R  00  9
                                                             1 U  10

Aliases     Ref's

Date of Arrest     Crime     Age  3 3
Ht. about 5-7  Wt. abt. 150 lbs. Comp.     Hair  Drk Red Hair  Eyes  Blue     Build  Meduim
Occup.     Where Born     P.C. No.     Date     Judge
Result     Sup. C. Disp.     Date     Judge
Bertillon  no scars that could be located on the body  outside where rope cut neck
Arresting Officers  hole that looked like bullet hole
   en by Majerus     Date  11-12-1919     Classified by H.M. Smith     Date  11-12-1919
Prev. Records;     Prints taken in the Jail at Centralia Wash. room very dark to see any thing
   on the body in line  scars;
   rope was still around the neck of t he man
                                        Signature

*Everest's fingerprints and the police report on the examination of his corpse*
*(Luke May Papers, University of Washington Libraries)*

"Be ready for the command 'eyes right' or 'eyes left' when we pass the 'reviewing stand,'" Grimm told the platoon commanders just as the parade started.

The procession covered most of the line of march without incident. When the union hall was reached there was some craning of necks but no outburst of any kind. A few of the out-of-town paraders looked at the place curiously and several business men were seen pointing the hall out to their friends. There were some dark glances and a few long noses but no demonstration.

"When do we reach the reviewing stand?" asked a parader, named Joe Smith, of a man marching beside him.

"Hell, there ain't any reviewing stand," was the reply. "We're going to give the wobbly hall 'eyes right' on the way back."

The head of the columns reached Third avenue and halted. A command of "about face" was given and the procession again started to march past the union hall going in the opposite direction. The loggers inside felt greatly relieved as they saw the crowd once more headed for the city. But the Centralia and Chehalis contingents, that had headed the parade, was [*sic*] now in the rear—just where the "scorpion sting" of the 1918 parade had been located! The danger was not yet over.

### "LET'S GO! AT 'EM, BOYS!"

The Chehalis division had marched past the hall and the Centralia division was just in front of it when a sharp command was given. The latter stopped squarely in front of the hall but the former continued to march. Lieutenant Cormier of the secret committee was riding between the two contingents on a bay horse. Suddenly he placed his fingers to his mouth and gave a shrill whistle. Immediately there was a hoarse cry of "Let's go-o-o! At 'em, boys!" About sixty feet separated the two contingents at this time, the Chehalis men still continuing the march. Cormier spurred his horse and overtook them. "Aren't you boys in on this?" he shouted.

At the words "Let's go," the paraders from both ends and the middle of the Centralia contingent broke ranks and started on the run for the union headquarters. A crowd of soldiers surged against the door. There was a crashing of glass and a splintering of wood as the door gave way. A few of the marauders had actually forced their way into the hall. Then there was a shot, three more shots . . . and a small volley. From Seminary hill and the Avalon hotel rifles began to crack.

The mob stopped suddenly, astounded at the unexpected opposition. Out of hundreds of halls that had been raided during the past two years this was the first time the union men had attempted to defend themselves. It had evidently been planned to stampede the entire contingent into the attack by having the secret committeemen take the lead from both ends and the middle. But before this could happen the crowd, frightened at the shots, started to scurry for cover. Two men were seen carrying the limp figure of a soldier from the door of the hall. When the volley started they dropped it and ran. The soldier was a handsome young man, named Arthur McElfresh. He was left lying in front of the hall with his feet on the curb and his head in the gutter. The whole thing had been a matter of seconds.

. . . . . . . . . .

## WESLEY EVEREST

But Destiny had decided to spare one man the bitter irony of judicial murder. Wesley Everest still had a pocket full of cartridges and a forty-four automatic that could speak for itself. This soldier-lumberjack had done most of the shooting in the hall. He held off the mob until the very last moment, and, instead of seeking refuge in the refrigerator after the "paraders" had been dispersed, he ran out of the back door, reloading his pistol as he went. It is believed by many that Arthur McElfresh was killed inside the hall by a bullet fired by Everest.

In the yard at the rear of the hall the mob had already reorganized for an attack from that direction. Before anyone knew what had happened Everest had broken through their ranks and scaled the fence. "Don't follow me and I won't shoot," he called to the crowd and displaying the still smoking blue steel pistol in his hand.

"There goes the secretary!" yelled someone, as the logger started at top speed down the alley. The mob surged in pursuit, collapsing the board fence before them with the sheer force of numbers. There was a rope in the crowd and the union secretary was the man they wanted. The chase that followed probably saved the life, not only of Britt Smith, but the remaining loggers in the hall as well.

Running pell-mell down the alley the mob gave a shout of exultation as Everest slowed his pace and turned to face them. They stopped cold, however, as a number of quick shots rang out and bullets whistled and zipped around them. Everest turned in his tracks and was off again like a flash, reloading his pistol as he ran. The mob again resumed the pursuit. The logger ran through an open gateway, paused to turn and again fire at his pursuers; then he ran between two frame dwellings to the open street. When the mob again caught the trail they were evidently under the impression that the logger's ammunition was exhausted. At all events they took up the chase with redoubled energy. Some men in the mob had rifles and now and then a pot-shot would be taken at the fleeing figure. The marksmanship of both sides seems to have been poor for no one appears to have been injured.

## DALE HUBBARD

This kind of running fight was kept up until Everest reached the river. Having kept off his pursuers thus far the boy started boldly for the comparative security of the opposite shore, splashing the water violently as he waded out into the stream. The mob was getting closer all the time. Suddenly Everest seemed to change his mind and began to retrace his steps to the shore. Here he stood dripping wet in the tangled grass to await the arrival of the mob bent on his destruction. Everest had lost his hat and his wet hair stuck to his forehead. His gun was now so hot he could hardly hold it and the last of his ammunition was in the magazine. Eye witnesses declare his face still wore a quizzical, half bantering smile when the mob overtook him. With the pistol held loosely in his rough hand Everest stood at bay, ready to make a last stand for his life. Seeing him thus, and no doubt thinking his last bullet had been expended, the mob made a rush for its quarry.

"Stand back!" he shouted. "If there are 'bulls' in the crowd, I'll submit to arrest; otherwise lay off of me."

No attention was paid to his words. Everest shot from the hip four times,—then his gun stalled. A group of soldiers started to run in his direction. Everest was tugging at the gun with both hands. Raising it suddenly he took careful aim and fired. All the soldiers but one

*Everest's burial, with Wobbly prisoners under guard serving as gravediggers (from John McClelland Jr.,*
Wobbly War: The Centralia Story, *1987)*

wavered and stopped. Everest fired twice, both bullets taking effect. But the soldier did not stop. Two more shots were fired almost point blank before the logger dropped his assailant at his feet. Then he tossed away the empty gun and the mob surged upon him.

The legionaire who had been shot was Dale Hubbard, a nephew of F. B. Hubbard, the lumber baron. He was a strong, brave and misguided young man—worthy of a nobler death.

### "LET'S FINISH THE JOB!"

Everest attempted to fight with his fists but was overpowered and severely beaten. A number of men clamoured for immediate lynching, but saner council prevailed for the time and he was dragged through the streets towards the city jail. When the mob was half a block from this place the "hot heads" made another attempt to cheat the state executioner. A wave of fury seemed here to sweep the crowd. Men fought with one another for a chance to strike, kick or spit in the face of their victim. It was an orgy of hatred and blood-lust. Everest's arms were pinioned, blows, kicks and curses rained upon him from every side. One business man clawed strips of bleeding flesh from his face. A woman slapped his battered cheek with a well groomed hand. A soldier tried to lunge a hunting rifle at the helpless logger; the crowd was too thick. He bumped them

aside with the butt of the gun to get room. Then he crashed the muzzle with full force into Everest's mouth. Teeth were broken and blood flowed profusely.

A rope appeared from somewhere. "Let's finish the job!" cried a voice. The rope was placed about the neck of the logger. "You haven't got guts enough to lynch a man in the daytime," was all he said.

At this juncture a woman brushed through the crowd and took the rope from Everest's neck. Looking into the distorted faces of the mob she cried indignantly, "You are curs and cowards to treat a man like that!"

There may be human beings in Centralia after all.

Wesley Everest was taken to the city jail and thrown without ceremony upon the cement floor of the "bull pen." In the surrounding cells were his comrades who had been arrested in the union hall. Here he lay in a wet heap, twitching with agony. A tiny bright stream of blood gathered at his side and trailed slowly along the floor. Only an occasional quivering moan escaped his torn lips as the hours slowly passed by.

. . . . . . . . . .

But with the young logger [Everest] who had been taken out into the night things were different. Wesley Everest was thrown, half unconscious, into the bottom of an automobile. The hands of the men who had dragged him there were sticky and red. Their pant legs were sodden from rubbing against the crumpled figure at their feet. Through the dark streets sped the three machines. The smooth asphalt became a rough road as the suburbs were reached. Then came a stretch of open country, with the Chehalis river bridge only a short distance ahead. The cars lurched over the uneven road with increasing speed, their headlights playing on each other or on the darkened highway.

Wesley Everest stirred uneasily. Raising himself slowly on one elbow he swung weakly with his free arm, striking one of his tormentors full in the face. The other occupants immediately seized him and bound his hands and feet with rope. It must have been the glancing blow from the fist of the logger that gave one of the gentlemen his fiendish inspiration. Reaching in his pocket he produced a razor. For a moment he fumbled over the now limp figure in the bottom of the car. His companions looked on with stolid acquiescence. Suddenly there was a piercing scream of pain. The figure gave a convulsive shudder of agony. After a moment Wesley Everest said in a weak voice: "For Christ's sake, men; shoot me—don't let me suffer like this."

–*The Centralia Conspiracy* (Seattle, N.p., 1920), pp. 53–55, 57–60, 63

### Paul Bunyan
Dos Passos

When Wesley Everest came home from overseas and got his discharge from the army he went back to his old job of logging. His folks were of the old Kentucky and Tennessee stock of woodsmen and squirrel-hunters who followed the trail blazed by Lewis and Clark into the rainy giant forests of the Pacific slope. In the army Everest was a sharpshooter, won a medal for a crack shot.

(Since the days of the homesteaders the western promoters and the politicians and lobbyists in Washington had been busy with the rainy giant forests of the Pacific slope, with the result that:

*ten monopoly groups aggregating only one thousand eight hundred and two holders, monopolized one thousand two hundred and eight billion, eight hundred million,*
[1,208 ,800,000,000]
*square feet of standing timber, . . . enough standing timber . . . to yield the planks necessary [over and above the manufacturing wastage] to make a floating bridge more than two feet thick and more than five miles wide from New York to Liverpool;–*

wood for scaffolding, wood for jerrybuilding residential suburbs, billboards, wood for shacks and ships and shantytowns, pulp for tabloids, yellow journals,

editorial pages, advertizing copy, mailorder catalogues, filingcards, army paperwork, handbills, flimsy.)

Wesley Everest was a logger like Paul Bunyan.

The lumberjacks, loggers, shingleweavers, sawmill workers were the helots of the timber empire; the I.W.W. put the idea of industrial democracy in Paul Bunyan's head; wobbly organizers said the forests ought to belong to the whole people, said Paul Bunyan ought to be paid in real money instead of in company scrip, ought to have a decent place to dry his clothes, wet from the sweat of a day's work in zero weather and snow, an eight hour day, clean bunkhouses, wholesome grub; when Paul Bunyan came back from making Europe safe for the democracy of the Big Four, he joined the lumberjack's local to help make the Pacific slope safe for the workingstiffs. The wobblies were reds. Not a thing in this world Paul Bunyan's ascared of.

(To be a red in the summer of 1919 was worse than being a hun or a pacifist in the summer of 1917.)

The timber owners, the sawmill and shinglekings were patriots; they'd won the war (in the course of which the price of lumber had gone up from $16 a thousand feet to $116; there are even cases where the government paid as high as $1200 a thousand for spruce); they set out to clean the reds out of the logging camps;

free American institutions must be preserved at any cost;

so they formed the Employers Association and the Legion of Loyal Loggers, they made it worth their while for bunches of ex-soldiers to raid I.W.W. halls, lynch and beat up organizers, burn subversive literature.

On Memorial Day 1918 the boys of the American Legion in Centralia led by a group from the Chamber of Commerce wrecked the I.W.W. hall, beat up everybody they found in it, jailed some and piled the rest of the boys in a truck and dumped them over the county line, burned the papers and pamphlets and auctioned off the fittings for the Red Cross; the wobblies' desk still stands in the Chamber of Commerce.

The loggers hired a new hall and the union kept on growing. Not a thing in this world Paul Bunyan's ascared of.

Before Armistice Day, 1919, the town was full of rumors that on that day the hall would be raided for keeps. A young man of good family and pleasant manners, Warren O. Grimm, had been an officer with the American force in Siberia; that made him an authority on labor and Bolsheviks, so he was chosen by the business men to lead the 100% forces in the Citizens Protective League to put the fear of God into Paul Bunyan.

*Everest's grave marker, placed fifteen years after his death by the IWW, in Sticklin Greenwood Memorial Park, Centralia*
*(from John McClelland Jr.,* Wobbly War: The Centralia Story, *1987)*

The first thing the brave patriots did was pick up a blind newsdealer and thrash him and drop him in a ditch across the county line.

The loggers consulted counsel and decided they had a right to defend their hall and themselves in case of a raid. Not a thing in this world Paul Bunyan's ascared of.

Wesley Everest was a crack shot; Armistice Day he put on his uniform and filled his pockets with cartridges. Wesley Everest was not much of a talker; at a meeting in the Union Hall the Sunday before the raid, there'd been talk of the chance of a lynching bee; Wesley Everest had been walking up and down the aisle with his O.D. coat on over a suit of overalls, distributing literature and pamphlets; when the boys said they wouldn't stand for another raid, he stopped in his tracks with the papers under his arm, rolled himself a brownpaper cigarette and smiled a funny quiet smile.

Armistice Day was raw and cold; the mist rolled in from Puget Sound and dripped from the dark boughs of the spruces and the shiny storefronts of the town. Warren O. Grimm commanded the Centralia section of the parade. The exsoldiers were in their uniforms. When the parade passed by the union hall without halting, the loggers inside breathed easier, but on the way back the parade halted in front of the hall. Somebody whistled through his fingers. Somebody yelled, "Let's go . . . at 'em, boys." They ran towards the wobbly hall. Three men crashed through the door.

A rifle spoke. Rifles crackled on the hills back of the town, roared in the back of the hall.

Grimm and an exsoldier were hit.

The parade broke in disorder but the men with rifles formed again and rushed the hall. They found a few unarmed men hiding in an old icebox, a boy in uniform at the head of the stairs with his arms over his head.

Wesley Everest shot the magazine of his rifle out, dropped it and ran for the woods. As he ran he broke through the crowd in the back of the hall, held them off with a blue automatic, scaled a fence, doubled down an alley and through the back street. The mob followed. They dropped the coils of rope they had with them to lynch Britt Smith the I.W.W. secretary. It was Wesley Everest's drawing them off that kept them from lynching Britt Smith right there.

Stopping once or twice to hold the mob off with some scattered shots, Wesley Everest ran for the river, started to wade across. Up to his waist in water he stopped and turned.

Wesley Everest turned to face the mob with a funny quiet smile on his face. He'd lost his hat and his hair dripped with water and sweat. They started to rush him.

"Stand back," he shouted, "if there's bulls in the crowd I'll submit to arrest."

The mob was at him. He shot from the hip four times, then his gun jammed. He tugged at the trigger, and taking cool aim shot the foremost of them dead. It was Dale Hubbard, another exsoldier, nephew of one of the big lumber men of Centralia.

Then he threw his empty gun away and fought with his fists. The mob had him. A man bashed his teeth in with the butt of a shotgun. Somebody brought a rope and they started to hang him. A woman elbowed through the crowd and pulled the rope off his neck.

"You haven't the guts to hang a man in the daytime," was what Wesley Everest said.

They took him to the jail and threw him on the floor of a cell. Meanwhile they were putting the other loggers through the third degree.

That night the city lights were turned off. A mob smashed in the outer door of the jail. "Don't shoot, boys, here's your man," said the guard. Wesley Everest met them on his feet, "Tell the boys I did my best," he whispered to the men in the other cells.

They took him off in a limousine to the Chehalis River bridge. As Wesley Everest lay stunned in the bottom of the car a Centralia business man cut his penis and testicles off with a razor. Wesley Everest gave a great scream of pain. Somebody has remembered that after a while he whispered, "For God's sake, men, shoot me . . . don't let me suffer like this." Then they hanged him from the bridge in the glare of the headlights.

The coroner at his inquest thought it was a great joke.

He reported that Wesley Everest had broken out of jail and run to the Chehalis River bridge and tied a rope around his neck and jumped off, finding the rope too short he'd climbed back and fastened on a longer, one, had jumped off again, broke his neck and shot himself full of holes.

They jammed the mangled wreckage into a packing box and buried it.

Nobody knows where they buried the body of Wesley Everest, but the six loggers they caught they buried in the Walla Walla Penitentiary.

*—Nineteen-Nineteen, pp. 746–750*

*** 

## The Intellectual Left

*In addition to the working-class-based IWW, Dos Passos portrays in* U.S.A. *the role of the intellectual Left in arousing the nation to an awareness of the perils of unfettered capitalism. In this instance, apart from his self-portrait in the* Camera Eye *of the writer as aroused radical, he confined his depiction to several striking biographies. But although there are no university-educated intellectuals in the narratives except for the negatively portrayed Richard Savage, and little or none of the thinking of leftist intellectuals is reported in the newsreels, it can be argued that their indictment of American*

*society as reported in the biographies pervades the rendering of that society elsewhere in the trilogy.*

*Educated at Harvard, Jack Reed later participated in the 1913 Paterson, New Jersey, strike and sympathetically reported on the Mexican and Russian revolutions. Randolph Bourne was a Columbia University graduate who courageously attacked America's involvement in World War I. Thorstein Veblen, a university teacher of economics, wrote bitingly about the ways in which capitalism undermines efforts to achieve a productive and just society. As Dos Passos was later to do, Reed and Bourne lived in Greenwich Village in the period before and during the war, when it was a hotbed of radical causes, many of which were reflected in the magazine* The Masses. *Dos Passos had no direct links to Veblen, but as* John P. Diggins *argues in a seminal essay, Veblen's incisive critique of the effect of the nation's economic system on the way Americans lived and thought deeply influenced the central themes of the trilogy and especially those of* The Big Money.

## John Reed and Pancho Villa
Albert L. Michaels and James W. Wilkie

*The Harvard-educated Reed was a romantic and charismatic figure on the American Left. His participation in the Paterson strike, the 1914 Mexican Revolution, and the 1917 Russian Revolution and his vibrant reporting on these events—especially in* Insurgent Mexico *(1914) and* Ten Days That Shook the World *(1919)—made him nationally known. His early death in Russia in 1920, at the age of 33, added to his almost mythic image.*

John Reed's immediate and uncritical attraction to Villa and his cause now seems inevitable, particularly in the light of Reed's own career as an idealistic crusader in behalf of the Paterson strikers. In Paterson, Reed had found the forces of the state supporting the propertied interests arrayed against the miserable, oppressed workers. In Mexico, the poor had risen in arms against the state and the capitalists, both domestic and foreign. Reed had little difficulty in forgiving the cruelty, looting, and violence that accompanied the Mexican Revolution; he was satisfied with the excuse that the rebels were underdogs fighting for social justice against political tyrants and economic exploiters supported by the Church, one of the three principal villains he found in the Mexican situation.

Even in Paterson, Reed had identified the churchmen as staunch allies of the status quo against the poor:

The strikers told me how the combined clergy of the city of Paterson had attempted from their pulpits to persuade them back to work—back to wage slavery and the tender mercies of the mill owners on grounds of religion. . . . It was hard to believe that until I saw in

*General Pancho Villa (third from right) with military comrades, circa 1910*
*(Courtesy of Special Collections, University of Arizona Library)*

the paper the sermon delivered the previous day at the Presbyterian Church by the Reverend William A. Littell. He had the impudence to flay the strike leaders and advise workmen to be respectful of their employers . . . and this while living men were fighting for their very existence and singing of the Brotherhood of Man.[1]

Reed felt that the Mexican clergy had proved equally unresponsive to the plight of the poor.

In his discussions with Reed, Pancho Villa freely expressed the revolutionists' loss of patience with the priests and described the Catholic religion as "the greatest superstition that the world has ever known." This antireligious attitude gave Reed the hope that Villa would personally "settle the account" of the Mexican people with the Catholic Church. However, in his own prejudice and conviction that the Mexican Church has served as an opiate to the people, Reed may well have exaggerated Villa's hatred for religion.[2]

Another major target of Reed's condemnation was the Mexican military establishment, which had been a dead weight on the country since independence in 1821, absorbing huge shares of the national budget that were badly needed for education and the servicing

of the foreign debt. The army never won a war and usually behaved abysmally in defeat: its soldiers often deserted. Nevertheless, the army had turned its weapons upon almost every government that came to power and insisted on high pay and the maintenance of military courts outside the jurisdiction of the civil system.

Villa also realized the army's share of responsibility for the plight of the poor. He told Reed that after the Revolution there would be no more army in Mexico. He envisioned the revolutionary veterans established in colonies where they would drill for half the week and work for themselves the other half. All Mexican men would receive some military training, so that if the Yankees ever invaded again they would be met by a people in arms rather than the incompetent professionals they had faced in the War of 1846–1848. Villa's dream was never realized, however, and the army proved a continuing source of disunity through the 1920's, when several military rebellions nearly toppled the civil government.

The third main object of Reed's condemnation—in addition to the clergy and the military—were the large numbers of American businessmen residing in

Mexico. At the Robinson hacienda in Chihuahua, Reed met an entrepreneur who proved to be the stereotype of every capitalist who ever exploited the poor of a foreign nation. The American hacienda manager described his Mexican labor force as a "pretty filthy lot of people" incapable of ever becoming technically trained, and he threatened Reed with physical violence if he dared write anything that might discourage United States intervention against the Revolution. Ignoring the warning, Reed described the interview in detail in one of his stories, wryly noting that profits had remained high and wages low despite the Revolution.

At the time of Reed's visit in 1914, Villa could not afford to share his distrust of Americans, since he was receiving the support of both Woodrow Wilson and Secretary of State William Jennings Bryan (who had even called Villa a "Sir Galahad"). As Villa told Reed, "The last thing I want is war with the United States. I like Americans better than any other foreigners." Even when most Mexicans objected to the American seizure of Veracruz in 1914, though it had been calculated to topple Huerta, Villa refused to join the chorus of criticism. But in October, 1915, his attitude suddenly changed when the Wilson administration gave *de facto* recognition to the rival Carranza regime. Hurt and enraged, Villa became an archenemy of the United States. In January, 1916, his troops removed sixteen American mining engineers from a train and shot them in cold blood, and in March another *villista* force crossed the border at Columbus, New Mexico, and raided the town. The Columbus incident caused President Wilson to order General Pershing to enter Mexico at the head of an expeditionary force, which for about ten months attempted unsuccessfully to capture Villa in the mountains of Chihuahua. After the Columbus raid, even Reed admitted that he might have been mistaken about the extent of Villa's idealism, but he reaffirmed his admiration for Villa's personal qualities.[3]

Reed was perhaps fortunate to depart from Chihuahua without having doubts about Villa's glory. Another more famous American journalist was not so fortunate. According to a reliable account, Ambrose Bierce, author of the caustic *Devil's Dictionary,* visited Villa as a correspondent in 1913 and became a great favorite with Villa and his staff.[4] Bierce, however, was soon disillusioned and one night tactlessly described Villa's forces as a "band of thieves and assassins, who did not respect anything or anyone." Worse still, he announced his intention of joining Venustiano Carranza, Villa's nominal superior and later antagonist, "the only man of worth in all the republic." Villa embraced Bierce and wished him luck; but before Bierce left the room, Villa signaled to one of his men, who left with him. Bierce saddled his horse and rode away; shortly afterward shots rang out, and no one ever saw Bierce again, dead or alive.[5]

Reed's greatest exaggerations as a reporter resulted from his admiration of Villa's military ability. More than once he described Villa as a Napoleonic military genius, a master of tactics and improvisation. In fact, Villa was always dependent on the advice of professional soldiers such as Felipe Angeles, and many of his greatest victories were won over demoralized, poorly commanded and unwilling conscripts. Reed completely overlooked Obregón, the only genuinely Napoleonic figure the Revolution produced. Obregón appears only once in the pages of *Insurgent Mexico,* and then briefly.

Reed also missed the political genius of Carranza, the man who despite many setbacks was to emerge as victor in the long civil war. According to Reed, Carranza once deliberately kept six thousand of his troops virtually inoperative in Sonora while he watched bullfights and celebrated new national holidays. To Reed, Carranza's advisers appeared no more than a "throng of opportunist politicians . . . loud in their protestations of devotion to the Cause, liberal with proclamations, and extremely jealous of each other and of Villa."

Reed's glorification of Villa was later to involve him in a rancorous dispute with Lincoln Steffens, one of his intellectual mentors. Steffens, a celebrated muckraker, shared Reed's interest in Mexico, but his study of the Revolution had convinced him that Wall Street manipulators lay behind Villa, whom he described as "a grossly illiterate, unscrupulous bandit," and he urged the United States to support the honest and able nationalist, Carranza. Both Reed and Steffens clearly oversimplified complex personalities: Villa was certainly more than a cynical bandit (he was also far from illiterate), and Carranza was not the simple old man described in *Insurgent Mexico.* In Steffens' enthusiasm for Carranza's uncompromising nationalism, he overlooked the First Chief's debilitating social conservatism; while Reed, on the other hand, admired Villa's primitive idealism and rise from poverty but overlooked his cruelty and arbitrary use of power.

During the same period when Reed was covering the Revolution, two Mexican civilians, who were later to become leading literary figures, were serving under Villa. Martín Luis Guzmán and Mariano Azuela both gained fame from their descriptions of Villa's campaigns. Guzmán's *The Eagle and the Serpent,* originally published in 1928, is a classic account very favorable to Villa despite the author's reservations about Villa's cruelty and violence.[6] With time, however, Guzmán's memories of these shortcomings faded, and in writing Villa's memoirs after his assassination, Guzmán portrayed his former chief in the uncritical terms Reed might have used.[7]

Mariano Azuela's account of the *villista* movement significantly differs from both Reed's and Guzmán's. In his brilliant novel *The Underdogs,* originally published in 1915, Azuela, who had served as a medical doctor under Julio Medina, describes the combatants of both sides, confused peasants and unscrupulous intellectuals alike, as victims of a struggle beyond their comprehension.[8] Disillusioned by an ever-expanding civil war, Azuela condemned the excesses that compromised and confused the original goals of the Revolution. Whereas Guzmán and Reed wrote of heroes, Azuela portrays complex characters as neither simply good nor simply bad.

However, there is much in *Insurgent Mexico* that demonstrates Reed's innate reportorial ability. The conversation with a soldier who had a photo of Madero pinned to his coat could easily have appeared in Azuela's book: The soldier explained to Reed that though he did not know who Madero was, "My captain told me he was a great saint [and] I fight because it is not so hard as to work." In this, Reed clearly captured the essence of daily life among the revolutionary troops in Chihuahua, no matter what exalted claims he might make elsewhere for Villa and the Cause.

Perhaps the clearest explanation of Reed's uncritical sympathy is found in Granville Hicks' early biography *John Reed: The Making of a Revolutionary*:

Ultimately Reed's admiration for Villa rested upon the fact that he, too, wanted Mexico to be a happy place. . . . He had a deep, persistent distrust of industrialism, and he dreamed, as have so many of the radicals who have followed him to Mexico, of an agrarian paradise . . . He hated the American businessmen who were bringing the machine and machine slavery to Mexico, and he loved the peons. He hoped that they might escape from bondage to the land-owners without falling into the hands of Wall Street exploiters. At least the immediate step was their liberation, and it was their battle that Villa, himself a peon, was fighting.[9]

—Introduction to John Reed, *Insurgent Mexico* (New York: Simon & Schuster, 1969), pp. 23–28

### Notes

1. *The Education of John Reed: Selected Writings,* with an introductory essay by John Stuart (New York: International Publishers, 1955), pp. 45–46.

2. Martín Luis Guzmán, in the *Memoirs of Pancho Villa,* translated by V. H. Taylor (Austin: University of Texas Press, 1965), p. 285, quotes Villa as having suggested that God had put the Revolution on earth to carry on a struggle that included the punishment of bad priests.

3. Granville Hicks, *John Reed: The Making of a Revolutionary* (New York: Macmillan, 1936), pp. 207–208.

4. Ambrose Bierce, *The Devil's Dictionary* (New York: Saga-more Press, 1957), originally published in 1906 as *The Cynic's Word Book.*

5. Edward Larocque Tinker accepts this account of Bierce's death in his review of Richard O'Connor's *Ambrose Bierce: A Biography* in *The New York Times Book Review,* 23 July 1967, pp. 4–5. Tinker quotes Elías L. Torres, *Veinte Vibrantes Episodios de la Vida de Villa* (México, D.F.: Editorial Sayrols, 1934).

6. Translated by Harriet de Onís (New York: Doubleday, 1965).

7. Guzmán, *Memoirs of Pancho Villa.*

8. Mariano Azuela, *The Underdogs,* translated by E. Munguía, Jr., Signet Classics (New York: New American Library, 1963).

9. Hicks, *John Reed: The Making of a Revolutionary,* pp. 116–117.

### Review of Reed's *Insurgent Mexico*
Dos Passos

*Dos Passos's review of Reed's* Insurgent Mexico, *written during his junior year at Harvard, reveals not only his positive response to Reed's sympathetic depiction of the Mexican Revolution but suggests as well a degree of envy for Reed's "spirit of daring" and life of "danger and excitement."*

Ever since the beginning of the Mexican Revolution, we have been deluged with books about that unhappy country, each of which claims the final and ultimate solution of the problem of the land's pacification. Everyone who has spent ten days on Mexican soil, it seems, deems himself qualified to propound his pet idea as to the reasons for Mexico's unrest, or his favorite criticism of our government's policy in a long and tiresome book, or a lurid magazine article. In "Insurgent Mexico," a collection of sketches, consisting mainly of articles published in the *Metropolitan Magazine,* Mr. Reed, who is, by the way, a recent Harvard graduate, neither dogmatizes nor puts forward any panacea for the ills of Mexico; he is content to describe what he saw during the months he spent there as a correspondent.

The book as a whole contains some of the finest impressionistic descriptions of the life and scenery of Mexico that have ever appeared. The author has shown in his pictures a truly remarkable boldness and vividness; now and then, perhaps a little sensational, a little lurid, he is constantly redeemed by his accuracy of perception, and by his human, half-humorous, view. His startling vividness of description gives the sketches wonderful color and tangibility. To read them is to feel that you have been in Mexico, that you have felt the hot blast of the Mexican deserts, lived the passionate, picturesque life of the country.

"Insurgent Mexico" also deserves praise for its sympathetic understanding of the Mexicans. Since he writes neither as a disappointed monopoly seeker, nor as a jaded professional writer of books about the more disturbed parts of the world, Jack Reed reaches a com-

*Portrait of John Reed by his friend and Harvard classmate Robert Hallowell; the radical journalist
Louise Bryant, who married Reed and accompanied him to Russia in 1917
(Courtesy of the Fogg Art Museum, Harvard University)*

prehension of Mexican psychology denied to many a profounder student of this puzzling nation. He has the breadth to see a little the Mexican view, and his sympathy becomes at times almost admiration.

But the chief delight in "Insurgent Mexico" comes from a certain refreshing quality of adventurous youth. You find in all the adventures and descriptions the old spirit of daring and naive enjoyment of danger and excitement, altogether too rare in recent literature. This makes the book enjoyable even more for itself than for the knowledge of Mexico that can be gleaned from it.

–*Harvard Monthly,* 59 (November 1914): 67–68

### Playboy
Dos Passos

*In* Nineteen-Nineteen *Dos Passos provides a full recounting of Reed's life, with emphasis on the "American" roots of his radical beliefs: "Reed was a westerner and words meant what they said."*

Jack Reed
was the son of a United States Marshal, a prominent citizen of Portland Oregon.

He was a likely boy
so his folks sent him east to school
and to Harvard.

Harvard stood for the broad *a* and those contacts so useful in later life and good English prose . . . if the hedgehog cant be cultured at Harvard the hedgehog cant
at all and the Lowells only speak to the Cabots and the Cabots
and the Oxford Book of Verse.
Reed was a likely youngster, he wasnt a jew or a socialist and he didnt come from Roxbury; he was husky greedy had appetite for everything: a man's got to like many things in his life.
Reed was a man; he liked men he liked women he liked eating and writing and foggy nights and drinking and foggy nights and swimming and football and rhymed verse and being cheerleader ivy orator making clubs (not the very best clubs, his blood didn't run thin enough for the very best clubs)
and Copey's voice reading *The Man Who Would Be King,* the dying fall *Urnburial,* good English prose the lamps coming on across the Yard, under the elms in the twilight
dim voices in lecturehalls,

# INSURGENT MEXICO

BY

JOHN REED

NEW YORK AND LONDON

D. APPLETON AND COMPANY

1914

*Title page of Reed's book on the Mexican Revolution
(Lilly Library, Indiana University)*

the dying fall the elms the Discobulus the bricks of the old buildings and the commemorative gates and the goodies and the deans and the instructors all crying in thin voices refrain,

refrain; the rusty machinery creaked, the deans quivered under their mortarboards, the cogs turned to Class Day, and Reed was out in the world:

Washington Square!
Conventional turns out to be a cussword;
Villon seeking a lodging for the night in the Italian tenements on Sullivan Street, Bleecker, Carmine;
research proves R.L.S. to have been a great cocksman,
and as for the Elizabethans

to hell with them.
Ship on a cattleboat and see the world have adventures you can tell funny stories about every evening; a man's got to love . . . the quickening pulse the feel that today in foggy evenings footsteps taxicabs women's eyes . . . many things in his life.

Europe with a dash of horseradish, gulp Paris like an oyster;

but there's more to it than the Oxford Book of English Verse. Linc Steffens talked the cooperative commonwealth.

revolution in a voice as mellow as Copey's, Diogenes Steffens with Marx for a lantern going through the west looking for a good man, Socrates Steffens kept asking why not revolution?

Jack Reed wanted to live in a tub and write verses;

but he kept meeting bums workingmen husky guys he liked out of luck out of work why not revolution?

He couldnt keep his mind on his work with so many people out of luck;

in school hadnt he learned the Declaration of Independence by heart? Reed was a westerner and words meant what they said; when he said something standing with a classmate at the Harvard Club bar, he meant what he said from the soles of his feet to the waves of his untidy hair (his blood didnt run thin enough for the Harvard Club and the Dutch Treat Club and respectable New York freelance Bohemia).

Life, liberty, and the pursuit of happiness;
not much of that round the silkmills when
in 1913,
he went over to Paterson to write up the strike, textile workers parading beaten up by the cops, the strikers in jail; before he knew it he was a striker parading beaten up by the cops in jail;

he wouldn't let the editor bail him out, he'd learn more with the strikers in jail.

He learned enough to put on the pageant of the Paterson Strike in Madison Square garden.

He learned the hope of a new society where nobody would be out of luck, why not revolution?

The Metropolitan Magazine sent him to Mexico to write up Pancho Villa.

Pancho Villa taught him to write and the skeleton mountains and the tall organ cactus and the armored trains and the bands playing in little plazas full of dark girls in blue scarfs

and the bloody dust and the ping of rifleshots

in the enormous night of the desert, and the brown quietvoiced peons dying starving killing for liberty

for land for water for schools

Mexico taught him to write.

Reed was a westerner and words meant what they said.

The war was a blast that blew out all the Diogenes lanterns;

the good men began to gang up to call for machineguns. Jack Reed was the last of the great race of warcorrespondents who ducked under censorships and risked their skins for a story.

Jack Reed was the best American writer of his time, if anybody had wanted to know about the war they could have read about it in the articles he wrote

about the German front,

the Serbian retreat,

Saloniki;

behind the lines in the tottering empire of the Czar,

dodging the secret police,

jail in Cholm.

The brasshats wouldnt let him go to France because they said one night in the German trenches kidding with the Boche guncrew he'd pulled the string on a Hun gun pointed at the heart of France . . . playboy stuff but after all what did it matter who fired the guns or which way they were pointed? Reed was with the boys who were being blown to hell,

with the Germans the French the Russians the Bulgarians the seven little tailors in the Ghetto in Salonique,

and in 1917

he was with the soldiers and peasants
in Petrograd in October:
Smolny,
*Ten Days That Shook the World;*

no more Villa picturesque Mexico, no more Harvard Club playboy stuff, plans for Greek theatres, rhyming verse, good stories of an oldtime warcorrespondent,

this wasnt fun anymore
this was grim.

Delegate,

back in the States indictments, the Masses trial, the Wobbly trial, Wilson cramming the jails,

forged passports, speeches, secret documents, riding the rods across the cordon sanitaire, hiding in the bunkers on steamboats;

jail in Finland all his papers stolen,

no more chance to write verses now, no more warm chats with every guy you met up with, the college boy with the nice smile talking himself out of trouble with the judge;

at the Harvard Club they're all in the Intelligence Service making the world safe for the Morgan-Baker-Stillman combination of banks;

that old tramp sipping his coffee out of a tomatocan's a spy of the General Staff.

The world's no fun anymore,

only machinegunfire and arson

starvation lice bedbugs cholera typhus

no lint for bandages no chloroform or ether thousands dead of gangrened wounds cordon sanitaire and everywhere spies.

The windows of Smolny glow whitehot like a bessemer,

no sleep in Smolny,

Smolny the giant rollingmill running twentyfour hours a day rolling out men nations hopes millenniums impulses fears,

rawmaterial

for the foundations

of a new society.

A man has to do many things in his life.

Reed was a westerner words meant what they said.

He threw everything he had and himself into Smolny,

dictatorship of the proletariat;

U.S.S.R.

The first workers republic

was established and stands.

Reed wrote; undertook missions (there were spies everywhere), worked till he dropped,

caught typhus and died in Moscow.

—*Nineteen-Nineteen*, pp. 371–375

### The War and the Intellectuals (June 1917)
Randolph Bourne

*Aside from extreme left-wingers, Bourne was one of the few intellectuals to speak out against both America's growing war spirit and, after November 1917, the war itself. Severely crippled at birth, Bourne died in 1918 at the age of thirty-two.*

To those of us who still retain an irreconcilable animus against the war, it has been a bitter experience to see the unanimity with which the American intellectuals have thrown their support to the use of wartechnique in the crisis in which America found herself. Socialists, college professors, publicists, new-republicans, practitioners of literature, have vied with each other in confirming with their intellectual faith the collapse of neutrality and the riveting of the war-mind on a hundred million more of the world's people. And the intellectuals are not content with confirming our belligerent gesture. They are now complacently asserting that it was they who effectively willed it, against the hesitation and dim perceptions of the American democratic masses. A war made deliberately by the intellectuals! A calm moral verdict, arrived at after a penetrating study of inexorable facts! Sluggish masses, too remote from the world-conflict to be stirred, too lacking in intellect to perceive their danger! An alert intellectual class, saving the people in spite of themselves, biding their time with Fabian strategy until the nation could be moved into war without serious resistance! An intellectual class, gently guiding a nation through sheer force of ideas into what the other nations entered only through predatory craft or popular hysteria or militarist madness! A war free from any taint of self-seeking, a war that will secure the triumph of democracy and internationalize the world! This is the picture which the more self-conscious intellectuals have formed of themselves, and which they are slowly impressing upon a population which is being led no man knows whither by an indubitably intellectualized President. And they are right, in that the war certainly did not spring from either the ideals or the prejudices, from the national ambitions or hysterias, of the American people, however acquiescent the masses prove to be, and however clearly the intellectuals prove their putative intuition.

Those intellectuals who have felt themselves totally out of sympathy with this drag toward war will seek some explanation for this joyful leadership. They will want to understand this willingness of the American intellect to open the sluices and flood us with the sewage of the war spirit. We cannot forget the virtuous horror and stupefaction which filled our college professors when they read the famous manifesto of their ninety-three German colleagues in defense of their war. To the American academic mind of 1914 defense of war was inconceivable. From Bernhardi it recoiled as from a blasphemy, little dreaming that two years later would find it creating its own cleanly reasons for imposing military service on the country and for talking of the rough rude currents of health and regeneration that war would send through the American body politic. They would have thought any one mad who talked of shipping American men by the hundreds of thousands—conscripts—to die on the fields of France. Such a spiritual change seems catastrophic when we shoot our minds back to those days when neutrality was a proud thing. But the intellectual progress has been so gradual that the country retains little sense of the irony. The war sentiment, begun so gradually but so perseveringly by the preparedness advocates who came from the ranks of big business, caught hold of one after another of the intellectual groups. With the aid of Roosevelt,

the murmurs became a monotonous chant, and finally a chorus so mighty that to be out of it was at first to be disreputable and finally almost obscene. And slowly a strident rant was worked up against Germany which compared very creditably with the German fulminations against the greedy power of England. The nerve of the war-feeling centered, of course, in the richer and older classes of the Atlantic seaboard, and was keenest where there were French or English business and particularly social connections. The sentiment then spread over the country as a class-phenomenon, touching everywhere those upperclass elements in each section who identified themselves with this Eastern ruling group. It must never be forgotten that in every community it was the least liberal and least democratic elements among whom the preparedness and later the war sentiment was found. The farmers were apathetic, the small business men and workingmen are still apathetic towards the war. The election was a vote of confidence of these latter classes in a President who would keep the faith of neutrality. The intellectuals, in other words, have identified themselves with the least democratic forces in American life. They have assumed the leadership for war of those very classes whom the American democracy has been immemorially fighting. Only in a world where irony was dead could an intellectual class enter war at the head of such illiberal cohorts in the avowed cause of world-liberalism and world-democracy. No one is left to point out the undemocratic nature of this war-liberalism. In a time of faith, skepticism is the most intolerable of all insults.

Our intellectual class might have been occupied, during the last two years of war, in studying and clarifying the ideals and aspirations of the American democracy, in discovering a true Americanism which would not have been merely nebulous but might have federated the different ethnic groups and traditions. They might have spent the time in endeavoring to clear the public mind of the cant of war, to get rid of old mystical notions that clog our thinking. We might have used the time for a great wave of education, for setting our house in spiritual order. We could at least have set the problem before ourselves. If our intellectuals were going to lead the administration, they might conceivably have tried to find some way of securing peace by making neutrality effective. They might have turned their intellectual energy not to the problem of jockeying the nations into war, but to the problem of using our vast neutral power to attain democratic ends for the rest of the world and ourselves without the use of the malevolent technique of war. They might have failed. The point is that they scarcely tried. The time was spent not in clarification and education, but in a mulling over of nebulous ideals of democracy and liberalism and civilization which had never meant anything fruitful to those ruling classes who now so glibly used them, and in giving free rein to the elementary instinct of self-defense. The whole era has been spiritually wasted.

. . . . . . . . . .

–from Bruce Clayton, *Forgotten Prophet: The Life of Randolph Bourne* (Baton Rouge: Louisiana State University Press, 1984), pp. 205–208

### Randolph Bourne
Dos Passos

Randolph Bourne
came as an inhabitant of this earth
without the pleasure of choosing his dwelling or his career.

He was a hunchback, grandson of a congregational minister, born in 1886 in Bloomfield, New Jersey; there he attended grammarschool and highschool.

At the age of seventeen he went to work as secretary to a Morristown businessman.

He worked his way through Columbia working in a pianola record factory in Newark, working as proofreader, pianotuner, accompanist in a vocal studio in Carnegie Hall.

*Randolph Bourne (Courtesy of the Rare Book and Manuscript Library, Columbia University)*

At Columbia he studied with John Dewey,
got a travelling fellowship that took him to England Paris Rome Berlin Copenhagen,
wrote a book on the Gary schools.
In Europe he heard music, a great deal of Wagner and Scriabine
and bought himself a black cape.

This little sparrowlike man,
tiny twisted bit of flesh in a black cape
always in pain and ailing,
put a pebble in his sling
and hit Goliath square in the forehead with it.

*War,* he wrote, *is the health of the state.*

Half musician, half educational theorist (weak health and being poor and twisted in body and on bad terms with his people hadn't spoiled the world for Randolph Bourne; he was a happy man, loved die Meistersinger and playing Bach with his long hands that stretched so easily over the keys and pretty girls and good food and evenings of talk. When he was dying of pneumonia a friend brought him an eggnog; Look at the yellow, it's beautiful, he kept saying as his life ebbed into delirium and fever. He was a happy man.) Bourne seized with feverish intensity on the ideas then going around at Columbia, he picked rosy glasses out of the turgid jumble of John Dewey's teaching through which he saw clear and sharp
the shining capitol of reformed democracy,
Wilson's New Freedom;
but he was too good a mathematician; he had to work the equations out;
with the result
that in the crazy spring of 1917 he began to get unpopular where his bread was buttered at the New Republic;
for *New Freedom* read *Conscription,* for *Democracy, Win the War,* for *Reform, Safeguard the Morgan Loans*
for Progress Civilization Education Service,
Buy a Liberty Bond,
Straff the Hun,
Jail the Objectors.
He resigned from *The New Republic;* only *The Seven Arts* had the nerve to publish his articles against the war. The backers of *The Seven Arts* took their money elsewhere; friends didn't like to be seen with Bourne, his father wrote him begging him not to disgrace the family name. The rainbowtinted future of reformed democracy went pop like a pricked soapbubble.
The liberals scurried to Washington;
some of his friends plead with him to climb up on Schoolmaster Wilson's sharabang; the war was

great fought from the swivel chairs of Mr. Creel's bureau in Washington.

He was cartooned, shadowed by the espionage service and the counter-espionage service; taking a walk with two girl friends at Wood's Hole he was arrested, a trunk full of manuscript and letters was stolen from him in Connecticut. (Force to the utmost, thundered Schoolmaster Wilson)

He didn't live to see the big circus of the Peace of Versailles or the purplish normalcy of the Ohio Gang.

Six weeks after the armistice he died planning an essay on the foundations of future radicalism in America.

> If any man has a ghost
> Bourne has a ghost,
> a tiny twisted unscared ghost in a black cloak
> hopping along the grimy old brick and brownstone streets still left in downtown New York,
> crying out in a shrill soundless giggle:
> *War is the health of the state.*
>     —*Nineteen-Nineteen*, pp. 447–449

## Dos Passos to Edmund Wilson, 24 September 1934

*Dos Passos shared his rediscovery of Thorstein Veblen, whom he had first read in the 1920s, with his friend Edmund Wilson. Dos Passos's call slips from the New York Public Library for two of Veblen's later studies,* Absentee Ownership and the Business Enterprise in Recent Times *(1923) and* The Engineers and the Price System *(1921), date from this period.*

Since I've been in bed I've been reading a good deal of Veblen. He takes a good deal of reading. I admire his delicate surgeon's analysis more and more. In spite of the fact that everything he deals with is abstracted for classroom use, I shouldn't wonder if he were the only American economist whose work had any lasting value. His work is a sort of anthropological footnote to Marx. If you haven't read him recently you should read him—The Vested Interests or the Nature of Peace on Business Enterprise—(I think The Leisure Class is more or less of a side issue, though it will always be considered the type Veblen satire). Imperial Germany makes an excellent prelude to Hitler Over

*Front cover and political cartoon from the magazine published in Greenwich Village that was the principal vehicle of expression for the intellectual Left in the period before America's entrance into World War I. In the cartoon a Paterson silk manufacturer tramples basic rights, declaring his disdain for human-rights laws and his intention to punish IWW leaders Haywood and Flynn. The editors of* The Masses *were prosecuted for their antiwar views in November 1917, but the magazine was revived as the* New Masses *in 1926, with Dos Passos serving on its editorial board (from Robert E. Humphrey,* Children of Fantasy, *1978).*

Europe [Henri] and The Berlin Diaries [Klotz]–before you finish the series you are working on now. There certainly seems to me to be more ammunition in his analysis than in any other for us, because he seems to have been the only man of genius who put his mind critically to work on American capitalism–Stuart Chase and Howard Scott got all their analysis directly from him. And certainly he's of an entirely different stature than the purely literary critics, like Van Wyck Brooks and Randolph Bourne who have the same before-thewar limitations. Its amazing how fresh his clinical picture remains.

–Townsend Ludington, ed., *The Fourteenth Chronicle: Letters and Diaries of John Dos Passos* (Boston: Gambit, 1973), pp. 443–444

### The Bitter Drink
Dos Passos

*Dos Passos's biography of Veblen is similar to his accounts of other naysayers who refused to accept the weaknesses in American society: These figures led lives of pain and apparent failure, but they were also beacons of truth and hope.*

Veblen,

a greyfaced shambling man lolling resentful at his desk with his cheek on his hand, in a low sarcastic mumble of intricate phrases subtly paying out the logical inescapable rope of matteroffact for a society to hang itself by,

dissecting out the century with a scalpel so keen, so comical, so exact that the professors and students ninetenths of the time didn't know it was there, and the magnates and the respected windbags and the applauded loudspeakers never knew it was there.

Veblen

asked too many questions, suffered from a constitutional inability to say yes.

Socrates asked questions, drank down the bitter drink one night when the first cock crowed,

but Veblen

drank it in little sips through a long life in the stuffiness of classrooms, the dust of libraries, the staleness of cheap flats such as a poor instructor can afford. He fought the boyg all right, pedantry, routine, timeservers at office desks, trustees, collegepresidents, the plump flunkies of the ruling businessmen, all the good jobs kept for yesmen, never enough money, every broadening hope thwarted. Veblen drank the bitter drink all right.

. . . . . . . . .

*Thorstein Veblen, circa 1907 (from Carlton C. Qualey, Thorstein Veblen, 1968)*

Thorstein spoke English with an accent. He had a constitutional inability to say yes. His mind was formed on the Norse sagas and on the matteroffact sense of his father's farming and the exact needs of carpenterwork and threshingmachines.

He could never take much interest in the theology, sociology, economics of Carleton College where they were busy trimming down the jagged dogmas of the old New England bibletaught traders to make stencils to hang on the walls of commissionmerchants' offices.

Veblen's collegeyears were the years when Darwin's assertions of growth and becoming were breaking the set molds of the Noah's Ark world,

when Ibsen's women were tearing down the portieres of the Victorian parlors,

and Marx's mighty machine was rigging the countinghouse's own logic to destroy the countinghouse.

When Veblen went home to the farm he talked about these things with his father, following him up and down at his plowing, starting an argument while they were waiting for a new load for the wheatthresher. Thomas Anderson had seen Norway and America; he had the squarebuilt mind of a carpenter and builder, and an understanding of tools and the treasured elabo-

*Dos Passos's call slips from the New York Public Library for two books by Veblen (Albert and Shirley Small Special Collections Library, University of Virginia Library)*

rated builtupseasonbyseason knowledge of a careful farmer,

a tough whetstone for the sharpening steel of young Thorstein's wits.

At Carleton College young Veblen was considered a brilliant unsound eccentric; nobody could understand why a boy of such attainments wouldn't settle down to the business of the day, which was to buttress property and profits with anything usable in the debris of Christian ethics and eighteenth-century economics that cluttered the minds of collegeprofessors, and to reinforce the sacred, already shaky edifice with the new strong girderwork of science Herbert Spencer was throwing up for the benefit of the bosses.

People complained they never knew whether Veblen was joking or serious.

. . . . . . . . . .

In '91 Veblen got together some money to go to Cornell to do postgraduate work. He turned up there in the office of the head of the economics department wearing a coonskin cap and grey corduroy trousers and said in his low sarcastic drawl, "I am Thorstein Veblen,"

but it was not until several years later, after he was established at the new University of Chicago that had grown up next to the World's Fair, and had published *The Theory of the Leisure Class,* put on the map by Howells' famous review, that the world of the higher learning knew who Thorstein Veblen was.

. . . . . . . . . .

His friend Davenport got him an appointment at the University of Missouri. At Columbia he lived like a hermit in the basement of the Davenports' house, helped with the work round the place, carpentered himself a table and chairs. He was already a bitter elderly man with a grey face covered with a net of fine wrinkles, a vandyke beard and yellow teeth. Few students could follow his courses. The college authorities were often surprised and somewhat chagrined that when visitors came from Europe it was always Veblen they wanted to meet.

These were the years he did most of his writing, trying out his ideas on his students, writing slowly at night in violet ink with a pen of his own designing. Whenever he published a book he had to put up a guarantee with the publishers. In *The Theory of Business Enterprise, The Instinct of Workmanship, The Vested Interests and the Common Man,*

he established a new diagram of society dominated by monopoly capital,

etched in irony

the sabotage of production by business,

the sabotage of life by blind need for money profits,

pointed out the alternatives: a warlike society strangled by the bureaucracies of the monopolies forced by the law of diminishing returns to grind down more and more the common man for profits,

or a new matteroffact commonsense society dominated by the needs of the men and women who did the work and the incredibly vast possibilities for peace and plenty offered by the progress of technology.

These were the years of Debs's speeches, growing laborunions, the I.W.W. talk about industrial democracy: these years Veblen still held to the hope that the workingclass would take over the machine of production before monopoly had pushed the western nations down into the dark again.

War cut across all that: under the cover of the bunting of Woodrow Wilson's phrases the monopolies cracked down. American democracy was crushed.

The war at least offered Veblen an opportunity to break out of the airless greenhouse of academic life. He was offered a job with the Food Administration, he sent the Navy Department a device for catching submarines by trailing lengths of stout bindingwire. (Meanwhile the government found his books somewhat confusing. The postoffice was forbidding the mails to *Imperial Germany and the Industrial Revolution* while propaganda agencies were sending it out to make people hate the Huns. Educators were denouncing *The Nature of Peace* while Washington experts were clipping phrases out of it to add to the Wilsonian smokescreen.)

For the Food Administration Thorstein Veblen wrote two reports: in one he advocated granting the demands of the I.W.W. as a wartime measure and conciliating the workingclass instead of beating up and jailing all the honest leaders; in the other he pointed out that the Food Administration was a businessman's racket and was not aiming for the most efficient organization of the country as a producing machine. He suggested that, in the interests of the efficient prosecution of the war, the government step into the place of the middleman and furnish necessities to the farmers direct in return for raw materials;

but cutting out business was not at all the Administration's idea of making the world safe for democracy,

so Veblen had to resign from the Food Administration.

He signed the protests against the trial of the hundred and one wobblies in Chicago.

After the armistice he went to New York. In spite of all the oppression of the war years, the air was freshening. In Russia the great storm of revolt had broken, seemed to be sweeping west, in the strong gusts from the new world in the east the warsodden multitudes began to see again. At Versailles allies and enemies, magnates, generals, flunkey politicians were slamming the shutters against the storm, against the new, against hope. It was suddenly clear for a second in the thundering glare what war was about, what peace was about.

In America, in Europe, the old men won. The bankers in their offices took a deep breath, the bediamonded old ladies of the leisure class went back to clipping their coupons in the refined quiet of their safedeposit vaults,

the last puffs of the ozone of revolt went stale
in the whisper of speakeasy arguments.

Veblen wrote for the *Dial*,
lectured at the New School for Social Research.

He still had a hope that the engineers, the technicians, the nonprofiteers whose hands were on the switchboard might take up the fight where the working-class had failed. He helped form the Technical Alliance. His last hope was the British general strike.

Was there no group of men bold enough to take charge of the magnificent machine before the pigeyed speculators and the yesmen at office desks irrevocably ruined it

and with it the hopes of four hundred years?

No one went to Veblen's lectures at the New School. With every article he wrote in the *Dial* the circulation dropped.

Harding's normalcy, the new era was beginning;
even Veblen made a small killing on the stockmarket.

He was an old man and lonely.

His second wife had gone to a sanitarium suffering from delusions of persecution.

There seemed no place for a masterless man.

Veblen went back out to Palo Alto
to live in his shack in the tawny hills and observe from outside the last grabbing urges of the profit system taking on, as he put it, the systematized delusions of dementia praecox.

There he finished his translation of the *Laxdaela-saga*.

He was an old man. He was much alone. He let the woodrats take what they wanted from his larder. A skunk that hung round the shack was so tame he'd rub up against Veblen's leg like a cat.

He told a friend he'd sometimes hear in the stillness about him the voices of his boyhood talking Norwegian as clear as on the farm in Minnesota where he was raised. His friends found him harder than ever to talk to, harder than ever to interest in anything. He was running down. The last sips of the bitter drink.

He died on August 3, 1929.

Among his papers a penciled note was found:

*It is also my wish, in case of death, to be cremated if it can conveniently be done, as expeditiously and inexpensively as may be, without ritual or ceremony of any kind; that my ashes be thrown loose into the sea or into some sizable stream running into the sea; that no tombstone, slab, epitaph, effigy, tablet, inscription or monument of any name or nature, be set up to my memory or name in any place or at any time; that no obituary, memorial, portrait or biography of me, nor any letters written to or by me be printed or published, or in any way reproduced, copied or circulated;*

but his memorial remains
riveted into the language:
the sharp clear prism of his mind.
                    —*The Big Money*, pp. 845–855

### Dos Passos and Veblen's Villains
John P. Diggins

*Diggins trenchantly examines the impact of Veblen's beliefs about America as a business civilization on Dos Passos's work, particularly* The Big Money.

. . . . . . . . . .

During the depression decade it was common for writers on the Left to discern Marxist overtones in Dos Passos' writings. A more valid approach to understanding his social thought, it seems to me, may be found in the strong vein of Veblen that runs through a good many of his novels. Examined in the light of Veblen's thesis concerning the antagonism between industry and business, the fiction of Dos Passos, starting with the trilogy *U.S.A.* (1930–1936), reveals an abiding admiration for the technician and workman, for the craftsman and mechanic, for those who are close to the productive operations of society. Beginning in the thirties Dos Passos made the problem of the worker his primary concern. "To tell truly," he advised in a 1934 *New Republic* article, "about the relation between men and machines and to describe the machine worker, are among the most important tasks before the novelists today." The workers, proletariat and professional, became his heroes. Imaginative and constructive, they were interested in productivity rather than profit. Guided by what Veblen called the beneficent "instinct of workmanship," they led meaningful lives worthy of dignity. The role of the businessman, in contrast, was that of the antagonist in a number of Dos Passos' earlier works. Pecuniary gain as his sole objective, the businessman manipulated destructively the productive processes in order to profit. And since he was far removed from the source of production, the acquisitive businessman became one of Dos Passos' blackest villains in *U.S.A.*

. . . . . . . . . .

We can begin with J. Ward Moorehouse. Nowhere in modern American literature is the profile of the businessman so bitterly repulsive as in the figure of Moorehouse. His rise to wealth, which is traced through the three novels in *U.S.A.*, is a biting satire on the self-made man myth ("By gum, I can do it!"). Born in the late nineteenth century, Moorehouse represents Veblen's "new captain of industry," the salesman who is concerned neither with the "technical conduct" nor with the "tangible performance" of the industrial system. He finds no satisfaction working at the Bessemer plant, claiming the position is too mechanical and "routine." What he has in mind is a public relations program which will "educate the public" by creating a favorable image of the business community and by stimulating demand for consumer goods. Thus the pleasures of craftsmanship do not interest Moorehouse. Completely removed from the human source of work, he becomes obsessed with "ideas, plans, stockquotations unrolling in an endless tickertape in his head." His every action is spurred by base ambition cloaked with a pretentious idealism. When his public relations outfit begins to lag in 1916, the advice of his partner does not go unheeded: "Whoever wins, Europe will be economically ruined. This war is America's great opportunity." With a display of patriotic bravado he goes off to Europe as a publicity director for the Red Cross. Throughout the trilogy Moorehouse is motivated by what Veblen described as the "pecuniary calculus." Even as all Paris is celebrating the announcement of the Armistice, he remains capable of only one reaction: "J. W. was preoccupied and wanted to get to a telephone. . . . He must get in touch with his broker."

It is through such calculated cupidity that Moorehouse achieves eminence in American society and becomes, in Veblen's words, the pompous "prince and priest" of the business world. The personification of the captain of finance, he is institutionalized with deference ("After all J. W. Moorehouse isn't a man, it's a name"). The irony is that Moorehouse, like Veblen's "prehensile businessman," believes himself and his ilk to be the life force of the economy. The point is made when Dick Savage, Moorehouse's protege who, as the name implies, represents the predatory creatures of capitalism, attempts to defend the role of his alter-ego.

Whether you like it or not the molding of the public mind is one of the most important things that goes on in this country. If it wasn't for that American business would be in a pretty pickle. . . . It's only through public relations work that business is protected from wildeyed cranks and demagogues who are always ready to throw a monkeywrench into the industrial machine.

Although subtle, the irony in Savage's speech is clear enough. For while Moorehouse and Savage proudly look upon themselves as the driving force behind the industrial system, Dos Passos has made it clear that their role is one of price and profit rather than production. Their propensity to manipulate and "mold" is essentially destructive. They, in short, comprise the "monkeywrench." They are what Veblen called the "saboteurs" of the economy.

If Moorehouse was the ubiquitous villain of *U.S.A.*, Charley Anderson was the tragic victim. Anderson possessed a choice. As a skilled mechanic and aviator he found satisfaction in his craft and tried to remain loyal to his profession. "Hell, I ain't no boss. . . . I belong with the mechanics . . . don't I Bill? You and me, Bill, the mechanics against the world." Yet the lure of the "Big Money" was too strong. "I don't know what it is, but I got a kind of feel for the Big Money." Hopelessly he succumbs to the gaudy spree of speculation. Driven by a blind obsession for the tinsel and gloss of wealth and conspicuous leisure, he realizes he is caught and cannot return to his craft. "Aw Christ, I wish I was still tinkering with that damn motor and didn't have to worry about money all the time." The passion for acquisitive emulation overcame the instinct of workmanship. Anderson forsook his craft, thereby sealing his fate, and his drunken smashup at the conclusion of the novel served to point up what in his biographical sketch of Veblen Dos Passos called "the sabotage of life by the blind need for money."

A lesser character, Bill Cermak, Anderson's mechanic, presents an interesting contrast. Indeed, like Terry Bryant of *Midcentury,* he is one of the healthiest of all Dos Passos' characters. A rare specimen in *U.S.A.*, Cermak is content with his workmanship, his imaginative tinkering and "idle curiosity." He is the independent engineer who takes pride in his trade. Yet Cermak, speaking for Dos Passos, soon perceived that new production methods were alienating the worker from the use of his skills. The massive industrial machine was causing his men to lead lives of automated desperation. When Cermak complains to Anderson about the hectic mechanization of work he is told that the "oldtime shop" is obsolete and that from now on every department must "click like a machine." Cermak's protests [are] futile, for Anderson no longer has what Veblen called the "engineer's conscience." Interested only in making money, he subordinates production to profit. And such destructive manipulation not only sabotages the economy but also ruins the men who go to make the industrial machine.

The Veblen theme is the leitmotif for *U.S.A.*, particularly in the third novel, *The Big Money*. Implicit in much of the characterization, the theme became explicit in many of the "Newsreel" devices which provided a chorus of social protest (PIGIRON OUTPUT SHARPLY REDUCED). Similarly in the biographies, Dos Passos shifted from the lonely, defeated champions of labor and intellectual rebels (Taylor, LaFollette, Bourne, etc.) of the first two novels and gave more attention to industrial leaders and masters of the machine (Taylor, Ford, Wright Brothers, etc.). For it was during the thirties when he was writing the last part of the trilogy that the novelist became deeply interested in the precarious future of the individual workman. Given this background, one might well ask whether the New Deal provided any kind of solution for Dos Passos. He apparently approved of some of Roosevelt's programs during the thirties. In 1936 he voted for F.D.R. with "enthusiasm" and in 1940 he did likewise but later regretted it. Yet perhaps it was inevitable that Dos Passos would turn against the welfare state. For while Veblen had seen the dignity of work being undermined by the savagery of the business world, Dos Passos discerned a new threat to his independent artisan in the activities of the federal government. Just as the businessman could thwart the craftsman, so too could the politician. If the financier was interested in profit, the politician was preoccupied with power. In either case the workman's life would be truncated by institutions remote from the individual source of creative exertion. With the publication of *The Grand Design* (1949) Dos Passos made clear his hostility to this new form of organized power.

. . . . . . . . . .

More than the appeal of Communism, the influence of Veblen explains the politics of Dos Passos during the depression. Instead of looking forward to a collective upheaval, he hoped for some kind of structural transformation of corporate capitalism which would eliminate the leeches of leisures and the parasites of profit. Communism for Dos Passos meant the dislodging of Veblen's anti-Christ rather than the triumph of the proletariat. This position was implied in his articles written in 1930 in the *New Republic* and the *New Masses*. Expressed in the form of an appeal, Dos Passos called upon "engineers, scientists, independent manual craftsmen, artists, actors, writers, experts of one kind or another" to remain neutral in order to cushion a possible class struggle in America. He believed that the

"owning classes" could not be appealed to in a class war. But more significantly, he maintained that the "non-radical" segment of labor would fail to come to the aid of the Left, realizing, as did Veblen, that there was little revolutionary potential in the working class. Only the "intellectual proletariat," the craftsmen and artists, could be appealed to because this group had no stake in the capitalist system. This is just another way of saying that it was in Veblen's heroes that Dos Passos placed his hopes. Three decades later he restates this position in the Introduction to the Buckley book. He was not trying to change society radically but to "conserve the independence of the average citizen we felt the power of organized money was bent to destroy." His "radical" role was merely an extension of the Populist and Progressive spirit, he reflects, for he too wanted "somehow to restore the dignity of the man who did the work." And it is this persistent effort to liberate the workman which is at the core of Dos Passos' social protest, explaining his past radicalism as well as his present conservatism.

The strange political career of John Dos Passos becomes less a riddle when the philosophy of work implicit in his writings is given proper emphasis. With Veblen, Dos Passos propounded a social philosophy of salvation through craftsmanship. Like Veblen, moreover, he distinguishes between pecuniary and industrial occupations. Indeed, Dos Passos as novelist and Veblen as social scientist have much in common. The affinity is evident in *U.S.A.* where in the most extended and respectful of all the biographies Dos Passos expressed a sympathetic identification with the scholar who, because of the "sharp clear prism of his mind," could not "get his mouth around the essential yes." Dos Passos' veneration of Veblen relates to his own philosophy of literature, which considers the function of the novelist and the social scientist as one: that is, to "put the acid test to existing institutions, and strip the veils off them," to "peel the onion of doubt," and to "ponder the course of history." What remains to be noted, however, is the significant fact that to Dos Passos the idea of Veblen must be just as perilous as those of Marx. True, Dos Passos, Veblen, and Marx all grappled with the basic problem of the alienation of the worker. Yet their solutions are incompatible. While Marx accepted industrialism as an inevitable but painful blessing, Veblen saw in the "discipline of the machine" the salutary nurturing of a scientific habit of mind. For Marx, in short, industrialism created the revolutionary material in the proletariat, for Veblen the revolutionary mentality in the scientist. For Dos Passos, on the other hand, industrialism was the original sin of modern science. Hostile to the mechanization of society from the beginning of his literary life, he always remained skeptical of the cult of technology. The theme pervades his works. Frederick Winslow Taylor, the genius of efficiency who died "with his watch in his hand," is shown in *U.S.A.* to be less the master of his scientific American plan than its inevitable victim. In *Midcentury* Dos Passos' suspicion of technology has turned to alarm. Here the worship of science is satirized, the "advances" in behavioral engineering and biocontrol mockingly attacked as a dehumanization of personality and a violation of sovereignty. Freudianism comes in for bitter scorn as an escape from individual responsibility, an escape which, together with the dialectical determinism of Marx, has brought about the "disintegration of the Western will." Everyone is going under, surrendering his will to the false gods of science, psychology, and ideology. Even the engineer, the cherished hero of Veblen and Dos Passos, has become the product rather than the producer ("Send your key technical people / TOP MEN FOR SALE"). The machine is taking over, the novelist fretfully implies. Self-reliance has given way to scientific infallibility, even though in the final analysis "numbers fail." The individual has sold out his independence for the comfortable conditioned security of science. Modern man is becoming an idle man. Above all, the work ethic no longer operates. And so with sad irony Dos Passos carries the Veblen theme to its ultimate conclusion. Work has become automated and man dispensable. The modern scientist and the engineer, Veblen's heroic emancipators, have now alienated the worker and deprived him of his sole source of salvation—his workmanship. Veblen's hero has become Dos Passos' new villain.

That work is a source of moral nourishment is a notion that has its roots deep in American history: in the Puritan ethic and the Jeffersonian yeoman idea, in the preachings of Andrew Carnegie and the protests of Henry George. Dos Passos rightly regards himself as part of this tradition, a tradition which has been shared by the Right as well as the Left, by thinkers as politically diverse as Herbert Hoover and Thorstein Veblen. The novelist's dictum, succinctly stated thirty years ago in his introduction to *Three Soldiers*, that "every type of work has its own vigor inherent in it," is no less true for him today. In our age of affluence and leisure John Dos Passos remains the sensitive social conscience of the gospel of work.

–*Antioch Review*, 23 (Winter 1963): 485–500

\* \* \*

# Communism

*One of the effects of the founding of the Soviet Union upon world radicalism was the increased importance of the American Communist Party during the 1920s. The appeal of the party was also related to its combination of high idealism and strict discipline, a mix*

*that promised to deliver the working-class equality that the IWW had failed to produce.*

*In* The Big Money *Dos Passos devotes a good deal of Mary French's narrative to the party's central role in American radicalism during the 1920s, using especially the figures of Ben Compton and Don Stevens. Compton, who has his own narrative segment in* Nineteen-Nineteen, *in which his engagement as an IWW activist at Paterson, New Jersey, and Everett, Washington, is dramatized, has now transferred his loyalties to the Communists and plays a major role in the 1926 Passaic, New Jersey, textile strike. (Dos Passos based this portion of Ben's career on that of Albert Weisbord, a fiery young Communist.) Later, Compton falls victim to the vicious internal struggles of the party, in which any independent thinking is labeled "deviationism," and he is expelled. In Ben's career, and in the beliefs and actions of the Communist leader Stevens, Dos Passos sums up the history of the American Left from the perspective of the early 1930s, when he had become disillusioned with its efforts to return America to its "storybook democracy." Ben, the idealist, has moved from the inept IWW to the doctrinaire Communist Party to isolation. The party, and thus the Left as a whole, is now controlled by ruthless party functionaries such as Stevens.*

## The Communists and the Passaic Strike
Irving Howe and Lewis Coser

*Howe and Coser describe the Communists' role in the famous Passaic textile strike of 1926. Dos Passos was a member of a group of New York writers who visited the strike area.*

At its fourth national convention, in August, 1925, the Workers (Communist) Party passed a resolution urging the unionization of the textile workers by "strengthening the existing organization and the creation of new unions where none exist. . . ."[1] This formula was ambiguous: its first half suggested support to the AFL union, its second half left the door open to dual unionism. And the ambiguity was to be characteristic of the entire Passaic adventure.

In 1926 the party moved into action. When the Botany Mills at Passaic announced a 10 percent wage cut in October, the party's Needle Trade Committee, headed by Benjamin Gitlow, decided that the time was ripe for a strike.[2] It is important to note that from the very beginning the party leadership was divided as to the advisability of having Communists openly lead a strike. The Foster group warned that to organize new unions might immediately raise the danger of sliding into dual unionism, and such party leaders as Cannon and Dunne expressed the fear that for Communists *publicly* to lead a strike in so difficult a situation as that in Passaic might doom the workers to defeat.

Brushing aside such doubts, the party leadership dispatched Albert Weisbord, a Harvard law student

*Scene from the 1926 movie* The Passaic Textile Strikes, *produced by the Communist-front organization Workers' Aid International, in which two unidentified actors portray workers discussing their situation before the strike (Film Stills Archive, Museum of Modern Art, New York)*

recently converted from the young Socialists, to prepare for a strike in Passaic. Like most Communist missionaries to the American working class, Weisbord was enormously articulate and had an unlimited fund of energy but knew very little about trade unionism in general or the textile workers in particular. Since he was to work under the close supervision of the party's Needle Trade Committee, the party felt that these handicaps would not prove too serious; what it wanted most from Weisbord was his flamboyant oratory.[3]

A United Front Textile Committee was quickly organized, consisting mainly of party members and sympathizers. On January 23, 1926, a committee of forty-five workers presented Botany Mills with a demand that a wage cut be restored; the company replied by firing the entire committee; and immediately thereafter 5,000 Botany workers struck. The strike quickly spread to other Passaic mills, until 16,000 workers had walked out. But as was to happen repeatedly when the Communists took over strikes, a large proportion of the skilled workers remained on the job.[4]

The strike was bitter, bloody, merciless. Police and deputy sheriffs attacked strikers with clubs, fire hose, tear gas, guns.[5] Injunctions were issued, picket lines broken, union halls closed. Nearly a thousand arrests were made during the strike. Mayors, magistrates, United States Senators, a local "Citizens Committee," the U.S. Secretary of Labor–the whole apparatus of "public opinion"–joined against the strikers.[6] But most harmful of all was the AFL denunciation. As *The Christian Century* wrote at the time, "It is within the truth to say that, if the strike is broken, the AFL will have borne a conspicuous part in breaking it."[7] The AFL United Textile Workers Union accepted, in the June, 1926, issue of its paper, large display ads from three firms that were being struck; about the men on the picket lines it said not a word.

Though aware that their leadership of the strike furnished the enemy with major ammunition, the Communists refused to relinquish control. Weisbord was unambiguously told by the Central Executive Committee of the party that neither he nor the general strike committee commanded decisive power in formulating strike policy; the real decisions were to be taken by the party. As Benjamin Gitlow has testified–and in this case there is every reason to credit his testi-

# PASSAIC

*the Story of a Struggle*

## Against Starvation Wages

*and for*

## The Right to Organize

*Told by*

### Albert Weisbord

Price 15c

Published for the
WORKERS (COMMUNIST) PARTY
by the
DAILY WORKER PUBLISHING CO.

299                    1926

*Title page of the book on the 1926 Passaic textile workers'*
*strike by a young Communist activist who was a model*
*for the character Ben Compton in U.S.A.*
*(Collection of Donald Pizer)*

mony: "The most intimate questions of strike policy were settled without even consulting the general strike committee, let alone the strikers."[8] Weisbord received enormous quantities of national publicity and grew vain to the point where the local Passaic Communists protested against his dictatorial manner; but in actuality he was only a figurehead. The real decisions were taken in New York.

One thing the Communists did arrange with great efficiency: they set into motion an impressive machine for popularizing the strike and raising relief funds. Passaic was swamped with left-wing and liberal journalists who wrote passionate reports favorable to the strikers. Mary Heaton Vorse, Art Shields, Robert W. Dunn—either party members or sympathizers—held conferences, tried to influence public figures, congressmen, clergymen. Whenever strikers were clubbed, prominent liberals arrested simply for talking to pickets, parades organized of veterans and young girls, there quickly followed a barrage of stories and pictures favorable to the strikers. Simultaneously, the relief committee was raising sizable sums of money with which to support the destitute strikers—and, less honorably, to help pay

the salaries of a number of party functionaries who had been "attached" to the strike organization.[9]

The strike dragged on for almost a year. Workers began to drift back to the mills or to leave Passaic entirely. In September—much too late—the Communist leadership finally decided that a settlement could not be reached and that the strike had reached the point of exhaustion. There seemed only one solution: to persuade the AFL Textile Workers Union to take over. It was a hard step for the Communists, but they took it. After much negotiating, the AFL union agreed to become a sort of receiver for the strikers, but at a heavy price: that the Communist leaders, particularly Weisbord, leave Passaic. The party winced, the leaders quarreled and hesitated, the strike committee succumbed to demoralization. Finally the Communists surrendered and Weisbord left.

The strike had been lost: completely, pitiably, and at enormous cost. Even after the AFL reached an agreement, many of the strikers were denied their old jobs. Within two years less than 100 Passaic textile workers remained in the AFL union. The Communists had managed to gain national publicity; they had been able to preen themselves as courageous leaders who did not fear to tackle enemies that the AFL avoided; but they failed to win a permanent foothold in the industry. The party's isolation in textile was now greater than ever, and the price the Passaic workers had paid for the party's insistence upon exploiting their needs was incalculable. Having hesitated between working through the AFL and creating a dual union in textile, the Communists had ended without the organizational benefits of either course. A sense of realism as to their own powers, to say nothing of a regard for the immediate interests of the workers, should have taught the Communists that when they led strikes openly, in the most violently anti-union industries and in blunt opposition to the AFL, the overwhelming likelihood was that they would lead the workers to grief.

*—The American Communist Party: A Critical History, 1919–*
*1957 (Boston: Beacon, 1957), pp. 240–243*

## Notes

1. *The Fourth National Convention,* Workers (Communist) Party, Chicago, 1925, p. 101.

2. Benjamin Gitlow, *I Confess* (New York: Dutton, 1940), p. 363.

3. *Ibid.*

4. Albert Weisbord, *The Conquest of Power* (New York: Covici-Friede, 1937), II: 1115.

5. Gitlow, *op. cit.,* p. 366.

6. Cf. Mary Heaton Vorse, *The Passaic Textile Strike,* New York, 1927.

7. *The Christian Century,* 5 August 1926.

8. Gitlow, *op. cit.,* pp. 370–371.

9. Ibid., p. 372 ff.

## Passaic–A Left Wing Victory
Albert Weisbord

*Weisbord's conclusion to his account of the Passaic strike reveals those aspects of Communist engagement in social agitation that eventually disturbed Dos Passos greatly. The strike was lost, but Weisbord declares it a "victory" because Communists played a major role in it; because the AFL, a conservative craft union, had been defeated; and because the Marxist doctrine of the "class struggle" had been vindicated.*

In the meantime, whatever the outcome of the strike may be, certain conclusions can already be established. One conclusion is that the Passaic strike is a great victory for the Left Wing. It has shown that the policies and the tactics of the Left Wing are correct. The red banner of the class struggle again has been unfurled and spread to the breeze. The wage-cutting campaign has been definitely stopped. A smashing blow has been given to the "company union." "In Self Defense" the A. F. of L. reactionaries have been forced to begin to organize the unorganized and take in masses of unskilled foreign-born workers into their unions. The United Front of the workers has become the slogan and ideal which is driving the reactionaries more and more to move aside craft barriers that have hitherto made the workers impotent. The Left Wing, through the Passaic strike, has forced the bureaucrats into action against the bosses.

Passaic means organization of the unorganized. It means amalgamation, trade union unity, the united front of the workers against the united front of the bosses. It means the class struggle. It means war on the bureaucrats in the unions that help the bosses crush the workers.

*–Passaic: The Story of a Struggle Against Starvation Wages and for the Right to Organize* (New York: Daily Worker, 1926), p. 64

## Weisbord at Passaic
Melvin Landsberg

*Ben Compton's political career in* The Big Money *is in part based on Albert Weisbord's. Both are New York Jews and staunch Communists; both are sent by the party to help lead various strikes in order to exert party influence on their outcome; and both are dismissed by the party for their failure to accept party discipline unequivocally.*

To understand the subsequent history of the strike, we must look at the Communist strategy. The United Front Textile Committee, which seemed to be running the strike, was an instrument of the Communist party. To prevent the A.F.L. from interfering, the party had the Committee apply for affiliation with the United Textiles Workers (A.F.L.). The A.F.L., however, imposed the condition that Weisbord resign as strike leader. When it became clear that the strikers could not win, the Communist party decided to let the United Textile Workers take the responsibility for defeat.[1] Weisbord, who had avoided discussing politics at mass meetings, resigned on September 2, 1926. *New York Times* accounts gave the impression that his decision was voluntary.[2] Years later, Weisbord divulged how much had gone on behind the scenes: "The Communist Party leadership terminated the Passaic Strike in a disgraceful fashion, all the principal leaders of the Party voting that the independent union formed enter the A. F. of L., despite the fact that the communist union leaders were to be expelled. Only two members of the committee voted against, of whom the author is one."[3]

Textile industry leaders cared no more to negotiate with the A.F.L. than with a Communist-directed union. The strike dragged on and on, finally ending on a piecemeal basis. The companies yielded nothing substantial except the right of the workers to organize, and the last hold-out conceded nothing at all.[4]

The character of Weisbord the strike leader interested Dos Passos the novelist and playwright; he heard Weisbord speak, read about him, and may have met him.[5] Weisbord was, the *New York Times* reported, a "thin and frail" young man who did not look older than his twenty-five years. It added that observers attributed the duration of the strike to his personality and that the mill owners admitted his hold on the strikers was extraordinary. Gitlow, whom Weisbord antagonized during the strike, resented what he believed to be his narrowness, sectarianism, vanity, and ambition. After Gitlow left the Communist party, he described Weisbord as "thoroughly saturated with Marxist-Leninist lore, including all the exegeses and homilies thereof." "It was not unusual for him to address ten meetings a day and be twenty hours a day on the job. . . . Fanatical in his zeal, he literally ate, slept and talked nothing but the strike and Communism."[6]

After his role in Passaic was over, Weisbord was active in organizing Communist textile unions in the South and elsewhere. He was expelled from the central committee of the Communist party in October 1929 and suspended from the party for a year that December–for, in the words of the central control committee, "maintaining an unpermissible non-communistic attitude toward the party and its decisions, taking upon himself to decide which decisions of the party he will

*Two scenes from documentary footage used in* The Passaic Textile Strikes
*(Film Stills Archive, Museum of Modern Art, New York)*

carry out and which other decisions he will fight." In April of the next year the Communist International completely expelled him from the party. Weisbord organized a splinter group, the Communist League of Struggle, in March 1931.[7]

*–Dos Passos' Path to U.S.A.: A Political Biography, 1912–1936* (Boulder: Colorado Associated University Press, 1972), pp. 130–131

### Notes

1. Benjamin Gitlow, *I Confess* (New York: Dutton, 1940), pp. 315–377.

2. *New York Times,* 18 April 1926, sec. 1, p. 24; 28 July, p. 3; 14 August, p. 18; 3 September, p. 19.

3. Albert Weisbord, *The Conquest of Power* (New York: Covici-Friede, 1937), II: 115n.

4. *New York Times,* 12 November 1926, p. 14; 14 December 1926, p. 1; 15 February 1927, p. 12; 17 February 1927, p. 12; 1 March 1927, p. 46.

5. Letters from Dos Passos to M. L., 1 February and 23 September 1957.

6. *New York Times,* 18 April 1926, sec. 1, p. 24; Gitlow, *I Confess,* pp. 366–370 (quotations, pp. 363, 369 respectively).

7. *New York Times,* 17 December 1929, p. 20, and 8 April 1930, p. 7; Daniel Bell, in *Socialism and American Life,* I: 366.

### Mary French, Ben Compton, and Don Stevens
Dos Passos

*In scenes from* The Big Money *involving Communist Party activities, Ben serves as a leader during the Passaic strike and later tells Mary French how he was expelled from the party. For party functionary Don Stevens, the imminent execution of Nicola Sacco and Bartolomeo Vanzetti is principally a means toward furthering party goals.*

She [Mary French] never knew when Ben was going to turn up. Sometimes he'd be there every night for a week and sometimes he would be away for a month and she'd only hear from him through newsreleases about meetings, picketlines broken up, injunctions fought in the courts. Once they decided they'd get married and have a baby, but the comrades were calling for Ben to come and organize the towns around Passaic and he said it would distract him from his work and that they were young and that there'd be plenty of time for that sort of thing after the revolution. Now was the time to fight. Of course she could have the baby if she wanted to but it would spoil her usefulness in the struggle for several months and he didn't think this was the time for it. It was the first time they'd quarreled. She said he was heartless. He said they had to sacrifice their personal feelings for the workingclass, and stormed out

of the house in a temper. In the end she had an abortion but she had to write her mother again for money to pay for it.

She threw herself into her work for the strikecommittee harder than ever. Sometimes for weeks she only slept four or five hours a night. She took to smoking a great deal. There was always a cigarette resting on a corner of her typewriter. The fine ash dropped into the pages as they came from the multigraph machine. Whenever she could be spared from the office she went around collecting money from wealthy women, inducing prominent liberals to come and get arrested on the picketline, coaxing articles out of newspapermen, traveling around the country to find charitable people to go on bailbonds. The strikers, the men and women and children on picketlines, in soupkitchens, being interviewed in the dreary front parlors of their homes stripped of furniture they hadn't been able to make the last payment on, the buses full of scabs, the cops and deputies with sawedoff shotguns guarding the tall palings of the silent enormouslyextended oblongs of the blackwindowed millbuildings, passed in a sort of dreamy haze before her, like a show on the stage, in the middle of the continuous typing and multigraphing, the writing of letters and working up of petitions, the long grind of officework that took up her days and nights.

She and Ben had no life together at all any more. She thrilled to him the way the workers did at meetings when he'd come to the platform in a tumult of stamping and applause and talk to them with flushed cheeks and shining eyes talking clearly directly to each man and woman, encouraging them, warning them, explaining the economic setup to them. The millgirls were all crazy about him. In spite of herself Mary French would get a sick feeling in the pit of her stomach at the way they looked at him and at the way some big buxom freshlooking woman would stop him sometimes in the hall outside the office and put her hand on his arm and make him pay attention to her. Mary working away at her desk with her tongue bitter and her mouth dry from too much smoking would look at her yellowstained fingers and push her untidy uncurled hair off her forehead and feel badlydressed and faded and unattractive. If he'd give her one smile just for her before he bawled her out before the whole office because the leaflets weren't ready, she'd feel happy all day. But mostly he seemed to have forgotten that they'd ever been lovers.

After the A. F. of L. officials from Washington in expensive overcoats and silk mufflers who smoked twentyfivecent cigars and spat on the floor of the office had taken the strike out of Ben's hands and settled it, he came back to the room on Fourth Street late one night just as Mary was going to bed. His eyes were

*Labor activists Vera Buch Weisbord, Ellen Dawson, Albert Weisbord, and Fred Beal at the 1929 Gastonia,*
*North Carolina, textile strike (from Vera Buch Weisbord,* A Radical Life, *1977)*

redrimmed from lack of sleep and his cheeks were sunken and grey. "Oh, Ben," she said and burst out crying. He was cold and bitter and desperate. He sat for hours on the edge of her bed telling her in a sharp monotonous voice about the sellout and the wrangles between the leftwingers and the oldtime socialists and laborleaders, and how now that it was all over here was his trial for contempt of court coming up. "I feel so bad about spending the workers' money on my defense. . . . I'd as soon go to jail as not . . . but it's the precedent. . . . We've got to fight every case and it's the one way we can use the liberal lawyers, the lousy fakers. . . . And it costs so much and the union's broke and I don't like to have them spend the money on me . . . but they say that if we win my case then the cases against the other boys will all be dropped. . . ." "The thing to do," she said, smoothing his hair off his forehead, "is to relax a little." "You should be telling me?" he said and started to unlace his shoes.

—*The Big Money,* pp. 1144–1146

Next morning she was in the middle of drinking her coffee out of a cracked cup without a saucer, feeling bitterly lonely in the empty apartment when the telephone rang. At first she didn't recognize whose voice it was. She was confused and kept stammering, "Who is it, please?" into the receiver. "But, Mary," the voice was saying in an exasperated tone, "you must know who I am. It's Ben Compton . . . bee ee enn . . . Ben. I've got to see you about something. Where could I meet you? Not at your place." Mary tried to keep her voice from sounding stiff and chilly. "I've got to be uptown today. I've got to have lunch with a woman who may give some money to the miners. It's a horrible waste of time but I can't help it. She won't give a cent unless I listen to her sad story. How about meeting me in front of the Public Library at two thirty?" "Better say inside. . . . It's about zero out today. I just got up out of bed from the flu."

Mary hardly knew Ben he looked so much older. There was grey in the hair spilling out untidily from under his cap. He stopped and peered into her face querulously through his thick glasses. He didn't shake hands. "Well, I might as well tell you . . . you'll know it soon enough if you don't know it already . . . I've been expelled from the party . . . oppositionist . . . exceptionalism . . . a lot of nonsense. . . . Well, that doesn't matter, I'm still a revolutionist . . . I'll continue to work outside of the party."

"Oh, Ben, I'm so sorry," was all Mary could find to say. "You know I don't know anything except what I read in the *Daily*. It all seems too terrible to me." "Let's go out, that guard's watching us." Outside Ben began to shiver from the cold. His wrists stuck out red from his frayed green overcoat with sleeves much too short for his long arms. "Oh, where can we go?" Mary kept saying.

Finally they went down into a basement automat and sat talking in low voices over a cup of coffee. "I didn't want to go to your place because I didn't want to meet Stevens. . . . Stevens and me have never been friends, you know that. . . . Now he's in with the comintern crowd. He'll make the centralcommittee when they've cleaned out all the brains."

"But, Ben, people can have differences of opinion and still . . ."

"A party of yesmen . . . that'll be great. . . . But, Mary, I had to see you . . . I feel so lonely suddenly . . . you know, cut off from everything. . . . You know if we hadn't been fools we'd have had that baby that time . . . we'd still love each other. . . . Mary, you were very lovely to me when I first got out of jail. . . ."

– *The Big Money*, pp. 1221–1222

In a crowd that had just been unloaded from the wagon on the steep street outside the policestation she caught sight of a tall man she recognized as Donald Stevens from his picture in the *Daily*. A redfaced cop held on to each of his arms. His shirt was torn open at the neck and his necktie had a stringy look as if somebody had been yanking on it. The first thing Mary thought was how handsomely he held himself. He had steelgrey hair and a brown outdoorlooking skin and luminous grey eyes over high cheekbones. When he was led away from the desk she followed his broad shoulders with her eyes into the gloom of the cells. The woman next to her whispered in an awed voice that he was being held for inciting to riot instead of sauntering and loitering like the rest. Five thousand dollars bail. He had tried to hold a meeting on Boston Common.

Mary had been there about a halfhour when little Mr. Feinstein from the office came round with a tall fashionablydressed man in a linen suit who put up the bail for her. At the same time Donald Stevens was bailed out. The four of them walked down the hill from the policestation together. At the corner the man in the linen suit said, "You two were too useful to leave in there all day. . . . Perhaps we'll see you at the Bellvue . . . suite D, second floor." Then he waved his hand and left them. Mary was so anxious to talk to

Donald Stevens she didn't think to ask the man's name. Events were going past her faster than she could focus her mind on them.

Mary plucked at Donald Stevens' sleeve, she and Mr. Feinstein both had to hurry to keep up with his long stride. "I'm Mary French," she said. "What can we do? . . . We've got to do something." He turned to her with a broad smile as if he'd seen her for the first time. "I've heard of you," he said. "You're a plucky little girl . . . you've been putting up a real fight in spite of your liberal committee." "But they've done the best they could," she said.

"We've got to get the entire workingclass of Boston out on the streets," said Stevens in his deep rattling voice.

"We've gotten out the garmentworkers but that's all."

He struck his open palm with his fist. "What about the Italians? What about the North End? Where's your office? Look what we did in New York. Why can't you do it here?" He'd leaned over towards her with a caressing confidential manner. Right away the feeling of being tired and harassed left her, without thinking she put her hand on his arm. "We'll go and talk to your committee; then we'll talk to the Italian committee. Then we'll shake up the unions." "But, Don, we've only got thirty hours," said Mr. Feinstein in a dry tired voice. "I have more confidence in political pressure being applied to the governor. You know he has presidential aspirations. I think the governor's going to commute the sentences."

At the office Mary found Jerry Burnham waiting for her. "Well, Joan of Arc," he said, "I was just going down to bail you out. But I see they've turned you loose." Jerry and Donald Stevens had evidently known each other before. "Well, Jerry," said Donald Stevens savagely, "doesn't this shake you out of your cynical pose a little?"

"I don't see why it should. It's nothing new to me that collegepresidents are skunks."

Donald Stevens drew off against the wall as if he were holding himself back from giving Jerry a punch in the jaw. "I can't see how any man who has any manhood left can help getting red . . . even a pettybourgeois journalist."

"My dear Don, you ought to know by this time that we hocked our manhood for a brass check about the time of the first world war . . . that is if we had any . . . I suppose there'd be various opinions about that." Donald Stevens had already swung on into the inner office. Mary found herself looking into Jerry's reddening face, not knowing what to say. "Well, Mary, if you have a need for a pickup during the day . . . I should think you would need it . . . I'll be at the old

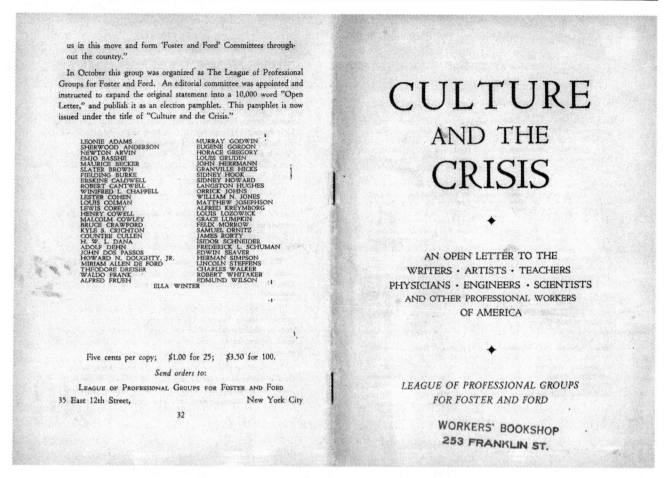

us in this move and form 'Foster and Ford' Committees throughout the country."

In October this group was organized as The League of Professional Groups for Foster and Ford. An editorial committee was appointed and instructed to expand the original statement into a 10,000 word "Open Letter," and publish it as an election pamphlet. This pamphlet is now issued under the title of "Culture and the Crisis."

LEONIE ADAMS
SHERWOOD ANDERSON
NEWTON ARVIN
EMJO BASSHE
MAURICE BECKER
SLATER BROWN
FIELDING BURKE
ERSKINE CALDWELL
ROBERT CANTWELL
WINIFRED L. CHAPPELL
LESTER COHEN
LOUIS COLMAN
LEWIS COREY
HENRY COWELL
MALCOLM COWLEY
BRUCE CRAWFORD
KYLE S. CRICHTON
COUNTEE CULLEN
H. W. L. DANA
ADOLF DEHN
JOHN DOS PASSOS
HOWARD N. DOUGHTY, JR.
MIRIAM ALLEN DE FORD
THEODORE DREISER
WALDO FRANK
ALFRED FRUEH

MURRAY GODWIN
EUGENE GORDON
HORACE GREGORY
LOUIS GRUDIN
JOHN HERRMANN
GRANVILLE HICKS
SIDNEY HOOK
SIDNEY HOWARD
LANGSTON HUGHES
ORRICK JOHNS
WILLIAM N. JONES
MATTHEW JOSEPHSON
ALFRED KREYMBORG
LOUIS LOZOWICK
GRACE LUMPKIN
FELIX MORROW
SAMUEL ORNITZ
JAMES RORTY
ISIDOR SCHNEIDER
FREDERICK L. SCHUMAN
EDWIN SEAVER
HERMAN SIMPSON
LINCOLN STEFFENS
CHARLES WALKER
ROBERT WHITAKER
EDMUND WILSON

ELLA WINTER

Five cents per copy;   $1.00 for 25;   $3.50 for 100.

*Send orders to:*

LEAGUE OF PROFESSIONAL GROUPS FOR FOSTER AND FORD
35 East 12th Street,                                   New York City

32

# CULTURE
## AND THE
# CRISIS

♦

AN OPEN LETTER TO THE
WRITERS · ARTISTS · TEACHERS
PHYSICIANS · ENGINEERS · SCIENTISTS
AND OTHER PROFESSIONAL WORKERS
OF AMERICA

♦

*LEAGUE OF PROFESSIONAL GROUPS
FOR FOSTER AND FORD*

WORKERS' BOOKSHOP
253 FRANKLIN ST.

*Covers of a pamphlet signed by Dos Passos and others supporting the Communist Party ticket
in the 1932 presidential elections (Collection of Richard Layman)*

stand." "Oh, I won't have time," Mary said coldly. She could hear Donald Stevens' deep voice from the inner office. She hurried on after him.

The lawyers had failed. Talking, wrangling, arguing about how a lastminute protest could be organized Mary could feel the hours ebbing, the hours of these men's lives. She felt the minutes dripping away as actually as if they were bleeding from her own wrists. She felt weak and sick. She couldn't think of anything. It was a relief to be out in the street trotting to keep up with Donald Stevens' big stride. They made a round of the committees. It was nearly noon, nothing was done. Down on Hanover Street a palefaced Italian in a shabby Ford sedan hailed them. Stevens opened the door of the car. "Comrade French, this is Comrade Strozzi . . . he's going to drive us around." "Are you a citizen?" she asked with an anxious frown. Strozzi shook his head and smiled a thinlipped smile. "Maybe they give me a free trip back to Italy," he said.

Mary never remembered what they did the rest of the day. They drove all over the poorer Boston suburbs. Often the men they were looking for were out. A

great deal of the time she spent in phonebooths calling wrong numbers. She couldn't seem to do anything right. She looked with numb staring eyes out of eyelids that felt like sandpaper at the men and women crowding into the office. Stevens had lost the irritated stinging manner he'd had at first. He argued with tradeunion officials, socialists, ministers, lawyers, with an aloof sarcastic coolness. "After all they are brave men. It doesn't matter whether they are saved or not any more, it's the power of the workingclass that's got to be saved," he'd say. Everywhere there was the same opinion. A demonstration will mean violence, will spoil the chance that the governor will commute at the last moment. Mary had lost all her initiative. Suddenly she'd become Donald Stevens' secretary. She was least unhappy when she was running small errands for him.

Late that night she went through all the Italian restaurants on Hanover Street looking for an anarchist Stevens wanted to see. Every place was empty. There was a hush over everything. Death watch. People kept away from each other as if to avoid some contagion. At the back of a room in a little upstairs speakeasy she saw

Jerry Burnham sitting alone on a table with a jigger of whiskey and a bottle of gingerale in front of him. His face was white as a napkin and he was teetering gently in his chair. He stared at her without seeing her. The waiter was bending over him shaking him. He was hopelessly drunk.

It was a relief to run back to the office where Stevens was still trying to line up a general strike. He gave her a searching look when she came in. "Failed again," she said bitterly. He put down the telephone receiver, got to his feet, strode over to the line of hooks on the grimy yellow wall and got down his hat and coat. "Mary French, you're deadtired. I'm going to take you home."

They had to walk around several blocks to avoid the cordon of police guarding the State House. "Ever played tug of war?" Don was saying. "You pull with all your might but the other guys are heavier and you feel yourself being dragged their way. You're being pulled forward faster than you're pulling back. . . . Don't let me talk like a defeatist. . . . We're not a couple of goddamned liberals," he said and burst into a dry laugh. "Don't you hate lawyers?" They were standing in front of the bowfronted brick house where she had her room. "Goodnight, Don," she said. "Goodnight, Mary, try and sleep."

Monday was like another Sunday. She woke late. It was an agony getting out of bed. It was a fight to put on her clothes, to go down to the office and face the defeated eyes. The people she met on the street seemed to look away from her when she passed them. Death watch. The streets were quiet, even the traffic seemed muffled as if the whole city were under the terror of dying that night. The day passed in a monotonous mumble of words, columns in newspapers, telephone calls. Death watch. That night she had a moment of fierce excitement when she and Don started for Charlestown to join the protest parade. She hadn't expected they'd be so many. Gusts of singing, scattered bars of the *International* burst and faded above the packed heads between the blank windows of the dingy houses. Death watch. On one side of her was a little man with eyeglasses who said he was a musicteacher, on the other a Jewish girl, a member of the Ladies' Full-fashioned Hosiery Workers. They linked arms. Don was in the front rank, a little ahead. They were crossing the bridge. They were walking on cobbles on a bad-lylighted street under an elevated structure. Trains roared overhead. "Only a few blocks from Charlestown jail," a voice yelled.

This time the cops were using their clubs. There was the clatter of the horses' hoofs on the cobbles and the whack thud whack thud of the clubs. And way off the jangle jangle of patrolwagons. Mary was terribly scared. A big truck was bearing down on her. She jumped to one side out of the way behind one of the girder supports.

Two cops had hold of her. She clung to the grimy girder. A cop was cracking her on the hand with his club. She wasn't much hurt, she was in a patrolwagon, she'd lost her hat and her hair had come down. She caught herself thinking that she ought to have her hair bobbed if she was going to do much of this sort of thing. "Anybody know where Don Stevens is?" Don's voice came a little shakily from the blackness in front. "That you, Mary?" "How are you, Don?" "O.K. Sure. A little battered round the head an' ears." "He's bleedin' terrible," came another man's voice. "Comrades, let's sing," Don's voice shouted. Mary forgot everything as her voice joined his voice, all their voices, the voices of the crowds being driven back across the bridge in singing:

*Arise ye prisoners of starvation . . .*
—*The Big Money*, pp. 1151–1155

## BIG BUSINESS

*In* U.S.A. *Dos Passos indicts the large corporate entities controlling the American economy during the early twentieth century both for an ethic of unbridled self-interest and for the conscious deception by which they sought to disguise this motive. This indictment included the great tycoons of the period—Andrew Carnegie, J. P. Morgan, Henry Ford, and William Randolph Hearst—figures who combined a ruthless acquisitiveness with various seemingly beneficent public activities (philanthropy, art collecting, and political leadership, for example), as well as the increasingly prominent public-relations and advertising industries, which molded public opinion into accepting a society controlled by the dictates of big business.*

*President Calvin Coolidge famously declared during the boom decade of the 1920s that "the business of America is business." Thus, it is not surprising that Dos Passos titled the novel in the* U.S.A. *trilogy devoted to that decade* The Big Money *and that he devoted much attention in its narratives and biographies to the character of a society in which the quest for wealth threatens the conditions making a humane society possible. Within this general concern he focused on several aspects of American capitalism that were increasingly prominent in the 1920s: the rise of new industries, such as aircraft manufacture, as vehicles for corporate manipulation; the wide-scale adoption of the "American plan" of workforce efficiency, in which the workers' well-being is sacrificed for the sake of increased production; the speculative crazes of the period, as illustrated by the brash mix of greed and phoniness in the Florida land boom; and the polishing of public deception into an art form by the advertising industry.*

*Aside from the biographies of the principal icons of twentieth-century American capitalism, Dos Passos's major means for dramatizing the impact of big money on American life are the narratives of Charley Anderson and J. Ward Moorehouse. Anderson, who begins his career (like Ford) as a mechanic; becomes a major player in the aircraft industry; is caught up in the corporate infighting of his firm; willingly adopts the "American plan" of workplace efficiency and the public-relations language created to defend it; and ends his career (with Margo Dowling) attempting to recoup his fortunes in the Florida land boom. Moorehouse, however, appears to epitomize, as several critics have claimed, the hypocritical greed at the core of the American system. Wherever he appears—as a land salesman, as an apologist for the railroads, as a defender of the war, or (in* The Big Money*) as the head of an advertising firm—he perverts the "old words" of the American Dream in order to mask the suspect motives of those employing him.*

### Prince of Peace
Dos Passos

*As with many of his narratives, in his biography of Carnegie, Dos Passos undermines the common association between a fulfillment of the American dream of success and the moral life by means of a telling final irony. The idealism of Carnegie's "millions for peace" fails to survive the test of his desire that America enter World War I in order that Germany be defeated.*

Andrew Carnegie
was born in Dunfermline in Scotland,
came over to the States in an immigrant
ship worked as bobbinboy in a textile factory
fired boilers
clerked in a bobbin factory at $2.50 a week
ran round Philadelphia with telegrams as a Western Union messenger
learned the Morse code was telegraph operator on the Pennsy lines
was a military telegraph operator in the Civil War and

always saved his pay;
whenever he had a dollar he invested it.
Andrew Carnegie started out buying Adams Express and Pullman stock when they were in a slump;
he had confidence in railroads,
he had confidence in communications,
he had confidence in transportation,
he believed in iron.
Andrew Carnegie believed in iron, built bridges Bessemer plants blast furnaces rolling mills;
Andrew Carnegie believed in oil;
Andrew Carnegie believed in steel;
always saved his money
whenever he had a million dollars he invested it.
Andrew Carnegie became the richest man in the world
                                    and died.
Bessemer Duquesne Rankin Pittsburgh Bethlehem Gary

*Andrew Carnegie, subject of the biography "Prince of Peace" in* The 42nd Parallel *(Underwood & Underwood)*

Andrew Carnegie gave millions for peace
and libraries and scientific institutes and endowments and thrift
whenever he made a billion dollars he endowed an institution to promote universal peace
always
except in time of war.
                        —The 42nd Parallel, *pp. 230–231*

### The House of Morgan
Dos Passos

*Dos Passos is at pains in this biography to make evident the archetype of the American multimillionaire represented by J. P. Morgan: religious conviction, vast economic power, and the economic exploitation of human misery.*

*I commit my soul into the hands of my savior,* wrote John Pierpont Morgan in his will, *in full confidence that having redeemed it and washed it in His most precious blood, He will present it faultless before my heavenly father, and I intreat my children to maintain and defend at all hazard and at any cost of personal sacrifice the blessed doctrine of complete atonement for sin through the blood of Jesus Christ once offered and through that alone,*

and into the hands of the House of Morgan represented by his son,

he committed,

when he died in Rome in 1913,

the control of the Morgan interests in New York, Paris and London, four national banks, three trust companies, three life insurance companies, ten railroad systems, three street railway companies, an express company, the International Mercantile Marine,

power,

on the cantilever principle, through interlocking directorates

over eighteen other railroads, U.S. Steel, General Electric, American Tel and Tel, five major industries;

the interwoven cables of the Morgan Stillman Baker combination held credit up like a suspension bridge, thirteen percent of the banking resources of the world.

. . . . . . . . .

The panic of 1907 and the death of Harriman, his great opponent in railroad financing, in 1909, had left him the undisputed ruler of Wall Street, most powerful private citizen in the world;

an old man tired of the purple, suffering from gout, he had deigned to go to Washington to answer the questions of the Pujo Committee during the Money Trust Investigation: Yes, I did what seemed to me to be for the best interests of the country.

So admirably was his empire built that his death in 1913 hardly caused a ripple in the exchanges of the world: the purple descended to his son, J. P. Morgan.

who had been trained at Groton and Harvard and by associating with the British ruling class

to be a more constitutional monarch: *J. P. Morgan suggests . . .*

By 1917 the Allies had borrowed one billion, ninehundred million dollars through the House of Morgan: we went overseas for democracy and the flag;

and by the end of the Peace Conference the phrase *J. P. Morgan suggests* had compulsion over a power of seventyfour billion dollars.

J. P. Morgan is a silent man, not given to public utterances, but during the great steel strike he wrote Gary: *Heartfelt congratulations on your stand for the open shop, with which I am, as you know, absolutely in accord. I believe*

*J. P. Morgan, subject of "The House of Morgan" in* Nineteen-Nineteen *(photograph by Edward Steichen, 1903). When Dos Passos refused to delete the biography of Morgan, Harper and Brothers, who had published* The 42nd Parallel, *declined to publish* Nineteen-Nineteen *because a loan from Morgan's bank had saved the publisher from bankruptcy.* Nineteen-Nineteen *and* The Big Money *were published by Harcourt, Brace (National Portrait Gallery).*

American principles of liberty are deeply involved, and must win if we stand firm.

(Wars and panics on the stock exchange,
machinegunfire and arson,
bankruptcies, warloans,
starvation, lice, cholera and typhus:
good growing weather for the House of Morgan.)
—*Nineteen-Nineteen,* pp. 644, 647–648

### Poor Little Rich Boy
Dos Passos

*The great newspaper magnate William Randolph Hearst had become increasingly conservative by the time Dos Passos was writing* The Big Money. *Hearst's garish and ornate estate on the California coast was roughly comparable, Dos Passos believed, to his cheap exploitation in his newspapers of public taste for his own power and aggrandizement.*

. . . . . . . . .

*San Simeon, William Randolph Hearst's California estate (from John K. Winkler,* William Randolph Hearst, *1955)*

He arrived home in California, a silent soft smiling solemneyed young man

dressed in the height of the London fashion.

When his father asked him what he wanted to do with his life,

he said he wanted to run the *Examiner* which was a moribund sheet in San Francisco which his father had taken over for a bad debt. It didn't seem much to ask. The old man couldn't imagine why Willie wanted the old rag instead of a mine or a ranch, but Mrs. Hearst's boy always had his way.

Young Hearst went down to the *Examiner* one day

and turned the office topsyturvy. He had a knack for finding and using bright young men, he had a knack for using his own prurient hanker after the lusts and envies of plain unmonied lowlife men and women (the slummer sees only the streetwalkers, the dopeparlors, the strip acts and goes back uptown saying he knows the workingclass districts); the lowest common denominator;

manure to grow a career in,

the rot of democracy. Out of it grew rankly an empire of print. (Perhaps he liked to think of himself

as the young Caius Julius flinging his millions away, tearing down emblems and traditions, making faces at togaed privilege, monopoly, stuffedshirts in office;

Caesar's life like his was a millionaire prank. Perhaps W.R. had read of republics ruined before;

Alcibiades, too, was a practical joker.)

The San Francisco *Examiner* grew in circulation, tickled the prurient hankers of the moneyless man

became *The Monarch of the Dailies.*

. . . . . . . . . .

In spite of enormous expenditures on forged documents he failed to bring about war with Mexico.

In spite of spraying hundreds of thousands of dollars into moviestudios he failed to put over his favorite moviestar as America's sweetheart.

And more and more the emperor of newsprint retired to his fief of San Simeon on the Pacific Coast, where he assembled a zoo, continued to dabble in movingpictures, collected warehouses full of tapestries, Mexican saddles, bricabrac, china, brocade, embroidery, old chests of drawers, tables and chairs, the loot of dead Europe,

built an Andalusian palace and a Moorish banquethall and there spends his last years amid the relaxing adulations of screenstars, admen, screenwriters, publicitymen, columnists, millionaire editors,

a monarch of that new El Dorado

where the warmedover daydreams of all the ghettos

are churned into an opiate haze

more scarily blinding to the moneyless man

more fruitful of millions

than all the clinking multitudes of double eagles

the older Hearst minted out of El Dorado County in the

old days (the empire of the printed word continues powerful by the inertia of bigness; but this power over the dreams

of the adolescents of the world

grows and poisons like a cancer),

and out of the westcoast haze comes now and then an old man's querulous voice

advocating the salestax,

hissing dirty names at the defenders of civil liberties for the workingman;

jail the reds,

praising the comforts of Baden-Baden under the blood and bludgeon rule of Handsome Adolph (Hearst's own loved invention, the lowest common denominator come to power

out of the rot of democracy)

complaining about the California incometaxes,

shrilling about the dangers of thought in the colleges.

Deport; jail.

Until he dies
the magnificent endlesslyrolling presses will pour out print for him, the whirring everywhere projectors will spit images for him,
a spent Caesar grown old with spending never man enough to cross the Rubicon.
—*The Big Money*, pp. 1163–1164, 1168–1169

\* \* \*

# Frederick W. Taylor and the American Plan

### The American Plan
Dos Passos

*Frederick W. Taylor founded and popularized the concept of industrial engineering, in which factories were designed and labor employed to achieve the maximum efficient use of both. His ideas were widely adopted in the period before World War I, both in America and elsewhere. Dos Passos's final detail in this biography, of Taylor dying with a stopwatch in his hand, was noted by Taylor's biographer.*

The early years he was a machinist with the other machinists in the shop, cussed and joked and worked with the rest of them, soldiered on the job when they did. Mustn't give the boss more than his money's worth. But when he got to be foreman he was on the management's side of the fence, *gathering in on the part of those on the management's side all the great mass of traditional knowledge which in the past has been in the hands of the workmen and in the physical skill and knack of the workman.* He couldn't stand to see an idle lathe or an idle man.

Production went to his head and thrilled his sleepless nerves like liquor or women on a Saturday night. He never loafed and he'd be damned if anybody else would. Production was an itch under his skin.

He lost his friends in the shop; they called him niggerdriver. He was a stockily built man with a temper and a short tongue.

*I was a young man in years but I give you my word I was a great deal older than I am now, what with the worry, meanness and contemptibleness of the whole damn thing. It's a horrid life for any man not being able to look any workman in the face without seeing hostility there, and a feeling that every man around you is your virtual enemy.*

That was the beginning of the Taylor System of Scientific Management.

He was impatient of explanations, he didn't care whose hide he took off in enforcing the laws he believed inherent in the industrial process.

*When starting an experiment in any field question everything, question the very foundations upon which the art rests, question the simplest, the most selfevident, the most universally accepted facts; prove everything,*

except the dominant Quaker Yankee (the New Bedford skippers were the greatest niggerdrivers on the whaling seas) rules of conduct. He boasted he'd never ask a workman to do anything he couldn't do.

He devised an improved steamhammer; he standardized tools and equipment, he filled the shop with college students with stopwatches and diagrams, tabulating, standardizing. *There's the right way of doing a thing and the wrong way of doing it; the right way means increased production, lower costs, higher wages, bigger profits:* the American plan.

He broke up the foreman's job into separate functions, speedbosses, gangbosses, timestudy men, order-ofwork men.

The skilled mechanics were too stubborn for him, what he wanted was a plain handyman who'd do what he was told.

. . . . . . . . . .

He was called in by Bethlehem Steel. It was in Bethlehem he made his famous experiments with handling pigiron; he taught a Dutchman named Schmidt to handle fortyseven tons instead of twelve and a half tons of pigiron a day and got Schmidt to admit he was as good as ever at the end of the day.

He was a crank about shovels, every job had to have a shovel of the right weight and size for that job alone; every job had to have a man of the right weight and size for that job alone; but when he began to pay his men in proportion to the increased efficiency of their work,

the owners who were a lot of greedy smalleyed Dutchmen began to raise Hail Columbia; when Schwab bought Bethlehem Steel in 1901

Fred Taylor

inventor of efficiency

who had doubled the production of the stamping-mill by speeding up the main lines of shafting from ninetysix to two-hundred and twentyfive revolutions a minute

was unceremoniously fired.

After that Fred Taylor always said he couldn't afford to work for money.

He took to playing golf (using golfballs of his own design), doping out methods for transplanting huge boxtrees into the garden of his home.

At Boxly in Germantown he kept open house for engineers, factorymanagers, industrialists;

he wrote papers,

lectured in colleges,

appeared before a congressional committee,

everywhere preached the virtues of scientific management and the Barth slide rule, the cutting down of waste and idleness, the substitution for skilled mechanics of the plain handyman (like Schmidt the pigiron handler) who'd move as he was told

and work by the piece:

production;

more steel rails more bicycles more spools of thread more armorplate for battleships more bedpans more barbedwire more needles more lightningrods more ballbearings more dollarbills;

(the old Quaker families of Germantown were growing rich, the Pennsylvania millionaires were breeding billionaires out of iron and coal)

production would make every firstclass American rich who was willing to work at piecework and not drink or raise Cain or think or stand mooning at his lathe.

Thrifty Schmidt the pigiron handler can invest his money and get to be an owner like Schwab and the rest of the greedy smalleyed Dutchmen and cultivate a taste for Bach and have hundredyearold boxtrees in his garden at Bethlehem or Germantown or Chestnut Hill,

and lay down the rules of conduct;

the American plan.

But Fred Taylor never saw the working of the American plan;

in 1915 he went to the hospital in Philadelphia suffering from a breakdown.

Pneumonia developed; the nightnurse heard him winding his watch;

on the morning of his fiftyninth birthday, when the nurse went into his room to look at him at fourthirty,

he was dead with his watch in his hand.

—*The Big Money*, pp. 784–785, 786–787

## The Principle of Worker Efficiency
Frederick W. Taylor

*This passage from Taylor's most influential book suggests the aspect of "scientific management" that most troubled Dos Passos. To pursue "maximum productivity" at the worker's "fastest pace," Dos Passos and other critics believed, was to ignore the effects of this principle of "efficiency" on the human mind and body.*

No one can be found who will deny that in the case of any single individual the greatest prosperity can exist only when that individual has reached his highest state of

*Frederick W. Taylor, the work-efficiency expert profiled in "The American Plan" in* The Big Money *(from Frank Barkley Copley,* Frederick W. Taylor, *1923)*

efficiency; that is, when he is turning out his largest daily output.

The truth of this fact is also perfectly clear in the case of two men working together. To illustrate: if you and your workman have become so skilful that you and he together are making two pairs of shoes in a day, while your competitor and his workman are making only one pair, it is clear that after selling your two pairs of shoes you can pay your workman much higher wages than your competitor who produces only one pair of shoes is able to pay his man, and that there will still be enough money left over for you to have a larger profit than your competitor.

In the case of a more complicated manufacturing establishment, it should also be perfectly clear that the greatest permanent prosperity for the workman, coupled with the greatest prosperity for the employer, can be brought about only when the work of the establishment is done with the smallest combined expenditure of human effort, plus nature's resources, plus the cost for the use of capital in the shape of machines, buildings, etc. Or, to state the same thing in a different way: that the greatest prosperity can exist only as the result of the greatest possible productivity of the men and machines of the establishment— that is, when each man and each machine are turning out the largest possible output; because unless your men and

# TIME-NOTE.

Machine Shop,........................................ 188......

Order ...........................    TIME .....................

Name ..........................................................

| WORK DONE. | No. | Rate in cents. | Amt. | Time |
|---|---|---|---|---|
| Enter tires in records from standing orders, . . . | . . | 0.25 | . . . | . . . |
| Enter tire time-notes on white sheets, . . . . . . | . . | 0.5 | . . . | . . . |
| Post tire records from time-notes, . . . . . . . . | . . | 0.3 | . . . | . . . |
| Enter weights of tires on white sheet and add up weights of tires from tire mill, | . . | 0.3 | . . . | . . . |
| Post wages earned by men on mills and fix bonus, . . . | . . | 0.2 | . . . | . . . |
| File and put away records of finished tires, . . . | . . | 5.0 | . . . | . . . |
| Assort tire records and put in final file, . . . . . . | . . | 10.0 | . . . | . . . |
| Make out standing orders I. S. F. tires, . . . . . | . . | 1.5 | . . . | . . . |
| Make out standing orders ordinary tires, . . . . . | . . | 0.5 | . . . | . . . |
| Enter miscellaneous time-notes on white sheet, . . . | . . | 0.3 | . . . | . . . |
| Post miscellaneous time-notes in records, . . . . . | . . | 0.85 | . . . | . . . |
| Check off white and yellow sheets from register for men, to see if all time is correct, . . . . | . . | 5.0 | . . . | . . . |
| Enter axles (standing orders) in records, . . . . . | . . | 0.3 | . . . | . . . |
| Post records of axles from time-notes, . . . . . . | . . | 0.3 | . . . | . . . |
| Take out standing orders to boxes, . . . . . . . . | . . | 5.0 | . . . | . . . |
| Make out standing orders for I. S. F. tires, . . . . | . . | 1.5 | . . . | . . . |
| Make out standing orders for ordinary tires, . . . | . . | 0.5 | . . . | . . . |

Time out ..........................    Total time.......................

Time in.............................    Total amount earned...............

I have inspected the above work and find that it is all done as per order.

........    Signed, ....................

*An early Frederick W. Taylor work form (circa 1885), on which each action of a worker was carefully measured in relation to its cost and the time it took to complete ( from Frank B. Copley,* Frederick W. Taylor, *1969)*

your machines are daily turning out more work than others around you, it is clear that competition will prevent your paying higher wages to your workmen than are paid to those of your competitor. And what is true as to the possibility of paying high wages in the case of two companies competing close beside one another is also true as to whole districts of the country and even as to nations which are in competition. In a word, that maximum prosperity can exist only as the result of maximum productivity. Later in this paper illustrations will be given of several companies which are earning large dividends and at the same time paying from 30 per cent. to 100 per cent. higher wages to their men than are paid to similar men immedi-

ately around them, and with whose employers they are in competition. These illustrations will cover different types of work, from the most elementary to the most complicated.

If the above reasoning is correct, it follows that the most important object of both the workmen and the management should be the training and development of each individual in the establishment, so that he can do (at his fastest pace and with the maximum of efficiency) the highest class of work for which his natural abilities fit him.

–*The Principles of Scientific Management* (New York: Harper, 1911), pp. 11–12

*A Ford Model T in 1914. Between 1908 and 1927 more than fifteen million "Tin Lizzies" were produced by Ford (Reproduced through the courtesy of the Ford Motor Company).*

### Tin Lizzie
Dos Passos

*Henry Ford's adoption of the Taylor plan led directly to his great breakthrough: the assembly-line mode of production, which permitted his company to produce a cheap, efficient car–the Model T–in vast numbers. It was also a process in which the workingman himself became a standardized, easily replaceable "part" within the production process.*

Henry Ford had ideas about other things than the designing of motors, carburetors, magnetos, jigs and fixtures, punches and dies; he had ideas about sales,

that the big money was in economical quantity production, quick turnover, cheap interchangeable easilyreplaced standardized parts;

it wasn't until 1909, after years of arguing with his partners, that Ford put out the first Model T.

Henry Ford was right.

That season he sold more than ten thousand tin lizzies, ten years later he was selling almost a million a year.

In these years the Taylor Plan was stirring up plantmanagers and manufacturers all over the country. Efficiency was the word. The same ingenuity that went into improving the performance of a machine could go into improving the performance of the workmen producing the machine.

In 1913 they established the assemblyline at Ford's. That season the profits were something like twentyfive million dollars, but they had trouble in keeping the men on the job, machinists didn't seem to like it at Ford's.

—*The Big Money*, pp. 808–809

### Charley Anderson
Dos Passos

*Charley Anderson, now a principal investor in an airplane factory, and his foreman and friend, Bill Cermak, face the realities of the American Plan. Charley notes that Ford is also building planes and that they must be "efficient" to compete; Bill responds that the new mode of labor drains all the energy from the men.*

One night when he'd taken Bill Cermak, who was now a foreman at the Flint plant, over to a roadhouse the other side of Windsor to talk to him about the trouble they were having with molders and diemakers, after they'd had a couple of whiskies, Charley found himself instead asking Bill about married life. "Say, Bill, do you ever have trouble with your wife?"

"Sure, boss," said Bill, laughing. "I got plenty trouble. But the old lady's all right, you know her, nice kids good cook, all time want me to go to church."

*A Ford assembly line in 1913 or 1914 (Reproduced through the courtesy of the Ford Motor Company)*

"Say, Bill, when did you get the idea of callin' me boss? Cut it out."

"Too goddam rich," said Bill.

"S–t, have another whiskey." Charley drank his down. "And beer chasers like in the old days. . . . Remember that Christmas party out in Long Island City and that blonde at the beerparlor. . . . Jesus, I used to think I was a little devil with the women. . . . But my wife she don't seem to get the idea."

"You have two nice kids already; what the hell, maybe you're too ambitious."

"You wouldn't believe it . . . only once since little Peaches was born."

"Most women gets hotter when they're married a while. . . . That's why the boys are sore at your damned efficiency expert."

"Stauch? Stauch's a genius at production."

"Maybe, but he don't give the boys any chance for reproduction." Bill laughed and wiped the beer off his mouth.

"Good old Bill," said Charley. "By God, I'll get you on the board of directors yet."

Bill wasn't laughing any more. "Honestly, no kiddin'. That damn squarehead make the boys work so hard they can't get a hard on when they go to bed, an' their wives raise hell with 'em. I'm strawboss and they all think sonofabitch too, but they're right."

Charley was laughing. "You're a squarehead yourself, Bill, and I don't know what I can do about it, I'm just an employee of the company myself. . . . We got to have efficient production or they'll wipe us out of business. Ford's buildin' planes now."

"You'll lose all your best guys. . . . Slavedrivin' may be all right in the automobile business, but buildin' an airplane motor's skilled labor."

—*The Big Money,* pp. 1026–1027

\* \* \*

## J. Ward Moorehouse and E. R. Bingham

### The Source of J. Ward Moorehouse
Dos Passos

*Dos Passos met Ivy Lee (1877–1934), often considered the founder of the American public-relations industry, in Moscow in August 1927. Much of his portrait of J. Ward Moorehouse is based on Lee's career.*

There were no tourists in those days. A grim young woman from Voks settled me in a vast room at the old Moscow Hotel. The first American I found myself talking to there was Ivy Lee. What the man who was devoting his life to giving eyeappeal to old John D. Rockefeller was doing in Moscow I never learned, but lacking anybody to talk English with, he used to waylay me in the lobby and tell me tales of his early life. He was a southerner. He had no trace of humor but I couldn't help admiring his dedication to his trade. I was sorry when he left.

—*The Best Times: An Informal Memoir* (New York: New American Library, 1966), p. 178

### Ivy Lee and J. Ward Moorehouse
Melvin Landsberg

Examination of historical sources for Moorehouse's career and activities is both possible and enlightening (although the story and descriptions of any illegal deeds are fictitious). The public relations man Edward L. Bernays writes that the muckrakers originally drove businessmen to employ "whitewash." ("Whitewash" is Bernays' own term, which he distinguishes from "publicity based on informa-

tion and disclosure.") First those businessmen whom muckrakers had attacked and then other businessmen initiated programs of concealing or defending their activities. "Engineering of consent on a mass scale was ushered in in the 1914–18 period," says Bernays, recalling that he like his colleagues "found new public relations horizons being opened by the requirements of the war." The war led directly to an expansion and refinement of propaganda for peacetime.[1]

Moorehouse's public career is in many ways similar to that of Ivy Lee; Dos Passos, in fact, acknowledged a probable influence. When Lee "was a young New York newspaper man thirty-odd years ago," the *New York Times* wrote after his death in 1934, "there were numerous press agents in town who promoted theatres and stage stars, but there was no specialist in publicity who conferred on terms of equality with the boards of directors of great corporations. His life spanned that change, and he had much to do with the change."[2]

After several years as assistant to the president of the Pennsylvania Railroad, Lee, in January 1915, became publicity counsel to John D. Rockefeller, gaining this position through work for the multimillionaire's son, John D. Rockefeller, Jr. A major stockholder in the Colorado Fuel and Iron Company, the son was a severely harassed man when in 1914 he first summoned Lee to his aid. Violent outbreaks had attended a year-old strike by Colorado miners. At Ludlow, militia firing into tents had killed seven men, two women, and eleven children. Pickets led by Upton Sinclair and "Sweet Marie Ganz" demonstrated before the younger Rockefeller's offices at 26 Broadway, driving him to his estate at Pocantico Hills. I.W.W. men pursued him even there.[3]

Lee's publicity work on his behalf so outraged the reformer-journalist George Creel (later chairman of the wartime Committee on Public Information) that he attacked the Colorado Fuel and Iron Company. Lee subsequently had to make some discomfiting admissions before a Commission on Industrial Relations. In a bulletin of his, the annual wages of strike leaders had been represented as their pay for only nine weeks; one man receiving $4,052.92 had been listed as getting $32,000.[4]

Lee worked as publicity counsel to John D. Rockefeller until April 1916, when he established a business of his own. He remained Rockefeller's adviser, however, and his firm enjoyed Standard Oil's patronage. During World War I, Lee (like the fictitious Moorehouse) served as unsalaried publicity director for the Red Cross. His clients during a career which ended only in 1934 included the Copper and Brass Research Association, the Bethlehem Steel Company, and the Guggenheim and Chrysler interests.[5]

Moorehouse's client Bingham bears some resemblance in his showmanship and product line to Bernarr Macfadden, the picturesque hawker of "Physcultopathy" and the *New York Evening Graphic.* "Like so many other big New Yorkers," Henry F. Pringle declared of Macfadden in 1928, "he has recently engaged a press agent. Having first considered engaging Ivy Lee, he later turned to Edward L. Bernays, only slightly less renowned in the public relations field."[6]

> *–Dos Passos' Path to U.S.A.: A Political Biography, 1912–1936* (Boulder, Colo.: Associated University Press, 1972), pp. 210–212

### Notes

1. Edward L. Bernays, *Public Relations* (Norman: University of Oklahoma Press, 1952), pp. 64–66, 78. The last two quotations are on pp. 71 and 73 respectively.

2. David Sanders, typescript of interview with John Dos Passos, in the University of Virginia Library; *New York Times*, 10 November 1934, p. 15.

3. *New York Herald Tribune*, 10 November 1934, p. 13.

4. Henry F. Pringle, *Big Frogs* (New York: Macy-Masius, 1928), p. 107.

5. Alvin F. Harlow, "Ivy Ledbetter Lee," *Dictionary of American Biography*, XXI (Supplement One), pp. 489–490; *New York Times*, 10 November 1934, p. 15; *New York Herald Tribune*, 10 November 1934, p. 13; Pringle, *Big Frogs*, pp. 93–114.

6. Pringle, *Big Frogs*, p. 132.

### Language and Persuasion
Ivy Lee

*Lee explains that a publicist affects public belief about railroads or any other large business enterprises less by resorting to logic than by appealing to emotion. In other words, to make propaganda work, truth must often be sacrificed to achieve the desired effect.*

The problem of influencing the people en masse is that of providing leaders who can fertilize the imagination and organize the will of crowds. Moses painted a picture of the promised land, and he induced the Israelites to spend forty years of

*Ivy Lee, the public-relations expert who served as the model for J. Ward Moorehouse in* U.S.A.
*(from Ray E. Hiebert,* Courtier to the Crowd, *1966)*

## Ivy Lee's Philosophy

"This is not a secret press bureau. All our work is done in the open. We aim to supply news."

"This is not an advertising agency. If you think any of our matter ought properly to go to your business office, do not use it."

"Our matter is accurate. Further details on any subject treated will be supplied promptly, and any editor will be assisted most carefully in verifying directly any statement of fact. . . ."

"In brief, our plan is frankly, and openly, on behalf of business concerns and public institutions, to supply the press and public of the United States prompt and accurate information concerning subjects which it is of value and interest to the public to know about."

–Ivy Lee, *Declaration of Principles* (1906)

extraordinary hardship under his leadership. Caesar drew a picture of the conquest of Gaul, and so infused the imagination of the Roman populace that they thrice offered him a crown. Napoleon's uncanny power in France was due to his resourcefulness in the appeal to these same elementary crowd-impulses.

These are some of the mainsprings of crowd stimulation. They are factors which statesmen, preachers and soldiers have from time immemorial recognized when they sought to lead peoples. My point is that in working out the railroad problem we must take account of these same principles of crowd psychology.

We must, for example, replace with sound phrases and symbols those symbolic words, symbolic terms and phrases that have gotten into the public mind and created a false impression. We have heard a great deal about "full crew" laws. The labor people were very happy in their selection of that term "full crew." Now, if we had referred to that from the beginning as the "extra crew" it seems to me we would have made considerably more headway than we did.

The phrase, "What the traffic will bear," has done as much to hurt the railroads as any expression ever used. It is scientifically correct, no doubt, but it conveys a most unfortunate suggestion to the popular mind—the thought that the rate is "*all* the traffic will bear," a suggestion absolutely contrary to the fact.

We can never be too careful in the terms we use. Sometime ago, a certain public service corporation was in great financial difficulties; it could not pay its bond interest. Its skillful president induced its bondholders to agree to a reduction of the rate of interest on the bonds. The president then announced to the public that there was to be "a readjustment" of the finances of the company. Now "readjustment of finances" is so much better than saying, "Your company is bankrupt," and no one ever suggested that his company was bankrupt. It was a matter of terms, and we must be careful of the terms we allow to be lodged in the public mind. There is often talk of "educating the public." Now, railroad officers themselves are getting a good deal of very helpful "education." It is not a question of "educating the public"; it is a very real question for the railroad man of understanding the public and having the public understand him.

What we say to the public, it seems to me, must be with reference to its effect, and not primarily with reference to its logical sequence. You cannot argue with the public. To illustrate, Mr. Roosevelt in his speeches gives us holes through which one can drive a coach and four. Mr. Bryan doesn't reason, but he moves multitudes powerfully. Such men, and quite legitimately, say what they have to say with a view to its effect, the emotional effect upon the imagination of the people they are seeking to reach.

–*Human Nature and the Railroads* (Philadelphia: Nash, 1915), pp. 16–18

## J. Ward Moorehouse
Stanley Geist

*Geist offers a spirited interpretation of Moorehouse as "the high-priest of the new national religion: Publicity."*

J. WARD MOOREHOUSE. Personage of the three-volume "novel," *U.S.A.* (1930–37), by the American writer, John Dos Passos (1896– ). The disciple upon whom falls the mantle of this messiah *à l'américaine* says of him that he has "perhaps done more than any one living man, whether you like what he does or not, to form the public mind in this country." Perhaps. Perhaps, also, recent American literature has created no figure so extraordinary in its symbolic resonance and so terrifying in its symbolic truth. Devoid of everything that, in the Christian and humanistic traditions of Europe, makes up the "identity" of a human person—except a body (which he wants to forget) and a name (which is false)—he incarnates a "metaphysic" of a new kind of world. He makes his appearance in the first volume as one of the work's twelve "typical" Americans; the generic nature of their lives, defined through the figure of Mac, achieves in Moorehouse a bizarre perfection; his presence soon dominates them and the work.

Born in the east, of petit-bourgeois, 100% American parents, he has an uneventful childhood–there are no "events" in *U.S.A.*, only incidents. He graduates from high-school as class orator; helps the family budget as a traveling book-salesman; goes for a short time to college; and takes a job in a real-estate office. At twenty, he is an ordinary, good-looking, blonde-headed, "bright," enterprising young American who does not smoke or drink and is "keeping himself clean for the lovely girl" whom he shall some day no doubt marry. He marries twice, into wealth; works as a newspaper reporter, as advertising manager for a hardware company, and, during the first World War, as a European publicity agent for the Red Cross; opens an office in New York; becomes a ubiquitous go-between in financial, industrial, and governmental affairs; rises to success as an advertising executive and "Public Relations Counsel"; and disappears from the book, in old age, as a powerful and mysterious "man behind the scenes" of American public life.

But the "success" is not of this earth, the "power" is theocratic, the "mystery" sacerdotal. A religious vocation that resembles both genius and a blind physiological reflex–and into which enters neither a will to power nor a desire for personal gain–summons him, as the voice of the Lord summons Biblical prophets, to do its supernatural bidding: to liberate man in America from all sensual or spiritual intimacy with the gross malodorous substance of human life. Practising–though not understanding–a system of tribal magic whose origins go back at least to Benjamin Franklin, the tribal wizard, Moorehouse, transforms the base ore of human experience into Byzantium's celestial gold: into "conventions" of verbal formulas which, because they have nothing to do with the nature of experience, can not be tried against it, are absolutely pure, and have the force of magic charms. Subjecting to his will the impure, harmful facts of human experience, rendering them by his magic impotent to touch the body or penetrate the mind except as he has transformed them, he realizes a dream, older than Franklin, of freeing mankind from its immemorial bondage to the human condition. He does not knowingly aim so high. His boyhood ambition is merely to be a writer of popular songs. But in the age of Moorehouse the "popular song" has begun to be something different from an expression, more or less formal, in rhymed verses and music, of popular sentiments. It has become, on the one hand, a mass-produced article of commerce, like the household gadget, which does not so much satisfy a need as create a need for itself; and on the other hand a product–often ingenious and sometimes brilliant, but neither expressing nor issuing from any sentiment actually felt–of an inventive fantasy devoted to fabricating new "sentiments" in order that they may be, if not felt, entertained. The writing of popular songs–though Moorehouse does not become a song-writer–is his apprenticeship in the variety of popular magic that he will later practise. He performs the same magic operation, without rhyme, as the author of a rhapsodic brochure for a real-estate development; and it is to the perfecting of this operation, which becomes in time a veritable *operatio spiritualis,* that he dedicates the rest of his career. Difficult to describe, like all forms of magic, it consists, roughly, in substituting for every possible intimate (hence contaminating) relation between flesh or spirit and the sentiments, thoughts, persons, places, things, events, movements, processes, acts that are the traditional substance of their lives, a mass of pure conventions, verbal formulas, ritual artefacts, and magic charms. These he assembles, as if composing a Surrealist canvas, from the junk heaps of human civilizations: broken phrases, tangled metaphors, rusty fragments of ideas, pieces of sentiment twisted like old bed-springs, fossil relics of rhetorical and dramatic organisms, shattered bottles that had once held scents of the world's body, torn bits of newspaper, pages of sheet-music, water-soaked calendars showing Christmas on the farm, plaster of ruined churches, cracked concrete posts from the gates of Heaven and Hell. Whatever was not yet in a junk-heap becomes junk when Moorehouse finds it, and promptly thereafter, gold. As the scope of this operation widens to embrace every aspect of American life and culture, Moorehouse becomes the high-priest of a new national religion: Publicity. Its worship takes various forms; the most "formalized" of them–oratory, song-writing, salesmanship, "promotion," journalism, advertising, "public relations" (though not the films)–are those practised by him. All have a common "metaphysical" basis and a common system of tactical manoeuver (serving a common "moral" ideal) for preventing the contamination of the faithful by human life: the conversion of human life, past and present, at home and abroad, into "pure conventions"; the substitution of these both for a direct experience of things and for those impure conventions–impure because they express or conceal some "reality" behind themselves– without which no experience is possible; the creation, from these pure elements of a hermetic, suspended, supernatural "other world," which has for the Americans of Dos Passos a reality superior to that of any world–natural, supernatural, or conventional–previously known to man. At the center of this world, continuously renewing it, keeping it in motion, is Moorehouse—messiah, prophet, wizard, high-priest, and mediating god. The Americans of Dos Passos, having no lives and no identities of their own through which they might communicate with one another, may nevertheless, through Him, enjoy the sense of communicating: the conventions and formulas that he interposes among them are in effect a common language available to all. Nothing, to be sure, is "expressed" in this language by anyone to anyone about anything—except the language itself; but the semblance of communication is maintained. No one questions it but "Intellecutals," who reject the messiah as a fraud—"a big bluff . . . a goddam megaphone . . . a damn publicity agent." But the scoffers, having no language or religion that is more valid, drink themselves to death in bewilderment and despair. For businessmen, industrialists, financiers and workers, for statesmen, politicians, diplomats, for readers of magazines and newspapers, he creates possibilities of "agreement"; through him they "contact" (even the word is new) but do not touch or contaminate one another; he redeems them from discord or from solitude with an illusion of speaking in the same tongue. No more than the public that he serves can he dispense with his publicity. Only through the opaque screen of his magic formulas can he "see" or interpret what is before him, what happens to him, what he himself does: which is to say, he sees nothing and interprets nothing but Publicity. A sacred obligation requires that he transform, like all else, the data of his own existence—even his rudimentary animal needs—into pure conventions (which may be conventional images of himself as a mediating god); he offers them to a public that may be his wife, his mistress, his secretary, his clients, ten million readers of a weekly magazine, or himself; and he is liberated from the human reality that might otherwise take diabolical possession of him and call into question the absolute authority of his will. His "interpretations," however grotesque their incongruity with the facts known to an outsider—to the author and reader of *U.S.A.*—are in no sense hypocritical; for the complex moral action that bears the name "hypocrisy" is beyond his power to execute as it is beyond his power to conceive; his moral innocence (which is to say, his inaccessibility to moral knowledge) is perfect. The gap between his perfectly non-moral actions and the righteous morality of his words, between the facts that he confronts and the formulas or conventions with which he designates them, soon widens to a gulf across which neither of the two parties to this strange double game has the smallest communication with the other: his right hand, in all good faith, would not

dream of asking what his left hand is up to. Each, as the book advances, becomes more and more pure, more and more independent of the other; and the play of their irrelevance to each other becomes a vast metaphysical comedy. Unlike certain of his literary antecedents (e.g. Babbitt), he is never troubled by a vestigial human longing to feel within himself the reality of his own life. The formula of convention has indeed, for him, an exclusive claim upon the real—and a real force—so evident as to render merely querulous any counter-claim that facts might have the presumption to advance. The notion that his life might have any reality other than that of the conventional words and images he substitutes for it does not occur to him. Not less than his external public does he "believe" his own publicity; his belief is an unfaltering religious faith: *Credo quia absurdum.* But between the believer and the objects of his belief—between Moorehouse and his conventions, his interpretations, his formulas, his images—there is, notwithstanding, a distance as great as that which separates both him and them from the traditional "reality" for which they have been substituted. The words spoken by his mouth are none of his concern; detached from them as from all else, he is not responsible for them and has no obligation to them. Since they are no more and no less than Words, nothing is to be gained if (as sometimes happens) they turn out to be descriptions of the truth, nothing lost if events prove them to be false: the question of truth or falsehood is simply beside the point. His detachment, indeed—his freedom from the bondage of the human condition—would also be perfect, were not its Byzantine purity marred by the exasperating persistence of his flesh: by the shameful indignities of hunger, desire, digestion, indigestion, excretion, seasickness, corpulence, and physical decay. The physiological details that serve as points of reference for the discontinuous narrative of his life are, however, the only details of this "life" that have an internal relation to one another or that give to it an organic continuity: the blonde hair turns white, the large body takes on fat, the cheeks fall into jowls. Apart from them, the "life" of Moorehouse is wholly a public fact—a creation of Publicity. He exists from childhood only as a sequence of names and images in other minds. Christened John Ward, he grows up as Johnny, introduces himself to social superiors as John, passes the war years as Major Moorehouse, is married to his "aristocratic" first wife as J. Ward (so much more "distinguished"), is known to her as Ward ("John" is awfully plebian, isn't it?), adopts J. Ward as his final and definitive name, and allows trusted employees or important clients to call him "J. W." Each name is accompanied by one or more conventional public masks; he "memorizes" for each, and in turn creates for it, a conventional lexicon of manners, costumes, formalities, phrases, opinions, intonations, and gestures. He discovers, as a young man, that he has a usable "pair of bright blue eyes" and can put on at will "an engaging boyish look." He learns as he grows older how to wear Scotch tweeds or a uniform, how to dictate speeches in a private railroad car, how to play golf with "executives," smoke cigars at a conference table, order tea from a French valet, surround himself with telephones and stenographers, talk with the quiet drawl of a Southern senator, frown thoughtfully, nod doubtfully, smile faintly, and twinkle knowingly his now pale and bovine eyes. Unaware of any distinction between himself and the roles he plays–a *comédien malgré lui*–he plays them with the dedicated but effortless pertinacity of a man divinely chosen and divinely gifted with absolute freedom of choice: the "personage" named Moorehouse is the sum of the rôles that he plays, the magic operation that he performs, and the supernatural "necessity" of which he is the chosen instrument. The name "J. Ward Moorehouse" once fixed, the nondescript individual born Moorehouse once wholly consumed by his sacred office, he indulges in small harmless lapses from priestly rigor: mitigates the religious austerity of his presence in the public mind by creating images of himself that are less awesome and mysterious and remote; cultivates for the delectation of privileged fellow-tribesmen (and himself) "characteristic" foibles by which they may identify him, and a repertoire of conventional sentiments–nostalgia, regret, loneliness, arcadian longing, parental solicitude, marital distress–by which they may grasp him as a creature like themselves after all. Not less detached from these than if he knew them to be fictions, he does not doubt that they are true. They are as true as the fact that, having no humanly conceivable existence, he exists.

–"Fictitious Americans," *Hudson Review*, 5 (Summer 1952): 206–211

## J. Ward Moorehouse
Dos Passos

*In three vignettes from* U.S.A., *Moorehouse composes a real-estate brochure in which "scorched sandlots" are elevated to "the tonic breath of the pines"; expertly manipulates the language of political obfuscation at Versailles; and offers American values as a basis for buying a patent medicine in the booming postwar 1920s.*

It was a hot August, the mornings still, the afternoons piling up sultry into thundershowers. Except when there were clients to show about the scorched sandlots and pinebarrens laid out into streets, Johnny sat in the office alone under the twoflanged electric fan. He was dressed in white flannels and a pink tennis shirt rolled up to the elbows, drafting the lyrical description of Ocean City (Maryland) that was to preface the advertising booklet that was the Colonel's pet idea: "The life-giving surges of the broad Atlantic beat on the crystalline beaches of Ocean City (Maryland) . . . the tonic breath of the pines brings relief to the asthmatic and the consumptive . . . nearby the sportsman's paradise of Indian River spreads out its broad estuary teeming with . . ." In the afternoon the Colonel would come in sweating and wheezing and Johnny would read him what he had written and he'd say, "Bully, ma boy, bully," and suggest that it all be done over. And Johnny would look up a new batch of words in a dogeared "Century Dictionary" and start off again.

–*The 42nd Parallel*, pp. 164–165

J.W. had come in by the other door and was moving around the room shaking hands with men he knew, being introduced to others. A young fellow with untidy hair and his necktie crooked put a paper in Dick [Savage]'s hand. "Say, ask him if he'd answer some of these questions." "Is he going to campaign for the League of Nations?" somebody asked in his other ear.

Everybody was settled in chairs; J.W. leaned over the back of his and said this was going to be an informal chat, after all, he was an old newspaper man himself. There was a pause. Dick glanced around at J.W.'s pale slightly jowly face just in time to catch a flash of his blue eyes around the faces of the correspondents. An elderly man asked in a grave voice if Mr. Moorehouse cared to say anything about the differences of opinion between the President and Colonel House. Dick settled himself back to be bored. J.W. answered with a cool smile that they'd better ask Colonel House himself about that. When somebody spoke the word oil everybody sat up in their chars. Yes, he could say definitely an accord, a working agreement had been reached between certain American oil producers and perhaps the Royal Dutch-Shell, oh, no, of course not to set prices but a proof of a new era of international cooperation that was dawning in which great aggregations of capital would work together for peace and democracy, against reactionaries and militarists on the one hand and against the bloody forces of bolshevism on the other. And what about the League of Nations? "A new era," went on J.W. in a confidential tone, "is dawning."

–*Nineteen-Nineteen*, pp. 752–753

Next day at noon when J.W. came back from church with the children Dick was dressed and shaved and walking up and down the flagged terrace in the raw air. Dick's eyes felt hollow and his head throbbed but J.W. was delighted with the work. "Of course self-service, independence, individualism is the word I gave the boys in the beginning. This is going to be more than a publicity campaign, it's going to be a campaign for Americanism. . . . After lunch I'll send the car over for Miss Williams and get her to take some dictation. There's more meat in this yet, Dick." "Of course," said Dick, reddening. "All I've done is restore your original conception, J.W."

*—The Big Money, p. 1183*

## Charley Anderson
Dos Passos

*Charley Anderson, once a mechanic but now in management, relies on typical Moorehouse public-relations language when management is faced with labor problems: The firm has "a responsibility toward our investors" and is also "the first line of national defense."*

While Charley pulled a suit of overalls on the mechanics pushed the new ship out onto the grass for Bill to make his general inspection. "Jesus, she's pretty." The tiny aluminum ship glistened in the sun out on the green grass like something in a jeweler's window. There were dandelions and clover on the grass and a swirling flight of little white butterflies went up right from under his black clodhoppers when Bill came back to Charley and stood beside him. Charley winked at Bill Cermak standing beside him in his blue denims stolidly looking at his feet. "Smile, you sonofabitch," he said. "Don't this weather make you feel good?"

Bill turned a square bohunk face towards Charley. "Now look here, Mr. Anderson, you always treat me good . . . from way back Long Island days. You know me, do work, go home, keep my face shut." "What's on your mind, Bill? . . . Want me to try to wangle another raise for you? Check."

Bill shook his heavy square face and rubbed his nose with a black forefinger. "Tern Company used to be good place to work good work good pay. You know me, Mr. Anderson, I'm no bolshayvik . . . but no stoolpigeon either."

"But damn it, Bill, why can't you tell those guys to have a little patience . . . we're workin' out a profit-sharin' scheme. I've worked on a lathe myself. . . . I've worked as a mechanic all over this goddam country. . . . I know what the boys are up against, but I know what the management's up against too. . . . Gosh, this thing's in its infancy, we're pouring more capital into the business all the time. . . . We've got a responsibility towards our investors. Where do you think that jack I made yesterday's going but the business of course. The old-time shop was a great thing, everybody kidded and smoked and told smutty stories, but the pressure's too great now. If every department don't click like a machine we're rooked. If the boys want a union we'll give 'em a union. You get up a meeting and tell 'em how we feel about it but tell 'em we've got to have some patriotism. Tell 'em the industry's the first line of national defense. We'll send Eddy Sawyer down to talk to 'em . . . make 'em understand our problems."

*—The Big Money, pp. 1030–1031*

## E. R. Bingham
Laura Browder

*Dos Passos drew heavily on the career of Bernarr Macfadden (1868–1955) for his portrait of E. R. Bingham in* The Big Money. *An early advocate of physical culture, Macfadden stressed that exercise and diet were the keys to good health, sexual vigor, and longevity. Although Macfadden, unlike Bingham, was not active in the manufacturing of patent medicines, he displayed the same mix of charlatanism, showmanship, and pruriency.*

Bingham's reappearance at this late date in the trilogy is significant. He shows up as Dos Passos is using his strongest ammunition to blast away at ineffectual or morally corrupt forms of discourse. Doc Bingham is both one of the most amusingly sleazy characters in the trilogy and, perhaps, the character with the greatest rhetorical skill. For example, when he first meets Mac, his young employee in *The 42nd Parallel*, Doc Bingham eschews log-cabin imagery and instead uses Progressive Era slogans of modernity and liberation: "Oh, religion, what crimes are committed in your name? I'm an agnostic myself. . . . No sir, my God is the truth, that rising ever higher in the hands of honest men will dispel the mists of ignorance and greed, and bring freedom and knowledge to mankind" (*FP*, 55). Bingham's ability to use effectively such a wide range of rhetorical styles has the result of somehow cheapening all the styles. If the progressive talk of the importance of education and freedom from prejudice is a coded sales pitch, if Shakespeare (whom he quotes incessantly) can so easily be used to advertise the self and to drown out debate, and if Jacksonian rhetoric is a cover for Barnum-style hucksterism, then it is clear that none of this speech is inherently strong enough to withstand abuse by its speakers. Bingham is one of Dos Passos's most effective characters in that he is granted such a great facility for slippage. The comic effect of his appearance lightly makes the serious point that no speech is sacred and, more importantly, that "virtuous"—that is, culturally or politically sound—rhetoric can easily be put to nefarious uses and thus should never be taken for granted. The fact that Bingham has, of course, no such

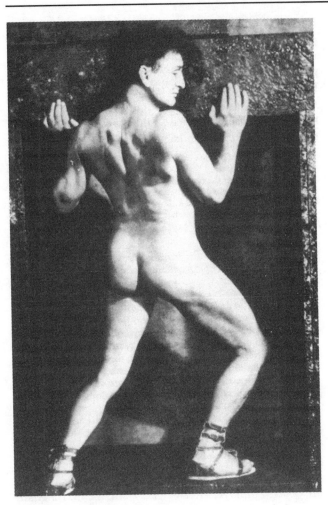

*Bernarr Macfadden, at age sixty, a model for the character E. R. Bingham in* The Big Money *(from Robert Ernst,* Weakness Is a Crime: The Life of Bernarr Macfadden, *1991)*

virtuous past as he claims in his patent-medicine-king guise calls into question the soundness of this rhetoric to begin with: Was the image of America painted now by Bingham ever an accurate one, or has it always been as much of a lie as it is now in the mouth of this con artist? One thing is clear, however, and that is that the rhetoric of patriotism is now particularly liable to exploitation.

We see this patriotic rhetoric being used to its fullest extent when Moorehouse and Savage go to Washington to try to fight the progressive legislation that would put Bingham and others like him out of business. Disputing the value of the pure food legislation, J. W. says,

> Once government interference in business is established as a precedent, it means the end of liberty and private initiative in this country. . . . What this bill purports to do is to take the right of selfmedication from the American people. A set of lazy government employees and remittancemen will be able to tell you what lax-

atives you may take and what not. Like all such things, it'll be in the hands of cranks and busybodies. Surely the American people have the right to choose what products they want to buy. It's an insult to the intelligence of our citizens. (*BM,* 505)

Moorehouse's ease in turning the language of Jacksonian Democracy to commercial uses is disturbing. It's not necessarily that this linguistic corruption is anything new—as James Harvey Young points out in his essay "Patent Medicines and the Self-Help Syndrome," "Learned physicians also lost caste, along with members of other educated professions, during the cultural climate associated with Jacksonian democracy. As leaders of opinion lost this traditional role, each common man had to decide for himself." It is this Jacksonian tradition that Moorehouse is exploiting in using terminology like "liberty," "private initiative," and "government interference," as well as in questioning the right of "experts" to make decisions for common people.

As one of his lobbyists said, "all these so-called pure food and drug bills are class legislation in favor of the medical profession. Naturally the doctors want us to consult them before we buy a toothbrush or a package of licorice powder" (*BM,* 506). Thus these reactionaries are managing to use the language of the class struggle to oppose legislation that will regulate quacks. Similarly, when Moorehouse resumes, it is to speak to the American mythology of individualism: "The tendency of the growth of scientifically prepared proprietary medicine has been to make the layman free and self-sufficient, able to treat many minor ills without consulting a physician" (506). Thus the reader is not surprised when his lobbyist tells the assembled company that "Mr. Moorehouse is about to launch one of the biggest educational drives the country has ever seen to let people know the truth about proprietary medicines. . . . He will roll up a great tidal wave of opinion that Congress will have to pay attention to. I've seen him do it before" (506).

—*Rousing the Nation: Radical Culture in Depression America* (Amherst: University of Massachusetts Press, 1998), pp. 57–59

**Bingham**
Dos Passos

Dick was surprised by the wrench the handshake gave his arm. He found himself standing in front of a gaunt loose-jointed old man with a shock of white hair and a big prognathous skull from which the sunburned skin hung in folds like the jowls of a bird-dog. J.W. seemed small and meek beside him. "I'm very glad to meet you, sir," E. R. Bingham said. "I have often said to my girls that had I grown up in your generation I would have found happy and useful work in the field of publicrelations. But alas in my day the path was harder for a young man entering life with nothing but the excellent tradition of moral fervor and natural religion I absorbed if I may say so with my mother's milk. We had to put our shoulders to the wheel in those days and it was the wheel of an old muddy wagon drawn by mules, not the wheel of a luxurious motorcar."

E. R. Bingham boomed his way into the diningroom. A covey of palefaced waiters gathered round, pulling out chairs, setting the table, bringing menucards. "Boy, it is no use handing me the bill of fare," E. R. Bingham addressed the headwaiter. "I live by nature's law. I eat only a few nuts and vegetables and drink raw milk. . . . Bring me some cooked spinach, a plate of grated carrots and a glass of unpasteurized milk. . . . As a result, gentlemen, when I went a few days ago to a great physician at the request of one of the great lifeinsurance companies in this city he was dumbfounded when he examined me. He could hardly believe that I was not telling a whopper when I told him I was seventyone. 'Mr. Bingham,' he said, 'you have the magnificent physique of a healthy athlete of fortyfive' . . . Feel that, young man." E. R. Bingham flexed his arm under Dick's nose. Dick gave the muscle a prod with two fingers. "A sledgehammer," Dick said, nodding his head. E. R. Bingham was already talking again: "You see I practice what I preach, Mr. Moorehouse . . . and I expect others to do the same. . . . I may add that in the entire list of remedies and proprietary medicines controlled by Bingham Products and the Rugged Health Corporation, there is not a single one that contains a mineral, a drug or any other harmful ingredient. I have sacrificed time and time again hundreds of thousands of dollars to strike from my list a concoction deemed injurious or habitforming by Dr. Gorman and the rest of the splendid men and women who make up our research department. Our medicines and our systems of diet and cure are nature's remedies, herbs and simples culled in the wilderness in the four corners of the globe according to the tradition of wise men and the findings of sound medical science."

"Would you have coffee now, Mr. Bingham, or later?"

"Coffee, sir, is a deadly poison, as are alcohol, tea and tobacco. If the shorthaired women and the longhaired men and the wildeyed cranks from the medical schools, who are trying to restrict the liberties of the American people to seek health and wellbeing, would restrict their activities to the elimination of these dangerous poisons that are sapping the virility of our young men and the fertility of our lovely American womanhood I would have no quar-rel with them. In fact I would do everything I could to aid and abet them. Someday I shall put my entire fortune at the disposal of such a campaign. I know that the plain people of this country feel as I do because I'm one of them, born and raised on the farm of plain godfearing farming folk. The American people need to be protected from cranks."

"That, Mr. Bingham," said J.W., "will be the keynote of the campaign we have been outlining." The fingerbowls had arrived. "Well, Mr. Bingham," said J.W., getting to his feet, "This has been indeed a pleasure. I unfortunately shall have to leave you to go downtown to a rather important directors' meeting but Mr. Savage here has everything right at his fingertips and can, I know, answer any further questions. I believe we are meeting with your sales department at five."

*—The Big Money*, pp. 1187–1188

\* \* \*

## The Aircraft Industry and the Florida Land Boom

### The Beginnings of the Aircraft Industry on Long Island
John B. Rae

*Although the aircraft industry was later concentrated on the West Coast, several small firms were active on Long Island in the period during and following World War I. Thus, Dos Passos is historically correct in placing Charley Anderson's fledgling business in Long Island City and, given the company's proximity to the New York financial market, in indicating the important role that corporate structure and methods play in the firm's activities.*

A more obscure firm at this period was the Lewis and Vought Corporation, which, like Loening, was established in New York. It was formed in 1917 by Chance Milton Vought, aeronautical engineer and pilot, and his friend Birdseye Lewis, who provided the capital and the business management. The company, whose original quarters were a third floor in a loft building in Astoria, Long Island, began by building trainers for both Army and Navy but soon specialized in naval aircraft, particularly reconnaissance planes designed for catapult launching. Thus the company, while small, was making aircraft of a type that had not been produced in quantity during the war and was therefore not subject to competition from war surplus. It became the Chance Vought Corporation in 1922.

*—Climb to Greatness: The American Aircraft Industry,
1920–1960* (Cambridge, Mass.:
MIT Press, 1968), pp. 7–8

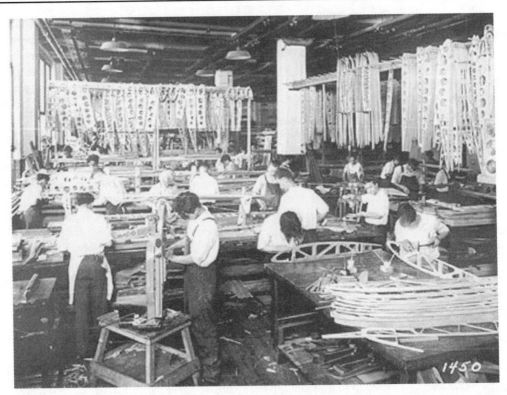

*O2U Corsair airplane assembly (circa 1926–1929) at the Chance Vought Corporation factory in Long Island City,
New York, where the airplane-manufacturing business in which Charley Anderson has
a stake is established in* The Big Money *(Vought Photograph files)*

*Engine run-up and ground testing of a Vought XF2U-1 at the Chance Vought headquarters in
Long Island City, 1929 (Vought Photograph files)*

## Charley Anderson
Dos Passos

They had lunch with Merritt, who turned out to be a greyfaced young man with a square jaw, at the Yale Club. Charley still had a pounding headache and felt groggily that he wasn't making much of an impression. He kept his mouth shut and let Joe do the talking. Joe and Merritt talked Washington and War Department and Navy Department and figures that made Charley feel he ought to be pinching himself to see if he was awake.

After lunch Merritt drove them out to Long Island City in an open Pierce Arrow touringcar. When they actually got to the plant, walking through the long littered rooms looking at lathes and electric motors and stamping and dyemaking machines, Charley felt he knew his way around better. He took out a piece of paper and started making notes. As that seemed to go big with Merritt he made a lot more notes. Then Joe started making notes too. When Merritt took out a little book and started making notes himself, Charley knew he'd done the right thing.

They had dinner with Merritt and spent the evening with him. It was heavy sledding because Merritt was one of those people who could size a man up at a glance, and he was trying to size up Charley. They ate at an expensive French speakeasy and sat there a long time afterwards drinking cognac and soda. Merritt was a great one for writing lists of officers and salaries and words like capitalization, depreciation, amortization down on pieces of paper, all of them followed by big figures with plenty of zeros. The upshot of it seemed to be that Charley Anderson would be earning two hundred and fifty a week (payable in preferred stock) starting last Monday as supervising engineer and that the question of percentage of capital stock he and Joe would have for their patents would be decided at a meeting of the board of directors next day. The top of Charley's head was floating. His tongue was a little thick from the cognac. All he could think of saying, and he kept saying it, was, "Boys, we mustn't go off half-cocked."

When he and Joe finally got Merritt and his Pierce Arrow back to the Yale Club they heaved a deep breath. "Say, Joe, is that bird a financial wizard or is he a nut? He talks like greenbacks grew on trees."

"He makes 'em grow there. Honestly . . ." Joe Askew took his arm and his voice sunk to a whisper, "that bird is going to be the Durant of aviation financing." "He don't seem to know a Liberty motor from the hind end of a blimp." "He knows the Secre-tary of the Interior, which is a hell of a lot more important."

Charley got to laughing so he couldn't stop. All the way back to the Chatterton House he kept bumping into people walking along the street. His eyes were full of tears. He laughed and laughed. When they went to the desk to ask for their mail and saw the long pale face of the clerk Charley nudged Joe. "Well, it's our last night in this funeral parlor."

The hallway to their rooms smelt of old sneakers and showers and lockerrooms. Charley got to laughing again. He sat on his bed a long time giggling to himself. "Jesus, this is more like it; this is better than Paree." After Joe had gone to bed Charley stuck his head in the door still giggling. "Rub me, Joe," he yelled. "I'm lucky."

Next morning they went and ate their breakfast at the Belmont. Then Joe made Charley go to Knox's and buy him a derby before they went downtown. Charley's hair was a little too wiry for the derby to set well, but the band had an expensive englishleathery smell. He kept taking it off and sniffing it on the way downtown in the subway. "Say, Joe, when my first paycheck comes I want you to take me round and get me outfitted in a soup an' fish. . . . This girl, she likes a feller to dress up." "You won't be out of overalls, boy," growled Joe Askew, "night or day for six months if I have anything to say about it. We'll have to live in that plant if we expect the product to be halfway decent, don't fool yourself about that." "Sure, Joe, I was only kiddin'."

They met at the office of a lawyer named Lilienthal. From the minute they gave their names to the elegantlyupholstered blonde at the desk Charley could feel the excitement of a deal in the air. The blonde smiled and bowed into the receiver. "Oh, yes, of course. . . . Mr. Anderson and Mr. Askew." A scrawny officeboy showed them at once into the library, a dark long room filled with calfbound lawbooks. They hadn't had time to sit down before Mr. Lilienthal himself appeared through a groundglass door. He was a dark oval neckless man with a jaunty manner. "Well, here's our pair of aces right on time." When Joe introduced them he held Charley's hand for a moment in the smooth fat palm of his small hand. "Andy Merritt has been singing your praises, young fellah, he says you are the coming contactman." "And here I was just telling him I wouldn't let him out of the factory for six months. He's the bird who's got the feel for the motors." "Well, maybe he meant you birdmen's kind of contact," sad Mr. Lilienthal, lifting one thin black eyebrow.

The lawyer ushered them into a big office with a big empty mahogany desk in the middle of it and a blue

Chinese rug on the floor. Merritt and two other men were ahead of them. To Charley they looked like a Kuppenheimer ad standing there amid the blue crinkly cigarettesmoke in their neatlycut dark suits with the bright grey light coming through the window behind them. George Hollis was a pale young man with his hair parted in the middle and the other was a lanky darkfaced Irish lawyer named Burke, who was an old friend of Joe Askew's and would put their patents through Washington for them, Joe explained. They all seemed to think Charley was a great guy, but he was telling himself all the time to keep his mouth shut and let Joe do the talking.

They sat round that lawyer's mahogany desk all morning smoking cigars and cigarettes and spoiling a great deal of yellow scratchpaper until the desk looked like the bottom of an uncleaned birdcage and the Luckies tasted sour on Charley's tongue. Mr. Lilienthal was all the time calling in his stenographer, a little mouselike girl with big grey eyes, to take notes and then sending her out again. Occasionally the phone buzzed and each time he answered it in his bored voice, "My dear young lady, hasn't it occurred to you that I might be in conference?"

The concern was going to be called the Askew-Merritt Company. There was a great deal of talk about what state to incorporate in and how the stock was to be sold, how it was going to be listed, how it was going to be divided. When they finally got up to go to lunch it was already two o'clock and Charley's head was swimming. Several of them went to the men's room on their way to the elevator and Charley managed to get into the urinal beside Joe and to whisper to him, "Say, for crissake, Joe, are we rookin' those guys or are they rookin' us?" Joe wouldn't answer. All he did was to screw his face up and shrug his shoulders.

–*The Big Money*, pp. 840–843

### The Miami Real-Estate Boom
Dana L. Thomas

*The Florida land boom of the late 1920s was similar to the stock-market boom of the same period in that it was driven by a speculative craze rather than by the intrinsic worth of the object purchased. The center of this craze in Florida was Miami and the beach towns just north of it.*

*A Miami, Florida, real-estate office, 18 March 1926 (Photo by W. A. Fishbaugh, Florida Photographic Collection, Florida State Archives)*

Prices of Miami real estate started climbing in 1925. Stories cropped up in newspapers about people who were becoming rich in land deals. One Miamian paid $1.75 million for three hundred thousand acres of swampland and forest in three counties south of Tallahassee, then turned around and peddled it within a week for a $250,000 profit. Another Miamian unloaded ten acres on Northwest Thirty-sixth Street to an ex-sheriff for $175,000. The seller had paid $250 for the property thirty years previously. A certain Ike Jones sold land near the Coco Lobo Kay Club for $250,000. He had bought it for $212. A shopkeeper peddled his store and surrounding land for $2 million and retired to enjoy his wealth. A month after the deal, his property was leased out for ninety-nine years on a $3 million appraisal. The president of the Miami Jockey Club bid $2 million for sixty thousand acres in Sumter and Hernando counties. The syndicate had bought the land unseen, believing it was located near Tampa several hundred miles away.

As early as February 1925, magazines around America were reporting that ordinary men and women with little or no capital were suddenly getting rich in Florida. The state census that year disclosed there were 103,000 year-round residents in greater Miami, but the city fathers predicted the population would jump to at least a million in ten years or less.

The speculative contagion mounted. Even the U.S. War Department became infected with it and decided to throw Chapman Air Field onto the market after giving a portion of it to the Department of Agriculture to use as an experimental farm. Leading Miami businessmen convinced the government it was wiser to keep the field as an air base in case of another war.

A phenomenon that mushroomed as a by-product of the speculative fever was the so-called "binder boys." Swarms of them poured into Florida to reap an overnight buck on land options. They jumped off trains, arriving from all directions, clad in golf knickers, rolled up their sleeves and went to work on the gullible. Knickers became the universal attire for the Miami hustlers.

The headquarters for the "binder boys" was the Biscayne Hotel, which was close to the major real estate offices. By the summer of 1925, the schedule of the hustlers was well established. They jumped from the train, looked around. "Is this Miami?" they asked. Then, "Where can I rent an office?" "What is the price of acreage?"

The binder strategy was highly lucrative. People contracting to buy a lot usually put up 10 percent or less of the established price until the arrangements could be undertaken to tie up the bargain formally. The purchaser received the binder and at the end of thirty days would pay another 15 to 20 percent upon the receipt of the lot after the title had been searched and the deed recorded.

But as the speculative craze spiraled, the county clerk became overwhelmed with work and there were long intervals between the down payment and the next one. During these interims, speculators could trade in options without putting up more cash, and the binder boys reaped a windfall. Initially they made small profits on the binders themselves, then they began working the business of running up the price of the lot through several transactions, while it was still on one binder. Properties were sold dozens of times before the first large payment fell due.

Profits mounted as the binder boys set a dizzier and dizzier pace. It wasn't unusual for a lot to change hands a half-dozen times from the day the first buyer received his binder until the deal was finally sealed. Often when the final buyer received the deed, there were a dozen mortgages attached to it "like ticks on a cow," each representing the profit of one of the traders along the way. The binder boys went around peddling from nine o'clock in the morning until two in the afternoon when the banks shut their doors. They rushed their checks immediately to depositories for the cash. Many a seat-pants plunger who had only enough money to buy a binder brazenly issued a subdivision brochure and sold enough lots to meet his first installment payment. He was careful to sell his lots only on the installment plan, for if a buyer had offered the total cash for a deal, he would have had to turn it down since he hadn't yet acquired the deed to sell it. He had to move quickly to stay one step ahead of his customers.

Meanwhile Americans poured in from all over. Asked by reporters why they came to Florida, they invariably replied they were seeking a way to "better themselves." Florida was the place where one could dine on lotus forever.

Newspapers around the country were crammed with reports on how ordinary folks living next door had suddenly struck it rich and would never have to work again. One newspaper wrote about a boilermaker from Buffalo who had worked hard all his life and despaired of getting ahead. He scraped up $1,000 and rushed to Florida in December 1924. There he accumulated $90,000 in cash and lots valued at $100,000. His employer offered him his job back. He wired, "Go to hell. I don't have to work!"

"The rush to Florida," argued one journalist, "has its rise in deep dissatisfaction with our economic situation, with the state of labor, with the physical limitations cities impose on the way we earn and spend our leisure."

The stories of people who had hit the jackpot continued to pour from the press. Around dinner tables, families discussed the latest tidbits—how the neighborhood butcher had shut up shop and moved his family to Florida, making $30,000 overnight in a property speculation. There was a story of a Columbia, South Carolina, stenographer who paid $350 for a Miami lot five years before and sold it—too soon alas—for a mere $65,000. There was the tale of James, a wealthy family misfit, whom relatives were sure would never amount to anything. He went to Florida in 1924, and, convinced millions could be made there, put $40,000 into property deals. When his family learned of this, they decided James must be saved from his disastrous speculation. They dispatched a battery of lawyers to Florida to extricate him from his binders, managing to free him after alienists testified he was insane. The $40,000 worth of land was released to another buyer who subsequently resold it for $400,000.

One minister was induced by the town undertaker to put his $2,000 of life's savings into Florida land. The mortician's son had just made $40,000 there in a month and had wired for $10,000 cash to swing more deals.

Exuberance in Miami was unbounded. One fellow called to see the head of a business concern. While he was waiting in the outer office, he overheard the office boy ask a stenographer if she thought the boss would pay their salaries on time this week. "Gee, I hope so," said the girl. "I got to make another payment on those two lots I bought."

By the end of 1925, $7 billion worth of Florida real estate had changed hands. A full-page advertisement was carried in periodicals around the country showing a ragged breadwinner fighting off a pack of wolves while leading his wife and children toward a beacon light blazing from the doorway of a Miami real estate broker. The Miami newspapers churned out propaganda for the Chamber of Commerce. They played up the remarks of one New York businessman on Miami's precipitous growth. "Your skyline reminds me of New York." What the visitor had actually said was, "It compares with the skyline of *lower* New York."

A high-powered public relations machine headed by Steve Hannigan, who later turned up as President Franklin Roosevelt's press secretary, grounded out testimonials, interviews and speeches, and magazine articles to keep the ballyhoo going. Boasted Florida's Governor Martin, "We have a population of a hundred thousand, but we can support five million." Queried how long the Florida boom would last, a member of the Sarasota Chamber of Commerce replied, "As long as the sun shines, the birds sing and the children

"Mr. Miami Beach," businessman and real-estate developer Carl G. Fisher, who spearheaded the Miami land boom in the 1920s (I.M.S.)

laugh and play." Financial pundits nodded their heads in agreement. Roger Babson, the investment adviser, predicted in *Forbes* magazine that the boom would persist for another five years at the very least.

The euphoria was breathtaking. Charles L. Apfel of Miami bought the entire town of Olympia in Martin County to use as the future capital of the world's movie industry. Eminent scientists had tipped him off, he explained, that a treacherous Arctic current had been discovered off the coast of California and in a few years it would freeze the California climate so severely that filmmakers would have to quit Hollywood and ship their studios to Florida.

For more than thirteen months, in 1925 and 1926, the *Miami Herald,* thanks to a flood of real estate advertising, became the world's largest newspaper in business volume, beating the *New York Times,* the *Chicago Tribune,* and the *Los Angeles Times* by a wide margin.

The boom brought to Miami a host of vaudeville headliners, opera singers, and jazz bands. Real estate promoters put on lavish shows to entice crowds away from rival operators. Land peddlers and subdividers hired songwriters to compose music and lyrics, ballyhooing their properties. The offices of the bigger real

*A real-estate auction at the Brickell Hammock townsite, Miami, 1 February 1923 (Photo by W. A. Fishbaugh, Florida Photographic Collection, Florida State Archives)*

estate promoters had the atmosphere of cabarets, with elaborate vaudeville acts presented between sales pitches.

Evelyn Nesbit, the ex-show girl who had been Stanford White's sweetheart, was hired to sing and lure the crowds into a leading real estate office. Feodor Chaliapin, the celebrated Russian opera basso who was touring the United States in *Boris Godunov,* was enticed by a fat salary offer to sing jazz songs for tired Miami businessmen relaxing after a hectic day's trading. Paul Whiteman, the band impresario, was hired to play fox-trots and pep up the flagging spirits of pitchmen. Gene Tunney, while awaiting his title fight with Jack Dempsey, entered the real estate business to reap a few dollars, becoming sales manager of an outfit called Hollywood Pines Estates.

William Jennings Bryan, the former secretary of state and perennial seeker of the presidency, turned up in Miami after a bruising Democratic Party convention which nominated John Davis instead of him. From the bandshell of the Royal Palms Park Hotel, Bryan made a tub-thumping pitch on the glories of Florida real estate, unloading 280 acres of property he owned in Dade County for $73,000. This erstwhile leader of the Free Silver Movement, the idol of Western liberals who headed

the State Department in the Wilson presidency, now became a $100,000-a-year hustler for George Merrick, the Coral Gables land promoter.

The boom accelerated. By the middle of August 1925, real estate values on Miami's Flagler Street soared to $50,000 a front acre. Two weeks later a front acre went for $70,000. One businessman, I. C. Richmond, unloaded ten acres at N. W. Seventeenth Avenue and Thirty-third Street for $218,000. He had bought them twenty years before for $100.

*—Lords of the Land: The Triumphs and Scandals of America's Real Estate Barons, from Early Times to the Present* (New York: Putnam, 1977), pp. 192–196

## Margo Dowling
Dos Passos

*Following Charley Anderson's death in a Florida automobile accident, Margo, thrown on her own, decides to parlay her resources in cash and good looks into possible success in the Miami land boom. In this passage, as in his biography of William Jennings Bryan in* The 42nd Parallel, *Dos Passos includes the striking scene of the former 1890s Populist radical hawking real estate from a lagoon float.*

Neither of them said anything for a while. They'd reached the end of the causeway and turned past yellow frame wharfbuildings into the dense traffic of the Miami waterfront. Everywhere new tall buildings iced like layercake were standing up out of scaffolding and builder's rubbish. Rumbling over the temporary wooden bridge across the Miami River in a roar of concretemixers and a drive of dust from the construction work, Margo said, turning a roundeyed pokerface at the judge, "Well, I guess I'll have to hock the old sparklers." The judge laughed and said, "I can assure you the bank will afford you every facility. . . . Don't bother your pretty little head about it. You hold some very considerable options right now if I'm not mistaken." "I don't suppose you could lend me a couple of grand to run on the strength of them, judge."

They were running on a broad new concrete road through dense tropical shrub. "Ma dear young lady," said Judge Cassidy in his genial drawl, "I couldn't do that for your own sake . . . think of the false interpretations . . . the idle gossip. We're a little oldfashioned down here. We're easygoin' but once the breath of scandal . . . Why, even drivin' with such a charmin' passenger through the streets of Miamah is a folly, a very pleasant folly. But you must realize, ma dear young lady . . . A man in ma position can't afford . . . Don't misunderstand ma motive, ma dear young lady. I never turned down a friend in ma life. . . . But ma position would unfortunately not be understood that way. Only a husband or a . . ."

"Is this a proposal, judge?" she broke in sharply. Her eyes were stinging. It was hard keeping back the tears.

"Just a little advice to a client. . . ." The judge sighed. "Unfortunately I'm a family man."

"How long is this boom going to last?"

"I don't need to remind you what type of animal is born every minute."

"No need at all," said Margo gruffly.

They were driving into the parkinglot behind the great new caramelcolored hotel. As she got out of the car Margo said, "Well, I guess some of them can afford to lose their money but we can't, can we, judge?" "Ma dear young lady, there's no such word in the bright lexicon of youth." The judge was ushering her into the diningroom in his fatherly way. "Ah, there are the boys now."

At a round table in the center of the crowded diningroom sat two fatfaced young men with big mouths wearing pinkstriped shirts and nilegreen wash neckties and white suits. They got up still chewing and pumped Margo's hand when the judge presented them. They were twins. As they sat down again one of them winked and shook a fat forefinger. "We used to see you at the Palms, girlie, naughty naughty."

"Well, boys," said the judge, "how's tricks?" "Couldn't be better," one of them said with his mouth full. "You see, boys," said the judge, "this young lady wants to make a few small investments with a quick turnover. . . ." The twins grunted and went on chewing.

After lunch the judge drove them all down to the Venetian Pool where William Jennings Bryan sitting in an armchair on the float under a striped awning was talking to the crowd. From where they were they couldn't hear what he was saying, only the laughter and handclapping of the crowd in the pauses. "Do you know, judge," said one of the twins, as they worked their way through the fringes of the crowd around the pool, "if the old boy hadn't wasted his time with politics, he'da made a great auctioneer."

Margo began to feel tired and wilted. She followed the twins into the realestateoffice full of perspiring men in shirtsleeves. The judge got her a chair. She sat there tapping with her white kid foot on the tiled floor with her lap full of blueprints. The prices were all so high. She felt out of her depth and missed Mr. A to buy for her, he'd have known what to buy sure. Outside, the benches on the lawn were crowded. Bawling voices came from everywhere. The auction was beginning. The twins on the stand were waving their arms and banging with their hammers. The judge was striding around behind Margo's chair talking boom to anybody who would listen. When he paused for breath she looked up at him and said, "Judge Cassidy, could you get me a taxi?" "Ma dear young lady, I'll drive you home myself. It'll be a pleasure." "O.K.," said Margo. "You are very wise," whispered Judge Cassidy in her ear.

As they were walking along the edge of the crowd one of the twins they'd had lunch with left the auctioneer's stand and dove through the crowd after them. "Miss Dowlin'," he said, "kin me an' Al come to call?" "Sure," said Margo, smiling. "Name's in the phonebook under Dowling." "We'll be around." And he ran back to the stand where his brother was pounding with his hammer. She'd been afraid she hadn't made a hit with the twins. Now she felt the tired lines smooth out of her face.

"Well, what do you think of the great development of Coral Gables?" said the judge as he helped her into the car. "Somebody must be making money," said Margo dryly.

*—The Big Money,* pp. 1090–1093

## WORLD WAR I

*World War I, the principal historical event of the early twentieth century, dominates* Nineteen-Nineteen. *Although Dos Passos's anger at America's participation in the conflict, still potent after fifteen years, colored his entire depiction of the event, it is perhaps most evident in his representation of three of its aspects: the role of Woodrow Wilson in propelling the nation into the war; the horror and ugliness of the war itself, especially at Verdun; and the failure of the peace to achieve any of the lofty goals earlier proclaimed by the victors.*

*Dos Passos's major vehicle for the expression of these themes, aside from the biographies of Wilson and the Unknown Soldier, is Richard Savage's narrative. Drawn in part from his own war experiences and those of his Harvard friend Robert Hillyer, Dos Passos's portrait of Savage is almost an allegory of the corruption of the American spirit by the war. Initially a high-minded (but also ambitious and weak-willed) pacifist, Savage is at first horrified by the carnage of Verdun. But the war also provides an opportunity for advancement, and by the time of the Versailles Peace Conference he*

*is an officer much at home in a luxurious Paris setting and is about to be drawn into the orbit of J. Ward Moorehouse, who is himself acting for various oil interests seeking to profit from decisions made at the conference.*

Nineteen-Nineteen *ends with perhaps the most widely reprinted portion of U.S.A., "The Body of an American." This mordant recasting of the ceremonial burial of the Unknown Soldier at Arlington Cemetery in November 1921 recapitulates in lyric form Dos Passos's essential charge that a war corrupt both in its origin and outcome principally injures the innocent.*

### Meester Veelson
Dos Passos

*Dos Passos's biography of Wilson relies on the basic rhetorical device apparent in many of his accounts of World War I: Wilson's high-minded language in defense of American participation is juxtaposed against the reality of the war.*

*"President Wilson: 'But I don't want them—there isn't any enemy to fight.' Morgan, Schwab & Co.: 'You buy these guns and we'll get you an enemy.'" A cartoon from the January 1916 issue of* The Masses *expressing the belief that Woodrow Wilson was drawing the United States into the war on behalf of the Morgan banking interests, which had supported both the Allies and the international armaments industry in general (National Archives).*

*We are witnessing a renaissance of public spirit, a reawakening of sober public opinion, a revival of the power of the people the beginning of an age of thoughtful reconstruction . . .*

but the world had started spinning round Sarajevo.

First it was *neutrality in thought and deed,* then *too proud to fight* when the *Lusitania* sinking and the danger to the Morgan loans and the stories of the British and French propagandists set all the financial centers in the East bawling for war, but the suction of the drumbeat and the guns was too strong; the best people took their fashions from Paris and their broad "a's" from London, and T.R. and the House of Morgan.

Five months after his reelection on the slogan *He kept us out of war,* Wilson pushed the Armed Ship Bill through congress and declared that a state of war existed between the United States and the Central Powers:

*Force without stint or limit, force to the utmost.*

Wilson became the state (war is the health of the state), Washington his Versailles, manned the socialized government with dollar a year men out of the great corporations and ran the big parade

of men munitions groceries mules and trucks to France. Five million men stood at attention outside of their tarpaper barracks every sundown while they played *The Star Spangled Banner.*

War brought the eight hour day, women's votes, prohibition, compulsory arbitration, high wages, high rates of interest, cost plus contracts and the luxury of being a Gold Star Mother.

If you objected to making the world safe for cost plus democracy you went to jail with Debs.

Almost too soon the show was over, Prince Max of Baden was pleading for the Fourteen Points, Foch was occupying the bridgeheads on the Rhine and the Kaiser out of breath ran for the train down the platform at Potsdam wearing a silk hat and some say false whiskers.

With the help of *Almighty God, Right, Truth, Justice, Freedom, Democracy, the Selfdetermination of Nations, No indemnities no annexations,*

and Cuban sugar and Caucasian manganese and Northwestern wheat and Dixie cotton, the British blockade, General Pershing, the taxicabs of Paris and the seventyfive gun

we won the war.

—*Nineteen-Nineteen,* pp. 567–568

\* \* \*

## Richard Savage

### Robert Hillyer and Richard Savage
Donald Pizer

*Pizer examines Dos Passos's reliance on his Harvard friend Robert Hillyer for his depiction of Richard Ellsworth Savage.*

Dos Passos wished to depict in Savage what he believed to be the worst potential of his own background—that of a youth whose Harvard aestheticism reflected both his superficial rebelliousness and his weak posturing and whose later experiences confirmed the uselessness of rebellion and the advantages of deception and conformity. In a sense, the model for this figure was Dos Passos' entire generation of literary aesthetes at Harvard—the group that had dominated the *Harvard Monthly* and that had collaborated on *Eight Harvard Poets,* a small book of verse that had been published with the aid of Dos Passos' father. This was the group that had combined art interests with antiwar sentiment, had gone overseas in the ambulance corps, and had drifted into various kinds of postwar middle-class roles. It was also a group with a strong homoerotic current, though seldom any overt homosexuality. But Dos Passos also chose a far more specific model in his friend Robert Hillyer. He and Hillyer had been friends at Harvard and had deepened their association when they collaborated on the early portion of "Seven Times Round the Walls of Jericho" while serving in the ambulance corps at Verdun during the summer of 1917. Indeed, Dos Passos worked so much of his awareness of Hillyer's life into the portrait of Savage that Hillyer reacted with shocked indignation when he finally came to read *Nineteen-Nineteen* in 1944. Dos Passos' reply to his old friend—that Savage was principally a "synthetic character" and that he didn't think "there's much Hillyer in Savage"—disguises the extent of Dos Passos' use of Hillyer as a model.[1] Like Hillyer, Savage was born in New Jersey, was an Episcopalian with a family military background, went to Kent School, wrote poetry at Harvard, and served overseas—first in the ambulance corps and later as an officer and army courier during the peace conference.[2] Dos Passos' principal departure from the external events of Hillyer's life in the portrait of Savage to 1919 was in placing Savage on the Italian front as an ambulance driver during the winter and spring of 1917–18. (Here Dos Passos drew upon his own experiences.) And there is no evidence of Hillyer having an affair in Europe resembling that between Savage and Daughter. As far as later careers are concerned, Hillyer was to become a conventional and conservative minor poet and a Harvard instructor, activities that Dos Passos perhaps found roughly equivalent in verbal texture to Savage's career in public relations. But given Dos

*Dos Passos's Harvard classmate Robert Hillyer in 1917 (By permission of George Arents Library, Syracuse University)*

Passos' portrayal of Savage in *Nineteen-Nineteen* as the deserter of a pregnant sweetheart, as a latent homosexual, and as essentially dishonest and self-serving, Hillyer did not need to reach into Savage's postwar career for material in the characterization to object to.

—*Dos Passos' U.S.A.: A Critical Study* (Charlottesville: University Press of Virginia, 1988), pp. 143–144

### Notes

1. Dos Passos to Robert Hillyer (responding to Hillyer's complaints), October 1944 and 3 November 1944, in Townsend Ludington, ed., *The Fourteenth Chronicle: Letters and Diaries of John Dos Passos* (Boston: Gambit, 1973), pp. 543–544.

2. There is no biography of Hillyer, but see the entry by David D. Anderson in the *Dictionary of American Biography*, supplement 7 (1981), pp. 346–347.

## Richard Ellsworth Savage
Dos Passos

*Dos Passos emphasizes the thin personal morality underlying Dick Savage's seemingly rebellious Harvard aestheticism. Dick gives his antiwar poem "a note of hope" in order to have it published, and his enlistment in the ambulance corps is accompanied by a bout of self-pity. In a second passage Dick's experiences at Verdun closely resemble those both of Hillyer and Dos Passos.*

In the Easter vacation, after the Armed Ship Bill had passed Dick had a long talk with Mr. Cooper who wanted to get him a job in Washington, because he said a boy of his talent oughtn't to endanger his career by joining the army and already there was talk of conscription. Dick blushed becomingly and said he felt it would be against his conscience to help in the war in any way. They talked a long time without getting anywhere about duty to the state and party leadership and highest expediency. In the end Mr. Cooper made him promise not to take any rash step without consulting him. Back in Cambridge everybody was drilling and going to lectures on military science. Dick was finishing up the four year course in three years and had to work hard, but nothing in the courses seemed to mean anything any more. He managed to find time to polish up a group of sonnets called Morituri Te Salutant that he sent to a prize competition run by *The Literary Digest*. It won the prize but the editors wrote back that they would prefer a note of hope in the last sestet. Dick put in the note of hope and sent the hundred dollars to Mother to go to Atlantic City with. He discovered that if he went into war work he could get his degree that spring without taking any exams and went in to Boston one day without saying anything to anybody and signed up in the volunteer ambulance service.

The night he told Ned that he was going to France they got very drunk on orvieto wine in their room and talked a great deal about how it was the fate of Youth and Beauty and Love and Friendship to be mashed out by an early death, while the old fat pompous fools would make merry over their carcasses. In the pearly dawn they went out and sat with a last bottle on one of the old tombstones in the graveyard, on the corner of Harvard Square. They sat on the cold tombstone a long time without saying anything, only drinking, and after each drink threw their heads back and softly bleated in unison Blahblahblahblah.

—*Nineteen-Nineteen*, p. 441

Provincetown Mass
Nov. 3 – 1944

Dear Robert –

It serves you right for departing from your resolution not to read your friends' books. But really you've got it wrong. Savage was a synthetic character as all the characters in my novels are. In developing him a few little touches of Hillyer may have crept in. In fact I put in some of your inimitable stories about the late General Hillyer – Zonos. But there was never any intention of producing a portrait or a caricature of my friend Robert Hillyer. You've written novels yourself & you know how you start out with a few notions and anecdotes about somebody you know and then other scraps of the lives of other people get in and a large slice of your own life and then if you are lucky the mash begins to ferment and becomes something

*First page of 3 November 1944 letter from Dos Passos to Hillyer in which the novelist insisted that the character Richard Savage was not strictly based on Hillyer (Albert and Shirley Small Special Collections Library, University of Virginia)*

There were two other fellows in the section who liked to drink wine and chatter bad French; Steve Warner, who'd been a special student at Harvard, and Ripley who was a freshman at Columbia. The five of them went around together, finding places to get omelettes and pommes frites in the villages within walking distance, making the rounds of the estaminets every night; they got to be known as the grenadine guards. When the section moved up onto the Voie Sacrée back of Verdun and was quartered for three rainy weeks in a little ruined village called Erize la Petite, they set up their cots together in the same corner of the old brokendown barn they were given for a cantonment. It rained all day and all night; all day and all night camions ground past through the deep liquid putty of the roads carrying men and munitions to Verdun. Dick used to sit on his cot looking out through the door at the jiggling mudspattered faces of the young French soldiers going up for the attack, drunk and desperate and yelling à bas la guerre, mort au vaches, à bas la guerre. Once Steve came in suddenly, his face pale above the dripping poncho, his eyes snapping, and said in a low voice, "Now I know what the tumbrils were like in the Terror, that's what they are, tumbrils."

Dick was relieved to find out, when they finally moved up within range of the guns, that he wasn't any more scared than anybody else. The first time they went on post he and Fred lost their way in the shellshredded woods and were trying to turn the car around on a little rise naked as the face of the moon when three shells from an Austrian eightyeight went past them like three cracks of a whip. They never knew how they got out of the car and into the ditch, but when the sparse blue almondsmelling smoke cleared they were both lying flat in the mud. Fred went to pieces and Dick had to put his arm around him and keep whispering in his ear, "Come on, boy, we got to make it. Come on Fred, we'll fool 'em." It all hit him funny and he kept laughing all the way back along the road into the quieter section of the woods where the dressing station had been cleverly located right in front of a battery of 405s so that the concussion almost bounced the wounded out of their stretchers every time a gun was fired. When they got back to the section after taking a load to the triage they were able to show three jagged holes from shellfragments in the side of the car.

Next day the attack began and continual barrages and counterbarrages and heavy gasbombardments; the section was on twentyfour hour duty for three days, at the end of it everybody had dysentery and bad nerves. One fellow got shellshock, although he'd been too scared to go on post, and had to be sent back to Paris. A couple of men had to be evacuated for dysentery. The grenadine guards came through the attack pretty well, except that Steve and Ripley had gotten a little extra sniff of mustard gas up at P2 one night and vomited whenever they ate anything.

In their twentyfour hour periods off duty they'd meet in a little garden at Récicourt that was the section's base. No one else seemed to know about it. The garden had been attached to a pink villa but the villa had been mashed to dust as if a great foot had stepped on it. The garden was untouched, only a little weedy from neglect, roses were in bloom there and butterflies and bees droned around the flowers on sunny afternoons. At first they took the bees for distant arrivés and went flat on their bellies when they heard them. There had been a cement fountain in the middle of the garden and there they used to sit when the Germans got it into their heads to shell the road and the nearby bridge. There was regular shelling three times a day and a little scattering between times. Somebody would be detailed to stand in line at the Copé and buy south of France melons and four franc fifty champagne. Then they'd take off their shirts to toast their backs and shoulders if it was sunny and sit in the dry fountain eating the melons and drinking the warm cidery champagne and talk about how they'd go back to the States and start an underground newspaper like *La Libre Belgique* to tell people what the war was really like.

What Dick liked best in the garden was the little backhouse, like the backhouse in a New England farm, with a clean scrubbed seat and a half moon in the door, through which on sunny days the wasps who had a nest in the ceiling hummed busily in and out. He'd sit there with his belly aching listening to the low voices of his friends talking in the driedup fountain. Their voices made him feel happy and at home while he stood wiping himself on a few old yellowed squares of a 1914 *Petit Journal* that still hung on the nail. Once he came back buckling his belt and saying, "Do you know? I was thinking how fine it would be if you could reorganize the cells of your body into some other kind of life . . . it's too damn lousy being a human . . . I'd like to be a cat, a nice comfortable housecat sitting by the fire."

"It's a hell of a note," said Steve, reaching for his shirt and putting it on. A cloud had gone over the sun and it was suddenly chilly. The guns sounded quiet and distant. Dick felt suddenly chilly and lonely. "It's a hell of a note when you have to be ashamed of belonging to your own race. But I swear I am, I swear I'm ashamed of being a man . . . it will take some huge wave of hope like a revolution to make me feel any selfrespect ever again. . . . God, we're a lousy cruel vicious dumb type of tailless ape." "Well, if you want to earn your selfrespect, Steve, and the respect of us other apes, why don't you go down, now that they're not shelling, and buy us a bottle of champagny water?" said Ripley.

—*Nineteen-Nineteen,* pp. 518–520

* * *

## The Peace

*Meester Veelson*
Dos Passos

*The conclusion of the Wilson biography centers on the failure of the Versailles Peace Conference. The idealistic "Fourteen Points" plan that Wilson had brought to the Conference as a basis for world peace and justice was soon neglected in the struggle by the great European powers to maintain their nationalistic self-interest in land, markets, and raw material, a struggle that indeed was a principal cause of the war. Wilson was a kind of innocent in this hurly-burly and returned home a defeated man.*

On December 4th, 1918, Woodrow Wilson, the first president to leave the territory of the United States during his presidency, sailed for France on board the *George Washington,*
the most powerful man in the world.

In Europe they knew what gas smelt like and the sweet sick stench of bodies buried too shallow and the grey look of the skin of starved children; they read in the papers that Meester Veelson was for peace and freedom and canned goods and butter and sugar;

he landed at Brest with his staff of experts and publicists after a rough trip on the *George Washington.*

La France héroïque was there with the speeches, the singing schoolchildren, the mayors in their red sashes. (Did Meester Veelson see the gendarmes at Brest beating back the demonstration of dockyard workers who came to meet him with red flags?)

*The Big Four at the Versailles Peace Conference, June 1919: David Lloyd George of England, Vittorio Orlando of Italy, Georges Clemenceau of France, and Woodrow Wilson of the United States (from August Heckscher,* Woodrow Wilson, *1991)*

At the station in Paris he stepped from the train onto a wide red carpet that led him, between rows of potted palms, silk hats, legions of honor, decorated busts of uniforms, frockcoats, rosettes, boutonnières, to a Rolls Royce. (Did Meester Veelson see the women in black, the cripples in their little carts, the pale anxious faces along the streets, did he hear the terrible anguish of the cheers as they hurried him and his new wife to the hôtel de Mûrat, where in rooms full of brocade, gilt clocks, Buhl cabinets and ormolu cupids the presidential suite had been prepared?)

While the experts were organizing the procedure of the peace conference, spreading green baize on the tables, arranging the protocols,

the Wilsons took a tour to see for themselves: the day after Christmas they were entertained at Buckingham Palace; at Newyears they called on the pope and on the microscopic Italian king at the Quirinal. (Did Meester Veelson know that in the peasants' wargrimed houses along the Brenta and the Piave they were burning candles in front of his picture cut out of the illustrated papers?) (Did Meester Veelson know that the people of Europe spelled a challenge to oppression out of the Fourteen Points as centuries before they had spelled a challenge to oppression out of the ninetyfive articles Martin Luther nailed to the churchdoor in Wittenberg?)

January 18, 1919, in the midst of serried uniforms, cocked hats and gold braid, decorations, epaulettes, orders of merit and knighthood, the High Contracting Parties, the allied and associated powers met in the Salon de l'Horloge at the quai d'Orsay to dictate the peace,

but the grand assembly of the peace conference was too public a place to make peace in

so the High Contracting Parties

formed the Council of Ten, went into the Gobelin Room and, surrounded by Rubens's History of Marie de Medici,

began to dictate the peace.

But the Council of Ten was too public a place to make peace in

so they formed the Council of Four.

Orlando went home in a huff

and then there were three:

Clemenceau,

Lloyd George,

Woodrow Wilson.

Three old men shuffling the pack,

dealing out the cards:

the Rhineland, Danzig, the Polish corridor, the Ruhr, self determination of small nations, the Saar, League of Nations, mandates, the Mespot, Freedom of the Seas, Transjordania, Shantung, Fiume and the Island of Yap:

machine gun fire and arson

starvation, lice, cholera, typhus;

oil was trumps.

Woodrow Wilson believed in his father's God

so he told the parishioners in the little Lowther Street Congregational church where his grandfather had preached in Carlisle in Scotland, a day so chilly that the newspaper men sitting in the old pews all had to keep their overcoats on.

On April 7th he ordered the *George Washington* to be held at Brest with steam up ready to take the American delegation home;

but he didn't go.

On April 19 sharper Clemenceau and sharper Lloyd George got him into their little cosy threecardgame they called the Council of Four.

On June 28th the Treaty of Versailles was ready

and Wilson had to go back home to explain to the politicians who'd been ganging up on him meanwhile in the Senate and House and to sober public opinion and to his father's God how he'd let himself be trimmed and how far he'd made the world safe

for democracy and the New Freedom.

From the day he landed in Hoboken he had his back to the wall of the White House, talking to save his faith in words, talking to save his faith in the League of Nations, talking to save his faith in himself, in his father's God.

He strained every nerve of his body and brain, every agency of the government he had under his control; (if anybody disagreed he was a crook or a red; no pardon for Debs).

In Seattle the wobblies whose leaders were in jail, in Seattle the wobblies whose leaders had been lynched, who'd been shot down like dogs, in Seattle the wobblies lined four blocks as Wilson passed, stood silent with their arms folded staring at the great liberal as he was hurried past in his car, huddled in his overcoat, haggard with fatigue, one side of his face twitching. The men in overalls, the workingstiffs let him pass in silence after all the other blocks of handclapping and patriotic cheers.

In Pueblo, Colorado, he was a grey man hardly able to stand, one side of his face twitching:

*Now that the mists of this great question have cleared away, I believe that men will see the Truth, eye for eye and face to face. There is one thing the American People always rise to and extend their hands to, that is, the truth of justice and of liberty and of peace. We have accepted that truth and we are going to be led by it, and it is going to lead us, and through us the world, out into pastures of quietness and peace such as the world never dreamed of before.*

That was his last speech;

on the train to Wichita he had a stroke. He gave up the speaking tour that was to sweep the country for the League of Nations. After that he was a ruined paralysed man barely able to speak;

the day he gave up the presidency to Harding the joint committee of the Senate and House appointed Henry Cabot Lodge, his lifelong enemy, to make the formal call at the executive office in the Capitol and ask the formal question whether the president had any message for the congress assembled in joint session;

Wilson managed to get to his feet, lifting himself painfully by the two arms of the chair. "Senator Lodge, I have no further communication to make, thank you . . . Good morning," he said.

In 1924 on February 3rd he died.

—*Nineteen-Nineteen*, pp. 568–571

*The dining room of the fashionable Hotel Crillon, the headquarters of the American delegation to the Versailles Peace Conference*

## Richard Ellsworth Savage

Dos Passos

*Dick Savage moves into Moorehouse's orbit in the context of the elegant salon established by Eleanor Stoddard in Paris during the Versailles Peace Conference. In a sense, Savage will be bought by "big oil" just as Wilson's ideals were undermined by it.*

When he got back to Paris, Dick and Colonel Edgecombe went to tea at Miss Stoddard's. Her drawingroom was tall and stately with Italian panels on the walls and yellow and orange damask hangings; through the heavy lace in the windows you could see the purple branches of the trees along the quai, the jade Seine and the tall stone lace of the apse of Nôtre Dâme. "What a magnificent setting you have arranged for yourself, Miss Stoddard," said Colonel Edgecombe, "and if you excuse the compliment, the gem is worthy of its setting." "They were fine old rooms," said Miss Stoddard, "all you need do with these old houses is to give them a chance." She turned to Dick: "Young man, what did you do to Robbins that night we all had supper together? He talks about nothing else but what a bright fellow you are." Dick blushed. "We had a glass of uncommonly good scotch together afterwards . . . It must have been that." "Well, I'll have to keep my eye on you . . . I don't trust these bright young men."

They drank tea sitting around an ancient wroughtiron stove. A fat major and a lanternjawed Standard Oil man named Rasmussen came in, and later a Miss Hutchins who looked very slender and welltailored in her Red Cross uniform. They talked about Chartres and about the devastated regions and the popular enthusiasm that was greeting Mr. Wilson everywhere and why Clemenceau always wore grey lisle gloves. Miss Hutchins said it was because he really had claws instead of hands and that was why they called him the tiger.

Miss Stoddard got Dick in the window: "I hear you've just come from Rome, Captain Savage . . . I've been in Rome a great deal since the war began . . . Tell me what you saw . . . tell me about everything . . . I like it better than anywhere." "Do you like Tivoli?" "Yes, I suppose so; it's rather a tourist place, though, don't you think?" Dick told her the story of the fight at the Apollo without mentioning Ed's name, and she was very much amused. They got along very well in the window watching the streetlamps come into greenish bloom along the river as they talked; Dick was wondering how old she was, la femme de trente ans.

As he and the Colonel were leaving they met Mr. Moorehouse in the hall. He shook hands warmly with Dick, said he was so glad to see him again and asked him to come by late some afternoon, his quarters were at the Crillon and there were often some interesting people there. Dick was curiously elated by the tea, although he'd expected to be bored. He began to think it was about time he got out of the service, and, on the way back to the office, where they had some work to clean up, asked the Colonel what steps he ought to take to get out of the service in France. "Well, if you're looking for that, this fellow Moorehouse is the man for you . . . I believe he's to be in charge of some sort of publicity work for Standard Oil . . . Can you see yourself as a public relations counsel, Savage?" The Colonel laughed. "Well, I've got my mother to think of," said Dick seriously.

*—Nineteen-Nineteen, pp. 680–681*

\* \* \*

## The Body of an American

### Our Unknown Warrior Buried, The World Honoring Him. . . .
*New York Times*

*The exalted language and sentiments of this report of the burial of the Unknown Soldier at Arlington National Cemetery were characteristic of the reporting of the event throughout the United States.*

WASHINGTON, Nov. 11.–America buried her Unknown Warrior today–placed in the earth the body of that boy whose very namelessness symbolized 50,000 others who had given their lives for America on the field of battle in the World War.

Surrounded by the world's great, with none of them too great to bow in homage, this dead boy's funeral was still no pageant, no spectacular drama, no worldly show. It was more a benediction, a spiritual something whose very realities were less apparent than the thoughts they conjured.

Washington has witnessed many notable ceremonials, but never one like this. Its people saw the bodies of Lincoln and Garfield borne along the broad streets, and under cover of darkness, through a drizzling rain, had watched the solemn progress of that procession which followed the dead McKinley to the White House. There were tears of sorrow then. There were tears today, but most of those who shed them were carried away by the emotion of the symbolism of patriotism which this unknown American embodied.

Taken from that central spot in the Capitol's rotunda where before this only the bodies of Presidents had lain in state, and where it had been designed to place the body of George Washington, this fighting boy whose coffined figure stood for sacrifice to honor and patriotism was followed to his body's final resting place by statesmen, law-makers, law-givers, soldiers, sailors and many others, led by the President of the United States, all walking for part of that solemn journey close to the funeral caisson.

At Arlington, the nation's military Valhalla, in the low Virginia hills which form a background for the capital city, the Unknown Warrior was placed in a marble sarcophagus, designed to be a national shrine like that under the Arc de Triomphe in Paris, where an unknown poilu's body rests, and Westminster Abbey, where Britain's Unknown lies.

The place of burial is a lawn with grass still green overlooking the Potomac and the city beyond, the white dome of the Capitol and the tall shaft of the Washington Monument standing out conspicuously among the mass of buildings.

. . . . . . . . . .

*—New York Times,* 12 November 1921, p. 1

### The Body of an American
Dos Passos

*In perhaps the best-known excerpt from* U.S.A., *Dos Passos initially juxtaposes the public language of the national celebration of the Unknown Soldier and an imagined re-creation of the actualities of his background. Dos Passos then follows the soldier's career in the army until his death. The intent of the whole is not to diminish the pain and anguish of death on the battlefield but to indict the falsification of its nature for suspect motives.*

Whereasthe Congressoftheunitedstates byaconcurrentresolutionadoptedon the 4thdayofmarch lastauthorizedthe Secretaryofwar to cause to be brought to theunitedstatesthe body of an Americanwhowasamemberoftheamericanexpeditionaryforcesineurope wholosthislifeduringtheworldwarandwhoseidentityhas notbeenestablished for burial inthememorialamphitheatreofthe nationalcemeteryatarlingtonvirginia

In the tarpaper morgue at Chalons-sur-Marne in the reek of chloride of lime and the dead, they picked out the pine box that held all that was left of

enie menie minie moe plenty other pine boxes stacked up there containing what they'd scraped up of Richard Roe

and other person or persons unknown. Only one can go. How did they pick John Doe?

make sure he aint a dinge, boys,

make sure he aint a guinea or a kike,

how can you tell a guy's a hundredpercent when all you've got's a gunnysack full of bones, bronze buttons stamped with the screaming eagle and a pair of roll puttees?

. . . and the gagging chloride and the puky dirt-stench of the yearold dead . . .

The day withal was too meaningful and tragic for applause. Silence, tears, songs and prayer, muffled drums and soft music were the instrumentalities today of national approbation.

John Doe was born (thudding din of blood in love into the shuddering soar of a man and a woman alone indeed together lurching into

and ninemonths sick drowse waking into scared agony and the pain and blood and mess of birth). John Doe was born

and raised in Brooklyn, in Memphis, near the lakefront in Cleveland, Ohio, in the stench of the stockyards in Chi, on Beacon Hill, in an old brick house in Alexandria Virginia, on Telegraph Hill, in a halftimbered Tudor cottage in Portland the city of roses,

in the Lying-In Hospital old Morgan endowed on Stuyvesant Square,

across the railroad tracks, out near the country club, in a shack cabin tenement apartmenthouse exclusive residential suburb;

scion of one of the best families in the social register, won first prize in the baby parade at Coronado Beach, was marbles champion of the Little Rock grammarschools, crack basketballplayer at the Booneville High, quarterback at the State Reformatory, having saved the sheriff's kid from drowning in the Little Missouri River was invited to Washington to be photographed shaking hands with the President on the White House steps;—

though this was a time of mourning, such an assemblage necessarily has about it a touch of color. In the boxes are seen the court uniforms of foreign diplomats, the gold braid of our own and foreign fleets and armies, the black of the conventional morning dress of American statesmen, the varicolored furs and outdoor wrapping garments of mothers and sisters come to mourn, the drab and blue of soldiers and sailors, the glitter of musical instruments and the white and black of a vested choir

—busboy harveststiff hogcaller boyscout champeen cornshucker of Western Kansas bellhop at the United States Hotel at Saratoga Springs office boy callboy fruiter telephone lineman longshoreman lumberjack plumber's helper,

worked for an exterminating company in Union City, filled pipes in an opium joint in Trenton, N. J.

Y.M.C.A. secretary, express agent, truckdriver, fordmechanic, sold books in Denver Colorado: Madam would you be willing to help a young man work his way through college?

President Harding, with a reverence seemingly more significant because of his high temporal station, concluded his speech:

*We are met today to pay the impersonal tribute;*
*the name of him whose body lies before us took flight with his imperishable soul . . .*

*as a typical soldier of this representative democracy he fought and died believing in the indisputable justice of his country's cause . . .*

by raising his right hand and asking the thousands within the sound of his voice to join in the prayer:

*Our Father which art in heaven hallowed be thy name . . .*

Naked he went into the army;

they weighed you, measured you, looked for flat feet, squeezed your penis to see if you had clap, looked up your anus to see if you had piles, counted your teeth, made you cough, listened to your heart and lungs, made you read the letters on the card, charted your urine and your intelligence,

gave you a service record for a future (imperishable soul)

and an identification tag stamped with your serial number to hang around your neck, issued O D regulation equipment, a condiment can and a copy of the articles of war.

Atten'SHUN suck in your gut you c———r wipe that smile off your face eyes right wattja tink dis is a choirch-social? Forwar-D'ARCH.

John Doe
and Richard Roe and other person or persons unknown

drilled hiked, manual of arms, ate slum, learned to salute, to soldier, to loaf in the latrines, forbidden to smoke on deck, overseas guard duty, forty men and eight horses, shortarm inspection and the ping of shrapnel and the shrill bullets combing the air and the sorehead woodpeckers the machineguns mud cooties gasmasks and the itch.

*Say feller tell me how I can get back to my outfit.*

John Doe had a head

for twentyodd years intensely the nerves of the eyes the ears the palate the tongue the fingers the toes the armpits, the nerves warmfeeling under the skin charged the coiled brain with hurt sweet warm cold mine must dont sayings print headlines:

Thou shalt not the multiplication table long division, Now is the time for all good men knocks but once at a young man's door, It's a great life if Ish gebibbel, The first five years'll be the Safety First, Suppose a hun tried to rape your my country right or wrong, Catch 'em young, What he dont know wont treat 'em rough, Tell 'em nothin, He got what was coming to him he got his, This is a white man's country, Kick the bucket, Gone west, If you dont like it you can croaked him

*Say buddy cant you tell me how I can get back to my outfit?*

Cant help jumpin when them things go off, give me the trots them things do. I lost my identification tag swimmin in the Marne, roughhousin with a guy while we was waitin to be deloused, in bed with a girl named Jeanne (Love moving picture wet French postcard dream began with saltpeter in the coffee and ended at the propho station);–

*Say soldier for chrissake cant you tell me how I can get back to my outfit?*

John Doe's
heart pumped blood:
alive thudding silence of blood in your ears
down in the clearing in the Oregon forest where the punkins were punkincolor pouring into the blood through the eyes and the fallcolored trees and the bronze hoopers were hopping through the dry grass, where tiny striped snails hung on the underside of the blades and the flies hummed, wasps droned, bumblebees buzzed, and the woods smelt of wine and mushrooms and apples, homey smell of fall pouring into the blood,
and I dropped the tin hat and the sweaty pack and lay flat with the dogday sun licking my throat and adamsapple and the tight skin over the breastbone.

The shell had his number on it.

The blood ran into the ground.

The service record dropped out of the filing cabinet when the quartermaster sergeant got blotto that time they had to pack up and leave the billets in a hurry.
The identification tag was in the bottom of the Marne.

The blood ran into the ground, the brains oozed out of the cracked skull and were licked up by the trenchrats, the belly swelled and raised a generation of bluebottle flies,
and the incorruptible skeleton,
and the scraps of dried viscera and skin bundled in khaki

they took to Chalons-sur-Marne
and laid it out neat in a pine coffin
and took it home to God's Country on a battleship
and buried it in a sarcophagus in the Memorial Amphitheatre in the Arlington National Cemetery
and draped the Old Glory over it
and the bugler played taps

and Mr. Harding prayed to God and the diplomats and the generals and the admirals and the brasshats and the politicians and the handsomely dressed ladies out of the society column of the *Washington Post* stood up solemn
and thought how beautiful sad Old Glory God's Country it was to have the bugler play taps and the three volleys made their ears ring.

Where his chest ought to have been they pinned
the Congressional Medal, the D.S.C., the Medaille Militaire, the Belgian Croix de Guerre, the Italian gold medal, the Vitutea Militara sent by Queen Marie of Rumania, the Czechoslovak war cross, the Virtuti Militari of the Poles, a wreath sent by Hamilton Fish, Jr., of New York, and a little wampum presented by a deputation of Arizona redskins in warpaint and feathers. All the Washingtonians brought flowers.

Woodrow Wilson brought a bouquet of poppies.
—*Nineteen-Nineteen,* pp. 756–761

## An Elegy for the Unknown Soldier
Melvin Landsberg

*Landsberg carefully examines the ways in which "The Body of an American" often makes ironic use of the conventions of the pastoral elegy to achieve its effect.*

Ninety thousand people filed past the body of the American Unknown Soldier as it lay in the Rotunda of the Capitol in Washington, D.C. on November 10, 1921. First, in Europe, a soldier's body had been chosen from each of the four permanent U.S. cemeteries there, taken to Châlons-sur Marne, and brought to a small room in the City Hall. An American sergeant then went into that room and placed flowers on one of the four coffins.[1] Amid ceremony, that coffin was then brought to the United States on the *Olympia,* flagship of the late Admiral George Dewey.

At 8:30 A.M. on November 11 the coffin was carried to a caisson in the Capitol Plaza. Huge crowds watched as a military funeral procession accompanying the body passed down Capitol Hill and Pennsylvania Avenue to the White House. Immediately behind the caisson marched President Harding, with General Pershing at his left. Behind these two marched Vice President Coolidge and a ranking admiral, then Chief Justice Taft and another ranking admiral. Following them came the associate justices of the U.S. Supreme Court, more military, governors of the States, members of the Cabinet, the U.S. Senators, eight abreast, then the U.S. House of Representatives. Former President Woodrow Wilson, who had suffered a stroke, was unable to march. He rode with his wife in an open victoria, wearing a poppy on the left lapel of his coat.

Behind the military and the civilian notables from the government, representatives of many organizations–from the Grand Army of the Republic, the Confederate Veterans, the Colored Veterans of the War, the Red Cross through the Rotary Club and the Georgetown Cadets–marched in columns. When the funeral procession, after going seventeen blocks, passed the White House, the enfeebled Wilson returned to his residence, and the U.S. government officials left to ride by automobile to Arlington National Cemetery. But the military escorting the caisson proceeded on foot to the cemetery, as did thousands of members of the patriotic societies.

Admission to the amphitheater at Arlington was by ticket only. Perhaps five thousand people were admitted, and tens of thousands of others gathered outside. From the main entrance to the amphitheater, body bearers carried the coffin to the stage and placed it on a catafalque there. Seated on the stage were many notables, including Marshal Foch of France, General Jacques of Belgium, General Diaz of Italy, Arthur James Balfour of Great Britain, Premier Briand of France, and U.S. Secretary of State Hughes. Still other notables occupied boxes. Three sections of the amphitheater directly fronting the stage were filled with U.S. Senators and Representatives and their families, and other sections held wounded soldiers, Congressional Medal of Honor winners, and Gold Star mothers.[2]

We turn to the ceremonies at the amphitheater, relying, as above, on the *Washington Post* and the *New York Times* for our material. The *Post,* the only newspaper that Dos Passos mentions in his piece on the Unknown Soldier, "The Body of an American," had on its front page a long feature article by George Rothwell Brown, a political journalist, who wrote of the Soldier's being honored by "the mighty country for which he gladly gave his life." When Harding came up to the flag-covered casket, Brown wrote, a noteworthy event transpired: "A light, thin haze had hung in the sky nearly all morning, but now, as the President began speaking, the sun for the first time scattered away the clouds and fell full upon his face, softly illuminating it, a very happy omen, it seemed."[3]

The *Washington Post's* lead article made similar use of the sun: "Just as the cortege reached the tomb," it reported, "the clouds that had hung low all day, parted and the feeble rays of an autumnal sun filtered down on the casket. It was as if the heavens had opened to receive the spirit of the dead hero."[4]

Reading "The Body of an American" in *Nineteen-nineteen* (1932) one is fascinated by Dos Passos' effrontery in satirizing the august commemoration

of November 11, 1921. Actually, he was in Baghdad on November 11, having sailed for Europe in March and, after a stay there, gone on a writer's journey to Turkey, the Soviet Caucasus, Iran, and some of the Arab lands.

However his novel *Three Soldiers* appeared in 1921 and was being reviewed in October of that year.[5] Although the novel's close antecedence to the November 11 ceremonies was coincidental, it struck a note of opposition to officially sustained versions of wartime service. In his elegy "The Body of an American" Dos Passos struck that note again but now more specifically. He placed the elegy, strategically, at the very end of *Nineteen-nineteen,* the second volume of *U.S.A.,* which deals with the war years.

"The Body of an American" is a brilliantly written modernist elegy, with some of its roots in the traditional pastoral elegy–e.g., Milton's "Lycidas" and Shelley's "Adonais," in English literature. As we shall see, it fictionalizes details, and should not be read as factual history.

The work is a montage, juxtaposing and interweaving four voices:

1. An initial voice giving a slurring, perfunctory rendition of President Harding's proclamation on bringing the body of an American back for burial in the memorial amphitheater of Arlington National Cemetery.[6]

2. The author's narrative voice.

3. A newspaper account of the memorial service, alternating glib patriotism with pleasure in the pageantry.

4. The imagined voice of the Unknown Soldier, shortly before his death.

The voice reciting Harding's proclamation has all the concern of a courtroom clerk asking: "Doyou solemnly swearto tell the truth the whole truth, and nothing butthetruth?" It is Dos Passos' introduction to what is being played out as an outpouring of national emotion.

Without transition we are in a "tarpaper morgue" in Châlons-sur-Marne, where several American soldiers endure the stench to choose a corpse. The soldier directing the operation is saying:

Make sure he ain't a dinge, boys.
make sure he ain't a guinea or a kike . . .

But, asks the author's voice in mimicry, how can the soldiers tell? There is so little left of these dead.

Without transition again, we are reading a newspaper account of the ceremony:

The day withal was too meaningful and tragic for applause. Silence, tears, songs, and prayer, muffled drums and soft music were the instrumentalities today of national approbation.

We go on to some of Dos Passos' biography of the Unknown Soldier. The narrating voice is tough and clipped, and his account is made up entirely of specifics, in contrast to the syrupy abstractions found in the newspaper account: "meaningful," "tragic," "national approbation."

The narrator's list of the Soldier's possible identities may remind us of sections 15 and 16 of Walt Whitman's "Song of Myself."[7] It is interrupted by the newspaper account:

> though this was a time of mourning, such an assemblage necessarily has about it a touch of color. In the boxes are seen the court uniforms of foreign diplomats, the gold braid of our own and foreign fleets and armies, the black of the conventional mourning dress of American statesmen, the varicolored furs and outdoor wrappings of mothers and sisters come to mourn . . .

The list of the Soldier's possible identities then is taken up again, and then again followed by the newspaper account. Then Dos Passos' narration continues with the Unknown Soldier's life:

> Naked he went into the army;
> they weighed you, measured you . . . charted your urine and your intelligence . . .

In the same clipped language the narrator proceeds to recount typical experiences in a U.S. soldier's basic training and typical phrases to which the Unknown Soldier would have been subjected during his brief life. These are contrasted with the primary biological sensations of a human being. Narrator's voice and Soldier's voice merge as Dos Passos gives us likely and possible circumstances of the Soldier's death. The account is interrupted three times by a refrain in the Soldier's voice, the first instance being: "Say feller tell me how I can get back to my outfit," and the third a frightened: "Say soldier for chrissake can't you tell me how I can get back to my outfit?"

The Soldier's primal animal sensations (e.g., heart pumping blood) are matched by his experiences in nature ("tiny striped snails hung on the underside of the blades"). But "the shell had his number on it," says the narrator, using an item from the wartime bag of clichés. In Washington, D.C., mourners with their own agendas subject the remnants of the body to their rites and oratory.

I have spoken of "The Body of an American" as an elegy. But, one could ask, may we call it a poem at all? I believe so. Much of it is written in free verse,

whether line by line or run together in prose paragraphs. Like Whitman, Dos Passos makes extensive use of parallelism. Dos Passos' piece is rhythmic, except in the first paragraph, where he deliberately has discord. And at points where the still-alive Soldier speaks for himself, his lines are not only a refrain, but also one with incremental repetition.

Richard P. Adams, in an essay "Whitman's 'Lilacs' and the Tradition of the Pastoral Elegy," says: "Of seventeen devices commonly used in pastoral elegies from Bion to [Matthew] Arnold, seven appear in 'Lilacs.'"[8] Going through Adams' list of all seventeen, I find that nine appear in "The Body of an American"–I use Adams' words in listing them:

1. "The dramatic framework" (here used partially)
2. "The announcement that the speaker's friend or alter ego is dead and is to be mourned"
3. "the funeral procession with other mourners"
4. "the eulogy of the dead man"
5. "The dead man's biography"
6. "The account of when and how the man died"
7. "The account of the dying speech and death"
8. "The placing of flowers on the bier"
9. "The resolution of the poem in some formula of comfort or reconciliation"

Of course, some of these devices are used ironically or sardonically, for "The Body of an American" is a satirical exposé of the State's myth, as it was expressed in the orations of government officials and in the columns of establishmentarian newspapers. From the start, Dos Passos' method is to depict facade and reality.

We begin our illustration of this method with the announcement that the speaker's friend or alter ego is dead and is to be mourned. But the announcement is President Harding's proclamation, offered without thought or emotion. For the narrator, who shared in the Soldier's experiences and might have encountered him (as the reader knows from "The Camera Eye" in *Nineteen-nineteen*), the Soldier is a military acquaintance.

Dos Passos gives us, we have said, historical fiction, not history. Never mind that only one soldier, a sergeant, chose among four coffins, not four visible bodies, at Châlons-sur-Marne.[9] "Enie menie minie moe," says the narrator, using a racist counting formula.

A listing of the soldier's possible identities is interrupted by the newspaper "excerpt" on dress and color at the amphitheater.[10] Following a resumption of the listing, the newspaper article again interrupts by describing and quoting President Harding as he concludes his speech. The Chief Executive is introduced by the fatuous comment: "President Harding with a reverence seemingly

*President Warren G. Harding placing the Medal of Honor on the casket of the Unknown Soldier, 11 November 1921*
*(from Gene Gurney,* Arlington National Cemetery, *1965)*

more significant because of his high temporal station . . ." (Might this be in mockery of Brown's report of the "very happy omen"?) Harding makes the problematic assertion: "As a typical soldier of this representative democracy he fought and died believing in the indisputable justice of his country's cause." Then he offers the Lord's Prayer. For officialdom this is the elegiac resolution in a formula of comfort or reconciliation.

Dos Passos' refutation of this formula will come with his comment on the Soldier's death:

> The blood ran into the ground, the brains oozed out of the cracked skull and were licked up by the trench-rats, the belly swelled and raised a generation of blue-bottle flies . . .

But we have moved ahead of ourselves. After Harding's Lord's Prayer passage, the narrator resumes his account of the Soldier's life. He describes the young man going into the army, where recruits are processed as if on a conveyer belt. The President's eulogy of the dead man is mocked by the depiction of the processing of the man's body and mind. Never do we find the Soldier genuinely thinking.

Though we do not have a procession of mourners from the Capitol–for artistic purposes, Dos Passos foreshortened events–mourners we have aplenty towards

the end of Dos Passos' piece: Harding and "the diplomats and the generals and the admirals and the brasshats and the politicians and the handsomely dressed ladies out of the society column of the *Washington Post.*"

We conclude with what in the traditional pastoral elegy is the "placing of flowers on the bier." But we have, instead, mostly the bestowal of medals. In reality the medals were pinned or placed on the flag draping the Unknown Soldier's coffin. Dos Passos renders this bitterly and unforgettably with "Where his chest ought to have been they pinned. . . ."

After the coffin was put into the sarcophagus, Hamilton Fish, Jr. (a conservative congressman and prominent anti-Communist in 1932) placed a wreath on the tomb. A U.S. war mother, who had lost a son, and a British war mother, who had lost three sons, also placed wreaths there. The Chief of the Crow nation, Plenty Coops, then placed his feathered war bonnet and his coup stick on the sarcophagus.

Dos Passos describes this selectively and sardonically in the final lines of the elegy, and combines medals, wreaths, and Indian wampum in the pinning. "All the Washingtonians brought flowers," he says in the penultimate line.

A final section, of only a single line, concludes the elegy: "Woodrow Wilson brought a bouquet of poppies." We have seen that Wilson, incapacitated by a stroke, returned home when the funeral procession reached the White House. But Dos Passos did not wish to allow any sympathy for "Meester Veelson,"[11] whom he saw as betraying his anti-interventionist followers and leading the United States into war. In the elegy, Wilson makes an appearance at Arlington Cemetery, and the poppy on his lapel has turned into a bouquet.

Bitterness is absent in Whitman's "When Lilacs Last in the Dooryard Bloom'd," a greater American elegy, which in its mood of national reconciliation provides a contrast to "The Body of an American." But bitterness is an element in "Lycidas" and "Adonais." Milton in honoring Edward King, refers to English bishops as "blind mouths." Shelley thus addresses the anonymous reviewer whom he represents as having killed John Keats: "Thou noteless blot on a remembered name." Dos Passos seems even more bitter than Milton and Shelley, and his bitterness is expressed in the very strategy of the elegy—he exposes the chief mourners as the veritable killers.

– *John Dos Passos Newsletter*, no. 2 (June 1998): 1–4

### Notes

1. *New York Times*, 24 October 1921, p. 5.

2. On the funeral procession from the Capitol and on the ceremonies at Arlington, see *New York Times*, 12 November 1921, pp. 1–2; *Washington Post*, 11 November 1921, p. 2; 12 November 1921, pp. 1, 4, 6.

3. George Rothwell Brown, *Washington Post*, 12 November 1921, pp. 1, 6.

4. *Washington Post*, 12 November 1921, p. 4.

5. Melvin Landsberg, *Dos Passos' Path to U.S.A.: A Political Biography, 1912–1936* (Boulder: Colorado Associated University Press, 1972), pp. 67–77.

6. For the text of Harding's proclamation, see *New York Times*, 1 October 1921, p. 15.

7. In the ninth edition (1891–1892) of *Leaves of Grass*.

8. Richard P. Adams, "Whitman's 'Lilacs' and the Tradition of the Pastoral Elegy," *Publications of the Modern Language Association of America*, 72 (June 1957): 479–487. All the quotations are on p. 479.

9. For the selection of the body, see *New York Times*, 24 October 1921, pp. 1, 5.

10. I dutifully searched the *Washington Post* (the only newspaper mentioned in Dos Passos' piece) and the *New York Times* to see whether the excerpts might have come from one of their columns, and ascertained that they had not. I might have searched further; but in view of the fictions in Dos Passos' piece, of his gift for parody, and of the excerpts not being credited, I take them to be parodic fiction.

Some of the actual newspaper reporting in the *Times* and *Post* was so far from communicating grief that Dos Passos in his parody may have thought it best to subdue the resulting irony. Consider the subject of clothing. The *New York Times*, in paragraph after paragraph listing notables in the amphitheater, described their dress and decorations in

detail (12 November 1921, p. 2). The *Washington Post* offered a society-type article, on over two thousand women marching to Arlington, with a subhead declaring: "Salvation Lassies Lend Picturesque Color." Contrasting the marchers with some other women, the *Post* reported: "Those who stepped out of limousines and occupied reserved seats held for notables and representatives of organizations within the amphitheater would have honored any fashion parade ever held on Connecticut Avenue"–and it went on to give details (12 November 1921, p. 4).

11. Title of Dos Passos' biography of Wilson in *Nineteen-Nineteen*. On Dos Passos' view of Wilson, see also Landsberg, *Dos Passos' Path to U.S.A.: A Political Biography, 1912–1936*, pp. 194–195.

## THE POPULAR ARTS

*Dos Passos devotes considerable attention in* U.S.A., *and especially in* The Big Money, *to the nature of the popular arts in twentieth-century America. His basic intent in the narrative of Margo Dowling's Hollywood movie career and in the biographies of Rudolph Valentino, Isadora Duncan, and Frank Lloyd Wright is to dramatize the role of the popular arts in the general cheapening of values in a society that also cheapened the specific meaning of the "old words." Whatever the original integrity or strength of purpose of the artist, the powerful opposition to innovative art and the need for success in the marketplace determined the nature of the art produced, as in the cases of Duncan and Valentino. Only a heroic figure such as Wright, one willing to sacrifice for his beliefs, could produce meaningful work.*

*It is not surprising, given this theme, that Dos Passos chose to emphasize the motion picture as the dominant popular art form of the 1920s. The Hollywood ethos, in which the phony is the coin of the realm and the meretricious is the eventual product, served as an excellent vehicle for his broadly satiric account of the movie as popular art.*

### Hollywood and Margo Dowling

*Dos Passos's brief screenwriting stint during the summer of 1934 on a Josef von Sternberg movie starring Marlene Dietrich supplied him with the prototypes of Sam Margolies and Margo in her Hollywood phase. Something of Jean Harlow, the archetypal sexy blond of this period of moviemaking, also appears to enter into the mix.*

**Dos Passos in Hollywood, Summer 1934**
Dos Passos

*Dos Passos spent a little more than two months in Hollywood in the summer of 1934, supposedly working on the movie* The Devil Is a Woman *(1935), directed by Josef von Sternberg and starring Marlene Dietrich, but in fact Dos Passos was ill much of the time. He nevertheless absorbed a great deal of the Hollywood ethos during this period, no doubt much of it colored by the cynicism toward the motion-picture industry shared by many of his New York theatrical friends then working in Hollywood.*

*Nineteen Nineteen* hadn't sold any better than *The 42nd Parallel*. What with my rheumatics and enforced winter trips I was running into debt. When I got a bid from Josef von Sternberg to work with him on a Spanish picture he was getting up for Marlene Dietrich I accepted the dare. Everybody I knew had taken a whack at Hollywood. Even Gerald Murphy had spent a month there on the invitation of King Vidor. I had to see what it was like.

Flying out to Los Angeles, for some reason you had to change planes at Salt Lake City. The end of the trip was in an old Ford trimotor that seemed to flap its

*Gary Cooper and Dietrich in the 1934 movie* Morocco, *which resembles the movie project that the Sternberg-based character Sam Margolies describes to Margo Dowling in* The Big Money *(from Homer Dickens,* The Films of Marlene Dietrich, *1974)*

*Josef von Sternberg and Marlene Dietrich (1934), models for Sam Margolies and Margo Dowling in* The Big Money *(from Herman G. Weinberg,* Josef von Sternberg, *1967)*

wings like a buzzard. It was the roughest flight I ever had. I felt pretty rocky when I staggered off at the airport.

Von Sternberg was something. Of course he was born Joe Stern in Brooklyn, but he exuded a faint—only hinted at—flavor of Austrian nobility with such gusto that I found myself playing up to it. I'd never been to Vienna either, but we spent as much time talking about the Ring and wine festivals in the old days and the Spanish riding school as we did about Pierre Louÿs' silly *La Femme et le Pantin,* which he was trying to turn into a vehicle for Marlene. Since singing German ballads was what she did best he was determined not to let her sing.

It was an instructive few weeks. The whole thing turned out a mess. When I took sick (rheumatics again) at the hotel, Marlene, who was just the nicest German hausfrau you ever met, sent me flowers. Francis Faragoh insisted on moving me to his house. My old companions of New Playwrights' Theatre days who foregathered there in the evening to play poker amused me by putting aside a tithe of their winnings for the Party. Communism for the highsalaried screenwriters had become a secret solemn rite.

—*The Best Times: An Informal Memoir* (New York: New American Library, 1966), pp. 214–215

## Margo Dowling
Dos Passos

*In a "real" Hollywood setting of drink and sex, Margolies describes a ludicrously empty romantic movie scenario filled with self-sacrifice and heroism to Margo.*

Margolies came back with a tray with bottles and glasses and set it on an ebony stand near the couch. "This is where I do my work," he said. "Genius is helpless without the proper environment. . . . Sit there." He pointed to the couch where Cathcart was lying. "I shot that lion myself. . . . Excuse me a moment." He went up the stairs to the balcony and a light went on up there. Then a door closed and the light was cut off. The only light in the room was over the pictures. Rodney Cathcart sat up on the edge of the couch. "For crissake, sister, drink something. . . ." Margo started to titter. "All right, Si, you can give me a spot of gin," she said and sat down beside him on the couch.

He was attractive. She found herself letting him kiss her but right away his hand was working up her leg and she had to get up and walk over to the other side of the room to look at the pictures again. "Oh, don't be silly," he sighed, letting himself drop back on the couch.

There was no sound from upstairs. Margo began to get the jeebies wondering what Margolies was doing up there. She went back to the couch to get herself another spot of gin and Rodney Cathcart jumped up all of a sudden and put his arms around her from behind and bit her ear. "Quit that caveman stuff," she said, standing still. She didn't want to wrestle with him for fear he'd muss her dress. "That's me," he whispered in her ear. "I find you most exciting."

Margolies was standing in front of them with some papers in his hand. Margo wondered how long he'd been there. Rodney Cathcart let himself drop back on the couch and closed his eyes. "Now sit down, Margo darling," Margolies was saying in an even voice. "I want to tell you a story. See if it awakens anything in you." Margo felt herself flushing. Behind her Rodney Cathcart was giving long deep breaths as if he were asleep.

"You are tired of the giddy whirl of the European capitals," Margolies was saying. "You are the daughter of an old army officer. Your mother is dead. You go everywhere, dances, dinners, affairs. Proposals are made for your hand. Your father is a French or perhaps a Spanish general. His country calls him. He is to be sent to Africa to repel the barbarous Moors. He wants to leave you in a convent but you insist on going with him. You are following this?"

*The platinum blond Jean Harlow, who often played tough but sympathetic working-class movie roles and may have served as one of Dos Passos's models for Margo Dowling (from David Stenn,* Bombshell, *1993)*

"Oh, yes," said Margo eagerly. "She'd stow away on the ship to go with him to the war."

"On the same boat there's a young American collegeboy who has run away to join the foreign legion. We'll get the reason later. That'll be your friend Si. You meet. . . . Everything is lovely between you. Your father is very ill. By this time you are in a mud fort besieged by natives, howling bloodthirsty savages. Si breaks through the blockade to get the medicine necessary to save your father's life. . . . On his return he's arrested as a deserter. You rush to Tangier to get the American consul to intervene. Your father's life is saved. You ride back just in time to beat the firingsquad. Si is an American citizen and is decorated. The general kisses him on both cheeks and hands his lovely daughter over into his strong arms. . . . I don't want you to talk about this now. . . . Let it settle deep into your mind. Of course it's only a rudimentary sketch. The story is nonsense but it affords the director certain opportunities. I can see you risking all, reputation, life itself to save the man you love. Now I'll take you home. . . . Look, Si's asleep. He's just an animal, a brute blond beast."

—*The Big Money,* pp. 1114–1115

\* \* \*

## Rudolph Valentino, Isadora Duncan, and Frank Lloyd Wright

### *Adagio Dancer*
Dos Passos

*Like Margo, Rudolph Valentino was transformed by Hollywood into a marketable popular image—in his case, that of the romantic Latin lover. Dos Passos was also intrigued by the mass hysteria illustrated by Valentino's idolization by millions of women and by the response to his death.*

The nineteenyearold son of a veterinary in Castellaneta in the south of Italy was shipped off to America like a lot of other unmanageable young Italians when his parents gave up trying to handle him, to sink or swim or maybe send a few lire home by international postal moneyorder. The family was through with him. But Rodolfo Guglielmi wanted to make good.

He got a job as assistant gardener in Central Park but that kind of work was the last thing he wanted to do; he wanted to make good in the brightlights; money burned his pockets.

He hung around cabarets doing odd jobs, sweeping out for the waiters, washing cars; he was lazy handsome wellbuilt slender goodtempered and vain; he was a born tangodancer.

Lovehungry women thought he was a darling. He began to get engagements dancing the tango in ballrooms and cabarets; he teamed up with a girl named Jean Acker on a vaudeville tour and took the name of Rudolph Valentino.

*Rudolph Valentino, subject of "Adagio Dancer" in* The Big Money, *in the title role as* The Sheik *(1921), one of his most popular movies (from Irving Shulman,* Valentino, *1967)*

Stranded on the Coast he headed for Hollywood, worked for a long time as an extra for five dollars a day; directors began to notice he photographed well.

He got his chance in *The Four Horsemen* and became the gigolo of every woman's dreams.

. . . . . . . . . .

When the doctors cut into his elegantlymolded body they found that peritonitis had begun; the abdominal cavity contained a large amount of fluid and food particles; the viscera were coated with a greenishgrey film; a round hole a centimeter in diameter was seen in the anterior wall of the stomach; the tissue of the stomach for one and onehalf centimeters immediately surrounding the perforation was necrotic. The appendix was inflamed and twisted against the small intestine.

When he came to from the ether the first thing he said was, "Well, did I behave like a pink powderpuff?"

His expensivelymassaged actor's body fought peritonitis for six days.

The switchboard at the hospital was swamped with calls, all the corridors were piled with flowers, crowds filled the street outside, filmstars who claimed they were his betrothed entrained for New York.

*Valentino's funeral procession, New York, August 1926 (George Eastman House)*

*Late in the afternoon a limousine drew up at the hospital door (where the grimyfingered newspapermen and photographers stood around bored tired hoteyed smoking too many cigarettes making trips to the nearest speak exchanging wisecracks and deep dope waiting for him to die in time to make the evening papers) and a woman, who said she was a maid employed by a dancer who was Valentino's first wife, alighted. She delivered to an attendant an envelope addressed to the filmstar and inscribed From Jean, and a package. The package contained a white counterpane with lace ruffles and the word Rudy embroidered in the four corners. This was accompanied by a pillowcover to match over a blue silk scented cushion.*

Rudolph Valentino was only thirtyone when he died.

His managers planned to make a big thing of his highlypublicized funeral but the people in the streets were too crazy.

While he lay in state in a casket covered with a cloth of gold, tens of thousands of men, women, and children packed the streets outside. Hundreds were trampled, had their feet hurt by policehorses. In the muggy rain the cops lost control. Jammed masses stampeded under the clubs and the rearing hoofs of the horses. The funeral chapel was gutted, men and women fought over a flower, a piece of wallpaper, a piece of the broken plateglass window. Showwindows were burst in. Parked cars were overturned and smashed. When finally the mounted police after repeated charges beat the crowd off Broadway, where traffic was tied up for two hours, they picked up twentyeight separate shoes, a truckload of umbrellas, papers, hats, tornoff sleeves. All the ambulances in that part of the city were busy carting off women who'd fainted, girls who'd been stepped on. Epileptics threw fits. Cops collected little groups of abandoned children.

The fascisti sent a guard of honor and the antifascists drove them off. More rioting, cracked skulls, trampled feet. When the public was barred from the undertaking parlors hundreds of women groggy with headlines got in to view the poor body

claiming to be exdancingpartners, old playmates, relatives from the old country, filmstars; every few minutes a girl fainted in front of the bier and was revived by the newspapermen who put down her name and address and claim to notice in the public prints. Frank E. Campbell's undertakers and pallbearers, dignified wearers of black broadcloth and tackersup of crape, were on the verge of a nervous breakdown. Even the boss had his fill of publicity that time.

It was two days before the cops could clear the streets enough to let the flowerpieces from Hollywood be brought in and described in the evening papers.

The church service was more of a success. The policecommissioner barred the public for four blocks round.

Many notables attended.

America's Sweetheart sobbing bitterly in a small black straw with a black band and a black bow behind, in black georgette over black with a white lace collar and white lace cuffs followed the coffin that was

covered by a blanket of pink roses

sent by a filmstar who appeared at the funeral heavily veiled and swooned and had to be taken back to her suite at the Hotel Ambassador after she had shown the reporters a message allegedly written by one of the doctors alleging that Rudolph Valentino had spoken of her at the end

as his bridetobe.

A young woman committed suicide in London.

Relatives arriving from Europe were met by police reserves and Italian flags draped with crape. Exchamp Jim Jeffries said, "Well, he made good." The champion himself allowed himself to be quoted that the boy was fond of boxing and a great admirer of the champion.

The funeral train left for Hollywood.

In Chicago a few more people were hurt trying to see the coffin, but only made the inside pages.

The funeral train arrived in Hollywood on page 23 of the New York *Times*.

—*The Big Money*, pp. 926–930

### Art and Isadora
Dos Passos

*Dos Passos's biography of the dancer Isadora Duncan is colored by his sympathy for the tragic condition of the free artistic spirit who is driven to excess and posturing by a society incapable of accepting the artist, and especially the woman artist, on any other terms.*

. . . . . . . . .

Isadora's earliest memories were of wheedling grocers and butchers and landlords and selling little things her mother had made from door to door,

helping hand valises out of back windows when they had to jump their bills at one shabbygenteel

*Isadora Duncan (Photo by Jacob Schloss, courtesy of the Dance Collection of the New York Public Library for the Performing Arts, Astor, Lenox and Tilden Foundations)*

boardinghouse after another in the outskirts of Oakland and San Francisco.

The little Duncans and their mother were a clan; it was the Duncans against a rude and sordid world. The Duncans weren't Catholics any more or Presbyterians or Quakers or Baptists; they were Artists.

. . . . . . . . .

In London at the British Museum
they discovered the Greeks;
the Dance was Greek.

Under the smoky chimneypots of London, in the sootcoated squares they danced in muslim tunics, they copied poses from Greek vases, went to lectures, artgalleries, concerts, plays, sopped up in a winter fifty years of Victorian culture.

Back to the Greeks.

. . . . . . . . .

Isadora was the vogue.

She arrived in St. Petersburg in time to see the night funeral of the marchers shot down in front of the Winter Palace in 1905. It hurt her. She was an American like Walt

*Poster for the famous American dancer, attributed to Kees van Dongen (Roger Viollet Collection)*

Whitman; the murdering rulers of the world were not her people; the marchers were her people; artists were not on the side of the machineguns; she was an American in a Greek tunic; she was for the people.

In St. Petersburg, still under the spell of the eighteenthcentury ballet of the court of the Sunking,

her dancing was considered dangerous by the authorities.

In Germany she founded a school with the help of her sister Elizabeth who did the organizing, and she had a baby by Gordon Craig.

She went to America in triumph as she'd always planned and harried the home philistines with a tour; her followers were all the time getting pinched for wearing Greek tunics; she found no freedom for Art in America.

. . . . . . . . . .

The rest of her life moved desperately on

in the clatter of scandalized tongues, among the kidding faces of reporters, the threatening of bailiffs, the expostulations of hotelmanagers bringing overdue bills.

Isadora drank too much, she couldn't keep her hands off goodlooking young men, she dyed her hair

various shades of brightred, she never took the trouble to make up her face properly, was careless about her dress, couldn't bother to keep her figure in shape, never could keep track of her money

but a great sense of health
filled the hall

when the pearshaped figure with the beautiful great arms tramped forward slowly from the back of the stage.

She was afraid of nothing; she was a great dancer.

. . . . . . . . . .

*– The Big Money,* pp. 896–901

### Architect
Dos Passos

*Frank Lloyd Wright is a key figure in Dos Passos's depiction of the many thinkers, artists, and leaders who were "not without honor except in [their] own country." During most of his career, and certainly in the mid 1930s, when Dos Passos wrote this biography, Wright's sensational personal life and radical designs made him more a figure of contempt than of honor.*

. . . . . . . . . .

His training in architecture was the reading of Viollet le Duc, the apostle of the thirteenth century and of the pure structural mathematics of gothic stonemasonry, and the seven years he worked with Louis Sullivan in the office of Adler and Sullivan in Chicago. (It was Louis Sullivan who, after Richardson, invented whatever was invented in nineteenthcentury architecture in America.)

When Frank Lloyd Wright left Sullivan he had already launched a distinctive style, prairie architecture. In Oak Park he built broad suburban dwellings for rich men that were the first buildings to break the hold on American builders' minds of centuries of pastward routine, of the wornout capital and plinth and pediment dragged through the centuries from the Acropolis, and the jaded traditional stencils of Roman masonry, the halfobliterated Palladian copybooks.

Frank Lloyd Wright was cutting out a new avenue that led towards the swift constructions in glassbricks and steel

foreshadowed today.

Delightedly he reached out for the new materials, steel in tension, glass, concrete, the million new metals and alloys.

The son and grandson of preachers, he became a preacher in blueprints,

projecting constructions in the American future instead of the European past.

Inventor of plans,

*One of the best-known of Frank Lloyd Wright's domestic designs, the Robie house (Chicago, 1909), which
illustrates the architect's belief that a home should be organic to its setting—in this case,
the flat Midwestern prairie (Historic American Buildings Survey)*

plotter of tomorrow's girderwork phrases,

he preaches to the young men coming of age in the time of oppression, cooped up by the plasterboard partitions of finance routine, their lives and plans made poor by feudal levies of parasite money standing astride every process to shake down progress for the cutting of coupons:

*The properly citified citizen has become a broker, dealing chiefly in human frailties or the ideas and inventions of others, a puller of levers, a presser of buttons of vicarious power, his by way of machine craft . . . and over beside him and beneath him, even in his heart as he sleeps, is the taximeter of rent, in some form to goad this anxious consumer's unceasing struggle for or against more or less merciful or merciless money increment.*

To the young men who spend their days and nights drafting the plans for new *rented aggregates of rented cells upended on hard pavements,*

he preaches

the horizons of his boyhood,

a future that is not the rise of a few points in a hundred selected stocks, or an increase in carloadings,

or a multiplication of credit in the bank or a rise in the rate on callmoney,

but a new clean construction, from the ground up, based on uses and needs,

towards the American future instead of towards the painsmeared past of Europe and Asia. Usonia he calls the broad teeming band of this new nation across the enormous continent between Atlantic and Pacific. He preaches a project for Usonia:

*It is easy to realize how the complexity of crude utilitarian construction in the mechanical infancy of our growth, like the crude scaffolding for some noble building, did violence to the landscape. . . . The crude purpose of pioneering days has been accomplished. The scaffolding may be taken down and the true work, the culture of a civilization, may appear.*

. . . . . . . . . .

He works in Wisconsin,

an erect spare whitehaired man, his sons are architects, apprentices from all over the world come to work with him, drafting the new city (he calls it Broadacre City).

Near and Far are beaten (to imagine the new city you must blot out every ingrained habit of the past, build a nation from the ground up with the new tools). For the architect there are only uses:

the incredible multiplication of functions, strength and tension in metal,

the dynamo, the electric coil, radio, the photoelectric cell, the internalcombustion motor,

glass
concrete;

and needs. (Tell us, doctors of philosophy, what are the needs of a man. At least a man needs to be notjailed notafraid nothungry notcold not without love, not a worker for a power he has never seen

that cares nothing for the uses and needs of a man or a woman or a child.)

Building a building is building the lives of the workers and dwellers in the building.

The buildings determine civilization as the cells in the honeycomb the functions of bees.

Perhaps in spite of himself the arrogant draftsman, the dilettante in concrete, the bohemian artist for wealthy ladies desiring to pay for prominence with the startling elaboration of their homes has been forced by the logic of uses and needs, by the lifelong struggle against the dragging undertow of money in mortmain,

to draft plans that demand for their fulfillment a new life;

only in freedom can we build the Usonian city. His plans are coming to life. His blueprints, as once Walt Whitman's words, stir the young men:–

Frank Lloyd Wright,

patriarch of the new building,

not without honor except in his own country.

–*The Big Money*, pp. 1129–1132

\* \* \*

# "The Practical Mechanics":
# Luther Burbank, Thomas A. Edison,
# Charles Proteus Steinmetz,
# and the Wright Brothers

*In his December 1929 review of books on Thomas A. Edison and Charles Proteus Steinmetz, Dos Passos noted the American capacity to produce, nurture, and make vast economic use of the kinds of inventive brilliance illustrated by these two figures as well as by Henry Ford. In* U.S.A. *Dos Passos continued to explore this theme, especially in the biographies of Luther Burbank, Edison, Steinmetz, and Wilbur*

*and Orville Wright, and in the narrative of Charley Anderson. Running through these accounts is Dos Passos's belief that the inventor, whether he stands aloof from or participates in the exploitation of his genius, cannot escape the consequences of an economic system that thrives on technological advance but often fails to acknowledge the human element in this process.*

*Perhaps the clearest instance of this theme is present in Anderson's narrative. A Midwesterner from a poor background, he reads* Popular Mechanics *as a boy, tinkers with automobiles, and after World War I (in* The Big Money*) contributes to various inventions that rapidly make commercial and military airplanes a valuable commodity. But Anderson, in an almost allegorical representation of Veblen's beliefs, is drawn by the promise of big money out of inventive technology and into production and sales, despite his lack of ability in these areas, and is eventually used up and discarded by the industry he helped to found.*

## Edison and Steinmetz: Medicine Men
Dos Passos

*Dos Passos's review illustrates both his contempt for the conventional superficial biographies of America's great scientists and his fascination with the life of the socialist scientist Steinmetz, a figure who preserved his integrity in a system that often crushes the individual.*

The book on Edison is the old-fashioned perfunctory two-volume life, evidently first published about 1910 and now revamped. In spite of much meaningless bombast and chapters so badly written that they convey no idea whatsoever, it has a full account of Edison's inventions, and contains much information (a little too much on the Horatio Alger side, perhaps) about Edison's early life that should be interesting to anybody who wants to know about the personalities that created the world we live in today. "Loki" is the up-to-date version of the same sort of thing. It attempts to be pithy and epigrammatic and to have the fashionable air that now seems to be considered necessary in biographies. The book contains some extremely interesting photographs that make it almost worth owning, and are indefinitely more informative than the text. A good deal of time is spent in glossing over Steinmetz's eccentricities, of which Socialism seems to have been the most sinful and glaring.

"Forty Years with General Electric" is as uninstructive as a book could well be. Still, the report of several conversations with Steinmetz gives it a certain historical value.

If the foregoing paragraphs seem grouchy and impertinent, it is due to the bitterness of a great many futile hours spent grubbing in the literature of the last fifty years of American industrial development. You have to read these books to believe how muddle-headed, ill-written and flatly meaningless they can be. You'd think that any youngster in a high-school composition course could do better with the material in hand.

For one thing, the writing was usually left to hired hacks and publicity men. The people who were actually doing the work had no time and no inclination to put themselves down on paper. But even if they had, I doubt if the result would have been very different. The men who counted in our national development during the last half-century seem hardly to have used the analytic or coordinating centers of their brains at all. They carried practicality to a point verging on lunacy.

Thomas Edison, who played the lead the other day in that amazing charade at Dearborn, where in the presence of Henry Ford and Harvey Firestone and Mr. Hoover and Mr. Schwab and Mr. Otto Kahn, and the regimented microphones of the world, he reconstituted the incandescent lamp as he had first built it at Menlo Park fifty years ago, is one of the two or three individuals most responsible for the sort of world we live in today. It would be more exact to say that thousands of men of the Ford and the Edison type are its builders. Politicians made more noise, financiers and industrial organizers and bankers got more personal power and ate bigger dinners, but it was the practical mechanics who were rebuilding the city the capitalists lived in while they blustered and gambled with the results of other men's labor. When you think that Edison was partially or exclusively connected with putting on the market the stock ticker, the phonograph, the moving picture camera, the loudspeaker and microphone that make radio possible, electric locomotives, vacuum electric lamps, storage batteries, multiple transmission over the telegraph, cement burners, it becomes obvious that there is no aspect of our life not influenced by his work and by the work of men like him. Reading his life, you feel that he never for a moment allowed himself to envisage the importance of the changes in the organization of human life that his inventions were to bring about. And he would have resented it if anyone had suggested to him that his work would destroy homes, wreck morals, and help end the individual toiler's world he was brought up in. Henry Ford, less the mechanic and more the organizer, seems equally unconcerned with the results of his work in human terms. The newspaper accounts of the goings-on at Dearborn at the jubilee of the incandescent lamp, the press statements and the kittenish skipping-about in the lime-

*Thomas Edison and Charles Proteus Steinmetz*
*(Courtesy of General Electric)*

light of all involved, make that appallingly clear. These men are like the sorcerer's apprentice who loosed the goblins and the wonder-working broomsticks in his master's shop and then forgot what the formula was to control them by.

I don't mean to minimize their achievements, which are among the greatest in history.

Good writing is the reflection of an intense and organized viewpoint towards something, usually towards the value and processes of human life. The fact that the writing that emanates even from such a powerful institution as General Electric is so childish is a measure of proof that the men directing it are muddled and unclear about their human aims. They know in a vague sort of way that they want to make money and to make good; most of them want to play the game according to the rules of their time and not to be a worse son-of-a-bitch than the next man, but the problem of the readjustment of human values necessary to fit their world is the last thing they think about. I suppose they would say it was none of their business.

That is why the little crumpled figure of Steinmetz stands out with such extraordinary dignity against this background of practical organizers, rule-of-thumb inventors, patent-office quibblers. Steinmetz felt every moment what his work meant in the terms of the ordinary human being.

Steinmetz was a hunchback, the son of a hunchback, a railroad lithographer in Breslau. He was born in 1865, and grew up under the pressure of the Bismarck steamroller that was grinding down the jumble of cities, states, nationalities, idealistic creeds and caste prejudices that was Germany, into a smoothly integrated empire for his masters, the Hohenzollerns. Steinmetz was a bright boy; mathematics for him was a compensation for poverty, for being deformed, for being a member of the under-dog class in the university. It was a closed garden, free from corruption and death as the New Jerusalem of the early Christians, where he was absolute god and master. If he'd been a less warm-blooded man, that would have been enough, but he wanted real life, too. So it was inevitable that he should become a social revolutionist. Chased out of Breslau, he fled across the border to Zurich; there he studied at the Politechnik and shook up the institution considerably with his ideas about electricity. He met a young Dane named Asmussen and with him came to America, in the flood-tide of European immigration to the Promised Land, in the days when men used to fall on their knees and kiss the soil of liberty when they landed in Castle Garden. He had the good luck to get a job with Rudolf Eichemeyer, who was an old German forty-eighter, electrical theorist and practical inventor, who had a plant in Yonkers for building dynamos and hat-making machinery. From then on, Steinmetz had no life outside of the laboratory—when General Electric bought out Eichemeyer, Steinmetz went along with the rest of the apparatus, first to Lynn and then to Schenectady.

At Schenectady for many years he was the bad boy of G.E. The directors of that organization soon realized that apart from enormous value as a technician, Steinmetz was a publicity asset. So the Sunday papers were filled with his gila monsters and his cactus plants and his unconventional ideas on various subjects, and they let him teach and talk Socialism and even write offering his services to Lenin. He was the little parlor-magician who made toy thunderstorms for the reporters and took dignitaries out to his summer camp and dumped them out of his canoe with all their clothes on. It was largely his work with the mathematics of electricity that made the large-scale use of alternating current possible and the use of high-tension electricity safe and easy. The transformers you see hunched in their lit-

tle gabled houses along the lines of high-tension wires are all monuments to Steinmetz's formulas. The officials of G.E. had the attitude of Edison, who when he was asked whether he'd ever studied mathematics, said "No . . . I can hire a mathematician any time, but the mathematicians can't hire me." G.E. had hired its mathematician, and it was a funny, rare little animal and had to be allowed to range a good deal to be kept happy and contented.

Finally, he wore out and died. If he'd been living, he'd probably have been at Dearborn with his toy thunderstorm, grinning in the limelight with the rest of the grand old men.

On the whole, it's fitting that he should not have been there. Edison, Ford, Firestone have cashed in gigantically on the machine. They have achieved a power and a success undreamed of by Tamerlane or Caesar. America has cashed in gigantically on the machine, has attained in these fifty years since the day when Edison—having tried everything, even a red hair out of a Scotchman's beard, finally settled on the paper carbon filament for the electric light bulb—a degree of wealth and prosperity absolutely new in history. Steinmetz was not of the temperament to cash in on anything.

Reading Hammond's life and Leonard's and the various notes and articles published about Steinmetz since his death, you feel more and more that the men around him were not of the caliber to understand and appreciate him. They thought of him as a pet oddity and let it go at that. He was a man of a different race, the race of those who do not cash in. The average European view is that America does not produce first-rate men—men who do not cash in. We had Franklin and Jefferson, but that's a long time ago. In the great industrial parades of our day, it is the cashers-in who are at the wheel. Are the Europeans right?

That brings me to the preachment I started in with. The woods are full of young men who have enough sense of human value, who have in their veins enough of the blood of those who don't cash in, to be pretty good writers; it seems a shame that instead of picking up the easy garbage of European bellelettristic small-talk, they don't try harder to worm their way in among the really compelling events and personalities that are molding lives.

It's about time that American writers showed up in the industrial field where something is really going on, instead of tackling the tattered strawmen of art and culture.

—New Republic, 61 (18 December 1929): 103–105

### The Plant Wizard
Dos Passos

*Luther Burbank's brilliant Darwinian-based plant experimentation was often attacked by religious fundamentalists.*
Luther Burbank was born in a brick farmhouse in Lancaster Mass,

    he walked round the woods one winter
    crunching through the shinycrusted snow
    stumbled into a little dell where a warm spring was
    and found the grass green and weeds sprouting
    and skunk cabbage pushing up a potent thumb,
He went home and sat by the stove and read Darwin
    Struggle for Existence Origin of Species Natural
    Selection that wasn't what they taught in church,
so Luther Burbank ceased to believe moved to Lunenburg,

    found a seedball in a potato plant
    sowed the seed and cashed in on Mr. Darwin's Natural
    Selection
    on Spencer and Huxley
    with the Burbank Potato.

*Young man go west;*
Luther Burbank went to Santa Rosa
    full of his dream of green grass in winter ever-
    blooming flowers ever-
    bearing berries; Luther Burbank
    could cash in on Natural Selection Luther Burbank
    carried his apocalyptic dream of green grass in winter
    and seedless berries and stoneless plums and thornless roses brambles cactus—
        winters were bleak in that bleak
        brick farmhouse in bleak Massachusetts—
    out to sunny Santa Rosa;
    and he was a sunny old man
    where roses bloomed all year
    everblooming everbearing
    hybrids.
    America was hybrid
    America should cash in on Natural Selection.
He was an infidel he believed in Darwin and Natural
    Selection and the influence of the mighty dead
    and a good firm shipper's fruit
    suitable for canning.
He was one of the grand old men until the churches
    and the congregations
    got wind that he was an infidel and believed
    in Darwin.
Luther Burbank had never a thought of evil,

    selecting improved hybrids for America
    those sunny years in Santa Rosa.
But he brushed down a wasp's nest that time;
    he wouldn't give up Darwin and Natural Selection
    and they stung him and he died
    puzzled.
They buried him under a cedartree.
    His favorite photograph
    was of a little tot
    standing beside a bed of hybrid
    everblooming double Shasta daisies
    with never a thought of evil
    And Mount Shasta
    in the background, used to be a volcano
    but they don't have volcanos
    any more.
            —*The 42nd Parallel,* pp. 77–79

### The Electrical Wizard
Dos Passos

*In a 1929 book review Dos Passos called Edison "one of the two or three individuals most responsible for the world we live in today." He again paid tribute to the inventor in this biography from* The 42nd Parallel.

    . . . . . . . . . .

    Thomas Edison only went to school for three months because the teacher thought he wasn't right bright. His mother taught him what she knew at home and read eighteenth century writers with him, Gibbon and Hume and Newton, and let him rig up a laboratory in the cellar.

    Whenever he read about anything he went down cellar and tried it out.

    When he was twelve he needed money to buy books and chemicals; he got a concession as newsbutcher on the daily train from Detroit to Port Huron. In Detroit there was a public library and he read it.

    He rigged up a laboratory on the train and whenever he read about anything he tried it out. He rigged up a printing press and printed a paper called *The Herald,* when the Civil War broke out he organized a newsservice and cashed in on the big battles. Then he dropped a stick of phosphorus and set the car on fire and was thrown off the train.

    By that time he had considerable fame in the country as the boy editor of the first newspaper to be published on a moving train. The London *Times* wrote him up.

    . . . . . . . . . .

*Thomas Edison, Luther Burbank, and Henry Ford in 1915 at Burbank's ranch near Santa Rosa, California*
*(Courtesy of Luther Burbank Museum, Santa Rosa)*

He rented a shop in Newark and worked on an automatic telegraph and on devices for sending two and four messages at the same time over the same wire.

In Newark he tinkered with Sholes on the first typewriter, and invented the mimeograph, the carbon rheostat, the microtasimeter and first made paraffin paper.

Something he called etheric force worried him, he puzzled a lot about etheric force but it was Marconi who cashed in on the Hertzian waves. Radio was to smash the ancient universe. Radio was to kill the old Euclidian God, but Edison was never a man to worry about philosophical concepts;

he worked all day and all night tinkering with cogwheels and bits of copperwire and chemicals in bottles, whenever he thought of a device he tried it out. He made things work. He wasn't a mathematician. I can hire mathematicians but mathematicians can't hire me, he said.

In eighteen seventysix he moved to Menlo Park where he invented the carbon transmitter that made the telephone a commercial proposition, that made the microphone possible

he worked all day and all night and produced
    the phonograph
        the incandescent electric lamp

and systems of generation, distribution, regulation and measurement of electric current, sockets, switches, insulators, manholes. Edison worked out the first system of electric light using the direct current and small unit lamps and the multiple arc that were installed in London Paris New York and Sunbury Pa.,
    the threewire system,
      the magnetic ore separator,
        an electric railway.

He kept them busy at the Patent Office filing patents and caveats.

To find a filament for his electric lamp that would work, that would be a sound commercial proposition he tried all kinds of paper and cloth, thread, fishline, fibre, celluloid, boxwood, cocoanut-shells, spruce, hickory, bay, mapleshavings, rosewood, punk, cork, flax, bamboo and the hair out of a redheaded Scotchman's beard;
    whenever he got a hunch he tried it out.

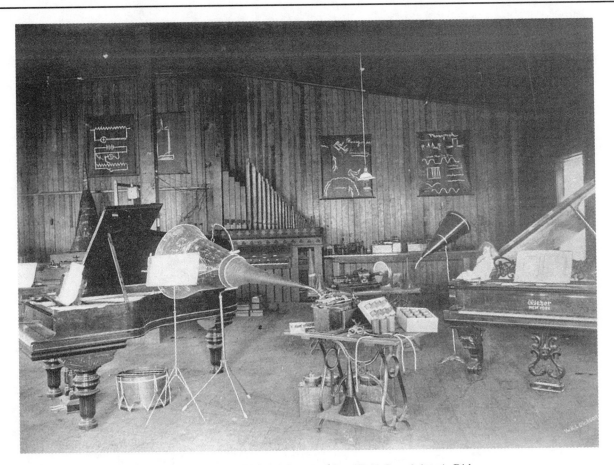

*The phonograph room at Edison's laboratory (from W. K. L. and Antonia Dickson,*
The Life and Inventions of Thomas Alva Edison, *1894)*

In eighteen eightyseven he moved to the huge laboratories at West Orange.

He invented rockcrushers and the fluoroscope and the reeled film for movie cameras and the alkaline storage battery and the long kiln for burning out portland cement and the kinetophone that was the first talking movie and the poured cement house that is to furnish cheap artistic identical sanitary homes for workers in the electrical age.

. . . . . . . . . .

–*The 42nd Parallel,* pp. 258–261

### *Proteus*
Dos Passos

*Dos Passos juxtaposes Steinmetz's rich and complex nature with his role at General Electric as a "piece of apparatus."*

Steinmetz was a hunchback,
son of a hunchback lithographer.

He was born in Breslau in eighteen sixtyfive, graduated with highest honors at seventeen from the Breslau Gymnasium, went to the University of Breslau to study mathematics;

mathematics to Steinmetz was muscular strength and long walks over the hills and the kiss of a girl in love and big evenings spent swilling beer with your friends;

on his broken back he felt the topheavy weight of society the way workingmen felt it on their straight backs, the way poor students felt it, was a member of a socialist club, editor of a paper called *The People's Voice.*

Bismarck was sitting in Berlin like a big paperweight to keep the new Germany feudal, to hold down the empire for his bosses the Hohenzollerns.

Steinmetz had to run off to Zurich for fear of going to jail; at Zurich his mathematics woke up all the professors at the Polytechnic;

but Europe in the eighties was no place for a penniless German student with a broken back and a big head filled with symbolic calculus and wonder about electricity that is mathematics made power
and a socialist at that.

*Charles Proteus Steinmetz at Camp Mohawk, his rural retreat near Schenectady, New York, circa 1920*
*(Hall of History Foundation, Schenectady, N.Y.)*

With a Danish friend he sailed for America steerage on an old French line boat *La Champagne,*

lived in Brooklyn at first and commuted to Yonkers where he had a twelvedollar a week job with Rudolph Eichemeyer who was a German exile from fortyeight an inventor and electrician and owner of a factory where he made hatmaking machinery and electrical generators.

In Yonkers he worked out the theory of the Third Harmonics

and the law of hysteresis which states in a formula the hundredfold relations between the metallic heat, density, frequency when the poles change places in the core of a magnet under an alternating current.

It is Steinmetz's law of hysteresis that makes possible all the transformers that crouch in little boxes and gableroofed houses in all the hightension lines all over everywhere. The mathematical symbols of Steinmetz's law are the patterns of all transformers everywhere.

In eighteen ninetytwo when Eichemeyer sold out to the corporation that was to form General Electric, Steinmetz was entered in the contract along with other valuable apparatus. All his life Steinmetz was a piece of apparatus belonging to General Electric.

First his laboratory was at Lynn, then it was moved and the little hunchback with it to Schenectady, the electric city.

General Electric humored him, let him be a socialist, let him keep a greenhouseful of cactuses lit up by mercury lights, let him have alligators, talking crows and a gila monster for pets and the publicity department talked up the wizard, the medicine man who knew the symbols that opened up the doors of Ali Baba's cave.

Steinmetz jotted a formula down on his cuff and next morning a thousand new powerplants had sprung up and the dynamos sang dollars and the silence of the transformers was all dollars, and the publicity department poured oily stories into the ears of the American public every Sunday and Steinmetz became the little parlor magician,

who made a toy thunderstorm in his laboratory and made all the toy trains run on time and the meat stay cold in the icebox and the lamp in the parlor and the great lighthouses and the searchlights and the revolving beams of light that guide airplanes at night towards Chicago, New York, St. Louis, Los Angeles,

and they let him be a socialist and believe that human society could be improved the way you can improve a dynamo and they let him be pro-German and write a letter offering his services to Lenin because mathematicians are so impractical who make up formulas by which you can build powerplants, factories, subway systems, light, heat, air, sunshine but not human relations that affect the stockholders' money and the directors' salaries.

Steinmetz was a famous magician and he talked to Edison tapping with the Morse code on Edison's knee

because Edison was so very deaf

and he went out West

to make speeches that nobody understood

and he talked to Bryan about God on a railroad train

and all the reporters stood round while he and Einstein

met face to face,

but they couldn't catch what they said

and Steinmetz was the most valuable piece of apparatus General Electric had

until he wore out and died.

–*The 42nd Parallel*, pp. 282–284

### The Campers at Kitty Hawk
Dos Passos

*Wilbur and Orville Wright remarkably remain "practical mechanics" in the face of the revolution in transportation and warfare introduced by the airplane.*

On December seventeenth, nineteen hundred and three, Bishop Wright of the United Brethren one-time editor of the *Religious Telescope* received in his frame house on Hawthorn Street in Dayton, Ohio, a telegram from his boys Wilbur and Orville who'd gotten it into their heads to spend their vacations in a little camp out on the dunes of the North Carolina coast tinkering with a homemade glider they'd knocked together themselves. The telegram read:

SUCCESS FOUR FLIGHTS THURSDAY MORNING ALL AGAINST TWENTYONE MILE WIND STARTED FROM LEVEL WITH ENGINEPOWER ALONE AVERAGE SPEED THROUGH AIR THIRTYONE MILES LONGEST FIFTYSEVEN SECONDS INFORM PRESS HOME CHRISTMAS

The figures were a little wrong because the telegraph operator misread Orville's hasty penciled scrawl

but the fact remains

that a couple of young bicycle mechanics from Dayton, Ohio

had designed constructed and flown

for the first time ever a practical airplane.

. . . . . . . . . .

They were home for Christmas in Dayton, Ohio, where they'd been born in the seventies of a family who had been settled west of the Alleghenies since eighteen fourteen, in Dayton, Ohio, where they'd been to grammarschool and highschool and joined their father's church and played baseball and hockey and worked out on the parallel bars and the flying swing and sold newspapers and built themselves a printingpress out of odds and ends from the junkheap and flown kites and tinkered with mechanical contraptions and gone around town as boys doing odd jobs to turn an honest penny.

The folks claimed it was the bishop's bringing home a helicopter, a fiftycent mechanical toy made of two fans worked by elastic bands that was supposed to hover in the air, that had got his two youngest boys hipped on the subject of flight

so that they stayed home instead of marrying the way the other boys did, and puttered all day about the house picking up a living with jobprinting,

bicyclerepair work,

sitting up late nights reading books on aerodynamics.

Still they were sincere churchmembers, their bicycle business was prosperous, a man could rely on their word. They were popular in Dayton.

In those days flyingmachines were the big laugh of all the crackerbarrel philosophers. Langley's and Chanute's unsuccessful experiments had been jeered down with an I-told-you-so that rang from coast to coast. The Wrights' big problem was to find a place secluded enough to carry on their experiments without being the horselaugh of the countryside. Then they had no money to spend;

they were practical mechanics; when they needed anything they built it themselves.

. . . . . . . . . .

*Orville Wright piloting the first airplane flight as Wilbur Wright looks on at Kitty Hawk, North Carolina, 17 December 1903*
*(from Tom D. Crouch,* The Bishop's Boys: A Life of Wilbur and Orville Wright, *1989)*

As the flights got longer
the Wright brothers got backers,
engaged in lawsuits,
lay in their beds at night sleepless with the whine
of phantom millions, worse than the mosquitoes at
Kitty Hawk.

In nineteen seven they went to Paris,
allowed themselves to be togged out in dress suits
and silk hats,
learned to tip waiters
talked with government experts, got used to gold
braid and postponements and vandyke beards and the
outspread palms of politicos. For amusement
they played diabolo in the Tuileries gardens.
They gave publicized flights at Fort Myers, where
they had their first fatal crackup, St. Petersburg, Paris,
Berlin; at Pau they were all the rage,
such an attraction that the hotelkeeper
wouldn't charge them for their room.
Alfonso of Spain shook hands with them and was
photographed sitting in the machine,
King Edward watched a flight,
the Crown Prince insisted on being taken up,
the rain of medals began.

They were congratulated by the Czar
and the King of Italy and the amateurs of sport,
and the society climbers and the papal titles,

and decorated by a society for universal peace.

Aeronautics became the sport of the day.
The Wrights don't seem to have been very much
impressed by the upholstery and the braid and the gold
medals and the parades of plush horses,
they remained practical mechanics
and insisted on doing all their own work themselves,
even to filling the gasolinetank.

. . . . . . . . . .

*–The Big Money,* pp. 1001–1006

\* \* \*

## The Condition of Women

*As a 1918 entry in his diary suggests, Dos Passos shared
with many artists and intellectuals of his age a conviction that women
had to win greater freedom if they were to contribute to the achievement of a civilization beyond that which had produced World War I.
On the one hand, Dos Passos's concern with the condition of women
in twentieth-century America is represented by his devoting six of the
twelve narratives in* U.S.A. *to female characters. On the other hand,
all these narratives appear to be negative portraits in the sense that
the protagonists function largely within limiting feminine stereotypes.
The following essays are part of a lively debate on the significance of
this paradox. Was Dos Passos participating, knowingly or not, in the
perpetuation of these stereotypes or do his portrayals ask readers,
through various devices, to reject them?*

## The Lost Girls of *U.S.A.*: Dos Passos's '30s Movie
Eleanor Widmer

*Widmer argues that since Dos Passos's women narrative characters all fulfill movie stereotypes of the feminine, he himself is guilty of perpetuating these stereotypes.*

. . . . . . . . . .

Nowhere is the undercutting of character for naturalistic effect more in evidence than in the heroines of *U.S.A.*, those sad victims of female biology. Purportedly dealing with the "new woman" and the influence of World War I and its aftermath on what roughly used to be talked of as "female emancipation," Dos Passos nevertheless handles women with a gentility closely akin to Edwardianism and defeats them by stock situations, lugubrious determinism, and his particular brand of social consciousness *cum* caricature.

In this non-gorgeous, naturalistic bestiary, the most easily disposed of are the extremely wealthy to whom Dos Passos lends neither patience nor authenticity. The two wealthy wives of J. Ward Morehouse [*sic*] veer toward aristocratic idiocy, the first, Annabelle, by her indiscriminate licentiousness, the second, Gertrude, by quickly retiring behind the veil of "female trouble" after the birth of her second child. This malady causes Gertrude to withdraw almost entirely from Morehouse; despite her salmon colored dressing gown and her occasional threats to withhold her money from her husband's public relations interests, she moves like a quickly forgotten shadow out of Morehouse's life.

Dos Passos takes curious delight in the ruse of after-birth illness, for not content to apply it to Gertrude Morehouse, he consigns this exact malady to Gladys Wheatley, the wealthy woman who marries Charley Anderson. No sooner does she bear her second child than Gladys propels Charley into a separate bedroom, and soon into a separate domicile. A carry-over from the 19th century novel, where a dreaded female indisposition eradicated women in droves (most blatantly in Dickens), it becomes an anti-naturalistic device in *U.S.A.*, a creaking *modus vivendi* for disposing of extraneous female characters.

Except for the millionaire's daughters who hide behind their locked bedroom doors, the heroines of *U.S.A.* share in the American Dream of pursuing their identities in cities far away from home, and in their desire "to do good" and to change and re-shape the world. Yet their modernity proves ironic, for their victimization stems from the oldest "system" and the most expected quarter of "waste"—men. Anne Elizabeth, also known as Daughter, one of the prominent heroines of *1919,* meets her downfall, in spite of some exotic trappings, in a manner similar to heroines of gaudy "penny

---

### "The New Feminism"

*In this diary entry made while he was serving as an ambulance driver at the Italian front, Dos Passos expresses his hope that women's participation in the actualities of war will free them at last from the harmful false stereotypes associated with the "Ideal."*

*Jan 8th* [1918]

Women & the war—The new feminism—And the more women who get mixed up in it the better. Its an education in gall & wormwood and flesh and hate and the varied hideousnesses and beauties of life. The idea that a woman is a high fallutin' uncarnal creature, that, if she has any mind she must keep it resolutely fixed on the Ideal, whatever that is, refusing to look at things as they are. Out of things as they are are ideals made, worthwhile ones, not out of the waxwork figures that stand about on clouds of pink sentimentality in the woman's world. The sad part of it is that its from the women of a generation that the next generation gets its all-important things—life, attitudes, sensibilities & revulsions—The men make a great jabber, but they are awfully incidental parts of the machine of reproduction. Its on the women, that the men to come, as well as the women to come, depend. That's why it seems to me so infernally necessary for women to be mixed up in the holocaust. American women, especially, for in America lies the future, the menace & the hope—At present more of menace than of hope. Our whole life is a childish failure—our inane attitudes towards the war, our ignorance & stupidity, our womanish sentimentality stored up like a vat of dye, ready to be poured over whatever those who pull the strings of our ideas & emotions want disguised.

And on this question of wars & nations the future depends—Whether it shall be the old round of greedy miseries—of sacrifices to ancient blood tainted tribal gods—or something new—with hope in it.

—Townsend Ludington, ed., *The Fourteenth Chronicle: Letters and Diaries of John Dos Passos* (Boston: Gambit, 1973), pp. 122–123

---

dreadfuls." Born into a monied Texas family, Daughter persuades her father to allow her to study journalism in New York. Presently, she makes headlines by participating in a New Jersey strike, is rushed home to Texas, idles restlessly until she joins a missionary group in Europe. In Italy, she falls in love with Richard Savage, a sometime poet turned opportunist, and though a virgin, Daughter gives herself to him stirred by his observation, ". . . Do you know what we are, Anne

Elizabeth? we're the Romans of the Twentieth Century."

Roman or not, Daughter's first encounter impregnates her, for though Dos Passos may be a political radical he unimaginatively indulges in the standard, historical pitfall for women: illicit love equals pregnancy. While this affair takes place in Rome and Naples, the consequences are no different than for Hardy's milkmaids. Unmoved by Daughter's plight, her lover drops her, and bereft of solutions–illegitimacy does not appear an option for the Dos Passos heroine–Daughter compels a drunken friend to take her up in an airplane which inevitably crashes. The inevitability of defeat in *U.S.A.* is irking enough, but when combined with stock causes, such as an unwanted pregnancy, it moves away from its possibilities for tragedy into melodrama.

Though less dramatic in her defeat, the plight of Mary French of *The Big Money* illustrates Dos Passos' intrinsic design–the indifferent cruelty of men towards women and destiny towards the dedicated. Breaking with her clubwoman mother and identifying with her doctor father who treats the impoverished, homely Mary French throws up her education at Vassar to become a social worker at Hull House. Dogged by bitter frustrations–her ardent efforts for the striking mill hands in Pittsburgh end in a sell-out by the union and the various good works to which she commits herself fail–Mary drifts into an affair with the hypocritical labor leader, George Barrow. Though Barrow prides his knowledge of contraceptives, Mary instantly becomes pregnant and chooses abortion. But her greatest involvements collapse simultaneously: Sacco and Vanzetti are executed despite the efforts of her committee, and Don Stevens, the "comrade" whom she loves and who scorns "bourgeois marriage," marries a co-worker in Russia. To these disasters Mary reacts characteristically–by preparing for a new relief committee and a mass protest rally in Madison Square Garden. Loveless, homeless, as much a replaceable part in the infernal machine of good causes as Ward Morehouse and Charley Anderson are in the machine of high finance, Mary neither questions nor struggles against her heavy-handed fate.

The background against which Mary French operates appears contemporary enough, and the free discussions of her affairs and abortion conveys [*sic*] a deceptively revolutionary texture to *The Big Money,* but Mary French can no more exercise choice than the ill-used Marion Yule of Gissing's *New Grub Street,* or turn principled dedication to anything less savage than that encountered by Maggie Tulliver in Eliot's *Mill on the Floss.* Thus, Don Passos' thousand and one naturalistic details about Mary French can not truly modernize her fundamentally 19th century story.

This ambiguous modernity is re-enforced by the somewhat colorless figure of Janey Williams, the young secretary from Georgetown, who initially reads Arnold Bennett, shortens her skirts and considers herself an advanced bachelor girl, but who inexplicably settles into a dronish existence. No sooner does she become Morehouse's assistant than she relinquishes all thoughts except work, and by the time she reaches Paris during the war, she complains because Parisians sit around cafes and get nothing done. Slavishly devoted to every ridiculous detail of Morehouse's career, Janey Williams represents the Protestant work ethic in its most selfless and leveling form, a creed that sustained cottage industries and early industrialization a half century before.

Dos Passos fares somewhat better with his so-called artistic types, Eleanor Stoddard and her friend Eveline Hutchins, but only in the limited sense, that like the men of *U.S.A.,* they are not so much individuals as cinematic types. Of Eleanor Stoddard we are told, "When she was small, she hated everything." Driven by ambition, she becomes a successful interior decorator, first in Chicago, then in New York, and commences a lifetime, platonic relationship with Ward Morehouse. The archetypal frigid woman, Eleanor Stoddard invariably wears elegant grey dresses with pearls, presides over equally elegant apartments in both New York and Paris, and moves among the wealthy and powerful as if they provided the true patina to her otherwise grey existence. We see Eleanor presiding over endless teas, "her place . . . glittering with chandeliers and cutglass . . . her narrow face smooth and breakable as a piece of porcelain. . . ." When she finally decides to marry after the war, she selects a Russian prince, "the last word in the decorating business," and her soirées become dominated by "a houseful of Russian emigrees in tiaras."

The role of Eleanor Stoddard has appeared in dozens of the Thirties society movies, played by the cool Joan Fontaine or her earlier prototypes, the self-contained, highly motivated social climber whose esthetics are bound up with costly household trivia. We know Eleanor Stoddard only from the outside, by a series of visual tableaux in which we are conscious of the postures and the gestures that represent an illusory, rather than flesh-and-blood, woman.

Eveline Hutchins, on the other hand, though more genuine in her struggle for self-achievement, never manages to discover the hard core of her needs. Like most of the figures in *U.S.A.* she appears victimized by the fortuitous and incapable of coping with each minor defeat that finally compels her to suicide. A dab-

*Mary French returning by train to Vassar, a scene from* The Big Money *illustrated by Reginald Marsh for the 1946 Houghton Mifflin edition of* U.S.A. *(© 1946 by Houghton Mifflin Co. © renewed by Houghton Mifflin Co. Reprinted by permission of Houghton Mifflin Co.)*

bler, Eveline starts and soon drops painting, interior decorating, socialism, war relief, free love. Never deeply in love, never out of love, she marries Paul Johnson because he makes her pregnant, returns to New York from Paris where she entertains the *au courant,* and goes from affair to affair in the same haphazard way that she attempts to produce stage plays or sponsor ballets. When her writer-lover of long standing leaves her, she takes an overdose of sleeping pills. Yet her romantic escape into death is no more surprising than her flirtations with art and the arty; neither she nor her commitments are serious, and her melodramatic end, on the very night when she has crowned her achievement as a hostess by entertaining a famous movie star, smacks of the historic cinema, the camera pulling away from the prone body as the party conversation dissolves in the still air.

Perhaps this is why the character of Margo Dowling, the orphan turned movie star is the most successful in the trilogy, for here conception and technique are united—the movie star plays herself, her screen image, and the personification of the American Dream simultaneously. Margo Dowling begins her career under the aegis of her stepmother's second husband who soon rapes her, elopes with a young entertainer from Havana who not only proves to be a homosexual but gives her syphilis, loses her

baby, leaves her husband, resumes her career and becomes Charley Anderson's mistress—all before the age of twenty-one. The true whore-with-the-golden-heart, golden-headed Margo rarely complains, and when Charley's death leaves her penniless in Miami, she packs up her stepmother and with her foolish husband disguised as her chauffeur drives to the golden land, California. A chance meeting with her former photographer, now director, proves a double boon: he turns her both into a movie star and into his wife, encouraging her affair with her male co-star for its publicity value. Our last view of Margo is at Eveline Hutchins' party, accompanied by husband and lover, where it is already whispered that her high, reedy voice will cause her failure in "talkies."

Because of its stereotyped elements—the child orphan, the teenage-rape and marriage, the period of mistress before success—it would be possible to take this portrayal of Margo Dowling as satire, except that Dos Passos means it for real. Neither by temperament nor act does Margo ever behave selfishly; her generosity and ability to forgive are indicative of her easy going role. At the same time she is an American, and she believes in getting ahead and in the simple precepts of opportunity. She lives with Charley because he's rich, and marries the director, Margolies, because he's powerful. Vulnerable, corruptible, without standards or scruple, and because and in spite of these, dazzling, she symbolizes and becomes the *U.S.A.*, the big money, the system and the waste of which Dos Passos despairs.

Since the very premise of movie stardom is the synthetic, since the very quality of the American Dream is its false bravura, we can accept in the portrayal of Margo Dowling what is indefensible in Eleanor Stoddard, the interior decorator, or Eveline Hutchins, the dilettante. Perhaps Dos Passos intended socialist Mary French as the outstanding heroine, for she is the last one of whom he wrote before his epilogue, "Vag." But for all her worthiness, Mary French does not have the glamour, the toughness, the resilience and the immorality of Margo Dowling, who is America.

The heroines, lost girls all, as well as the heroes of *U.S.A.* rest on 19th century types and naturalistic techniques which culminate in our standard cinematic images. Inadequately individualized and lacking complex and subtle development, the stereotypes nonetheless merge into a revealing vision of this country. The sordid patterns of defeat and the harsh cadences of the style, with their hypervisuality of place, poeticize the U.S.A., providing us with an America as recognizable and painfully endearing as an old movie. The experience of reading *U.S.A.* represents just this poetic and cinematic image of America, and in this Dos Passos does not fail.

–Warren French, ed., *The Thirties: Fiction, Poetry, Drama* (Deland, Fla.: Everett Edwards, 1967), pp. 14–19

## Romancing the Revolution: Dos Passos' Radical Heroines
Clara Juncker

*In a close study of Mary French, Dos Passos's "radical heroine," Juncker offers a more nuanced reading than Widmer of Dos Passos's depiction of a 1930s feminine type, though in the end she finds much of the portrait indebted to the traditional sentimental narrative of seduction and betrayal.*

. . . . . . . . . .

Although the Radical Woman had occasionally appeared in his writings before the publication of *The Big Money*, Mary French is the most fully developed revolutionary heroine in Dos Passos' works. In creating perhaps the only character in the *U.S.A.* trilogy endorsed by its author, Dos Passos built on his own experiences in radical circles–from the Passaic textile strike in 1926 and the Sacco-Vanzetti case in 1927 to the mid-thirties, when Party intrigues, recent developments in the Soviet Union and his impatience with communist phraseology caused him to resign from his

position as "Dos Passos the revolutionary writer, the comrade" ("To John Dos Passos"). Just as importantly, however, he modeled the well-intentioned but ultimately ineffective Mary French on a standard type of revolutionary femininity.

Like the *Life* cartoon of matronly militants, Mary is physically unattractive. As a child she wears spectacles and a band to straighten her teeth; in addition, she suffers from a slight lisp, freckles, and "hair that wasn't red or blond but just sandy" (*The Big Money* 110). At Vassar, the students find her "homely as a mud fence but a darling" (*Money* 113). And in her adult life as a social worker, the bespectacled radical heroine must make her way with untidy, usually uncurled hair, yellow-stained fingers, and faded cheeks and clothes (*Money* 448).

Mary shares with the women confessing their political faith in the *New Masses* a solid middle-class background: she is the product of a union between a Colorado physician and his ambitious wife. The tension between Mary's class background and her political inclinations, a tension that dominates the *New Masses* columns as well, is dramatized in the relationship between her ill-matched parents. As a child in Trinidad, Mary associates "Poor Daddy" with lack of sleep and whitefaced miners at the back door, "Mother" with orders not to play with miners' children. Significantly, Dr. French supports Eugene V. Debs, while his wife joins an anti-suffrage campaign. With little hesitation, Mary sides with her father against what Le Sueur designated "the decaying pool" of the bourgeoisie. Like the typical Radical of her time, the adolescent Mary distances herself from a life characterized by "parties and the Country Club and the sets of tennis and summer hotels and automobiles and friends in finishingschools in the East" (*Money* 110). She grows increasingly hostile to her conventional mother and her Bohemian counterparts, who, Mary observes, frequent New York art galleries "to be seen appreciating art" (*Money* 439).

Initially, however, Mary's own approach to radicalism has a decidedly intellectual bent. Like her author and other activist writers and artists of post-war America, Dos Passos' young heroine finds inspiration in books and lectures. She devours *The Harbor* and *The Jungle*, dreams over *The Promise of American Life* and "The Man with the Hoe," and defies her elegant mother with *The Theory of the Leisure Class*.

In a parallel to the Radical's fantasies about the proletariat, Mary associates the working-class with satisfaction and vitality. With a recurring lexical matrix, she desires "to be connected with something real," and, again like Le Sueur in "The Fetish of Being Outside," she immerses herself in America's poor. Her first attempt at social activism follows the path of earlier middle-class women: she joins Jane Addams at Hull House in Chicago. Apart from settlement work, Mary slaves as a cafeteria countergirl in Cleveland, writes on working-class issues for the International Ladies Garment Workers, joins the Sacco-Vanzetti Defense, and runs a succession of strike committees. Denouncing the "waste" of the decadent bourgeoisie, Mary, like Rose Pastor Stokes, envisions a new Radical America.

Dos Passos' depiction of Mary's political career draws on a readily-available revolutionary iconography. At the Sacco-Vanzetti deathwatch outside the Charlestown jail, Mary feels a sudden shot of excitement as she joins with fellow protestors in singing the "International"—a moment of power reminiscent of Lola Ridge's Russian electricity. Like the *New Masses* confessionals, Dos Passos moreover casts Mary's development in images of sunlight/darkness, death/rebirth, and drought/wetness. Yet he injects the standard images with ideas of his own, thus rewriting the triumphant conversion narratives into a story of dejection and disillusion.

Initially, little Mary associates her own class with sunshine, the working-class, with darkness—in a linguistic register that indicates Mrs. French's prejudiced influence and Mary's middle-class roots:

> Whenever anybody said Denver it made her think of sunny. Now they lived in Trinidad where everything was black like coal, the scrawny hills tall, darkening the valley full of rows of sooty shanties, the minetipples, the miners most of them greasers and hunkies and the awful saloons and the choky smeltersmoke and the little black trains. In Denver it was sunny, and white people lived there, real clean American children. . . . (*Money* 107)

The blackness of the proletariat is not, however, of the throbbing, sensual variant imagined by Le Sueur. With his clear distinction between life on the sunny side and elsewhere, Dos Passos emphasizes the split between the haves and the have-nots that dominates *The Big Money*. Yet when the young social worker crosses a symbolic bridge to Pittsburgh to mingle with the working class, she sees the sun of promise, perhaps of revolution, breaking over the smoking factory chimneys (*Money* 131). The "brownish dark gloom" of the station nonetheless forebodes a different reality. Throughout Mary's political struggles, a sooty darkness rests over the working-class Revolution, while the sun appears as soon as the radical heroine attempts to cultivate her own interests. When Mary rents herself a room in Boston and decides to write a novel, the winter days are sunny, reminiscent of "oldtime" America (*Money* 450). In Dos Passos' interpretation, then, hope rests with the Individual, with the American traditions, rather than with the Party and the Revolution.

Le Sueur's romantic-idealistic vision of rebirth, to come about by stepping into the fecund darkness of the proletariat, becomes in Dos Passos' representation a vision of death. On the eve of the Sacco-Vanzetti electrocution, Mary feels "the minutes dripping away as actually as if they were bleeding from her own wrists" (*Money* 457). Perhaps because of the magnitude of the class enemy, Mary's fight for the "underdog" ends in weakness, sickness, and emotional death. In our last glimpse of Mary, she has turned into a petrified hard-core Radical, indistinguishable from the communist commissars around her. Ultimately, she has lost her femininity and her individuality to the Party, which is dominated by emotionally thwarted males.

Dos Passos' negative view of the Communist Party manifests itself in the wasteland imagery with which he writes about Party politics. While the *New Masses* radicals spoke of the dead bourgeoisie, Dos Passos associates the Party itself with dryness and rot. As Mary French and Don Stevens, a calculating C. P. official, make a series of phone calls in behalf of Sacco and Vanzetti, Mary looks "with numb staring eyes out of eyelids that [feel] like sandpaper" (*Money* 458); at the end of their endeavors, Stevens "burst[s] into a dry laugh" (*Money* 459). While alcohol flows destructively over the pages of *U.S.A.* and into Mary's life, the fecund humidity of Le Sueur's proletarian vision is missing. Indeed, the Party literally destroys Mary's fertility: because her Leftist partners need to devote their full strength to the Revolution, Mary has a series of abortions.

The subtext of eroticism characteristic of the communist conversion accounts surfaces in Dos Passos' text as a plot of seduction and betrayal. In a parallel to the *New Masses* militants, whose ardent political commitment frequently originated in unconscious sexual and emotional needs, Dos Passos casts the political struggle of his romantic radical heroine in the pattern of traditional sentimental fiction. Obviously, the seduction-abandonment plot lent itself to a presentation of the private and political treachery which, in Dos Passos' view, characterized the radical Left.

Whether in the eighteenth-century "feminocentric" novel (Miller), or in its modern-day Harlequin successor, the sentimental plot revolves around a young woman defending her chastity against the attacks of a ruffian, often her superior in terms of age, class, and power. In the Harlequin variant, the romantic heroine suffers from the hero's confusing behavior: despite his love interest, he is hostile, contemptuous, even cruel. In the end, however, the heroine's pain, temptation, and sacrifice are rewarded with a ring and a home, as misunderstanding makes way for love (Modleski 36; Mattelart 139). In *The Heroine's Text*, Miller clarifies the sentimental formula by defining two female-centered plots: one "euphoric," the other "dysphoric." The euphoric text climaxes with the heroine's social integration: over the course of the novel, she ascends from "nothing" to "all." The dysphoric text, however, ends in unhappiness and death, as the heroine descends from "all" to "nothing" (xi). Needless to say, Dos Passos dramatizes Mary French's political betrayal in a dysphoric paradigm, as the idealistic young heroine moves through a succession of militant lovers to despair.

The melodramatic plot, preoccupied with inserting the self into the social frame, spends limited narrative energy on childhood and parentage, but enough to establish the heroine's familial and social context. As Mattelart explains, the family dynamics frequently include "social pathology and individual problems—unhappy homes, incurable diseases, illegitimate children, alcoholism, incestuous or quasi-incestuous cohabitation, and so on" (139). While Mary would not be able to check all items on Mattelart's list, her own background is nonetheless riddled by her parents' unhappy marriage and eventual divorce, Mary's Oedipal attachment to her father (*Money* 112), a Spanish influenza epidemic, Dr. French's alcoholism and untimely death, and Mary's own flight from college. At this point, Dos Passos' romantic heroine embarks on the psycho-sexual journey that constitutes the feminocentric novel. The central narrative paradigm unfolds in the confrontation between feminine innocence and masculine experience, with the (ab)uses of chastity as the all-encompassing signifier in "the grammar of seduction." In Miller's formulation, "the textual socialization of a female self is eroticized in a particularly insistent way" (4). It is thus Mary's sexual relationships which most significantly determine her political development.

With her plain looks, Mary may seem an unlikely sentimental heroine. Whenever she is within traditional feminine folds, however—usually in connection with a new love interest—she curls her hair, takes off her glasses, and buys new clothes. Moreover, Dos Passos' Radical qualifies for femininity as defined by popular romance: emotionality, innocence, credulity. Whatever discrepancy might exist between the ideal sentimental heroine and Mary French signals, ultimately, "the power of the female code to inflect the life story of any woman" (Miller 12).

The revolutionists who come to determine Mary's sexual/political quest appear in a climactic structure of insensitivity, even cruelty. Most likeable is Gus Moscowski, a blue-eyed strike leader, who stimulates in Mary dreams of "big black rows of smoke-gnawed clapboarded houses" and "the hard fuzzy bearcub feel of him when his arm brushed against her arm . . ." (*Money* 136). George Barrow, an oily-mouthed labor leader, inspires the idealistic Hull House volunteer to break her remaining middle-class ties. The newly released Ben Compton, an influential Party speaker and organizer, finds in his girl comrade a willing comforter and, more importantly, a hard-working publicity and research assistant. Despite the inhuman political burdens and the political squabbles which eventually dissolve her relationship with Compton, Mary once again blends private attraction and political activism by becoming the mistress of Don Stevens, a wobbly turned Party official who epitomizes Dos Passos' notion of the iron-hearted communist.

In the first manifestation of the seduction/betrayal pattern which will dominate her life, Mary realizes after a season of slaving away at the Amalgamated office with the handsome Gus Moscowski "that the highpaid workers weren't coming out" (*Money* 139) and that the object of her fancy is not coming across either. The end of Mary's political innocence coalesces with her loss of sexual innocence. During a period as George Barrow's secretary, Mary eventually submits to his attentions, only to find that "sleeping with a man didn't make as much difference in her life as she'd expected it would" (*Money* 144). Stripped of romantic illusions, Mary also becomes aware of the insincerity of Barrow's loyalty towards labor and decides to abort the child they are expecting. When she later finds herself pregnant by Compton, her communist lover declares that "they had to sacrifice their personal feelings for the workingclass" and makes clear that "it would destroy her usefulness in the struggle for several months . . ." (*Money* 447). The end of this affair significantly coincides with the end of the strike and with the sell-out of the workers by cigar-smoking American Federation of Labor officials. But Don Stevens' secret and sudden departure for Russia speaks most eloquently of Party treachery. Though Mary has shared her apartment with the communist leader for months and eagerly awaits his return, it is from another Party member that Mary is informed of Stevens' marriage to a beautiful English comrade while in Russia. Thus, Dos Passos' romantic Radical loses all her private and political battles. She reacts like a true sentimental heroine by succumbing to "the heroine's disease"—a mysterious fever that primarily serves to dramatize misery (Miller 107).

Interestingly, Dos Passos follows the popular romance in coding illicit sex as the germ of disaster. As Mattelart points out, melodrama rewards marital love, while mere passion brings suffering and punishment (139). Mary thus becomes a negative pole to valorized femininity, in the sentimental genre epitomized by the maternal instinct (Miller 14). Through her abortions and her attempts at becoming a desiring self, Mary violates the romantic script, in which the hero is the signifier of power and lust. In a sense, then, Dos Passos' Radical writes herself as a negative heroine, a hardened outlaw existing in the margins of social discourse. The result is a restoration of masculine privilege and a romantic heroine who, seduced and abandoned, is a heroine no more.[1]

. . . . . . . . . .

—*Works and Days,* 8 (Spring 1990): 56–61

## Note

1. Dos Passos' use of seduction as a repressive strategy contrasts with Jean Baudrillard's celebratory interpretation of seduction in *De la séduction* (1979, repr. 1981). In this polemical, anti-feminist work, Baudrillard privileges seduction, read as a playful subversion, over the productive and utilitarian order. He envisions an alternative, symbolic universe, "which is no longer interpreted in terms of psychic or psychological relations, nor in terms of repression or of the unconscious, but in terms of play, of challenge and defiance, of duelling relations and the strategy of appearances: that is, in terms of seduction" (*De la séduction* 18, trans. Douglas Kellner).

## Works Cited

Dos Passos, John. *The Big Money*. New York: Harcourt, Brace, 1936.

Le Sueur, Meridel. "The Fetish of Being Outside." *New Masses,* 14 (26 February 1935): 22–23.

Mattelart, Michele. "Women and the Cultural Industries." Translated by Keith Reader. *Media, Culture and Society,* 4 (1982): 133–151.

Miller, Nancy. *The Heroine's Text*. New York: Columbia University Press, 1980.

Modeleski, Tania. *Loving with a Vengeance: Mass-Produced Fantasies for Women*. Hamden, Conn.: Archon, 1982.

"To John Dos Passos." *New Masses,* 10 (6 March 1934): 8–9.

## Historicizing the Female in *U.S.A.*: Re-Visions of Dos Passos's Trilogy

Janet G. Casey

*Casey believes that a full examination of Dos Passos's depiction of women in the newsreels, biographies, and Camera Eye portions of the* U.S.A. *trilogy is necessary to realize that his female characters are not mere stereotypes but rather tragic figures who struggle against conventional roles.*

The elaborate structural design of Dos Passos's *U.S.A.* has the effect of splintering our sympathies, forcing us to divide our attention among not only a broad cast of characters but also a rich, and sometimes distracting, array of novelistic devices. The bulk of this three-volume work (*The 42nd Parallel* [1930], *1919* [1932], *The Big Money* [1936]), which depicts Americans in the first thirty years of this century, consists of the conventional narratives of twelve characters whose stories are told, via free indirect discourse, from their own points of view. These individual narratives are frequently interrupted, however, by three other voices that together form a kind of Greek chorus, commenting, if somewhat obliquely, on the characters and the world in which they live. The alternative voices—the discourses of the Newsreels, Biographies, and Camera Eye sections—have long been recognized as integral to our understanding of the fictional narratives, presenting "outside" information that contextualizes and colors their "inner" reality. Meaning in *U.S.A.* is created by the complex interactions among these varied narrative modes (to use Donald Pizer's term)—the ways in which the Newsreels, Biographies, and Camera Eye sections comment on each other as well as how they singly and collectively illuminate the larger body of the fictional narratives. As Carl Darryl Malmgren observes, the act of reading becomes one of synthetic creation, "concertedly mobiliz[ing] a variety of readerly activities and thus exercis[ing] what Barthes terms the "lexeographical muscles" (141).

One of the primary effects of this formal complexity is to provide a sense of the limitless possibilities of perspective—of character, of narrator, of author, of reader, of history. Ironically, it seems that this aspect of *U.S.A.* has been stifled even by those who have celebrated it. Specifically, Dos Passos scholars have interpreted *U.S.A.* almost exclusively as a socialist text that highlights, through the various "visions" embodied by the different narrative modes as well as the individual characters, the devastating effects of capitalistic greed. It is not so much this particular reading, but rather the exclusive emphasis on this reading, that has clouded the vigor of Dos Passos's work by failing to admit the possibilities of other themes that might draw equally on *U.S.A.*'s complex interrelation of forms and perspectives. Indeed, a closer examination of what we might call the peripheral modes—the Newsreels, Biographies, and Camera Eye sections—reveals another preoccupation, one that is complementary to the proletarian theme: namely, the theme of gender dominance. Once this idea has been isolated and highlighted, it irrevocably colors our interpretation of the power struggles depicted in the fictional narratives that form the novel's core. Even more important, however, is the way such a reading may alter our understanding of the *function* of the fictional narratives: it appears that they offer an imaginative challenge to the pseudo-factual, pseudo-historical representation of women in the Biographies and Newsreels, and that they are in part a symbol of the new and all-encompassing social awareness of the Camera Eye persona. In short, an understanding of the presentation of women and women's issues in the peripheral modes leads us to see the fictional narratives as an alternative discourse in which women become speaking subjects rather than silent objects.

An important issue raised by the interrelation of *U.S.A.*'s structural elements is that of the amorphous line dividing fact from fiction, and the shifting realm somewhere between the two that is generally termed "history." All four of *U.S.A.*'s structural modes demonstrate the equivocality of historicity. The narratives, although peopled by fictional characters, nevertheless center on such historical events as the World War and the Sacco-Vanzetti trials, and frequently exploit the real-life careers of individuals such as Ivy Lee, the public-relations entrepreneur upon whom the character of J. Ward Moorehouse is largely based. Similarly, the Camera Eye, an openly lyrical *Bildungsroman*, traces the subjective development of the "real" John Dos Passos as he personally experiences the events through which the fictional characters live. The Biographies are filled with factual information from the pages of *Who's Who* while simultaneously revealing, in their selection as well as their presentation, the individual prejudices of their author—prejudices which are inherent, although perhaps less obvious, in any compilation of "significant" figures in history. Subjectivity is also betrayed by the Newsreels, collections of journalistic clippings and popular song lyrics that are ostensibly the most factual of the novel's four structural elements. Yet Dos Passos's juxtaposition within the Newsreels is anything but random, and the implied lesson of the Camera Eye and Biographies extends to the "objective" realm of journalism as well: all accounts of history are intrinsically biased.

Hence the creative act of reading and synthesizing the different modes not only encourages us to construct our own idea of the history presented, but also suggests the highly idiosyncratic nature—despite the addition of fact—of Dos Passos's portrait of modern America. Dos Passos himself clearly recognized this subjectivity, and thought of his trilogy more as a factualized fiction than a fictionalized history. In talking about the addition of the biographical sketches, he explained his process of attempting to add a sense of historical objectivity to what was first and foremost a novel: "I was trying to get different facets of my subject and trying to get something a little more accurate than fiction, at the same time to work those pieces into the fictional picture. The aim was always to produce fiction" (Sanders 82). Dos Passos's "history" is therefore a novelistic one, and necessarily subjective. Indeed, critics have repeatedly pointed to *U.S.A.*'s historical falsity by remarking on such issues as its tone of unrelenting despair (e.g., Whipple, Cowley) and its lack of full class and race representation (e.g., Pizer, Rosen).

History is employed, then, in the service of fiction. Historical events provide a backdrop for the action of the fictional characters, and the Newsreels, Biographies, and Camera Eye sections—which present varying amounts of historical fact—reinforce and extend the themes and events of the narratives, lending the fictional world a validity and verisimilitude not otherwise possible. For a social novelist such as Dos Passos, this method is particularly effective. By incorporating historical elements into a work that is essentially fictional, he creates the illusion of historical truth even as he subjectively refashions history. In *U.S.A.* Dos Passos provides his own version of history by filtering certain facts about American society through the refracting prism of his artistic consciousness, and also by actively multiplying and diversifying the traditional voices of historical representation.

The delineation of women throughout *U.S.A.* suggests precisely this sense of historicity. One of the first things we notice about the novel is that the modes that essentially record public action—the Biographies and the Newsreels—devalue women: the former mode acknowledges their overall lack of influence in history, and the latter records their inferior and often debased social status. The Camera Eye persona, however, is an acutely sensitive observer who develops into not just a political radical but a writer whose mission will be the championing of the disenfranchised; as he says in his last appearance, "we have only words against / POWER SUPERPOWER" (*Big* 523).[1] This writer, the implied composer of the trilogy, will form a world of his own making in which women's lives and perspectives will be as significant as men's. In short, he will recreate reality, reinstating women in their rightful place in history.

The fictional narratives of *U.S.A.* represent that recreation. They are divided evenly among six men and six women, allowing women an equal voice in relating and interpreting the individual's response to the modern world. Much of what the women have to "say" about that experience suggests their shared oppression in a social structure that privileges men. The quasi-suicide of Daughter, impregnated and abandoned by the man she loves (*1919*), is merely the most obvious manifestation of the insidious gender/power relations that repeatedly victimize the female characters of *U.S.A.* What is fascinating is not merely Dos Passos's rendering of such relations, but his determination to fictionally challenge them: throughout the trilogy he rescues women from their gender-imposed degradation by providing a vehicle through which their history, individual and collective, is heard, empowering them with the dignity of representation that traditional versions of history have denied them. Moreover, Dos Passos orchestrates a suggestive growth pattern among his major female characters, who progress from those who are largely defined by their fear of male victimization (e.g., Janey and Eleanor of *The 42nd Parallel*) to those who overcome sexual injustice and humiliation to lead lives that effect history (Mary and Margo of *The Big*

*Money*). By positing a place of voice and of growth for these women in the larger landscape of historical oppression represented by the peripheral modes, Dos Passos metaphorically creates for them a new reality, a new history. Since this creation depends for its fulfillment on the negative context provided by the Newsreels, Biographies, and Camera Eye sections, it is necessary to closely analyze the presentation of women in these modes before we can begin to appreciate the complexity of Dos Passos's historicization of the female.

*U.S.A.*'s Newsreels are, as Charles Marz puts it, "cemeteries and museums" of "verbal artifacts"—signifiers of an "outside" world in which all is decontextualized and public (406). Yet the "outsideness" of the Newsreels is of a dual nature. On one hand, these sections are merely "outside" the world of the fictional narratives, calling attention to the ways in which public media echo private life; in this sense the Newsreels have a novelistic function, acting as an intrinsic part of the overall fictional work. On the other hand, the Newsreels are, in a sense, "outside" the realm of fiction. Because Dos Passos painstakingly constructed these sections from real-life headlines, popular songs, and advertisements, they are as much a part of his contemporary reality as they are of the "reality" occupied by the fictional characters. They thus form an integral link between the fictional world and the world of history, acting as a kind of pivoting mirror which simultaneously reflects the worlds outside and inside the novel. They are particularly important to Dos Passos's dual conception of history, for they record society's actual preoccupations and also provide a general setting against which the author can play out his more overtly personal version of American life.

In many ways the presentation of women throughout the Newsreels is predictable, given the era from which they were gleaned. Throughout the three volumes of the trilogy the Newsreels record the limitedness of female participation in the influential realms of business and politics, and emphasize woman's restriction to the domestic sphere. Independence for the female is relegated largely to the innocuous realms of dress and courtship:

the bride's gown is of charmeuse satin with a chiffon veiled lace waist. The veil is of crepe lisse edged with point de venise a departure from the conventional bridal veil and the bouquet is to be lilies of the valley and gardenias (*42nd* 165).

conventions of one sort or another are inevitably sidestepped or trod upon during the languid or restful days of summer, and because of the relaxation just now there are several members of the younger set whose debutante days lie in the distance of two or even three seasons hence enjoying the glory of (277)

*Janey Williams taking dictation, a scene from* The 42nd Parallel *illustrated by Marsh for the 1946 Houghton Mifflin edition of* U.S.A. *(© 1946 by Houghton Mifflin Co. © renewed by Houghton Mifflin Co. Reprinted by permission of Houghton Mifflin Co.)*

References to the female world frequently point out its absurdity and emptiness, as well as the desperation with which women attempt to infuse the domestic with significance. One headline screams out, "SOCIETY WOMEN SEEK JOBS IN VAIN AS MAIDS TO QUEEN" (*Big* 269). Other clippings chart women's attempts to maintain dominance, or merely security, within the domestic realm: "HER WOUNDED HERO OF WAR A FRAUD SAYS WIFE IN SUIT" (*1919* 222); "PITEOUS PLAINT OF WIFE TELLS OF RIVAL'S WILES" (345).

Yet this apparently random "history" of women is subtly shaped by Dos Passos; specifically, his selective hand forces the Newsreels to give way to an increasing emphasis on violence against the female sex. Rape, physical abuse, sexual harassment, and murder of women become increasingly commonplace as the Newsreels progress:

the crime for which Richardson was sentenced to die in the electric chair was the confessed murder of his former sweetheart nineteen-year-old Avis Linnell of

Hyannis a pupil in the New England Conservatory of Music at Boston.

The girl stood in the way of the minister's marriage to a society girl and heiress of Brookline both through an engagement that still existed between the two and because of a condition in which Miss Linnell found herself.

The girl was deceived into taking a poison given her by Richardson which she believed would remedy that condition and died in her room at the Young Women's Christian Association. (*42nd* 185–186)

ARMY WIFE SLASHED BY ADMIRER (*1919* 223)

YOUNG WOMAN FOUND STRANGLED IN YONKERS (*1919* 416)

TWO WOMEN'S BODIES IN SLAYER'S BAGGAGE (*Big* 169)

BROADWAY BEAUTY BEATEN (386)

according to the police the group spent Saturday evening at Hillside Park, a Belleville amusement resort, and about midnight went to the bungalow. The Bagley girls retired, they told the police, and when the men entered their room one of the girls jumped from a window (386)

WOMAN SLAIN MATE HELD (441)

Even more alarming, perhaps, is the female's self-inflicted violence, for any suicides mentioned are invariably committed by women: "KILLS HERSELF AT SEA" (*1919* 118); "UNHAPPY WIFE TRIES TO DIE" (*Big* 178, 268); "RUSSIAN BARONESS SUICIDE AT MIAMI" (205). The suggestion of the Newsreels is that women are not only physically ravaged by men; in at least some instances they are miserable enough to seek death by their own hands.

The grim vision of female existence created by this persistent evidence of women's physical ruination is reinforced by innumerable examples of the ways in which women are objectified, and thus trivialized, by male culture. Popular music, snatches of which are also contained in the Newsreels, proves to be one of the most significant vehicles for this diminishment. Although a song such as "Oh You Beautiful Doll" seems harmless enough when it appears early in *The 42nd Parallel* (148), the pattern that it inaugurates makes it less innocent in retrospect. Later in the same volume, for instance, Dos Passos inserts a telling bit from another popular song in which a woman will find happiness in a marriage that promises her "rings on [her] fingers / And bells on [her] toes" (226). While such songs represent women as trifling ornaments, the songs in *1919*'s Newsreels are much more offensive, focusing on women as instru-

ments for the sexual satisfaction of men. One song asks, "Avez vous fiance," then "cela ne fait rien / Voulez vous coucher avec moi ce soir?" (189), while another crassly revels in the glories of the sexual conquest:

Oh Mademoiselle from Armentieres
  Parleyvoo
Hasn't been——for forty years
  Hankypanky parleyvoo. . . .
Oh he took her upstairs and into bed
And there he cracked her maidenhead
  Hankypanky parleyvoo (345–346)

In both cases these song snippets are interspersed with references to the war, suggestively commingling military and sexual domination. With similar irony, one of the late *1919* Newsreels, otherwise highlighting the socialist-oriented journalistic clippings concerning the demand for "freedom of speech" and protection from "domination and exploitation," quotes a song about "that tattooed French Lady" in which woman is celebrated as symbolic object, in this case a personified map: "what I loved best was across her chest / My home in Tennessee." Especially pointed is the final entry of this Newsreel (XXXVII, 396). A fragmented newspaper report alludes to the exploits of the infamous Landru, a French con artist who was executed in 1922 for the alleged murder of eleven women; he was known to have used his romantic wiles to bilk nearly three hundred others, mostly lonely widows and spinsters, out of money and property (Birkenhead). The position of this clipping–at the end of the Newsreel, and immediately following explicit references to bolshevism and labor unrest–offers a scathing commentary on the previous excerpts, highlighting the hypocrisy of a culture that fights to insure freedom for all men while it sanctions the perpetual violation of women.

This tone continues in the Newsreels of *The Big Money*. In Newsreel LIV, Dos Passos follows a headline about a female suicide with a song that speaks of "the kind of girl that men forget / Just a toy to enjoy for a while" (205). Still later in the volume, "If you can't tell the world / She's a good little girl / Then just say nothing at all"; these lyrics give way to allusions to poison, a mining "death pit," and a devastating hurricane (LXII, 385–386). The juxtapositional irony of these examples is neither accidental nor subtle; many of the songs quoted in the Newsreels are interpolated with other elements in ways that echo this satiric tone. Taken together, they suggest that American society unselfconsciously views women as sexual playthings and/or idealized aesthetic possessions, resulting in the systemic ravagement of women and pointing to the shallowness of male culture's concern for peace and justice.

287

Within this overwhelmingly negative presentation of society's view of women, however, the Newsreels also manage to suggest the female's gradual political and social development. As early as Newsreel XV in *The 42nd Parallel,* a woman not only speaks out on a social issue, but also seems concerned with marshaling the support of her sex: "I'm against capital punishment as are all levelminded women. I hate to think any woman would attend a hanging. It is a terrible thing for the state to commit murder" (276). In *1919* Dos Passos begins to stress more heavily the political and social gains of women, as well as their potential collective power:

STRIKING WAITERS ASK AID OF WOMEN (27)
WOMEN VOTE LIKE VETERAN POLITICIANS (117)
JERSEY TROOPS TAKE WOMAN GUNNERS (122)

This emphasis on women's growing influence is most marked in *The Big Money,* in which women are shown to have gained increased employment opportunities in the aftermath of the war. While Newsreel XLVII, which occurs early in the volume and is culled from advertisements, is entirely devoted to career options for males, it is countered by the female-centered Newsreel LI, which presents an equal array of job offers for women:

positions that offer quick, accurate, experienced, well-recommended young girls and young women . . . good chance for advancement . . .

canvassers . . . caretakers . . . cashiers . . . chambermaids . . . cleaners . . . file clerks . . . companions . . . comptometer operators . . . collection correspondents . . . cooks . . . dictaphone operators . . . gentlewomen . . . multigraph operators . . . Elliott Fisher operators . . . bill and entry clerks . . . gummers . . . glove buyers . . . governesses . . . hairdressers . . . models . . . good opportunity for stylish young ladies . . . intelligent young women (123)

But while Newsreel XLVII presents remunerative work for men as completely positive, an untainted "OPPORTUNITY" (53), it is significant that Newsreel LI combines the concept of economic independence for females with insidious suggestions of failure and even death. The line "GIRLS GIRLS GIRLS" hints at less reputable employment, and a song about a dead woman "all stretched out on a table" is also interpolated throughout this Newsreel. In this way Dos Passos tempers his presentation of female success, capturing through metaphor and suggestive apposition the complex cultural dilemma of female progress: economic independence does not necessarily result in a corresponding improvement in social status, and, ultimately, such efforts may even have dire consequences. For

all their advancements, the Newsreels suggest, women are still far from enjoying full equality with men.

What is remarkable and particularly effective is the manner in which Dos Passos's careful editing of the Newsreels creates this dual sense of stasis and development. While women are still used and abused in the final Newsreel of the trilogy ("PLAY AGENCIES IN RING OF SLAVE GIRL MARTS" [*Big* 520]), we are also aware throughout *The Big Money* of subtle changes that have propelled women from the domestic sphere and into the world of independent action. A half-humorous, half-serious inclusion in Newsreel LVII—which, significantly, records the state visit of a Queen—tells of a man's rejection by a woman: "ABANDONED APOLLO STILL HOPES FOR RETURN OF WEALTHY BRIDE" (269). By the end of the trilogy's Newsreels, the suggestion is that women could be on their way to enjoying an increased social, political, and economic influence that was conspicuously absent in the earliest of these sections; yet it also seems clear that the culture as a whole continues to resist such progress. This scheme of the Newsreels is highly suggestive as a contextualization device for *U.S.A.*'s fictional narratives, as it draws attention simultaneously to the growing female desire for self-realization and the continuing cultural denial of that desire.

In contrast, the Biographies present a more persistent view of women's general lack of influence in society: of twenty-seven biographical sketches scattered throughout the trilogy, only one is of a woman, Isadora Duncan. Robert C. Rosen questions this lack of notable women, suggesting that Margaret Sanger, pioneer advocate of birth control, might have been a likely candidate, especially given the number of female characters in the trilogy who find themselves unexpectedly and undesirably pregnant. It may be, as Rosen suggests, that Dos Passos's choices reflect his own "unexamined assumptions" as well as "the sexism of the society [he] depicts" (85).[2] Yet this explanation seems unsatisfactory in light of the author's apparently pointed scrutiny of society's sexism in other parts of the text; it seems more likely, therefore, that his lack of explicit attention to women in the Biographies stems from more complex objectives. Pizer explains in detail Dos Passos's careful selection of biographical subjects, and points out that those eventually chosen "are present because of their specific relevance to narrative figures or to central themes in the trilogy as a whole." Moreover, for obvious reasons the author wanted to use "public figures"—people with name recognition (*Dos Passos'* 75). In trying to fit females into this scheme, Dos Passos would have been faced with a daunting, if not impossible, task: prominent influential female figures were relatively scarce, and within the realms of labor disputes, big business, and war—all acknowledged as central issues of the trilogy—they were virtually nonexistent.

Viewed in another way, then, the actual *lack* of female biographies may have been more efficacious for Dos Passos's larger purpose of creating, as he put it, "a contemporary commentary on history's changes" ("Desperate"). Barry Maine argues that the function of *U.S.A.*'s Biographies is to emphasize the author's belief in the power of individuals to affect society: the purpose of these sketches is "to draw attention to, not away from, the significance of individual *men* in history" (32, my emphasis). If so, the absence of women is clearly appropriate, for women have traditionally had little influence on the processes of historical change. Furthermore, even as Dos Passos presents this fact via the Biographies, he argues for its contrary in the fictional world he has created: in *The Big Money* he shows, specifically through the character of Mary French, that women have the sympathies and the capabilities to effect change for the good of the common person. As the male biographical subjects symbolically thrash out the issue of social versus personal commitment, Mary French, a woman—and not coincidentally the single effective radical figure of the entire trilogy—fictionally and practically demonstrates those ideals that are so positively represented in Biographies of, for example, Big Bill Haywood and Eugene Debs.

The placement of the single female biography in the last volume of the trilogy is therefore apt, for its position reinforces the concept of women's growing independence, a development that is suggested through both the fictional narratives and the Newsreels of that volume. The particular choice of Isadora Duncan, notwithstanding the complexity of her presentation, further supports this idea. Melvin Landsberg comments on the expedience of Dos Passos's inclusion of Duncan, observing that she was considered "both the greatest living dancer and the symbol of the body's deliverance from mid-Victorian taboos" (196). Dos Passos's admiration for Duncan's convention-jarring individuality is clear throughout the Biography (*Big* 170–176), although his attitude toward her is hardly unmixed. In many ways the entire Duncan family is made to seem rather ludicrous ("leading the Greek life of nature in a flutter of unpaid bills"), and Isadora is perhaps as much an unabashed icon of self-absorption as she is a self-conscious social progressive. Yet as such she seems insistently multi-dimensional, confounding the more traditional, essentialist, versions of womanhood that might threaten to flatten her into an unblemished ideal or an insipid victim. And, ultimately, this rather ironic presentation of her valorizes—despite her absurdities—her energetic will and her belief in the immense power of Art ("She was afraid of nothing; she was a great dancer"). Particularly highlighted are Duncan's social attitudes: "When the war broke out she danced the *Marseillaise,* but it didn't seem quite respectable and she gave offense by refusing to give up Wagner or to show the proper respectable feelings of satisfaction at the butchery." Even within the context of a certain ridiculousness, she is depicted, above all, as a Whitmanesque American of the type Dos Passos respected:

> She arrived in St. Petersburg in time to see the night funeral of the marchers shot down in front of the Winter Palace in 1905. It hurt her. She was an American like Walt Whitman; the murdering rulers of the world were not her people; the marchers were her people; artists were not on the side of the machineguns; she was an American in a Greek tunic; she was for the people.

The symbolic import of Isadora Duncan's biography is further underscored by comparison with that of Rudolph Valentino, which follows it (206–209). Valentino is depicted as an equally famous "artist," but, in contrast to Duncan, his narcissism and superficiality are not mitigated by a social consciousness. Most of Valentino's sketch is devoted to his death and the subsequent riots; Duncan's death, on the other hand, marks the end of her sketch, the final statement on a life that, if not entirely praiseworthy, has been complex and, in some way, meaningful. Dos Passos underscores Valentino's status as merely a pretty face, a "powder puff" with little substance, whose death seems somehow more significant than his life. Valentino, the "lazy handsome wellbuilt slender goodtempered and vain" sex idol who merely wants "to make good in the bright lights," cannot compete with Duncan, who, despite her outlandishness, is depicted as having a genuine reverence for art and a certain sense of personal integrity.

Duncan's biography is also crucial because it stresses, again within a somewhat ironic context, the concept of art as a kind of religion that engenders its own followers: "The Duncans weren't Catholics any more or Presbyterians or Quakers or Baptists; they were Artists" (171). Dos Passos writes that "Art was whatever Isadora did," implying that, despite (or perhaps because of) her bizarreness, she somewhat redefined art, instructing her followers not only in dancing but in the freedom and individuality intrinsic to artistry. This belief in the transformational powers of art is central not only to the *U.S.A.* trilogy, but to all art involving the elevation of social consciousness. It is particularly interesting that the only female biographical subject in all of *U.S.A.* is presented as the embodiment of this aesthetic. In this sense Isadora Duncan is more closely connected than any of the male biographical subjects to the guiding spirit of the trilogy, an artistic, socially responsible ego that is primarily represented through the mediating consciousness of the Camera Eye persona.

The narrator of the Camera Eye eventually comes to believe in the power of art–specifically, the art of the word. Although he laments the weakening of language's inherent potency, he acknowledges the possibility of its revitalization: "rebuild the ruined words worn slimy in the mouths of lawyers districtattorneys collegepresidents" (444). Ultimately, language is our only hope, for "we have only words against / POWER SUPERPOWER" (523). These are the sentiments of the boy turned into not just a man, but a radical of intense social awareness and, most important, an artist. This artist, we realize, is the implied creator of the novel *U.S.A.*, the wielder of artistic power used to render life, as Pizer observes, "with virile honesty and full attention to the frequent ugliness and injustice of experience" ("Camera" 425).

Although the primary exposure in *U.S.A.* will be that of the economically advantaged who suck the life from the working class, there is room for the condemnation of sexism as well, and the Camera Eye sections reveal an interest in this issue. The frequent incidents of war and class violence, carefully detailed by George Spangler (426–427), lead the Camera Eye persona to a general sensitivity toward the oppressed. More specifically, however, several Camera Eyes record the narrator's budding awareness of the various manifestations of gender inequality, even as he is dealing with his own emerging desires, both sexual and otherwise. In Camera Eye 19, for example, Dos Passos presents an abridged version of his short story "July" (first published in 1924), in which a minister's wife speaks of her discontent with her life, including, interestingly, her dashed literary ambitions. The Camera Eye narrator reveals his sympathy: "she talked awful sad about the things she had hoped for and you thought it was too bad" (*42nd* 254). The narrator is exposed to similar female sentiments of constriction in Camera Eye 41, in which he is ensconced in "the thirdclass car" with "a fine girl her father she said never let her go out alone never let her see any young men it was

*Marsh illustration of an episode from* The 42nd Parallel *in which J. Ward Moorehouse and the aesthete Eleanor Stoddard view art (© 1946 by Houghton Mifflin Co. © renewed by Houghton Mifflin Co. Reprinted by permission of Houghton Mifflin Co.)*

like being in a convent she wanted liberty fraternity equality and a young man to take her out" (*1919* 418). In an ironic way, the very limitedness of this young woman's sense of "rebellion" is particularly effective in highlighting the extent to which she is constrained both physically and psychologically.

But the narrator learns the most about society's sexism in the several Camera Eyes which relate his growing awareness of the male's hypocritical demand for, and condemnation of, prostitutes. In Camera Eye 24, on a visit to Quebec, the narrator is warned that "there were bad girls in a town like this and boys shouldn't go with bad girls" (*42nd* 295), although by Camera Eye 28 he apparently has had his own experience with such women, as he recalls "grinding the American Beauty roses to dust in that whore's bed" (*1919* 34). The juxtaposition of this memory with unpleasant memories of war (including the narrator's K.P. duties and the "almond smell of high explosives sending singing eclats through the sweetish puking grandiloquence of the rotting dead") achieves two things: it reinforces our sense that the narrator recalls the event with distaste, and shares in the pregnant association of sexual and military domination that is a prominent aspect of *1919*'s Newsreels. Most suggestive, however, is the final line of this Camera Eye, immediately following these sex/war reminiscences: "tomorrow I hoped would be the first day of the first month of the first year." The narrator's desire to be reborn, to put such events behind him, seems to be reinforced by subsequent Camera Eyes which, although they don't remove him from the scene of war, record his lack of participation in the sordid sexual enterprises that are routine among the troops. While it would be inaccurate to suggest that the narrator comes to openly oppose the sexual exploitation of women, his stance as detached observer—the essential role of the artist—leads him to record this exploitation with a mindfulness that can only be interpreted as activism in a culture that so routinely sanctions and deemphasizes it.

In Camera Eye 33, for instance, the narrator is told that the streets of Marseilles are "infest[ed]" with "eleven thousand registered harlots"; his description of these women as "slot machines undressed as Phocean figurines posted with their legs apart around the scummy edges of the oldest port" makes clear the economic nature of their exploitation in a world that disallows more financially advantageous employment for females (*1919* 164–165). Later, in Camera Eye 37, the narrator quietly witnesses the exploitation of yet another ignominious woman: "in the dark hallway to the back room the boys are lined up waiting to get in to the girl in black from out of town to drop ten francs and hurry to the propho station." In the very next paragraph he reveals his understanding that such exchanges indicate the male equation of women with other consumable goods: "outside it's raining on the cobbled town inside we drink vin rouge parlezvous froglegs may wee couchez avec and the old territorial at the next table drinks illegal pernod" (258).

Nor is the narrator's keen awareness of the exploitation of women limited to his knowledge of prostitution. He knows that even "nice girls" suffer from a sexual system that objectifies women, allowing them to be bartered and purchased as symbols of capitalistic success: in Camera Eye 46, for instance, a businessman, to sweeten his offer, adds, "And I have daughters." Such women are little more than ornamental trophies of wealth: "money in New York (lipstick kissed off the lips of a girl fashionably-dressed fragrant at five o'clock careening down Park Avenue)" (*Big* 168). Although the Camera Eye narrator does not comment overtly on this issue, his growing file of observations concerning the perpetual objectification, trivialization, and victimization of women becomes an important part of his repertoire of images, the compilation of faces and events that will be transformed into a coherent vision of American society.

The late Camera Eye sections center increasingly on the growth of the narrator's radical consciousness. For a while he is unsure of his political and social identity ("hat pulled down over the has he any? face" [212]), but he comes to realize that his proper role consists in using language to mold a social vision: "pencil scrawls in my notebook the scraps of recollection the broken halfphrases the effort to intersect word with word to dovetail clause with clause to rebuild out of mangled memories unshakably (Old Pontius Pilate) the truth" (444). Ultimately the narrator will write the *U.S.A.* trilogy. Since his growing awareness of his function coincides with his political activism during the trials of Sacco and Vanzetti, it is clear that a primary theme of the resulting work will be society's persistent oppression of the proletariat, especially its denial of a worker-based political system to counteract the exploitative nature of capitalism. This does not, however, preclude an interest in the corresponding victimization of women, a theme that similarly draws upon the complex structure of *U.S.A.* for its fulfillment.

Malmgren explains that there is little reason to limit our conception of the trilogy based on the Camera Eye's final, Marxian, sentiments: he argues that each Camera Eye section is "idiosyncratic" and that therefore these particular Camera Eyes merit "no special privilege." What is important, Malmgren asserts, is not the Camera Eye's "validity as a judgement" but its growth "from perception through reflection to evaluation. This is a course that the reader is encouraged to take" (140). One issue calling for reflection and evaluation in the pages of *U.S.A.* is that of the status of the female. The championing of the underclass may be a primary—perhaps even the dominant—theme of the trilogy, but it finds an insistent echo in a complementary theme concerning society's sexism, a sexism that is subtly (and sometimes not so subtly) critiqued in not only the Camera Eye sections, but also the Newsreels and Biographies. Most important is the way in which such a reading may affect our perception of the fictional narratives.

Reading the peripheral modes with an eye toward the depiction of women irrevocably alters our perspective of the fictional female characters of *U.S.A.* The suicides of Daughter and Eveline and the repressed sexuality of Janey and Eleanor take on more tragic, and universal, dimensions, and even the smaller tribulations of minor female characters achieve new coherence. Yet while these women are both defined and illuminated by the female "reality" presented through the peripheral structural modes, they also transcend it. As the alternative aspect of Dos Passos's dual historical vision, they form a counterpoint to the Newsreels, Biographies, and Camera Eyes, the mere *rendering* of the "objective" female history wherein women are systematically silenced, ignored, or abused. The female characters in the fictional narratives embody, rather, their creator's imaginative *refashioning* of female history: a "herstory" wherein women's voices are heard, their experiences of humiliation and degradation are validated, and they are provided the figurative opportunity—notably through the character of Mary in the final volume—to break free of conventional societal limitations. In short, Dos Passos's intricate, multifaceted approach allows him to deconstruct, and then reconstruct, the story of women in American society. Further examination of his treatment of the female in *U.S.A.* can only deepen our appreciation of the subtleties of his historical vision.

### Notes

1. Since Dos Passos's use of italics is often idiosyncratic, and since their notation or lack thereof is not generally relevant here, I have eliminated italics from all quotations.

2. Rosen does admit, however, that Dos Passos's even-handed inclusion of female fictional characters, and his positive depiction of Mary French, redeem his failure to include more women in the Biographies. Rosen argues that, although the "radical social criticism" of the trilogy is "male as well as white," Dos Passos's is not "a misogynist's vision of the world."

### Works Cited

Birkenhead, Frederick Edwin Smith, Earl of. "Landru." *More Famous Trials.* New York: Doubleday, 1929.

Cowley, Malcolm. "John Dos Passos: The Poet and the World." *Dos Passos: A Collection of Critical Essays.* Ed. Andrew Hook. Englewood Cliffs, N.J.: Prentice-Hall, 1974.

Dos Passos, John. "The Desperate Experiment." *Book Week,* 15 (September 1963): 3.

Dos Passos. *U.S.A.* (*The 42nd Parallel* [1930], *1919* [1932], *The Big Money* [1936]). Rep. New York: New American Library, 1969.

Landsberg, Melvin. *Dos Passos' Path to U.S.A.: A Political Biography, 1912–1936.* Boulder: Colorado Associated University Presses, 1972.

Maine, Barry. "Representative Men in Dos Passos's *The 42nd Parallel.*" *Clio,* 12, 1 (1982): 31–43.

Malmgren, Carl Darryl. "Dos Passos's *U.S.A.:* The Polymorphous Novel." *Fictional Space in the Modernist and Postmodernist American Novel.* Cranbury, N.J.: Associated University Presses, 1985.

Marz, Charles. "*U.S.A.:* Chronicle and Performance." *Modern Fiction Studies,* 26 (Autumn 1980): 398–415.

Pizer, Donald. "The Camera Eye in *U.S.A.:* The Sexual Center." *Modern Fiction Studies,* 26, no. 3 (Autumn 1980): 417–430.

Pizer. *Dos Passos's U.S.A.: A Critical Study.* Charlottesville: University Press of Virginia, 1988.

Rosen, Robert C. *John Dos Passos: Politics and the Writer.* Lincoln: University of Nebraska Press, 1981.

Sanders, David. "Interview with John Dos Passos." *Writers at Work,* Fourth Series. Ed. George Plimpton. New York: Viking, 1976.

Spangler, George M. "The Idea of Degeneration of American Fiction: 1880–1940." *English Studies,* 70 (October 1989): 407–435.

Whipple, T. K. "Dos Passos and the U.S.A." *Dos Passos: A Collection of Critical Essays.* Ed. Andrew Hook. Englewood Cliffs, N.J.: Prentice-Hall, 1974.

# CHAPTER 4:

# PUBLICATION AND CRITICAL RESPONSE

## *U.S.A.:* INITIAL PUBLICATION, LATER EDITIONS, AND ADAPTATION

*Of special interest in the publication history of* U.S.A. *are the two versions of* The 42nd Parallel; *the significant editions in English of the complete trilogy, including the 1946 limited edition illustrated by Reginald Marsh; the many translations of individual novels and of the trilogy as a whole; and the successful Broadway adaptation of the trilogy in 1959.*

### The Publication of *U.S.A.:* An Overview
Donald Pizer

*Pizer reviews the publication history of each of the novels of* U.S.A. *as well as the trilogy as a whole, with special emphasis on Dos Passos's revision in 1937 of the 1930 first edition of* The 42nd Parallel.

*The 42nd Parallel* was published by Harper and Brothers in February 1930. Dos Passos had begun *Nineteen-Nineteen* even before this event, and he completed it in the summer of 1931. He and Harpers then became involved in a controversy over the biography of J. P. Morgan in *Nineteen-Nineteen*. Morgan had come to the aid of Harpers some years earlier, and the firm was reluctant to publish Dos Passos' extremely sardonic portrait of "The House of Morgan." Dos Passos sought another publisher, and it was Harcourt, Brace that published *Nineteen-Nineteen* in March 1932.

. . . . . . . . . .

With the publication of *The Big Money* by Harcourt, Brace in August 1936, Dos Passos could undertake the preparation of the three novels as a single-volume trilogy. He felt that the work as a whole had an integral character and force, and he wished to make these apparent both to those who had read the novels as they appeared and to a new generation of readers by making the entire work available in a single volume. The first task in the preparation of such a volume was to reconcile the different formats of the three novels. As I have noted, *The 42nd Parallel* was published by Harpers, while *Nineteen-Nineteen* and *The Big Money* were published by Harcourt, Brace. Whether through editorial influence, house styling, or Dos Passos' own insistence, the last two novels differed sufficiently from the first in typography and format to constitute a major anomaly if the three books were to appear together unchanged in a single volume. Most obviously, in *The 42nd Parallel* each new modal segment (except the biographies) begins on a new page, while in the last two novels the format is that of continuous run-on from segment to segment. In addition, the type size for the various modes in *The 42nd Parallel* is completely different from the same modes in the last two novels. *The 42nd Parallel*, in short, had to be completely reset to bring it into conformity with *Nineteen-Nineteen* and *The Big Money*.

This resetting in fact occurred before the appearance of the single-volume trilogy when—apparently in anticipation of that event—*The 42nd Parallel* was published in the Modern Library series in November 1937. The significance of this new edition of *The 42nd Parallel* is that Dos Passos took advantage of the need to reset to make a number of changes in the novel, including an extensive cutting of the Newsreels. The Newsreels were far more prominent in the first edition of *The 42nd Parallel* than in the other two novels, both because they are longer and because of the large type font used in their printing. In Dos Passos' revision, no one Newsreel was omitted entirely, but almost all were cut, some by as much as a third.[1] In addition, their typography was brought into conformity with that of the Newsreels in the last two novels. Late in his life, when questioned by a graduate student who had discovered the editing of the Newsreels, Dos Passos expressed surprise and denied any participation in or authorization of the cuts.[2] But this was a lapse of memory. In a letter to his agent Brandt and Brandt in late July 1937, he enclosed a blurb for a Harcourt, Brace house newsletter in which it was noted that "*The 42nd Parallel* by John Dos Passos will be reprinted this fall in the Modern Library. Mr. Dos Passos . . . has made many corrections in this forthcoming edition of his novel."[3]

The 42^{ND}
PARALLEL

BY JOHN DOS PASSOS

HARPER & BROTHERS PUBLISHERS
NEW YORK AND LONDON 1930

THE 42ND PARALLEL
COPYRIGHT, 1930, BY JOHN DOS PASSOS
PRINTED IN THE U. S. A.
FIRST EDITION
A-E

*Title page and copyright page for the first edition of the first novel
in the U.S.A. Trilogy (Collection of Richard Layman)*

THE 42^{ND}
PARALLEL

BY
JOHN DOS PASSOS

WITH AN INTRODUCTORY NOTE BY THE AUTHOR

THE MODERN LIBRARY
NEW YORK

Copyright, 1930, by JOHN DOS PASSOS
Introductory Note Copyright, 1937, by
RANDOM HOUSE, INC.

First Modern Library Edition
1937

THE MODERN LIBRARY
IS PUBLISHED BY
RANDOM HOUSE, INC.
BENNETT A. CERF · DONALD S. KLOPFER · ROBERT K. HAAS

*Manufactured in the United States of America*
Printed by Parkway Printing Company　　Paper by Richard Bauer & Co.
Bound by H. Wolff　　End sheets designed by Rockwell Kent

*Title page and copyright page for the revised second edition of the first novel
in the U.S.A. Trilogy (Collection of Richard Layman)*

### The Camera Eye (5)

And we played the battle of Port Arthur in the bathtub and the water leaked down through the drawing-room ceiling and it was altogether too bad but in Kew Gardens old Mr Garnet who was still hale and hearty although so very old came to tea. We saw him first through the window, red face and John Bull whiskers and aunty said it was a sailor's rolling gait. He was carrying a box under his arm and Vickie and Pompom barked and here was Mr Garnet come to tea. He took a gramaphone out of a black box and put a cylinder on the gramaphone and they pushed back the teathings off the corner of the table. Be careful not to drop it now, they scratch rather heasy. Why a hordinary sewin needle would do maam but I ave special needles;

and we got to talking about Hadmiral Togo and the Banyan and how the Roosians drank so much vodka and killed all those poor fisherlads in the North Sea and he wound it up very carefully so as not to break the spring and the needle went rasp rasp Yes I was a bluejacket miself miboy from the time I was a little shayver not much bigger'n you, rose to be bosun's mite on the first British hironclad the Warrior and I can dance a ornpipe yet maam. He had a mariner's compass in red and blue on the back of his hand and his nails looked black and thick as he fumbled with the needle and the needle went rasp rasp and far away a band played and out of a grindy noise in the little black horn came God Save the King and the little dogs howled.

54

## THE CAMERA EYE (5)

and we played the battle of Port Arthur in the bath-tub and the water leaked down through the drawing-room ceiling and it was altogether too bad but in Kew Gardens old Mr. Garnet who was still hale and hearty although so very old came to tea and we saw him first through the window with his red face and John Bull whiskers and aunty said it was a sailor's rolling gait and he was carrying a box under his arm and Vickie and Pompom barked and here was Mr. Garnet come to tea and he took a gramophone out of a black box and put a cylinder on the gramophone and they pushed back the tea-things off the corner of the table    Be careful not to drop it now they scratch rather heasy    Why a hordinary sewin' needle would do maam but I ave special needles

and we got to talking about Hadmiral Togo and the Banyan and how the Roosians drank so much vodka and killed all those poor fisherlads in the North Sea and he wound it up very carefully so as not to break the spring and the needle went rasp rasp    Yes I was a bluejacket miself miboy from the time I was a little shayver not much bigger'n you rose to be bosun's mite on the first British hironclad the *Warrior* and I can dance a ornpipe yet maam    and he had a mariner's compass in red and blue on the back of his hand and his nails looked black

*55*

*Camera Eye (5) from the 1930 Harper edition of* The 42nd Parallel *(left) and the first page of the same Camera Eye from the reset 1937 Modern Library edition of* The 42nd Parallel *(Collection of Richard Layman)*

NEWSREEL IV

*I met my love in the Alamo*
*When the moon was on the rise*
*Her beauty quite bedimmed its light*
*So radiant were her eyes*

SHARP ADVANCE IN WHEAT PRICES dervish dancer breaks spinning record making 2400 revolutions in 32 minutes.

during the forenoon union pickets turned back a waggon loaded with 50 campchairs on its way to the fire engine house at Michigan Avenue and Washington street. The chairs it is reported, were ordered for the convenience of policemen detailed on strike duty

FLEETS MAY MEET IN BATTLE TODAY
WEST OF LUZON

three big wolves were killed before the dinner.
A grand parade is proposed here in which President Roosevelt shall ride so that he can be seen by citizens. At the head will be a caged bear recently captured after killing a dozen dogs and injuring several men. The bear will be given an hour's start for the hills then the packs will be set on the trail and President Roosevelt and the guides will follow in pursuit
three Columbia students start auto trip to Chicago on wager

GENERAL STRIKE NOW THREATENS

*It's moonlight fair tonight upon the Wa-abash*

OIL KING'S HAPPYESTDAY

one cherub every five minutes market for all classes of real estate continues to be healthy with good demand for factory sites residence and business properties court bills break labor

BLOODY SUNDAY IN MOSCOW

lady angels are smashed troops guard oilfields America tends to become empire like in the days of the Caesars $5 poem gets rich husband eat less says Edison rich poker player falls dead when he draws royal flush charges graft in Cicero STRIKE MAY

55

and thick as he fumbled with the needle and the needle went rasp rasp and far away a band played and out of a grindy noise in the little black horn came *God Save the King* and the little dogs howled

NEWSREEL IV

*I met my love in the Alamo*
*When the moon was on the rise*
*Her beauty quite bedimmed its light*
*So radiant were her eyes*

during the forenoon union pickets turned back a wagon loaded with 50 campchairs on its way to the fire engine house at Michigan Avenue and Washington street. The chairs it is reported, were ordered for the convenience of policemen detailed on strike duty

FLEETS MAY MEET IN BATTLE TODAY
WEST OF LUZON

three big wolves were killed before the dinner.
A grand parade is proposed here in which President Roosevelt shall ride so that he can be seen by citizens. At the head will be a caged bear recently captured after killing a dozen dogs and injuring several men. The bear will be given an hour's start for the hills then the packs will be set on the trail and President Roosevelt and the guides will follow in pursuit
three Columbia students start auto trip to Chicago on wager

GENERAL STRIKE NOW THREATENS

*It's moonlight fair tonight upon the Wa-abash*

56

*First page of Newsreel IV from the 1930 Harper edition of* The 42nd Parallel *(left) and the first page of the same Newsreel from the Modern Library edition of 1937 (right) (Collection of Richard Layman)*

Three other revisions of *The 42nd Parallel* for the Modern Library resetting are worth noting. Since the other two novels in the trilogy have no interior divisions, the division of the novel into five parts was dropped.[4] Dos Passos also discarded the epigraph, in which he cited a passage from a book on the American climate as a partial explanation of the title of the novel. (Storms in North America move from West to East along several paths; the 42nd parallel latitude is the most central of these paths.) This omission has caused considerable perplexity to later readers of the trilogy, who have been left without a clue as to the relevance of the title of its first novel. (It is also of some interest that the dust jacket of the 1930 Harper edition of *The 42nd Parallel* depicted a map of the United States marked with longitude and latitude lines and indicating that the 42nd parallel crossed the east coast at approximately Plymouth, Massachusetts. This would have had a private symbolic meaning for Dos Passos.) The third significant revision of *The 42nd Parallel* consisted of a juggling of the order of the segments of the novel from Newsreel XVI through the Proteus biography (pp. 274–328 of the revised edition). Nothing is omitted in this revision, but the order in which we encounter the ten segments is much altered. The importance of this revision is less its effect on this portion of the novel than its reflection of Dos Passos' basic cast of mind in the shaping of the trilogy. The task of finding a satisfactory juxtapositional balance did not end even with publication if an opportunity was provided for yet a further refinement of the effort.[5]

The Harcourt, Brace edition of *U.S.A.*, published in January 1938, used the plates of the 1937 Modern Library edition of *The 42nd Parallel* and the plates of the 1932 and 1936 editions of *Nineteen-Nineteen* and *The Big Money,* which means that Dos Passos made no further changes in the text of the trilogy for its single-volume edition.[6] Nevertheless, for this initial publication of the entire trilogy, Dos Passos had two additional tasks. One was to devise a title for the work as a whole, which, as I have noted, he did in the summer of 1937. The other was to write an introduction to the trilogy. This, after many drafts, he completed in late 1937 and also titled "U.S.A." Since the final segment of *The Big Money,* "Vag," was itself a late addition to Dos Passos' plan for the novel, and since "U.S.A." and "Vag" have a number of striking similarities in structure and theme, the two appear to be Dos Passos' conscious effort to frame the work as a whole within a prologue and an epilogue.

Dos Passos made no changes in the text or format of *U.S.A.* after its 1938 Harcourt, Brace publication. The later publication history of the work, however, contains two notable events. The first was the reprinting of the Harcourt, Brace edition in the Modern Library in 1939; several generations of readers encountered the trilogy in this form. The second was the resetting of the trilogy in a deluxe edition by Houghton Mifflin in 1946, with illustrations by Reginald Marsh that sought to render the element of caricature in Dos Passos' narrative style.

—*Dos Passos' U.S.A.: A Critical Study* (Charlottesville: University Press of Virginia, 1988), pp. 32–35

### Notes

1. See Donald G. England, "The Newsreels of John Dos Passos' *The 42nd Parallel:* Sources and Techniques," dissertation, University of Texas, 1970.

2. Dos Passos to England, 7 March 1969, cited in England, "The Newsreels of John Dos Passos' *The 42nd Parallel,*" p. 6.

3. Dos Passos to Brandt and Brandt, 15 July 1937, Dos Passos Collection, University of Virginia Library.

4. The decision to divide the 1930s Harper edition into parts was apparently made late in the preparation of the novel for the press. The divisions are not present in any of the surviving manuscripts of the novel, and no divisions are indicated in the copy of unrevised proof of the novel in the Barrett Collection of the University of Virginia Library.

5. In addition to the changes noted above, Dos Passos also made some minor verbal changes and corrections and brought the punctuation of the Camera Eye and the biographies into greater conformity with his practice in *Nineteen-Nineteen* and *The Big Money.*

6. One anomaly in the format of *U.S.A.* that Dos Passos failed to rectify was that of the varying type fonts and indentation conventions of the tables of contents for the three novels. In its first edition, each novel had a different format for its table of contents. For the second edition of *The 42nd Parallel* in 1937, Dos Passos regularized its table of contents to conform to that of *The Big Money.* But he either neglected or was not permitted to regularize the contents pages of *Nineteen-Nineteen* on its second printing as part of the *U.S.A.* trilogy in 1938.

### Epigraph to the 1930 edition of *The 42nd Parallel*

*This epigraph was omitted from all later editions of* The 42nd Parallel *as well as all editions of* U.S.A., *leaving many readers confused about the meaning of the title of the novel.*

*These general storms have been a subject of inexhaustible interest in all American meteorological research and great labor has been expended on the various hypotheses in regard to their laws. Some of these laws, and particularly those relating to exterior features and general movements, may be regarded as very well determined; their general phenomena have been so conspicu-*

*ous and so frequent of occurrence that some conclusions of this sort could not fail to result from the most imperfect observation . . .*

*In short, these storms follow three paths or tracks from the Rocky Mountains to the Atlantic Ocean of which the central tracing roughly corresponds with the 42nd parallel of latitude; all phenomena travel eastward in all cases at a rate not less than twenty miles an hour and usually at thirty or forty in the season of high west winds or in winter.*

−AMERICAN CLIMATOLOGY
E. W. Hodgins, Chicago, 1865
−*The 42nd Parallel* (New York: Harper, 1930), p. [ix]

## Introductory note to the 1937 Modern Library edition of *The 42nd Parallel*
John Dos Passos

*In this preface, which appears only in the Modern Library edition of* The 42nd Parallel, *Dos Passos seeks not only to explain briefly his innovative techniques in the novel but also to place them firmly in the post–World War I modernist movement.*

*The 42nd Parallel* is the first volume of *U.S.A.*, a long narrative which deals with the more or less entangled lives of a number of Americans during the first three decades of the present century. The volumes that follow are called *1919* and *The Big Money*.

In an effort to take in as much as possible of the broad field of the lives of these times, three separate sequences have been threaded in and out among the stories. Of these *The Camera Eye* aims to indicate the position of the observer and *Newsreel* to give an inkling of the common mind of the epoch. Portraits of a number of real people are interlarded in the pauses in the narrative because their lives seem to embody so well the quality of the soil in which Americans of these generations grew.

This method was used with the idea of coping with the particular job in hand rather than from any generalized theory about novelwriting. In fact I don't think any such theory holds water. The shape of a piece of work should be imposed, and in a good piece of work always is imposed, by the matter. That's more or less of a commonplace of a considerable body of literary criticism.

The difficulty comes when you try to put into words how this occurs. If several people describe the same scene, say a man and a woman sitting at a table in a room and talking, the results are sure to be very different. Through a bunch of such descriptions a number of identical stereotypes will appear which will reveal the commonplace attitudes and the common grounds of the human group the narrators belong to. But there will also be found here and there in the accounts an occasional phrase or mental slant that tends to break the stereotype and to give some added insight or breadth to the event and to relate it in some new or fresh way to the experience of the group. That's the point where creative writing becomes of permanent value, as absolute discovery is of value in science. At the same time that's the point where many readers will feel annoyance and strain. Leaving the groove hurts. An effort of adjustment is demanded of the brain. People feel pain when the stereotype is broken, at least at first. Then gradually they become accustomed to the discovery and it in turn becomes a stereotype. There are long periods in history when no such breaking of stereotypes occurs and time-honored attitudes and phrases take on a liturgical insignificance and the standard of excellence becomes the exactness with which the stereotypes are repeated.

It may be that we are entering such a period now after a period of considerable fertility and tolerance of invention. Or it may be that we are merely in a lull to be followed by a new outburst of inventiveness and a new broadening of the field of language on the part of a young generation forced to make a fresh set of adjustments to a changed world. At any rate one thing is certain, the great advance made in American writing which can be roughly dated from Dreiser's final overthrow of the genteel tradition, has now become a commonplace of journalism, advertising and the applied arts of the trade, much as many of the discoveries of cubists and surrealists in painting have become the commonplace of the windowdresser and designer. There certainly has been no period in history when every slight imaginative advance has been so fast exploited and absorbed by the great mass of the population. For proof all you need is to compare the text of contemporary advertising in *Fortune* or *Life* with that of, say, the *Saturday Evening Post* of the years around 1910.

This does not mean that a limit has been reached, but it means that, like the pioneers who had to move west into the prairie as soon as the farm they'd just cleared could grow a good crop of corn, writers who want to do primary inventive work will have to keep moving forward into the wilderness. The pure scientist has to do the same thing.

No one will thank them for their work. Age and fatigue will overcome them with no roof over their heads; they'll come to bad ends. But so long as men are found among us who, confronted by welltilled fields yielding a rich harvest to the second generation of exploiters, can't help feeling an intolerable itch to push on beyond, to test continually slogans, creeds and commonplaces in the light of freshly felt experience, American writing will continue alive. When that race dies out or is forcibly extinguished by the pressure of civil war or robotmaking organization we shall settle down to the routine and sterility that seems in certain periods of low vitality so congenial to the race.

Provincetown, July, 1937.
−*The 42nd Parallel* (New York: Modern Library, 1937), pp. vii–ix

*Margo Dowling fending off the advances of a drunken real-estate broker in an episode from* The Big Money *illustrated by Marsh for the 1946 Houghton Mifflin edition of* U.S.A. *(© 1946 by Houghton Mifflin Co. © renewed by Houghton Mifflin Co. Reprinted by permission of Houghton Mifflin Co.)*

## Caricatures in Crisis: The Satiric Vision of Reginald Marsh and John Dos Passos

Richard N. Masteller

*Masteller reprints and discusses many of the illustrations by Reginald Marsh for the 1946 Houghton Mifflin edition of Dos Passos's* U.S.A., *with emphasis on the shared satiric vision of the two figures.*

. . . . . . . . . .

Throughout the thirties, while Marsh was creating his version of cultural satire, Dos Passos was publishing the individual volumes of his trilogy, *The 42nd Parallel* (1930), *Nineteen-Nineteen* (1932), and *The Big Money* (1936). These first appeared as the trilogy *U.S.A.* in 1938. When Marsh took up pen and ink to illustrate the trilogy in 1945, he adapted his cultural satire to the meaning and method of Dos Passos's prose; the fluid medium of ink drawing was as appropriate to Dos Pas-

sos's panoramic vision of contemporary life as etching had been to Marsh's individual scenes of Manhattan.

In about one month Marsh conceived and completed, without preliminary sketches, more than 500 ink drawings, 470 of which appear in the published volumes. Some dismissed these sketchy illustrations as simple hack work. Ernest Hemingway called them "absolutely atrocious," and completing 500 of them in approximately one month does suggest a lack of polish. Undeniably, some of them resemble the jottings in the sketchbooks Marsh carried on his daily excursions.

But some reviewers were more sympathetic than Hemingway. One called the illustrations "appropriately satirical"; another asserted, "the choice of illustrator was admirable . . . Marsh has caught perfectly in his sketches the harried, uneasy existence of the trilogy's multitude of characters." A third suggested that the illustrations *look as though they had been tossed off in haste and indignation. Yet these seemingly careless sketches . . . have the very considerable value of a spontaneous appreciation of the mood of the story itself. . . . The acid of Marsh's irony is exactly like that of Dos Passos' own; it eats into every line, showing that the pageant of the "boom" years which was supposed to be notable for its brilliance and exuberance was actually one of terrible disintegration and decay.[1]*

As these reviewers discerned, shifting from etchings and lithographs to pen-and-ink drawings enabled Marsh not only to produce more images in less time, but also to create images especially suited to Dos Passos's themes. In his prints Marsh focused on the psychological depth of a specific moment of time; in his drawings he heightened the sense of superficiality and constant change. In essence, he replaced the characters of his engravings with the caricatures of his drawings. His treatment of backgrounds supports this altered view of the people—the claustrophobic urban world circumscribed by iron girders, the burlesque theaters with their enclosing proscenium arches, and the sideshows with their shallow backgrounds of banners hemming in the performers have all disappeared. In their place is open white space, or the barest sketch of a setting, or occasionally a minimal delineation of seascape or landscape or horizon toward which various people gaze. As his characters became caricatures, they lost the oppressive contexts that had once helped to define them, but they failed to gain any new foundations or roots. In short, as quickly rendered records Marsh's illustrations visually replicated the themes of superficiality, transience, and spiritual poverty that pervaded Dos Passos's trilogy.

Numerous critics have underscored the superficiality of the characters who populate Dos Passos's novel.[2] Like Marsh, the literary satirist reduces his characters to caricatures, sacrificing psychological depth and depicting flat characters defined by repetitive phrases or recurrent, one-dimensional behavior patterns. In *Nineteen-Nineteen* Teddy Roosevelt repeats "bully," and Joe Williams first appears as an outsider on the run—a pattern that identifies him throughout the novel. As these characters career through their days and nights, their thoughts and words careen through an accumulation of phrases and simple sentences joined by the coordinating conjunction *and*. Particularly in the narrative sections of the trilogy, this inconsequential, rarely reflective prose levels all experience to a single dimension, although Dos Passos usually saves an anticlimactic detail for the conclusion of the sentence. For example, when *Nineteen-Nineteen*'s Richard Savage, Eveline Hutchins, and Eleanor Stoddard gather in Paris and chat about Woodrow Wilson's visit to Rome, we read: "They talked about Chartres and about the dev-

*Marsh illustration of J. W. Moorehouse in his Red Cross uniform in* Nineteen-Nineteen *(Illustration © 1946 by Houghton Mifflin Co. © renewed by Houghton Mifflin Co. Reprinted by permission of Houghton Mifflin Co.)*

astated regions and the popular enthusiasm that was greeting Mr. Wilson everywhere and why Clemenceau always wore gray lisle gloves."[3] When subordinate clauses or other qualifiers appear, they tend to fill in trivial details or to trivialize important information

*Marsh illustration for* Nineteen-Nineteen *of Dick Savage and his friend Ned Wigglesworth getting drunk on the eve of Dick's departure for Europe to join the ambulance service (Illustration © 1946 by Houghton Mifflin Co. © renewed by Houghton Mifflin Co. Reprinted by permission of Houghton Mifflin Co.)*

rather than demonstrate judicious evaluation. Moreover, such clauses usually tend to be replaced quickly by the simple coordinating conjunction offering yet more evidence of stunted emotions and empty lives. For example, Eleanor and Eveline have a dinner party for Jerry Burnham and Major Appleton, "who was in Paris doing something about tanks":

> *It was a fine dinner, duck roasted with oranges, although Jerry, who was sore about how much Eveline talked to Lemonnier, had to get drunk and use a lot of bad language . . . and after everybody had left [Eleanor] and Eveline had quite a quarrel. . . . "You're a darling, Eveline dear, but you have the vulgarist friends. I don't know where you pick them up, and that Felton woman drank four cocktails, a quart of beaujolais, and three cognacs, I kept tabs on her myself." Eveline started to laugh and they both got to laughing. But Eleanor said that their life was getting much too bohemian and that it wasn't right with the war on and things going so dreadfully in Italy and Russia and the poor boys in the trenches and all that.*[4]

As Dos Passos's emotionally and intellectually vacuous prose skims the surface of a kaleidoscopically shifting experience, many of Marsh's sketches similarly outline characters who have very little dimension or depth. Using an economical, even skimpy, line, his cartoonlike caricatures underscore the emptiness and inconsequence of their lives. Thus, when *Big Money*'s Mary French throws herself into the workers' struggle by "collecting money from wealthy women" and "inducing prominent liberals to come and get arrested on the picketline," Marsh depicts two such representatives, but neither seems deeply involved in the struggle: each carries a blank placard (in contrast to Marsh's well-known use of signs, slogans, headlines, and banners in other works); and the woman, a purse dangling from her arm, is wearing a coat that appears to have a fur collar. Marsh's drawing thus suggests the superficial engagement of these "prominent liberals" as they parade across the page, even as the prose goes on to indicate that the strikers themselves return to "dreary front parlors of their homes stripped of furniture they hadn't been able to make the last payment on." At another point in the novel, Margo Dowling "gave [Ed] a poke" for breaking into her room while she was changing her clothing. Marsh's cartoon underscores the farce of the episode and its protagonists by including those impact lines used in newspaper comic strips, as fist hits nose.[5]

The correspondence between prose and sketch also holds when these caricatures attempt to act. Having reduced his subjects to easily comprehended, one-dimensional models, Dos Passos presents people whose characteristic actions are more often than not reactions. Rather than agents of social change (as progressive myths about "the people" suggested), they are more often opportunists, such as Richard Savage and J. Ward Moorehouse, and most often victims of social change. The nature of this change is also important: ceaseless and largely mindless motion pervades these novels, and the details of this movement are always governed by Dos Passos's satiric strategy. As Alvin Kernan, Barbara Foley, Townsend Ludington, and others have noted, the narrative line in most satire tends to be disjunctive and non-progressive; rather than ranging across a broad spectrum of time, the satirist slices into one moment or into separate moments of a relatively compressed period, thereby gaining opportunities to elaborate satirically on recurring flaws.[6] As we encounter the various biographies, newsreels, narratives, and camera-eye sections in the trilogy, our sense of rationally ordered experience—our sense of beginning, middle, and end—is assaulted by what Alfred Kazin has called a "literature of empiricism," comprising an abundance of detail that does not so much lead toward the future as exhaust the present.[7] Dos Passos's satiric prose thus undermines the ideology of progress so important in the rhetoric of the New Deal era.

To echo this general sense of motion in the trilogy Marsh sketches a fair number of cars and trains, and many ships. But he adopts a more complex strategy to accentuate visually the absence of progress behind all this motion. Marsh chooses to depict actions that are, first of all, largely trivial: café rendezvous, much drinking, and many parties appear among his sketches, visually echoing these recurrent motifs in the prose of the novel. And it is the redundancy of these sketches that drives home his satiric point: as he details these activities he simultaneously undercuts any sense of fundamental change. Thus, Marsh's repetitious images only underscore the absence of progress toward some meaningful future.

Although many of Marsh's characters are engaged in constant motion with little direction, he also includes many characters who simply stand around a lot. In these instances Marsh's line tends to be firmer and more elaborate: he begins to fill in the outline of his caricatures. But even as he tends toward portraiture, Marsh's satiric strategies continue to illuminate Dos Passos's satiric themes. These are portraits of people in waiting. Don Stevens, Webb Cruthers, G. H. Barrow, Homer Cassidy: each stands with a hand in his pocket. Their satiric poses suggest their relative helplessness before forces beyond their control.

Besides suggesting the psychological passivity of these more fully drawn characters, Marsh seems to underscore their posturing—their affectations—in a world of facades, charades, and clichés. Thus, he chooses to illustrate Mr. Dreyfus from *42nd Parallel*, taking his cues from Dos Passos's description:

*Mr. Dreyfus was a small thinfaced man with a small black mustache and small black twinkly eyes and a touch of accent that gave him a distinguished foreign diplomat manner. He carried yellow wash gloves and a yellow cane and had a great variety of very much-tailored overcoats.*[8]

In *Nineteen-Nineteen* a nameless "longfaced English officer" in a bar in Genoa repeats "bloody" seven times in the brief conversation he has with Dick Savage, blabs about an important "secret mission [to] trace an entire carload of boots that had vanished between Vintimiglia and San Raphael," concludes that, "It's a bloody melodrama that's what it is, just like Drury Lane," says "cheeryoh," and hustles out. Although this particular character never reappears in the trilogy, the cliché he embodies nevertheless warrants a Marsh illustration.[9]

J. W. Moorehouse, who arrives in Paris to take charge of the publicity department for the Red Cross, provides Marsh with yet another opportunity. Dos Passos describes him as having "blue eyes and hair so light it was almost white. His uniform fitted well and his Sam Browne belt and his puttees shone like glass." Dos Passos goes on, however, to accentuate not what Moorehouse looks like, but what he says and does. He makes "a little speech about the importance of the work the Red Cross was doing to keep up the morale of civilians and combatants":

*"Even at this moment, my friends, we are under fire, ready to make the supreme sacrifice that civilization shall not perish from the earth." Major Wood leaned back in his swivelchair and let out a squeak that made everybody look up with a start and several people looked out of the window as if they expected to see a shell from Big Bertha hurtling right in on them. "You see," said Major Moorehouse eagerly, his blue eyes snapping, "that is what we must make people feel . . . the catch in the throat, the wrench to steady the nerves, the determination to carry on."*[10]

*Marsh illustration for "Vag," the vignette of an unnamed hitchhiker that serves as an epilogue to* U.S.A. *(Illustration © 1946 by Houghton Mifflin Co. © renewed by Houghton Mifflin Co. Reprinted by permission of Houghton Mifflin Co.)*

Marsh depicts J. Ward Moorehouse with an open mouth as he spouts rhetoric that the rest of the novel discredits.

Like Dos Passos's prose, therefore, Marsh's caricatures depend on strategies of satiric exaggeration and diminution. He isolates a stance or gesture, thereby defining the one-dimensionality of the caricatures on the page before us. But even when he fills in and distinguishes some of these personalities, he continues to qualify their individuality, using recurrent devices—drinks in hands or hands in pockets—to link them with the mass of named and nameless human beings who populate the trilogy.

Given the frenetic, trivial activities, the fatuous reactions, the curious combination of passivity and posturing, and the jaded emotions so pervasive in these novels, how can one expect these caricatures to face anything resembling a true crisis? Rather, what sort of crises do these caricatures face and how do they face them?

Because many of the crises are never deeply felt, they are easily resolved—or rather, dismissed. For example, when *Nineteen-Nineteen*'s Richard Savage, aspiring poet soon to become public relations hack, volunteers for the ambulance service to avoid final exams at Harvard, he and roommate Ned spend the night getting drunk and talking

*a great deal about how it was the fate of Youth and Beauty and Love and Friendship to be mashed out by an early death. . . . In the pearly dawn they went out and sat with a last bottle on one of the old tombstones in the graveyard, on the corner of Harvard Square. They sat on the cold tombstone a long time without saying anything, only drinking, and after each drink threw their heads back and softly bleated in unison Blahblahblahblah.*[11]

One could argue that this is one of the more spiritual crises in the novel, for many of the other crises are more properly described as physical conflicts, and to these Marsh was especially drawn.

When Marsh's men do take their hands out of their pockets, they often throw a punch, hoist a drink, or grab a woman's leg. If battles occur in the streets, the enemy is usually the police, but even here the visual conflict derives from Marsh's lavishing more attention on the horses than on the supposed victims of oppression. His relative neglect of the people underscores their unimportance and undercuts what one might expect to be a moment of crisis.

As for the woman's leg, here Marsh touches a more dramatic crisis in the trilogy, one that echoes an obsessive theme in his art: over and over Marsh highlights the fundamental male-female tensions pervading the trilogy. Men repeatedly stare across a distance at women, and generally his many images of men and women together emphasize their distance rather than their intimacy—even in intimate situations. As he did in his *Merry-Go-Round* fifteen years earlier, Marsh uses facial expressions to underscore these sexual conflicts. While *42nd Parallel*'s Mr. Barrow appears a grotesque caricature of male desire, Daughter is less distorted. Here again Marsh juxtaposes the cool composure of the woman against the awkward passions of the male. Even in the few idyllic images of togetherness in his trilogy, Dos Passos's satiric prose provides the impetus for Marsh's mock romantic moonlight:

> there was a little moon behind fleecy clouds and they sat down in the new grass where it was dark behind stacks of freshcut lumber laid out to season. She let her head drop on his shoulder and called him "baby boy."[12]

Such moments are rare and fleeting in Dos Passos's prose. More often, even when physical distance narrows, psychological distance does not. In both the prose and the sketches confrontation is the normal mode of encounter between the sexes. Even caricatures can have this kind of crisis because it is rooted not in spiritual agony, but in elemental and elementary relationships of brute power.

Death is certainly another kind of crisis in the trilogy. Significantly, Marsh avoids illustrating the trilogy's single most powerful death—the "Body of an American" at the end of *Nineteen-Nineteen*—and focuses instead on two of the most ludicrous, presenting them in a manner wholly befitting Dos Passos's narrative treatment. In *42nd Parallel* Dos Passos describes the death of Miss Perkins:

> Then one day Eleanor got home late to supper and the old clerk at the hotel told her that Miss Perkins had been stricken with heartfailure while eating steak and kidney pie for lunch and had died right in the hotel diningroom and that the body had been removed to the Irving Funeral Chapel and asked her if she knew any of her relatives that should be notified.[13]

Dos Passos treats Jules Piquot's death with a similar satiric touch in *Big Money*:

> Then one Monday morning she [Margo Dowling] got down to Piquot's late and found the door locked and a crowd of girls milling shrilly around in front of it. Poor Piquot had been found dead in his bathtub from a dose of cyanide of potassium and there was nobody to pay their back wages.[14]

In the two minimal line drawings describing these events Marsh's cartoon style mirrors the slapstick comedy of the prose. Such images may have been, as Marsh wrote, "great fun to draw," but their frivolity also fosters a sense of the inescapable ridiculousness of the human condition. Both picture and prose turn crisis into bathos.

The energetic quality of Marsh's line throughout his *U.S.A.* trilogy drawings most clearly captures the essence of Dos Passos's satiric themes and style. Marsh's distortion of facial features, his exaggeration of the differences between men and women, and his use of frenetic action alternated with static posturing deny or oversimplify the complexities of human behavior and subvert popular myths about the nobility and heroism of "the people." Usually, his lightly drawn, thin ink line momentarily arrests characters against a background of undefined white space. When he provides an immediate setting or occasional elements of a wider landscape, he effectively reduces all these elements—character, setting, and scene—to the same level of impermanence and inconsequentiality.

There is however, one significant exception to this air of transience. A watercolor frontispiece appearing only in volume one of the 1946 edition of the trilogy echoes some themes of Marsh's earlier prints, while adumbrating the nature of the crises so many of the characters in the trilogy will face. This scene records an encounter of a man and a woman in the detritus of an industrial environment. The two garbage cans, the indistinguishable debris surrounding them, the rectangular door frame and wooden facade, and the factory spewing its smoke in the background combine to create a symbolic environment suggesting enclosure and entrapment—any hope for the future is destroyed by an insistent industrial present. The couple's tense, urgent demeanor, moreover, undercuts any presumption that a mutual attraction or alliance might act as a counterforce sufficient to mitigate the scene in which they find themselves. Thus, although this relatively complex image differs from the openness and lack of setting common in many of the drawings, Marsh again portrays not so much a crisis as a condition of being. As with the ludicrous deaths, the sexual encounters, the vain and manipulative attitudes, the anti-heroic brawls and riots, Marsh's frontispiece presents humanity largely defeated by its limited circumstances and thus forever unable to change them.

Marsh's prints of the 1930s and his illustrations for *U.S.A.* present two different views of the American scene, but each is shaped by his cultural satire. His vision is more trenchant than lighthearted social satire, less angry than political satire. Many of his etchings, born of a cumulative, incremental working and reworking of the copper plate, possess dark tonalities that present a dense mass of human beings enclosed in shallow space. His more rapidly executed drawings diminish this oppressive atmosphere with their more abundant white space, but only to suggest a fragile and ephemeral world. Marsh had other impulses, affirmative ones included. As Richard Cox has suggested, Marsh's "optimism for urban culture" despite its vulgarities prevented him from condemning the subjects he depicted.[15] But cultural satire by its very nature precludes such condemnation, just as it precludes offering explicit solutions to improve the human condition. Instead, it details the way things have gone wrong—the way "we, the people" are not so much initiators as products of events and processes beyond our control. Cultural satire shows us how far we have come, even as it doubts what more we can do.

Marsh's final image in the *U.S.A.* trilogy, the only drawing, excluding endpapers and the watercolor frontispiece, not tied to one of the longer narrative sections, corresponds to Dos Passos's final paragraphs detailing the wanderings of everyman Vag:

> The young man waits at the edge of the concrete, with one hand he grips a rubbed suitcase of phony leather, the other hand almost making a fist, thumb up
>
> that moves in ever so slight an arc when a car slithers past, a truck roars, clatters; the wind of cars passing ruffles his hair, slaps grit in his face.

The passage continues by emphasizing the vagrant's hunger and headache, then shifts to a transcontinental airplane carrying "the big men with bankaccounts" who will reach Los Angeles before the hitchhiker moves a hundred miles.[16] Marsh captures the mood fairly well. Although he excludes the rubbed suitcase and sketches instead one last hand-in-the-pocket, he foregrounds the hunched and rumpled Vag as the road, truck, and plane recede in the background, white space enforcing the separation.

The myth of "the people" argued the continuity of experience and the people's ability to direct that experience toward some common goal. Subverting this myth and moving beyond political and social satire, Dos Passos and

Marsh employed cultural satire to depict frenetic slices of life characterized by discontinuity, dissension, and loss of control. When only caricatures remained to endure the crises thrust upon them, the loss of depth and dimension—the loss of human integrity—was obvious, not only in the prose, but also in the graphic art of *U.S.A.*

—*Smithsonian Studies in American Art,* 3 (Spring 1989): 31–45

**Notes**

1. Martha MacGregor, *New York Post,* 9 December 1946; "New Edition of *U.S.A.,*" *Southwest Review* (Winter 1947): 111; James Gray, *Chicago Daily News,* 4 December 1946. These and other reviews are located in the John Dos Passos Papers, #5406, Manuscripts Division, Special Collections Department, University of Virginia Library, Charlottesville.

2. See especially Charles T. Ludington, "The Neglected Satires of John Dos Passos," *Satire Newsletter,* 7 (Spring 1970): 128–129, 133; Blanche Gelfant, *The American City Novel,* 2nd ed. (Norman: University of Oklahoma Press, 1970), pp. 159–166, 173–174; John Lydenberg, "Dos Passos' *U.S.A.*: The Words of the Hollow Men," in *Essays on Determinism in American Literature,* ed. Sydney J. Krause (Kent, Ohio: Kent State University Press, 1964), pp. 97–107. Lydenberg's essay is reprinted in Allen Belkind, ed., *Dos Passos, the Critics, and the Writer's Intention* (Carbondale: Southern Illinois University Press, 1971), pp. 93–105. Also, Alfred Kazin, *On Native Grounds* (1942; reprint, Garden City, N.Y.: Doubleday, 1956), pp. 276–282; and Kazin, "Introduction," *1919* (New York: New American Library, 1969), pp. xii–xiv.

3. *Nineteen-Nineteen* (Boston: Houghton Mifflin, 1946), pp. 433–444.

4. Ibid., pp. 251–252.

5. *The Big Money* (Boston: Houghton Mifflin, 1946), pp. 454, 520.

6. Alvin B. Kernan, *The Cankered Muse: Satire of the English Renaissance* (New Haven: Yale University Press, 1959), pp. 30–36, and *The Plot of Satire* (New Haven: Yale University Press, 1965), p. 100; Barbara Foley, "History, Fiction, and Satirical Form: The Example of John Dos Passos' *1919,*" *Genre,* 12 (Fall 1979): 363–364.

7. Kazin, *On Native Grounds,* p. 381.

8. *The 42nd Parallel* (Boston: Houghton Mifflin, 1946), pp. 174–175.

9. *Nineteen-Nineteen,* pp. 223–225.

10. Ibid., pp. 252–254.

11. Ibid., pp. 108–109.

12. *The 42nd Parallel,* p. 454.

13. Ibid., p. 269.

14. *The Big Money,* p. 390.

15. Richard Cox, "Coney Island, Urban Symbol in American Art," *New York Historical Society Quarterly,* 60 (1976): 49.

16. *The Big Money,* pp. 642–644.

\* \* \*

## Stage Adaptation

### Production Notes For "U.S.A."
Paul Shyre

*Paul Shyre was a theatrical director, writer, and actor who collaborated with Dos Passos on* U.S.A.: A Dramatic Revue *(1959). The play received largely positive reviews and ran for a little more than seven months.*

There are many ways the imaginative director can stage "U.S.A." I am merely giving a few notes on the production I originally staged in New York, and hope they will be of some value to other directors.

I have kept the cast to six actors, all of whom, with the exception of the one who plays Moorehouse, play several roles. The actors were always kept on the stage throughout the play, upstage on six high stools which were at the top of a small ramp. Behind them was a backdrop of a simple design, which did not in any way interfere with visual attraction of other scenes. The only props used were three chairs and a small round table. One of the chairs had arms; the others were armless, and in the second act a fourth chair was brought on. The table and chairs were lightweight, and were continuously moved into various positions by the actors. The use of lighting was most important as well as the proper choice of lighted areas.

The newsreels were done as follows: an appropriate tune of the period would play and as the music dropped the actors would be standing before their stools, and proclaim the larger headlines. For this there would be little or no special characterization. For the longer headlines or feature bits, the actor would step forward and deliver with a full characterization, according to the tone of the material. Each newsreel would end in a rising finale of music and blackout.

There were two points of narration on the left and right of the stage, where actors related the stories of the major characters as the action progressed.

Major narrations such as the ones on Isadora Duncan and Valentino were done stage center.

Costuming for the men remained basically the same throughout the play: stiff white collars, striped shirts under them, simple suits with vests. The women in the first act wore dresses of the 1900 to 1918 period. In the second act they returned in short, almost flapper type garments of the twenties period, all in accordance with the characters they portrayed.

"The Body of an American" section at the end of Act One can be staged in a variety of ways, and

*U. S. A.*

A DRAMATIC REVUE

*By Paul Shyre and John Dos Passos*

Based on the novel by John Dos Passos

SAMUEL FRENCH, INC.
45 WEST 25TH STREET    NEW YORK 10010
7623 SUNSET BOULEVARD HOLLYWOOD 90046
LONDON                          TORONTO

*Title page of the 1960 edition of the 1959 dramatic adaptation of Dos Passos's trilogy (Collection of Richard Layman)*

there is a slow drum roll towards the end of it. The imagination of the director can take over here.

The background music for the newsreel numbers should be appropriate songs of the periods depicted.

The Newsreel Number III number is sung by the cast in the early nineteen hundreds musical comedy style. Act Two opens with the cast pairing off in couples and dancing a fox trot reminiscent of 1918. The Charleston number is danced in the newsreel position by the cast in a typical 1920's way. The final newsreel has a 1929 Black Bottom rhythm, which is also danced by the cast.

Again, let me say these are suggestions, and to remember that the pacing of the play is important as well as the spirit of the periods as we enter them. It is called a dramatic revue, and should be played as such.

May 1963
–Paul Shyre and John Dos Passos, *U.S.A.:
A Dramatic Revue* (New York: S. French,
1963 [c. 1960]), pp. 1, 3–6

"U. S. A." was first presented by Howard Gottfried and Nick Spanos at the Martinique Theatre, New York City, on October 28, 1959, with the following cast:

PLAYER A
MOOREHOUSE
ORVILLE WRIGHT } . . . . . . . . . . . . . . . . .*Lawrence Hugo*

PLAYER B
McGILL
DEBS
JOE WILLIAMS } . . . . . . . . . . . . . . . . .*William Windom*
EDGECOMBE
BINGHAM
etc.

PLAYER C
DICK SAVAGE } . . . . . . . . . . . . . . . . .*William Redfield*
OLLIE TAYLOR
etc.

PLAYER D
JANEY WILLIAMS } . . . . . . . . . . . . . . . . .*Peggy McCay*
PAT DOOLITTLE
etc.

PLAYER E
GERTRUDE } . . . . . . . . . . . . . . . . .*Joan Tetzel*
JANEY'S MOTHER

PLAYER F
ELEANOR STODDARD } . . . . . . . . . . . . . .*Sada Thompson*
ISADORA
etc.

Directed by: Paul Shyre

Setting and costumes: Robert Ramsey

Lighting: Lee Watson

Orchestrations: Robert Cobert

Musical direction and continuity: Herbert Harris

Associate producer: Richard Rosen

The action of the play takes place between the turn of the Century and 1930. The play is in Two Acts.

*Cast list and credits from the 1963 publication of* U.S.A.: A Dramatic Revue
*(Collection of Richard Layman)*

## Reflections on *U.S.A.* as Novel and Play
Jules Chametzky

*Chametzky admires the technical virtuosity of the dramatic version of* U.S.A. *but also feels that it mutes the radical intensity of the novel.*

The off-Broadway production of *U.S.A.*, "a new dramatic review" written by John Dos Passos and Paul Shyre and based on Dos Passos' novel, has been running in the theatre of New York's Hotel Martinique for several months, so that it seems to have won popular acceptance along with the critical praise that greeted its appearance. I am more than usually interested in this fact, since I recently taught Dos Passos' novel and found that its reception by intelligent students nurtured in the Eisenhower years was an equivocal and conditioned one. To be crude about it,

my students responded to the technique of the novel, not to its content; after seeing the dramatization based on it, I wonder if the same—or worse—may not be true of the contemporary theatre audience. "Worse" because it seems to me that in this production the aspect of communion and revelation which the theatrical experience always contains, intensified in this instance by the technically brilliant sense of immediacy evoked, is in the service of a content that is only superficially and momentarily challenging, disturbing, *felt*. The production is, finally, the occasion for a species of audience self-congratulation.

. . . . . . . . . .

The play at the Martinique is by no means a sad one, a fact which, as a paying customer, I will admit to be pure gain; yet, from another standpoint, this may represent a loss. The sadness—or bitterness—in the novel had the

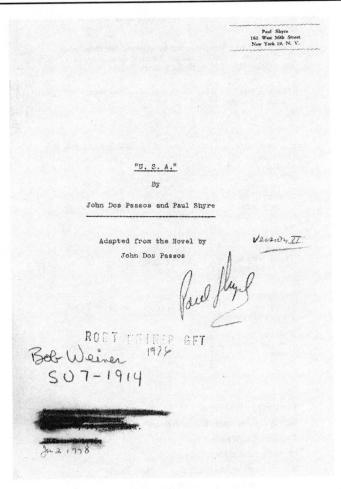

Title page of Paul Shyre's typescript of his and Dos Passos's 1959 dramatic adaptation of U.S.A.
(Collection of Richard Layman)

power to inform and transform; the play—which as the program notes, is only "based" on the novel—strikes an occasional sombre note that promises to penetrate to the heart, but these turn out to be only titillations, and the object has been only entertainment, after all.

Let me say at once that the production is excellent and, I would guess, superior to almost anything on Broadway this season. The virtuosity of the actors, writers, and director in fashioning a smooth-flowing continuous action that embodies a recognizable point-of-view is remarkable. In view of this, one soon abandons the skeptical idea that so panoramic a novel cannot be adapted to the dimensions of an evening's drama. Mr. Shyre proves once again that through a daring use of theatrical resources requiring only mind and talent, very little is outside the province of theatre. Our audiences are ready for almost anything, technically. On the other hand, there is a good deal lost in the transition from the novel (as I read it) to the play. What I should like to suggest is that this loss is due less to the requirements of the dramatic form than to the demands of the "here and now"—in this case, to the real or supposed expectations of the well-dressed, well-cushioned, well- coifed audience that

helps the play keep going. The reduction—especially the excision of almost everything "radical" (Debs is kept: the image of the saint deserted by the workers)—may also reflect Dos Passos' own changed social philosophy.

The setting is simple, geared to the work's demand for fluidity. The audience is seated on three sides of a small theatre; the fourth wall is covered with a large yellow backdrop on which is sketched a jagged mural suggesting aspects of the years between 1900 and 1930. Six wire-backed high stools are placed against this wall for the actors—three men and three women. From here the actors step forward to play their various parts in the narratives (the props down front are reduced to essentials: several chairs, a table or two), chant the headlines of the Newsreel portions, or address the audience directly in the Biography and Camera Eye sections. This is no concert reading, such as Mr. Shyre has successfully prepared with the work of O'Casey: the overall result represents a successful synthesis of Living Newspaper techniques, Epic theatre, a variety show, a review. The production is exciting.

Unfortunately, I do not feel that the content of the play and the conception behind it evenly fulfill the high expectations generated by its technical excellence. While the play was in rehearsal I have been told, Dos Passos reminded the actors that scenes are like icebergs and that they must always be aware of all that does not show. With the exception of some memorable moments, however, I had the uncomfortable feeling that I was seeing an inverted iceberg–almost everything *was* surface–the sense of depth was missing. This was perhaps due to the unrelieved sense of the actors "playing" their parts. The frequency of change in person and situation tended to force the actors into stock mannerisms in order to convey quickly a character and mood, so that the portrayals were too often caricatures. As a way of forcing the audience to achieve an ironic detachment and cool intellectuality towards the characters this is commendable, but the objects of our deliberation must be complex enough to justify the effort. Where the range of irony is limited, where, for example, only a few examples of spurious attitudes and personalities are isolated from the richness and complexity of the novel, the technique wears a little thin. We are repeatedly urged to consider the same absurdities–self-importance, self-infatuation, mindless reliance on cant and jargon, hypocrisy–until, finally, their concrete embodiments are only illustrations, not realities. And when the satirical treatment of these "humors" is not too general, it goes off in search of dead or dying horses.

By heavily underlining the inane aspects of the popular and official culture, the Newsreel portions attempt to locate these absurdities in the society as a whole. But soon the play of voices takes on a pattern: the politicians all begin to sound like Senator Claghorn; the sole radical demonstrator in the play is given a comically whining Brooklyn accent; Gertrude Ederle lumbers down to deliver her headlines in a tough male voice. The actress who plays Gertrude gets a deserved laugh as she bangs the water from her ear, but too much of this sort of thing has the effect, finally, of reducing the whole social scene to a kind of cartoon. The audience laughs, and is comfortably assured that there can be no connection between them and *them*. It's all good clean fun. And nice to be reminded how we've outgrown those dear, dead days of long ago–and the funny clothes, and the funny dances.

The chief burden of the play is carried in the stories of Janey Williams, J. Ward Moorehouse, and Richard Ellsworth Savage. The problem is not that *everyone* in the novel could not be in the play; the problem is, why these three? They each begin as touching or promising people, and each becomes, in one way or another, hollow, corrupt, opportunistic. Although individual corruption is surely an important aspect of the thematic structure in the novel, the play lacks the corrosive effect of a whole society hell-bent on the big money and futility. Of course, Moorehouse and Savage occupy positions of power in society and are not merely its victims, so that as products and carriers of our society's illness they could be doubly ominous. But the actors have such fun making fun of these self-evidently absurd characters that the threat to our composure they might represent is minimized. The iceberg does not seem so deep or so treacherous. It seems significant that the people selected for sharp focus are in the public relations game. Moorehouse and Savage are early Madison Avenue–which may be an effective symbol of general emptiness at that, but the rest of us *know* we're not Madison Avenue, so that as an all-inclusive symbol it is bound to fail. The play ends with Dick Savage settling smugly and cynically into his new role as a titan in the field. I suppose that is the "message" for the "here and now"–here is the menace in American life. This is certainly part of the truth–but is such a *fashionable* thing to attack.

Greater depths are hinted at in the play: the wonderfully comic World War I private soldier–an American Schweik–bombarded on all sides by voices filling the air with platitudes and patriotic slogans, plaintively asking, "Can't anyone tell me how to get back to my outfit?"; the unutterably sad scenes between Joe and Janey Williams amidst the shabby-genteel pretensions of Georgetown; the savage irony in the passages dealing with the selection of an Unknown Soldier. The raw bitterness is occasionally there–the play still says more than most contemporary works–but for the most part it serves as a counterpoint, teasing the imagination.

The emphasis in the Biographies is necessarily selective and interestingly slanted. Five biographies are offered: the Wright Brothers, Debs, Valentino, Henry Ford, Isidora Duncan. Isidora's portrait is last and receives the fullest and most "dramatic" treatment, as if it were intended to be the symbolic center of the play. The note that a society is hostile to its most sensitive people is certainly a serious one and should be sounded clearly and unambiguously, to lodge implacably in our minds and hearts and do its transforming work. But here, too, the effect is muffled: Isidora, after all, was terribly eccentric (and who can say she was driven to it by our hostility?), and her mode of life too remote to make a full assault upon the audience's sensibilities. Everyone knows we have treated an occasional artist shabbily–but times have changed, and besides, Isidora had her glory.

I think there are Biographies in the book, and stories, that would lie upon us like open wounds, but they were not done. Instead, a narrator reminds us at the close of the play that "U.S.A. is the lives of its people,"–forgetful of all those who did not receive a hearing–and smiles at us. We smile back. The lights go up; the playing is over.

–*Massachusetts Review,* 1 (Winter 1960):
60–61, 64–67

# INITIAL CRITICAL RECEPTION

Three Soldiers *(1921) and* Manhattan Transfer *(1925) had provided Dos Passos with a reputation as one of the most innovative and striking members of the postwar generation of new American novelists. All three novels of* U.S.A. *were therefore widely reviewed in major magazines and newspaper book-review sections of the day, often by reviewers and critics of considerable prominence. The reviews selected for inclusion are those that constitute characteristic contemporary responses, both positive and negative, to each of the novels in the trilogy and that also suggest— often with surprising insight, given the pressures of periodical reviewing—permanent issues in the interpretation of the work. Except in a few instances, all reviews are presented in their entirety.*

## Reviews of *The 42nd Parallel* (1930)

*Many reviewers were mystified by* The 42nd Parallel. *Some questions, either posed directly or implicit in the reviewer's irritation with the unusual form of the work, were: Was* The 42nd Parallel *the first in a series of novels? What relationship did its distinctive parts (its four modes) have to the overall intent of the work? What, indeed, was that intent? A few reviewers usefully turned back to* Manhattan Transfer *for guidance, while others struggled to site the innovative form of the novel in a modernistic aesthetic. The notes struck in this effort were to characterize much of the criticism of* U.S.A. *during the near decade between the appearance of* The 42nd Parallel *and the publication of the full trilogy in 1938.*

*Almost all reviewers of* The 42nd Parallel, *for example, felt a need to describe and explain each of the four modes making up the work, with frequent agreement that the narratives were thin in characterization, the newsreels amusing but perhaps unnecessary, the Camera Eye incomprehensible, and the biographies admirable in their tart conciseness. As for the larger meaning of the work, comments ranged from complete bafflement (its only unity, one reviewer noted, was "that suggested by its binding") to a facile linking of the work to the "futilitarian" naturalistic school of American fiction (in short, little "affirmation" could be found in its portrayal of modern American life). Yet, there was on the whole a recognition that Dos Passos was attempting to write a novel of depth and importance about the nature of twentieth-century American experience. As Edmund Wilson trenchantly put it, Dos Passos "seems to be the only novelist of his generation who is concerned with the large questions of politics and society."*

## Where Storms Meet the Ocean
Mary Ross

*English born and educated, Mary Ross was principally a poet. In 1932 she also reviewed* Nineteen-Nineteen *for the* New York Herald Tribune.

From an old book on American climatology John Dos Passos draws his title. General storms, says its author, travel eastward across the United States from the Rockies to the Atlantic along three paths or tracks, of which the central corresponds roughly to the forty-second parallel of latitude. And at the end of the path, where the storms meets the ocean, rests New York. In this book, a brave experiment in dynamic fiction, Mr. Dos Passos shows the eddying currents of individual lives that ultimately blow through or into the metropolis.

Though four years have passed since the author's preceding novel, "Manhattan Transfer," I can still feel beating in my memory its bright, sharp rhythms, the jangled, unorderly music of the Manhattan of dusty or rain-swept streets, taxis, trucks, steam riveting, jazz and symphonies. Behind its hurrying beat lay only the dim backgrounds that fed their youth into it. "The terrible thing about having New York go stale on you," said one of the people in "Manhattan Transfer," "is that there's nowhere else. It's the top of the world. All we can do is to go round and round in a squirrel cage."

Here Mr. Dos Passos starts not at the center of the maelstrom but out on its periphery, in small towns, on lonely farms, with flickering glimpses of Paris, London, Pittsburgh, San Francisco, Mexico, Chicago, Washington, showing the devious ways in which human atoms are finally drawn into the spinning circle.

There is Mac, who learned printing in Chicago, peddled tracts and pornography from a buggy in Michigan, fought with the wobblies on the west coast, married because he had to and made an honest try at domesticity in Los Angeles, followed revolution in Mexico and found himself running a bookstore till revolution came too realistically his way. There is Eleanor Stoddard, who swore she would die if ever a man touched her, and became an interior decorator in Chicago and a devoted (platonic) friend of a public relations counselor in New York and went to France with the American Red Cross. And then Ward Moorehouse, who started in Wilmington, promoted real estate at a Maryland beach, married the unhappily adventurous daughter of an innocent Philadelphia doctor, divorced her, rose to eminence in publicity on the fortunes of a Pittsburgh heiress and finally helped regulate the war from New York with the services of Janey and inspiration of Eleanor. And, finally, Charlie [*sic*] Anderson, whose mother kept a railroad boarding house near the

*Dust jacket for the first edition of the first volume in the U.S.A. trilogy, published in 1930 (Collection of Richard Layman)*

station at Fargo, N.D., who learned to tinker with Fords, eluded matrimony by a hairbreadth, hopped and worked his way through Milwaukee, Chicago, St. Louis and finally on to New Orleans at the time of the Mardi Gras and cleared out to New York in time to join the Ambulance Corps. And about these five the multitude of people whom they passed, ate or flirted with, fought, pursued or fled from.

Behind them, by an intricate structure of breaks in the narratives, Mr. Dos Passos suggests the evolution of America from the '90s on to the start of the Great War. The book has five main sections, each in turn subdivided into sections that deal respectively with Mac, Eleanor, Janey and the rest, into a series of passages headed "The Camera Eye," "Newsreel" and isolated portraits of Americans. "The Camera Eye" in a succession of flashes, twenty-seven in all, carrying the thread of time subjectively in the recollections of a boy as he grows on from childhood through adolescence—bright fragments of memory of walks, cabs, boats, vistas and visitors, on to college, war meetings in Madison Square Garden, the steamer going to France. "Newsreel" is another series of snatches, carried out in contemporary newspaper headlines, the doggerel of popular songs, fragments from the accounts of passing events, all jumbled together. And interspersed among these and the narratives are passages of a page or two set apart from the rest typographically on "Lover of Humanity," Eugene Debs, "The Plant Wizard," Luther Burbank, "Big Bill" Haywood, Bryan, Minor C. Keith ("Emperor of the Caribbean"), Andrew Carnegie, Edison, Steinmetz and "Fighting Bob" La Follette.

Such a book abandons the ordinary structures of fiction for a form as intricate as that of a symphony. It gives no satisfaction at all for those who would know how the story "comes out." Its main theme would seem to be nothing less than life in America through three decades, with a range from coast to coast, from top to bottom of the economic scale, from the sublime to the ridiculous in emotions. It is often excessively irritating in its demands on the reader's attention and imagination—and absorbing in the vividness and diversity of full moments of living it beckons from hither and yon. Like all of Mr. Dos Passos's writing, it has the poet's acuteness of sensuous perception—sights, sounds, smells, tastes, that fairly leap from the print to engulf you. Occasionally a whole page comes as clear and true as a lyric—for example, "The Camera Eye (25)," the nostalgia of spring night in Harvard Square.

Yet if "Manhattan Transfer" was baffling in the almost indiscriminate richness of its texture, "The 42nd Parallel" is doubly so, in its added range of time and place, its bombardment of ideas, types, social movements and individual lives. One cannot but admire the range of perception and sympathy that makes possible such a book, the stimulating courage that essays a synthesis of time, class, geography and social theory. For I believe the author's intention is not encyclopedic, as the listing of the substance of his book implies; nor yet a self-conscious attempt to startle and impress by doing The Big Thing in a big way. Mr. Dos Passos is groping toward some new approach that would catch life whole and living without the little frames that one's individual limitations and traditions impose on it. Despite its weight of concreteness, "The 42nd Parallel" becomes in the end a search for generalization, as a spectrum whirled on a disk shows solid white. All these sights and sounds and flavors, realized so acutely, seem to be means to an end—an end which is not clear. And because of this unasked and unanswered question—the bafflement which seems to me inherent in the book itself—the reader, too, ends with a sense of confusion. In attempting through the individual to wipe out the individual, going "round and round in a squirrel cage," searching for an end in a circle, "The 42nd Parallel" attains a brave and often stirring futility.

—*New York Herald Tribune Books*,
13 February 1930,
pp. 3–4

### John Dos Passos Satirizes an America "On the Make"
John Chamberlain

*John Chamberlain had a lengthy career as a literary and social critic. In 1930 he was an assistant editor of* The New York Times Book Review. *His widely read* Farewell to Reform *was published in 1932.*

This novel is a satire on the tremendous haphazardness of life in the expansionist America we all have known, the America which came into birth with the defeat of Jefferson's dream of an agricultural democracy, which grew by leaps and bounds and railroad scandals after the Civil War, and which flowered in the period between the Spanish-American War and the stock market crash of last Autumn, which Stuart Chase regards as a sort of punctuation mark. It is an America distinctly "on the make" that Mr. Dos Passos satirizes, an America filled with people with vague hopes of success—no matter what success. There are no "old" Americans in the book—"old," that is, in the sense that Justice Holmes is an "old" American; and there are no "new" Americans in it of the breed that, happily, one discerns here and there already—"new" Americans whose ideals are not wholly of the counting house. There have been intimations that the book—called "The 42nd Parallel" after a mythical line on the maps that cuts through the

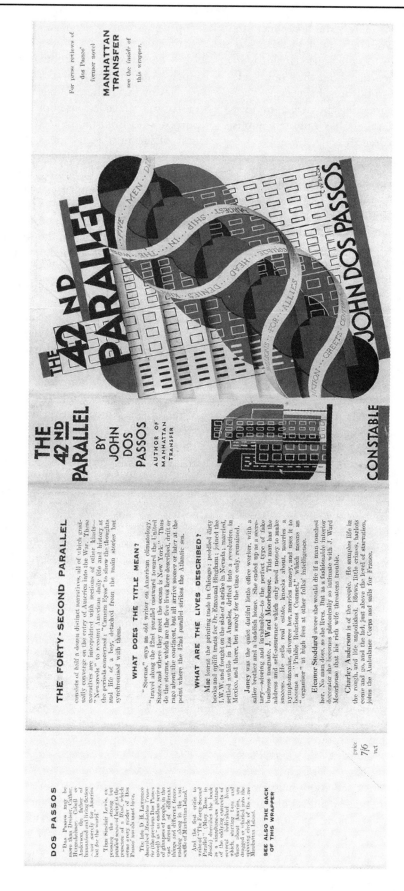

*Dust jacket for the first British edition of the first volume in the U.S.A. trilogy, published in 1930 (Collection of Richard Layman)*

heart of the United States—is merely the first panel in a series of novels that will, ultimately, attempt to satirize the effect of Americanization on the world. If this is so (and the generally unfinished air about the book leads us to believe it is so), the publishers have done their author a disservice in not spreading the news, for, as it now stands, "The 42nd Parallel" has only a tenuous sort of unity; it does not coalesce.

The technique of the novel owes something to Joyce, and something to the expressionism that John Howard Lawson has made familiar to theatregoers, the expressionism of "Processional." Fortunately, however, Mr. Dos Passos has stopped a long way short of going the whole hog with the authors who contribute to transition; he has realized that effective art must draw a balance between expression and communication. The actual stories of his five characters are all told in straightaway prose with overtones of satire, a satire that is kindly where Mr. Dos Passos deems kindliness to be in order, and decidedly acidulous in the case of J. Ward Moorehouse, who became an "eminent Public Relations Counsel" (John Dewey's symbol of the present-day America) with the aid of his wife's fortune.

Between the stories of Mac, the "wobbly"; of Janey, the congenial private secretary from Washington, D.C.; of the egregious Mr. Moorehouse who "used to be a newspaper man himself once"; of Eleanor, the interior decorator from Chicago, and of Charley, the drifting young man from the Farmer-Laborite stronghold of the Northwest, Mr. Dos Passos has inserted some "trick stuff" designed to draw his readers into the mood of his book. He has divided the trick stuff into three sorts of features, one a "newsreel" feature, which jumbles up newspaper headlines and snatches of popular song; one a "camera eye" feature which, with its memories of the visitation of Halley's Comet and of days in the Harvard Yard, is evidently intended to inform the reader of Mr. Dos Passos's stations of observation during the period spanned by the novel; and the third—and most effective, from a philosophical standpoint—a series of Whitmanesque biographies of famous Americans, Steinmetz, Edison, Burbank and La Follette, with cross reference to Henry Ford. This last feature is carried out in rough, chanting lines, but instead of singing of brotherly love, as Whitman did, Dos Passos points his rude song to bring out social ironies. Edison and Ford, as leaders, never "worried about mathematics or the social system or generalized philosophical concepts," in Mr. Dos Passos's opinion, and this lack of worry in the leaders has, the novel implicitly states, filtered down until it has affected all the characters in the book, even Mac, who isn't a "wobbly" for any burning love of humanity, but simply because it gives his energy scope for activity when he and his wife have come to a parting of the ways.

The stories of the five characters do not all touch—which is one indication that Mr. Dos Passos has not finished with them. While one realizes that Mr. Dos Passos may have left his book at loose ends for esthetic purposes—to bring home to the reader the haphazardness of life in a social milieu that shifts as the sands shift—one is left dissatisfied. One feels that his novel is still in a state of nature, that his own point of view, his own philosophical approach, has not been clearly indicated.

As for Americanization and the world, Mr. Dos Passos touches on this in the Mexico City interlude of Mac, in the visit of Moorehouse to Mexico, and points the way, perhaps, to more on this subject by shipping Charley, his last character, off to France on his penultimate page. The various people of the book, all of whom are thrown from pillar to post and none of whom has any clear idea of the end involved in taking any particular step, are made palpable, but only roughly and objectively so. The book being satire, Mr. Dos Passos has "interpreted" his people in terms of irony to emphasize aimlessness, and probably not one of them would recognize his or her portrait in Mr. Dos Passos's pages. The book, therefore, falls short of being sheerly creative, but it remains, in extenuation, very effective social castigation. And in writing of people who are not unduly troubled by ideas, Mr. Dos Passos has not made the mistake of John Herrmann or Morley Callaghan, for, while his prose is far from the shapely sort of prose that distinguishes Glenway Wescott, and Miss Roberts, it does not run into the deadly "tum tum tum" formula. It could hardly be as shapely as the prose cultivated by Wescott and Roberts, because he is dealing not with an older (and saner?) America, but with a newer American world whose matrix is often rough and out at the edge.

—*New York Times Book Review,* 2 March 1930, p. 5

### Kaleidoscope
### Henry Hazlitt

*Henry Hazlitt was literary editor of* The Nation *in 1930. He later became an editor for* The New York Times *and had a long career as a writer on economic issues.*

The most striking quality about "The 42nd Parallel" is its structure. It is built after the manner of Aldous Huxley's "Point Counter Point" and of Mr. Dos Passos's own "Manhattan Transfer," but in one or two respects it is more intricate than either. It is really five novels shuffled together; among these are also shuffled excerpts called The Camera Eye and Newsreel. One reads, say, forty pages about the adventures of Mac, then a camera eye, then a newsreel, then a three-page biography of Debs, then thirty pages about the adventures of Janey, then another newsreel, then more about Mac, and so on. Toward the end the paths of two or three of the main characters cross, but haphazardly; there is no general drawing together of the threads, no climax, no rounding-out of anyone's story; things simply leave off, arbitrarily, anywhere.

It would be difficult to point to any unity in the book except that supplied by the binding. The forty-second parallel, as the reader will recall, is that imaginary circle of latitude which passes roughly through Chicago and slightly north of New York. But many of the events in the present volume happen in Mexico, New Orleans, and Paris. Apart from style and treatment, the themes have chiefly in common the fact that they represent various aspects of life in these United States. We begin with Mac, who picks up a job peddling Boccaccio and "The Queen of the White Slaves," gets a girl into trouble, marries her, deserts her, becomes a wobbly, drifts to Mexico, lives with a Mexican girl, runs a bookstore for a time. Next we follow Janey, who ends by becoming the adoring secretary of J. Ward Moorehouse, a go-getter and platitudinarian who has risen from a real-estate salesman and reporter to a public-relations counsel, and has married first the dissolute daughter of a nose-and-throat specialist and then, having divorced her, a Pittsburgh heiress, after he has spent the night with the latter on the day following her father's death. Next we come to Eleanor, who as a girl swears that she will kill herself if a man ever touches her; she becomes an interior decorator and enters into a platonic friendship with Moorehouse. We end with Charley, who drifts around as a garage mechanic, and doesn't marry his girl after she has been seduced by his friend. He winds up on a boat off for the war in France.

Mr. Dos Passos is a writer of extraordinary talent; he knows American cities, he knows a great deal about life, he has a shrewd insight into men and women. "The 42nd Parallel" is full of amusing incidents, and at times, particularly in the early pages, it is absorbing. But it leaves one wondering whether Dos Passos's present method is not more a handicap than a help to him. This kaleidoscopic shaking of the fragments of several novels into one no longer has the attraction of novelty and its other advantages are not always clear. Dos Passos's present prose, too, seems to me greatly inferior to the prose of his "Three Soldiers." What he does here is simply to omit commas from their conventional places, link his statements together with the conjunction "and" as a substitute, and run phrases, nouns, and adjectives into single words, such as (all of

JOHN DOS PASSOS

# DER 42. BREITEN- GRAD

ROMAN

S. FISCHER VERLAG

*Title page for the first German translation of* The 42nd Parallel, *published in 1930 (Collection of Richard Layman)*

these are from his first paragraph) "fourfamily," "whaleoil," "cavechested," "blondegrey," "nightwatchman."

The net result of these mannerisms, which have already become stereotyped in the writing of the whole school of "new barbarians," is that the style of one member of the school has become almost indistinguishable from that of another. It is a prose that rapidly tends to become monotonous. It may be said in defense of such undistinguished writing that it is perfectly adapted to record, as it does here, the adventures of undistinguished people. But where the characters are so aimless and unimportant the novel itself may come to seem aimless and unimportant. Dos Passos's men are interested only in women, liquor, and money; nearly all of them pass through the same weary cycles. Even the reds and revolutionists that he presents with sympathy are so much driftwood, without persistence, ambition, emotional or intellectual discipline. The reader sees the tired cynical smile on the face of the narrator, and begins to feel almost as tired himself. "The 42nd Parallel," in brief, shares the capital danger of all futilitarianism in fiction: the fiction is apt to seem as futile as the events it records.

I must, however, bear witness to the fascination of the nineteen "newsreels" scattered through the book. Here the kaleidoscopic method achieves some brilliant effects. Newspaper headlines, fragments of contemporary speeches, snatches of popular songs of each year, are splattered on the page apparently at random but actually with great skill. These newsreels, which begin with the dawn of the present century and end with the year of America's entrance into the World War, not only indicate the cultural background of each period of the story, but supply an amazingly compact history that combines the merits of Thomas Beer and Mark Sullivan. They reveal admirably the mores of each year, and are so arranged that one news item becomes a subtly ironic commentary on the next.

—*Nation*, 130 (12 March 1930): 298

## Dahlberg, Dos Passos, and Wilder
Edmund Wilson

*Edmund Wilson was to become a major American literary and social critic and perhaps the last man of letters in America. From 1926 to 1931 he was an associate editor of* The New Republic. Axel's Castle, *his first significant literary study, was published in 1931. During the late 1930s he and Dos Passos shared a common disassociation from the Left. Wilson's review also includes discussions of Thornton Wilder's* The Woman of Andros *(1930) and Edward Dahlberg's* Bottom Dogs *(1930), which are here omitted.*

. . . . . . . . .

Now Dos Passos, in "The 42nd Parallel," has consciously and deliberately worked out a literary medium curiously and strikingly similar to Dahlberg's. "The 42nd Parallel," which it seems to me Dos Passos's publishers have made a great mistake in not announcing for what it is: the first section of a novel on a large scale, is to deal with the role of the United States in the western world during the first years of the present century; but though it is written from the point of view of an unusually internationally minded American of unusually complete culture, the author has been able to immerse himself in the minds and the lives of his middle-class characters, to identify himself with them, to a degree which must astonish any reader of Dos Passos's other novels. In this respect, "The 42nd Parallel" is quite different from "Manhattan Transfer" and marks a striking advance beyond it. "Manhattan Transfer," after all, might almost

have been written by a very intelligent and well documented foreigner: the characters are seen from the outside and, in consequence, seem sometimes scarcely human. But in his new novel, Dos Passos has abandoned all the literary baggage which encumbered his exploration of New York—there are no elaborately painted descriptions and no Joycian prose poems. Dos Passos has studied Anita Loos and Ring Lardner for the method of "The 42nd Parallel," and he is perhaps the first really important writer to have succeeded in using colloquial American for a novel of the highest artistic seriousness. This has enabled him to keep us close to the characters as we never were in "Manhattan Transfer." Dos Passos, in "The 42nd Parallel," is not without his characteristic moments of allowing his people to lapse into two-dimensional caricatures of qualities or forces which he hates; but, in general, he has made us live their lives, see the American world through their eyes.

The characters of "The 42nd Parallel" almost all belong to the white-collar class—almost all begin as obscure and sufficiently commonplace-appearing people who are anxious to improve their condition from the point of view of ordinary American ideals. The stenographer from Washington, the publicity director from Wilmington, the interior decorator from Chicago, have no intimation of any other values than those of the American business offices, of the American advertising game, of the American trade in luxury, where they make their salaries and conceive their ambitions. Only the nephew of the radical Irish printer finds himself discontented with the life of the white-collar class and tends to identify his interests with those of a proletariat. The author introduces each of his five main characters separately—we read the complete continuous history of each from childhood. Dos Passos has hit upon a method of swift close narration which enables him to present an immense amount of material with astonishing ease and speed—we seem to know all about his people's lives: all the members of their families, all their friends, all their amusements and periods of stagnation, all the places where they work and how much they get, all the meals they eat, all the beds they sleep in. And without any explicit commentary of the author, each of these series of incidents and details creates an unmistakable character. Eleanor Stoddard's cold-blooded shrewdness and passionate appetite for refinement, J. Ward Moorhouse's well-meaning and unconscious charlatanry, are presented entirely in terms of *things*. And when these commonplace individuals, who have been introduced independently of one another, are finally put into relation with one another, further significances begin to appear—we realize that what we have been witnessing is the making of our own contemporary society. And as Dos Passos marks in masterly fashion—always without explicit comment—the shift from one American city to another, so that we understand, without, apparently, having been told, the difference between the way people behave and feel in Chicago and the way they behave and feel in New York, in Washington, Minneapolis, Pittsburgh or Mexico City; so—also without, apparently, being told—we finally begin to understand the national character of America. Dos Passos has sandwiched in between the sections of the life-histories of his characters "newsreels" which are medleys of newspaper-clippings and which remind us of the American public consciousness contemporary with the private events of which we have just been hearing, and brief biographies (very well done) of eminent contemporary Americans, all hampered or perverted or stunted by that same middle-class commercial society in which the characters of the novel are submerged. And at the end of this first instalment of his story, with the entrance of the United States into the War and the introduction of the last of the characters, a young garageman from North Dakota, who in his wanderings around the country has fallen in with a rich and drunken cracker from Okechobee City and been persuaded that he ought to go over and see the fun "before the whole thing goes belly-up"—Dos Passos, in the perfectly aimed final paragraphs, shows us this character suddenly as a symbol of the United States, provincial, adventurous, well-intentioned, immature, going out from its enormous country into a world of which it knows nothing:

A week later they were on the Chicago of the French Line steaming out through the Narrows. They had hangovers from their farewell party and felt a little sick from the smell of the boat and still had the music of the jazz band on the wharf ringing through their heads. . . . They had wine with their first meal. There was a whole tableful of other guys going over in the ambulance service.

After dinner Doc went down to the cabin to go to sleep. Charley roamed around the ship with his hands in his pockets without knowing what to do with himself. In the stern they were taking the canvas cover off the seventyfive gun. He walked round the lowerdeck full of barrels and packingcases and stumbled across coils of big fuzzy cable to the bow. In the bow there was a little pinkfaced French sailor with a red tassel on his cap stationed as a lookout.

The sea was glassy, with dirty undulating patches of weed and garbage. There were gulls sitting on the water or perched on bits of floating wood. Now and then a gull stretched its wings lazily and flew off crying.

The boat's bluff bow cut two even waves through dense glassgreen water. Charley tried to talk to the lookout. He pointed ahead, "East," he said, "France."

The lookout paid no attention. Charley pointed back toward the smoky west. "West," he said and tapped himself on the chest. "My home Fargo North Dakota." But the lookout just shook his head and put his finger to his lips.

"France very far east . . . submarines . . . war," said Charley. The lookout put his hand over his mouth. At last he made Charley understand that he wasn't supposed to talk to him.

"The 42nd Parallel," when it is finished, may well turn out to be the most important novel which any American of Dos Passos's generation has written. Dos Passos seems the only novelist of this generation who is concerned with the large questions of politics and society; and he has succeeded in this book in bridging the gap, which is wider in America than anywhere else and which presents itself as a perpetual problem to American literature and thought, between the special concerns of the intellectual and the general pursuits and ideas of the people. The task of the intellectual is to make his symbols and his ideas *seem* relevant to the common life even when they actually are—to express them in terms of the real American world without either cheapening them or rendering them vacuous. Dos Passos, who has read as much and traveled as widely as Wilder, does not always avoid spinning literature—especially in the first Huckleberry Finn section of "The 42nd Parallel"—when he should give us a first-hand impression of reality; and, in consequence, he is sometimes flimsy, where Dahlberg dealing with a similar subject, would be authentic and hard. But though in intensity and execution "The 42nd Parallel" is not superior to Hemingway, for example, from the point of view of its literary originality and its intellectual interest, it seems to me by far the most remarkable, the most encouraging American novel which I have read since the War.

—*New Republic,* 62 (26 March 1930): 157–158

**The 42nd Parallel**
Unsigned review

Like *Manhattan Transfer,* this book is experimental in form. It contains four series of compositions, arranged like a scrapbook with no apparent order. These are: (1) short biographies of noted Americans, told in a form bordering on free verse, with considerable seasoning of Menckenesque irony; (2) "news-reel"; (3) "the camera eye"; and (4) five tales, told in excerpts, about two hobos, a publicity man, and two working girls.

The nineteen sections of the "news-reel" are arranged chronologically within the years 1900–1917. They are pastiches of scraps of headlines and news-stories and popular songs, and must represent considerable grubbing in old files. In expressionistic style they give vivid ironical pictures of the times they represent.

In the "camera eye" Mr. Dos Passos once again indulges in Joycean expressionism. These twenty-seven short passages present scoops from the stream of consciousness of some youth—perhaps the author?—from infancy to manhood. Here the author carefully shuns hyphens and coherency.

But these are mere interludes in Mr. Dos Passos's vaudeville program. The reader finds real interest, if anywhere, in the five tales. These are told in that carefully naïve condensed, colloquial style that Ernest Hemingway, among the followers of Stein and Joyce, has most successfully affected. They are, in pleasant contrast to the interludes, perfectly coherent, and contain abundance of vivid and convincing observations of life, particularly on its seamy side. The five characters' peregrinations take them all over the North American continent, and display, on the part of the author, an extraordinary knowledge of local color, particularly that tint seen in bawdy houses and saloons.

Despite the vividness of detail, however, the total effect is disappointment. In *Manhattan Transfer* one felt a unified theme: an attempt to portray the disordered complexity of the life of a great city. The author's scrapbook technique was, in view of this theme, justified. Here there is no such justification. From the title and the opening quotation on meteorology one is led to hunt a geographical motif, and one is unsuccessful. Such a motif would seem *a priori* rather futile; and as a matter of fact the characters range from Winnipeg to Mexico City. At the end we willingly suspect the author of a not very funny joke at our expense.

Apart from the title, the characters, though some of them meet, lead unrelated and insignificant lives, and not one of their stories has, in an artistic sense, an ending. Perhaps the author has given himself to that naturalistic creed which denies the existence of ends in life, and hence refuses to make endings in fiction. It remains a fact about human nature, however, that readers most enjoy stories which, in Aristotle's phrase, have a beginning, a middle—and an end. Finally, the very absence of any coherent scheme and of any explicit underlying idea, coupled with the author's bitter naturalism, yields an impression of futility. One must conclude that here again we have a sample of the naturalistic pessimism and spiritual anarchy which mark our age.

                                        —*Bookman*, 72 (April 1930): 210–211

## John Dos Passos: American Writer
Upton Sinclair

*Upton Sinclair achieved fame in 1906 with the publication of* The Jungle, *his socialist-inspired fictional exposé of the Chicago meatpacking industry. He remained throughout his life a socialist activist and novelist. The* New Masses *was the principal literary organ of the American Left during the 1930s.*

Two or three years ago I stood on a street corner in New York for half an hour, arguing with John Dos Passos about the form of the novel. It was the right sort of place, the sort he likes, with plenty of rattle of machinery, honk of automobile horns, and other evidences of mass activity. I was trying to make an impression on him. What I said was, in brief this:

"I have just been reading *Manhattan Transfer*. You have put into it the material for several great novels, and also the talent, insight, and knowledge of our times. But for me you spoiled it by that kaleidoscope form you put it into; giving me little glimpses of one character after another—and so many characters, and switching them back and forth, so fast, that I lost track of the stories, and half the time couldn't be sure which was which. It is my belief that if you would put into a plain, straightaway narrative the passion and humor that is lost in *Manhattan Transfer,* you would have a great novel."

I didn't know if I produced any impression; so I looked into *The 42nd Parallel* with no little curiosity. What I found this time is a sort of compromise between the two forms. The jazz effects are still here, but we get larger chunks of story, and so we don't lose track of them. What we have really is five novelettes, tied together with frail and slender threads. In between the chapters is a lot of vaudeville material, some of it funny, and some of it interesting, and some of it just plain puzzling to my old-fashioned mentality. Let us dispose of this vaudeville material first.

Some of the sections are called "Newsreel," and consist of a jumble of newspaper headlines. All newspaper headlines are absurd, as soon as they become a year or two old. They are like our fashions: revealing a stupid and vicious people trying to appear magnificent and important to themselves. We are willing to see them ridiculed, just so soon as they are out of date—that is, when they no longer touch our present delusions. Anyone may laugh at "Teddy" Roosevelt and at Harding; but of course he mustn't laugh at the great engineer who is curing unemployment by blowing blasts of false statistics.

Another set of interpolations tells us about some of the leaders of that time: Debs, Bryan, Burbank, Lafollette, Bill Haywood, etc. These are interesting enough, and as they are short, we don't mind them especially. But I cannot say the same about the third variety called "The Camera Eye." These are queer glimpses of almost anything, having nothing to do with the story or stories, and told as if they were fragments from an author's notebook, or perhaps from his dreams. Maybe they are what happened to Dos Passos himself as he grew up through this period of his novel. Maybe he will tell me some day. He hasn't told in this book.

Now for the five main stories. First, Mac, a working- boy who turns Wobbly, and gets into the Mexican revolution. Second, Janey, a girl whose home life is unhappy, and who becomes a stenographer. Third, J. Ward Moorehouse, a lad who is bound to rise in the world, and becomes a "public relations counsel," one of those magnificent, "Poison Ivy" Lee creatures who for a hundred thousand dollars or two will cause the American public to believe that glycerine mixed with toilet perfume will cure pyorrhea, or that high wages are bad for public morality. Fourth, Eleanor Stoddard, a young lady seeking culture, who learns to decorate homes for the rich. And fifth, Charley, another working-boy, who goes to the war.

The ties which bind these five into the narrative are of the very thinnest. Mac sees and hears about Moorehouse while the latter is doing his stuff on behalf of the American oil crowd in Mexico. Janey is there as Moorehouse's stenographer. Eleanor does some decorating for Moorehouse, and becomes his high-minded friend. As for Charley, who comes in at the very end, all he does is to hear about Moorehouse. One can imagine Dos Passos saying to himself: "Go to, I am sick of these closely knit novels, which are viciously contrived. I am going to write a novel that is like life itself, in which most of the boys whom Moorehouse helped send to war don't ever do any more than just hear him mentioned."

All right, Dos, that is according to reality. But then, I point out to you that it is also according to reality that the great J. Ward Moorehouse knows a whole lot of people, and why couldn't we have had these in the novel, just as well as those who didn't know him? The point of my kick is not any delusion about the ancient "unities" of a work of art, but merely the fundamental fact of human psychology, that when we have got interested in a person we want to know more about him; and if, after you have got our interest all worked up, you just shunt us off to some other character, we are not clear in our minds why you should have introduced us to either one. J. Ward Moorehouse is, I venture to assert, one of the most convincing characters in modern fiction, a real creation, simply gorgeous, and I am grumbling because, instead of telling me all I want to know about him, you switch me off to Charley, who is all right too, only less so, and who comes in at the very end, when there isn't room to tell me much about him.

If Dos Passos won't take my word, maybe he will take the example of Theodore Dreiser. When it comes to writing, Dos can make circles around Dreiser—who is, I firmly believe, the very worst great writer in the world. Also Dos has a clearer mind, he knows the revolutionary movement, which puts him a whole generation ahead of Dreiser's old-fashioned muddlement and despair. Furthermore, Dos has an impish humor, a quite heavenly impishness, if you know what I mean. All these gifts ought to make him our greatest novelist, and the one reason they don't is that he is so afraid of being naive that he can't bring himself to sit down and tell us a plain straight story, that we can follow without having to stand on our heads now and then, or else turn the page upside down. Dreiser is not afraid to be naive, he is willing to take a common ordinary bell-hop, and tell us about him to the extent of some four hundred thousand words—miserably written words, many of them—and yet, at the end he gets hold of us so that he was able to make a best seller out of a story that ends with the electric chair.

While I am registering my kicks, I want to beg Dos Passos to use a dictionary. His book is full of the sort of errors which publishers and printers' readers usually take care of. Molasses gets an extra "l" while Lafollette loses one. Such common names as Bismarck, Folkestone and Dick Whittington each lose a letter. Bill Haywood is Heywood four times and Haywood only twice. Sometimes there are errors which may be jokes, who can say? On page 79 "Mac dosed off to sleep," and on the same page "a dog barked at him and worried his angles." That is the sort of thing with which James Joyce is amusing himself in his new effusion—only you have to know twenty or thirty languages, and all history, ancient and modern, to appreciate the Joyce puns—and I am never going to.

Also, I want to know, just as a matter of curiosity, why the punctuation mark known as the hyphen should be considered counter-revolutionary. I noted one or two in the book, but I think they got in by accident. Dos Passos runs his compound words together, and when first our eye lights on them, we may not sort out the syllables correctly; I didn't, and got some funny effects—such as "riverbed" and "gass-tove" and "teaser-vice" and "co-algas" and "musicle-ssons."

Enough with fault finding. I want Dos Passos to be the great American novelist, as he is entitled to be. I want him to "become as a little child" again, and tell us a good, straight, bedtime story, to keep us awake all night. The reason I take the trouble to write this discourse, is because, in spite of all the handicaps he takes upon himself, he has written the most interesting novel I have read in many a long day. I happened recently to read the last volume of Paul Elmer More, in which that very august academic gentleman, leader of the so-called "Humanist" movement, condescends to refer to *Manhattan Transfer* as "an explosion in a sewer." Well, there is a little of the sewer in this new book also but not proportionately as much as there is in America and the lives of its people. I will conclude my review of *The 42nd Parallel* by the prophesy that they will be teaching this book in high schools in future years, when the teacher will have to go to some old encyclopedia to look up Paul Elmer More and the "humanists," in order to find out when they lived and what they taught.

—*New Masses*, 5 (April 1930): 18–19

## The 42nd Parallel
Unsigned review

The American novelists who are in rebellion against the standards of taste and conduct prevailing in the United States seem to be more and more bent on ruling the aesthetic element out of their novels. It is therefore difficult to understand upon what they base their appeal. Mr. John Dos Passos's last work THE 42ND PARALLEL (Constable, 7s. 6d. net) presents this problem in its starkest form. Though styled a novel, this book is a deliberate hotch-potch, to which the fanciful title—derived from the meteorological statement that storms from the American continent generally follow the 42nd parallel eastward—gives but an arbitrary unity. The fact that some of the characters finally drift eastwards to the War in France is not of any essential importance. What the author is obviously attempting is to extend the technique of that imaginative reporting which, together with Mr. Dreiser and Mr. Hemingway, he is aiming to substitute for the poetic unity of the traditional novel-form. The general object of this reporting is the swarming, hurried, material, amorphous life of the United States; and the method here employed by Mr. Dos Passos is to cut up life-stories of certain major characters into sections and sandwich them between interludes of several kinds—the "News-reel," which is a conglomeration of disparate news headings roughly illustrating a date; the "Camera Eye," which is in every instance a chunk of subjective mental flux from the brain-pan of an unnamed boy; and the pocket biographies of certain outstanding American personalities, drawn satirically to illustrate how heroes and geniuses are used in this world.

The major characters include Fainy McCreary, a boy of the people, who knocks about picking up a living as a printer, joins the I.W.W., marries at Los Angeles, and finally lives a somewhat joyously chequered life in Mexico; Charley Anderson, another boy of the people, who also drifts, satisfying his desires freely when he can, starving when he is "flat," and carousing at every opportunity till he finds himself bound for France as mechanic to an ambulance unit; J. Ward Moorhouse, the typical getter-on, who turns his brains into money by assiduous organizing and advertising till he becomes a "Public Relations Counsel," which means a big business intriguer in league with international finance; Janey, a nice little typist out of a poor home, with a rough but honest brother, who ends as Moorhouse's adoring secretary; and Eleanor Stoddard, a sexless but ambitious woman, who makes a living as an internal decorator of advanced taste and becomes the Platonic Egeria of Moorhouse. About the stories of these typical Americans there is nothing new to be said, just as there is nothing new in the method of their telling. Uncompromising, typical series of events, cleverly but unbeautifully told, about people who arouse few sparks of sympathy—that is all. The most effective sections, for their ruthlessness and the bitter contempt for contemporary standards which burns through them, are the biographical ones. Those of Luther Burbank, Big Bill Heywood, Eugene Debs, Andrew Carnegie, Edison, and Steinmetz are better reading than all the rest. In fact, poetry enters this novel, paradoxically enough, in the portions that are least fictitious; whereas the lives of Janey, Charley, and the rest are devoid of climax, rhythm, or proportion. This over-production of "life" unadorned by the modernist American novelists is surely bringing its own slump with it.

—*Times Literary Supplement*,
4 September 1930,
p. 698

\* \* \*

## Reviews of *Nineteen-Nineteen* (1932)

*Since reviewers of the second volume of* U.S.A. *now had in hand a fuller representation of the nature and intent of the project, they often attempted a more elaborate definition of its genre. Dos Passos was seeking to write a "news novel" (that is, a documentary record of contemporary life); or his effort was "collectivistic"—to render American society as a whole; or he was motivated above all by his desire to contribute to the emerging genre of the "proletarian novel," a form that rendered American life from the perspective of the working class. What almost all reviewers agreed upon, however, was that* Nineteen-Nineteen *made even more apparent than had* The 42nd Parallel *Dos Passos's leftist sympathies. To many reviewers, in a reaction that was to characterize responses to his writing for the remainder of his long career, Dos Passos's seeming political allegiances were indeed the litmus test for the acceptability of his work. Thus, an affirmation of his radical sympathies in* U.S.A. *invariably included an endorsement of the power and quality of the novel (see Malcolm Cowley, for example), while a rejection of his "Communism" was usually accompanied by a denial of the artistry of the work (see Francis Fergusson, for example).*

### A Sad "Big Parade"
Matthew Josephson

*Matthew Josephson's* Zola and His Time *was published in 1928. During the 1930s he was a left-wing sympathizer and wrote regularly for* The New Republic *and* New Masses. *His extremely popular* The Robber Barons *(1934) was an exposé of the ruthless practices of nineteenth-century-American entrepreneurial capitalism.*

John Dos Passos has distinguished himself among contemporary novelists for ambition, resolution, and fecundity. Reading "1919" as a companion-piece to "The 42nd Parallel," as the second volume of a tetralogy—or is it to be perhaps an American "Comédie Humaine"?—one is enabled to glimpse much more of the hull of a huge literary cargo vessel, in the process of building, and to guess at the form of its upper decks and bridges. One tends to liken this series of historical novels, based upon the recent World War period, to Balzac's long work rather than to Zola's twenty-volume epic of "The Rougon-Macquarts" or to Thomas Mann's "Buddenbrooks," because both of the latter were confined to a single family, although Zola's, to be sure, was a family of a thousand members spreading into every corner of nineteenth century Europe. Proust, on the other hand, devoted himself solely to the upper class of French society.

JOHN DOS PASSOS

# 1919

HARCOURT, BRACE AND COMPANY

NEW YORK

*Title page for the first edition of the second novel in the U.S.A. trilogy, published in 1932. For the first edition of U.S.A. in 1938, the title was spelled out (Collection of Richard Layman).*

The size of the author's framework, his social-historical objective, must be borne in mind if one would not be confused by the quick, episodic shifting of scenes and characters. The hero of "1919" is not a single person, but a great crowd, and more specifically a group of types out of the crowd. From one to another of these types the eye of the novelist moves back and forth: now he records the fictive biography of a "wobbly" in the American Northwest, now of a hypocrite, Harvard intellectual, now of a common, drifting sailor, or of a big publicity agent, or a middle-class Chicago flapper. These chronicles are systematically interlarded with a section of "newsreel," which is composed of a picturesque summation of newspaper headlines of the period; also with brief "biographies" of period characters, as likely to be of

*Dust jacket for the 1932 edition of the second novel in the U.S.A. trilogy, which maintains the geographical motif of the dust jacket for the first edition of* The 42nd Parallel *(Collection of Richard Layman)*

underground revolutionary fame, like John Reed or Wesley Everest, as of wider public note, like J. P. Morgan or "Meester Veelson." The style of the historical digression, a loose, dithyrambic, occasionally brilliant (through imagery) free verse, offers a marked contrast to that of the main narrative, soberly colloquial, behavioristic, almost monosyllabic. Besides lending some artistic relief, the digressions also serve as a sort of vivid backdrop against which the characters pass in procession. Yet the general reader should not be greatly disturbed by the impressionistic and experimental interruptions; for each chapter of narrative is often a finished episode in itself, or a character portrait in action. Sometimes, as in the long opening chapter upon the sailor, Joe Williams, they form complete and absorbing novelettes in themselves.

If we feared, in reading "The 42nd Parallel," that we were watching too many disconnected characters and scenes falling apart, this fear subsides before the increased effectiveness of "1919." We sense the "collective" character of the various world-historical developments which, driving the characters of the Dos Passos epic before them, move toward the climax of the war's end.

The whole work is further unified by the author's consistent view of the history he deals with: this, it is perhaps embarrassing to relate, is nothing less than Marx's materialist conception of history as determined by the means of production. Indeed, the consistency of Dos Passos is his shining distinction. Ever since the World War, it seems to me, Dos Passos has stubbornly refused to believe either in the benevolence of American capitalism or in the wonders of American prosperity. Rather, he has been numbered among those who longed to see the present order exchanged for that of a socialist and proletarian state. And although such principles may seem vexing to many citizens who are perfectly aware that this is a free country, in which everyone is free to find a job and save money, it is necessary to touch upon them in passing so that the particular, grim color of Dos Passos's novel may be better understood.

It is a matter of little surprise, then, that the account of Dos Passos's troop of American characters in no way resembles a Horatio Alger fable. Here in "1919" there are only driven beasts, eating, drinking, fornicating, sliding always toward the line of least resistance. This qualification goes for the types who represent learning or heavy industry, as for the sailors, "wobblies," and up-to-date stenographers. Many gently bred readers may possibly be forced to shut their eyes and stop their noses at certain pages, since the novelist writes with so much deliberate "bad taste." On the other hand, Earl Carroll and a few movietones selected at random have left this reviewer wondering what there is that the American public may still be shocked by. The fecal is left—and Dos Passos does use this occasionally, like a naughty boy, to rouse us or horrify us out of our indifference.

In any case, Dos Passos, energetic and impassioned novelist, is leading the way—while groping at times—toward a proletarian literature; that is, a literature of revolution, something which certain of our critics have been calling for. His novels strike one as being far richer than those of the pedestrian Upton Sinclair (whom, however, he has resembled enough in point of view upon America to have won a considerable European success). He is more imaginative than Dreiser, more intelligent than Sinclair Lewis, and exceeds both these able *tendenz* novelists in natural culture. Dos Passos is little more than thirty-five; has written a dozen volumes of prose fiction and drama, and is improving in power. He has his pronounced limitations, over which, one hopes, his courage and will may prevail.

One may well quarrel with his style, for one thing. In the direct narrative of "1919" there is, plainly enough, a systematic avoidance of all rhetorical elegance, adherence only to bare, factual chronicle of outward movements, which admits of no "inwardness" in the characters. In this behavioristic manner certain of our modern neo-realists believe they approach their subject more closely than ever before, and without the intervention of sentiment. Yet it cannot be denied that such a method gives at times a monotonous and unlovely texture to the literary monolith which Dos Passos is building, however respectable his motives may be. Besides, he contradicts these motives in his digressive interludes which are done, as I have pointed out, in a picturesque and impressionistic free verse. On the whole, Dos Passos's innovations of language (ugly neologisms) and of style (a heedless colloquialism introduced into the text, a pell-mell syntax), seem neither appetizing nor important. Tolstoy wrote epic novels designed for universal reading without holding himself to a nearly monosyllabic vocabulary; Zola, save for the instance of one early novel, wrote a tolerably pure French; and both of them have been read by millions of proletarians.

One still has the feeling, finally, that Dos Passos portrays types rather than characters, though he does seem to work out the destiny of each type within the logical limits of heredity and background. One could wish that he had Hemingway's shrewd eye for character and the special accidents thereof, with which a bullfighter is pictured as so thoroughly a bullfighter. Yet if Dos Passos had such an eye, perhaps he would not have so remarkable a bird's-eye view for the collective and panoramic drama which he evokes in "1919."

*—Saturday Review*, 8 (19 March 1932): 600

## The Poet and the World
Malcolm Cowley

*Like Dos Passos, Malcolm Cowley went from Harvard to ambulance service on the western front and then spent several years as an expatriate before returning to America. He succeeded Edmund Wilson as literary editor of* The New Republic *and during the 1930s became one of the principal American Marxist literary critics. Cowley's* Exile's Return *(1934) is an autobiographical account of the expatriate movement of the 1920s. His distinction between two strains in Dos Passos's fiction, the poetic and radical, was extremely influential and became a commonplace in later discussions of Dos Passos's work.*

John Dos Passos is in reality two novelists. One of them is a late-Romantic, an individualist, an esthete moving about the world in a portable ivory tower; the other is a collectivist, a radical historian of the class struggle. These two authors have collaborated in all his books, but the first had the larger share in "Three Soldiers" and "Manhattan Transfer." The second, in his more convincing fashion, has written most of "The 42nd Parallel" and almost all of "1919." The difference between the late-Romantic and the radical Dos Passos is important not only in his own career: it also helps to explain the recent course of American fiction.

The late-Romantic tendency in his novels goes back to his years in college. After graduating from a good preparatory school, Dos Passos entered Harvard in 1912, at the beginning of a period which was later known as that of the Harvard esthetes. I have described this period elsewhere, in reviewing the poems of E. E. Cummings, but I did not discuss the ideas which underlay its picturesque manifestations, its mixture of incense, patchouli and gin, its erudition displayed before barroom mirrors, its dreams in the Cambridge subway of laurel-crowned Thessalian dancers. The esthetes themselves were not philosophers; they did not seek to define their attitude; but most of them would have subscribed to the following propositions:

That the cultivation and expression of his own sensibility are the only justifiable ends for a poet.

That originality is his principal virtue.

That society is hostile, stupid and unmanageable: it is the world of the philistines, from which it is the poet's duty and privilege to remain aloof.

That the poet is always misunderstood by the world. He should, in fact, deliberately make himself misunderstandable, for the greater glory of art.

That he triumphs over the world, at moments, by mystically including it within himself: these are his moments of *ecstasy,* to be provoked by any means in his power—alcohol, drugs, madness or saintliness, venery, suicide.

*Dust jacket for Melvin Landsberg's 1972 study that explores Dos Passos's life in relation to* U.S.A.
*(Collection of Richard Layman)*

That art, the undying expression of such moments, exists apart from the world; it is the poet's revenge on society.

That the past has more dignity than the present.

There are a dozen other propositions which might be added to this unwritten manifesto, but the ideas I have listed were those most generally held, and they are sufficient to explain the intellectual atmosphere of the young men who read "The Hill of Dreams," and argued about St. Thomas in Boston bars, and contributed to The Harvard Monthly. The attitude was not confined to one college and one magazine. It was often embodied in The Dial, which for some years was almost a postgraduate edition of The Monthly; it existed in earlier publications like The Yellow Book and La Revue Blanche; it has a history, in fact, almost as long as that of the upper middle class under capitalism. For the last half-century it has furnished the intellectual background of poems and essays without number. It would seem to preclude, in its adherents, the objectivity that is generally associated with good fiction; yet the esthetes themselves sometimes wrote novels, as did their predecessors all over the world. Such novels, in fact, are still being published, and favorably criticized: "Mr. Zed has written the absorbing story of a talented musician tortured by the petty atmosphere of the society in which he is forced to live. His wife, whom the author portrays with witty malice, prevents him from breaking away. After an unhappy love affair and the failure of his artistic hopes, he commits suicide. . . ."

Such is the plot forever embroidered in the type of fiction that ought to be known as the Art Novel. There are two essential characters, two antagonists, the Poet and the World. The Poet—who may also be a painter, a violinist, an inventor, an architect or a Centaur—is generally to be identified with the author of the novel, or at least with the novelist's ideal picture of himself. He tries to assert his individuality in despite of the World, which is stupid, unmanageable and usually victorious. Sometimes the Poet triumphs, but the art novelists seem to realize, as a class, that the sort of hero they describe is likely to be defeated in the sort of society which he must face. This society is rarely presented in accurate terms. So little is it endowed with reality, so great is the author's solicitude for the Poet, that we are surprised to see him vanquished by such a shadowy opponent. It is as if we were watching motion pictures in the dark house of his mind. There are dream pictures, nightmare pictures; at last the walls crash in and the Poet disappears without ever knowing what it was all about; he dies by his own hand, leaving behind him the memory of his ecstatic moments and the bitter story of his failure, now published as a revenge on the world of the philistines.

The art novel has many variations. Often the World is embodied in the Poet's wife, whose social ambitions are the immediate cause of his defeat. Or the wife may be painted in attractive colors: she is married to a mediocre Poet who finally and reluctantly accepts her guidance, abandons his vain struggle for self-expression, and finds that mediocrity has its own consolations, its country clubs and business triumphs—this is the form in which the art novel is offered to readers of The Saturday Evening Post. Or again the Poet may be a woman who fights for the same ambitions, under the same difficulties, as her male prototypes. The scene of the struggle may be a town on the Minnesota prairies, an English rectory, an apartment on Washington Square or Beacon Hill; but always the characters are the same; the Poet and the World continue their fatal conflict; the Poet has all our sympathies. And the novelists who use this plot for the thousandth time are precisely those who believe that originality is a writer's chief virtue.

Many are unconscious of this dilemma. The story rises so immediately out of their lives, bursts upon them with such freshness, that they never recognize it as a familiar tale. Others deliberately face the problem and try to compensate for the staleness of the plot by the originality of their treatment. They experiment with new methods of story-telling—one of which, the stream of consciousness, seem peculiarly fitted to novels of this type. Perhaps they invest their characters with new significance, and rob them of any real significance, by making them symbolic. They adopt new manners, poetic, mystical, learned, witty, allusive or obfuscatory; and often, in token of their original talent, they invent new words and new ways of punctuating simple declarative sentences. Not all their ingenuity is wasted. Sometimes they make valuable discoveries; a few of the art novels, like "The Hill of Dreams," are among the minor masterpieces of late-Romantic literature; and a very few, like "A Portrait of the Artist as a Young Man," are masterpieces pure and simple.

Dos Passos's early books are neither masterpieces nor are they pure examples of the art novel. The world was always real to him, painfully real; it was never veiled with mysticism and his characters were rarely symbolic. Yet consider the plot of a novel like "Three Soldiers." A talented young musician, during the War, finds that his sensibilities are being outraged, his aspirations crushed, by society as embodied in the American army. He deserts after the Armistice and begins to write a great orchestral poem. When the military police come to arrest him, the sheets of music flutter one by one into the spring breeze; and we are made to feel that the destruction of this symphony, this ecstatic song choked off and dispersed on the wind, is the real tragedy of the War. Some years later, in writing "Manhattan Transfer," Dos Passos seemed to be undertaking a novel of a different type, one which tried to render the color and movement of a whole city; but the book, as it proceeds, becomes the story of Jimmy Herts (the Poet) and Ellen Thatcher (the Poet's wife), and the Poet is once again frustrated by the World: he leaves a Greenwich Village party after a last drink of gin and walks out alone, bareheaded, into the dawn. It is obvious, however, that a new conflict has been superimposed on the old one: the social ideas of the novelist are now at war with his personal emotions, which remain those of The Dial and The Harvard Monthly. Even in "1919," this second conflict persists, but less acutely; the emotional values themselves are changing, to accord with the ideas; and the book as a whole belongs to a new category.

"1919" is distinguished, first of all, by the very size of the project its author has undertaken. A long book in itself, containing 473 pages, it is merely the second chapter, as it were, of a novel which will compare

# TWENTY INDISPENSABLE BOOKS

## A Short List of Suggested Reading for Those Who Want Radical Change in America

*The very latest books are not always by any means the best books, nor is there any special virtue in old books. Most magazines are content to review and discuss the latest books only, leaving to incidental mention or to other services, the presentation of books of past years. In an effort to bring together a coherent list of radical books, old and new, the Editors of "Common Sense" prepared a list of representative volumes and submitted it to a group of informed writers for criticism; Benjamin Stolberg, John Chamberlain, John Carter, J. B. S. Hardman, Robert S. Allen, Upton Sinclair, Henry Hazlitt, H. L. Mencken, Louis M. Hacker, V. F. Calverton, Harry Elmer Barnes, Roger Baldwin, Matthew Josephson, Reinhold Niebuhr, Carleton Beals, Lewis Mumford, John Dewey, Malcolm Cowley, Edmund Wilson and Senator Bronson D. Cutting. Taking heed of the comments and suggestions of these men, the following list has been compiled. It offers, so to speak, a minimum list of required reading for radicals. Most of the volumes mentioned will be found in any good public library, or they can be purchased, new or second-hand, for nominal sums. From time to time the Editors will discuss the volumes mentioned, make additional suggestions and publish lists by individuals which seem to them to have a particular interest and value.*

1. EDWARD BELLAMY. *LOOKING BACKWARD.*
   This classic has recently come into notice once more because of its apparent anticipation of technocracy. Apart from that, it is one of the most brilliantly prophetic utopias of all time.

2. KARL MARX. *CAPITAL AND OTHER WRITINGS.* Edited by Max Eastman.
   Those who prefer to take their Marx straight can go to his own books, here analyzed and presented in selections by a "revisionist" student. The volume includes the "Communist Manifesto."

3. JOHN STRACHEY. *THE COMING STRUGGLE FOR POWER.*
   Readers who want to know how the contemporary world appears to a Communist whose technique of interpretation does not clutter up his pages, should turn to Strachey's brilliant book. A work of the first importance and required reading on the depression.

4. THOMAS PAINE. *COMMON SENSE.*
   In addition to being the source of the title of our magazine, this little book is a keen and cogent statement of the reasons for the first great American revolution, that of the rising middle class in the American colonies against the British crown.

5. HENRY THOREAU. *ESSAY ON CIVIL DISOBEDIENCE.*
   Thoreau's essay is probably the most permanently valuable of the many documents which grew out of the agitation for freeing the slaves. Somewhat anarchistic in tone, it teaches one not to take the government too seriously.

6. CHARLES BEARD. *RISE OF AMERICAN CIVILIZATION.*
   A comprehensive knowledge of the history of the United States is absolutely indispensable to an understanding of present conditions.

7. LEWIS COREY. *THE HOUSE OF MORGAN.*
   This story of a financial house of tremendous symbolic significance, is quite the best study yet written and is thoroughly rooted in the social setting. A case history of the first importance.

8. JOHN CHAMBERLAIN. *FAREWELL TO REFORM.*
   Chamberlain reviews the efforts of the reformers to patch up and clean up the American system and concludes that the story leads to socialism or cynicism. A vivid book, easy to read.

9. LINCOLN STEFFENS. *AUTOBIOGRAPHY.*
   Steffens's story complements Chamberlain's book. It is the personal history of one of the chief figures of the reforming period in American radicalism, intensely human and very honest.

10. THORSTEIN VEBLEN. *THE THEORY OF THE LEISURE CLASS.*
    Veblen founded a school of economic thinking the primary principle of which is to keep both eyes on reality. Indispensable to an understanding of the beneficiaries of the capitalistic system.

11. SCOTT NEARING. *WAR.*
    In the enormous literature of war and peace, Nearing's book stands out for its clarity and incisiveness. Demonstrates that the opponents of war must also be social revolutionists.

12. HENRY GEORGE. *PROGRESS AND POVERTY.*
    Of all the radical social theorists who have appeared in America from time to time, Henry George has had the widest influence and has remained an active force for the greatest length of time. Whatever objections may be raised to his system, the fact remains that George demonstrated the evil consequences of private property in land.

13. DANIEL DE LEON. *TWO PAGES FROM ROMAN HISTORY.*
    De Leon was an uncompromising radical who scattered his energies among the socialists, the I. W. W. and in various other directions. A man who should not be forgotten, here represented by his most frequently recalled book.

14. UPTON SINCLAIR. *THE JUNGLE.*
    Sinclair, the most prolific radical writer in American history, novelist, playwright, pamphleteer, produced a classic in The Jungle. This study of life and labor in the Chicago stockyards created a furor on its appearance and still is vital. It is the earliest of the permanently interesting stories of "wage slavery."

15. BERTRAND RUSSELL. *PROPOSED ROADS TO FREEDOM.*
    The celebrated English mathematician and social philosopher here examines a variety of proposals for liberating mankind. A brief lucid book.

16. JOHN REED. *TEN DAYS THAT SHOOK THE WORLD.*
    A Harvard graduate who turned Communist, Reed wrote a vivid eye-witness account of the Russian revolution. Carries a preface by Lenin.

17. LEON TROTSKY. *MY LIFE and HISTORY OF THE RUSSIAN REVOLUTION.*
    Trotsky's name is imperishably joined to Lenin's as a leader of the Bolshevik revolution. His own story is a fascinating case history of the radical intellectual and his History is both a study of the event and, in part, a defense of his part in it.

18. NICOLAI LENIN. *STATE AND REVOLUTION.*
    A statement of the case for revolution by the great engineer of revolution. Recognized as a classic by all students.

19. JOHN DOS PASSOS. *1919.*
    A panoramic study of American life as seen through the eyes of the best of the left-wing novelists.

20. SINCLAIR LEWIS. *BABBITT.*
    What we have now by way of leaders, bitingly portrayed and so memorably that Babbitt has become a generic as well as a specific term.

*COMMON SENSE*

24

*List of "indispensable books" from the March 1933 issue of* Common Sense, *with the second volume in the* U.S.A. *trilogy listed as number nineteen (Collection of Richard Layman)*

in length with "Ulysses," perhaps even with "Remembrance of Things Past." Like the latter, it is a historical novel dealing with the yesterday that still exists in the author's memory. It might almost be called a news novel, since it uses newspaper headlines to suggest the flow of events, and tells the story of its characters in reportorial fashion. But its chief distinction lies in the author's emphasis. He is not recounting the tragedy of bewildered John Smith, the rise of ambitious Mary Jones, the efforts of sensitive Richard Robinson to maintain his ideals against the blundering malice of society. Such episodes recur in this novel, but they are seen in perspective. The real hero of "The 42nd Parallel" and "1919" is society itself, American society as embodied in forty or fifty representative characters who drift along with it, struggle to change its course, or merely to find a secure footing–perhaps they build a raft of wreckage, grow fat on the refuse floating about them; perhaps they go under in some obscure eddy– while always the current sweeps them onward toward new social horizons. In this sense, Dos Passos has written the first American collective novel.

The principal characters are brought forward one at a time; the story of each is told in bare, straightforward prose. Thus, J. Ward Moorehouse, born in Wilmington, Delaware, begins his business career in a real-estate office. He writes songs, marries and divorces a rich woman, works for a newspaper in Pittsburgh–at the end of fifty-seven pages he is a successful public- relations counselor embarked on a campaign to reconcile labor and capital at the expense of labor. Joe and Janey Williams are the children of a tugboat captain from Washington, D.C.; Janey studies shorthand; Joe plays baseball, enlists in the navy, deserts after a brawl and becomes a merchant seaman. Eleanor Stoddard is a poor Chicago girl who works at Marshall Field's; she learns how to speak French to her customers and orders waiters about "with a crisp little refined moneyed voice." All these characters, first introduced in "The 42nd Parallel," reappear in "1919," where they are joined by others: Richard Ellsworth Savage, a Kent School boy who goes to Harvard and writes poetry; Daughter, a warm-hearted flapper from Dallas, Texas; Ben Compton, a spectacled Jew from Brooklyn who becomes a Wobbly. Gradually their careers draw closer together, till finally all of them are caught up in the War.

"This whole goddam war's a gold brick," says Joe Williams. "It ain't on the level, it's crooked from A to Z. No matter how it comes out, fellows like us get the s——y end of the stick, see? Well, what I say is all bets is off . . . every man go to hell in his own way . . . and three strikes is out, see?" Three strikes is out for Joe, when his skull is cracked in a saloon brawl at St. Nazaire, on Armistice night. Daughter is killed in an airplane accident; she provoked it herself in a fit of hysteria after being jilted by Dick Savage–who for his part survives as the shell of a man, all the best of him having died when he decided to join the army and make a career for himself and let his pacifist sentiments go hang. Benny Compton gets ten years in Atlanta prison as a conscientious objector. Everybody in the novel suffers from the War and finds his own way of going to hell–everybody except the people without bowels, the empty people like Eleanor Stoddard and J. Ward Moorehouse, who stuff themselves with the proper sentiments and make the right contacts.

The great events that preceded and followed the Armistice are reflected in the lives of all these people; but Dos Passos has other methods, too, for rendering the sweep of history. In particular he has three technical devices which he uses both to broaden the scope of the novel and to give it a formal unity. The first of these consists of what he calls "Newsreels," a combination of newspaper headlines, stock-market reports, official communiqués and words from popular songs. The Newsreels effectively perform their function in the book, that of giving dates and atmospheres, but in themselves, judged as writing, they are not successful. The second device is a series of nine biographies interspersed through the text. Here are the lives, briefly told, of three middle-class rebels, Jack Reed, Randolph Bourne and Paxton Hibben; of three men of power, Roosevelt, Wilson and J. P. Morgan; and of three proletarian heroes. All these are successful both in themselves and in relation to the novel as a whole; and the passage dealing with the Wobbly martyr, Wesley Everest, is as powerful as anything Dos Passos has ever written.

The Camera Eye, which is the third device, introduces more complicated standards of judgment. It consists in the memories of another character, presumably the author, who has adventures similar to those of his characters, but describes them in a different style, one which suggests Dos Passos's earlier books. The Camera Eye gives us photographs rich in emotional detail:

Ponte Decimo    in Ponte Decimo ambulances were parked in a moonlit square of bleak stone workingpeople's houses    hoarfrost covered everything    in the little bar the Successful Story Writer taught us to drink cognac and maraschino half and half

havanuzzerone

it turned out he was not writing what he felt he wanted to be writing    What can you tell them at home about the war?    it turned out he was not wanting what he wrote he wanted to be feeling cognac and maraschino    was no longer young    (It made us damn sore we greedy for what we felt we wanted tell 'em all they lied see new towns go to Genoa)

havanuzzerone?    it turned out that he wished he

was a naked brown shepherd boy sitting on a hillside playing a flute in the sunlight

Exactly the same episode, so it happens, is described in Dos Passos's other manner, his prose manner, during the course of a chapter dealing with Dick Savage:

That night they parked the convoy in the main square of a godforsaken little burg on the outskirts of Genoa. They went with Sheldrake to have a drink in a bar and found themselves drinking with the Saturday Evening Post correspondent, who soon began to get tight and to say how he envied them their good looks and their sanguine youth and idealism. Steve picked him up about everything and argued bitterly that youth was the lousiest time in your life, and that he ought to be goddam glad he was forty years old and able to write about the war instead of fighting in it.

The relative merit of these two passages, as writing, is not an important question. The first is a good enough piece of impressionism, with undertones of E. E. Cummings and Gertrude Stein. The style of the second passage, except for a certain conversational quality, is almost colorless; it happens to be the most effective way of recording a particular series of words and actions; it aspires to no other

virtue. The first passage might add something to a book in which, the plot being hackneyed or inconsequential, the emphasis had to be placed on the writing, but "1919" is not a novel of that sort. Again, the Camera Eye may justify itself in the next volume of this trilogy—or tetralogy—by assuming a closer relation to the story and binding together the different groups of characters; but in that case, I hope the style of it will change. So far it has been an element of disunity, a survival of the art novel in the midst of a different type of writing, and one in which Dos Passos excels.

He is, indeed, one of the few writers in whose case an equation can accurately and easily be drawn between social beliefs and artistic accomplishments. When he writes individualistically, with backward glances toward Imagism, Vorticism and the Insurrection of the Word, his prose is sentimental and without real distinction. When he writes as a social rebel, he writes not flawlessly by any means, but with conviction, power and a sense of depth, of striking through surfaces to the real forces beneath them. This last book, in which his political ideas have given shape to his emotions, and only the Camera Eye remains as a vestige of his earlier attitude, is not only the best of all his novels; it is, I believe, a landmark in American fiction.

—*New Republic*, 70 (27 April 1932): 303–305

*Dust jacket for the first British edition of the second volume in the* U.S.A. *trilogy, published in 1932*
*(Collection of Richard Layman)*

## War and Peace and Revolution
Unsigned review

*Nineteen Nineteen* is the second part of a big novel in a new manner. Readers of *The 42nd Parallel,* the first part of this novel, will remember the scope of the book–to give a cross-section of American life; and the curious technique employed–a sort of verbal camera-work. The narratives of a number of individual lives ran separately, alternating in strips, and then converged or touched by accident; a newsreel flickered intermittently; there was the further background of public figures memorialised in odd brief biographies. Mr. dos Passos continues this technique in *Nineteen Nineteen.* It is possible now to judge the success of his method, and the magnitude of the undertaking, for though there may be other volumes to follow (Russia seems likely to come under the lens), *Nineteen Nineteen* sets a limit of expansion beyond which a sequel can hardly go.

Mr. dos Passos has attempted a modern *War and Peace,* but a *War and Peace* in which the disintegration of society has already begun below the surface, in which the march of American solidarity–God's Own Country first keeping out of the war and then with a rocket of stars going into it–is only an Independence Day procession from which blacklegs are absent because they are being batoned round the corner. It is not the public structure that interests him, but the cross-section underneath; he gives us, instead of the distant view, these glimpses of vivid swarming units. Thus his picture lacks the emphasis and design of the panoramic novel, and he relies on the vividness, the quick change of the shifting camera. His object is to portray the disintegration of American life in 1900–30, the reverse of the newspaper story, and he uses a method which will reflect disintegration.

*The 42nd Parallel* ended with America's entry into the war. *Nineteen Nineteen* covers the war and the beginning of the peace. Europe as well as America occupies the scene. They come pouring over, the doughboys, war workers, secretaries, publicity men, Red Cross nurses, heralded by the image of President Wilson and sanctified afterwards by the Fourteen Points; and Mr. dos Passos catches the life of this circulating colony with astonishing zest. The addition of a patter of European languages to his rich American is excellent. He has succeeded in doing what Mr. Hemingway is supposed all along to have done, but actually only hinted at: he has really made Americans talk on paper–not an isolated remark that we seize on as typical or a carefully-set Mutt-and-Jeff dialogue–but the continuous, vigorous, appropriate talk of his own narrative. It is in the Marx Brothers jokes, the "grenadine guards" and the "cross red nurses"; in the picture of couples sitting along the Seine frozen in "the strangleholds of l'amour"; the "crinkly cigarette smoke" in a Paris restaurant and a party of evening-dress Americans crossing the floor looking like "plush horses," while an American girl in the corner says "I think the French are wonderful"; the four American sailors in Liverpool:

> They went to another fried fish shop; couldn't seem to get a damn thing to eat in this country except fried fish, and then they all had some more drinks and were the four of them Americans feeling pretty good in this lousy limejuicer town. A runner got hold of them because it was closing time on account of the war and there wasn't a damn thing open and very few street-lights and funny little hats over on the street-lights on account of the zeppelins. The runner was a rat-faced punk and said he knowed a house where they could 'ave a bit of beer and nice girls and a quiet social time.

That is Mr. dos Passos running on level gear. He has no big scenes, no big characters, no crescendos or diminuendos. But he can change his atmosphere. Here, for contrast, is the childhood of a clergyman's daughter in Chicago:

> Little Eveline and Arget and Lade and Gogo lived on the top floor of a yellow brick house on the North Shore Drive. Arget and Lade were little Eveline's sisters. Gogo was her little brother littler than Eveline. On the floor below was Dr. Hutchins's study where Yourfather mustn't be disturbed, and Dearmother's room where she stayed all morning painting dressed in a lavender smock. On the ground floor was the drawingroom and the diningroom, where parishioners came and little children must be seen and not heard, and at dinnertime you could smell good things to eat and hear knives and forks and tinkly companyvoices and Yourfather's booming scary voice and when Yourfather's voice was going all the companyvoices were quiet. Yourfather was Dr. Hutchins but Our Father art in heaven. . . .

As a background to these individual narratives, which gurgle on with extraordinary ease and rapidity and a completely convincing earthiness, there are the newsreels, snippets from newspapers ludicrously isolated and juxtaposed, and the advertisement biographies of Wilson, Roosevelt, Edison, and other public men–the charade of public events. Wilson appears once at close-hand, addressing a select convoy of Italians near the ruins of the Temple of Romulus, assuring them of the immense love of humanity borne in American hearts–"a grey stony cold face grooved like columns, very long under the silk hat: the little smile around the mouth looked as if it had been painted on afterwards. The group moved on." The one ludicrous and pathetic appearance of the Napoleon of this *War and Peace* is typical and effective.

How far then do the halves of the picture—the private lives and the public show, so violently contrasted—join? Well, they give the effect of simultaneity rather than unity; the mere contrast is effective and gives the book breadth. Mr. dos Passos has succeeded in splitting the one hundred per cent. American. He is a Communist (there is a strong undercurrent of the I.W.W. throughout these volumes) and this fact perhaps has decided the shape of his book. When Communism becomes his positive theme it may give him the larger momentum needed for a novel of this scope. *Nineteen Nineteen* leaves the impression that Mr. dos Passos is essentially master of a small art, like Mr. Hemingway, but possessed of immense zest for life and an incomparable native vigour in expressing it. *Nineteen Nineteen* has a mass of life of its own—vivid, restless, vernacular—and that after all is most important.

—*New Statesman and Nation*
(London), new series 3
(11 June 1932): 770

### John Dos Passos—*1919*
Carey McWilliams

*Carey McWilliams was an attorney and author who wrote extensively on western subjects and, later in his career, on civil rights. Contempo, a "little magazine" of the period, was published in Chapel Hill, North Carolina.*

Mr. Paul Elmer More once characterized a novel by Dos Passos as "an explosion in a sewer." If one thinks of modern civilization as a sewer,—by no means an extravagant request,—then the reference takes on a note of accuracy that was not intended. For Dos Passos' work explodes, ignites, blazes. It is purposely eruptive. *1919* (Harcourt, Brace, $2.50) carries forward the rushing narrative of *The 42nd Parallel* in the spirit and manner of the latter volume. Keyed to the point of hysteria, the force and impact of the novel is extraordinary. It is designed to be read at a great speed, and, if read in this manner, it does give an unforgettable picture of the wild insanity of 1919.

*The 42nd Parallel* covered the period, roughly, from the close of the Spanish-American War to the outbreak of the World War. The range covered by the present volume, in the space of a single year, is amazing: the various stories that are interwoven in the narrative cross back and forth on the Atlantic, reach down into Italy and the Mediterranean, and touch the shores of South America. There is little effort to picture the war in the manner attempted by so many contemporary novelists. The scenes everywhere impinge upon the war zone yet one never gets to the front line trenches. It is rather a back-stage war: nurses, ambulance drivers, publicity experts, sailors on transports, and peace negotiators. As much as anything, the novel is designed to show the break-down of an accumulated bourgeois tradition in the cataclysmic shake-up of the war. It is not only the profound desolation in individual lives worked by the war that the book depicts: it is the destruction of values in the giddy tumultuous period when the world went mad, that forms its real substance. As such it is a successful and memorable document. The totality of its effect, when read in the manner that I have indicated, is about what Dos Passos intended. Yet, considered in detail, each section being read slowly and with care, it fails to be quite as impressive.

Writing of the work of E. E. Cummings in *The Dial* some years ago, Dos Passos said: "We'll have to forget the hissing of the safety-valve and stroke like beavers if we are to get off the sticky shoals into the deeper reaches beyond." He has always striven with rather unnecessary intensity to achieve this end. Dos Passos has always been profoundly afraid that he might accidentally step inside the pale of convention, that he might inadvertently affirm a bourgeois value, or that he might for a perceptible interval cease to yell against the world at large. His work has always been characterized by a radical experimentation for the reason that he is a rebel not only against existing institutions but against convention and tradition in the arts. He looks, both in his thinking and in his writing, from the present to the future and never for a moment does he gaze into the past. In an essay in *The New Republic,* as early as October 14th, 1915, he was writing that "the only substitute for dependence on the past is dependence on the future." He was at that period, and he has since remained, something of a futurist in manner.

The innovations in the form of the novel which appear in *The 42nd Parallel* and *1919* are, of course, the use of the news-reel, the camera eye, and the interpolated prose sagas. The news-reel devise is unquestionably effective; the jerky irrelevancy of the thing does suggest the flash of events. The portions of the story involved in "The Camera Eye" are obviously autobiographical. For this reason, it is quite appropriate that they should be fragmentary, and given as glimpses into the past, as brief reminiscences. The sagas in this volume are devoted to Theodore Roosevelt, Randolph Bourne, Paxton Hibben, Woodrow Wilson, J. P. Morgan (page the House of Harper!), and Joe Hill. They are interesting and readable enough, but their inclusion in a novel seems a piece of fortuitous silliness. Dos Passos sets them up in a staccato manner, as though they were meant to be declaimed as entr'actes.

As a novelist, Mr. Dos Passos' merits are obvious and have received sufficient praise. His limitations seem to have escaped attention. For one thing, he is as emotional and impulsive as a school-girl. Consider his neologisms. By what actual necessity is he driven to concoct such terms as "manuresmelling," "leadentired," "washed-out," "dollarproud," "squashysweet," "fragillycut," "cindergritty," and "sicklytingling"? These, I must confess, are from *Manhattan Transfer;* the later volumes show a creditable diminution of this tendency. It would seem, in most cases, that he jotted the impression down in an impetuous manner in mortal fear that its vividness would fade. Then, too, one often detects in his neologisms an animus toward the objects or persons described, a violent desire to lather them with a frothy foam of words. This tendency often detracts from the impression attempted to be conveyed. The passage in *1919* called "The Body of an American" is overdone, in this way, with almost sophomoric lavishness.

The same emotional unrest, apparent in his style, appears also in his grotesque attempts to create characters. With the possible exceptions of Ben Compton and Anne Trent, there is scarcely a single character in *1919* drawn with an eye for clarity. Even these two are rather blotched in the telling. His characters are creatures who live and move on a monotonous plane to which he arbitrarily assigns them. In one sense most of Dos Passos' characters are caricatures: he permits his feeling to get the better of his powers of discernment. You recognize the type, but you do not meet a recognizable individual. Occasionally this inability to draw character is a positive advantage, as in the case of Joe Williams, meant to be an anonymous figure, representative of thousands. I also appreciate that Dos Passos is not particularly interested in character in the sense that the conventional novelist must be.

To understand the lush naturalism of Passos, one should read *Streets of Night*. It is a study of the unbearable placidity of pre-war Harvard and an excellent account of the Harvard aesthetes. Three young people, Nan, Wendell, and Fanshaw are caught in a web of gentility, gagged by tradition, and positively ill from an overdose of culture. To step

from such an atmosphere into the War, and the post-War world, must have been a disturbing experience. The reaction has been rather too violent.

And his father, a Philadelphia lawyer, (the phrase is proverbial) wrote tracts defending Imperialism, Capitalism, and the rights of "large aggregations of capital"!

—*Contempo*, 2 (5 July 1932): 5

## The War Generation
Francis Fergusson

*Francis Fergusson, a professor of drama at Rutgers and then Princeton, was the author of the well-known* The Idea of a Theater *(1949).*

Mr. Dos Passos's new novel takes the characters we first met in *42nd Parallel,* and a few new ones, through the War and into the Peace. His method is the same as in *42nd Parallel;* he tells the stories of about a dozen "real Americans," intertwining them apparently quite mechanically, and breaking them off from time to time, seemingly quite arbitrarily, to make room for "Newsreel," "Camera Eye," and "Biographies." The Newsreels are collections of newspaper headlines, posters, snatches from popular songs, and so on, intended to give the atmosphere of the public events of the time. The Biographies are sketches of conspicuous figures, such as John Reed the radical, Woodrow Wilson, J. P. Morgan. They are in the style of *New Masses* cartoons: loud, simplified and somewhat heavy: we see the elder Morgan with his magpie eye and his big black cigar clutching the loot of empire. The Camera Eyes contain the best writing in the book; they are lyrical and impressionistic. The dust cover informs you that they give Mr. Dos Passos's "own memory of the events and years recorded in the novel," and they are indeed *intermittences du coeur,* like Hemingway's famous homesick trout-fishing trips, and jaunts to Spain. The uprooted generation likes to dwell on its memories, while

With Ernest in the streets of Saragossa
Our mouths are hard, we say *qué cosa,*

as Mr MacLeish chants.

The stories of the "real Americans" take up most of the book, and constitute its best claim to being a novel, if there still is such a thing. As stories they are very monotonous, but as snapshots of the War Generation they are excellent. The Texas flapper Daughter; the seaman Joe Williams; and the Harvard undergraduates, all come to life. Mr. Dos Passos is supposed to have studied Joyce; perhaps it was by reading *Ulysses* that he trained his ear to catch the dialects of various trades, localities, and social strata—at any rate, his book is full of authentic voices and rhythms of speech. But at this point the similarity to *Ulysses* ends. Joyce revivified a myth in contemporary terms; *1919* has no more structure than a show at the New Playwrights' Theatre, now defunct. And, of course, Mr. Dos Passos has a different intention: he is a propagandist for Communism.

"It will take some huge wave of hope like a revolution to make me feel any selfrespect ever again," says Richard Savage, the Harvard man, in one of his moods of good-fellowship and self-hatred. This seems to be what the Revolution means to the author, or perhaps what it meant to him in *1919*. But in *1919* the Revolution was thwarted on all sides. The honest young people who might have made Dos Passos-Communists are all premature victims of the System. Those who belong to the "Capitalist Class" but have some capacity for receiving the new faith, relapse into cynicism and disillusionment. Democratic Idealism, it is true, perishes with Woodrow Wilson, but Mass Action goes to Atlanta with Ben Compton or is mutilated and then murdered in the person of Wesley Everest. And all the while Mr. Dos Passos asks us to believe that the Revolution would have made self-respecting men out of the boys, and that all the furtive, selfish love-affairs he shows us would grow clean and fine under Communism. Under Communism a woman can have a baby if she wants one, as Helen Mauer remarks, when she sends Ben out for contraceptives. Meanwhile, she accepts the painful realities of the Capitalist regime. Something like this seems to be the moral of the tale. The Chosen People are to mortify themselves with dust and ashes during the Dispersion.

It is evident that this new faith, or "new wave of hope," is a mob excitement just as much as the parades of returning soldiers which Mr. Dos Passos scorns so bitterly. The blaring of brass, whether by the 7th Regiment Band or Mr. Dos Passos, stirs up enough ill-defined emotion to make you forget for the moment the sub-human stupidity of the marchers. Mr. Dos Passos's book is as exciting as Armistice Day on Fifth Avenue, or the Sunday Rotogravure. The question arises, is Mr. Dos Passos really interested in the enthusiasm itself, or in the Marxian dogma which is supposed to be its object?—In Marxian dogma, he would probably answer. But the picture he shows us is a picture of a crowd of boys and girls, Whitman's "tan-faced children," "you rough, you twain!" looking with their "slow honest eyes" for oblivion in excitement, whatever the slogan. Here I believe is the fundamental confusion in the book. Mr. Dos Passos would like to have us think of him as pretty grim—a steel-grey figure weeping at the Proletarian woes, yet clear-eyed; an intellectual who has outgrown the last two thousand years of civilization, bearing the Five-Year Plan in one hand and Martyrdom in the other. What his book shows us is a talented story-writer, the spiritual heir of Stephen Crane and Jack London, with a sentimental attachment to the great quality of American Innocence, which is the innocence of his own adolescence never outgrown.

—*Hound and Horn*, 6 (January–March 1933): 342–344

\* \* \*

## Reviews of *The Big Money* (1936)

*As is signified by Dos Passos's appearance on the cover of the 6 August 1936 issue of* Time *magazine, accompanied by a lengthy article in the journal itself, the publication of* The Big Money *was greeted as a major literary event. Critics of all literary and political persuasions took the opportunity afforded by the appearance of the last volume in the U.S.A. trilogy to review the nature and success of the work as a whole, with such leading literary voices of the period as Bernard De Voto and Malcolm Cowley participating in the effort.*

*Most of these commentators agreed that the trilogy constituted a significant effort to create an American epic, and Dos Passos was also usually afforded equal stature with such other figures of the period as Theodore Dreiser, Sinclair Lewis, and Ernest Hemingway. But America, and indeed the entire world, was still in the midst of the Depression, and thus* The Big Money, *which dealt specifically with the decade preceding the Depression, raised the question of the stance of the trilogy toward the civilization that had produced this disaster. Some reviewers asked whether the work was too pessimistic in its diagnosis of the capitalist system, while others, from a different angle of approach, questioned whether Dos Passos's unsympathetic portrayal of the Communist Left in* The Big Money *indicated that he had lost hope in the Left as an alternative to capitalism.*

*Some strains of earlier criticism remained constant. The Newsreels and Camera Eye remained the bugbear of some critics, the biographies a favored mode of others. But emerging as well, with the perspective gained by three novels and six years, were several significant new areas of insight and interpretation that were to bear much fruit in the future—that the trilogy was constructed in a form of cinematic montage; that U.S.A. as a whole and the narratives in particular were efforts to represent America as a language system; that Dos Passos's essential values were rooted in the American past; and that his social beliefs owed more to Thorstein Veblen than to Karl Marx.*

### Mr. Dos Passos' Newsreel, Continued
Clifton Fadiman

*A literary jack-of-all-trades, Clifton Fadiman was an editor at* The New Yorker *from 1925 to 1935; he was later the master of ceremonies for many years of* Information Please, *a popular radio quiz show.*

The French are a grave race who have spent centuries carefully cultivating a profitable reputation for frivolity. They disclose the core of their character, one often thinks, when they talk of a *maison sérieuse,* one which is established, keeps its responsibilities constantly in mind, or, as we brisk Americans would put it, really "means business." In this sense certain writers are *sérieux,* too, and others, often quite good ones, are not. Thus, Hervey Allen or Margaret Mitchell would hardly be considered *vraiment sérieux,* whereas John Dos Passos would rate full marks for true seriousness. And I dare say he is one of a scant half-dozen American novelists who would.

A great writer he is not; not even, like his friend and contemporary, Ernest Hemingway, a brilliant one. But he means business. He is less interested in striking attitudes, however memorable, of his own, than in noting the far more memorable attitudes of whole classes and generations. He is not, like that gloomily picturesque castaway, Mr. Faulkner, marooned within his own sensibility. When he grasps American life it is always at its center. He works with cross-sections, but the cross-sections are of maximum density. When he fails, as he does on occasion, it is with major material. Hence, if you lean to the exquisite and prefer small things done perfectly, Dos Passos is not your man, nor are you his.

In "The 42nd Parallel" and "1919" he began to work seriously at the oversized job of pinning his and our America on paper. "The Big Money" (561 pages, $2.50) adds another panel to the picture. The general subject is America in the twenties. The personal slant, kept severely in check, is founded on

JOHN DOS PASSOS

# The Big Money

*Title page of the last volume in the* U.S.A. *trilogy with a note by Dos Passos to Malcolm Cowley, who edited* The New Republic, *the magazine that published "Vag" in July 1935, the month before publication of* The Big Money *(Collection of Richard Layman)*

Dos Passos' sympathy for the disinherited, whom he thinks of as comprising the true America. The motifs are concrete and, if you will, checkable: financial inflation, Big Business, mass production, the withering of the American libertarian tradition (legal assassination of Sacco and Vanzetti), the Speakeasy Culture, the frustration of the Bright Young Men, the sharpening of class lines, the development of various mass-entertainment narcoses (Hollywood), and the feverish search for The Big Money, the Holy Grail of the period. The fourfold technique of portraiture is that made familiar by "1919" and "The 42nd Parallel": the biographies of a few crucially representative imagined Americans; the life-histories of a few equally representative actual ones; the Newsreel, made up of scraps of popular songs, newspaper headlines, ads, speeches—all this meant to serve as a recall-device; and the Camera Eye, consisting of lyric flashbacks from the author's own experience during the decade. Of these four devices, the first two seem to me sound, the third a plain bore, the fourth a bit arty and not worth the effort Dos Passos puts into it. The interweaving is loose, and often gives an almost random or crazy-quilt effect. But life in the Twenties, if you can remember your American history, was like that.

The central, the fundamental experiences of the Boom Decade are reflected for us in the lives of four young people: Charley Anderson, an ex-aviator who gets into the big money via luck, good looks, and a rising stock market, and ruins himself via the ladies, rye whiskey, and plain stupidity; Mary French, the social worker who becomes a social revolutionary; Margo Dowling, geared slickly to the period, rising from nothing to Hollywood stardom; and Richard Ellsworth Savage, the bright publicity man, a product of Bruce Barton plus the East Fifties. By skilfully moving these four counter-around, Dos Passos establishes a hundred and one lines of relation. The criss-cross of these lines maps the general pattern of the life of the era.

But Dos Passos is newspaper-trained. For him The Fact is all-important. Therefore he is not satisfied with his imaginary symbols; he needs real men and real women. He does with fair success what Mr. Sheean failed to do in "Sanfelice"—weld history to fiction. The effect is achieved by sandwiching in short biographies of ten Americans, these biographies being, for me, the high points of the book. The ten are cunningly chosen. Four of them—Frederick Winslow Taylor, Henry Ford, and the Wright brothers—provided the technical framework of ideas and inventions which made possible the lunatic industrial expansion of the decade. Two—Samuel Insull and William Randolph Hearst—represent the kind of success the decade most valued. The arts yield a shrewdly selected trio: Rudolph Valentino, whose own life was of not the remotest importance, but who, by the adoration in which he was held, revealed in a clear mirror the emotional poverty of the lives of millions of others; Isadora Duncan, the spurious rebel who had nothing to give but her talent for personal surrender; and Frank Lloyd Wright, the real rebel who has all to give, but few takers. The final exhibit is Thorstein Veblen, who understood the whole period in terms of its basic economic weaknesses. Many of the others were after The Big Money; Veblen alone knew what it was all about. He was perhaps the greatest American of his period and one of the most scorned and rejected. Won't someone please do a book pointing out that

the very greatest Americans—and I mean the really great ones, not the schoolbook heroes—are precisely the greatest "failures"? We will tolerate and even admire the merely outstanding, but when something superbly tops comes along we either kick it to death (Veblen) or don't know it's there (Herman Melville, Willard Gibbs). Any arguments?

Getting back to "The Big Money," I feel that it does not have quite the drive and go of its two predecessors, being looser and more cluttered with pedestrian stretches. But it represents the American social novel at its most serious and conscientious, and hence is decidedly worth reading. Dos Passos is no Romains, but he is trying to do the Romains kind of thing. And that is just about enough to tax the capacities of any novelist of our time.

—*New Yorker*, 12 (8 August 1936): 52–53

## John Dos Passos: Anatomist of Our Time
Bernard De Voto

*Bernard De Voto, a Western-born novelist and critic, taught at such universities as Northwestern and Harvard. He is best known for his* Mark Twain's America *(1932).*

John Dos Passos has developed more consistently than any other American novelist of his time. With the exception of "Streets of Night," which fell far below "Three Soldiers" and is surely one of the worst novels of the generation, every book he has written has been distinctly better than its predecessors. "The Big Money" is better than "1919," which came out four years ago and was then easily his best novel. Whether it is the end of a trilogy, or whether it will be succeeded by a volume carrying the anatomy of our times still closer to today's headlines, cannot be made out—the method of discontinuity does not permit endings but only terminations, and there is no reason why the surviving Richard Savage, Margo Dowling, and Mary French should not move on into the depression years. But at any rate the enterprise, the most ambitious one that American fiction has embarked on since Frank Norris's unfinished trilogy of the wheat, has gone far enough to justify a few conclusions.

. . . . . . . . . .

Mr. Dos Passos was interested in depicting mass man, the mass experience obliterating the individual. The war carried the theme in "Three Soldiers," the metropolis in "Manhattan Transfer." In the trilogy it is identified with the mighty currents of American life during the prewar years, the war, and the boom. He set an ambitious goal: to convey the movement of continental United States during more than a quarter of a century. In the maturity of his powers he has splendidly succeeded. In scope and in multiplicity no comparable achievement exists in our fiction. "The Big Money," for instance, gives us not only New York but Detroit, Miami, and Hollywood as well; not only a Minnesota rural community but a Colorado mining town; not only brokers, promoters, publicity men, engineers, movie directors, inventors, senators, and salesmen, but labor leaders, social workers, literary socialists, communist organizers, and a counter-revolutionary; not only the insipid daughters of millionaires, hostesses of salons, wealthy widows, and suburban wives, but cabaret entertainers and a movie queen. This scale is maintained throughout the trilogy, and it is supported by a truly amazing fecundity of incident, and by a rushing narrative that is one of the finest technical accomplishments of our time. Mr. Dos Passos does indeed cover the continent from ocean to ocean, from farm to factory, from mine to mill, from proletariat to the master class. And he has mastered his details. He knows the provinces and geographies of America, the rituals and etiquettes, the creeds and superstitions, the avenues of tradition, the lines of force, the flowing shape of things. He has got a greater variety of them into fiction than any other novelist of his time.

"1919" was a better novel than "The 42nd Parallel," and "The Big Money" is better still, more in the round, more nearly three-dimensional, more mature and finished. It carries J. Ward Moorehouse, the Ivy Lee image, up to collapse and invalidism; and Richard Savage, his faintly poetic, faintly homosexual understudy, up to a partnership in his firm. Eveline Hutchins works through a series of adulteries to suicide. Ben Compton gets out of Atlanta and is excommunicated from the Party, in whose councils Don Stevens has risen so high that he makes a secret trip to Moscow. G. H. Barrow makes a good thing out of the trades unions. But the main burden of the book is carried by Mary French, a Vassar girl from Colorado who sleeps and weeps her way into the Party and finally into dedication to its purposes; by Margo Dowling, whose career takes her from a vaudeville act to Hollywood by way of a Cuban marriage and the most extensive whoring anyone has yet done in the series; and especially by Charley Anderson, who makes his first appearance since the end of "The 42nd Parallel." Charley, whom we had seen as a farmer, garage mechanic, and hobo, has meanwhile been, it now appears, a member of the LaFayette Escadrille and something of an inventor. He patents improvements in airplane design, falls in with promoters and makes several killings on the stock market, boozes his way through his first partnership, through his marriage, and through a number of affairs,

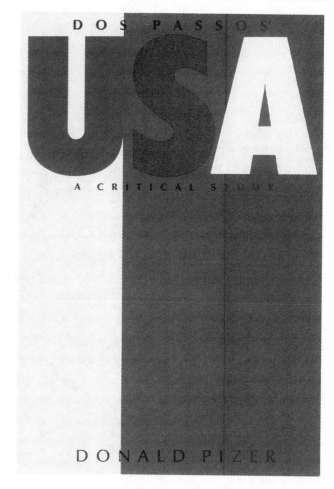

Dust jacket for Donald Pizer's 1988 study of Dos Passos's trilogy (Collection of Richard Layman)

ending with Margo Dowling, and finally, bankrupt and burnt out, drives his car in front of an express train while drunk.

Accompanying all this are the rockets and pinwheels of Mr. Dos Passos's fantasia on the boom years, with the fateful shadow of collapse moving close. There are also a number of genre pieces, such as Margolies, the movie director, who gives the author a field day of caricature: he is done to a turn and he will not be forgotten. And there are—innovations. When Charley Anderson, getting drunk, passes himself off as Charles Edward Holden, the writer, he precipitates the first joke in more than a thousand pages of fiction. Irony Mr. Dos Passos has plentifully provided before, suave or corrosive at need, and a fine sardonic quality runs through most of his work, but this is the first bit of fun. It seems lonely in all that expanse of mechanized behavior. But there is another novelty: in Mary French's Daddy, in Charley Anderson's partner Joe Askew, and in the treatment of the death of Charley's mother one

*Dust jacket for the 1936 edition of the final novel in the U.S.A. trilogy (Collection of Richard Layman)*

comes upon something recognizable as human emotion. It has not been perceptible in any of the death, violence, or torture that has gone before. Looking back over the trilogy, one can remember only one small incident when any of the characters seemed to be feeling anything at all, the passage in "1919" where the reluctant Sister, during a mountain rainstorm, was putting off Richard Savage to another time. She seemed to be feeling a genuine emotion at the time, which is more than she did when, pregnant and drunk, she started on the airplane ride that killed her. That incident in the rain stuck out as sharply as a metaphysician would in a novel by Ernest Hemingway.

With that realization we come to Mr. Dos Passos's principal deficiency as a novelist. How far it is also a deficiency of the fiction of mass man is indeterminable. It may be that the rigorous behaviorism of his method is what deprives his characters of intellectual life. It may be that you cannot show the interests and passions of the mind, its reveries, its analyses, its preoccupations, its satisfactions and anxieties, when you limit yourself to exhibiting only motor and verbal behavior. Certainly, no character in the trilogy thinks at all, none of them follows an idea for none has an idea to follow, and no intellectual value affects any of them in the least. But if that complete atrophy of the cerebrum must be charged to technical rigorousness, surely something other than technique is responsible for the atrophy of the emotions. A technique of fiction is only a means of presenting human beings—and human beings feel. But the automatons of Mr. Dos Passos do not feel.

They have no emotions of any kind. It is not only that the more complex pleasures and pains pass them by, so that they are not stimulated by anything aesthetic or depressed by anything spiritual—but that all pleasures and pains pass them by. They sleep with each other every page or two and they drink enough liquor to make this the most eloquent temperance tract since "The Beautiful and Damned." But they seem to enjoy neither the flesh nor the devil; they invoke both in a nerveless and even bodiless lethargy that looks like an abstract concept being mathematically worked out. They feel no lust and no love, nor any other of the common experiences of mankind. From page 1 of "The 42nd Parallel" to page 561 of "The Big Money" there is neither anger nor hate, neither loyalty nor admiration, neither affection nor fellowship, neither jealousy nor envy. Violent stresses are laid on the characters, their ambitions are frustrated, their bodies are mangled, savage cruelties and repulsive deaths are inflicted on them—but though they grimace they do not suffer. Oppress them and they do not cry out, cut them and they do not bleed.

But that is to say that one essential of fiction is slighted, that the atoms blown about the universe by Mr. Dos Passos's intergalactic winds remain atoms, remain symbols, and do not come alive. And so the reader does not much care what happens to them—interesting, spectacular, kaleidoscopic, pyrotechnic, expertly contrived, a fine movie, but you remain untouched. Compared to Mr. Dos Passos, Mr. Sinclair Lewis, for instance, is an unsophisticated technician—but his people have nervous systems. More life resides in even the minor characters of a Lewis novel than ever gets between the covers of this trilogy. You remember what Fran Dodsworth was doing in 1929—what was Eleanor Stoddard doing a year later? J. Ward Moorehouse is a stylized statement of a conception—George F. Babbitt is a living man. Or, for an exact parallel, consult the Benda mask of E. R. Bingham in "The Big Money" and reflect on the hideousness, but the living hideousness, of Dr. Almus Pickerbaugh. . . . Not Mr. Lewis alone need be invoked. In the six novels of Mr. Dos Passos there is no one with blood and flesh comparable to Catherine Barkley, or Maidy Forrester, or Jean Marie Latour, or Jay Gatsby, or Dr. Bull, or Clyde Griffiths, or Studs Lonigan, or Oliver Gant. Whatever power and brilliance his art may have, it is only imperfectly an art of giving life to fictitious characters.

Now it may be that there are reciprocal forces in fiction—that if you want mass man, the movement of classes and groups and geographies, you must reconcile yourself to doing without individuals. And certainly it is the essence of Mr. Dos Passos's intention to reduce personality to a mere pulsation of behavior under the impersonal and implacable drive of circumstance. But it may be also that in opening to fiction the area which Mr. Wolfe calls the manswarm you risk depriving it of its preëminent value—the exploration of individual human nature that has been the unifying theme in all the diverse kinds of fiction. And it may be that the intricate and dazzling technique that has produced this trilogy rationalizes a personal inadequacy and veils an inability to come to grips with experience. Why otherwise would the short biographies of real people interspersed through the narrative of imaginary ones have so much more feeling and so much more vitality? And certainly, when the individual disappears from fiction the most powerful means of enlisting the reader has gone also, and in achieving a map-survey of America through a quarter-century, you may forfeit your touch with the Americans.

And that map-survey—how accurate is it? Granted its brilliant effects, its breathlessness, intensity, and force, how closely does it follow experience? Well, not very. It is a mature interpretation of our times, integrated throughout, interknit, and consistent, symphonically marshalling its themes to an indictment, a judgment, and even an obsequy. And yet . . . however cruel life in the United States may have been these thirty years it has not been so dreary as all that. The Americans have not had this stolidity, they have not so nervelessly gone down before so dull a destiny. Mr. Dos Passos sees them as noisy, drunken, and lecherous from a kind of tropism. But, really, they are rowdy because they enjoy rowdiness, they drink because liquor makes them feel good, they fornicate because they find fornication fun. They do not go on debauches from a sense of obligation, and they enormously enjoy the business, the bargaining, the sports, the contention, the boisterousness, the daily routine that he depicts as no more than cellular irritability. They sing a lot. They laugh a lot. They enjoy themselves. Millionaires and hoboes, strikers and scabs, they are incurable hedonists. They have gusto. You need only look out of your window, turn on your radio, or listen in the street. . . . What kind of interpretation is this that leaves out gusto and delight to say no more of anger and pain? What kind of interpretation, especially, of the expanding years? Those years had plenty of hangovers in them, but the way to a hangover has not led through solemnity. No, when you give us the Americans as a mere mass of contractile tissue quivering in a fog, you have turned inward from the street. You are in an atelier, and a damned odd one.

Literature is the richer for any interpretation so sincere and eloquent as this one, and its brilliance, its novelty, and the intensity of its conviction go far to compensate its distortion and the anemia of its characters. Nevertheless both weaknesses must tell against it in any final judgment, and that distortion is ominous in the one remaining aspect of Mr. Dos Passos that is inescapable in any discussion of his work. His sympathies are proletarian, but the proletarian critics have had difficulty with him, sometimes accepting him as orthodox, sometimes rejecting him as a social fascist. "The Big Money" will not ratify his orthodoxy. Talk about the "rot of democracy" is disturbing, the presentation of two Party workers as saps will not be comforting, the frustration and defeat of them all run counter to the mythology of proletarian fiction, and though the treatment of the craven capitalists conforms more to precedent it is a counsel of folly. For the Movement, the whole importance of Charley Anderson is that, in general, he does not end as a drunken letch—but that he stays sober, perfects his directorates, and more securely rivets his system on the dispossessed. The whole importance of the United States Senate is that it is not composed of homosexuals and cheap grafters—the Movement would have much easier going if it were. The whole importance of J. Ward Moorehouse is not that he is a fatuous fool—but that he is a highly intelligent man formidably skilled in the busi-

ness of evil. And though throughout the trilogy, the proletarians, such as have not betrayed their class, have got the dirty end of the stick, they have also been presented with something of a theoretical argument, originating in formula, the aroma of a syllogism lingering round them, the warm and living reality ignored.

That is what it comes to, from whichever angle you approach the six novels. Experimentation, technical versatility, imagistic brilliance, the perfection of an advanced theoretical system of composition, and an advanced theoretical system of analysis and argument, all these exist almost to surfeit. But the thing lacks something in warmth, in a knowledge of life that is experienced rather than theorized about. A vast amount of fascinating substance, but in the midst of it an artist who remains intensely individualistic and incurably solipsistic, and builds his structure out of logic rather than blood and breath.

–*Saturday Review*, 14 (8 August 1936): 3–4, 12–13

## Dos Passos Completes His Modern Trilogy
Horace Gregory

*Horace Gregory, a poet and critic, taught at Sarah Lawrence College.*

It was perhaps inevitable that the Dos Passos trilogy, the work of some half dozen years, should at last betray concern for the problem of truth. I quote the forty-ninth installment of "The Camera Eye" which appears in "The Big Money":

> pencil scrawls in my notebook the scraps of recollection the broken half-phrases the effort to intersect word with word to dovetail clause with clause to rebuild out of mangled memories unshakably (Oh Pontius Pilate) the truth

I suspect that the truth toward which Mr. Dos Passos reaches is of protean structure and not the least considerable of its influences has been the wise and saturnine instruction of Thorstein Veblen's Theory of the Leisure Class. Meanwhile we have the cumulative force of three novels, each complete in itself which in time read as one entire work.

It has been characteristic of Mr. Dos Passos never to stand still, never to take for granted those truths and realities accepted by other novelists. That is why "The Big Money," with its rapidly moving scenes of action in New York, Washington, Detroit, Hollywood and Miami seems to reflect an energy which has its source in a fresh point of view. He has chosen the places where big money seems to pour in an unending stream, among politicians, movie mag-

*Dust jacket for the first British edition of the final volume in the U.S.A. trilogy, published in 1936 (Collection of Richard Layman)*

nates, the automotive industries, and real estate speculators. The people in "The Big Money" are ex-war aces, movie stars, promoters from Wall Street, social workers, reformers, Communist leaders and United States Senators—and all are influenced by the kind of living that demands the quick reward, the millions that are made today and lost tomorrow. "The Big Money" proves again that the popularity of Mr. Dos Passos's novels in Europe is well deserved, for here, as in his earlier work, he has caught the reckless speed at which the big money is made, lost, wasted in America; he, more than any other living American writer, has exposed to public satire those peculiar contradictions of our poverty in the midst of plenty. And in each of the narratives which carry the theme of the novel to its conclusion the reader shares the sensations of speed and concentrated union. Only the most unresponsive reader would fail to appreciate the humor which is the force behind the keen stroke of Mr. Dos Passos's irony.

To those who have read "The 42nd Parallel" and "1919" Mr. Dos Passos's devices of "the camera eye" and "newsreel" are familiar properties of a technic which has been skillfully borrowed from the motion picture. "The camera eye" as he employs it is usually a subjective, soft-focus close-up and the "newsreel" time sequence throughout the progress of thirty-five years, from 1900 to 1935, and contained within these thousand four hundred odd pages. But what was not clear in the earlier sections of the trilogy and which now emerges in "The Big Money" is the fact that the entire work may be described as an experiment in *montage* as applied to modern prose. We may assume that the work is a scenario of contemporary American life, and to appreciate its eloquence the trilogy should be read in three successive sittings quite as one might witness three successive performances of a single motion picture. I would almost insist that the three novels be read as fast as one can *see,* for here we are to be concerned with the stream of action in social history; no single character dominates the picture, no single force drives toward a conclusion; it is rather the cumulative forces, characters, episodes that are gathered together under the shifting lens of the camera; images of action are superimposed and from the long rolls of film Mr. Dos Passos (to complete the analogy), like another Griffith, Pabst or Eisenstein, has made a selection of cell units in news, subjective observation, biography and fictional narrative.

It is significant, I believe, that the trilogy opens on board a train going west to Chicago and closes in "The Big Money" with a flash of a large passenger plane in transcontinental flight far overhead speeding westward from the Atlantic seaboard to the Golden Gate. The first observation is made from the point of view of a small boy who was to share the poverty of his family in a Chicago slum; the last is seen through the eyes of a young man, jobless, distinctly one of the unemployed, hitchhiking his way to anywhere, still following the forty-second parallel cross country to the Pacific Coast. Between the two we have news of events at home and abroad, short biographies of American heroes, and the life history of more than a dozen characters of which the most important are Mac, J. Ward Morehouse, Richard Ellsworth Savage, Anne Elizabeth ("Daughter") Eveline Hutchins, Joe Williams, Ben Compton, Mary French, Margo Dowling and Charley Anderson.

We are introduced to Morehouse in "The 42d Parallel"; the shadow of his success story lengthens in "1919" (ex-advertising man, public relations counsel, dollar-a-year man, adviser to Woodrow Wilson at the Peace Conference in Paris) and the figure dwindles to a neurotic tangle of nerves and dyspepsia, half-dead from overwork in "The Big Money." The blue-eyed charm is gone; the rosy platitudes now roll into heavy, sententious, oily phrases; his assistant, Richard Ellsworth Savage, now does most of his work, high pressure work with periodic release in violent drinking.

Savage (we remember), once the handsome Harvard poet of "1919," was an ambulance driver during the war (he resented the war, but at its close was made secure by appointment under Morehouse). We are led to assume that he will inherit the Morehouse rewards, the well oiled platitudes, the loss of energy.

Morehouse and Savage are good type specimens of the American success story on the upper middle class level, but I believe the careers of Joe Williams ("1919") and Charley Anderson ("The 42nd Parallel" and "The Big Money") are equally if not more significant. In these two lives we have the ironic recital of a fable in contemporary American ethics: both boys start at the bottom of the social scale. Joe is a sailor, rises to second mate rating, then slips back to able seaman, and never dares to play for large stakes—perhaps his greatest crime is stealing a pair of women's silk stockings—and he is killed in a drunken brawl. Anderson, garage mechanic, enlists for war service, emerges from it an aviator, drifts home to the Middle West, drifts back to New York and enters airplane manufacturing. He then plays for larger stakes, dabbles in Wall Street speculation (the slow corruption of his character is vividly revealed in the succeeding episodes); he betrays his friends and climbs high into the infinities of paper profits; like Williams he is destined to complete his career in violent death, and it is important to remember that Anderson, like Williams, dies without a cent left to his name. Neither Williams nor Anderson escapes the threat of danger always near; from the very start their lives were insecure, and when at last they realize (however dimly, however subconsciously) that danger which surrounds them, they step forward to meet it, fulfilling their social destiny. Like the heroes in Stephen Crane's "War Is Kind," "These men were born to drill and die"; and it is one of Mr. Dos Passos's great merits that there are no tears wasted over their remains and we soon learn from him that such violence which seems so casual, so accidental, is actually a form of half-willed suicide.

I find Mr. Dos Passos's women less clearly defined than his men; they seem to follow the course of sex adventure with too much repetition, and in that sense they all seem too much alike. I would say that his detailed study of Eveline Hutchins ("1919," "The Big Money") is a shade too logical. We recognize her as the archetype of war heroine who wears short skirts, who possesses the restlessness as well as the kind of half-ironic despair which made her choose colorless, weak Paul Johnson as a father for a baby; but her disintegration throughout the narrative of "The Big Money" is all too obvious. Anne Elizabeth ("1919") with her embarrassing aggressiveness, her helplessness and her death in dramatic suicide, is far more interesting; I suspect that she is an ironic portrait of the "new woman," one of those millions sacrificed to the "new freedom" who were the girls who talked too loud, who believed too literally in the hope of a single standard and lost; it is her honesty which gives her a touch of awkward dignity. In "The Big Money" it is Margo Dowling who is most interesting as a typical American phenomenon; she is the shrewd little chorus-girl-dress-model who rises to the rewards of our bi-annual American sweethearts in Hollywood; she is the face behind that smooth close-up reflected from a million silver screens. Mr. Dos Passos's subtlety in recording her conversation saves him from the mere repetition of Anita Loos's earlier success in "Gentlemen Prefer Blondes." It is Mr. Dos Passos's refusal to caricature Hollywood that makes his portrait of Margo and her associates convincing; they are both comic and terrifying and they are given the semblance of reality through understatement.

Granting that the origins of Mr. Dos Passos's technic may be found in the art of the motion picture, it is not surprising that some of the best passages in "The Big Money" should deal with Hollywood directly; and it is significant that Mr. Dos Passos's final commentary on the American success story should leave Wall Street and Hollywood with the few victories to be gained in the making of big money. There can be no doubt about *that* conclusion, that segment of the picture is perfectly

clear. But it is also clear that the conclusion is a concrete statement of the ironic generalities contained in Veblen's "Theory of the Leisure Class," and we must not confuse Mr. Dos Passos's objectives with those of the strictly Marxian critics. Mr. Dos Passos's trilogy is as important to them as Veblen's own work, no more, no less; but they must supply the means by which his work may be applied to fit Marxian theory.

By this route we return at last to Mr. Dos Passos's concern for truth which for the most part remains a split objective; on one side lies esthetic truth; on the other, the truth of social observation. The present work is an attempt to create a synthesis out of untractable material within a new technic (which has already resulted in a number of flattering imitations by younger novelists). In one sense the present trilogy has been a record of Mr. Dos Passos's own learning process, a record of unhasty knowledge in the use of the "newsreel" and biography devices. Contrast the inadequate biographies of "The 42d Parallel" with the brilliant sketches of Henry Ford, Frederick Winslow Taylor, Isadora Duncan, Frank Lloyd Wright and Thorstein Veblen in "The Big Money." What was mere time notation in the earlier "newsreels" is a well integrated instrument of commentary in "newsreels" XLVII and LV. In these the potentialities of the device are excellently realized. But for a very few exceptions the problem of the "camera eye" remains unsolved; in these Mr. Dos Passos always seems uncomfortably arty rather than artful–they seem to move contrary to that final truth, that final integration of method and content toward which Mr. Dos Passos is moving. There is still some doubt as to whether the Dos Passos method of recording social history (despite its accuracy in stating the truth of our present defeat in radical activity which is illustrated by the stories of Ben Compton and Mary French) can bring a satisfactory conclusion to the trilogy. There would be little to prevent a fourth volume being written to the refrain of the echo now heard in motion picture theaters: "Time Marches On!" Yet while admitting these flaws in the structure of Mr. Dos Passos's trilogy it is also plain that the work is one of the most impressive contributions made to the literature of our time. The speed at which it travels is a cleansing force, dismissing the "destructive elements" in our civilization as transitory and unreal. Mr. Dos Passos offers no consolations of prophecy. He continues to perceive the realities of the life around him and in that sense he remains one of the most important of our contemporary poets. "The Big Money" establishes his position as the most incisive and direct of American satirists. It has been his hope "to rebuild . . . unshakably (Oh Pontius Pilate) the truth" and in that hope discover the truth that makes men free.

*–New York Herald Tribune Books,* 9 August 1936, p. 1

## The End of a Trilogy
Malcolm Cowley

Most of the characters in "The Big Money" had been introduced to us in the two earlier novels of the series. Charley Anderson, for example, the wild Swedish boy from the Red River Valley, had first appeared at the end of "The 42nd Parallel," where we saw him drifting over the country from job to job and girl friend to girl friend, then sailing for France as the automobile mechanic of an ambulance section. Now he comes sailing back as a bemedaled aviator, hero and ace. He helps to start an airplane manufacturing company (like Eddie Rickenbacker); he marries a banker's daughter, plunges in the stock market, drinks, loses his grip and gets killed in an automobile accident. Dick Savage, the Harvard esthete of doubtful sex, had appeared in "1919" as an ambulance driver. Now he is an advertising man, first lieutenant of the famous J. Ward Moorehouse in his campaign to popularize patent medicines as an expression of the American spirit, as self-reliance in medication. Eveline Hutchins, who played a small part in both the earlier novels, is now an unhappy middle-aged nymphomaniac. Don Stevens, the radical newspaper man, has become a Communist, a member of the Central Executive Committee after the dissenters have been expelled (and among them poor Ben Compton, who served ten years in Atlanta for fighting the draft). New people also appear: for example, Margo Dowling, a shanty-Irish girl who gets to be a movie actress by sleeping with the right people. Almost all the characters are now tied together by love or business, politics or pure hatred. And except for Mary French, a Colorado girl who half-kills herself working as the secretary of one radical relief organization after another—except for Mary French and poor honest Joe Askew, they have let themselves be caught in the race for easy money and tangible power; they have lost their personal values; they are like empty ships with their seams leaking, ready to go down in the first storm.

Read by itself, as most people will read it, "The Big Money" is the best of Dos Passos' novels, the sharpest and swiftest, the most unified in mood and story. Nobody has to refer to the earlier books in order to understand what is happening in this one. But after turning back to "The 42nd Parallel" and "1919," one feels a new admiration for Dos Passos as an architect of plots and an interweaver of destinies. One learns much more about his problems and the original methods by which he has tried to solve them.

His central problem, of course, was that of writing a collective novel (defined simply as a novel without an individual hero, a novel of which the real protagonist is a social group). In this case the social group is almost the largest possible: it is the United States from the Spanish War to the crash of 1929, a whole nation during thirty years of its history. But a novelist is not a historian dealing with political tendencies or a sociologist reckoning statistical averages. If he undertakes to depict the national life, he has to do so in terms of individual lives, without slighting either one or the other. This double focus, on the social group and on the individual, explains the technical devices that Dos Passos has used in the course of his trilogy.

It is clear enough that each of these devices has been invented with the purpose of gaining a definite effect, of supplying a quality absent from the narrative passages that form the body of the book. Take the Newsreels as an example of these technical inventions. The narratives have dealt, necessarily, with short-sighted people pursuing their personal aims—and therefore the author intersperses them with passages consisting of newspaper headlines and snatches from popular songs, his purpose being to suggest the general or collective atmosphere of a given period. Or take the brief biographies of prominent Americans. The narrative selections have dealt with people like Charley Anderson and Dick Savage, fairly typical Americans, figures that might have been chosen from a crowd—and therefore the author also gives us life-sketches of Americans who were representative rather than typical, the leaders or rebels of their age.

The third of Dos Passos' technical devices, the Camera Eye, is something of a puzzle and one that I was a long time in solving to my own satisfaction. Obviously the Camera Eye passages are autobiographical, and obviously they are intended to represent the author's stream of consciousness (a fact that explains the lack of capitalization and punctuation). At first it seemed to me that they were completely out of tone with the hard and behavioristic style of the main narrative. But this must have been exactly the reason why Dos Passos introduced them. The hard, simple, behavioristic treatment of the characters has been tending to oversimplify them, to make it seem that they were being approached from the outside—and the author tries to counterbalance this weakness by inserting passages that are written from the inside, passages full of color and warmth and hesitation and little intimate perceptions.

I have heard Dos Passos violently attacked on the ground that all these devices—Newsreels and biographies and the Camera Eye—were presented arbitrarily, without relation to the rest of the novel. This attack is partly justified as regards "The 42nd Parallel," though even in that first novel there is a clearer interrelation than most critics have noted.

For instance, the Camera Eye describes the boyhood of a well-to-do lawyer's son and thereby points an artistically desirable contrast with the boyhood of tough little Fainy McCreary. Or again, the biography of Big Bill Haywood is inserted at the moment in the story when Fainy is leaving to help the Wobblies win their strike at Goldfield. Many other examples could be given. But when we come to "1919," connections of this sort are so frequent and obvious that even a careless reader could not miss them; and in "The Big Money" all the technical devices are used to enforce the same mood and the same leading ideas.

Just what are these ideas that Dos Passos is trying to present? . . . The question sounds more portentous than it is in reality. If novels could be reduced each to a single thesis, there would be no reason for writing novels: a few convincing short essays would be all we needed. Obviously any novelist is trying to picture life as it is or was or as he would like it to be. But his ideas are important in so far as they help him to organize the picture (not to mention the important question of their effect on the reader).

In Dos Passos' case, the leading idea is the one implicit in his choice of subject and form: it is the idea that life is collective, that individuals are neither heroes nor villains, that their destiny is controlled by the drift of society as a whole. But in what direction does he believe that American society is drifting? This question is more difficult to answer, and the author doesn't give us much direct help. Still, a certain drift or progress or decline can be deduced from the novel as a whole. At the beginning of "The 42nd Parallel" there was a general feeling of hope and restlessness and let's-take-a-chance. A journeyman printer like Fainy McCreary could wander almost anywhere and find a job. A goatish but not unlikable fraud like old Doc Bingham could dream of building a fortune and, what is more, could build it. But at the end of "The Big Money," all this has changed. Competitive capitalism has been transformed into monopoly capitalism; American society has become crystallized and stratified. "Vag"—the nameless young man described in the last three pages of the novel—is waiting at the edge of a concrete highway, his feet aching in broken shoes, his belly tight with hunger. Over his head flies a silver transcontinental plane filled with highly paid executives on their way to the Pacific Coast. The upper class has taken to the air, the lower class to the road; there is no longer any bond between them; they are two nations. And we ourselves, if we choose the side of the defeated nation, are reduced to being foreigners in the land where we were born.

That, I suppose, is the author's thesis, if we reduce it to a bald statement. Dos Passos prefers to keep it in the background, suggesting it time and again. The tone of his last volume is less argumentative than emotional—and indeed, we are likely to remember it as a furious and somber poem, written in a mood of revulsion even more powerful than that which T. S. Eliot expressed in "The Waste Land." Dos Passos loves the old America; he loathes the frozen country that the capitalists have been creating—and when he describes it he makes it seem like an inferno in which Americans true to the older spirit are crushed and broken. But for the hired soldiers of the conquering nation—for J. Ward Moorehouse and Eleanor Stoddard and Dick Savage and all their kind—he reserves an even sharper torture: to be hollow and enameled, to chirp in thin squeaky voices like insects with the pulp of life sucked out of them and nothing but thin poison left in their veins. Rich, empty, frantic, they preside over an icy hell from which Dos Passos sees no hope of our ever escaping.

—*New Republic,* 88 (12 August 1936): 23–24

*Dust jacket for the 1938 Swiss edition of* The Big Money, *translated by Klaus Lambrecht (Collection of Donald Pizer)*

## The America of John Dos Passos
Max Lerner

*A Ph.D. in economics and an influential, though undoctrinaire, Marxist critic, Max Lerner was an editor at* The Nation *from 1935 to 1937. His* America as a Civilization *(1957) was greeted as a major study.*

One's impulse is to write about John Dos Passos as he has himself in his novel-trilogy written about other Americans who have been etched on our consciousness. That is to say, to write a prose-poem telling of those early impressionable days when he was carted around the world in the shelter of a well-to-do-family, his dawdling at Harvard, his "one man's initiation" into the disenchantment of the war, his attempt to apply a novelist's scalpel to murder on an organized scale in "Three Soldiers" and to the entire anatomy of a diseased social system in the more firmly wrought novels that have followed. One would set down the contradictions of a sensitive (almost shy) personality, an acid intelligence, and a gusto for life which scoops up experience with both hands. Failing a prose-poem it is none the less worth saying that with "The Big Money" Dos Passos emerges the most considerable and serious of our American writers.

His talent is expansive rather than concentrated. There is little of the creative frenzy about him. There is no tone of philosophic brooding about his books, and few of the flashing insights by which Malraux, for example, can distill a lifetime into a phrase. But there is a massiveness about Dos Passos' work, as about that of Dreiser or Lewis, that places it squarely in the path of our attention.

His aim has been to capture in three novels the whole spirit and movement of American life from the beginning of the century to the end of the boom period of the twenties. There is a central group of characters that runs through the whole trilogy. There are interlacing individual lives and destinies, but the central theme and destiny belong to America itself. The first book, "The 42d Parallel," shows America in a mood of nascent strength and recklessness, with business enterprise finding itself and expanding into new domains, with labor going through the adolescent crudeness of its I.W.W. phase on the one hand and its dreams of capital-labor cooperation on the other, with the whole complex of American life rushing into the World War. The second book, "1919," deals not with the war itself but with the fringes of it, for the author's concern is not with what happened to the cannon-fodder, but with the war as a phase of our culture. It is a study in individual rootlessness

and group hysteria, and it is only at the end of the book that the magnificent lyric on the Unknown Soldier hurtles us back ironically into a consciousness of what price we had paid as a culture for the dalliance of our Eleanor Stoddards and our J. Ward Moorehouses and our Eveline Hutchinses in Paris. The last book, "The Big Money," deals with the sequel of the war in the period of boom capitalism in the twenties. It is the era of stock speculation, mushroom real estate values, advertising and marketing, paradise on the instalment plan, the flowering of junior vice-presidents. Dos Passos has caught unforgettably the flow of American life at its high point—just before the Ice Age of the depression set in. The three books together form as complete a record as we have in fiction of the crest of American capitalist culture. If America is ever destroyed by war or overwhelmed by fascist barbarism, later generations may dig up these books and read what manner of lives we led.

Dos Passos, as is well known, is not an anatomist of the individual but a historian of the collective mentality. What he seeks to build up always is the climate of opinion—the milieu of emotion, aspiration, and shibboleth in which individuals move. That is what gives unity to each of the books. In "The Big Money" the dominating mood is the feverish desire to be where the sluices of wealth are running free and strong. The principal characters—Charley Anderson, Mary French, Margo Dowling, and Richard Ellsworth Savage—are either possessed by this desire or have to reckon with it. Charley Anderson will be remembered as the western boy whose mother ran a railroad boarding house and who had roughed it about a good deal before going to war. He comes back restless but determined to get at the big money, turns his mechanical sense to aviation, grows wealthy, marries a banker's daughter. But although he boasts of being mechanically "the boy with the knowhow," the boys at the pecuniary end outsmart him; he is stripped of most of his money, and the only love and pleasure he gets are what he buys. His tragedy is the tragedy of the technician in a money age, and of fine impulses in a shoddy culture. In fact the whole character may be regarded as a footnote to Veblen's "The Engineers and the Price System." Dick Savage does, on the surface at least, a good deal better. Harvard-bred, he comes back from a soft berth behind the lines in France to become J. Ward Moorehouse's right-hand man in the publicity racket. He is cruelly drawn. His life, no less than Charley Anderson's, is stripped of any real satisfactions—a sacrifice to the Moloch of the big money. But while Charley Anderson in going to his ruin adds something at least to the industrial arts, Savage adds nothing except marvelous ideas for getting Bingham's Patent Medicines across to the country.

There is a similar contrast between Mary French and Margo Dowling. Mary, after a middle-class girlhood in Colorado, wanders into social work, meets up with some steel strikers, falls in love with a succession of radicals and near-radicals, and learns that love can be just as frustrate on the fringes of the revolutionary movement as anywhere else. But despite the frustration she does throw her energies into organizing work which may some day have meaning for America. Margo Dowling on the other hand throws hers into building the illusion of glamour on the screen. She is the ruthless career girl on whom the boom decade smiles most kindly. She learns how to sleep her way to success, and her path carries her to Charley Anderson's arms, to the Miami land boom, and finally across the country to Hollywood where her smooth heartless face makes her exactly the person for director Samuel Margolies to exalt to stardom.

To portray the collective mood and the mass culture requires technical innovation in the novel. To my knowledge Dos Passos has never formulated a theory about it, as Jules Romains has done with his *unanisme*. But it is clear that he has in the realm of the novel-form what H. G. Wells has called in another connection the "skepticism of the instrument." He has played havoc with spelling and his punctuation has given the traditionalists among the critics some acute distress. More important, he has selected out of the stream of American living speech a new American language which for its vitality and usableness should delight Mr. Mencken. Most important, he has contrived a film technique for giving perspectives, close-ups, rapid sequences difficult for the orthodox narrative.

The problem was this. Here are people neither sensitive nor complex, living a good part of their lives not far from the level of animal behavior. Here is a culture shot through with complex currents and cross- currents of influence which touch the lives and destinies of even the simplest people. Experience is no longer the tidy unity it was once believed. How can the author catch up the splintered fragments of experience and hold them up to view while at the same time getting something like a total effect? The answer was a fourfold technique. The *narrative* of individual fictional lives is told in an unadorned hard-surfaced manner—a modern picaresque that gives the barest details of overt behavior. The *newsreel,* made up of newspaper headlines, speeches, popular songs, tries to depict the mass consciousness and furnishes a backdrop against which the individual

lives are enacted. The *biography* deals with historical Americans who summed up and expressed in their lives the main forces of their day. Finally, the *camera eye* turns the searchlight of the author's own intense brooding gaze at the set of events being discussed: it is a chaotic flow of consciousness, strangely subjective and lyrical amidst the expanse of objectivity elsewhere in the book, warm and intimate with the remembered rush of personal incident. Mechanically used, these four devices may merely make the problem of communication so much more complex. Skilfully interwoven they may go to form a unity that does not simplify, and hence falsify, the reality. There is a good deal of both—mechanical and skilful—in the trilogy. But in the last book Dos Passos has written with a passion that welds his material together as never before. The improved cunning of his hand is governed by a real heat of the brain. This book is therefore easily the best of the whole series.

The America of John Dos Passos that is presented in these pages is not a lovely America. How could it be? Dos Passos is one of the few novelists writing today who are truly literate. He knows things. He knows the force of institutions and mass ideas, he knows by what impulsions people are moved, he knows what things are first things in a social system and what things are derivative, he knows the ways and the speech of common people. He is part of the America that he depicts, and he bestows upon the portrait that desperate tenderness that can only flow from love and solicitude turned into satire. His social analysis owes much to Marx, but essentially he is the Veblen of American fiction, sharing Veblen's rebelliousness, his restless questing mind, his hatred of the standardized middle class culture and of the leisure class aesthetic, his insight into American traits, his divided feeling about the underlying population. But beyond social analysis he has the qualities of the great novelist—tenderness, humanity, fertility. He is never at a loss to people his world, and already his world has come to have an existence of its own in the reader's mind, apart from the America it depicts.

One thing is certain—he will keep moving. His social beliefs are still fluid, his sense for innovation still has a sharp edge. But what will carry him farthest is his belief in American life. A sentence from one of his Camera Eyes (46) contains affirmation as well as irony: "I go home after a drink and a hot meal and . . . ponder the course of history and what leverage might pry the owners loose from power and bring back (I too Walt Whitman) our storybook democracy."

*—Nation,* 143 (15 August 1936): 187–188

## Greatness
Isidor Schneider

*Isidor Schneider, a Communist Party spokesman on literary matters throughout the 1930s, wrote frequently for the* New Masses *and* The Daily Worker. *He was one of the co-editors (with Granville Hicks and Mike Gold, among others) of the influential collection* Proletarian Literature in the United States *(1935).*

*The 42nd Parallel,* the first volume in the series of which *The Big Money* is the third, was published in 1930 and must have been begun at least a year earlier. Jules Romains's vast novel, *Men of Good Will,* is perhaps a more recent conception but his short novel, *The Death of a Nobody,* published in the early twenties, almost as the manifesto of a movement then called Unanism, foreshadowed what is now called the "collective novel." The point I want to make is that a shift in interest from the individual to society had already begun some years before the present concentration upon social subjects. Nor are these instances solitary. The same direction may be discerned in other work, for example even in Hemingway's *The Sun Also Rises,* which depends relatively little upon studied individual characterization, but seeks to give a personality to a whole generation. There was already growing in the consciousness of writers, before the crisis had made the class struggle clinically visible, an awareness that in contemporary life the fate of the individual was more than ever determined by the fortunes of his class.

By this I do not want to be understood as announcing the decline and fall of the novel of individual characterization and the rise of the collective novel, examples of which are still scarce. Many novelists are very ably doing what they wish to do (even where it is the illumination of the class struggle) from the focus of individual character. There is little likelihood that the interest in individual character will ever end or that its technical advantages will be lost sight of. It is to be noted that in Dos Passos's novels, separate characters are, through the use of concentrated narrative, given as full a development as in most novels. I have attempted here only to indicate the historical place of the collective novel, to show that it is not merely an experiment in technique but an expression of the time spirit and a significant response to social change.

In the three novels, *The 42nd Parallel, 1919,* and *The Big Money,* we have, in the main, a fictionized history of the American middle class in the last generation. From this class most of the characters are drawn; and the crises in their lives reflect their class fortunes. The class is a frustrated one, and the omens of its defeat are visible in hours of apparent triumph.

The defeat is the special theme of *The Big Money,* the scenes of which shift to and fro between New York, Detroit, Hollywood, and Miami, wherever the big money comes easy; sweated out on the factory belt, water-bloated in Wall Street, alchemized out of Florida sunshine, stamped out of merchandised sex-appeal in Hollywood. The defeat is on two fronts—in the bid for economic power, and in the undertaking to set up a special civilization of the middle-class intelligentsia. For it was middle-class intellectuals, many of them artists buried in commerce—newspaper men, advertising men, commercial artists, and so on—who nurtured the modern arts now blooming in Rockefeller's Radio City, and who sought to establish as common rights the anarchy of conduct formerly held as the privilege of the rich.

The first is powerfully shown in the career of Charley Anderson, one-time garage mechanic who comes back from France with two exploitable assets, his reputation as an aviation ace and his invention of a new airplane starter. The developing aviation industry makes use of both. Charley has a swift career, upward. Part owner in a small plant, then executive in a big plant, he gets in the money. He plays the stock market in a sort of frenzied tasting of the sense of money power. He is dazzled by the slender daughters of aristocratic families whose arrogance is as pure as an essence. He marries one of them, to be used by her as heartlessly as a male by an insect queen. But he never feels more than naturalized in the class he has risen into. His happiest moments and memories, his truest loyalty, is with the Czech mechanic whose company he resorts to in the search for genuine human contact. He becomes what might be termed a lumpen millionaire, retreating into drink and high living to bury his confusion. He is being frozen out of his holdings, and his elimination is only a matter of time, when he does the job for his enemies. He kills himself driving a car while drunk. I say "kills himself" deliberately, for the heedless life he had been leading had in it a yearning for and a standing invitation to death.

Another key figure is that of Eveline Hutchins, intelligent, charming, and restless, living on sensation, swept by vague ambitions which sediment down into a taste for notoriety, and finally into maintaining a salon for the purpose of providing a setting for, and of holding her lover. She becomes one of the most successful hostesses in the Greenwich Village that, during the twenties, cut the stock patterns of "civilized" living in America. In her studios you could always count on finding an awesome collection of celebrities. Her affairs were public. Her patiently modern husband stood it for a time; then, through a hushed divorce, he quietly removed himself and the anachronous decoration of marriage from her menage. Her lover, however, marries another woman and Eveline brings her problem to a stale solution with an overdose of veronal. Shocked friends remember that it climaxed one of her best parties; that she had looked tired; and that she had been amused by the exclamations of sophisticated guests over the presence of so many authentic celebrities.

The companion pieces are the careers of Richard Ellsworth Savage, the publicity man, putting a sensitive and keen intelligence to degenerate uses and anaesthetizing his sense of futility in alcohol; Margulies, the "art" photographer who becomes a movie solon, shutting up banalities in mystifying phrases, a verbal dark room in which they develop into banalities focused and highlighted. Hollywood has often been satirized but never so mordantly, never from the angle that Hollywood, besides being a triumph of money adventurism, is a realization of mutilated dreams of art.

In these and, in fact, in most of the other characters, the portraiture, that of the individual faces and the composite face they blend into, is superb. Passages in the book are among the surest realistic writing I have ever read. The scenes with Charley Anderson's family are truer Main Street than Sinclair Lewis's; Eveline Hutchins's last party reaches a point of ironic tragedy not attained by any other portrayer of the lost generation.

However, in his characterization of Mary French, the middle-class liberal sympathizer who steps out of her class to work with the labor movement, and still more in the characterization of the revolutionists, Ben Compton and Don Stevens, Dos Passos falls short. Mary French is noticeably a stock character of Dos Passos. Daughter, in *1919,* was a variant of the type. She is eager, sincere, and over-credulous. Her life is an automatic function of sympathetic response. Especially in the later sections where she is involved with Compton and Stevens, the drive of Dos Passos's narrative, always so concentrated and swift, seems to fall into the hum of a machine, the action is so dehumanized.

Compton and Stevens are unreal. They are twenty-four-hour-a-day revolutionists. Humanity is replaced in them by a sort of mechanism for revolutionary activity that permits at the same time automatic operation of the vital functions. It is a common enough concept of the revolutionary, the usual rationalization of this challenging exception in society, who seeks to make it over in the image of his ideals. Dos Passos is sympathetic; he seeks to arouse respect instead of horror; but his concept is nevertheless the dehumanized figure of tradition. There is an attempt to restore balance by giving Compton and Stevens love affairs, but the affairs have a super-Bohemian quality. One can only add that revolutionists do not love, as they do not talk and work, like Ben Compton and Don Stevens. In

a writer of Dos Passos's sensitiveness such a failure is a great disappointment.

There has been considerable controversy over Dos Passos's use of his especially developed literary devices, the *newsreels* in which he makes a mosaic of the news headlines, advertising catchlines, song-hit choruses of the period, the *camera eyes* in which he seeks to capture the mood of the period, and the brief biographies of significant characters of the period, in whose notoriety and influence contemporary forces in America are symbolized. Some critics regard these passages, in spite of the universally admitted eloquence and beauty of the writing, as unessential, even as excrescences. Such an attitude fails to understand their functions in Dos Passos's narrative.

In the first place the tempo of his narrative is so swift and its material is so concentrated that it provides no room for the asides, the speculations, the psychological analyses, the set descriptions, and back-ground layouts which most novelists incorporate as essential textual elements. This material which other novelists scatter through their writing, Dos Passos separates out, organizes, gives distinct forms and functions to. And this specialization justifies itself in the effectiveness with which they do their work. The *newsreels,* for instance, give continuity and the time sense; the brief biographies which, in *The Big Money,* include Ford, Insull, Hearst, Veblen, Taylor, innovator of belt-line production, the Wright Brothers, Isadora Duncan, Rudolf Valentino, and the architect, Frank Lloyd Wright, fix the historical symbols; the *camera eye* not only fixes moods, but provides what might be regarded as a stream of social consciousness. These devices provide necessary stops and relaxations in the swift, powerful flow of narrative, point directions, and intensify insights.

The limitation I have spoken of, the failure in the presentation of revolutionary figures, is serious. Yet, in spite of it, *The Big Money* is so powerful as a presentation of the American middle class in its testing years, so mature and trickless in its portrayal of character, so large, so comprehensive, and so deep-feeling in its treatment of humanity in motion that it establishes itself and the work of which it is a part as one of the major achievements of American fiction. It is a particular distinction in this achievement that, with the exception noted, the principal characters rise into symbolic life without, as individuals, dropping into types, and that the characters of this collective novel are therefore among the finest realized individuals in our literature.

*–New Masses,* 20 (11 August 1936): 40–41

## The Big Money
Unsigned review

In this novel of the 1920s, Mr. Dos Passos continues the technique of his other fictional studies of the United States of our times. He uses newspaper headlines, bits of popular song, odd typographical arrangements, the "camera eye", and so on, and those who are interested in such experiments will probably be absorbed by the tricks.

As for me, I am frankly no more impressed than if the publishers had announced that Mr. Dos Passos had written the book while standing on his head. This would have proved him to be an acrobat, but not necessarily a good novelist.

The body of the book is concerned with a number of characters—an aviator, an actress, a wife, and so on. They are supposed to represent the evil influences of capitalism, I believe; but they are more accurate presentations of people who drink too much gin when anything goes wrong, and, having thrown up, drink some more. This pleasant habit they alternate with sleeping in strange beds.

I found the novel tiresome because the people never seemed to matter in the least; they would have gone down under any system, so why blame capitalism for their complete and appalling lack of character?

Mr. Dos Passos's America seems to me a figment of his own imagination, and I doubt the value of his reportage of our period.

The present novel breaks the world's record for the number of times the people in it give up their meals because of too much liquor.

—*Review of Reviews*, 94 (September 1936): 12

## Novelists Who Explore
Theodore Spencer

*Theodore Spencer, a poet, critic, and scholar, taught at Harvard.*

*The Big Money* is the third and last of John Dos Passos's novels describing the American scene in the years after the war. As in its predecessors, we are shown a wide panorama of American life, through snatches of typical news headlines, through more or less lyrical interpolations, through brief and admirable biographies of significant public figures, and most of all through the interweaving stories of several representative people: a war ace who gets into big business and is ruined, a girl who becomes a movie star, an earnest social worker, a public relations man—all of them people whose lives have been directly conditioned by the circumstances of their time.

No one concerned with the health of the novel as a living form can fail to sympathize with the ambitious task Mr. Dos Passos has set himself; no one can fail to regard his achievement with respect. He writes from a wise and comprehending point of view; his construction is firm; his narrative is swift, realistic, and interesting. There are few novelists in this country to-day whose craftsmanship is as secure, and whose sense of American life as understanding and awake.

Yet both the subject matter and the technique of this novel raise some important doubts and problems. Fundamentally its method is the method of journalism: the book, to use a familiar distinction, is a record of what *did* happen,—rationalized, sorted, and typified, to be sure,—but not, in spite of its sometimes vivid characterization, an imaginative reconstruction of what *might* happen. It is description rather than interpretation. Consequently, and this is its fundamental weakness as a work of art, there is nothing inevitable in what happens to the main figures. The case of Charley Anderson, his chief hero, is typical. Charley is a man without character, almost without personality. Nothing that he does is the result of his own determination; he makes money by accident, he gets married by accident, he gets killed by accident. He is an unconscious victim of the society which produced him.

Now this is all very well if Mr. Dos Passos's aim is to sonality; Mr. Dos Passos gives us a most convincing picture of its meaningless stupidity. But in the hero of a novel we want more than an illustration of a society. The trouble with Charley Anderson as a character is that there is nothing about him which is dramatic; his awareness of himself is so rudimentary that a conflict, such as there was in George F. Babbitt, is impossible. The crude and cruel circumstances, of which he is only childishly conscious, are his destruction.

There is both contrast and similarity in the work of Huxley and Dos Passos. In a sense their weaknesses are the opposites of each other: Huxley tries to interpret—to explain and possibly to solve—too much; Dos Passos does not try to interpret enough. But their virtues are the same; they are both honest and sincere craftsmen, and they both vividly describe two different aspects of a civilization which, however decadent or blind it seems, may perhaps be better because they have so faithfully shown us what it is like.

—*Atlantic Monthly*, 158 (October 1936), n.p.

* * *

## Reviews of *U.S.A.* (1938)

*The publication of Dos Passos's trilogy in a single volume, with the three novels subsumed for the first time under an epic-suggesting title, did not attract the large number of reviews one might expect. Apparently, most journals, especially newspapers, felt that since each of the novels had been reviewed when first published, a review of what constituted, in a sense, a reprinting was not necessary. Nevertheless, the reviews that did appear were exceptional in their substantiality and importance, as major literary spokesmen of the period, recognizing the significance of the trilogy as a whole, took the opportunity of its publication in one volume to discuss the issues raised by the work as a whole.*

*One such issue was the political standing of the trilogy in the turbulent arena of late-1930s left-wing infighting. Dos Passos's apostasy from the far Left, signaled by his negative portrayal of the Communist zealot Don Stevens in* The Big Money, *had been confirmed in 1937 by his criticism of Communist actions in the conduct of the Spanish Civil War. The negative reviews of* U.S.A. *by Granville Hicks and especially by the party hack Mike Gold anticipate Dos Passos's exclusion for some decades from serious consideration by a large body of critical opinion.*

*Of far greater lasting importance are the major reviews by T. K. Whipple and Lionel Trilling. Both critics accept the vitality and significance of the trilogy and thus seek to define the qualities that contribute to and detract from its possible claim to greatness. Is the thinness of the inner lives of Dos Passos's narrative figures, for example, a sign of his commitment to a vitiating naturalism, or is it a reflection of his penetrating moral vision of American life as a whole? In affording the trilogy the advantage of full-ranging scrutiny on this level, this group of critics provided the basis for much of the vital criticism of* U.S.A. *that was to come.*

**Dos Passos and the U.S.A.**
T. K. Whipple

*T. K. (Thomas King) Whipple was a professor of English at the University of California, Berkeley, and a frequent contributor to literary journals. His* Spokesmen: Modern Writers and American Life *(1928) was well received.*

The choice of the ambitious title "U.S.A." for the volume which brings together Dos Passos's "The 42nd Parallel," "Nineteen-Nineteen," and "The Big Money" looks as if it might be intended to stake out a claim on the fabulous "great American novel." And Dos Passos's claim is not a weak one. A single book could hardly be more inclusive than his: in the stories of his main characters he covers most parts of the country during the first three decades of the twentieth century. His people have considerable social diversity, ranging from Mac, the I.W.W. type-

setter, and Joe Williams, the feckless sailor, to Ben Compton, the radical leader, Eleanor Stoddard, the successful decorator, Margo Dowling, the movie star, and J. Ward Moorehouse, the big publicity man. The background of the panorama is filled out with "newsreels" of newspaper headlines, popular songs, and the like, with the autobiographic "camera eye" which gives snatches of Dos Passos's own experience, and with a series of biographical portraits of representative men—Debs, Edison, Wilson, Joe Hill, Ford, Veblen, Hearst, and twenty more. Probably no other American novel affords a picture so varied and so comprehensive.

Furthermore, the picture is rendered with extraordinary vividness and brilliance of detail, especially of sensory detail. Sights and sounds and above all smells abound until the reader is forced to wonder that so many people, of such different sorts, are all so constantly aware of what their eyes and ears and noses report to them: might not some of

# U. S. A.

1. THE 42*nd* PARALLEL

2. NINETEEN NINETEEN

3. THE BIG MONEY

*John Dos Passos*

Harcourt, Brace and Company

NEW YORK

*Title page of the first single-volume edition of Dos Passos's trilogy, published in 1938 (Collection of Richard Layman)*

them, one asks, more often get absorbed in meditation or memory or planning or reverie? But it is no part of Dos Passos's scheme to spend much time inside his characters' heads; he tells, for the most part, what an outsider would have seen or heard–gestures, actions, talk, as well as the surroundings. The result is a tribute to the keenness of the author's observation–not only of colors, noises, and odors but, even more important, of human behavior and of American speech. People as well as things are sharp and distinct.

Nor does the presentation lack point and significance. As the book goes on, the U.S.A. develops, with the precision of a vast and masterly photograph, into a picture of a business world in its final ripeness, ready to fall into decay. Though Dos Passos does not call himself a Marxist–and would seem in fact not to be one–his point of view is unmistakably radical. The class struggle is present as a minor theme; the major theme is the vitiation and degradation of character in such a civilization. Those who prostitute themselves and succeed are most completely corrupted; the less hard and less self-centered are baffled and beaten; those who might have made good workers are wasted; the radicals experience internal as well as external defeat. No one attains any real satisfaction. Disintegration and frustration are everywhere. The whole presentation leads to the summary: "Life is a shambles." Perhaps there are implications that it need not be; but no doubt is left that actually it is.

These generalities, when stated as generalities, have of course become the trite commonplaces of a whole school of literature. But actual people shown going through the process of victimization can never become trite or commonplace; the spectacle must always be pitiful and terrible. And no one, I should suppose, could look on Dos Passos's picture wholly untouched and unmoved. But still one might ask whether he has quite achieved the tragic effect which presumably he aimed at.

To complain that the picture is one-sided may appear captious and unreasonable, and in one sense of "one-sided" it is. The whole truth about a hundred million people throughout thirty years cannot be told in fifteen hundred–or in fifteen million–pages. The novelist has to select what he considers representative and characteristic persons and events, and if Dos Passos has chosen to omit big business men, farmers, and factory workers and to dwell chiefly on midway people in somewhat ambiguous positions–intellectuals, decorators, advertising men–perhaps that is his privilege. The question is whether this picture of his, which is surely extensive enough as novels go, is entirely satisfactory within the limitations which must be granted. How

close does "U.S.A." come to being a great American novel? That it comes within hailing distance is proved by the fact that it has already been so hailed; indeed, it comes close enough so that the burden of proof is on those who would deny the title. Yet to grant it offhand would be premature.

On one point at least everyone probably agrees: that the biographical portraits are magnificent, and are the best part of the book. But wherein are they superior? Is it not that these portraits have a greater depth and solidity than Dos Passos's fictional characterizations–a more complete humanity? If so, the implication must be that his creation of character is not complete. And indeed when Mac is put beside Big Bill Haywood or Ben Compton beside Joe Hill and Jack Reed, or Margo Dowling beside Isadora Duncan, the contrast is unflattering to Dos Passos's powers as a novelist. There is more human reality in the 10 pages given to Henry Ford than in the 220 given to Charley Anderson. Nor is the explanation that the real people are exceptional, the fictitious ones ordinary, satisfactory: some of the fictitious ones are supposed to be leaders; and besides it is a novelist's business so to choose and treat his imagined characters as to reveal his themes in their utmost extension, not at their flattest. No, the contrast has nothing to do with the positions people occupy; it is a fundamental matter of the conception of human nature and the portrayal of it in literature.

In thinking of this contrast, one notices first that the real men have a far better time of it in the world, that they do find a good many genuine satisfactions, that even when they fail–when they are jailed like Debs or shot down like Joe Hill–they are not wholly defeated. Inside them is some motive power which keeps them going to the end. Some of them swim with the stream and some against it, but they all swim; they all put up a fight. They all have persistent ruling passions. Furthermore, they are all complex and many-sided, full of contradictions and tensions and conflicts. They have minds, consciousness, individuality, and personality.

Not that all these things are entirely lacking in the fictitious characters–Dos Passos is too good a novelist for that–but they do appear only in a much lower degree, played down, degraded, reduced to a minimum. As a result, the consciousness of these people is of a relatively low order. True, they are aware with an abnormal keenness of their sensations, but is not this sensory awareness the most elementary form of consciousness? On the other hand, these folk can hardly be said to think at all, and their feelings are rather sharp transitory reactions than long-continuing dominant emotions. Above all, they are devoid of will or purpose, helplessly impelled hither and yon by the circumstances of the moment. They have no strength of resistance. They are weak at the very core of personality, the power to choose. Now it may be that freedom of choice is an illusion, but if so it is an inescapable one, and even the most deterministic and behavioristic novelist cannot omit it or minimize it without denaturing human beings. When the mainspring of choice is weakened or left out, the conflicts and contradictions of character lose their virtue and significance, and personality almost disappears. Dos Passos often gives this effect: that in his people there is, so to speak, nobody much at home, or that he is holding out on us and that more must be happening than he is willing to let on. This deficiency shows itself most plainly in the personal relations of his characters—they are hardly persons enough to sustain real relations with one another, any more than billiard balls do—and in his treatment of crises, which he is apt to dispose of in some such way as "They had a row so that night he took the train. . . ."

The final effect is one of banality—that human beings and human life are banal. Perhaps this is the effect Dos Passos aimed at, but that it is needless and even false is proved by the biographical portraits, in which neither the men nor their lives are ever banal. The same objection holds, therefore, to Dos Passos's whole social picture as to his treatment of individuals, that he has minimized something vital and something which ought to be made much of—namely, forces in conflict. Society is hardly just rotting away and drifting apart; the destructive forces are tremendously powerful and well organized, and so are the creative ones. Furthermore, they are inextricably intermingled in institutions and in individuals. If Dos Passos is forced, by sheer fact, to present them so when he writes of Ford and Steinmetz and Morgan, why should he make little of them in his fiction? Is it to illustrate a preconceived and misleading notion that life nowadays is a silly and futile "shambles?"

One might hope, but in vain, to find the answer in the autobiographic "camera eye." To be sure, the author there appears as the extremest type of Dos Passos character, amazingly sensitive to impressions and so amazingly devoid of anything else that most of the "camera eye" is uninteresting in the extreme. The effect of this self-portrait is further

*Dust jacket for the 1938 edition of Dos Passos's trilogy (Collection of Richard Layman)*

heightened by the brief prologue which introduces "U.S.A.": an account of a young man, plainly the author himself, who "walks by himself searching through the crowd with greedy eyes, greedy ears taut to hear, by himself, alone," longing to share everybody's life, finding his only link with other people in listening to their talk. If the obvious conclusion could be accepted that Dos Passos had been never a participant but always a mere onlooker hungry for participation, so that he had to depend only on observation from outside, it would explain much. But such is not the fact; he took part in the World War and in the Sacco-Vanzetti case and other activities. He has been no mere spectator of the world. Moreover, he must have had powerful and lasting purposes and emotions to have written his books, and it is hardly credible that he has done so little thinking as he makes out. His self-portrait must be heinously incomplete, if only because he is a real man. But it is possible that he may have chosen to suppress some things in himself and in his writing, and that he may have acquired a distrust of thought and feeling and will which has forced him back upon sensations as the only reliable part of experience. Some such process seems to have taken place in many writers contemporary with him, resulting in a kind of spiritual drought, and in a fear lest they betray themselves or be betrayed by life. Perhaps the disillusionment of the war had something to do with it, but more probably a partial view and experience of our present society are responsible.

According to any view, that society, in all conscience, is grim enough, but not banal, not undramatic. Dos Passos has reduced what ought to be a tale of full-bodied conflicts to an epic of disintegration and frustration. That reduction—*any* reduction—is open to objection, because it is an imperfect account of human beings and human society that does not present forces working in opposition. In that sense "U.S.A." is one-sided, whereas life and good literature are two-sided or many-sided. In a word, what we want is a dialectic treatment of people and the world. Dos Passos does not call himself a Marxist; if he were more of one, he might have written a better novel. The biographical portraits are the best part of his book because they are the most nearly Marxist, showing the dynamic contradictions of our time in the only way they can be shown—namely, as they occur in the minds and lives of whole men. Nothing will do, in the end, but the whole man.

                    —*Nation,* 146 (19 February 1938): 210–212

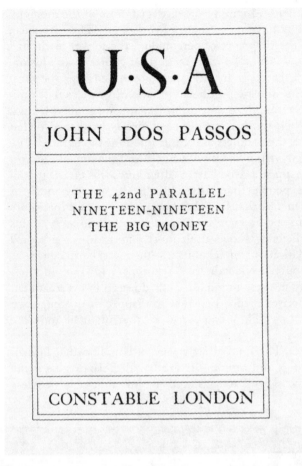

*Title page of the first one-volume British edition of Dos Passos's trilogy, published in 1938 (Collection of Richard Layman)*

### Change the World: The Keynote to Dos Passos' Works
Mike Gold

*Mike Gold (the pen name of Irving Granich) was a major spokesman for the Communist Party on literary matters throughout the 1920s and 1930s. His articles appeared often in the* New Masses *and* The Daily Worker.

Arnold Gingrich, a smart young entrepreneur who publishes Esquire and other magazines, sent me recently the trilogy by John Dos Passos, with a note saying in effect: "I think this the greatest book written in modern America, and would like to know whether you agree."

I've read the book but haven't answered the letter. There are feelings involved—political feelings you can't explain satisfactorily to the publisher of a magazine that has gotten rich by re-telling the dirty stories of travelling salesmen. Such publishers always have the loftiest private morals about art (with a capital A).

But the problem of Dos Passos remains, and needs to be explained to oneself and to the workers—at least for the record.

First problem: Only a few years ago Dos Passos was the hope of our left-wing literature in America. I myself wrote enthusiastically about him in the official magazine of English teachers and in other places. Granville Hicks capped his book on American literature with the figure of Dos Passos. We were all doing it. Even some of the Soviet writers and critics were doing it.

Second problem: Dos Passos falls among Trotsky-ites, and goes sour on us. The climax arrives with his visit to fighting Spain. He returns, not hating the fascism that has committed this crime against the people, but hating Communism.

From now on he displays the familiar lunacy of Trotskyite intellectuals: Stalin engineered the war in Spain. Stalin framed China to resist Japan. Stalin is trying to frame America into a war against Japan. Stalin framed up the "gentle old martyr" Trotsky, etc., etc.

Ernest Hemingway also went to Spain. He learned a different lesson. He and Dos Passos had been the most intimate friends since the World War. Now Hemingway, I understand, has completely broken off his old friendship with Dos Passos on the issue of Spain. Hemingway regards Franco as the enemy of Spain.

Third problem: How should one sit in "esthetic" judgment on a book by a man who has gone through this evolution?

Well, I got the clue, I think, in reading through the trilogy. The most frequent word in it is "merde," a French euphimism I shall use for the four-letter word, s—t, that Dos Passos so boldly scatters through his pages (Oh, the courage of it!).

The merde was there formerly when we praised Dos Passos. But we praised him as a fellow-traveller, not as a Communist. We were anxious to win the fellow-travellers and ignored the merde and looked for every gleam of the proletarian hope.

There was such hope Dos Passos was moving up from the bourgeois merde. It was right that we recognized in him a powerful if bewildered talent, tried to help free that talent from the muck of bourgeois nihilism.

He was going somewhere; it was right to hope to the limit and to ignore the merde. Now Dos Passos is going nowhere. On rereading his trilogy, one cannot help seeing how important the merde is in his psychology, and how, after a brief, futile effort, he has sunk back into it, as into a native element.

Like the Frenchman Celine, Dos Passos hates Communists because organically he seems to hate the human race. It is strange to see how little real humane-

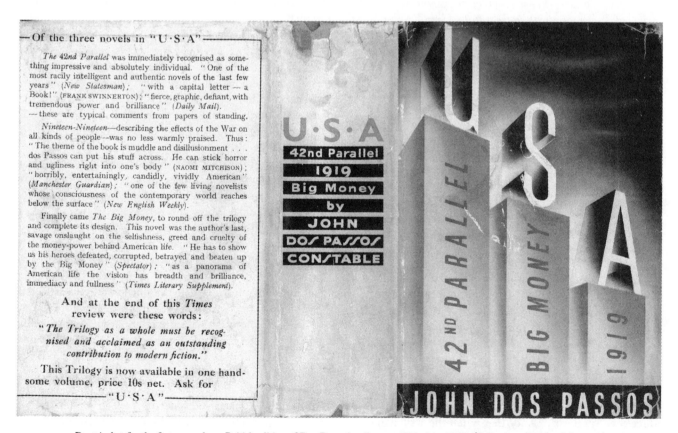

*Dust jacket for the first one-volume British edition of Dos Passos's trilogy, published in 1938 (Collection of Richard Layman)*

ness there is in his book. He takes a dull, sadistic joy in showing human beings at their filthiest, meanest, most degraded moments. They have no will power; they are amoeba, moved by chemistry. Everything about them is blah!

You cannot be a Communist on hate and disgust alone. Lenin "deeply loved the people," was his wife's final word upon him. There's not a spark of such dynamic love on the merde-writers like Dos Passos, Farrell, Dahlberg, et al. They reflect only the bourgeois decadence.

The transition to Trotzkyism is easy for such folks. It is only a new form of hatred of the people and of life, and of whatever human hope there is.

Celine, the French merde-writer, came for a brief spell close to Communism, then departed. Now Celine is an avowed fascist. From merde he came, to merde he has returned.

What is the future of Dos Passos? You tell me, Mr. Gingrich!

–*Daily Worker* (New York), 26 February 1938, p. 7

## The America of John Dos Passos
Lionel Trilling

*With Edmund Wilson one of the preeminent American literary critics from the 1930s to the 1960s, Lionel Trilling was a teacher at Columbia University for most of his career. He contributed frequently to the* Partisan Review, The Nation, *and* The New Republic. *His* The Liberal Imagination *(1950) is still widely discussed.*

*U.S.A.* is far more impressive than even its three impressive parts—*42nd Parallel, 1919, The Big Money*—might have led one to expect. It stands as the important American novel of the decade, on the whole more satisfying than anything else we have. It lacks any touch of eccentricity; it is startlingly normal; at the risk of seeming paradoxical one might say that it is exciting because of its quality of cliché: here are comprised the judgments about modern American life that many of us have been living on for years.

Yet too much must not be claimed for this book. To-day we are inclined to make literature too important, to estimate the writer's function at an impossibly high rate, to believe that he can encompass and resolve all the contradictions, and to demand that he should. We forget that, by reason of his human nature, he is likely to win the intense perception of a single truth at the cost of a relative blindness to other truths. We expect a single man to give us all the answers and produce the "synthesis." And then when the writer, hailed for giving us much, is discovered to have given us less

than everything, we turn from him in a reaction of disappointment: he has given us nothing. A great deal has been claimed for Dos Passos and it is important, now that *U.S.A.* is completed, to mark off the boundaries of its enterprise and see what it does not do so that we may know what it does do.

One thing *U.S.A.* does not do is originate; it confirms but does not advance and it summarizes but does not suggest. There is no accent or tone of feeling that one is tempted to make one's own and carry further in one's own way. No writer, I think, will go to school to Dos Passos, and readers, however much they may admire him will not stand in the relation to him in which they stand, say, to Stendhal or Henry James or even E. M. Forster. Dos Passos' plan is greater than its result in feeling; his book *tells* more than it *is*. Yet what it tells, and tells with accuracy, subtlety and skill, is enormously important and no one else has yet told it half so well.

Nor is *U.S.A.* as all-embracing as its admirers claim. True, Dos Passos not only represents a great national scene but he embodies, as I have said, the cultural tradition of the intellectual Left. But he does not encompass—does not pretend to encompass in this book—all of either. Despite his title, he is consciously selective of his America and he is, as I shall try to show, consciously corrective of the cultural tradition from which he stems.

Briefly and crudely, this cultural tradition may be said to consist of the following beliefs, which are not so much formulations of theory or principles of action as they are emotional tendencies: that the collective aspects of life may be distinguished from the individual aspects; that the collective aspects are basically important and are good; that the individual aspects are, or should be, of small interest and that they contain a destructive principle; that the fate of the individual is determined by social forces; that the social forces now dominant are evil; that there is a conflict between the dominant social forces and other, better, rising forces; that it is certain or very likely that the rising forces will overcome the now dominant ones. *U.S.A.* conforms to some but not to all of these assumptions. The lack of any protagonists in the trilogy, the equal attention given to many people, have generally been taken to represent Dos Passos' recognition of the importance of the collective idea. The book's historical apparatus indicates the author's belief in social determination. And there can be no slightest doubt of Dos Passos' attitude to the dominant forces of our time: he hates them.

But Dos Passos modifies the tradition in three important respects. Despite the collective elements of his trilogy, he puts a peculiar importance upon the individual. Again, he avoids propounding any sharp con-

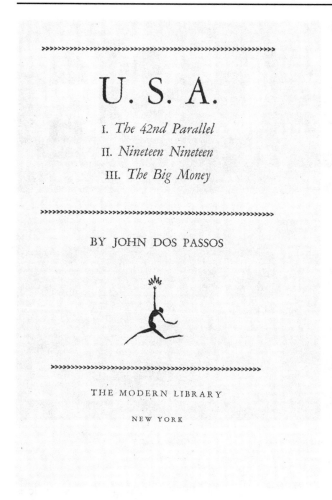

# U. S. A.

I. *The 42nd Parallel*

II. *Nineteen Nineteen*

III. *The Big Money*

BY JOHN DOS PASSOS

THE MODERN LIBRARY

NEW YORK

*Title page of the 1939 Modern Library publication of Dos Passos's trilogy, which was kept in print and was the version most commonly encountered by several generations of readers (Collection of Richard Layman)*

flict between the dominant forces of evil and the rising forces of good; more specifically, he does not write of a class struggle, nor is he much concerned with the notion of class in the political sense. Finally, he is not at all assured of the eventual triumph of good; he pins no faith on any force or party—indeed he is almost alone of the novelists of the Left (Silone is the only other one that comes to mind) in saying that the creeds and idealisms of the Left may bring corruption quite as well as the greeds and cynicisms of the established order; he has refused to cry "Allons! the road lies before us," and, in short, his novel issues in despair.—And it is this despair of Dos Passos' book which has made his two ablest critics, Malcolm Cowley and T. K. Whipple, seriously temper their admiration. Mr. Cowley says: "They [the novels comprising *U.S.A.*] give us an extraordinarily diversified picture of contemporary life, but they fail to include at least one side of it—the will to struggle ahead, the comradeship in struggle, the con-

sciousness of new men and new forces continually rising." And Mr. Whipple: "Dos Passos has reduced what ought to be a tale of full-bodied conflicts to an epic of disintegration."

These critics are saying that Dos Passos has not truly observed the political situation. Whether he has or not, whether his despair is objectively justifiable, cannot, with the best political will in the world, be settled on paper. We hope he has seen incorrectly; he himself must hope so. But there is also an implicit meaning in the objections which, if the writers themselves did not intend it, many readers will derive, and if not from Mr. Whipple and Mr. Cowley then from the book itself: that the emotion in which *U.S.A.* issues is negative to the point of being politically harmful.

But to discover a political negativism in the despair of *U.S.A.* is to subscribe to a naive conception of human emotion and of the literary experience. It is to assert that the despair of a literary work must inevitably engender despair in the reader. Actually, of course, it need do nothing of the sort. To rework the old Aristotelian insight, it may bring about a catharsis of an already existing despair. But more important: the word "despair" all by itself (or any other such general word or phrase) can never characterize the emotion the artist is dealing with. There are many kinds of despair and what is really important is what goes along with the general emotion denoted by the word. Despair with its wits about it is very different from despair that is stupid; despair that is an abandonment of illusion is very different from despair which generates tender new cynicisms. The "heartbreak" of *Heartbreak House,* for example, is the beginning of new courage and I can think of no more useful *political* job for the literary man today than, by the representation of despair, to cauterize the exposed soft tissue of too-easy hope.

Even more than the despair, what has disturbed the radical admirers of Dos Passos' work is his appearance of indifference to the idea of the class struggle. Mr. Whipple correctly points out that the characters of *U.S.A.* are all "midway people in somewhat ambiguous positions." Thus, there are no bankers or industrialists (except incidentally) but only J. Ward Morehouse, their servant; there are no factory workers (except, again, incidentally), no farmers, but only itinerant workers, individualistic mechanics, actresses, interior decorators.

This, surely, is a limitation in a book that has had claimed for it a complete national picture. But when we say limitation we may mean just that or we may mean falsification, and I do not think that Dos Passos has falsified. The idea of class is not simple but complex. Socially it is extremely difficult to determine. It cannot be determined, for instance, by asking individuals to what class they belong; nor is it easy to convince them that they belong to one class or another. We may, to be sure, demonstrate the

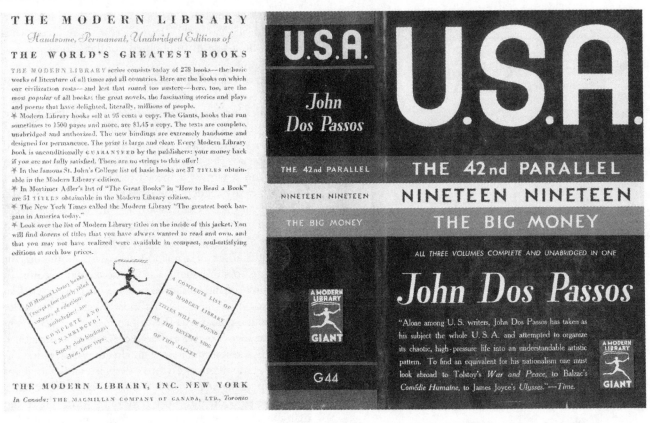

*Dust jacket for the 1939 Modern Library edition of Dos Passos's trilogy (Collection of Richard Layman)*

idea of class at income-extremes or function-extremes, but when we leave these we must fall back upon the criterion of "interest"–by which we must mean *real* interest ("real will" in the Rousseauian sense) and not what people say or think they want. Even the criterion of action will not determine completely the class to which people belong. Class, then, is a useful but often undetermined category of political and social thought. The political leader and the political theorist will make use of it in ways different from those of the novelist. For the former the important thing is people's perception that they are of one class or another and their resultant action. For the latter the interesting and suggestive things are likely to be the moral paradoxes that result from the conflict between real and apparent interest. And the "midway people" of Dos Passos represent this moral-paradoxical aspect of class. They are a great fact in American life. It is they who show the symptoms of cultural change. Their movement from social group to social group–from class to class, if you will–makes for the uncertainty of their moral codes, their confusion, their indecision. Almost more than the people of fixed class, they are at the mercy of the social stream because their interests cannot be clear to them and give them direction. If Dos Passos has omitted the class struggle, as Mr. Whipple and Mr. Cowley complain, it is only the external class struggle

he has left out; within his characters the class struggle is going on constantly.

This, perhaps, is another way of saying that Dos Passos is primarily concerned with morality, with personal morality. The national, collective, social elements of his trilogy should be seen not as a bid for completeness but rather as a great setting, brilliantly delineated, for his moral interest. In his novels, as in actual life, "conditions" supply the opportunity for personal moral action. But if Dos Passos is a social historian, as he is so frequently said to be, he is that in order to be a more complete moralist. It is of the greatest significance that for him the barometer of social breakdown is not suffering through economic deprivation but always moral degeneration through moral choice.

This must be said in the face of Mr. Whipple's description of Dos Passos' people as "devoid of will or purpose, helplessly impelled hither and yon by the circumstances of the moment. They have no strength of resistance. They are weak at the very core of personality, the power to choose." These, it would seem, are scarcely the characters with which the moralist can best work. But here we must judge not only by the moral equipment of the characters (and it is not at all certain that Mr. Whipple's description is correct: choice of action is seldom made as the result of Socratic dialectic) but by the novelist's idea

*Dust jacket for the first volume of the 1946 Houghton Mifflin edition of Dos Passos's trilogy, with illustrations by Marsh*
*(Illustration © 1946 by Houghton Mifflin Co. © renewed by Houghton*
*Mifflin Co. Reprinted by permission of Houghton Mifflin Co.)*

of morality—the nature of his judgments and his estimate of the power of circumstance.

Dos Passos' morality is concerned not so much with the utility of an action as with the quality of the person who performs it. *What* his people do is not so important as *how* they do it, or what they become by doing it. We despise J. Ward Morehouse not so much for his creation of the labor-relations board, his support of the war, his advertising of patent-medicines, though these are despicable enough; we despise him rather for the words he uses as he does these things, for his self-deception, the tone and style he generates. We despise G. H. Barrow, the labor-faker, not because he betrays labor; we despise him because he is mealy-mouthed and talks about "the art of living" when he means concupiscence. But we do not despise the palpable fraud, Doc Bingham, because, though he lies to everyone else, he does not lie to himself.

The moral assumption on which Dos Passos seems to work was expressed by John Dewey some thirty years ago; there are certain moral situations, Dewey says, where we cannot decide between the ends; we are forced to make our moral choice in terms of our preference for one kind of character or another: "What sort of an agent, of a person

shall he be? This is the question finally at stake in any genuinely moral situation: What shall the agent *be?* What sort of character shall he assume? On its face, the question is what he shall *do,* shall he act for this or that end. But the incompatibility of the ends forces the issue back into the questions of the kind of selfhood, of agency, involved in the respective ends." One can imagine that this method of moral decision does not have meaning for all times and cultures. Although dilemmas exist in every age, we do not find Antigone settling her struggle between family and state by a reference to the kind of character she wants to be, nor Orestes settling his in that way; and so with the medieval dilemma of wife vs. friend, or the family oath of vengeance vs. the feudal oath of allegiance. But for our age with its intense self-consciousness and its uncertain moral codes, the reference to the quality of personality does have meaning, and the greater the social flux the more frequent will be the interest in qualities of character rather than in the rightness of the end.

The modern novel, with its devices for investigating the quality of character, is the aesthetic form almost specifically called forth to exercise this modern way of judgment. The novelist goes where the law cannot go; he tells the truth where the formulations of even the subtlest ethical theorist cannot. He turns the moral values inside out to question the worth of the deed by looking not at its actual outcome but at its tone and style. He is subversive of dominant morality and under his influence we learn to praise what dominant morality condemns; he reminds us that benevolence may be aggression, that the highest idealism may corrupt. Finally, he gives us the models of the examples by which, half-unconsciously, we make our own moral selves.

Dos Passos does not primarily concern himself with the burly sinners who inherit the earth. His people are those who sin against themselves and for him the wages of sin is death—of the spirit. The whole Dos Passos morality and the typical Dos Passos fate are expressed in Burns' quatrain:

> I waive the quantum o' the sin,
>   The hazard of concealing;
> But, och! it hardens a' within
>   And petrifies the feeling!

In the trilogy physical death sometimes follows upon this petrifaction of the feeling but only as its completion. Only two people die without petrifying, Joe Williams and Daughter, who kept in their inarticulate way a spark of innocence, generosity and protest. Idealism does not prevent the consequences of sinning against oneself and Mary French with her devotion to the working class and the Communist Party, with her courage and "sacrifice" is quite as dead as Richard Savage who inherits Wardhouse's [*sic*] mantle, and she is almost as much to blame.

It is this element of blame, of responsibility, that exempts Dos Passos from Malcolm Cowley's charge of being in some part committed to the morality of what Cowley calls the Art Novel—the story of the Poet and the World, the Poet always sensitive and right, the World always crass and wrong. An important element of Dos Passos' moral conception is that, although the World does sin against his characters, the characters themselves are very often as wrong as the world. There is no need to enter the theological purlieus to estimate how much responsibility Dos Passos puts upon them and whether this is the right amount. Clearly, however, he holds people like Savage, Fainy McCreary and Eveline Hutchins accountable in some important part for their own fates and their own ignobility.

The morality of Dos Passos, then, is a romantic morality. Perhaps this is calling it a bad name; people say they have got tired of a morality concerned with individuals "saving" themselves and "realizing" themselves. Conceivably only Dos Passos' aggressive contemporaneity has kept them from seeing how very similar is his morality to, say, Browning's—the moment to be snatched, the crucial choice to be made, and if it is made on the wrong (the safe)

Frontispiece by Marsh for the 1946 Houghton Mifflin edition of U.S.A. (Illustration © 1946 by Houghton Mifflin Co. © renewed by Houghton Mifflin Co. Reprinted by permission of Houghton Mifflin Co.)

side, the loss of human quality, so that instead of a man we have a Success and instead of two lovers a Statue and a Bust in the public square. But too insistent a cry against the importance of the individual quality is a sick cry—as sick as the cry of "Something to live for" as a motivation of political choice. Among members of a party the considerations of solidarity, discipline and expedience are claimed to replace all others and moral judgment is left to history; among liberals, the idea of social determination, on no good ground, appears tacitly to exclude the moral concern: witness the nearly complete conspiracy of silence or misinterpretation that greeted Silone's *Bread and Wine*, which said not a great deal more than that personal and moral—and eventually political—problems were not settled by membership in a revolutionary party. It is not at all certain that it is political wisdom to ignore what so much concerns the novelist. In the long run is not the political choice fundamentally a choice of personal quality?

—*Partisan Review*, 4 (April 1938): 26–32

## The Moods and Tenses of John Dos Passos
Granville Hicks

*The journalist Granville Hicks was literary editor of the* New Masses *for a period during the 1930s and often wrote from a Communist Party standpoint. His* The Great Tradition *(1933) was a widely noted left-leaning literary history of America. In addition to* U.S.A., *Hicks is reviewing Dos Passos's* Journeys Between Wars *(1938).*

John Dos Passos' publishers are wisely doing their part to make the country conscious of him as a major literary figure, and they have accordingly issued two omnibus volumes of his work. *U.S.A.* is, of course, his famous trilogy: *The 42nd Parallel, 1919,* and *The Big Money. Journeys Between Wars* is made up of his travel books: much of *Rosinante to the Road Again* (1922), almost the whole of *Orient Express* (1927), and most of those sections of *In All Countries* (1934) that deal with foreign lands. It also contains some sixty pages on Dos Passos' visit to Spain a year ago.

Comparison of the two books makes it quite clear that Dos Passos' deeper experiences go into his novels, leaving his more casual impressions to be recorded in the travel essays. *Journeys Between Wars* shows that he is at his best when he is describing the persons he meets or recording his own moods. The *padrone* in the Spanish restaurant, the Sayid on the Orient express, the Danish accountant on his way home from America—these are effectively drawn. And the journal of the camel ride from Bagdad to Damascus is as pleasant a personal record as can be found in modern literature. But there is not much—and I have now read most of these essays twice—that the mind holds onto. Other novelists—Gide, Lawrence, Huxley—have written travel books that belong with their major works, but not Dos Passos.

The explanation, which has some importance for the understanding of Dos Passos as a writer, seems to me fairly clear. He deals, consistently and no doubt deliberately, with impressions—the specific scene, the precise emotions, the exact conversation. The seeing eye—even "the camera eye"—is admittedly the first virtue of the travel writer. But it is equally certain that the memorable travel writers have not been afraid to draw conclusions from what they saw. Don Passos is afraid: no milder word will do. What one feels in *Journeys Between Wars* is neither a casual holiday from the job of thinking nor a conscientious elimination of ideas for some literary purpose but a deep emotional unwillingness to face the intellectual implications of things seen and heard.

And the extraordinary thing is that this shrinking from conclusions is to be found even in the last section, the section dealing with Spain in 1937. Dos Passos tells of crossing the border from France, of a night on the road, of executions in Valencia, of a bombardment of Madrid, of a fiesta of the Fifteenth Brigade, of a trip through some villages, and of an interview with officials of the P.O.U.M. But there is not a word about the issues between the loyalists and the fascists, not a word about the differences between the loyalist government and the P.O.U.M. It seems incredible that any author, considering all that is involved in Spain today, could keep such silence. Do not suppose that Dos Passos is merely maintaining an artistic objectivity, holding back his own opinions so that the reader can arrive unhampered at the truth. He simply has refused to think his way through to clear convictions. He has sympathies—with the loyalists as against the fascists and apparently with the P.O.U.M. as against the government. But even the Spanish crisis cannot shake him into thought.

The only approximation to a conclusion comes as Dos Passos is leaving Spain, and, characteristically, it is in the form of a question: "How can they win, I was thinking? How can the new world of confusion and crosspurposes and illusions and dazzled by the mirage of idealistic phrases win against the iron combination of men accustomed to run things who have only one idea binding them together, to hold on to what they've got?" This passage has been quoted by almost every conservative reviewer of the book, and quoted with undisguised satisfaction. "We told you so," one could hear them saying. "There's no sense in trying to help Spain. It's all foolishness to hope for social justice anywhere. Let's make the best of things as they are."

The truth is that it is impossible to avoid having opinions, and the only question is whether or not they are based on adequate information and clear thinking. If Dos Passos had faced the responsibility of the writer, and especially the radical writer, to use his intellect as well as his eyes, if he had been concerned, not with avoiding conclusions, but with arriving at sound ones, I think he would have come out of Spain with something more to say than these faltering words of despair. Afraid to think, he has yielded to a mood, and the reactionaries are delighted with his surrender. Both that surrender and his flirtation with the P.O.U.M. are results of an essential irresponsibility.

Dos Passos' irresponsibility takes two forms: unwillingness to think and unwillingness to act. Several years ago, I remember, at the time when he was perhaps closest to the Communist Party, he said something to the effect that he was merely a camp-follower. In *Journeys Between Wars* there is a revealing passage. (It is, of course, creditably characteristic of Dos Passos to reveal himself.) When he was leaving the Soviet Union in 1928, the director and the actors of the Sanitary Propaganda Theatre came to see him off. The director said, "They want to know. They like you very much, but they want to ask you one question. They

*Cover of* The 42nd Parallel *from the 1978 Hungarian three-volume boxed edition of* U.S.A., *translated by Tibor Bartos (Thomas Cooper Library, University of South Carolina)*

want you to show your face. They want to know where you stand politically. Are you with us?" Dos Passos continues: "The iron twilight dims, the steam swirls round us, we are muddled by the delicate crinkly steam of our breath, the iron crown tightens on the head, throbbing with too many men, too many women, too many youngsters seen, talked to, asked questions of, too many hands shaken, too many foreign languages badly understood. 'But let me see. . . . But maybe I can explain. . . . But in so short a time . . . there's not time.' The train is moving. I have to run and jump for it."

The passage, so palpably sincere and so pleasant, reminds us that, even in a broader sense, Dos Passos has always been uncommonly detached. Indeed, detachment is almost the keynote of *Journeys Between Wars*. In the extracts from *Rosinante* Dos Passos is "the traveler"; in *Orient Express* he is "the eastbound American"; in the Russian section he is "the American Peesatyel." Perhaps it is no wonder that in writing about Spain in 1937 he is still merely an observer. It is no wonder that he has seldom tried to write about the revolutionary movement from inside, and when

he has tried, has failed. It is no wonder that he has never communicated the sense of the reality of comradeship, as Malraux, for example, communicates it in *Days of Wrath*.

Yet there was a time when Dos Passos seemed willing to try to think clearly and to feel deeply. His second play, *Airways, Inc.,* was bad dramatically, but in it Dos Passos at least made an attempt to be clear. There was a sharp difference between that play and *The Garbage Man,* and an even greater difference between *The 42nd Parallel,* first novel of his trilogy, and *Manhattan Transfer.* In *The 42nd Parallel* Dos Passos seemed for the first time to have mastered the American scene. The technical devices used in this novel and *1919* perplexed some readers, but Dos Passos himself appeared to be relatively clear about what he was trying to do.

*Airways, Inc.* was published in 1928, *The 42nd Parallel* in 1930, and *1919* in 1932. Here, then, are three or four years of comparative clarity. And in those years Dos Passos was close to Communism. At this time he actually believed in something like the Marxian analysis of history, and it worked. He also felt a stronger confidence in the working class. Communism did not make him a novelist, but it made him a better novelist.

What I failed to realize at the time of the publication of *1919* was the extent to which Dos Passos' interest in the Communist Party was a matter of mood. He had not sufficiently overcome his fear of conclusions to make a serious study of Marxism, and he had only partly subdued his passion for aloofness. Little things could—and, as it happened, did—disturb him. He was on the right track, but not much was required to derail him.

In the four years since he left the track Dos Passos has gone a long and disastrous way. Last summer, as has been said, he came out of Spain with nothing but a question mark, and committed himself to a hysterical isolationism that might almost be called chauvinistic. Last December he and Theodore Dreiser held a conversation that was published in *Direction.* Dos Passos' confusion—equaled, I hasten to say, by Dreiser's—is unpleasant to contemplate for anyone who expects some semblance of intellectual dignity in a prominent novelist. He is still looking for an impartial observer of the Soviet Union, and thinks he has found one in Victor Serge. His new-found devotion to the United States continues to run high: "America is probably the country where the average guy has got a better break." "You can't get anywhere," he says, "in talking to fanatic Communists." He talks about revolution: "A sensible government would take over industries and compensate the present owners, and then deflate the money afterwards." And this is his contribution to economics: "Every time there is a rise in wages, prices go up at the A. & P."

After one has noted the banality, the naiveté, and the sheer stupidity of most of Dos Passos' remarks in his talk with Dreiser, one knows that politically he is as unreliable as a man can be and is capable of any kind of preposterous vagary. But I am interested in Dos Passos' politics only insofar as they influence his writings, as of course they do. When *1919* appeared, I believed that Dos Passos had established his position as the most talented of American novelists—a position he still holds. As early as 1934, however, I was distressed by his failure to shake off habits of mind that I had thought—quite erroneously, as it turns out—were dissolving under the influence of contact with the revolutionary movement. At that time, reviewing *In All Countries,* I said: "Dos Passos, I believe, is superior to his bourgeois contemporaries because he is, however incompletely, a revolutionist, and shares, however imperfectly, in the vigor of the revolutionary movement, its sense of purpose, its awareness of the meaning of events, and its defiance of bourgeois pessimism and decay. He is also, it seems to me, superior to any other revolutionary writer because of the sensitiveness and the related qualities that are to be found in this book and, much more abundantly, in his novels. Some day, however, we shall have a writer who surpasses Dos Passos, who has all that he has and more. He will not be a camp-follower."

Now that Dos Passos is not in any sense a revolutionist and does not share at all in the vigor of the revolutionary movement, what about the virtues that I attributed to his association with the Communist Party? I am afraid the answer is in *The Big Money,* most of which was written after 1934. One figure dominates *The Big Money* to an extent that no one figure dominated either *The 42nd Parallel* or *1919.* It is Charley Anderson, the symbol of the easy-money Twenties, the working stiff who gets to be a big shot. ("America is probably the country where the average guy has got a better break.") His desperate money-making and drinking and fornicating take place against a background of unhappy rich people and their unhappy parasites. Further in the background are some equally unhappy revolutionists, who are either futile or vicious. ("You can't get anywhere in talking to fanatic Communists.")

It seems to me foolish to pretend that an author doesn't choose his material. Dos Passos didn't have to lay his principal emphasis on the hopeless mess that the capitalist system makes of a good many lives. He didn't have to make his two Communists narrow sectarians. He didn't have to make the strongest personal note in the book a futilitarian elegy for Sacco and Vanzetti. There must have been a good deal in the Twenties that he left out, for large masses of people did learn something from the collapse of the boom, and the Communist Party did get rid of factionalism, and the workers did save Angelo Herndon and the Scottsboro Boys, even though they failed to save Sacco and Vanzetti. *The Big Money,* in other words, grows out of the

same prejudices and misconceptions, the same confusion and blindness, as the conversation with Dreiser.

The difference is, of course, that there is a lot in *The Big Money* besides these faulty notions. I have written elsewhere about Dos Passos' gifts, and I need only say here that I admire them as strongly as ever. I know of no contemporary American work of fiction to set beside *U.S.A.* But I also know that, because of the change in mood that came between *1919* and *The Big Money, U.S.A.* is not so true, not so comprehensive, not so strong as it might have been. And, though I have acquired caution enough not to predict Dos Passos' future direction, I know that, if he follows the path he is now on, his claims to greatness are already laid before us and later critics will only have to fill in the details of another story of genius half-fulfilled.

—*New Masses,* 27 (26 April 1938): 22–23

## GENERAL ESTIMATES

*As is usually true of important works by major writers, significant criticism of* U.S.A. *has often consistently touched upon several overriding areas of importance in the interpretation of the trilogy while reflecting as well the more specific preoccupations of the age in which the critic lived.*

*Criticism of the larger dimensions of* U.S.A. *began in the 1930s with essays by Mike Gold and Jean-Paul Sartre, in which two permanent strains in the critical estimate of the trilogy—its political and social creed on the one hand and its artistic and philosophical depth and complexity on the other—received important discussion. For much of the 1940s and 1950s—as reflected in the essays by Alfred Kazin, Claude-Edmonde Magny, and John W. Aldridge, as well as in Paul Palmer's parody—a major critical concern, one appropriate to a period of American political and military dominance on the world scene, was to identify the specific character of* U.S.A. *as an epic depiction of twentieth-century American life. Many of the critics of this period, however, viewed the trilogy as above all negative in this portrayal—indeed, the tendency was to find its themes of moral decay and spiritual emptiness the fictional equivalent of T. S. Eliot's poetic rendering of the spiritual wasteland of modern life.*

*Beginning in the mid 1950s, much criticism of* U.S.A., *as in the essay by John H. Wrenn, responded to the New Criticism imperative requiring the discovery of theme through the close examination of form by fully exploring both the techniques of specific modes and the complex fictional architectonics of the work as a whole. Related to this effort was the somewhat later emergence of an important new element in the interpretation of* U.S.A., *as in the essays by John Lydenberg and David L. Vanderwerken, which located a powerfully rendered positive component in the trilogy in Dos Passos's weaving of the thematic thread of the "old words" throughout its various modes.*

Cover of the 1951 Italian edition of The 42nd Parallel, *translated by a noted postwar Italian novelist and translator of contemporary American fiction. The wide range of translations of the individual novels in U.S.A., as well as of the trilogy as a whole, reflects the worldwide interest in Dos Passos's work.* The 42nd Parallel, *for instance, has been published in at least fourteen editions and seven foreign languages (Collection of Donald Pizer).*

*Since Dos Passos's death in 1970 there have been several large-scale overview essays of* U.S.A. *that have sought to reaffirm its importance, as in those by Harry Levin and Donald Pizer. In addition, as in the earlier philosophically centered criticism of Sartre and Magny, such critics as Iain Colley and Thomas Strychacz have sought, using interpretive tools derived from a Marxist-based cultural criticism pervasive in the late twentieth century, to isolate the social philosophy underlying the trilogy.*

### The Education of John Dos Passos
Mike Gold

*Since it predates Dos Passos's later attacks on the far Left, Gold's essay is more positive than his 1936 review of* The Big Money *(see above).*

. . . . . . . . .

In 1930 John Dos Passos published his *42nd Parallel,* first novel of a trilogy which is to document American life for the two momentous decades, 1910–1930. The second volume, *1919,* appeared last year. These two books mark a turning point in the career of John Dos Passos, besides having won recognition as new landmarks in the history of American literature.

They extend the experiment begun in *Manhattan Transfer.* There he tried to portray all of the life of a great city; now he has tried to digest a continent.

The architecture of these novels is masterly, and has provoked discussion among the critics—I am not exaggerating—of all Europe, America, and Asia. The novel has always been the most fluid of all fiction forms, but Dos Passos has enlarged its range. James Joyce wrote in *Ulysses* the ultimate novel of the tormented consciousness of the bourgeois individual. Dos Passos has written one of the first collective novels. I envy his achievement rather than that of Joyce's, for Dos Passos leads to the future. The collective emotion is the new and inevitable hope of the world. In every land the young writers have been effected [*sic*] by the Communist movement which is building the new collective society, where men will be brothers, instead of bitter, futile, competitive individuals. And these young writers, trying to speak in art what they have felt in life, must find new forms. Dos Passos has hewed out at least one path for them.

There are really a dozen novels in these two books, fitted together in a continuity and context that makes each narrative a comment on the other. Dos Passos ranges through all the strata of the social order. He is the geologist and historian of American society. The characters whose lives are followed through war and peace are a stenographer, a publicity man, an I.W.W. migratory worker, an interior decorator, a sailor, a minister's daughter, a Harvard graduate, an impulsive Texan, a Jewish radical from New York.

Some of their stories interlock; in the last volume of the trilogy all the loose ends will probably be tied. What we have now is a cross-section of American humanity which, as much as any history, gives the authentic inside facts of the past twenty years.

To add historic poignancy to these individual lives, and to relate them to their background, there is a Greek chorus of newspaper headlines and Americans. This adds to the strangeness of the novels, yet, after careful reading, one finds them an organic part of the massive effect at which Dos Passos was aiming.

So, too, are the score or more of cameo biographies of significant Americans which Dos Passos has interpolated on his narrative. Bryan, Debs, John Reed, Bill Haywood, Burbank, La Follette, Edison—these terse bitter passionate portraits add an extraordinary flavor of historic truth to the novels, and contain, besides, germs of the future revolutionary growth of John Dos Passos.

It is a chaos again, but Nietzsche said "one must have chaos to give birth to a dancing star." In the complexity and confusion of these novels the drive is felt toward a new communist world; and, if the aesthetes and gin-soaked Harvard futilitarians are present, it is that they may serve as contrast to the obscure, almost unmarked hero of this epic canvas—the rising Proletaire.

. . . . . . . . . .

We can say now that the Harvard aesthete in Dos Passos is almost dead. The spiritual malady of tourism no longer drains his powers. He has entered the real world. He has definitely broken with capitalism, and knows it is but a walking corpse. He wars upon it, and records its degeneration. But he has not yet found the faith of Walt Whitman in the American masses. He cannot believe that they have within them the creative forces for a new world. This is still his dilemma; a hangover of his aristocratic past; yet this man grows like corn in the Iowa sun; his education proceeds; the future will find his vast talents, his gift of epic poetry, his observation, his daring experimentalism, and personal courage enlisted completely in the service of the co-operative society. He does not retreat; he goes forward. Dos Passos belongs to the marvelous future.

–*English Journal*, 22 (February 1933): 95–97

## John Dos Passos and "1919"
Jean-Paul Sartre

*Jean-Paul Sartre, who was later to become world-famous as one of the founders of existentialism, wrote extensively on modern American fiction during the 1930s. His essay on Dos Passos's fictional method was prompted by the publication of a French translation of* Nineteen-Nineteen *and appeared initially in the journal* Nouvelle Revue Française *in 1938.*

A novel is a mirror. So everyone says. But what is meant by *reading* a novel? It means, I think, jumping into the mirror. You suddenly find yourself on the other side of the glass, among people and objects that have a familiar look. But they merely look familiar. We have never really seen them. The things of our world have, in turn, become outside reflections. You close the book, step over the edge of the mirror and return to this honest-to-goodness world, and you find furniture, gardens and people who have nothing to say to you. The mirror that closed behind you reflects them peacefully, and now you would swear that art is a reflection.

There are clever people who go so far as to talk of distorting mirrors.

Dos Passos very consciously uses this absurd and insistent illusion to impel us to revolt. He had done everything possible to make his novel seem a mere reflection. He has even donned the garb of populism. The reason is that his art is not gratuitous; he wants to prove something. But observe what a curious aim he has. He wants to show us this world, our own—to *show* it only, without explanations or comment. There are no revelations about the machinations of the police, the imperialism of the oil kings or the Ku-Klux-Klan, no cruel pictures of poverty. We have already seen everything he wants to show us, and, so it seems at first glance, seen it exactly as he wants us to see it. We recognize immediately the sad abundance of these untragic

Cover of the first volume in the 1977 two-volume reprint of N. Guterman's 1949 French translation of The 42nd Parallel (Thomas Cooper Library, University of South Carolina)

lives. They are our own lives, these innumerable, planned, botched, immediately forgotten and constantly renewed adventures that slip by without leaving a trace, without involving anyone, until the time when one of them, no different from any of the others, suddenly, as if through some clumsy trickery, sickens a man for good and throws a mechanism out of gear.

Now, it is by depicting, as we ourselves might depict, these too familiar appearances with which we all put up that Dos Passos makes them unbearable. He arouses indignation in people who never get indignant, he frightens people who fear nothing. But hasn't there been some sleight-of-hand? I look about me and see people, cities, boats, the war. But they aren't the real thing; they are discreetly queer and sinister, as in a nightmare. My indignation against this world also seems dubious to me; it only faintly resembles the other indignation, the kind that a mere news item can arouse. I am on the other side of the mirror.

Dos Passos' hate, despair and lofty contempt are real. But that is precisely why his world is not real; it is a created object. I know of none—not even Faulkner's or Kafka's—in which the art is greater or better hidden. I know of none that is more precious, more touching or closer to us. This is because he takes his material from our world. And yet, there is no stranger or more distant world. Dos Passos has invented only one thing, an art of story-telling. But that is enough to create a universe.

We live in time, we calculate in time. The novel, like life, unfolds in the present. The perfect tense exists on the surface only; it must be interpreted as a present *with aesthetic distance,* as a stage device. In the novel the dice are not loaded, for fictional man is free. He develops before our eyes; our impatience, our ignorance, our expectancy are the same as the hero's. The tale, on the other hand, as Fernandez has shown, develops in the past. But the tale explains. Chronological order, life's order, barely conceals the causal order, which is an order for the understanding. The event does not touch us; it stands half-way between fact and law. Dos Passos' time is his own creation; it is neither fictional nor narrative. It is rather, if you like, historical time. The perfect and imperfect tenses are not used simply to observe the rules; the reality of Joe's or Eveline's adventures lies in the fact they are now part of the past. Everything is told as if by someone who is remembering.

"*The years Dick was little* he never heard anything about his Dad. . . ." "All Eveline thought about *that winter* was going to the Art Institute. . . ." "They waited two weeks in Vigo while the officials quarreled about their status and they got pretty fed up with it."

The fictional event is a nameless presence; there is nothing one can say about it, for it develops. We may be shown two men combing a city for their mistresses, but we are not told that they "do not find them," for this is not true. So long as there remains one street, one café, one house to explore, it is not yet true. In Dos Passos, the things that happen are named first, and then the dice are cast, as they are in our memories.

> Glen and Joe only got ashore for a few hours and couldn't find Marcelline and Loulou.

The facts are clearly outlined; they are ready for *thinking about.* Dos Passos never thinks them. Not for an instant does the order of causality betray itself in chronological order. There is no narrative, but rather the jerky unreeling of a rough and uneven memory, which sums up a period of several years in a few words only to dwell languidly over a minute fact. Like our real memories, it is a jumble of miniatures and frescoes. There is relief enough, but it is cunningly scattered at random. One step further would give us the famous idiot's monologue in *The Sound and the Fury.* But that would still involve intellectualizing, suggesting an explanation in terms of the irrational, suggesting a Freudian order beneath this disorder. Dos Passos stops just in time. As a result of this, past things retain a flavour of the present; they still remain, in their exile, what they once were, inexplicable tumults of colour, sound and passion. Each event is irreducible, a gleaming and solitary *thing* that does not flow from anything else, but suddenly arises to join other things. For Dos Passos, narrating means adding. This accounts for the slack air of his style. "And . . . and . . . and. . . ." The great disturbing phenomena—war, love, political movements, strikes—fade and crumble into an infinity of little odds and ends which can just about be set side by side. Here is the armistice:

> In early November rumours of an armistice began to fly around and then suddenly one afternoon Major Wood ran into the office that Eleanor and Eveline shared and dragged them both away from their desks and kissed them both and shouted, "At last it's come." Before she knew it Eveline found herself kissing Major Moorehouse right on the mouth. The Red Cross office turned into a college dormitory the night of a football victory: It was the Armistice.
> Everybody seemed suddenly to have bottles of cognac and to be singing, *There's a long trail awinding* or *La Madel-lon pour nous n'est pas sévère.*

These Americans see war the way Fabrizio saw the battle of Waterloo. And the intention, like the method, is clear upon reflection. But you must close the book and reflect.

Passions and gestures are also things. Proust analysed them, related them to former states and thereby made them inevitable. Dos Passos wants to retain only their factual nature. All he is allowed to say is, "In that place and at that time Richard was that way, and at another time, he was different." Love and decisions are great spheres that rotate on their own axes. The most we can grasp is a kind of *conformity* between the psychological state and the exterior situation, something resembling a colour harmony. We may also suspect that explanations are *possible,* but they seem as frivolous and futile as a spider-web on a heavy red flower. Yet, never do we have the feeling of fictional freedom: Dos Passos imposes upon us instead the unpleasant impression of an indeterminacy of detail. Acts, emotions and ideas suddenly settle within a character, make themselves at home and then disappear without his having much to say in the matter. You cannot say he submits to them. He experiences them. There seems to be no law governing their appearance.

Nevertheless, they once did exist. This lawless past is irremediable. Dos Passos has purposely chosen the perspective of history to tell a story. He wants to make us feel that the stakes are down. In *Man's Hope,* Malraux says, more or less, that "the tragic thing about death is that it transforms life into a destiny." With the opening lines of his book, Dos Passos settles down into death. The lives he tells about are all closed in on themselves. They resemble those Bergsonian memories which, after the body's death, float about, lifeless and full of odours and lights and cries, through some forgotten limbo. We constantly have the feeling that these vague, human lives are destinies. Our own past is not at all like this. There is not one of our acts whose meaning and value we cannot still transform even now. But beneath the violent colours of these beautiful, motley objects that Dos Passos presents there is something petrified. Their significance is fixed. Close your eyes and try to remember your own life, try to remember it *that way;* you will stifle. It is this unrelieved stifling that Dos Passos wanted to express. In capitalist society, men do not have lives, they have only destinies. He never says this, but he makes it felt throughout. He expresses it discreetly, cautiously, until we feel like smashing our destinies. We have become rebels; he has achieved his purpose.

We are rebels *behind the looking-glass.* For that is not what the rebel of this world wants to change. He wants to transform Man's *present* condition, the one that develops day by day. Using the past tense to tell about the present means using a device, creating a strange and beautiful world, as frozen as one of those Mardi-Gras masks that become frightening on the faces of real, living men.

But whose memories are these that unfold through the novel? At first glance, they seem to be those of the heroes, of Joe, Dick, Fillette and Eveline. And, on occasion, they are. As a rule, whenever a character is sincere, whenever he is bursting with something, no matter how, or with what:

> When he went off duty he'd walk home achingly tired through the strawberry-scented early Parisian morning, thinking of the faces and the eyes and the sweat-drenched hair and the clenched fingers clotted with blood and dirt. . . .

But the narrator often ceases to coincide completely with the hero. The hero could not quite have said what he does say, but you feel a discreet complicity between them. The narrator relates from the outside what the hero would have wanted him to relate. By means of this complicity, Dos Passos, without warning us, has us make the transition he was after. We suddenly find ourselves inside a horrible memory whose every recollection makes us uneasy, a bewildering memory that is no longer that of either the characters or the author. It seems like a chorus that remembers, a sententious chorus that is accessory to the deed.

> All the same he got along very well at school and the teachers liked him, particularly Miss Teazle, the English teacher, because he had nice manners and said little things that weren't fresh but that made them laugh. Miss Teazle said he showed real feeling for English composition. One Christmas he sent her a little rhyme he made up about the Christ Child and the three Kings and she declared he had a gift.

The narration takes on a slightly stilted manner, and everything that is reported about the hero assumes the solemn quality of a public announcement: ". . . she declared he had a gift." The sentence is not accompanied by any comment, but acquires a sort of collective resonance. It is a *declaration.* And indeed, whenever we want to know his characters' thoughts, Dos Passos, with respectful objectivity, generally gives us their declarations.

> Fred . . . said the last night before they left he was going to tear loose. When they got to the front he might get killed and then what? Dick said he liked talking to the girls but that the whole business was too commercial and turned his stomach. Ed Schuyler, who'd been nicknamed Frenchie and was getting very continental in his ways, said that the street girls were too naive.

I open *Paris-Soir* and read, "*From our special correspondent: Charlie Chaplin declares that he has put an end to Charlie.*" Now I have it! Dos Passos reports all his characters' utterances to us in the style of a statement to the Press. Their words are thereby cut off from thought, and become pure utterances, simple reactions that must be registered as such, in the behaviourist style upon which Dos Passos draws when it suits him to do so. But, at the same time, the utterance takes on a social importance; it is inviolable, it becomes a maxim. Little does it matter, thinks the satisfied chorus, what Dick had in mind when he spoke that sentence. What matters is that it has been uttered. Besides, it was not formed inside him, it came from afar. Even before he uttered it, it existed as a pompous sound, a taboo. All he has done is to lend it his power of affirmation. It is as if there were a Platonic heaven of words and commonplaces to which we all go to find words suitable to a given situation. There is a heaven of gestures, too. Dos Passos makes a pretence of presenting gestures as pure events, as mere exteriors, as free, animal movements. But this is only appearance. Actually, in relating them, he adopts the point of view of the chorus, of public opinion. There is no single one of Dick's or of Eleanor's gestures which is not a public demonstration, performed to a humming accompaniment of flattery.

> At Chantilly they went through the château and fed the big carp in the moat. They ate their lunch in the woods, sitting on rubber cushions. J.W. kept everybody laughing explaining how he hated picnics, asking everybody what it was that got into even the most intelligent women that they were always trying to make people go on picnics. After lunch they drove out to Senlis to see the houses that the Uhlans had destroyed there in the battle of the Marne.

Doesn't it sound like a local newspaper's account of an ex-servicemen's banquet? All of a sudden, as the gesture dwindles until it is no more than a thin film, we see that it *counts,* that it is sacred in character and that, at the same time, it involves commitment. But for whom? For the abject consciousness of "everyman," for what Heidegger calls "das Mann." But still, where does it spring from? Who is its representative as I read? *I* am. In order to understand the words, in order to make sense out of the paragraphs, I first have to adopt his point of view. I have to play the role of the obliging chorus. This consciousness exists only through me; without me there would be nothing but black spots on white paper. But even while I *am* this collective consciousness, I want to wrench away from it, to see it from the judge's point of view, that is, to get free of myself. This is the source of the shame and uneasiness with which Dos Passos knows how to fill the reader. I am a reluctant accomplice (though I am not even sure that I am reluctant), creating and rejecting social taboos. I am, deep in my heart, a revolutionary again, an unwilling one.

In return, how I hate Dos Passos' men! I am given a fleeting glimpse of their minds, just enough to see that they are living animals. Then, they begin to unwind their endless tissue of ritual statements and sacred gestures. For them, there is no break between inside and outside, between body and consciousness, but only between the stammerings of an individual's timid, intermittent, fumbling thinking and the messy world of collective representations. What a simple process this is, and how effective! All one need do is use American journalistic technique in telling the story of a life, and like the Salzburg reed, a life crystallizes into the Social, and the problem of the transition to the typical—stumbling-block of the social novel–is thereby resolved. There is no further need to present a working man type, to compose (as Nizan does in *Antoine Bloyé*) an existence which represents the exact average of thousands of existences. Dos Passos, on the contrary, can give all his attention to rendering a single life's special character. Each of his characters is unique; what happens to him could happen to no one else. What does it matter, since Society has marked him more deeply than could any special circumstance, since *he is* Society? Thus, we get a glimpse of an order beyond the accidents of fate or the contingency of detail, an order more supple than Zola's physiological necessity or Proust's psychological mechanism, a soft and insinuating constraint which seems to release its victims, letting them go only to take possession of them again without their suspecting, in other words, a statistical determinism. These men, submerged in their own existences, live as they can. They struggle; what comes their way is not determined in advance. And yet, neither their efforts, their faults, nor their most extreme violence can interfere with the regularity of births, marriages and suicides. The pressure exerted by a gas on the walls of its container does not depend upon the individual histories of the molecules composing it.

We are still on the other side of the looking-glass. Yesterday you saw your best friend and expressed to him your passionate hatred of war. Now try to relate this conversation to yourself in the style of Dos Passos. "And they ordered two beers and said that war was hateful. Paul declared he would rather do anything than fight and John said he agreed with him and both got excited and said they were glad they agreed. On his way home, Paul decided to see John more often." You will start hating yourself immediately. It will not take you long, however, to decide that you *cannot* use this tone in talking about yourself. However insincere you may have been, you were at least living out your insincerity, playing it out on your own, continuously creating and extending its existence from one moment to the next. And even if you got caught up in collective representations, you had first to experience them as personal resignation. We are neither mechanical objects nor possessed souls, but something worse; we are free. We exist either entirely *within* or entirely *without*. Dos Passos' man is a hybrid creature, an interior-exterior being. We go on living with him and within him, with his vacillating, individual consciousness, when suddenly it wavers, weakens, and is diluted in the collective consciousness. We follow it up to that point and suddenly, before we notice, we are on the outside. The man behind the looking-glass is a strange, contemptible, fascinating creature. Dos Passos knows how to use this constant shifting to fine effect. I know of nothing more gripping than Joe's death.

> Joe laid out a couple of frogs and was backing off towards the door, when he saw in the mirror that a big guy in a blouse was bringing down a bottle on his head held with both hands. He tried to swing around but he didn't have time. The bottle crashed his skull and he was out.

We are inside with him, until the shock of the bottle on his skull. Then immediately, we find ourselves outside with the chorus, part of the collective memory, ". . . and he was out." Nothing gives you a clearer feeling of annihilation. And from then on, each page we turn, each page that tells of other minds and of a world going on without Joe, is like a spadeful of earth over our bodies. But it is a behind-the-looking-glass death: all we really get is the fine *appearance* of nothingness. True nothingness can neither be felt nor thought. Neither you nor I, nor anyone after us, will ever have anything to say about our real deaths.

Dos Passos' world—like those of Faulkner, Kafka and Stendhal—is impossible because it is contradictory. But therein lies its beauty. Beauty is a veiled contradiction. I regard Dos Passos as the greatest writer of our time.

–*Literary and Philosophical Essays,* translated by Annette Michelson (London: Rider, 1955), pp. 88–96

## Alfred Kazin

*Alfred Kazin made his reputation at the age of twenty-seven with the publication of his widely read and influential study of modern American writing,* On Native Grounds *(1942). Although he later taught at several universities, he devoted himself principally to literary criticism. Among his later collections of essays are* The Inmost Leaf *(1955) and* Contemporaries *(1962).*

Technically *U.S.A.* is one of the great achievements of the modern novel, yet what that achievement is can easily be confused with its elaborate formal structure. For the success of Dos Passos's method does not

rest primarily on his schematization of the novel into four panels, four levels of American experience—the narrative proper, the "Camera Eye," the "Biographies," and the "Newsreel." That arrangement, while original enough, is the most obvious thing in the book and soon becomes the most mechanical. The book lives by its narrative style, the wonderfully concrete yet elliptical prose which bears along and winds around the life stories in the book like a conveyor belt carrying Americans through some vast Ford plant of the human spirit. *U.S.A.* is a national epic, the first great national epic of its kind in the modern American novel; and its triumph is not the pyrotechnical display that the shuttling between the various devices seems to suggest, but Dos Passos's power to weave so many different lives together in narrative. It is possible that the narrative sections would lose much of that power if they were not so craftily built into the elaborate framework of the book. But the framework holds the book together and encloses it; the narrative makes it. The "Newsreel," the "Camera Eye," and even the very vivid and often brilliant "Biographies" are meant to lie a little outside the book always; they speak with the formal and ironic voice of History. The "Newsreel" sounds the time; the "Biographies" stand above time, chanting the stories of American leaders; the "Camera Eye" moralizes shyly in a lyric stammer upon them. But the great thing about *U.S.A.* is that though it sweeps up so many human lives together and intones their waste and illusion and defeat so steadily, we seem to be swept along with them and to see each life perfectly at the moment it passes by us.

The brilliance of the structure lies therefore not so much in its external surface design as in its internal one, in the manifold rhythms of the narrative. Each of the various narrative sections has its dominant musical mode, as it were; each of the characters is encased in his characteristic prose. Thus at the very beginning of *The 42nd Parallel,* when the "Newsreel" blares in a welcome to the new century, while General Miles falls off his horse and Senator Beveridge's toast to the new imperialist America is heard, the story of Fenian McCreary, "Mac," begins with the smell of whale-oil soap in the printer's house in Middletown. That smell, the clatter of the presses, the political arguments, the muddy streets and saloons, give the tone of Mac's life from the first, as his life—Wobbly, tramp, working stiff—sounds the emergence of labor as a dominant force in the new century. So the story of Eleanor Stoddard begins with "When she was small she hated everything," a sentence that calls up the thin-lipped rebellion and superciliousness, the artiness and desperation, of her loveless life before we have gone into it. *The 42nd Parallel* is a study in youth, of the youth of the new century, the "new America," and of all the human beings who figure in it;

and it is in the world of Mac's bookselling and life on freights, of Eleanor Stoddard's rebellion against her father and Janey Williams's picnic near the falls at Georgetown, of J. Ward Moorehouse's Wilmington and the railroad boarding house Charley Anderson's mother kept in North Dakota, that we move. The narrator behind his "Camera Eye" is a little boy holding to his mother's hand, listening to his father's boasts (at the end of the book he will be on his way to France); the "Newsreel" sings out the headlines and popular songs of 1900–16; the "Biographies" are of the magnates (Minor C. Keith, Carnegie), the wonder men of the new century (Steinmetz, Edison, Burbank), the rebels (Bryan, Debs, Bob La Follette, Big Bill Haywood).

We have just left the world of childhood behind us in *The 42nd Parallel,* but we can already hear the clatter of the conveyor belt pushing all these lives along. Everyone is sparring hard for position; the fences of life are going up. There is no expectancy in this youth, not even the sentimental poetry of adolescence. The "Newsreel" singing the lush ballads of 1906 already seems very far away; the "Biographies" are effigies in stone. The life in the narrative has become dominant; the endless pulsing drowns everything else out. Everything is hard, dry, and already a little outrageous. Johnny Moorehouse falls in love only to learn that the socially prominent girl whom he needs for his ambition is a whore. When Eleanor Stoddard's father announces his plan to marry again, he tells her it will be to a "Mrs. O'Toole, a widow with five children who kept a boardinghouse out Elsden way." Mac, after his bitterly hard youth, leaves the Wobblies with whom he has found comradeship and the joy of battle to marry a girl who drives him almost insane; then leaves her and is thrown into the Mexican revolutions of the period. Janey Williams's life has already taken on the gray color of the offices in which she will spend her life. There are no refuges in this world, no evasions, and above all no second starts. The clamps have been laid down early, and for all time.

Yet we can feel the toneless terror of all these lives, the oppression and joylessness that seem to beat down upon us from the first, only because every narrative section is so concrete and every sentence, as Delmore Schwartz pointed out, "can expand in the reader's mind to include a whole context of experience." *U.S.A.* is perhaps the first great naturalistic novel that is primarily a triumph of style. Everything that lives in the book is wound up on the spool of that style; from the fragments of popular songs in the "Newsreel" and the clean verse structure of the "Biographies" down to the pounding beat of the narrative, the book seems to be propelled by one dynamic rhythm. The Dos Passos prose, once so uncertain and self-conscious, has here

been whittled down to a sharpness that can kill; but it has by no means lost its old wistful rhetoric in *U.S.A.,* which is particularly conspicuous in the impressionist "Camera Eye" sections, and generally gives a kind of secret and mischievous color to the severely reportorial prose. Scrubby, slangy, with a kind of grim straightforwardness, it is the style of a very cunning artisan who seems to be working in these human materials as another might work in stone or wood—forever carving away, forever whittling, but never without subtle turns and a loving sense of design. It is never a "distinguished" style, beautiful in its own right; never as prismatic as Fitzgerald's or as delicately molded as Hemingway's, and there is always something fundamentally mechanical about it. But it is the style Dos Passos needs to turn the motor of the conveyor belt; it is the reportorial and satiric style needed to push along and circumscribe all these lives. With *The 42nd Parallel* we have entered into a machine world in which the rhythm of the machine has become the primal beat of all the people in it; and Dos Passos's hard, lean, mocking prose, forever sounding that beat, calling them to their deaths, has become the supreme expression of his conception of them.

Perhaps nowhere in the trilogy, save in the descending spiral of Charley Anderson's life in the first half of *The Big Money,* is Dos Passos's use of symbolic rhythm so brilliant as in the story of Joe Williams in *1919.* For Joe, Janey Williams's sailor brother, is the leading protagonist of the war and the early postwar period, as J. Ward Moorehouse's ambitiousness marked the pattern of *The 42nd Parallel.* Joe's endless shuttling between the continents on rotting freighters has become the migration and rootlessness of the young American generation whom we saw growing up in *The 42nd Parallel;* and the growing stupor and meaninglessness of his life became the leit-motif of the waste and death that hold everyone in the book as in a ghostly vise. The theme of death, of the false optimism immediately after the Armistice, are sounded immediately by the narrator behind his "Camera Eye" reporting the death of his mother and the notation on the coming of peace— "tomorrow I hoped would be the first day of the first month of the first year." The "Biographies" are all studies in death and defeat, from Randolph Bourne to Wesley Everest, mutilated and lynched after the Centralia shootings in Washington in 1919; from the prose poem commemorating the dozens of lives the Unknown Soldier might have led to the death's-head portrait of J. P. Morgan ("Wars and panics on the stock exchange,/ machinegunfire and arson/ . . . starvation, lice, cholera and typhus"). The "Camera Eye" can detect only "the almond smell of high explosives sending singing éclats through the sweetish puking grandiloquence of the rotting dead." And sounding its steady beat under the pub-

*Dust jacket for the 1970 reprint of the 1963 Polish edition of Nineteen-Nineteen, translated by Krzysztof Zarzecki (Thomas Cooper Library, University of South Carolina)*

lic surface of war is the story of Joe Williams hurled between the continents—Joe, the supreme Dos Passos cipher and victim and symbol, suffering his life with dumb unconsciousness of how outrageous his life is, and continually loaded and dropped from one ship to another like a piece of cargo.

> Twentyfive days at sea on the steamboat *Argyle*, Glasgow, Captain Thompson, loaded with hides, chipping rust, daubing red lead on steel plates that were sizzling hot griddles in the sun, painting the stack from dawn to dark, pitching and rolling in the heavy dirty swell; bedbugs in the bunks in the stinking focastle, slumgullion for grub, with potatoes full of eyes and mouldy beans.

All through *1919* one can hear death being sounded. Every life in it, even J. Ward Moorehouse's, has become a corrosion, a slow descent. Richard Ellsworth Savage goes back on his early idealism and becomes a cynical but willing abetter in Moorehouse's schemes. Eveline Hutchins and Eleanor Stoddard lose all their genteel pretense to art and grapple for Moorehouse's favor. "Daughter," the Texas girl Savage has betrayed, falls to her death in an airplane. Even Ben Compton, the New York radical, soon finds himself rotting away in prison. The war for almost all of them has become an endless round of drink and travel; they have brought nothing to it and learned nothing from it save a growing consciousness of their futility. And when they all slip into the twenties and the boom with *The Big Money*, the story of Charley Anderson's precipitate rise and fall becomes the last mad parable of their existence, a carnival of greed and corruption. Beginning with Dick Savage's life on ambulances and trains over France and Italy in *1919*, the pace of the trilogy has become faster and faster; now, as the war world empties into the pleasure world of *The Big Money*—New York and Detroit, Hollywood and Miami at the height of the boom—it has become a death ride. There is money in the air, money and power for Charley Anderson and Margo Dowling and Dick Savage; but as they come closer to this material triumph, their American dream, the machine has begun to spin them too rapidly. Charley Anderson can kiss the bright new century notes in his wallet, Margo can rise higher and higher in Hollywood, Dick Savage, having sold out completely, can enjoy his power at the hands of J. Ward Moorehouse; the machine has begun to strangle them; there is no joy here for anyone. All through *The Big Money* we wait for the balloon to collapse, for the death cry we hear in that last drunken drive of Charley Anderson's and his smashup.

What Waldo Frank said of Mencken is particularly relevant to Dos Passos: he brings energy to despair. Not merely does the writing in the trilogy become richer and firmer as the characters descend into the pit, but Dos Passos himself seems so imbued with an almost mystical conviction of failure that he rises to new heights in those last sections of *The Big Money* which depict the last futile efforts of the liberals and radicals to save Sacco and Vanzetti, and their later internecine quarrels. The most moving scene in all of *U.S.A.* is the scene in which Mary French, the only counterpoise to the selfishness of the other characters in *The Big Money*, becomes so exhausted by her labors for Sacco and Vanzetti that when she goes to bed she dreams that her whole world is forever coming apart, that she is climbing up a shaky hillside "among black guttedlooking houses pitching at crazy angles where steelworkers lived" and being thrown back. The conflicting hopes of Mary French, who wanted Socialism, and of Charley Anderson, who wanted the big money, have brought two different kinds of failure; but it is failure that broods over them and over everyone else in *U.S.A.* in the end—over the pompous fakes like J. Ward Moorehouse, the radicals like Ben Compton, the grasping little animals like Eleanor Stoddard and Eveline Hutchins, the opportunists like Richard Ellsworth Savage. The two survivors are Margo Dowling, supreme for the moment in Hollywood, and the homeless boy "Vag," who stands alone on the Lincoln Highway, gazing up at the transcontinental plane above winging its way west, the plane full of solid and well-fed citizens glittering in the American sun, the American dream. *All right we are two nations.* And like the scaffolding of hell in *The Divine Comedy*, they are frozen into eternity; for Dos Passos there is nothing else, save the integrity of the camera eye that must see this truth and report it, the integrity and sanctity of the individual locked up in the machine world of modern society.

With *The Big Money*, published at the height of the nineteen-thirties, the story of the twenties comes to a close; but even more does it bring the story of the lost generation to a close, that generation which has stood at the peak of modern time in America as no other has. Here in *U.S.A.*, in the most ambitious of all its works, is its measure of the national life, its conception of history—and it is a history of struggle that is vain, of failure that is irrevocable, and of final despair. There is strength in *U.S.A.*, Dos Passos's own strength, the strength of the craft that can weld so many lives together and make them live so intensely before us as they pass. But for the rest it is a brilliant hecatomb, and one of the coldest and most mechanical of tragic novels. By the time we have come to the end of *U.S.A.* we begin to feel what Edmund Wilson could detect in Dos Passos before it appeared, that "his disapproval of capitalistic society becomes a distaste for all the human beings who compose it." The protest, the lost-generation "I," has taken all of them into his vision; he has given us his truth. Yet if it intones anything affirmative in the end, it is the pronouncement of young Orestes Brownson— "There is no such thing as reforming the mass without reforming the individuals who compose it." It is this conviction, rising to a bitter crescendo in *Adventures of a Young Man,* this unyielding protest against modern society on the part of a writer who has now turned back to the roots of "our storybook democracy" in works like *The Ground We Stand On* and his projected life of Thomas Jefferson, that separates Dos Passos from so many of the social novelists who follow after him in the thirties. Where he speaks of sanctity, they speak of survival; where he lives by the truth of the camera eye, they live *in* the vortex of that society which Dos Passos has always been able to measure, with hatred but not in panic, from the outside. Dos Passos is the first of the new naturalists, and *U.S.A.* is the dominant social novel of the thirties; but it is not merely a vanished social period that it commemorates; it is an individualism, a protestantism, a power of personal disassociation, that seem almost to speak from another world.

— *On Native Grounds* (New York: Harcourt, Brace, 1942), pp. 353–359

### Orestes Rides Again, or, Little Electra and the Pulitzer Prize
Paul Palmer

*Paul Palmer was a journalist and writer of mystery novels.*

*Author's Note:* Recently re-reading Mr. Eugene O'Neill's *Mourning Becomes Electra,* the author was struck by the everlasting power of that deathless plot concerning the tragic fate of Electra, Clymenestra [*sic*], Agamemnon, Aegisthus, and Orestes. And then another thought—if the plot had so well served Aeschylus, Sophocles, Euripides, and Mr. O'Neill, how well might it also have served other distinguished authors? What would the classics of American literature be today if Mr. O'Neill's contemporaries had followed his example and hewed to the Greek line? The answer soon became some renderings of the Electra legend, each in the manner of a chef d'ouvre of Mr. O'Neill's period.

The customary, and most sincere, apologies are hereby offered to the talented writer whose name, one hopes, has not been taken in vain

— *Paul Palmer*

*As John Dos Passos Might Have Written It—*

### NYE-YENN, NYE-YENN, NYE-YENN

———

### NEWSREEL XLIV

*Twas Christmas in the harem, the eunuchs all were there
Watching the lovely maidens comb their golden hair*

### MAN BITES DOG

### DRED SCOTT MAKES TWELVE CONSECUTIVE PASSES N PRISON CELL

to the well known fact that Henry Ford, staunch friend of labor, will not allow his employees to drink beer. Mr. Ford also piloted The Peace Ship to Europe and was instrumental in imprisoning Matthew Arnold for having sold the West Point signals to Nathan Allen, the British spy

### SLAYS FATHER, MOTHER, TEN CHILDREN, BECAUSE THEY WERE UNHAPPY

*When in strode the Sultan and looked about the walls,
Said: "What do you want for Christmas, boys?"*

### J. P. MORGAN OPENS PRIVATE MUSEUM TO PUBLIC: MING VASE SOUVENIR TO EACH VISITOR

urgently advise the careful investor to take advantage of the present golden opportunity and buy Blue Chip securities. Prices may seem high at three and four hundred but that is nothing compared to what they will be in the future

### UNEMPLOYED OFFERED TEN-CENT BEDS AT WHITE HOUSE

### MISSING NEW YORK JUDGE WINS FIRST PRIZE AT ASBURY BABY PARADE

*And the eunuchs answered: "_____!"*

### JOE AGNEW

The years Joe was little he never heard anything about his Dad or his Mummy who were both in Leavenworth doing time, but when he was studying his homework evenings up in his little room in the attic he'd start thinking about them sometimes. He'd throw himself on the bed and lie on his back having erotic daydreams and trying to remember what Dad had been like and Bellingham and Mummy and everything before Aunt Mattie. There was a smell of bayrum and cigarsmoke and he was sitting in the barbershop watching Dad trim the customers; and he would climb up on Dad's back while Dad was shaving a Mr. Engberg and the back of Dad's neck was fat and red and when Dad laughed he could feel it rumble in his back. "Joey, keep your dirty feet offen Dad's white jacket," and he was on his hands and knees in the gaslight that poured down from the lamp trying to pick the grey hairs out of the brown hairs and the smell of armpits. And Mummy was saying, "Henry don't strike the child," and they stood hissing at one another behind the partition on account of customers while he got sicklyfeeling and rubbed against Mummy's puffy silk sleeves putting his teeth on edge and making him shudder all down his spine.

That summer he got a job as bellboy at The Greystone Hotel and Aunt Mattie told him he must keep himself pure for the lovely sweet girl he would someday marry and that anything else led only to madness and disease. Later that summer he found that Aunt Mattie was half right anyway. But a fella he knew showed him where the Y.M.C.A. would cure you of clap for twenty-five dollars and so he was all right till the next time.

The next summer he met an old tramp down by the railroad tracks when he was on his vacation and they hopped a fast freight out of Spokane on the Chicago, Milwaukee, and St. Paul. When they got to Cleveland Joe's friend borrowed a quarter from him and lammed. Joe never saw him again. That left Joe forty-five cents and he found a chink joint where you could get hamandeggs and french fries for thirty cents and with the other fifteen cents he bought *Snappy Stories* and went out under a pine tree and read all afternoon in the sunshine. It felt fine stretching out there under the blue sky.

Next winter he rode the rods to New York and got a job pearl diving in Moneta's restaurant but the food was too rich for him and he had to quit and he slung hash at Thompson's for a whole year. He didn't go out much nights, sticking around the Y and shooting a little pool with the guys and only going after the skirts Saturday nights. He was making seven-fifty a week and saving up for an accordion.

That summer a swell show was put on down at Miner's Bowery Theater and Joe decided to take it in. He went down to the theater on Tuesday, July 4th, in the afternoon, to get a good seat for that night and forked over seventy-five cents for Row C, Seat 1.

. . . . . . . . . .

–*New Directions IX,* edited by James Laughlin (Norfolk, Conn.: New Directions, 1946), pp. 218–225

## Time in Dos Passos
Claude-Edmonde Magny

*Claude-Edmonde Magny was a major French critic of the postwar years. Her study of the relationship between the modern American novel and motion pictures was initially published in 1948 as* L'Age du Roman Americain.

The special technique of *The Big Money* encompasses an entire, implicit metaphysic–the challenge of Being. It is important for another reason, too: thanks to this technique, Dos Passos's trilogy has a temporal structure. The several individual stories composing the trilogy, which are what one is first aware of, are not only different shots of a single reality but moments within a single development. This single development transcends each of them and exists only by virtue of the complex design they all form. It is possible to put them end to end and demonstrate their continuity; the occasional use of flashbacks when the author wants to present the past of a newly introduced character is no more frequent than it is in the movies. The nonnovelistic elements that frame the stories–the Newsreels, the Camera Eyes, the lyrical biographies–are thus seen to have a very important "linking" function: they assure the cosmic as well as the psychological continuity of the narrative. Because of them, the impersonal reality that is the subject of the book–the year 1919 or the economic inflation of the twenties–can unfold without interruption, independent of the individual consciousnesses in which it is embodied, and preserve the mythic quality Dos Passos wanted to achieve. They are like movie background music, which nobody listens to but everybody hears, and which prepares our subconscious for the images to come.

The Newsreels in particular have taken on the major role of the narrative–to measure the rhythm of time, to give us the uninterrupted sound that the film of life makes as it unrolls and winds off the reel behind the scenes. The Newsreels give us the unfolding world events that will have repercussions on the individual destinies of the characters. For example, J. Ward Moorehouse's story before and after his second marriage is cut in two not so much because of the marriage itself–which in no way interrupts a personal, emotional, and professional continuity–but because war is declared in Europe during his honeymoon. The war does not affect the characters' lives immediately, but it is destined to do so soon. Consequently, just as in Wagner's *Tristan and Isolde* the theme of Isolde's death is announced by a drum in the prelude long before it is taken up officially by the entire orchestra, so the "theme of war" is first presented longitudinally in the nonnovelistic elements of the book: a Newsreel filled with such headlines as "CZAR LOSES PATIENCE WITH AUSTRIA," "GENERAL WAR NEAR," "ASSASSIN SLAYS DEPUTY JUARES"; a biography of "Andrew Carnegie, Prince of

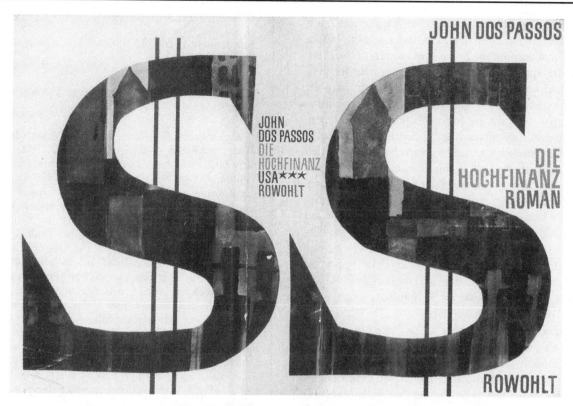

*Dust jacket for the 1962 West German edition of* The Big Money, *translated by Paul Baudisch*
*(Thomas Cooper Library, University of South Carolina)*

Peace"; and a Camera Eye that appears to be the interior monologue of an English sailor. Then the narrative resumes. Further on, America's entry into the war is announced through a Camera Eye–the interior monologue of a couple (or a group) of New York leftist intellectuals–and a Newsreel punctuated by the refrain "It's a long way to Tipperary" and including headlines like "JOFFRE ASKS TROOPS NOW."

Similarly, in *The Big Money,* the biography of Rudolph Valentino–symbol of the handsome young man who has made it, of the gigolo elevated by the movies to the stature of a myth that has become a reality in the collective consciousness–is interpolated into the story at the moment when Margo Dowling leaves for Cuba with her gigolo husband. The biography itself is introduced by the last news item in the preceding Newsreel: "Rudolph Valentino, noted screen star, collapsed suddenly yesterday in his apartment at the Hotel Ambassador. Several hours later he underwent. . . ." At this moment, just as on the radio, the voice suddenly changes and a new speaker "fades in" by announcing, in a completely different tone: "Adagio Dancer, The nineteenyearold son of a veterinary in Castellaneta . . ." And during all this time the story of Margo (and through her of an entire epoch) is going on uninterruptedly, though because of the novel's aesthetic we are only able to apprehend fragments of it.

Then a parenthesis begins–the story of Charley Anderson–followed by a new Newsreel and then by a Camera Eye that is the collective monologue of emigrants leaving for Havana, which brings us back to Margo's story. When Charley leaves for Detroit, where he will join a big airplane company and marry–in other words, where he will begin the series of adventures that will lead him to success, to his meeting with Margo, then to ruin and land speculations in Miami–we get a biography of the Wright brothers, aviation pioneers; a verse of "Valencia" and other songs evoking the charm of the South; a fragment of a speech by someone who has made a fortune in Miami; an excerpt from a brochure about installment buying; and so forth. The major events of Charley's life are prefigured in the evolution of society as a whole, which makes these events possible and determines their nature. His destiny is so little of his own making that it can be foretold and prophesied. Don Passos's characters do not have their own inner rhythm; its place is taken by the objective, mechanical rhythm of social facts, which replace at every moment the personal time, the "lived time," that Charley, Margo, and Mary French are incapable of possessing. It is social time, external time, that will carry them along in its inexorable unfolding.

One can now begin to see the profound connection at the heart of *U.S.A.* between the narrative technique of the stories and the objective elements that frame them. It is *necessary* that Dos Passos's characters have no positive inner existence, that they are not in the least masters of their fate, that they be equally incapable of controlling what happens to them and how they feel about it, that they marry for who knows what reason (Charley's marriage to Gladys and Margo's to Tony are from this point of view symbolic), and that they succeed or fail depending only upon whether they are being carried forward by the tide or left abandoned by it. And all of this is true even when, like Mary French, they *want* to give their lives a sense or meaning—by, for example, social action or self-sacrifice. Two of Dos Passos's later novels, *Adventures of a Young Man* and *Number One*, present us with a diptych of two equally absurd fates—that of Glenn Spotswood, martyr to the cause of the proletariat, and that of his brother Tyler, opportunist and dipsomaniac, the yes-man and tool of Chuck Crawford, the despicable boss of a Southern state, until Crawford decides to abandon him.

In modern society neither self-sacrifice nor ambition permits a man to be "captain of his soul, master of his fate," as the Victorian poets like Kipling or Henley had too naively hoped. And if Dos Passos has chosen to recount his characters' lives in that terrible preterit that *deadens* events as soon as they are so described to us; if he gives us their feelings and their states of consciousness by means of a third-person pseudo-inner monologue filled with clichés, adulterants that almost invariably come from a too-obvious hypocrisy, lacking every kind of reaction normal to an authentic and spontaneous life except for the lowest biological responses; if, thanks to the diabolic magic of his style, he thus pares modern man down to the bone to show him in his misery, his nakedness, his basic nothingness; if he does all these things, it is to prepare for the appearance, the display, the *epiphaneia*, of the major character of his book—Time: the inexorable and monstrous time of contemporary capitalist society as it incoherently unwinds in Newsreels; the time that elevates and casts down Margo, Charley, and Mary, with neither discernment nor justice, and rules over the empty consciousness it invades and tyrannizes.

"Time," says Schelling somewhere, "is the bad conscience of all barren metaphysics." It would not be at all arbitrary (or at least no more than it is to set forth any proposition) to begin to formulate an aesthetic of the novel by saying that Time is the main character of the novel; that the novel is the literary genre on which has devolved the task of exploring and explicating every aspect and every dimension of Time; and that the novel's current popularity and triumph is quite likely at least partly due to the unhappiness of the modern consciousness, one that has fallen away from its relationship with eternity—which it had successfully retained until the Renaissance—and is now wounded by a traumatism of Time, the presence of which is felt in most of the great contemporary novels from

---

### The Reach of *U.S.A.*
Frederick R. Karl

*Frederick R. Karl notes the influence of* U.S.A. *on major novelists of the post–World War II period.*

Dos Passos's *The 42nd Parallel, 1919*, and *The Big Money*, published respectively in 1930, 1932, 1936, were books that carried well past the Depression years into the postwar era, traveling as well as Hemingway's early stories and novels and Faulkner's major work, somewhat better than much of Fitzgerald or Wolfe. The Dos Passos novels, furthermore, could not be slighted for lack of technical daring; like Faulkner, Dos Passos incorporated modernist experiments into his work. Along with *The Sound and the Fury, Absalom, Absalom!* and "The Bear," the trilogy was a bona fide American experimental fiction. And because the novels were technically daring, their political message penetrated. As immediately after the war as Jones's *From Here to Eternity* and Mailer's first two novels, *The Naked and the Dead* and *Barbary Shore*, political aspects of *U.S.A.* are apparent. We can see the reach of the trilogy, also, in Richard Wright, John Horne Burns, Alfred Hayes, even in later writers like Pynchon, Doctorow, and Gaddis.

*—American Fictions, 1940–1980: A Comprehensive History and Critical Evaluation* (New York: Harper & Row, 1983), p. 77

---

Faulkner to Virginia Woolf. One of the functions of criticism would then be to bring this to light and analyze it, to expose the wound if a thoroughgoing cure is shown to be impossible.

Within a dialectic of Time, the short story corresponds to the instant. An essentially impressionistic genre, it is—from Mérimée to Katherine Anne Porter and from the calm garden of Balzac's *Secrets de la Princesse de Cadignan* (*A Princess's Secrets*) to those short stories of Faulkner through which a tumultuous storm sweeps—an incision at a specific instant. To the novel, on the other hand, belongs the third dimension—the opaque density of duration that is alone capable of integrating the two other dimensions. Obviously, this does not mean that the author has to show a character grow from birth to old age: the objective duration of the events he relates does not have to exceed the twenty-four hours of classical tragedy. Joyce's *Ulysses* and Virginia Woolf's *Mrs. Dalloway* are unquestionably the most famous (and the most deliberate) examples; a less well-known one is Louis Guilloux's *Le Sang noir*. And, of course, there is also Sterne's *Tristram Shandy*, which only manages to cover the first three days of the hero's life in its several hundred pages. But no one will be misled by appearances. The true time of the novel, its normal time, the time most often encountered (the very function of the genre seems to be to exploit it literally), is what Bergson, in one of those simple and superficial views so characteristic of him, called "lived time." One senses this "lived time" in George Eliot's *Mill on the Floss,* in Balzac, in Meredith (to say nothing of in Rosamund Lehmann). And this "lived time" is what is lacking in Zola (but not in the Maupassant of *Une Vie*), and so ostentatiously present in Proust.

What makes Dos Passos stand out from other novelists is undoubtedly that the characteristic time of his novels does not, to the slightest degree, have this organic rhythm, the dense continuity of living tissue. His characters move within "dead time"—or rather "deadened time"—with neither spurts nor continuity, where each instant comes to the fore only to be immediately replunged into nothingness. An atomic time, like that of a Cartesian universe no longer at every instant supported by continuous creation, God having defaulted once and for all. But the discontinuity is only in the detail, in the psychological awareness of the characters. If the five hundred pages of *The Big Money* are read without interruption, the reader, far from having an impression of perpetual rupture, of atomism (which would seem the inevitable result of the purposeful dislocation of the story and its multiplicity of perspectives), feels rather as if he is being carried along by a swift current. This is because the psychological time within which the charac-

ters' states of consciousness, and their acts, unfold—and the essence of which is fragmentation—is not Dos Passos's real or basic time.

His true time is the time of Society—objective, inexorable, and spatialized. The hidden mainspring of *U.S.A.* is this implacable and regular machine rhythm, already evidenced in *Manhattan Transfer*. The powerful impetus that carries us through these three volumes for 1500 pages is the thumping of the locomotive, the regular "chug-chug" of a ship's boilers, the whir of a taxi motor in front of a building, or the relentless circuits of those moving headlines around the big newspaper buildings—their hallucinating monotony hypnotizing the crowd, causing the stock market crash, and provoking a rash of Wall Street suicides whose repercussions would eventually reach the Scandinavian farmers of Minnesota and the plantation population of South Carolina. The inexorable pulsation at the heart of Dos Passos's work is that of the basic, regular rhythm of the transmission belt in the heart of a factory—invisible, omnipresent, all-powerful. The rhythm of the modern world itself.

. . . . . . . . . .

*—The Age of the American Novel: The Film Aesthetic of the Fiction Between the Two Wars,* translated by Eleanor Hochman (New York: Ungar, 1972), pp. 124–130

*Dust jacket for the 1980 East German edition of Baudisch's 1932 translation of* Nineteen-Nineteen
*(Thomas Cooper Library, University of South Carolina)*

**John Dos Passos: The Energy of Despair**
John W. Aldridge

*John W. Aldridge taught for many years at the University of Michigan and was a novelist as well as a critic. His* After the Lost Generation: A Critical Study of the Writers of Two Wars, *an account of American fiction of the 1930s and 1940s, remained an influential study for many years.*

It is generally believed that the bitterness engendered in Dos Passos by the injustice done to Sacco and Vanzetti provided him with the focus and purpose he needed to write his immense trilogy *U.S.A.* However true this may be, one can just as easily explain his achievement in that work in terms of natural creative evolution. As we have already seen, there were two distinct forces developing in Dos Passos' work up to the time of *U.S.A.* *One Man's Initiation* was primarily a record of his early disenchantment with the ideals of war and his emerging sympathy with the victims of war. *Three Soldiers* was an open protest against the evils of war at the same time that it indicated the futility of the individual's revolt against the system responsible for the making of wars. In *Manhattan Transfer* Dos Passos' social sympathies had broadened to such an extent that he was able to depict the futility he felt in terms of a dozen lives; but his disenchantment rendered those lives meaningless. They did not add up to a powerful denunciation of the system—because Dos Passos had still not found a way of centering his sympathies on an object more precise than that of the undifferentiated human mass. But as the result of the experiments he made in *Manhattan Transfer,* Dos Passos was able to return to the material he had begun to explore in that book and see in it implications which had previously escaped him. He sensed now that the real victims of the system were the working classes and that the real evils of the system stemmed from wealth and power. He was thus able to focus his sympathies upon a specific social group and set them against his hatred of another social group, just as in his earlier work he had focused his sympathies upon the individual aesthete and set them against his hatred of war. He was able to write now within the frame of two distinct and separate worlds, two nations, and to bring to his writing the full power of his protest (for he believed in the cause of the working classes as he had formerly believed in the cause of the aesthete) as well as the full power of his futility (for he knew, in spite of his belief in their cause, that the working classes under capitalism must always be defeated).

The dramatic intensity of *U.S.A.* derives from the perfect balance of these conflicting forces within Dos Passos. There is, on one side, the gradual corruption

# Dos Passos
# La grosse galette I

folio

Texte intégral

*Cover of the first volume in the two-volume 1980 French paperback reprint of Charles de Richter's 1946 translation of* The Big Money *(Thomas Cooper Library, University of South Carolina)*

and defeat of the characters whose lives are depicted in the straight-narrative sections. There is, on the other, the implicit indignation of the harsh, cutting style, which runs persistently counter to the drift of the narrative and comments upon it. Then, in the "Camera Eye" and "Biographies" sections the style picks up additional counterforce. The lyric meditations of the "Camera Eye" recast in poetic terms the negation expressed in the narrative and serve as a sort of moral center for the book. Through them the author periodically reenters the book and reminisces on moments out of the past when men fought, and were punished for fighting, for the cause of labor. During these moments, he seems to be saying, occurred the real tragedy of which the characters are now victims. The "Biographies" comment on the narrative in still other terms. This time the portraits are of real men who have been instrumental in shaping the system, either by rebelling against it or by trying to dominate it. Those who have rebelled are, for the most part, martyrs to the cause–Debs, Veblen, Big Billy Haywood, Randolph Bourne, Sacco and Vanzetti. Those who have sought power are, for the most part, tycoons like Hearst, Carnegie, and J. P. Morgan. But, however much their aims may have differed, the destiny of both groups is the same; the rebels are defeated by the system and the tycoons are corrupted by it.

This hypothesis of universal ruin, introduced lyrically through the "Camera Eye" and historically through the "Biographies," is given dramatic proof in the narrative proper. Here all the social classes of *U.S.A.* are represented. There are J. Ward Moorehouse, Charley Anderson, Richard Ellsworth Savage, Eveline Hutchins, Eleanor Stoddard, the prototypes of privilege; and Joe Williams, Ben Compton, Mary French, the prototypes of unprivilege. Each has a different story, but all come to the same end.

The career of J. Ward Moorehouse, the central symbol of Dos Passos' American-dream-become-nightmare, links the three volumes of the trilogy together into one continuous narrative. Born near the turn of the century, Moorehouse is the typical product of the new industrial Success Myth. Like Fitzgerald's Gatsby, he begins early in youth to build his life around the simple pioneer virtues of Horatio Alger: early rising, hard work, thrift, honesty, self-confidence–"By gum, I can do it." His story, beginning in *The 42nd Parallel,* is a perfect leitmotiv for the naive new century; and it is presented, fittingly enough, against a background of jubilantly patriotic headlines, "Biographies" of the new wonder men of science (Edison, Burbank, Steinmetz) and the new political rebels (Bryan, LaFollette, Debs, Big Bill Haywood), and lyric reveries of the "Camera Eye" narrator, who is still a child. But out of this background the stories of other youths also emerge. Mac, the boy who never had a chance, begins as a seller of pornographic books, drifts aimlessly over the country looking for work, gets a girl in trouble, leaves her to become a revolutionary comrade in Mexico; Janey Williams goes to work, gets lost in the gray office routine that is to be her life; Eleanor Stoddard, thin, sterile, hater of everything and everyone, struggles to get ahead as an interior decorator. And finally we see that the sickness which has begun to destroy these people almost from the moment of their birth has infected Moorehouse also. Now no longer the innocent trusting child of the new century, he has become a perversion of its ideals and a burlesque of his own earlier hopes. After divorcing his socially prominent wife because she is a whore, he begins to perfect his talent for exploiting the talents of others. Janey Williams as his secretary,

Eleanor Stoddard as his platonic mistress, and Eveline Hutchins as Eleanor's best friend all come under his influence and are carried forward by him toward a success that is to be their common grave.

As Moorehouse's ambition characterizes *The 42nd Parallel,* so the aimless drifting of Joe Williams, Janey's brother, sets the pattern for *1919,* the year that marked the beginning of the end of the Great American Dream for Dos Passos. As Joe wanders from continent to continent, getting drunk, whoring, fighting, hating, the generation he symbolizes plunges headlong into the violence of the Boom years. The "Biographies" now are studies in horror and destruction (Jack Reed, dead of typhus in Moscow; the ghost of Randolph Bourne "crying out in a shrill soundless giggle / *War is the health of the state*"; Woodrow Wilson, idealist and dreamer, broken on the cause of Peace; J. P. Morgan–"Wars and panics on the stock exchange,/ machinegunfire and arson,/ bankruptcies, warloans,/ starvation, lice, cholera, and typhus: / good growing weather for the House of Morgan"; Joe Hill executed). The "Camera Eye" narrator is no longer a child but a disillusioned ex-soldier "walking the streets rolling on your bed eyes sting from peeling the speculative onion of doubt if somebody in your head topdog? underdog? didn't (and on Union Square) say liar to you." Richard Ellsworth Savage, one-time idealist and poet, becomes a Moorehouse underling; Eveline Hutchins and Eleanor Stoddard fight for their share of the Moorehouse patronage; "Daughter," the reforming young Texas girl whom Savage has ruined, is killed in a plane crash; Ben Compton, the hard-working radical, is jailed. The forming patterns of *The 42nd Parallel* have now hardened into a mold, the pace has become faster and more frantic, and the hunger for success has become a mad lust for pleasure and power.

The corruption, greed, and spiritual torment of the years after the war shroud *The Big Money* in an atmosphere of chilly death. For nearly all the characters the American Dream has found a monstrous apotheosis in material triumph. Charley Anderson makes money, more money than he ever imagined existed in the world, but he finds no happiness. Margo Dowling, after a life of incredible sordidness culminating in high-class prostitution, rises to spectacular success in Hollywood; J. Ward Moorehouse, grown old and empty, finally perceives his failure, collapses, and dies; Savage, realizing too late that he has sold out his ideals, sinks into homosexual corruption. The "Biographies" too have become portraits of waste and misused success (Frederick Winslow Taylor, the efficiency expert, who "never saw the working of the American plan" and who died with his watch in his hand; Hearst, "a spent Caesar grown old with spending / never man enough to cross the Rubicon"; Henry Ford, the mechanical wizard, living a frightened old age surrounded by "thousands of millionaire acres, protected by an army of servicemen, secretaries, secret agents, dicks under orders of an English exprizefighter . . . ," attempting to "put back the old bad road, so that everything might be the way it used to be, in the days of horses and buggies"; Veblen, dying unrecognized, deliberately obliterating the last traces of his own memory–"It is also my wish . . . that no tombstone, slab, epitaph, effigy, tablet, inscription or monument be set up to my memory or name in any place or at any time; that no obituary, memorial, portrait, or biography of me . . . be printed or published"). Finally, at the end, in Charley Anderson's crack-up, the destruction is made pathetically complete and the last ideals of a great age are brought to ruin. There is only "Vag" now, the hopeless, embittered wanderer, hitchhiking, like Jimmy Herf, to nowhere on the big concrete highway; while overhead an air liner passes filled with transcontinental passengers thinking "contracts, profits, vacation-trips, mighty continent between Atlantic and Pacific, power, wires humming dollars, cities jammed, hills empty, the indian-trail leading into the wagonroad, the macadamed pike, the concrete skyway, trains, planes: history the billiondollar speedup. . . . *All right we are two nations.*"

The U.S.A. which Dos Passos describes is thus more than simply a country or a way of life. It is a condition of death, a wasteland of futility and emptiness. In it, the best and the worst must be defeated; for defeat can be the only answer for the inhabitants of a world in which all goals are unattainable and the most powerful gods are corrupt. Yet, although the thing he describes is death, Dos Passos brings to his description a savage kind of power which saves it from becoming dead too. Through it all, he has consistently hated and condemned; and he has expressed his hatred with great strength and purpose. This has given meaning to the meaninglessness of his characters, value to their valuelessness. His style has been the perfect instrument of that meaning, protesting at every step in its development against the horror of the thing it was disclosing. His "Camera Eye" and biographical devices have extended that meaning to the outermost limits of suggestion and elevated it to the stature of pure insight into the dilemma of our time. What was shadowy and unfocused in *Manhattan Transfer* is now brilliantly clear; the protest has broken free of the mere mass and become concentrated in a specific social phenomenon; and as this has occurred, Dos Passos has also been freed, to create the world of powerful despair which is his best and truest world.

–*After the Lost Generation: A Critical Study of the Writers of Two Wars* (New York: McGraw-Hill, 1951), pp. 71–76

## U.S.A.
John H. Wrenn

*John H. Wrenn was a professor of English at the University of Colorado. In addition to his study of Dos Passos, he has published books on Sherwood Anderson and Edgar Lee Masters.*

If Americans were to discover and develop their "own brand" of political idealism, they would have to refurbish their memories–as Dos Passos implied so strongly in his play *Airways*. If they could remember enough within the hectic years they had been living through, perhaps they could discover the elements of a scale of values, without which they would remain a "mindless and panicky mob." If Dos Passos as an artist were to help them, he would first have to stretch his own memory to its limits. In 1927 and 1928, while he was formulating these opinions, Dos Passos was already at work on his manuscript for *The 42nd Parallel*. Early in 1929, just back from Russia, he began digging in earnest into his own and his nation's past. By the fall of that year the stock-market crash had begun to make Americans' mindlessness and panic apparent even to themselves.

### I  A Book of Memories

*U.S.A.* is first of all a book of memories. These memories, all relating to the United States during the first third of the twentieth century, are presented and developed contrapuntally in autobiography, history, biography, and fiction. The form is that of the associational process of memory itself, by which perceptions are established in the mind and later recalled. And the purpose of the work is equivalent to the function of the memory: to establish in the mind perceptions which, in association with other perceptions from experience such as those of pleasure or pain, develop into attitudes toward certain kinds of experience, frames of reference, or standards by which we judge today.

Dos Passos' intent was to establish for himself and his audience a broad and pertinent framework of memory. This required a maximum selective recall of his own experience, supplemented by the general experience and that of other individuals recorded in documents of the times. It also required an imaginative organization of these materials into a mnemonic unity which could suggest appropriate attitudes toward related kinds of past, present, and future experience.

If he could get a sequence of enough memories, or even a characteristic segment of them, into focus in his camera's eye, he could develop it, edit it, and give it artistic form. Then he could run it through again, stop the motion for a moment if he wished, and present a

## The Influence of *U.S.A.*
### Alfred Kazin

*The permanent impact of* U.S.A. *on the depiction of American social life is discussed by Kazin.*

[Dos Passos's] one lasting book, *U.S.A.,* continued to dazzle readers as *the* American experimental novel of the 1920s. Dos Passos's fluid originality as a stylist, his ability to bring the whole new century into his trilogy, made it not at all ludicrous for Jean-Paul Sartre, a harshly demanding critic, to say in 1938: "Dos Passos has invented only one thing, an art of story-telling, and that is enough. I regard Dos Passos as the greatest writer of our time."

Whatever that meant in 1938—Hemingway in Toots Shors's talked about knocking Tolstoy out of the ring, but no one cared any longer about being or even naming "the greatest writer"—*U.S.A.* brilliantly succeeded as novel because it reflected the inventiveness of the twenties and the "religion of the word." Dos Passos had written a "collective" novel about "the march of history" with mass society as his protagonist. But with his gift for putting on display all the social events and stylistic novelties of his time, he made his trilogy seem the work of many American minds. In the gray and anxious 1930s, *U.S.A.* reflected the buoyant twenties as freshness and irreverence. It offered no bright hopes for the future, and the Communists were right to complain that it lacked a political direction—theirs. But like certain Elizabethan playwrights and Italian painters of the Renaissance, Dos Passos was less a great artist than one of several hinges operating the same great door. That door did open to "the great American thing." There would yet be an American literature and art equal to the promise of American life. Without Dos Passos's invention of his cinematic machine to record the momentum carrying an industrial mass society headlong into moral chaos, a good deal of our present sophistication in fiction, in the classy new journalism, even in the formal writing of American history, would not exist. Dos Passos was a writer whom other writers will always imitate without knowing it. He created a tight-lipped national style that was above all a way of capturing the million alternatives of experience in America.

*—An American Procession* (New York: Knopf, 1984), p. 382

the "exclusive presentations of the Mesmer Agency" containing comments on "the great and near great" and "a fund of racy anecdotes"—as Dos Passos later satirized the ballyhooing of his books in *The Prospect Before Us* (1950). But for himself, he would present it only as one man's attempt "to add his nickel's worth."

When it was ready, some risked their nickels; and almost the first thing they saw was the producer-director as a little child flitting across the screen, like Alfred Hitchcock sneaking into his own films. As autobiography Dos Passos presented his own story directly in the Camera Eye sequences, in stream-of-consciousness—or more accurately, stream-of-memory—narration. His story in *The 42nd Parallel* is almost entirely separate from the rest of his history of the country in the early years of the century; but, as the novel progresses through the three volumes, there is a continuous tightening in the relationship of its several parts—narrative, Camera Eyes, Newsreels, biographies—as the narrator becomes one with his subject.

In *1919* the autobiography of the Camera Eyes begins to merge with the fictional story of Dick Savage, especially at Harvard and in the war. Toward the end of the final volume, *The Big Money,* Camera Eyes Forty-nine and Fifty include indirect biography of Sacco and Vanzetti; and in between those two sequences Dos Passos' story merges with the fictional story of Mary French in her work for the Sacco-Vanzetti defense and with the history of the time as outlined in Newsreel LXVI. Finally, within the last twenty-five pages of the trilogy, the fictional Ben Compton (the prototype of Glenn Spotswood in his next novel, *Adventures* and of Jay Pignatelli in *Chosen Country*) expresses, peering "through his thick glasses," Dos Passos' relationship to the Communist Party: "oppositionist . . . exceptionalism . . . a lot of nonsense." And in the final sketch, "Vag," of the last two and a half pages, the Camera Eye has become the biography of the depression vagrant, a distinctive phenomenon of the times. It is also very nearly the picture of Jimmy Herf hitchhiking west out of Manhattan.

In *U.S.A.* Dos Passos placed himself securely within the history of his country in his time. But he emphasized the history above the importance of his relation to it. As an historian, he did not need to be told that his country's own brand of idealism was "democracy"; the problem was to discover what the word meant. It seemed to have pretty much lost its meaning at about the time the United States had fought a war to make the world safe for it. Taking the word at its pre-war value, Dos Passos devoted his trilogy to a history of the struggle for industrial democracy in America.

close-up or a flash-back: "Now who was that, could that have been me in that funny hat?" He could also give a tune or a speech on the sound track. The viewer might even leave the theater wiser than when he went in; at any rate, a few people might risk a nickel to see it. It would probably be misleadingly advertised as one of

As a critic Dos Passos has always been principally interested in the effects of phenomena upon individual men and women. This interest helped to make him a novelist; and it—and not simply his training as a novelist—focuses all of his histories upon personalities and traits of character. The focus of *U.S.A.,* therefore, is upon the twenty-six *actual* persons engaged in the struggle and the twelve principal *fictional* persons also engaged in it and affected by it. The actual people of the biographies are those who influenced the pattern of the struggle—labor leaders, politicians, artists, journalists, scientists, and business leaders. The fictional characters represent average men and women molded by the complex of forces about them.

The fictional characters illustrate more than anything else the dissolution of the once central cohesive institution in American society (the one Dos Passos first

Cover of 1982 Spanish paperback edition of The Big Money, translated by Jesús Zulaika (Thomas Cooper Library, University of South Carolina)

achieved with his marriage in 1929, as he began *U.S.A.*), the family. Although most of them come from fairly secure family units, they are unable to form them for themselves. The fictional narrative is filled with pathetic promiscuity, perversion, vague temporary alliances, divorces, abortions. Ben Compton, again, sums up the need at the end of *The Big Money*. Speaking to Mary French, who is one of the most sympathetically portrayed of the principal characters and whose maternal instincts have made her a devoted worker for the oppressed, Ben says, "You know if we hadn't been fools we'd have had that baby that time . . . we'd still love each other."

In Dos Passos' picture of the U.S.A., it was essential to reinstitute the family; but neither of the two larger institutions in which the forces of the times had become polarized—*laissez-faire* capitalism and Stalinist communism—appeared to permit its free growth. Until people achieved a social system which would give the average man a sense of participation—of responsibility for and pride in his work—the smaller, more vital social units would be ineffective. To achieve that system, the meaning of the old mercantile-agrarian democracy and its libertarian phraseology—liberty, equality, pursuit of happiness—must somehow be restored in the scientific, urban-industrial present.

The makers of that present and those who hoped to remake it are the subjects of the biographies. Toward each of the principal fictional characters, each of whom is seen as a child, the reader shares Dos Passos' affection, which turns to scorn or pity as they become mere cogs or pulp in the capitalist or communist machines, or to indignation as their individualism leaves them crushed and dead—like Joe Williams and Daughter, both killed by accident in France in the aftermath of the war—or stranded and alone like Ben Compton. Toward the biographies, however the reader's reaction is principally a sharing of the burning indignation with which most of them were written. Of the twenty-six, not counting the two portraits of the anonymous Unknown Soldier and "Vag," fourteen are sympathetic and twelve are not.

The criterion of judgment of them as of the fictional characters is the courage or will of the individual to maintain the faith that most of them were born to in the untarnished meanings of the democratic creed. By this criterion we recognize them as friends or strangers whatever their births or origins or ends. If their work is intended to uphold the dignity of the individual man or woman and the integrity of their language as Americans, they are friends. If they are scornful or even like Edison and Henry Ford merely "unconcerned with the results of [their] work in human terms," they are the "strangers" of Camera Eye Fifty, "who have turned our language inside out who have taken the clean words our fathers spoke and made them slimy and foul."

Dos Passos is not at all mysterious as to his purposes; he even states them directly in Camera Eyes Forty-seven and Forty-nine of *The Big Money:* ". . . shape words remembered light and dark straining    to rebuild yesterday    to clip out paper figures    to simulate growth    Warp newsprint into faces smoothing and wrinkling in the various barelyfelt velocities of time." Or again, reporting his reporting of the Sacco-Vanzetti case: "pencil scrawls in my notebook the scraps of recollection the broken halfphrases the effort to intersect word with word to dovetail clause with clause to rebuild out of mangled memories unshakably (Oh Pontius Pilate) the truth." Here is the meaning of the terms "straight writing" and "architect of history."

Yet the architect of history works not only "to rebuild yesterday" as the foundation of today, but to build of today a sound foundation for tomorrow. By straight writing and with the materials of contemporary speech, the writer provides contexts of meaning for today's speech, which will be the basis of tomorrow's memories. Dos Passos achieves his contexts through the use of dialogue and even of direct narration phrased in the colloquial language appropriate to the character he is treating. The reader sees and hears the speech in conjunction with actions and through the consciousness of the character concerned. We participate in the individual's attitudes toward events.

Further than this, Dos Passos has the reader share, at least for the moment, the attitudes of quite different individuals toward the same or similar events. We see the affair between Dick Savage and Daughter (Anne Elizabeth Trent), for instance, through the eyes and feelings of each of them. To Dick it is simply an affair which becomes awkward and threatens to embarrass him in his career when Daughter expects him to feel some responsibility for her pregnancy. To her it is a tremendous event which results in tragedy. The reader also sees and experiences a variety of attitudes toward business, labor, government, the war, the Sacco-Vanzetti case, and many other institutions and particular events. Since he cannot sympathetically entertain at the same time two opposing attitudes toward a single phenomenon, he is forced to choose, to criticize, to formulate standards.

As a realist Dos Passos reveals his characters in the historical framework of time, place, and social milieu which help to form them. These backgrounds, usually presented through the memories of the characters themselves, are various enough to provide a representative cross-section, geographically and socially, of American society. In the "Introduction" to *Three Soldiers,* Dos Passos remarked that "our beds have made us and the acutest action we can take is to sit up on the edge of them and look around and think." In describing his characters' beds, Dos Passos is an objective reporter of existing phenomena. But in portraying the individuals themselves and their attempts to sit up and look around and think, he is a selective critic. He controls our choice of attitude by creating characters with whom we must at first sympathize, for their beds and their wants are ours. We continue to sympathize as they struggle to express themselves and to satisfy their needs; but we become indignant at the Procrustean forces that chain them prone in their beds or at the individuals as they lose the courage to struggle, refuse to think, or prefer to crawl back under the sheets within the security of the familiar narrow limits of their bedsteads.

## II   *Tools of Language*

Half of the fictional characters of *U.S.A.* and nearly half of the subjects of the biographies have a special facility with the tools of language, the means with which to build or to restrict human freedom. Of the fictional ones, most are poor or careless keepers of their talents. J. Ward Moorehouse becomes a public-relations executive—a propagandist for big business who exploits language for profit; Janey becomes his expert private secretary and an efficient, warped old maid; Dick Savage degenerates from a young poet to Moorehouse's administrative assistant and contact-man—a sort of commercial pimp. Mac surrenders his principles as an itinerant printer for the labor movement and succumbs to the security offered by a girl and a little bookstore of his own in Mexico; Mary French and Ben Compton become pawns of communist politics. Only Ben emerges at the end, though rejected and alone, still looking around him and thinking.

In contrast, only three of roughly a dozen subjects of the biographies seem to misuse their gifts of language: Bryan, "a silver tongue in a big mouth"; Woodrow Wilson, "talking to save his faith in words, talking . . . talking"; Hearst, whose "empire of the printed word . . . this power over the dreams of the adolescents of the world grows and poisons like a cancer." Most of the heroes of Dos Passos' biographies are chosen from among the heroes and martyrs of the working-class movement: men who looked around, thought critically, and developed their abilities in an effort to restore the meanings rather than to exploit the phraseology of American democracy. They were men like Eugene Debs, Bill Haywood, La Follette, Jack Reed, Randolph Bourne, Paxton Hibben, Joe Hill, Thorstein Veblen.

Dos Passos' own handling of the language can be demonstrated in an example from his fictional narrative in *1919*. Dick Savage at the end of the war is still in Paris; Daughter, spurned by her "Dickyboy" and carrying his child, goes off alone in a taxi; Dick, now captain but angling for a public relations job after the war, goes to bed with a hangover; but he cannot get to sleep:

> Gradually he got warmer. Tomorrow. Seventhirty: shave, buckle puttees. . . . Day dragged out in khaki. . . . Dragged out khaki days until after the signing of the peace. Dun, drab, khaki. Poor Dick got to go to work after the signing of the peace. Poor Tom's cold. Poor Dickyboy . . . Richard . . . He brought his feet up to where he could rub them. Poor Richard's feet. After the signing of the Peace.

Dick is a Harvard graduate; he had intended to become a writer. He has nearly lost our sympathy because of his attitude toward Daughter. Here he gives up the struggle to sit up and think as he climbs literally and figuratively into bed, self-indulgent, self-pitying. "Poor Tom" suggests his subconscious awareness of his disguise—in part the uniform of an officer and a gentleman, in part his role of a dedicated poet; and it also suggests the contrast of his character with that of Edgar in *King Lear*. "Poor Dickyboy" reveals the transfer of his pangs of conscience into self-sympathy. "Poor Richard" indicates his falling from critical awareness into the thoughtless selfishness of the old American cliché of success (Franklin's Poor Richard and Horatio Alger's Ragged Dick), as he resumes the foetal position because he lacks the courage to think and to doubt; he has, in the vernacular, cold feet: "By the time his feet were warm he'd fallen asleep."

The picture is at once comic and pathetic and somewhat revolting. Up to about this point we have been sympathizing with Dick as another struggling, wanting human; suffering with him; and enjoying his occasional successes as our own. In this passage, Dos Passos' method prevents our suddenly ceasing to participate. We must share Dick's experience—after all a rather ordinary one, already familiar to us—at the same time that we reject it. We share from within his consciousness; we observe and reject from outside it. By the multiplication of such experiences Dos Passos attempts to establish in the reader something like what T. S. Eliot called the objective correlative of the work of art; but another name for it is a critical standard or part of a frame of reference. Once established, it exists outside of, even independent of, its original source. If Dick Savage's retreat from responsibility, for example, is established as symbolic of all retreat from responsibility, and if we are made to reject it here, then we must reject it whenever we encounter it.

This process Dos Passos once explained in a little-known "Introductory Note" to the first Modern Library edition of his *42nd Parallel* as the destruction and reconstruction of stereotypes. He was aware that it would probably lose him readers: "People feel pain when the stereotype is broken, at least at first." But it was the necessary method of the architect of history. The reaction from the reader is similar to the "grin of pain" that Dos Passos described as the essential response to satire in his essay about George Grosz in 1936.

Yet the reader's reaction to Dos Passos' novels is only remotely and occasionally one of mirth. To *U.S.A.* it is more nearly a grim realization of the sores and weaknesses of our culture which cry out for repair. To some readers, doubtless, it is too bad that Dos Passos is not more nearly the satirist than he is. Perhaps a leavening of humor that could change a grimace to a grin would make him more palatable to both readers and critics and, therefore, presumably more effective because more widely read. But Dos Passos' intent is vitally serious. He does not write to entertain but to communicate, to inform—in brief, to educate. He has always been too close to his materials, too involved personally, to be able to attain the special kind of detachment demanded of the satirist. Like Swift indeed, he heartily loves John, Peter, Thomas, and so forth; but he can by no means manage a principal hate and detestation for that animal called man.

### III  *Method of Tragedy*

Rather than satire—or rather including the satire and including also his naturalism—Dos Passos' method in *U.S.A.* is that of tragedy, a method based on an ironic attitude toward the past. *U.S.A.* is a great agglomerate tragic history. The protagonist, obviously enough, is the real U.S.A. in the first third of the twentieth century. Its tragic characters are the real subjects of the biographies: Debs, Luther Burbank, Bill Haywood, Bryan, Minor Keith, Carnegie, Edison, Steinmetz, La Follette, Jack Reed, Randolph Bourne, T. R., Paxton Hibben, Woodrow Wilson, and the rest. Merely to read their names is to sense the tragedy of their era: so much talent, ambition, love—all frustrated or misdirected or drained away into war, profits, prohibitions, intolerances, and oppressions.

In the background of the novel, democratic individualism and reliance on the future (pursuit of happiness) are the characteristics which gave the U.S.A. its greatness. A too narrow individualism, a too great reliance on the future—a loss of memory—and a warped interpretation of happiness in purely material terms: these are the characteristics which brought on its apparent downfall in the years Dos Passos wrote of. They are the tragic flaws of the society which rejects its best men.

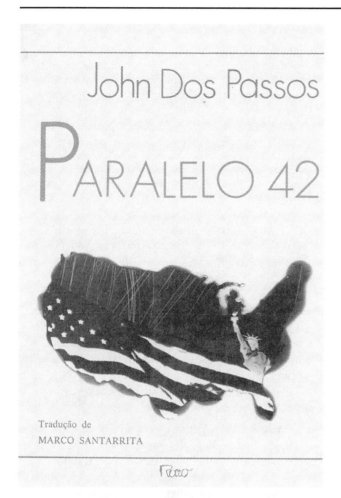

*Cover of the 1987 Brazilian paperback edition of* The
42nd Parallel *(Thomas Cooper Library,
University of South Carolina)*

But its failures and its worst men have their own equivalent flaws—Bryan's "silver tongue in a big mouth," Wilson's "faith in words," and the overweening ambition of the Morgans, Insull, and others.

The fictional characters—like the anonymous "Vag" and the Unknown Soldier and the narrator—have not the stature of tragic characters. They are the extras, the *demos* or ordinary citizens like ourselves, or the members of the chorus with whom we can participate as they work and suffer in the shadow of the struggle for industrial democracy. Yet, while we participate, we also watch; and for our capacity as objective audience, there is the more formal chorus of the Newsreels, in which the past provides its own ironic commentary about the past and reveals our recent idiocies to ourselves.

Many Americans in the audience have been unwilling to sit through Dos Passos' documentary tragedy. If they have come to it for entertainment or escape, they have been disappointed. But those who have

stayed to see and hear have been exposed to a unique dramatic experience. This experience is one of participating satire; for, as Dos Passos said of the painter Grosz, he "makes you identify yourself with the sordid and pitiful object." This identification, in turn, provides the catharsis, "a release from hatred"—in part because the reader or spectator cannot wholly hate himself and in part because the hatred is already expressed more adequately than most could express it through vitriolic portraits of the villains, real and fictional. The uniqueness, however, is in the partial nature of the catharsis: it might be said to be both catharsis and anti-catharsis. The reader is purged only of the self-indulgent emotions of hatred and self-love, which allow him to forget. He is denied complacency and forced to remember. The tragedy he has witnessed is that of the unfulfilled potential of the individual, including himself, in a society dedicated, ironically, to the possibilities of its fulfillment. He is left with a feeling of incompleteness.

—*John Dos Passos* (New York: Twayne, 1961),
pp. 154–163

## Dos Passos' *U.S.A.*: The Words of the Hollow Men
John Lydenberg

*John Lydenberg, in addition to this important essay on Dos Passos, wrote extensively on the works of Theodore Dreiser and edited* Dreiser: A Collection of Critical Essays *(1971). He taught at Hobart and William Smith College for most of his career.*

Because James Baldwin, like Tocqueville a decade or more ago, has now become so fashionable that one cannot decently take a text from him, I shall start with Yevgeny Yevtushenko, in the hope that he has not quite yet reached that point. In one of his poems appear the simple lines: "Let us give back to words/Their original meanings." My other non-Dos Passos text is so classic that it cannot be over-fashionable. In *A Farewell to Arms*, Gino says, "What has been done this summer cannot have been done in vain." And, as you all know, Hemingway has Frederic Henry reply: "I did not say anything. I was always embarrassed by the words sacred, glorious, and sacrifice and the expression in vain. . . . Abstract words such as glory, honor, courage, or hallow were obscene."

These quotations suggest the concern of writers with abstract words representing the ideals and values of their society. Both Yevtushenko and Hemingway say that these words have lost their glory, their true meaning. But they take diametrically opposed attitudes toward the role the words will play in their writings. Representing the party of Hope, Yevtushenko is the social and political idealist, the reformer, the artist who sees his art as a weapon in man's unceasing struggle for a better world. Representing the party of Despair, Hemingway abjures political concerns, makes his separate peace, and develops an art unconcerned with social ideals. Thus they symbolize two extremes: writers at one pole–Yevtushenko's–will utilize the words, will insist on doing so; writers at the other–Hemingway's–will dispense with them altogether, or try to do so, as did Hemingway in most of his early fiction.

Dos Passos falls between the extremes, but instead of presenting us with a golden mean he gives something more like an unstable compound of the two. Hemingway abandons the words because he can see no relation between them and the realities, and creates a world stripped of the values represented by the words. By contrast, reformers–who are equally insistent on the disparity between the ideals and the realities–are unwilling to reject the words and strive, like Yevtushenko, to give back to them their original meanings. Dos Passos can neither abandon nor revivify the words. Like Hemingway he feels that they have been made obscene and he can find no way in his art to redeem them. Yet like any reformer he puts them at the center of his work.

Critics have often held that the protagonist of *U.S.A.* is society. I could almost maintain that it is, instead, "the words." Dos Passos seems obsessed by them: he cares about them passionately and cannot abandon them, but at the same time he is made sick at heart–nay at stomach–by the way they have been spoiled. So he concerns himself with problems of social values, ever returning to the words, "as a dog to his vomit" (to use the inelegant but expressive Biblical phrase). *U.S.A.* tastes sour because the words are tainted and indigestible, but neither here nor in his other fiction can Dos Passos spew them forth once and for all as could the Hemingways of our literature.

In two well-known passages, Dos Passos makes explicit his feeling about the words. These–the most eloquent and deeply felt parts of *U.S.A.*–are the Camera Eyes focused on the execution of Sacco and Vanzetti. In the first, immediately preceding the Mary French section on the last desperate days before the executions, he asks:

> how make them feel who are your oppressors America
> rebuild the ruined words worn slimy in the mouths of lawyers districtattorneys collegepresidents judges without the old words the immigrants haters of oppression brought to Plymouth how can you know who are your betrayers America . . . ? (*Big Money*, 437)[1]

In the second, after the execution, he says:

> we the beaten crowd together . . . sit hunched with bowed heads on benches and hear the old words of the haters of oppression     made new in sweat and agony tonight
> our work is over     the scribbled phrases     the nights typing releases the smell of the printshop the sharp reek of newprinted leaflets     the rush for Western Union stringing words into wires the search for stinging words to make you feel who are your oppressors America
> America our nation has been beaten by strangers who have turned our language inside out who have taken the clean words our fathers spoke and made them slimy and foul (462)

Just as Dos Passos makes the Sacco-Vanzetti affair symbolic of his vision of the state of the nation, so, in talking about the "old words," "the clean words our fathers spoke," and "the old American speech," he is alluding to his ideals, to the American dream, and in describing the words now as "ruined," "slimy and foul," and "turned . . . inside out," he is expressing his sense of the betrayal of the dream.

"Mostly U.S.A. is the speech of the people," says Dos Passos to conclude the prose poem he added as preface to the trilogy. Maybe. But *U.S.A.*, the novel, in no way carries out that Sandburg-like suggestion of faith in the people and delight in their talk. It contains none of the salty talk, the boastful talk, the folksy talk, the "wise" talk that is the staple of much "realistic" American fiction. Actually, we discover, on re-examination of these novels, that dialogue plays a smaller role than we might have thought it did. What little talk there is is either purely functional, merely a way of getting on with the narrative: "Shall we go to bed?" "Where can I get a drink?" "God I feel lousy this morning." Or it is banal and stereotyped. Whenever his characters express anything resembling ideas they talk only in tired slogans; the words have been drained of meaning, and the characters mouthing them are empty puppets.

Here is one example. I would give many more, had I time, for the real effect is gained only through the continuous repetition of the vaporous phrases. This is from *1919*, the novel written during the time Dos Passos was presumably most favorably inclined toward Marxism and the Communists. One might have expected that here if anywhere the words of a communist, Don Stevens in this instance, would carry some conviction. Instead Dos Passos makes them sound mechanical, false, flat, like counterfeit coins. The effect is heightened here, as in many other places, by giving us the words in indirect dialog.

*Cover of the 1991 Dutch paperback edition of* The
42nd Parallel, *translated by Paul Syrier (Thomas
Cooper Library, University of South Carolina)*

He said there wasn't a chinaman's chance that the U.S. would keep out of the war; the Germans were winning, the working class all over Europe was on the edge of revolt, the revolution in Russia was the beginning of the worldwide social revolution and the bankers knew it and Wilson knew it; the only question was whether the industrial workers in the east and the farmers and casual laborers in the middle west would stand for war. The entire press was bought and muzzled. The Morgans had to fight or go bankrupt. "It's the greatest conspiracy in history." (131)

This is the way the words sound in passage after passage. The ruined words dribble from the mouths of Dos Passos' hollow men. Within is nothing but clichés, phrases having no meaning for the speaker and conveying none to the listener. *This* is the speech of the people in Dos Passos's *U.S.A.*, and it does much to establish the tone of the whole trilogy.

But if the words are often empty and meaningless, they often too have a very real meaning, vicious and perverted. The old words of the American dream have been "turned . . . inside out"; now they are the lies by which the new Americans live. The theme of the transformation of the clean words into lies had been baldly stated in Dos Passos's first novel, *One Man's Initiation*. Early in the book, Martin Howe dreams romantically of his mission as the ocean steamer carries him "over there": "And very faintly, like music heard across the water in the evening, blurred into strange harmonies, his old watchwords echo a little in his mind. Like the red flame of the sunset setting fire to opal sea and sky, the old exaltation, the old flame that would consume to ashes all the lies in the world, the trumpet-blast under which the walls of Jericho would fall down, stirs and broods in the womb of his grey lassitude" (14). Then as Martin is first going up to the front, he comes to adopt a new conception in which the lies are all-inclusive, his "old watchwords" now no different from the rest of the world's lies. A stranger appears and explains it to him: "Think, man, think of all the oceans of lies through all the ages that must have been necessary to make this possible! Think of this new particular vintage of lies that has been so industriously pumped out of the press and the pulpit . . . [The] lies are like a sticky juice over-spreading the world, a living, growing flypaper to catch and gum the wings of every human soul" (30). Finally, Martin talks in much the same way himself: "'What terrifies me . . . is their power to enslave our minds. . . . America, as you know, is ruled by the press. . . . People seem to so love to be fooled. . . . We are slaves of bought intellect, willing slaves'" (144). And a French anarchist takes up the theme and makes the moral explicit: "'Oh, but we are all such dupes. . . . First we must fight the lies. It is the lies that choke us'" (156).

In *U.S.A.*, Dos Passos does not *tell* us about the lies, he makes us feel them. The Newsreels are his most obvious device for showing us the "sticky juice" of lies in which Americans are caught. The opening lines of *The 42nd Parallel* are: "It was that emancipated race/ That was chargin up the hill;/Up to where them insurrectos/Was afightin fit to kill." The hill is not San Juan but a hill in the Philippines. And that first Newsreel ends with Senator Beveridge's lucid bluster: "The twentieth century will be American. American thought will dominate it. American progress will give it color and direction. American deeds will make it illustrious. . . . The regeneration of the world, physical as well as moral, has begun, and revolutions never move backwards" (5).

One recognizable pattern keeps recurring in the shifting kaleidoscope of the Newsreels: that is—the official lies disguised as popular truths. We see—and hear—

the rhetoric of the American Way drummed into the heads of the American public, by advertisements, newspaper headlines, newspaper stories, politicians' statements, businessmen's statements. In contrast to these standardized verbalizations about happy, prosperous, good America, the Newsreels give continual flashes of Dos Passos's "real" America—of fads and follies, hardships and horrors. More striking even than the contrasts within these collages are those between the shimmering surface of the Newsreels and the sardonic realities of the Portraits, and above all the dreary lives of his fictional characters.

The narratives of these lives take up the greater part of the book, of course, and our reaction to it depends to a great extent on our evaluation of the characters. My suggestion is that it is by their use of "the words" that we judge them. And here, *mirabile dictu,* we come at last to the theme of "determinism."

That *U.S.A.* is strongly naturalistic and deterministic is obvious to all. Readers who judge it a major work of fiction do so in part because of its success in portraying characters as helpless individuals caught in a world they have not made and can not control. Less admiring critics are apt to consider its weakness to be the weakness of the characters, sometimes even implying that Dos Passos's failure to create free, responsible heroes was a failure of execution. Whatever their assessment of the novel, all agree that *U.S.A.* is starkly deterministic. None of its characters has free will, none determines his fate, all move like automatons.

The chief way in which Dos Passos makes us feel that his characters—or non-characters—are determined is by showing their choices as non-choices. In *U.S.A.* Dos Passos's people do not make decisions. Or, if you insist that human beings all make decisions, choose one road over another, I will say instead that he presents his characters to us so that we do not feel their choices to be decisions. They simply are doing so and so, and continue thus until they find themselves, or we find them, doing something else.

Here are two examples. The first, a long one, includes two decisions, one a reversal of the other. Note here—for future reference—what the protagonist, Richard Ellsworth Savage, does with the words, and note also how the indirect dialogue accentuates the feeling of cliché and slogan. Dick is "deciding" what he should do about the war and about his college education.

In the Easter vacation, after the Armed Ship Bill had passed Dick had a long talk with Mr. Cooper who wanted to get him a job in Washington, because he said a boy of his talent oughtn't to endanger his career by joining the army and already there was talk of conscription. Dick blushed becomingly and said he felt it would be against his conscience to help in the war in any way.

---

## Dos Passos and Twentieth Century Literature
George Steiner

*George Steiner places the montage technique of the German novelist Günter Grass in a modernist tradition founded by Dos Passos.*

Thus one of the most astounding sections in [Günter Grass's] *Hundejahre* is a deadly pastiche of the metaphysical jargon of Heidegger. Grass knows how much damage the arrogant obscurities of German philosophic speech have done to the German mind, to its ability to think or speak clearly. It is as if Grass had taken the German dictionary by the throat and was trying to throttle the falsehood and cant out of the old words, trying to cleanse them with laughter and impropriety so as to make them new. Often, therefore, his uncontrolled prolixity, his leviathan sentences and word inventories, do not convey confidence in the medium; they speak of anger and disgust, of a mason hewing stone that is treacherous or veined with grit. In the end, moreover, his obsessed exuberance undermines the shape and reality of the work. Grass is nearly always too long; nearly always too loud. The raucous brutalities which he satirizes infect his own art.

That art is, itself, curiously old-fashioned. The formal design of the book, its constant reliance on *montage,* on fade-outs, and on simultaneities of public and private events, are closely modeled on *U.S.A.* The case of Grass is one of many to suggest that it is not Hemingway, but Dos Passos who has been the principal American literary influence of the twentieth century.

*—Language and Silence: Essays on Language, Literature, and the Inhuman* (New York: Atheneum, 1986), p. 116

---

They talked a long time without getting anywhere about duty to the state and party leadership and highest expediency. In the end Mr. Cooper made him promise not to take any rash step without consulting him. [Note that Dick has now "decided" that his "principles" forbid him to enter any war work.] Back in Cambridge everybody was drilling and going to lectures on military science. Dick was finishing up the four year course in three years and had to work hard, but nothing in the courses seemed to mean anything any more. He managed to find time to polish up a group of sonnets called Morituri Te Salutant that he sent to a prize competition run by *The Literary Digest.* It won the prize but the editors wrote back that they would prefer a note of hope in the last sestet. Dick put in the note of hope [so go the words!] and sent the hundred dollars to Mother to go to Atlantic City with. He discovered that if he went into war work he could get his degree that spring without taking any exams and went in to Boston one day without saying anything to anybody and signed up in the volunteer ambulance service. [Now he has "decided" that his "principles" no longer prevent him from war work.] (*1919*, 95–96)

And here is the sound of a Dos Passos character "deciding" to have an abortion:

Of course she could have the baby if she wanted to [Don Stevens said] but it would spoil her usefulness in the struggle for several months and he didn't think this was the time for it. It was the first time they'd quarreled. She said he was heartless. He said they had to sacrifice their personal feelings for the workingclass, and stormed out of the house in a temper. In the end she had an abortion but she had to write her mother again for money to pay for it. (*Big Money*, 447)

These examples of important decisions presented as simply something that the character happened somehow to do are not exceptional; they are typical. I think I can say safely that there are *no* decisions in the three novels that are presented in a significantly different way.

To this extent, then, *U.S.A.* is systematically, rigidly, effectively deterministic. But there is a fault in its rigid structure, a softness in its determinism, and—in opposition to both the friendly and unfriendly critics of Dos Passos—I would suggest that a large part of the book's success comes precisely from the author's failure to be as consistently deterministic as he thinks he wants to be. True as it is that we never identify with any of his characters as we do with conventionally free characters, it is equally true that we do not regard them all with the nice objectivity required by the deterministic logic. Some we consider "good" and some "bad," just as though they were in fact responsible human beings making free choices. And these judgments that we make, however illogically, we base largely upon the way in which the different characters treat those crucial abstract words.

Some characters are essential [*sic*] neutral—or perhaps I should say that we feel them to be truly determined. We look upon Margo Dowling, Eveline Hutchins, Eleanor Stoddard, and Charley Anderson with a coolly detached eye, even though we may feel that in their various ways the women are somewhat bitchy. And although Daughter, and Joe and Janey Williams tend to arouse our sympathies, we view them quite dispassionately. Certainly we do not consider any of these as responsible moral agents. And none of them shows any inclination to be concerned with the words.

In contrast to the neutral characters are Mac, Ben Compton, and Mary French. Dos Passos likes them and makes us like them because they affirm the values which he holds and wishes his readers to accept. Each of them uses the words, tries to uphold the true mean-

ing of the "old words," and fights to rebuild the ruined words. Although their decisions are described in the same way that all other decisions are, we feel that their choices of the words are deliberate, and are acts of freedom for which they take the responsibility. Mac leaves his girl in San Francisco to go to Goldfield as a printer for the Wobblies because he finds that his life is meaningless when he is not using and acting out the words. Later, after his marriage, he escapes again from the bourgeois trap because he can't bear not to be talking with his old comrades about their dream and ideals. Finally, unable to do anything but talk and unable to find a way to make the old words new or effective, he sinks back into the conventional rut of the other unfree characters. Ben Compton insists on talking peace and socialism after the United States has entered the war, freely choosing thereby to be taken by the police and imprisoned. During the war, it seems, the old words may not be used in public until they have been converted into the official lies.

Mary French is generally considered Dos Passos's most sympathetic character in *U.S.A.* She is certainly associated with the words throughout, and in her work with the 1919 steel strikers and the Sacco-Vanzetti committee she is actively engaged in the attempt to "renew" the words and make them effective in the fight for justice. But, significantly, she does not employ them much. Not only have they been worn slimy in the mouths of her enemies, but they are continually being perverted by her co-workers and supposed friends, the ostensible renovators of the words. So, in the final section of *The Big Money*, we find her collecting clothes for the struck coal miners, doing good, but not a good that goes beyond the mere maintenance of brute existence. Anything of more significance would demand use of the words, and at this point in his writing, the words, to Dos Passos, have been ruined beyond redemption.

And then there are the bad guys, J. Ward Moorehouse and Richard Ellsworth Savage. They are as hollow as any other Dos Passos men, their decisions, like all others, non-decisions. But where Joe and Janey Williams make us sad, these make us mad. We dislike them and blame them, just as though they had really chosen.

Dos Passos makes us feel that a character is responsible for the words he chooses. To explain just *how* Dos Passos does that is not easy, but I think it goes, in part, something like this. We don't blame Dick for drinking too much or for wenching, any more than we blame Charley Anderson or Joe Williams. These activities seem to be instinctive reactions, self-defeating but natural escapes from freedom. Part of the reason we feel Dick and the others determined in their dissipation, and consequently do not blame them, is because the characters blame themselves, regret what they do and

*Covers for the 1996 paperback reprint of the 1962 West German edition of Dos Passos's trilogy,*
*translated by Baudisch (Thomas Cooper Library, University of South Carolina)*

feebly resolve not to do it again. Thus when they fall back into their old, familiar ways, we feel that they are doing what they do not want to do, do not will to do. But when we come to another sort of action, the choice of words, no character is shown regretting the abstract words he uses. Thus the character implicitly approves his choice of words, he seems to be acting freely, and we tend to hold him responsible.

To get back to our bad guys, Moorehouse and Savage are the successful exploiters in the trilogy, and on first thought we might assume that that fact would suffice to make them culpable. But they are not the usual exploiters found in proletarian novels: big bad businessmen gouging the workers, manufacturers grinding the faces of the poor. Indeed they don't seem to hurt anyone. They exploit not people but words, or people, impersonally, by means of the words. Their profession is "public relations." (We might look at them as precursors of the Madison Avenue villains of post–World War II fiction, and infinitely superior ones, at that.) Their job is to persuade people to buy a product or to act in a particular way. Their means of persuasion is words. And the words they use are to a great extent "the words," the words of the American dream. They talk cooperation, justice, opportunity, freedom, equality.

Here are two brief quotations from J. Ward Moorehouse. He and Savage are preparing a publicity campaign for old Doc Bingham's patent medicines–now called "proprietary" medicines. (You will remember that Doc was Mac's first employer at the beginning of the trilogy, as owner-manager of "The Truthseeker Literary Distributing Co., Inc.") The first quotation is part of J. W.'s argument to a complaisant senator: "But, senator, . . . it's the principle of the thing. Once government interference in business is established as a precedent it means the end of liberty and private initiative in this country. . . . What this bill purports to do is to take the right of selfmedication from the American people" (505–506). And in this next one he is talking to his partner Savage about the advertising–no, publicity–campaign: "Of course self-service, independence, individualism is the word I gave the boys in the beginning. This is going to be more than a publicity campaign, it's going to be a campaign for Americanism" (494).

Here at last we have arrived at the source–or at least one major source–of the cancerous evil that swells malignantly through the books. Here we observe the manufacturers of the all-pervasive lies busily at work, here we see the words being deliberately perverted. And we cannot consider the perverters of the words as merely helpless automatons or innocents; they deliberately choose their words and we judge them as villains.

So, in conclusion, Dos Passos finds that the old words of the immigrant haters of oppression, which should have set Americans free, have instead been worn slimy in their mouths. And these words are in effect central actors in *U.S.A.* They determine our attitudes toward the characters who use and misuse them, establish the tone of hollow futility that rings throughout the trilogy, and leave in our mouths the bitter after-taste of nausea. The novels that followed, to make the *District of Columbia* trilogy, emphasize Dos Passos's sick obsession with these words. In the first, the humanitarian socialist dream comes to us in the clichés and jargon of American communists; in the second, the American dream is conveyed to us through the demagoguery of a vulgar Louisiana dictator; in the third the dream of New Deal reform has been turned into a nightmare by cynical opportunists and time-serving bureaucrats who exploit the old words anew.

No longer able to imagine a way of giving to words their original meanings, after *U.S.A.*, Dos Passos could still not abandon them for some more palatable subject. And so he seemed to take the worst part of the worlds of Yevtushenko and Hemingway. But in *U.S.A.* he could still write about Mac and Ben Compton and Mary French; he could still feel some hope that the ruined words might be rebuilt; he could still imagine the dream to be yet a possibility. In *U.S.A.* his despair was not yet total and his dual vision of the words brought to these novels a tension, a vitality, and a creative energy he would never be able to muster again.

–*Essays on Determinism in American Literature,* edited by Sydney J. Krause (Kent, Ohio: Kent State University Press, 1964), pp. 97–107

### Note

1. Page references documenting the quotations from *U.S.A.* are to the Modern Library Edition (1937); those for *First Encounter* (originally published as *One Man's Initiation*) are to the New York, 1945, edition.

### Dos Passos and the "Old Words"
David L. Vanderwerken

*David L. Vanderwerken, a professor of English at Texas Christian University, has published several essays on Dos Passos.*

From the Preface, where Dos Passos asserts that the United States is "the speech of the people,"[1] to the final Camera Eye of *The Big Money,* where Dos Passos affirms the "old American speech of the haters of oppression" (*BM*, p. 463), the *U.S.A.* trilogy focuses unceasingly upon the theme of the misuse of the "old words." In defining America as "the speech of the people," Dos Passos means, not "speech" in general, but the special American language that he calls the "old words"–the "old American speech of the haters of oppression." Understood this way, "American speech" is the language of our common heritage, which, for Dos Passos, unites us and identifies our uniqueness as a people: "the tendrils of phrased words" (p. vi), "the link that tingled in the blood; U.S.A." (p. vii). By "old words," Dos Passos means the great verbal propositions stated at the birth of the nation. "Life, liberty and the pursuit of happiness," "all men are created equal"–in short, the language embodying the idea and the promise of America–comprise Dos Passos's "old words." This term "old words" then, is, for Dos Passos, broad in its implications. It is akin to another shorthand phrase, which, umbrella-like, covers much of the same ground–the "American Dream."

The lonely, itinerant young man of the Preface–"No job, no woman, no house, no city" (p. vi)–searches for America with his ears attuned to the "speech that clung to the ears" (p. vii). But through his journey, the young man discovers that "America our nation has been beaten by strangers who have turned our language inside out" (*BM,* p. 462). Dos Passos' thesis in *U.S.A.* is that our special language, and thus America, has been betrayed; by examining the rhetoric and behavior of modern Americans, Dos Passos desperately tries to show us the fraudulent uses of our "old words." And he hopes to "rebuild the ruined words" (*BM,* p. 437), to reaffirm the real America, to "bring back (I too Walt Whitman) our storybook democracy" (*BM,* p. 150). *U.S.A.* is Dos Passos' "search for stinging words to make you feel who are your oppressors America" (*BM,* p. 462), and *U.S.A.* is Dos Passos' affirmation of faith in the recovery of our "storybook" nation: "If you hit the words Democracy will understand" (*1919,* pp. 102–103). And, in the four structural devices of the trilogy, Dos Passos finds a fully effective strategy for accomplishing his intentions.

Each of the four structural devices expresses the "old words" theme in its own special way, yet, taken together, they form a unified and harmonious vision. Dos Passos uses the Newsreels to illustrate a number of corruptions in language. In the Biographies, Dos Passos judges many of his subjects according to their fidelity, in their words and actions, to the "old words." Through the Camera Eye sections, Dos Passos constructs an explicit thematic framework for the trilogy by creating, defining, and meditating upon his central term–the "old words." Finally, Dos Passos examines the lives of nearly a score of contemporary Americans to see if the "old words" manifest themselves in daily behavior. Most of the narratives are concerned with the relationship of the characters to the language they use or to the swirl of language around them. And any gaps between Dos Passos' understanding of the original meanings of the "old words" and their current definitions become readily visible.

The main technique of the Newsreel device is simple but effective–juxtaposition. Headlines, snatches of feature articles, bits of editorials, items from columns, advertisements, and popular songs are scrambled and listed in seemingly random fashion. Dos Passos lets the contradictions, incongruities, and absurdities speak for themselves. And what they speak is Babel: "spectators become dizzy while dancer eats orange breaking record that made man insane" (*42P,* p. 54).

Yet a careful disorderliness amidst the Newsreels' apparent jumble reveals itself:

> Come on and hear
> Come on and hear
> Come on and hear

> In his address to the Michigan state . . . Legislature the retiring governor, Hazen S. Pingree, said in part: I make the prediction that unless those in charge and in whose hands legislation is reposed do not change the present system of inequality, there will be a bloody revolution in less than a quarter of a century in this great country of ours.

> CARNEGIE TALKS OF HIS EPITAPH
> Alexander's Ragtime Band
> It is the best
> It is the best

> the luncheon which was served in the physical laboratory was replete with novel features. A miniature blastfurnace four feet high was on the banquet table and a narrow gauge railroad forty feet long ran round the edge of the table. Instead of molten metal the blast-furnace poured hot punch into small cars on the railroad. Ice-cream was served in the shape of railroad ties and bread took the shape of locomotives.

> Mr. Carnegie, while extolling the advantages of higher education in every branch of learning, came at last to this conclusion: Manual labor has been found to be the best foundation for the greatest work of the brain. (*42P,* p. 23)

In this selection from Newsreel II, the first paragraph concerns "inequality" in America, while the headline and the two paragraphs devoted to Carnegie's conspicuous consumption present a clear example of just such "inequality." And the interwoven strains of "Alexander's Ragtime Band" color the news items with a touch of absurdity. Moreover, in light of the context of *U.S.A.,* this illustration of "inequality" in the land where "all men are created equal" bespeaks the present state of the "old words." The items thus juxtaposed contain more meaning than if they were isolated; the whole becomes more than the sum of its parts. Newsreel II, taken as a model for all the Newsreels, demonstrates the two main thematic effects Dos Passos gains by carefully arranging disparate and incongruous material: the items tend to modify and qualify one another by their positions in the Newsreel; the sum of the items comments on the present state of the "old words."

. . . . . . . . . .

While it is difficult to generalize about the twenty-seven capitalists, labor leaders, politicians, scientists, intellectuals, and artists whom Dos Passos spotlights in the Biographies, many seem to divide roughly into two camps—heroes and villains—in accord with the famous statement in Camera Eye (50): "all right we are two nations" (*BM*, p. 462). Simply, Dos Passos' heroes are those men whose lives and writings affirm and uphold the "old words." Debs, Haywood, Reed, Bourne, Hibben, La Follette, Hill, Everest, and Veblen are true Americans, faithful to the original idea of America, and, finally, members of the "beaten nation" (*BM*, p. 463). And, just as simply, the villains are those whose words and actions betray and deny the "old words." Keith, Carnegie, Wilson, Morgan, Ford, Hearst, Taylor, and Insull are un-American, "strangers who have turned our language inside out," and "who have bought the laws and fenced off the meadows and cut down the woods for pulp and turned our pleasant cities into slums and sweated the wealth out of our people and when they want to they hire the executioner to throw the switch" (*BM*, pp. 462–463). In the Biographies, Dos Passos uses one criterion for judgment: fidelity to the "old words" admits the subject into the hallowed circle of "us"; infidelity banishes the subject to the realm of "them."

. . . . . . . . . .

No figure in *U.S.A.*, not even the capitalists, receives more scornful treatment than Woodrow Wilson. Dos Passos' Wilson cloaks himself in the "old words" while his actions betray them. Dos Passos' Biography describes Wilson as a man living in a "universe of words" (*1919*, p. 241), and, indeed, Wilson's Biography is filled with speeches. An early speech of Wilson's concerning his "belief in the common man" is juxtaposed with his wartime utterances, "force without stint or limit" (*1919*, p. 243), to show how he betrays the sacred words he invokes. Several times Dos Passos contrasts Wilson's rhetoric with the reality:

"I wish to take this occasion to say that the United States will never again seek one additional foot of territory by conquest";
    and he landed the marines at Vera Cruz. (*1919*, p. 245) And,
    With the help of "Almighty God, Right, Truth, Justice Freedom, Democracy, the Selfdetermination of Nations, No indemnities or annexations,"
    and Cuban sugar and Caucasian manganese and Northwestern wheat and Dixie cotton, the British blockade, General Pershing, the taxicabs of Paris and the seventyfive gun
    we won the war. (*1919*, p. 246)

For Dos Passos, Wilson is a liar who holds out the hope of the "regeneration" (*1919*, p. 243) of the "old words," but whose actions result in their degeneration. While uttering "freedom," "truth," "justice," "democracy," and all the rest, Wilson turns America into a repressive and militaristic "State" (*1919*, p. 245): "If you objected to making the world safe for cost plus democracy you went to jail with Debs" (*1919*, p. 246). Wilson is no Washington or Jefferson or Adams but a "stranger," who takes their "clean words" and makes them "slimy and foul."

Furthermore, Dos Passos is extremely vitriolic in his condemnation of Wilson's performance at the Paris Peace Conference. Dos Passos charges that Wilson does not realize the significance of his words for the peoples of Europe: "(Did Meester Veelson know that in the peasants' wargrimed houses along the Brenta and the Piave they were burning candles in front of his picture cut out of the illustrated papers?) (Did Meester Veelson know that the people of Europe spelled a challenge to oppression out of the Fourteen Points as centuries before they had spelled a challenge to oppression out of the ninetyfive articles Martin Luther nailed to the churchdoor in Wittenberg?)" (*1919*, p. 247). Wilson allows himself to be "trimmed" by Lloyd George and Clemenceau at the

---

**U.S.A. and the Great American Novel**
Norman Mailer

John Dos Passos came closer to writing the Great American Novel than any other novelist. There is no doubt that *U.S.A.* is the largest, most ambitious, and most successful social portrait of America in the first half of the twentieth century that we have.

–"John Dos Passos: A Centennial Celebration,"
in *Dictionary of Literary Biography Yearbook: 1996*
(Detroit: Gale/Bruccoli Clark Layman, 1997),
p. 173

*Covers of the 1968 Romanian paperback editions of* The 42nd Parallel *and* Nineteen-Nineteen
*(Thomas Cooper Library, University of South Carolina)*

conference. The world is safe for democracy, but Europe gets the oil fields. Wilson's efforts to explain himself to the nation, "to save his faith in words" (*1919,* p. 249), finally kill him. For Dos Passos, Wilson offered the possibility of reaffirming the "old words," but the man's character was not adequate to the hope he inspired.

The oft-anthologized Biography, "The Body of an American," which completes *Nineteen-Nineteen,* is a crushing indictment of the false America. Dos Passos juxtaposes the solemn rhetoric of the ceremony of the dedication with a fantasized account of Everyman's experience in the war. The official rhetoric of the government is undercut by the hard realities of racism, oppression, exploitation, and death. Dos Passos renders the dedication ceremony of the unknown soldier as a mockery of the very words it is intended to affirm. It is blasphemy in Dos Passos' view, and the chief blasphemer of all is the subject of the final sentence of the novel: "Woodrow Wilson brought a bouquet of poppies" (*1919,* p. 473).

The fifty-one Camera Eye sections, which record the growth and development of the informing consciousness of *U.S.A.* from the Boer War to the Harlan County miners' strike of 1932, compose a kind of autobiographical novel within the trilogy. And the story that the Camera Eyes tell is the story of Dos Passos' becoming aware of the misuse of the "old words." Following the pattern of a *Bildungsroman,* the Camera Eye consciousness progresses from innocence in *The 42nd Parallel* through initiation in *Nineteen-Nineteen* to experience in *The Big Money.* The Camera Eyes of *The 42nd Parallel,* which portray the perceptions, impressions, and memories of a comfortable and sheltered upper-middle-class child, seem generally oblivious to the world beyond the self, although, upon examination, they do reveal an active and inquisitive mind curious about the tumultuous social and political world from which he is insulated, sensitive to contrasts, distinctions, and injustices, aware of much yet understanding little. However, in *Nineteen-Nineteen,* the Camera Eye speaker's cozy world is shattered by the First World War. Through his experiences in France, he begins to question his own assumptions about America; he begins to see a difference between the real nature of this war, supposedly fought "to make the world safe for democracy," and what "they taught us" (*1919,* p. 101) America stands for; he begins to realize that his idea of America, which he had considered as stable and enduring as the firmament, diverges from the actuality of contemporary America. Finally, in *The Big Money,* the disillusioned Camera Eye speaker's understanding of this discrepancy, which the war had initially revealed to him, increases

and matures, climaxed by his final judgments in the Camera Eye concerning Sacco and Vanzetti and the Harlan strike.

The Camera Eye sections, in tracing the speaker's path from ignorance to radicalization, provide *U.S.A.* with a clear and complete framework for understanding the "old words" theme. Essentially, the Camera Eyes recapitulate the stages in the development of Dos Passos' understanding of his own central theme; establish, through explicit authorial statement, an unambiguous attitude toward his materials; and furnish a context in which to judge the behavior portrayed in the narratives. And the Camera Eye speaker becomes, finally, a metaphor for three decades of modern American experience; he assumes the role of righteous spokesman for the original and sacred, and, therefore, the legitimate and true, idea of America.

. . . . . . . . . .

The galvanizing and climactic event, not only of the Camera Eyes, but of the entire trilogy, is the Sacco-Vanzetti case. The speaker's judgments and interpretations of the incident color every aspect of *U.S.A.* and tell us how to read the trilogy. Camera Eye (49) expresses the significances and implications of Sacco-Vanzetti for the nation. The speaker's method is to establish a historical context in which to place the affair. First, it is fitting that Bartolomeo Vanzetti lives in Plymouth where, 300 years before, "the immigrants landed the roundheads the sackers of castles the kingkillers haters of oppression this where they stood in a cluster after landing from the crowded ship that stank of bilge" (*BM,* p. 345). Second, Vanzetti is a spiritual descendant of this original tradition of freedom lovers who founded America: "this is where another immigrant worked hater of oppression who wanted a world unfenced." The speaker, convinced that he has arrived at Vanzetti's essential importance, agonizes to find the words to make America understand the truth of Vanzetti also: "pencil scrawls in my notebook the scraps of recollection the broken half-phrases the effort to intersect word with word to dovetail clause with clause to rebuild out of mangled memories unshakeably (Oh Pontius Pilate) the truth" (*BM,* p. 436). And the "truth," once understood, shall make America free:

accustomed the smoking car     accustomed the jumble of faces rumble cozily homeward toward Boston through the gathering dark     how can I make them feel how our fathers our uncles haters of oppression came to this coast how say Don't let them scare you how make them feel who are your oppressors America

rebuild the ruined words worn slimy in the mouths
of lawyers districtattorneys collegepresidents judges
without the old words the immigrants haters of oppression brought to Plymouth how can you know who are
your betrayers America

> or that this fishpeddler you have in Charlestown Jail
is one of your founders Massachusetts? (*BM*, p. 437)

From this passage it is clear that the key phrase "old
words" means everything that we traditionally associate with the promise and the idea of America–the
words which separate America from other nations,
which define our national purpose, which establish
our claim as the most noble experimental nation ever
conceived, which embody our moral worth. Everything that motivates a Swedish family to risk the haz-
ards of a 5000-mile journey in Jan Troell's *The
Emigrants* is contained in the "old words." The "old
words" are America, more so than the mere geo-
graphic location, and the Camera Eye speaker warns
that to murder Sacco and Vanzetti is to murder America and to hand America over to the "strangers." Furthermore, Camera Eye (49), through its method of
drawing historical analogy, is a paradigm that shows
us how to read *U.S.A.* Just as the Camera Eye speaker
measures the incident against the "old words," so
should the reader measure the events and incidents
and behavior of the narratives against the "old words"
framework of the Camera Eye.

Camera Eye (50), which records the speaker's
response to the execution, contains the famous declaration: "all right we are two nations." Despite the
obvious Marxist interpretation of the phrase, the most
significant implication is that there are two conflicting
attitudes toward the "old words." One nation is composed of apostates: "America our nation has been
beaten by strangers who have turned our language
inside out who have taken the clean words our fathers
spoke and made them slimy and foul" (*BM*, p. 462).
Anyone, "lawyers districtattorneys college presidents
judges," even United States Presidents, who mouths
the "old words" while betraying them in his actions is
a "stranger." In Camera Eye (51), the speaker further
defines the "strangers":

> (they have made us foreigners in the land where we
were born they are the conquering army that has filtered into the country unnoticed they have taken the
hilltops by stealth they levy toll they stand at the minehead . . . they stand by when the bailiffs carry the furniture of the family evicted from the city tenement out on
the sidewalk they are there when the bankers foreclose
on a farm they are ambushed and ready to shoot down
the strikers marching behind the flag up the switchback
road to the mine    those that the guns spare they jail
(*BM*, p. 524, ellipsis mine)

Much like the Snopes's invasion of Faulkner's county,
the "strangers" have taken over the land by infiltration.
The "strangers" have killed Sacco and Vanzetti, but
they have also made them martyrs. Their deaths have
"made the old words new" (*BM*, p. 463). Given the
speaker's tone in these Camera Eyes, it would not be
extreme to see in his words a call for a new American
Revolution in response to a new Boston Massacre. And
the other nation, faithful to the "old words," is the true
heir of the patriarchs. Like the children of Israel who
had only the Word of God to combat their Egyptian
oppressors, the true America has the words of the
fathers–and they are sufficient:

> but do they know that the old words of the immigrants
are being renewed in blood and agony tonight do they
know that the old American speech of the haters of
oppression is new tonight in the mouth of an old
woman from Pittsburgh of a husky boilermaker from
Frisco who hopped freights clear from the Coast to
come here in the mouth of a Back Bay socialworker in
the mouth of an Italian printer of a hobo from Arkan-
sas    the language of the beaten nation is not forgotten
in our ears tonight (*BM*, p. 463)

The "language of the beaten nation" and the language of the "strangers" are easy to spot in the narrative sections of *U.S.A.* The terms and definitions set
forth with such lucidity by the speaker in Camera
Eyes (49)–(51) influence our judgments of the characters. And ultimately, in his interpretations of the
Sacco-Vanzetti incidents, the Camera Eye speaker
erects a central thematic framework integral for
understanding all parts of *U.S.A.*

In the narratives, Dos Passos mainly concentrates on the language of the "strangers" to show us
the misuses and distortions and deceptions to which
the "old words" are being subjected. We see in the
narratives a host of hucksters and confidence men,
who will befoul and beslime any and all words–
including the "old words"–for their special interests.

Through the eight narrative sections of *The 42nd
Parallel* devoted to Fenian (Mac) McCreary, Dos Passos
presents two deceptive users of words in Doc Bingham
and J. Ward Moorehouse. Bingham is Dickensian in his
pomposity, garrulousness, and pseudo-intellectuality,
much like an unbenevolent Pickwick. He proclaims
himself to be a man whose God is truth and whose mission is to bring knowledge to the benighted world. As
Mac soon discovers, Bingham is merely an avaricious
hypocrite who sells pornography, hack romantic novels, and religious tracts, depending upon the tastes of
his customers. Bingham is nothing more than a crude
confidence man, who exploits the petty lusts of people
under the guise of bringing them enlightenment. The

fact that a character such as Bingham appears this early in *U.S.A.* indicates that language manipulation will be a central concern of the trilogy. Later, in Mexico, Mac meets a more sophisticated confidence man in Moorehouse, who can adapt to different rhetorical situations as easily as Bingham.

J. Ward Moorehouse has come to Mexico as an agent for American businessmen who have a special interest in Mexico's current social and political dissension. Moorehouse believes in reconciling Mexican and American interests through public relations. Dos Passos employs his useful method of indirect discourse to illustrate Moorehouse's words: "J. Ward Moorehouse explained that he had come down in a purely unofficial capacity you understand to make contacts, to find out what the situation was and just what there was behind Carranza's stubborn opposition to American investors and that the big businessmen he was in touch with in the states desired only fair play and that he felt that if their point of view could be thoroughly understood through some information bureau or the friendly cooperation of Mexican newspapermen . . ." (*42P*, p. 318). Moorehouse also wants everyone involved "to give each fresh angle of the situation its proper significance in the spirit of fair play and friendly cooperation, but he felt that the Mexican papers had been misinformed about the aims of American business in Mexico just as the American press was misinformed about the aims of Mexican politics." Mac's only response to Moorehouse's rhetoric is to exclaim in awe, "'that's a smooth bastard'" (*42P*, p. 319).

The "smooth" quality Mac notes precisely describes the unctuous tone of Moorehouse's speech. It is a language of pacification and placation, dedicated to the preservation of business interests and the status quo. Moorehouse's terms, "fair play," "point of view," and "friendly cooperation," confuse understanding in their very neutrality and blandness of tone. What Moorehouse really wants is for the Mexicans to tacitly agree to their own economic exploitation by American business. When "cooperation" means exploitation, language, as a tool of human communication and understanding, is destroyed. Furthermore, the conciliatory tone of the above speech is only one of the many tones Moorehouse has at his disposal. For each rhetorical situation, Moorehouse is ready with an appropriate style and tone; he uses whatever rhetorical stance is most expedient at a given moment. The truth, of course, is no factor in his choice of a rhetorical stance.

. . . . . . . . .

*–Twentieth-Century Literature,* 23 (May 1977): 195–197, 205–207, 212–216

**Note**

1. John Dos Passos, *U.S.A.* (New York: The Modern Library, 1937 [1938]), "Preface," p. vii. Subsequent references are from this edition and will be cited parenthetically, and I will use the following abbreviations before the page number: *42P* for *The 42nd Parallel, 1919* for *Nineteen-Nineteen, BM* for *The Big Money*.

## Iain Colley

*Iain Colley is an English writer and critic.*

One critic has argued that "Dos Passos does not call himself a Marxist, if he were more of one, he might have written a better novel." While this view is false– "Art must make its own hay and by its own way and by its own means. The Marxian methods are not the same as the artistic"[1]–it is central to critical misunderstandings of Dos Passos. The feeling persists that he *should* have been a Marxist. Marxism, after all, supplies a unique means of reconciling determinism and the exercise of free will–an antithesis which, under the specific terms of the dialectic, can be regarded as false. It states that there is a global tendency in history and that men can, by their own conscious efforts, help to realise it. Marxism insists that the behaviour of society can be understood and changed by using discoverable laws. To a writer like Dos Passos, instinctively drawn to the side of the governed and exploited, dealing with men in society, choosing as his protagonists men who lose hope and fail, Marxism ought, on the face of it, to be an attractive philosophy, both intellectually strenuous and optimistic. Yet the fiction of John Dos Passos persistently denies, in its atmosphere, situations and artistic logic, that human society can be rationally understood or that there is any reason to hope for radical improvements. The early heroes of Dos Passos had struggled to create a meaning for themselves in a hostile or indifferent universe, and all failed. Between the conditioning which limited their freedom and the illusory ideal of the self-realising individual, they lacked the will or energy to oppose the huge impersonal forces that defeated them–the army, New England morality, the pressures of metropolitan living. Ultimately, their failures are not *explained:* they are shown in some detail, and with increasing credibility as the author lays his hands on the tropes that enable him to render so vividly the constant engrammatic bombardment of social and personal defeats. *Manhattan Transfer* in particular stresses the adventitious nature of life: penalties and rewards are distributed by accident, but the direction of all events is towards loss and disappointment. On this evidence, life is a crooked gamble in which everyone is robbed. This is the outlook of romantic pessimism (the very opposite of Marxism) but it establishes its partial truth in *Manhattan Transfer* by the fast, vivid and dramatic pattern of its examples. The sea of circumstances in which Jimmy Herf drowns is portrayed in energetic detail, and in *The Forty-Second Parallel* the method of *Manhattan Transfer* is extended to portray the society of a whole nation.

This method, the method of "saturation," requires the sensitive exercise of a selective faculty. Accusations that this is just what Dos Passos lacks are balanced by contrary objections that he limits his scope to too narrow a segment of American society.[2] In fact, he has carefully selected characters of the lower-middle social strata, the ideal type of humbly-born American who is expected to "get on" and for whom, in the sanctified tradition, America is the supreme land of opportunity. The significance of the narrative passages is to show that this is a profound illusion, that the actual freedom of the individual is limited, and that whether or not he succeeds in "making it" he is lonely and doomed. Those who decline to make it suffer materially; in any case, they compromise; their humanity is diminished by victimisation and by their personal inability to realise their principles. Those who succeed sacrifice so much in doing so. There is no contradiction in this attitude, any more than there is in the belief that personality is shaped by a combination of various circumstances—background, heredity, metabolism, conscious ideas. Dos Passos refrains from explaining: his eclecticism is entailed in the behaviour of his characters and in the accompanying data which he has chosen to include in the Newsreels, Biographies and Camera Eyes.

Hence the often-noted "behaviourism" of his character-portrayal aims for a particular kind of truth: the truth as it is observed, the facts as they appear in immediate context. Dos Passos is not obliged to say whether he believes that men are alienated by the capitalist system of productive relations or by the nature of human life itself. Indeed, where capitalism rules, the two are effectively the same, and unless the novelist wants to play the social reformer he is not, as he works to produce a mirror of reality, required to distinguish between them. What he can do is to employ a rhetoric and imagery that expresses the shape of reality as he sees it, and for Dos Passos' purposes the imagery of class warfare could hardly be bettered. The force lines of class conflict within which his characters are drawn stand for the immediate everyday hardships of an unequal social system and for the permanent conditions of loneliness and misfortune under which mankind abides. Mac has three latent destinies corresponding to the three separate strands of his early life: ordinary sensual working guy, radical, wandering hedonist. He is incapable of making any final choice between them.

Circumstances uproot him, and his fate, at the end of his personal history, is not evil or tragic but disappointing. The total weight of the novel's rhetoric contrives to suggest that he should have chosen a life of greater discipline and purpose—yet Mac is scarcely free to choose. He is free, however, to hope, no matter how inexorably his hopes are denied. The philosophy of proletarian revolution stands for his highest hopes, just as the American self-help philosophy stands for Morehouse's central aspirations, and the disparity between sustaining cultural myths and the manifold setbacks of life as it is actually lived is the major unifying tension of the book. Mac is a victim rather than an active traitor to his own ideology; his normative destiny is symbolic. Equally, J. Ward Morehouse, in one sense a Titan of self-discipline who prostitutes his talents in an unworthy cause, is in reality another victim. Whatever motivates him—and it is not a *conscious* desire to advance the class interests of the American bourgeoisie—leads him into the trap of the ruined individual. Such correspondences disqualify Dos Passos as a Marxist writer: a Marxist might agree that capitalism alienates both those who serve it and those who oppose it, but he could not describe their fates as individuals so even-handedly.

The importance of the individual to Dos Passos is underlined by his use of the Biographies, of which there are eight in *The Forty Second Parallel*. Only two are unequivocally hostile—those of Minor C. Keith and Andrew Carnegie, though if the last line were omitted from the piece on Carnegie it would be a bare collection of facts about a very rich man. Bryan is treated with a faintly compassionate satire—in 1930 he was only five years dead, but he stood, quaintly, for a much older America. Debs and La Follette took the risk of speaking out against the "interests." Burbank, Steinmetz and to some extent Edison are Veblenian heroes, the men of practical genius forced to mortgage their talents to the financial system. Each of these men is revealed to have some secret flaw or failure, but each—as T. K. Whipple has pointed out—seems to possess some superhuman quality, and they all overshadow the bleak and jaded lives of the fictional characters. Together with the imposing figure of John Randolph Dos Passos as he appears in the Camera Eyes,[3] they furnish a living reproach to the modern Americans who hobble blindly through the novel's narrative portions. The lesson may be partly historical—that the Gilded Age gave freer rein to the drives of the forceful individual—and partly political—that in a democracy only a few can expect to shine—but the principal effect is to suggest a contrast between those who dominated circumstances and those who are pushed about by chance or social currents. Even Morehouse, the shrewd, plausible opportunist is a flannel-suited puppet beside Bryan or Carnegie.

The author is not, however, proposing that histori-cal progress depends on the activity of great men. Most of his biographical subjects were alive during the period cov-ered by *The Forty Second Parallel,* but their achievements generally belong to the century before. The artistic value of the Biographies is to suggest the importance in himself of the individual and the variety of ways in which individ-uality can be expressed. There is little mention, for instance, of the advantages they drew from propitious cir-cumstances or of how far each man represented a move-ment. La Follette is described as "a wilful man expressing no opinion but his own" whereas Wilson had called him *one* of a "group of wilful men," i.e. the Congressional rump of anti-war insurgents. The contrast is deepened by this emphasis, and the society in which Mac, Morehouse and the others exist is given the appearance of a vast, disturbed ants' nest. Following his creations' movements, Dos Pas-sos adopts the point of view of the dismayed ant who, observing the disaster at first hand but unable to deter-mine its cause, runs helplessly about. The crowded yet atomised world which he depicts—a world superbly rea-lised through the multifaceted techniques of the novel—is not a world explicable as the product of strict historical laws. In refusing to be a social theorist, while at the same time using the observable facts from which social theorists would draw their conclusions, Dos Passos remains faithful to his vision. By throwing together the individual in all the patient and commonplace detail of his life-effort, the collec-tive organism examined through its dominant beliefs and representative figures, and the subjective awareness of memory, he creates a nexus that refuses to explain or explicitly to judge, but which *displays* with energy and seri-ousness the developing life of a civilisation.

. . . . . . . . . .

*The Big Money* is a novel of defeat. The deaths of Sacco and Vanzetti mark the end of a chapter, not a new beginning. The concluding Biographies deal with two "rogue" millionaires who used the power of wealth to subvert the democratic process. Both Hearst and Insull were alive in 1936 (though Insull had been "rum-bled") and in the *ad hominem* reproaches Dos Passos addresses to each there is angry grief, as though they are the contemptible victors left on a battlefield of noble corpses. This, and the last famous picture of "Vag" trudging along the highway while above him soars an aeroplane carrying "big men with bank accounts, highly paid jobs, who are saluted by doormen,"[4] round off the work with an image of universal hopelessness. "Vag" is walking from nowhere to nowhere; the execu-tive vomiting his lunch in mid-air is no happier or more purposeful. The striving for faith has been cancelled out by the persistence of doubt and pessimism.

The coexistence of political imagery and a funda-mental scepticism in *U.S.A.* made it a needlessly compli-cated puzzle for critics: Lionel Trilling wrote:

> . . . to discover a political negativism in the despair of *U.S.A.* is to subscribe to a naive conception of human emotion and human experience. It is to assert that the despair of a literary work must inevitably engender despair in the reader . . . the word "despair" all by itself (or any other such general word or phrase) can never characterize the emotion the artist is dealing with. There are many kinds of despair and what is really important is what goes along with the general emotion denoted by the word. Despair with its wits about it is very different from the despair that is stupid; despair that is an abandonment of illusion is very different from despair which generates tender new cynicisms[5]

Yet any number of liberal categories of despair will not erase the fact that the typical feeling of *U.S.A.* is entropic despair. True enough, the man who felt despair-in-the-bone might never write at all, but the quality of the author's energising impulse is precisely the artist's commitment to record experience in a man-ner that honestly registers its significance. And Dos Pas-sos' conception of this duty is highly traditional—the selfsame conception that has underlain his work since the story of Martin Howe: ". . . pencil scrawls in my notebook the scraps of recollection the broken half-phrases the effort to intersect word with word to dove-tail clause with clause to rebuild out of mangled memories unshakably (Oh Pontius Pilate) the truth."[6]

Yes, what is truth? Dos Passos' art springs from the patent, empirical (and partial) observation of truth. This is not, though, simply the "inner truth" of the introspective writer seeking spiritual verities: it is cine-matically alert for all the detritus of experience—per-sonal, material, historical. America of the post-depression years, with its time-honoured myths exploded, offered to artists like Dos Passos the perfect landscape of devastation. As his fellow-author on the Harlan County investigations observed:

> Faster cars, more efficient machinery, more and more towering skyscrapers erected in record time, subway trains screeching the extreme necessity of speed, more and larger cities, more business, more cares and duties—as though we, of all people, were ordered not only to mechanize but to populate the world! But just why? For any known event or spiritual reason? Rather, it seems to me that in this atmosphere, the mental and physical condition of millions of people have already "blown up" or are about to. They live and die without tasting anything really worth while. The average indi-vidual today is really tortured; he is so numerous, so meaningless, so wholly confused and defeated.[7]

But to pass from the certainty of observation to the exhausting and contentious path of active opposition is no easy matter. The strength of *U.S.A.* lies in its honest, unflagging exegesis of the particular in a form that presents life with the brilliant yet limited accuracy of the novel; Dos Passos had dug into his native culture for the words and symbols to realise it in all its variety–and in its essential entropy. *U.S.A.* is not informed by the global philosophy of Marxism but by a view of human existence as ultimately planless. Dos Passos' treatment by critics on the left, at first effuse and later hypocritically savage and abusive, illustrates both the relevance of his chosen subject-matter and the necessary risks of being misunderstood that are run by an author who attempts to adapt the novel to the kind of reality so powerfully conveyed by the cinema–a graphically mimetic persuasiveness, a versatility of scope and angle, an ability to blend poetic and realistic modes. Whatever Dos Passos' extra-literary associations with the platforms of the left may have meant to him personally, they cannot be adduced as evidence in judging his trilogy, which is *sui generis*. The resonance of its protest, expressed in a chosen and practised medium, is not reducible to a foursquare political argument, and Dos Passos cannot say with Ruskin that "I feel the force of mechanism and the fury of avaricious commerce to be at present so irresistible, that I have seceded from the study not only of architecture, but nearly of all art: and have given myself as I would in a besieged city, to seek the best modes of getting bread and water for its multitudes."[8]

Even so, it is not possible to dismiss the question of politics. The rhetoric of radical dissent is an inseparable part of the content of *U.S.A.* It is relevantly there as a facet of the total reality surveyed, but additionally as a major element of structure and meaning. The most prominent of the fictional characters–Mac, Morehouse, Eveline, Richard Savage, Joe Williams, Charley Anderson, Mary French– lead lives that are heavily touched by defeat. They are not all losers of the same kind: some, in their own terms, succeed, but only at the cost of denying every worthwhile human impulse. Others–Joe, particularly–experience nothing but misery and injustice. Losing is so universal that it overlays the "two nations" theme. Yet one of the means of dramatising that boundless gulf between the legendary promise of what life in America ought to be and the hideous facts is to show the two in suspenseful interaction. As the trilogy progresses through its three stages the reader is enabled to contrast engrammatic defeat and disappointment with the national dream of individual opportunity; the lib-

eral dream of inspirational war-aims; and the supernational dream of the libertarian future. In this fashion, the lesson that life can never live up to the expectations men place in it, that men themselves cannot live up to their own aspirations and that the world cannot be meaningfully interpreted for our comfort emerges powerfully from the aesthetic data of the trilogy. In the rhetoric of *U.S.A.*, radical dissent contributes–especially in *The Big Money*–a provision for judging and placing the efforts of the various characters in their blind and futile struggles to redeem the absurdity of the world they inhabit. It also helps to substitute for the bleak neutrality of *Manhattan Transfer* the writer's protest against the entropy he must accept–a protest self-contained in the pages of the trilogy itself. For this reason, among others, *U.S.A.* must stand as a major work of defiant pessimism.

–*Dos Passos and the Fiction of Despair*
(Totowa, N.J.: Rowman & Littlefield, 1978),
pp. 80–84, 117–119

### Notes

1. Leon Trotsky, *Literature and Revolution* (Ann Arbor: University of Michigan Press, 1960), p. 218.

2. Lukacs, in *The Meaning of Contemporary Realism,* argues the former case; Lionel Trilling, in "The America of John Dos Passos" (*Partisan Review* iv, Apr 1938, 26–32), the latter. Trilling at least has noticed that the characters in *U.S.A.* occupy a relatively narrow social spectrum.

3. A good deal of the Camera Eye material on John Dos Passos Sr. can be relocated in the form of straightforward reminiscence in the author's "informal memoir," *The Best Times.*

4. *The Big Money*, in *U.S.A.* (New York: Modern Library, 1938), p. 560.

5. Trilling, "The America of Dos Passos," p. 28.

6. *The Big Money*, p. 436.

7. Theodore Dreiser, *Tragic America* (London: Constable, 1932) p. 9.

8. John Ruskin, "Ad Valorem."

### Revisiting Dos Passos' *U.S.A.*
Harry Levin

*Harry Levin was a distinguished professor of English and comparative literature at Harvard University. Among his many books are studies of James Joyce, Stendhal, and Christopher Marlowe.*

John Dos Passos' reputation reached its highest point in 1938, when Jean-Paul Sartre–reviewing the

French translation of *Nineteen Nineteen*—proclaimed him without reservation "the greatest writer of our time." Sartre's critical attitudes have always been dictated by the personal or dialectical use he could make of his subjects, and he went on to imitate Dos Passos' method in his own unfinished tetralogy, *Les Chemins de la liberté*. He might not have considered that method so uniquely experimental if he had had any firsthand acquaintance with *Ulysses* (and Joyce was then still alive). But much of *Nineteen Nineteen* had the advantage, from Sartre's point of view, of being set in France. Insofar as he was interested in the larger patterns of interrelated lives, of course he could have found a precedent within that strong tradition of French fiction which had its fountainhead in the *Comédie humaine* and its contemporary manifestation in Jules Romains' *roman-fleuve*. And, as Claude-Edmonde Magny would be pointing out in *L'Age du roman américain* (which in turn would influence the emergent *nouveau roman*), the novel had to register the impact of the cinema. Yet *Nineteen Nineteen*, doubtless because of its sharp confrontations between history and consciousness, fitted in particularly well with Sartre's existentialist position.

Born and nurtured as a romantic individualist, Dos Passos had to work his way toward facing the problems of modern collectivity. His development can be traced from his poems, plays, and travelogues through his two early war novels to his fictional encounters with the city in *Streets of Night* and *Manhattan Transfer*, which Lionel Trilling would hail as perhaps "the most important novel of the decade." When we recall that *An American Tragedy* and *The Great Gatsby* were also published in that same year, or that the decade had already produced *The Age of Innocence* and *Main Street* and would soon be producing *A Farewell to Arms* and *The Sound and the Fury*, we need make no further comment on the vicissitudes of taste. But it was probably *Manhattan Transfer* that went farthest to shock the traditionalists, provoking Paul Elmer More to dismiss it as "an explosion in a cesspool." The more salubrious reaction of Sinclair Lewis may help us to recapture the sense of novelty that it conveyed to sensibilities yet unblurred by nearly a century of metropolitan fiction. Here was, according to Lewis, "the first book to catch Manhattan. . . . Here is the city, the smell of it, the sound of it, the harsh and shining sight of it." After all, *The New Yorker* likewise made its first appearance in that *annus mirabilis*, 1925.

Sartre would set his seal of world acclaim on the middle volume of *U.S.A.*, and Dos Passos would win the Feltrinelli if not the Nobel Prize, which has been awarded to many a lesser figure. His decline in standing, during the latter part of his career, was dramatically paralleled by the 180-degree shift in his political orientation. He could scarcely be blamed for sometimes feeling that critics, most of them still more or less liberal, were penalizing him for his congealing conservatism. He rationalized his claims to consistency by restudying Jefferson and the civic fathers in such books as *The Ground We Stand On*. But, as F. O. Matthiessen was able to retort: "They are the ground we stood on a long time ago, before the industrial transformation of our modern world." Moreover, the actual effects of that transformation had been the primary themes of Dos Passos as a novelist. Certain resources of novelistic compassion seem to have withered away, in the process that turned a young man arrested for protesting the Sacco-Vanzetti decision into an old man condoning the Kent State shootings. His second trilogy, *District of Columbia*, is at best a dim sequel to the first; and although *Mid-Century* returns to the documentaries and biographies of *U.S.A.*, significantly it omits the lyrical self-intimations.

Yet there had to be some continuity in which *U.S.A.* was pivotal, if only because it had been poised at a turning point between idealism and disillusionment. The expressionistic play that he wrote in college, *The Moon Is a Gong*, was retitled *The Garbage Man* for its off-Broadway production. Edmund Wilson's novel, *I Thought of Daisy*, sketches out a sympathetic portrait of Dos Passos in his Greenwich Village days: earnest, honest, shy, myopic, dedicated, self-denying, a poetic aesthete by temperament, willing himself by force of conscience to be a radical activist. His period of active radicalism started with the trial of Sacco and Vanzetti and terminated with the defeat of the Loyalists in the Spanish Civil War, which for him was history's wrong turn, exacerbated by the Soviet betrayal of Marxist principles. That was precisely the interval that witnessed the writing of *U.S.A.* As late as 1939 he answered a questionnaire with this credo: "My sympathies lie with the private in the front line against the brass hat; with the hod-carrier against the straw-boss, or the walking delegate for that matter; with the laboratory worker against the stuffed shirt in a mortar-board; with the criminal against the cop." *The 42nd Parallel* contains a vignette from his Harvard days, contrasting the gentlemanly conformities with a millworkers' strike at Lawrence, Massachusetts.

He never strayed very far from such temperamental alignments, though his hatred of the bureaucracy would complicate them by making a bugbear out of the New Deal. Internal conflicts were bound to be reinforced by his mixed ancestry, his illegitimate birth,

*Dos Passos in the 1940s (© Bettman/CORBIS)*

these three novels were conjoined to form a trilogy, moves from the lonely mind of a young man walking "the night streets" to a collective memory of images and echoes: "But mostly U.S.A. is the speech of the people." This passage turns out to be nothing less than a poem in Whitman's magnanimous vein; and there are many other such fragments of poetry, notably the composite portrait of the Unknown Soldier that concludes the second volume, "The Body of an American." Dos Passos' democratic conception is rooted in a Whitmanesque unanimism, in the prefatory assumption of *Leaves of Grass* that the United States itself is potentially a great poem, worthy of "gigantic and generous treatment" within the total ambiance of its immediate present. *Manhattan Transfer* had comprised a kind of urban kaleidoscope. Now the panoramic subject matter, to be treated on a scale of 1500 pages, was a cross-section of the entire country during the first three decades of the twentieth century. Modestly conceiving himself as "a second-class historian," the author claimed firsthand access to his age through its language, and asked no more than that his novels be read as "contemporary chronicles."

One of his strengths was his keen reportorial talent for taking in and getting down a locale. Novelists do not have to be circumscribed by a single region, but most of them stick to certain particular backgrounds. Even Balzac hardly covered his lavishly chosen ground in such full detail and over so wide an area as Dos Passos did with his material. At an ever-accelerating pace he zigzags across the continent, with a dip into Mexico and Cuba and a fling at Europe. On the make, his personages gravitate toward a series of capitals, each of them a center for the powers that control American values, all described with atmospheric precision: finance (New York), politics (Washington), industry (Detroit), entertainment (Hollywood), recreation (Miami Beach). As with *Manhattan Transfer,* the titles are large connective symbols. *The 42nd Parallel* roughly runs through Chicago, where, incidentally, Dos Passos was born, eastward to Provincetown, where he did much of his writing, and westward to the Oregon forest, which flashes by in a last reminiscence of his Unknown Soldier. *Nineteen Nineteen* shifts the titular emphasis from a spatial latitude to a temporal axis. And climactically *The Big Money*, as a central metaphor, universalizes the profit motive and tightens the network of human relations through the cash nexus itself.

*The 42nd Parallel* begins, in a flush of expectation, by celebrating the turn of the century, and ends with the embarkation of troops for the First World War in 1917. *Nineteen Nineteen*, as the date suggests, is less preoccupied with the war itself (previously and more closely rendered in *One Man's Initiation* and *Three Soldiers)* than

his upper-class education—not to mention his exposure to war. He had taken his first public stand in 1916 at the age of twenty, with an article for *The New Republic* entitled "Against American Literature." Characteristically it was the establishment that he opposed, in this case the Genteel Tradition, counterposing to it the modernist stance of Walt Whitman. "Our only substitute for dependence on the past is dependence on the future," declared the youthful Dos Passos. "Here our only poet found his true greatness." Forty years later, after reading *Les Temps Modernes,* he commented to Wilson: "In that connection I read over half of *Democratic Vistas* last night and found it much more based on realities than Sartre." The irony was that when the future toward which Whitman had looked—"Years of the Modern!"—arrived with the twentieth century, Dos Passos found it harder to contemplate than did his admirer, Sartre. To an inquiring student Dos Passos replied that the original slant of his work was "more likely to stem from Whitman (and perhaps Veblen) than from Marx."

Leaving Marx aside as a marginal though by no means irrelevant interest, we proceed through *U.S.A.* from the tutelage of Whitman to that of Thorstein Veblen. The prologue spelling out the title, added after

with its side-effects and disillusioning aftermath, signalized by the Disarmament Conference at Versailles. *The Big Money* deals with the following decade, the razzle-dazzle of the Twenties, the perturbation beneath the debonair surfaces of the so-called Jazz Age, ending with the Wall Street crash of 1929, and portending the strikes and breadlines of the Depression. Hence "this lousy superannuated hypertrophied hell-invented novel," as Dos Passos deprecated it in a letter to Ernest Hemingway, was put together just a few years after the incidents it chronicles. Yet it was conceived and executed as a historical novel, bearing witness to its epoch. Like its greatest prototype in that mode, Tolstoy's *War and Peace, U.S.A.* is concerned with the interweaving and shaping of private existences by public events. Like Tolstoy, Dos Passos shows great respect for history, which is conscientiously presented—unlike E. L. Doctorow in *Ragtime,* who introduces historical figures and then irresponsibly casts them in fictitious roles.

Dos Passos' historicism sets up its social framework through a sequence of biographical sketches. Symmetrically spaced, there are nine of these in each volume, twenty-seven in all, related thematically as well as synchronically to the matter at hand. This assortment of highly typical and widely varied Americans ranges from international bankers ( J. P. Morgan) to intransigent radicals (Eugene Debs), from prolific inventors (Thomas Edison) to eccentric artists (Isadora Duncan), from critical thinkers (Randolph Bourne) to film stars (Rudolph Valentino). Technological development has its outstanding proponents: the Wright brothers at Kitty Hawk, the efficiency expert F. W. Taylor, an ambivalent Henry Ford between his "tin lizzie" and his antique collection. Journalism has its playboy in John Reed and its bullyboy in William Randolph Hearst. (Dos Passos' characterization of the latter, "Poor Little Rich Boy," clearly lent inspiration to *Citizen Kane.*) Two presidents are represented: a mock-heroic Theodore Roosevelt and a Woodrow Wilson who comes near to being the arch-villain. "Meester Veelson"—the European accent reflects the hopes for a just peace that he betrayed, after betraying his promise of keeping America out of the war. Dos Passos felt peculiarly embittered, as did Hemingway, because that betrayal debased the language, reducing trusted ideals to rhetorical slogans.

*U.S.A.* is further structured by two formalized devices: the "Newsreel" and "The Camera Eye." Sixty-eight intermittent Newsreels (modeled on a medium then vital but soon obsolescent) frame the time-scheme objectively with reverberating quotations from subtitles, headlines, and popular songs. At the opposite extreme, the fifty-one Camera Eyes are candidly subjective and autobiographical, revealing the mind of the author himself at the moment of his narration. Though the term sounds mechanical, the textures can be rhapsodic; taken together, these passages might constitute Dos Passos' "Song of Myself." James T. Farrell preferred them to all the others, whereas Hemingway's preference was for the portraits from life. The striking—and slightly dampening—implication is that, between the detailed reportage on the one hand and the introspective evocation on the other, the middle territory of sheer fiction seems less arresting or memorable. One wonders how much force it would have carried if the narrative had been straight, without the interventions of collage or montage. Through the trilogy Dos Passos has dispersed a dozen imaginary case histories, five in each volume: six men, six women. The numerical disparity is accounted for by the fact that some drop out, while others enter late. Yet those who cease to be protagonists have walk-on parts in other episodes, so that their life-stories are continued from other viewpoints than their own.

Novels are invariably progressions from innocence to experience, and not less so when—with Proust—they span decades and volumes. Born on the Fourth of July in the century's dewy youth, J. Ward Morehouse is originally viewed through his own eyes as an idealistic high-school debater. Step by step, we watch him from the outside, as he climbs the careerist's ladder: helping to break the Homestead Strike, profiteering as a Dollar-a-Year-Man, pompously and smugly manipulating the wiles of public relations. In a parallel movement, Janey, whom we meet as a lively tomboy, subsequently crushed by the loss of a boyfriend, will reappear as Miss Williams, a colorless old maid and perfect secretary to the important Mr. Morehouse. Mobility goes downward for her brother Joe, who, after wartime adventures with the navy and the merchant marine, is ironically killed in a tavern brawl on Armistice night. Fainy McCreary, the likeable Irish-American printer's devil, is radicalized on his trek to San Francisco, but somehow makes his Mexican peace and disappears from the cycle. Two aspiring girls from different backgrounds in Chicago, Eleanor Stoddard and Eveline Hutchins, pass on from the local Art Institute via an interior decorating studio to intrigues in New York and Paris. Though they get harder and harder to tell apart, one is destined to marry a Russian prince and the other to commit suicide.

The most poignant of these character-sketches, which might stand by itself as a novella, comprises the two sections entitled "Daughter." Anne Elizabeth Trent, a headstrong Texas belle, conscience-stricken after her brother's death as a pilot in training, gets into social work and goes abroad as a postwar Red Cross aide. Made pregnant by an American officer, who temporizes because of other ambitions, she wildly persuades a half-drunk French aviator into looping the loop with her at night, and loses not her baby but her life. A single section is devoted to the radicalization of Ben Compton, a Jewish law student from Brooklyn who goes to jail for his pacifist convictions. Incidental glimpses afterward reveal him as a loyal member of the Communist Party who is ultimately expelled in a doctrinal purge. The comparable case of Mary French, who briefly takes up with Ben Compton at one point, is more fully developed. Ill at ease with the pretentious gentility of her mother, she drops out of Vassar to nurse her beloved doctor-father, who dies of influenza contracted from his patients. After an apprenticeship among the poor at Hull House, she drifts farther leftward: to radical journalism in Pittsburgh, labor organization in Washington, party work as a fellow traveler. Having rejected her family background and been rejected by her Communist lover, she is left to carry on alone.

If the book has any heroine, it is this committed fighter for losing causes, and much of the Sacco-Vanzetti agitation is witnessed from Mary's standpoint. Her opposite number, who also makes her debut in the third volume, is indeed a mock-heroine, a movie queen: the hard-boiled and easygoing Margo Dowling. Sex provides her sordid education; but she learns to use it; and she manages to rise through vaudeville, chorus lines, and nightclubs to the precarious heights of Hollywood stardom. On her way up, she has good-naturedly tried to alleviate the fate of Charley Anderson, which dominates *The Big Money*. That stalwart mechanic from North Dakota was left boarding a troopship at the conclusion of *The 42nd Parallel*. He does not appear in *Nineteen Nineteen* at all; he is too busy fighting and learning all about airplanes. Disembarking at the outset of *The Big Money*, he is now a veteran, a war hero, an ace from the Lafayette Escadrille, trying to realize that the war is over. Demobilization means demoralization for a while. Basically skilled and hard-working, however, he invents a new airplane motor. But an invention must not only be patented; it must be exploited, promoted, and capitalized; stock must be issued, and companies formed. Charley's mechanical know-how would be wasted without the entrepreneurial intercession of shrewd financiers and savvy lobbyists.

His own function, supervising production, inevitably takes him to Detroit, where he is taken up by the country club set. He makes a sort of allegorical choice, when he throws over the engineer's to marry the banker's daughter. He is still most comfortable when tinkering, in his overalls, with his foreman Bill Cermak. But Bill is killed and Charley is badly injured when their plane crashes in taking off for a trial flight. That

crash on the runway is emblematic, not merely of Charley's anticlimactic fortunes, but of what will be happening in the stockmarket and throughout the business world. Things fall apart for Charley; his hollow marriage is wrecked; he himself becomes a human wreck, increasingly alcoholic and self-destructive. Drifting down to Florida, where Margo moves in and out of his careening existence, he is fatally injured in a drunken automobile accident, and rival claimants beleaguer his hospital bed as his internal monologue tapers off. In five years, he has promised his assistant, they would be "in the big money"—as everyone has promised everyone else. Unpeeling a roll of fresh hundred-dollar bills, he was tempted to kiss them. "Gosh," he had said to himself at one moment, "money's a great thing." At another he has wished that "he didn't have to worry about money all the time," that instead "he was still tinkerin' with that damn motor."

As Margo Dowling had an opposite number in Mary French, so Charley Anderson has an anti-heroic foil in Richard Ellsworth Savage. He has begun as a well-connected poor relation, a sensitive Harvard poet, who graduates into the war and gets attached to the brass. After a number of safe and easy assignments behind the lines, he goes through the peace negotiations as aide-de-camp to that ever-hustling arch-operator, J. Ward Morehouse, now in charge of opinion-molding for the postwar American public. Through that connection Dick is assured of a future, if not as a man of letters, then as heir apparent to a high-powered advertising agency, as a highly paid apologist for the ensuing materialistic boom. The moral crisis is underlined by his affair with Anne Elizabeth ("Daughter"); when he jilts her, his good faith lies among the casualties. When we take leave of him, in a cynical miasma of worldly success and self-hate, he is suffering the grimmest of hangovers, after a homosexual escapade in Harlem. Dos Passos' classmate, the poet Robert Hillyer, who actually returned to an academic post and took a narrowly traditional line, objected seriously to this character as a caricature of himself. Dos Passos responded, with the usual embarrassment prompted by such identifications *á clef*, that he had simply borrowed certain military associations, along with a few details from their common undergraduate memories.

We might come closer to the significance of Richard Ellsworth Savage if we consider him as an imaginary projection of Dos Passos himself—Dos Passos as he might have become, had he followed the code of snobbery and careerism, had his talent and integrity been compromised by the seductions of the big money, the acquisitive society, and the military-industrial complex. Edmund Wilson remarked that "humanity generally comes off badly" in *Manhattan Transfer,* and it would be hard to gainsay such an impression of *U.S.A.* All too many of its *dramatis personae* wind up as sellouts or losers, just as the war is sold out and the peace is lost. Sartre would interpret this permutation in Marxist terms: "In capitalist society, men do not have lives, they have only destinies." That is why these people seem shallow or two-dimensional, even when contrasted with their historic role-models. And, though we are not given profiles of Sacco or Vanzetti, we hear their voices out of the depths—quoted directly from their correspondence or, most powerfully, from the famous response of Bartolomeo Vanzetti to the death-sentence. Two Camera Eyes record Dos Passos' own emotions before and after the execution. In one he walks through Plymouth, where Vanzetti had worked, and likens those Italian immigrants to the earliest Pilgrim settlers. In the other, he angrily reacts to the defeat of justice: "all right we are two nations."

On a previous page a Camera Eye has recorded his insomniac misgivings, "peeling the speculative onion of doubt," as Peer Gynt did from layer to layer ("topdog? underdog?"). Against the natural grain of skeptical diffidence, "the internal agitator crazy to succeed" had forced Dos Passos to make a soapbox speech in Union Square. Painfully mulling it over, he confesses, "I go home after a drink and a hot meal and read (with some difficulty in the Loeb Library trot) the epigrams of Martial and ponder the course of history and what leverage might pry the owners loose from power and bring back (I too Walt Whitman) our storybook democracy." Here is a pungent contrast: from Whitman to Martial, whom Dos Passos coupled in a letter with Juvenal, read in the same bilingual edition. Both of those Roman poets attest the decline from the virtues of the old Republic to the corruptions of their present Empire. The nostalgia for Whitman's vistas completes the American analogy. His impetus toward panegyric and rhapsody has been transposed into epigram and satire. The keen attraction that this last form held for Dos Passos made itself felt in his introduction to a portfolio of drawings by Georg Grosz, "Satire as a Way of Seeing," where he equated the satirist with the moralist. He identified his own outlook when he accepted the Gold Medal for Fiction from the National Institute of Arts and Letters in 1957, responding to William Faulkner's citation:

I wonder if any of you have ever noticed that it is sometimes those who find most pleasure and amusement in their fellow man, and have most hope in his goodness, who get the reputation of being his most carping critics. Maybe it is that the satirist is so full of

the possibilities of humankind in general, that he tends to draw a dark and garish picture when he tries to depict people as they are at any particular moment. The satirist is usually a pretty unpopular fellow. The only time he attains even fleeting popularity is when his works can be used by some particular faction as a stick to beat the brains out of their opponents. Satirical writing is by definition unpopular writing. Its aim is to prod people into thinking. Thinking hurts.

Dreiser called his most portentous novel *An American Tragedy,* and I suppose that title might subsume many of the destinies—not to say the lives—interwoven through *U.S.A.* Yet it might raise classical questions regarding the stature of the protagonist, since the characters so often seem to be dwarfed by their very multiplicity, if not by the Swiftian perspectives of the author. "We're living in one of the damndest tragic moments in history," he wrote to F. Scott Fitzgerald at about the time he was completing this trilogy. Its tragedy is that of America, and of the world itself. But there are times, he would have read in Juvenal, if he had not felt it in his bones, when it is difficult not to write satire. If the latter-day imperialism could not evoke the verse of a Juvenal or a Martial, then it needed something like the prose of a Petronius or a Tacitus. Given the extraordinary scope of *U.S.A.,* there is an additional temptation—which Alfred Kazin has not resisted—to designate it as "a national epic." But critics should be able to discriminate, better than Hollywood press agents, among the fitting literacy genres. We might well claim *Moby-Dick* as a national epic, or conceivably the *Leatherstocking* romances. Other and later American novelists, sometimes rather self-consciously, have touched upon the heroic vein: Frank Norris, Theodore Dreiser, Willa Cather.

Not that *U.S.A.* is lacking in heroes, the underdogs to whom Dos Passos professed his own allegiance, and those who fought and spoke on their behalf: the Unknown Soldier, the legendary Joe Hill, the socialist Debs, the progressive Senator LaFollette, Big Bill Hayward [*sic*] of the I.W.W., Sacco, Vanzetti, and most incisively Veblen, who gradually becomes the presiding spirit. In a letter to Edmund Wilson, written during the composition of *The Big Money,* Dos Passos speaks of gathering ammunition from Veblen's socioeconomic analyses. As the ideologist of the fable, he had been situated to understand—much more comprehensively than Marx—the uses and abuses of technology, its relationship to human factors, and its vulnerability to sabotage at every level. His will included a caveat against any posthumous memoir, which Dos Passos has flouted in a brilliantly satirical psychograph, "The Bitter

Drink." That beverage is the hemlock of Socrates, though it has been sipped in small doses and in sporadic classrooms by this twentieth-century gadfly. As a Norwegian- American compatriot of Ibsen, he has not only peeled the onion of doubt; he has slashed out against a shapeless and all-enveloping monster, the Boyg–which Georg Brandes interpreted as the Spirit of Compromise. As a congenital nay-sayer, who "suffered from a constitutional inability to say yes," Veblen has his place with Hawthorne and Melville among the iconoclasts of American culture.

Coming closer to the United States than the Marxian class-struggle, the Veblenite antithesis is the tension between producing and consuming. The downfall of Charley Anderson, which Edmund Wilson regarded as "the best part" of the story, is exemplary in that respect. Charley is an inventor; he possesses Veblen's positive "instinct for workmanship." He has a flair for production, but no head for consumption, and consumption is the order of the day. Veblen's negative phrase, "conspicuous consumption," realizes itself in the national spree that Dos Passos satirizes. And, what is economically and politically worse, this is rooted in "conspicuous waste"–waste of energy, of resources, and of lives. "It's the waste," Mary French cries out bitterly in the last scene of the trilogy. "The food they waste and the money they waste while our people starve in tarpaper barracks." These conflicting issues are counterpoised in the epilogue, "Vag." Dos Passos, as a lifelong traveler, had played the vagabond. Here the valedictory young man, who hikes on the transcontinental highway as the young man in the prologue walked the city streets, could obviously be picked up and booked for vagrancy. The contrast, as he seeks to thumb a ride, is with the airline passengers overhead. There is no longer such a contrast today, when the norm of travel is by air, as there was forty years ago, when it was a luxury of the rich to be skyborne.

The decade of this work was the crucial one for commercial aviation, and one of Dos Passos' plays had been *Airways, Inc.* It is not a coincidence that the tragic fall of Charley Anderson or of "Daughter" should be literally enacted as an airplane crash. "Vag" is still vainly thumbing when the long-drawn-out chronicle draws to a close: "A hundred miles down the road." The road is still open nowadays, and the traffic has greatly increased. As a Harvard student, Dick Savage won a prize from *The Reader's Digest* for a sonnet sequence; but the editor wanted it to terminate on "a note of hope"; and he very readily supplied the amelioration, which may have been the first

of his many intellectual compromises. Writing back to Malcolm Cowley, who seems to have wanted something more affirmative from *The 42nd Parallel,* Dos Passos promised "a certain amount of statement of position in the later Camera Eyes"–possibly what came out in regard to Sacco and Vanzetti, or what would be made more emphatic by his Veblenite adherence. "But as for the note of hope," he concluded in his sincere and straightforward way, "gosh who knows?" No novelist is under obligation to offer reforms or remedies for the state of affairs he undertakes to expose, and Dos Passos would be far less effective in making such an attempt than was his illustrious and wrong-headed predecessor, Tolstoy.

Veblen could have taught him the futility of his hope "to rebuild the past," to recover the "storybook democracy" of Whitman and Jefferson, and consequently have spared him the embarrassment of campaigning for Barry Goldwater. "The American Dream: What Has Happened to It?" This inquiry was raised in a pair of articles by Faulkner, who lectured and planned a book about it. It has been pursued, in one way or another, by many of the other major novelists of our century. The readiest instance may be the concluding page of *The Great Gatsby,* with its realization that "the last and greatest of all human dreams" has receded from the future into the past. If history has truly become a nightmare, better to reveal it than to keep it veiled in outworn fantasy. Speaking to the students of Choate School, after having received its Alumni Prize, Dos Passos affirmed:

> Writing is and I guess it ought to be one of the hazardous professions. . . . The first thing a man–striving to come of age in any period of human history–has to do is to choose for himself what is true and what is not true, what is real and what is not real in the picture of society established for him by his elders. . . . In the search for truth there are no secret formulae that can be handed down from one generation to another. Truth I believe is absolute. Some things are true and some false. You have to find it.

No further explanation was necessary for presenting the panorama as he had found it in *U.S.A.* The achievement was that he had caught so very much of it, thereby enabling Lionel Trilling to say that the whole seemed greater than the sum of its parts. Dos Passos did not need to be–he should not have later become–an ideologue. He was always enough of a moralist to be a genuine satirist. As a reporter, he saw a story in everything, a connecting issue everywhere. As a technician, he developed his own new modes for expressing the complications of modernity.

–*Massachusetts Review,* 20 (Winter 1979): 401–415

*Dos Passos on the cover of the 10 August 1936 issue of*
Time, *at the time* The Big Money *was published,
completing the* U.S.A. *trilogy (Time, Inc.)*

## John Dos Passos: *U.S.A.*
Donald Pizer

*Donald Pizer is Pierce Butler Professor Emeritus of
English at Tulane University. He has published studies of the
novels of Frank Norris and Theodore Dreiser as well as* Dos
Passos's U.S.A.: A Critical Study *(1988).*

Criticism of Dos Passos' fiction is often colored
by the naive transparency of the Dos Passos we know
through his essays, reminiscences, and letters.[1] Here is a
man, it seems, who came to writing in the years after
World War I armed with a few conventional ideas of
his day, who during the 1920s gathered up and used,
like a literary magpie, the principal avant garde techniques of the period, and who produced a series of historically significant but imaginatively deficient works
culminating in *U.S.A.,* after which his work settled into
the permanent dullness which best reflects his fundamental mediocrity.

There is some truth to this estimate of Dos Passos
and his work. From his early Harvard essays to his late
fiction he was preoccupied with the theme of the con-

flict between the Sensitive Young Man and a mechanis-
tic world and with the related subject of the dangers to
individual freedom posed by modern political and
social institutions.[2] He seems never, in other words, to
have advanced in ideas beyond his early absorption in
Joyce's *Portrait of the Artist as a Young Man* (which he read
twice before the end of the war)[3] and his acceptance of
his father's late nineteenth Century Spencerian version
of Jeffersonian individualism.[4] In both frames of reference, the person seeking to preserve freedom of feeling
and action is good; the world outside is crass and
restrictive and thus ultimately destructive and evil. By
the late 1920s, after a decade of interest and experimentation in avant garde fiction, drama, poetry, and film,
Dos Passos found a suitable form for the expression of
these conventional ideas. Joycean stream-of-consciousness
and narrative discontinuity, German expressionistic
drama and film, impressionistic biography, experimental free verse—these and still other twenties enthusiasms
helped chart his development from the comparatively
conventional form of *Three Soldiers* in 1921 to the experimental techniques of *U.S.A.* in the early 1930s. *U.S.A.*
is thus assumed to be a novel in which a 1930s naturalistic intensification of a traditional romantic theme—the
oppressive nature of the world—is communicated in
several fashionable experimental modes. Our interest in
the novel is therefore in its form as a panoramic social
novel. Otherwise, we are led to believe, the narrative
portions are flat and dull, the newsreels obvious, and
the Camera Eye obscure; only the biographies, because
of their mordant satire, are of permanent interest.

This is, I think, a fair account of the conventional
estimate of Dos Passos' work and of *U.S.A.* in particular. Yet many readers have found that *U.S.A.* has a
holding power—the power to drive one to the conclusion of an extremely long book—which they associate
with the greatest fiction. They are absorbed in its characters and events because these seem to communicate
something moving about human nature and experience, not because the trilogy documents easily grasped
ideas in fashionably experimental forms. Their response
to *U.S.A.* as a work of fullness and depth suggests that
the trilogy is not a collection of fragments but rather a
powerful and complex unity—a unity which I propose
to describe as that of a naturalistic tragedy.

The surface impression of *U.S.A.,* however, is
indeed of miscellaneousness. The three novels—*The
42nd Parallel* (1930), *Nineteen Nineteen* (1934), and *The
Big Money* (1936)—contain twelve discontinuous fictional
narratives (in effect twelve different plots), twenty-seven
brief biographies of famous late nineteenth- and early
twentieth-century Americans, sixty-eight newsreels consisting of snippets from popular songs and newspaper
headlines and stories, and fifty-one Camera Eye passages

which use modified stream-of-consciousness material to render specific moments in the inner life of the author from his youth to the early 1930s. In addition, each of the novels has a distinctive subject matter. Mac dominates *The 42nd Parallel,* Joe Williams and Richard Savage *Nineteen Nineteen,* and Charley Anderson and Margo Dowling *The Big Money,* while the setting shifts in emphasis from small-town America in the first volume to Paris and Rome in *Nineteen Nineteen* to New York in the final novel.

Of course, there is a correspondingly superficial unity to this diversity of subject matter and form in that the trilogy (as most critics have observed) is a parody epic. The histories of twelve Americans of various backgrounds and occupations but of similarly unsatisfactory lives is a 1930s version of the twelve books or cantos devoted to the career of an epic hero. Epics demand the inclusion of much material involving the heroic past of the nation or race, and *U.S.A.* is therefore also a historical novel. The major political and cultural figures of the age are the subject of the biographies and several also appear in the narratives (Wilson, Bryan, and Big Bill Haywood, for example). A number of fictional figures are based on recognizable historical personages (the publicist Ivy Lee served as a model for J. Ward Moorehouse, as did Bernarr Macfadden for Doc Bingham).[5] The principal events of American life from approximately 1900 to 1931 figure prominently in all of *U.S.A.* and not merely in the newsreels. By "events" I mean not only such specific historical occasions as the outbreak of war or the Sacco and Vanzetti executions but such phenomena as Prohibition, political and labor radicalism, the Florida land boom, the rise of the aircraft industry and of Hollywood, and so on. We come to know, too, a great deal about such American cities as Chicago, New York, Washington, Philadelphia, Pittsburgh, and Los Angeles. The career of each fictional character therefore renders not only a representative type of modern American (the public relations man, the inventor-entrepreneur, the IWW radical) but a representative range of historical and social life. *U.S.A.* thus appears to be largely an obvious exercise in imitative form, in which the theme of the discontinuity, fragmentation, and miscellaneousness of American life is both epic theme and form.

Yet there is much in *U.S.A.* which conflicts with this seemingly inevitable conclusion and which suggests that we must look further and deeper for a full understanding of the relation of theme to form in the trilogy. For example, fictional characters frequently appear in narratives other than their own (a device I shall call "interlacing"), and specific historical events frequently control an entire group of narratives, biographies, news-

reels, and Camera Eye segments in a particular portion of the novel (a device I shall call "cross-stitching").

Interlacing occurs in a number of ways in *U.S.A.* Minor figures, for example, reappear in the narratives of several different major characters. (By "major character" I mean one of the twelve figures who have narratives devoted to them.) Doc Bingham in a sense frames the trilogy by his appearance in the opening narrative devoted to Mac and his reappearance at the close of *The Big Money* as a client of Moorehouse's advertising firm, while the labor faker George W. Barrow and the newspapermen Jerry Burnham and Don Stevens reappear frequently throughout the trilogy. Love affairs occur between a number of major figures and thus create a frequent interlacing effect. Among the most prominent of such relationships are Daughter and Dick Savage, Dick and Eveline, Moorehouse and Eveline, Moorehouse and Eleanor, Charley and Eveline, and Mary French and Ben Compton. J. Ward Moorehouse in particular pervades the trilogy in an interlacing role. He is an important figure in the narratives of Eleanor, Janey, Eveline, and Dick Savage, and he appears occasionally or is mentioned in those of Mac, Joe Williams, and Daughter. On two notable occasions (an evening in a Paris nightclub during the war, and a New York party in the late 1920s) four or five of the major characters are briefly interlaced. Occasionally there is a sense of forcing when two characters are interlaced under unlikely circumstances, as when Dick and Joe meet briefly in Genoa or when Mac learns of Moorehouse's presence in Mexico City. But in general the effect is curiously appropriate—curious because of the range of life surveyed in the trilogy, appropriate because the intertwining of the lives of so many diverse figures seems to confirm our feeling that there is a rich substrata of relatedness to their experience.

Cross-stitching occurs most obviously when a new major character and thus a new area of experience is introduced. So the initial appearance of Margo, who is to become a Hollywood star, is accompanied by biographies of Isadora Duncan and Valentino, much newsreel reporting of Hollywood high jinks, and the presence of the Camera Eye in New York art life. The inventor Charley Anderson and the radical Ben Compton have similar cross-stitched introductions. A second kind of cross-stitching consists of the frequent reappearance of a major social phenomenon in a number of narratives as well as in various biographies, newsreels and Camera Eye segments. The IWW-led strike, the stock market boom, and Greenwich Village art life are a few examples. The war, above all, is present in the trilogy as an event touching almost everyone. Of all the major figures, only Mac (who retreats to Mexico before it begins) and Mary

French and Margo (who are too young) are not in some significant way involved in the war. And the war dominates the newsreels, many of the biographies, and much of the Camera Eye of *Nineteen Nineteen* as well as major portions of the other two novels.

Through the interlacing of characters and cross-stitching of events Dos Passos appears to be saying that though we seem to be a nation of separate strands, we are in fact intertwined in a fabric of relatedness. Dos Passos was seeking, in short, to create a symbolic form to express the theme that though we lead many different lives in a multiplicity of experience, these lives are part of our shared national life; thus our meaning as individuals and as a nation lies in the meaning which arises out of the inseparable unity of individual lives and national character.

Dos Passos provides an introduction to this meaning in his comment that the basic theme of all his work is "man's struggle for life against the strangling institutions he himself creates."[6] What lends distinction and vitality to his fictional rendering of this conventional Jeffersonian concept is his ability to dramatize our life-denying institutions as the ideas, beliefs, and values which we unconsciously and habitually express in our thoughts and feelings and thus in our language. His method is both verbal (in the sense of the language people use) and ironic. Dos Passos has claimed that the novelist is "the historian of the age he lives in,"[7] but he has also noted that "the mind of a generation is its speech,"[8] and he concluded the opening sketch of his trilogy, the sketch itself entitled "U.S.A.," with the comment that "mostly U.S.A. is the speech of the people."[9] When Carl Sandburg, in 1936, sought in his book-length poem *The People, Yes* to express the same belief, he celebrated the innate wisdom and courage of the folk which are embodied in their language. Dos Passos, on the other hand, suggested by the powerful ironic current in his dramatization of "the voice of the people" that the language of democratic idealism in America, because it disguises various suspect values, subverts the very ideals this language purports to express and reflects instead a deep malaise at the heart of American life.

As several of Dos Passos' best critics have sensed, *U.S.A.* is a novel in which most of the conventional attributes of fiction—plot, character, setting, and symbol—are subordinated to a vast and complex exercise in verbal irony.[10] The narratives in *U.S.A.*, both because of their relative length within the trilogy as a whole and because of the inherent nature of narrative, are the fullest expression of Dos Passos' ironic method. His technique is to use a version of indirect discourse to reveal the underlying nature of his narrative figures and thus to reveal as well the important similarities among these figures.

In response to a question asked in 1965 about the source of his technique of indirect discourse, Dos Passos replied that he was uncertain but that he believed he may have derived it from Zola and Joyce.[11] If so, he modified his own practice greatly, since his indirect discourse lacks both the slangy raciness of Zola (or Farrell) and the disconnected flux of Joyce. Instead, Dos Passos suggests by a number of devices that it is the very texture of his narrative prose—its vocabulary and syntax as a whole—which reflects a character's habitual modes of thought and expression. The narratives in *U.S.A.* contain remarkably little dialogue or dramatic scene because the author's narrative voice is itself essentially a dramatic rendering of character.

Dos Passos supplies several verbal keys to remind us occasionally that we are reading the author's rhetorical reshaping of a character's habitual voice. One is to place eye-catching colloquialisms in his third-person prose ("ud" for "would," for example), another is to run together as single words phrases that are spoken as single words ("officeboy," for example). A third is to open a narrative which depicts the childhood of a character in a prose style which is obviously childlike. Here, for example, is most of the first paragraph of Eveline Hutchins' narrative:

> Little Eveline and Arget and Lade and Gogo lived on the top floor of a yellowbrick house on the North Shore Drive. Arget and Lade were little Eveline's sisters. Gogo was her little brother littler than Eveline; he had such nice blue eyes but Miss Mathilda had horrid blue eyes. On the floor below was Dr. Hutchins' study where Yourfather mustn't be disturbed, and Dearmother's room where she stayed all morning painting dressed in a lavender smock. On the groundfloor was the drawingroom and the diningroom, where parishioners came and little children must be seen and not heard, and at dinnertime you could smell good things to eat and hear knives and forks and tinkly companyvoices and Yourfather's booming scary voice.... (*NN*, 107)

The irony in this passage is readily apparent but gentle. Far more characteristic of Dos Passos' use of indirect discourse for ironic effect are the many occasions in the narrative when a character's thoughts are rendered in a blatantly clichéd verbal style which clearly reflects the painful inadequacy of his stereotyped beliefs. So, for example, when Joe Williams is arrested in wartime Liverpool for drunkenness, Dos Passos' account of the magistrate's lecture to him and his comrades captures both Joe's colloquial idiom and the magistrate's hackneyed jingoism.

And the magistrate in the little wig gave 'em a hell of a talking to about how this was wartime and they had no right being drunk and disorderly on British soil but had ought to be fighting shoulder to shoulder with their brothers, Englishmen of their own blood and to whom the Americans owed everything, even their existence as a great nation, to defend civilization and free institutions and plucky little Belgium against the invading huns who were raping women and sinking peaceful merchantmen. (*NN*, 45)

Somewhat different in technique, but similar in effect in reminding us that Dos Passos is engaging us in the minds of his characters through their verbal formulas, is the passage reporting J. Ward Moorehouse's thoughts when he discovers that the rich man's daughter he had hoped to marry has been sleeping with a Frenchman. Here it is the last phrase which brings us up short.

He walked down the street without seeing anything. For a while he thought he'd go down to the station and take the first train out and throw the whole business to ballyhack, but there was the booklet to get out, and there was a chance that if the boom did come he might get in on the ground floor, and this connection with money and the Strangs; opportunity knocks but once at a young man's door. (*FP*, 193)

In fact, however, the narrative prose style in *U.S.A.* is generally far less blatant than these examples in its indirect-discourse rendering of the platitudes and clichés which guide the lives of the characters. Rather, Dos Passos' more common method is to suggest by the jaded, worn, and often superficially flat language of the narratives the underlying failure of understanding of those who approach life without independent vision and who are therefore "strangled" by the hold of the conventional upon their minds. And yet—and this is the source of the strength of the narratives as satiric fiction—this pervasive flatness is subtly and often powerfully ironic, since it always points to some specific limitation in the character depicted. Here, for example, is a typical passage of narrative prose, one in which without any bold ironic touches Dos Passos describes Janey Williams' new position as secretary in a Washington law office just before America's entrance into the war.

Working at Dreyfus and Carroll's was quite different from working at Mrs. Robinson's. There were mostly men in the office. Mr. Dreyfus was a small thin-faced man with a small black moustache and small black twinkly eyes and a touch of accent that gave him a distinguished foreign diplomat manner. He carried yellow wash gloves and a yellow cane and had a great variety of very much tailored overcoats. He was the

brains of the firm, Jerry Burnham said. Mr. Carroll was a stout redfaced man who smoked many cigars and cleared his throat a great deal and had a very oldtimey Southern Godblessmysoul way of talking. Jerry Burnham said he was the firm's bay window. Jerry Burnham was a wrinklefaced young man with dissipated eyes who was the firm's adviser in technical and engineering matters. He laughed a great deal, always got into the office late, and for some reason took a fancy to Janey and used to joke about things to her while he was dictating. She liked him, though the dissipated look under his eyes scared her off a little. She'd have liked to have talked to him like a sister, and gotten him to stop burning the candle at both ends. (*FP*, 152)

On the one hand, the passage merely records Janey's impressions of the various members of the firm and thus renders in a mildly ironic manner several of her received opinions: that fine clothes represent distinction, that speech mannerisms signify character, and that there are clear physical stigmata of moral decay—in short, that life is as superficially apparent as she finds it. But the passage also records, with a far deeper and more significant irony, Janey's unconscious absorption in Jerry Burnham and her fear of that absorption, a conflict which she seeks to resolve by her adoption of the role of "sister" toward him. Janey thus reveals in the seemingly bland prose of this passage her fear of her own emotions and desires, a fear which leads her to erect barriers of conventional and life-denying attitudes and roles between herself and the world.

. . . . . . . . . .

The most important way in which the narratives as a group represent theme is through what I shall call narrative clusters. Some of these clusters parallel Dos Passos' interlacing device. That is, a number of major figures not only appear in each other's narratives but also have a basic similarity of character and fate. Other clusters evolve out of discrete narratives in which the major characters never mix but nevertheless share a common destiny. An example of the first kind of cluster is the group of major figures who revolve around J. Ward Moorehouse as patron or employer: Janey, Eleanor, and Dick Savage. All three are from white-collar backgrounds of minor clerks or officials and all three are intent on solidifying their position in settings of greater gentility, power, and wealth. To do so, however, requires a repression of those emotions or drives, particularly the sexual, which might jeopardize their advance. All three, at the close of the trilogy, are both successful and desperately unhappy, with the "unnaturalness" of their lives represented most of all by their sexual failures. Eleanor is frigid, Janey has channelled her sexuality into a fierce and paranoiac protectiveness toward Moorehouse, and Dick refuses to acknowledge his homosexuality.

Unlike the group of figures revolving around Moorehouse, Eveline, Joe Williams, and Daughter constitute a cluster in which the characters do not interlace. (Dick Savage, however, knows or meets all three.) Eveline, Joe, and Daughter share a tragic innocence. They are "open" characters in the sense that they acknowledge their emotional (and sexual) natures and seek personal fulfillment as much as their circumstances allow. Eveline and Daughter want love, Joe freedom. But they are without strength or shrewdness, and thus for them something ventured is all lost. Daughter's openhearted love for Dick and his desertion of her despite her pregnancy suggests the similar victimization of all three figures by the more ruthless and circumspect. So all three go to bitter and meaningless deaths, victims of a naively innocent failure to realize that to desire is to make oneself vulnerable.

Mac and Joe also never interlace but have basically similar characters and fates, even though Mac's fate is bourgeois respectability and Joe's is death. Both represent the life of the working man at its most empty and futile. Until Mac moves into the middle class at the close of his narrative, their lives are of constant movement—Mac throughout America as a laborer, Joe throughout the world as a seaman. They are archetypically rootless American workingmen, in permanent transit not because they wish to be but because their marginal lives prevent them from putting down roots. And because they are marginal and thus weak, Mac and Joe are beaten up and robbed and cheated and deceived wherever they go. Both are also victimized (in a Marxist sense) by sex. They marry because girls whom they desire withhold sex as leverage to gain a husband. After marriage, their wives struggle for the possessions which signify a rise in status. So both take the road again, with their ultimate destinies—Mac sinking into a mindless desire for security, Joe dying in a bar—representing the two extremes of defeat for the workingman.

Mac is occasionally active in the IWW, and Joe, while not politically conscious, resents America's participation in the war. Both figures belong to an early phase of American radicalism. Ben Compton and Mary French, however, play active roles in the more theoretically based and institutionally structured radicalism of the 1920s. Yet both share with Mac and Joe an essential naiveté which to Dos Passos is the tragic center of modern American radicalism. Ben is a textbook Marxist and Mary is responsive to the misery she sees around her in city slums and in factory and mine towns. Both therefore lack an appreciation of the maneuvering, compromise, and betrayal which are central to left-wing radicalism after the war. So Ben is dismissed from the party as a deviationist because he fails to accept that party discipline supercedes Marxist truth, and Mary labors fruitlessly in the trenches of the movement because her political innocence is suspect.

The most significant cluster of narratives in *U.S.A.* is that of Moorehouse, Charley Anderson, and Margo Dowling as inversions of the American myth of success. Moorehouse's life is an ironic fulfillment of an Alger-like rise. Born on the Fourth of July, a reader of *Success* magazine in his youth, he works hard and "didn't drink or smoke and was keeping himself clean for the lovely girl he was going to marry, a girl in pink organdy with golden curls and a sunshade" (*FP*, 177). But Moorehouse's good luck in twice marrying the boss's daughter (in his two marriages) also includes having to accept sexually soiled and neurotic women who make his life a misery. And his upward-moving career—from selling real estate to public relations work for steel and oil corporations to pushing the war effort and fighting the "radical element" and finally to Madison Avenue advertising—touches upon the major areas of American life in which a false rhetoric of Americanism can be used by the wealthy and powerful to exploit the poor and weak. Moorehouse has risen by pluck and luck to eminence because he has been able to manipulate the naive faiths by which most Americans live, including their faith in the Alger myth.

Charley Anderson represents a different kind of inversion of the American success myth. He aspires to be a Henry Ford or Thomas Edison, a tinkerer of genius. A country boy come to the city, he will work hard to build a better mousetrap (an airplane engine for him) and thus rise to fame and fortune while aiding mankind through his ingenuity. But Charley soon discovers that hard work and mechanical inventiveness alone do not bring the rewards promised by the myth. In an almost allegorically precise demonstration of one of Thorstein Veblen's principal theses, he learns that ruthlessness and deception are also required. Although Charley tries to ape these qualities, his essentially trusting and open nature makes him an easy mark for more skilled corporation in-fighters. Seeking the big money, he is almost casually devoured by more rapacious birds of prey, while he himself helps destroy those who are even more naively honest and faithful than he himself—notably his old mechanic friend Bill Cermak. So Charley becomes a garrulous and drunken hulk, a corrupted Honest Workman.

Like Charley, Margo Dowling is poor and likeable, and she too discovers that success requires the perversion of one's most salable commodity—mechanical skill for Charley, sex for Margo. Her rise to stardom is a parody of the Hollywood version of the rags-to-riches career of the movie star. As in a film, poverty and hardship in youth are followed by work as a Ziegfeld girl, pursuit by a wealthy Yale halfback, obscurity in Hollywood, and at last discovery by a famous European director and marriage to her handsome leading man. In Margo's case, however, this rise is achieved not by hard work and good luck but rather by the open exploitation of her sexuality and by her ability at every stage of her rise to achieve an effective level of phoniness. In Hollywood, for example, a rented Rolls-Royce, relatives who pose as servants, and a false foreign background win her the entry into films that her talent could not. And once in the door, it is only her willingness to play the sexual games demanded by her kinky director (himself a Margo kind of phony) and by a sexual-athlete male star which assures her rise. Margo ends as a Jean Harlow figure–blonde, hard, shrewd, someone who has what she wants and who accepts what she had to do to get it.

The ironic inversion of the myth of success in the Moorehouse, Anderson, and Margo narratives occurs as well in two other major strands of the complex fabric which is *U.S.A.* The first is found in the anonymous biographies at the opening, approximate middle, and close of the trilogy–"U.S.A.," "The Body of an American," and "Vag." The three figures recapitulate the failure of the American dream. The "young man" of the opening sketch seeks a Whitmanesque community of shared labor and finds only loneliness and "words telling about longago."[12] The Unknown Soldier has spilled his blood to save the Morgan loans. And the hungry hobo who walks the dusty road (while planes overhead carry the rich) recalls that "books said opportunity, ads promised speed, own your home, shine bigger than your neighbor" (*BM,* 561).

A second major analogue to Dos Passos' ironic portrayal of the myth of success in the narratives occurs in his full-scale attention in the trilogy to two of the major moments in the history of the American consciousness in the twentieth century–the war and the Sacco-Vanzetti case. Both events have the same configuration: vested authority believes that it is pursuing a course of action that is necessary to preserve American ideals, and particularly the ideal of freedom, but in fact is aiding in the corruption and destruction of these ideals. In both instances, the failure of the American dream is so massively evident that this failure takes on mythic resonance. It is not merely the super-patriots and the Massachusetts establishment who falsify the great words–democracy, freedom, happiness–but the nation as a whole. The end of the war in *Nineteen Nineteen* and the deaths of Sacco and Vanzetti at the close of *The Big Money* are thus the historical equivalents of the narratives of Moorehouse, Anderson, and Margo. In both

the historical event and the fictional life the American dream, including the dream of success, is not only false but is itself corrupting.

Although the biographies in *U.S.A.* appear to be radically different in theme and form from the narratives, they are in fact essentially similar. Of course, the biographies substitute a stylized impressionistic selectivity for fully extended narration. But in the biographies as in the narratives the principal mode is irony. Often the very title of the biography is ironic ("Meester Veelson" or–for Carnegie–"Prince of Peace"); or, as in the narratives, a key word is used to reflect an obsession ("righteousness" for Roosevelt, "ideas" for Ford). Most of all, irony oozes out of every phrase in the biographies because they are studies in reversal of received opinion. In them, the presumed great of American life are revealed to be betrayers of American values and the conventionally vilified to be heroic and noble. . . .

Dos Passos' biographies of the presumed great divide into clusters of analogous "life stories," clusters which offer a massive confirmation in public lives of the dramatization in the fictional narratives of the perversion of the American myth of success. There are three clusters of bitterly ironic biographies of the great in *U.S.A.*: the robber barons (Minor Keith, J. P. Morgan, and Samuel Insull); the misguided or hypocritical do-gooders (W. J. Bryan, Roosevelt, Carnegie, Wilson, and Hearst); and the callous industrialists (Frederick Taylor and Ford). Considerably less biting in tone are the biographies of a cluster of inventors and artists (Burbank, Edison, the Wright brothers, Steinmetz, Isadora Duncan, and Valentino) who, while themselves not directly culpable, have nevertheless permitted themselves or their work to be controlled by the powerful and wealthy of America. The robber barons and assembly-line industrialists–the open manipulators of the system for their own profit–are easy game for Dos Passos' irony, particularly when they display an interest in art or politics, and he dispatches them effectively. His deepest anger and longest biographies are reserved for those who have used the rhetoric of American idealism but who, in his view, have betrayed that idealism because of their class or religious bias (Roosevelt and Wilson) or ambition (Hearst). In contrast to the caustic tone of these biographies, Dos Passos' tone in his portraits of duped men and women of creative genius is more ambivalent and occasionally even sympathetic. Here the fault, as with Edison, is often of preoccupation, or, as with Valentino, of naiveté. Nevertheless, though used by the system, all–whether consciously or not–have also used the system to gain success. All are therefore portrayed ironically in that their fame as artists or inventors echoes the falseness and hollowness of the society which has rewarded them.

Since all four of these clusters of biographies are ironic success stories, they are evocatively related to the ironic success narratives of Moorehouse, Anderson, and Margo. The sanctimoniously self-righteous rhetoric of Wilson and the hypocritical "public interest" journalism of Hearst are powerful public parallels to the methods and career of J. Ward Moorehouse. Charley Anderson's life as a tinkerer is closely related to the lives of Ford, Taylor, and Edison. Like Taylor, he believes that his "responsibility to the shareholders" requires him to impose dehumanizing conditions upon his work force. But more significantly he differs from Edison and Ford (and thus gains a tragic dimension) in that he can neither retreat into his work room nor push single-mindedly toward the big money he craves. And Margo, who has been transformed into a star by the image-making capacity of Hollywood, has her analogues in Isadora Duncan and Valentino, two figures whose artificially enlarged public personalities tragically outrun their ability to fulfill them.

The newsreels in *U.S.A.* maintain the ironic technique of the trilogy as a whole. They consist of authentic snippets from contemporary headlines, news stories, speeches, and songs—contemporary in the sense that they roughly parallel the forward-moving chronology of the narratives and Camera Eye from approximately the turn of the century to the early 1930s. Their authenticity produces an immediate ironic effect, since the "real" world they depict is one of trivia and hysteria, of the significant reduced to the superficial by simplistic loading, and of the superficial bloated into importance because of its "human interest." The newsreels create an impression not of life but, as in the indirect discourse of the narratives, of life seen through a distorting lens which has failed to recognize the gap between events and the falsified language used to report them.

. . . . . . . . . .

The character of *U.S.A.* as a naturalistic tragedy derives not only from the "stranglehold" of falsified American ideals on American life and belief. It also arises from the presence in the trilogy of those who struggle through to an understanding of the corruption of the American dream and who seek to express this understanding in word and deed. This theme in *U.S.A.* appears most clearly and powerfully in the biographies and Camera Eye, though it is also obliquely present in the narratives.

Several biography clusters are devoted to the possibility of the heroic life in America—to the life dedicated to the pursuit of truth in words and action by those willing to be ignored or vilified or martyred because they run against the grain of American life

established by the powerful and corrupt. One such cluster is of fallen leaders: Big Bill Haywood, Robert La Follette, and Eugene Debs. These three pre-war leaders sought to express through a radical ideal—the IWW, progressivism, and socialism—a vision of a better life for all Americans. Each, in the more innocent days before the war, met with some success. But the career of each was destroyed as old enemies exploited the super-patriotism of war hysteria to crush all forms of liberalism. Another cluster consists of the martyred radicals, Jack Reed, Joe Hill, and Wesley Everest. Here, as in the narratives, Dos Passos depicts pre-war radicalism more affirmatively than its post-war communist version. Reed, Hill, and Everest are native Americans (westerners all—Reed's motif is that he is "a westerner and words meant what they said") (*NN,* 14) who seek to translate the old words into acts and who are killed or die in the effort. And finally there is the cluster of the vilified truth-sayers, writers and thinkers and artists such as Randolph Bourne, Thorstein Veblen, Paxton Hibben, and Frank Lloyd Wright. These are men who struggle to say something true about the war or economics or diplomacy or architecture. Each, like Veblen, finds that so much falsehood is accepted as truth that he "couldn't get his mouth around the essential yes" (*BM,* 98) and thus each, like Wright, is "not without honor except in his own country" (*BM,* 433).

There are several minor figures in the narratives who play a similar role—men whose careers as truth-sayers result in their being labeled as cynics or disruptive forces. Mr. Robbins, who works many years for Moorehouse, is such a character, but Jerry Burnham, the radical newspaperman who appears in the narratives of Janey, Eveline, and Mary French, is the more developed figure. Because Robbins and Burnham know the truth but lack the heroic strength of the biography figures, they sink into moroseness and drunken self-contempt. Yet they too reveal that some men can see and speak honestly, as Jerry does about the war, the peace conference, and the communist involvement in the left-wing movement.

Far more significant among the narrative figures similar to the truth-sayers of the biographies are the major characters who have the ability to see the truth but who betray their vision because of their commitment to the big money. Blanche Gelfant has written perceptively about the failures in identity among the characters of *U.S.A.,* that "their flatness and helplessly drifting quality is largely a result of their inability to find inner reality."[13] Several of the major characters in *U.S.A.,* however, do not so much fail to find their identity as suppress an identity which threatens their success. We sense in the early lives of Charley Anderson, Dick Savage, and Margo Dowling qualities of character and temperament which are their essential natures. Charley's love of engines, Dick's aesthetic sensibility, and Margo's responsiveness to others have sparks of life in their early careers which, if properly nurtured, might have grown into sustaining identities. But each lacks the courage to sacrifice and fight for what he is, and thus each, despite his ostensible success, lives an artificial and unhappy life. Our last glimpse of Margo is of a doll-like figure created to fulfill a public role. But it is the fates of Charley and Dick which most fully enforce the implicit theme of the truth-sayer biographies that it is better to be martyred or misunderstood than to suppress a truthful vision of oneself for the success that this suppression might bring. The drunken and whoring Anderson, prone to prolonged binges and self-destructive accidents, and the deceitful, treacherous, self-hating Dick Savage are biting studies in the spiritual malaise which a knowledge of self-betrayal can bring. Their narratives are intended to move us not so much to moral condemnation (though there is some of this) as to a sense of the tragic waste of a potential for vision and honesty.

Perhaps the fullest expression of the tragic theme in the narratives is contained in the character and life of Mary French. Mary's career is that of an average but enlightened American. A sensitive and insightful young woman (a key is that she reads and admires Veblen while at college), Mary sees at first hand in the Chicago slums and Pennsylvania mine and mill towns the degradation of working class American life. Her radicalism arises less from a political ideology than from a responsiveness to misery and pain. Yet Mary's ability to help the working class is constantly compromised by her disastrous love affairs with various left-wing leaders, affairs which allegorize the ways in which an aroused social conscience can be weakened and limited in America. Her first relationship is with Gus, an uneducated young Pittsburgh radical with whom she unconsciously falls in love. Then she meets George Barrow and lives with him for some time in Washington while serving as his secretary. In New York she takes in and nurses Ben Compton; they fall in love and live together while he continues his union organizing. And finally she lives with Don Stevens, a newspaperman turned communist leader. Each of the affairs ends poorly. Gus is beaten and sent to jail for his activities; Barrow, Mary realizes, is selling out the labor movement, and she leaves him; Ben decides that a family will handicap his work in the party and drifts away; and Stevens leaves her at party orders in order to marry a foreign comrade. In each instance, Mary's capacity to give of herself is cast aside or betrayed for reasons that constitute the fate of the informed sensibility which seeks to respond to the needs and conditions of most Americans. Her potential for truth-saying is not so much suppressed as prevented from full beneficial expression, and we leave her not guilt-ridden but worn and wasted by her constantly thwarted efforts to fulfill her love for man and mankind.

The most cogent depiction in *U.S.A.* of man's ability to see and act despite the stranglehold of institutions and institutionalized language in America occurs in the career of the authorial persona portrayed in the Camera Eye. With some recent exceptions, this portion of the novel has long been misunderstood. Adopting the position expressed by Dos Passos himself in a late interview,[14] many readers have considered the Camera Eye merely a device to "drain off" the subjective from the creative process and thus somehow ensure the greater objectivity of the remainder of the novel. Or it has been taken to be a device which seeks to demonstrate the ability of the private consciousness to survive in the modern world. Both of these views of the nature and function of the Camera Eye tend to ignore two of its principal qualities. First, the substance of the Camera Eye stream of consciousness is less similar to Molly's reverie at the close of *Ulysses* than to Bloom's thoughts as he wanders during the day. The stream-of-consciousness material is not "pure" interior monologue but consists of the constant intertwining of exterior event and interior reflection, in which the "world outside" plays an important role in the world of consciousness. Second, the consciousness depicted in the Camera Eye is not static. The fifty-one episodes form a kind of novel of development, in which the protagonist, after a number of false starts and difficulties, comes to see his proper role in life and begins to undertake it.[15]

The notion that Dos Passos intended the Camera Eye to dramatize his own intellectual and emotional development is supported by the presence in other portions of the novel of similar reflections of his changing attitudes and values. During the seven or eight years of the genesis and composition of *U.S.A.*, from approximately 1927 to 1935, Dos Passos' commitment to the radical left underwent considerable change. As Daniel Aaron has noted, Dos Passos' radicalism "simmered in the early twenties, boiled furiously between 1927 and 1932 [the period during which he wrote the first two novels of the trilogy], and began to cool thereafter."[16] This shift in Dos Passos' degree of endorsement of the Left can

*William Faulkner and Malcolm Cowley presenting Dos Passos with the Gold Medal in fiction*
*of the American Academy of Arts and Letters in 1957 (Wide World)*

be seen most clearly in his treatment of the radical newspaperman Don Stevens. Throughout the trilogy Stevens and George Barrow frequently appear together in complementary roles. Whether in Washington and New York before the war or Paris during and after it, Barrow is always the soft-centered and self-serving labor leader while Stevens is a sympathetically portrayed radical and, later, enthusiast of the Russian Revolution. When we encounter them in *The Big Money,* however, Barrow is unchanged but Stevens has become a coldly calculating and deceptive party functionary. The depiction of Marxism itself undergoes a similar change. In Mac's narrative in *The 42nd Parallel*—and particularly in the portrayal of Mac's radical printer uncle—Marxism is endorsed as offering an apt description of the nature of class warfare in America. But in his dramatization of the role of Marxism in Ben Compton's life in the close of *Nineteen Nineteen* and throughout *The Big Money,* Dos Passos suggests the baneful personal and social consequences of a programmatic and religiously held economic theory.

Dos Passos also incorporated into his portrayal of several of the biography and narrative figures themes which suggest his absorption in the possibility of growth in vision by someone of his own class.

Among the biographies, Jack Reed and Paxton Hibben are depicted as figures who despite "four years under the ethercone" (*FP,* 301) at Harvard and Princeton awake to an understanding of the world as it is rather than as the conventional lies of their class would have it be. Dick Savage's career as a Harvard aesthete and as an ambulance driver in France and Italy closely parallels Dos Passos' as caught in the Camera Eye. But Dick, though he does develop in insight, lacks the moral courage to fight the system and thus descends into self-hate and spiritual death.

The Camera Eye persona develops despite two related handicaps. He must escape the narrow vision both of his class and of a self-imposed aestheticism if he is to grow in an understanding of the world as it is and thereby assume his proper role in life. His "education" begins as a child when he skates on a pond near the mills. He is warned of the "muckers . . . bohunk and polack kids" and contrasts them with "we clean young American Rover Boys handy with tools Deerslayers played hockey Boy Scouts and cut figure eights in the ice Achilles Ajax Agamemnon" (*FP,* 81). The imagery here and frequently elsewhere in the Camera Eye portions of the trilogy expresses a condition which the Camera Eye persona finally

413

openly acknowledges in one of his last segments when he cries, "all right we are two nations" (*BM*, 462). It is an imagery of two classes divided not only by wealth and power but by the language of degradation on the one hand and of mythic prowess and nobility on the other. By the time the Camera Eye persona has reached Harvard, he has begun to awaken to social awareness but feels himself bound by the code of the gentleman aesthete: "don't be a grind be interested in literature but remain a gentleman don't be seen with Jews or Socialists" (*FP*, 302). His participation in the war, because European conditions vividly reveal the disparity between the strong and the weak and between language and reality, moves him toward involvement as well as insight. His war responses contain a biting edge of anger which presages action, as in the comment that "Up north they were dying in the mud and the trenches but business was good in Bordeaux" (*FP*, 364), or in the front-line vision of "the grey crooked fingers the thick drip of blood off the canvas the bubbling when the lungcases try to breathe the muddy scraps of flesh you put in the ambulance alive and haul out dead" (*NN*, 101).

After the war, however, the Camera Eye persona is attracted by the excitement of traveling and by Greenwich Village bohemianism. Not until the late 1920s does the "two nations" theme again move him deeply. At this point he faces a conflict between his newly activated social conscience and his personal doubts about his ability to play a role in the struggle. He is also troubled by the conflict between the high idealism of his thoughts about "the course of history and what leverage might pry the owners loose from power and bring back (I too Walt Whitman) our storybook democracy" (*BM*, 150) and the pull of more personal desires and needs, as is suggested by the images of "dollars are silky in her hair soft in her dress sprout in the elaborately contrived rosepetals that you kiss become pungent and crunchy in the speakeasy dinner" (*BM*, 151). So he "peel[s] the speculative onion of doubt" (*BM*, 151) until the crisis of the Sacco-Vanzetti case persuades him that personal and literary activism must be his course. Standing in Plymouth, where Vanzetti lived and the pilgrims landed, he thinks:

> how can I make them feel how our fathers our uncles haters of oppression came to this coast     how say Don't let them scare you     how make them feel who are your oppressors America
>
> rebuild the ruined words worn slimy in the mouths of lawyers districtattorneys collegepresidents judges without the old words the immigrants haters of oppres-

sion brought to Plymouth how can you know who are your betrayers America (*BM*, 437)

To "rebuild the old words," he now realizes, is his function and commitment—to speak truly and movingly about the misuse of the great and noble terms—liberty, freedom, democracy—and so to help recreate their meaning and potency.

The deaths of Sacco and Vanzetti lead to anger but also to a hardening of this commitment:

> America our nation has been beaten by strangers who have turned our language inside out who have taken the clean words our fathers spoke and made them slimy and foul. . . .
>
>     all right we are two nations. . . .
>
>     but do they know that the old words of the immigrants are being renewed in blood and agony tonight do they know that the old American speech of the haters of oppression is new tonight in the mouth of an old woman from Pittsburgh of a husky boilermaker from Frisco . . . the language of the beaten nation is not forgotten in our ears tonight (*BM*, 462–463)

"We stand defeated America," the Camera Eye persona cries out at the close of this segment, but he himself stands confirmed in his role. At Harlan County, in the last Camera Eye of the trilogy, he recounts the betrayal of the miners by owners, government, and conservative labor and concludes with a statement which announces both temporary defeat and continuing effort: "we have only words against" (*BM*, 525).

In effect, the Camera Eye persona has brought us to the point in the late 1920s when he committed himself to write *U.S.A.* He has accepted the premise that "two nations" exist in America in part because of the betrayal of the language of freedom and democracy and that he, as a writer, can help restore the "ruined words" through his art. The Camera Eye in *U.S.A.* is thus not only a typical nineteenth-century development story in which understanding is gained through experience. Like such nineteenth-century poems as Whitman's "Out of the Cradle Endlessly Rocking," it also embodies in its story of growth a preoccupation with the growth of an artist's imaginative power and poetic role, a preoccupation which has fulfilled itself in the work we are reading.

*U.S.A.* thus combines two nineteenth-century forms—the romantic poem of the development of an imaginative sensibility and the Victorian novel of plot. Dos Passos' pervasive interlacing and cross-stitching of character, event, and place in an extremely long work produce the equivalent of the

Victorian novel's effect of the presence of an organic authorial voice, of a voice in this instance which shapes through ironic analogues or clusters a coherent and powerful vision of life. The Camera Eye is not an anomaly within this organic voice but is rather a means toward confirming in the drama of an expanding consciousness the validity of the depiction of experience in the other modes.

　　Dos Passos' brilliant control of his technique and materials persuades us to accept the tragic view of American life portrayed in *U.S.A.* We are persuaded that America has been false to its traditional ideals, that these ideals are manipulated by the wealthy and powerful in order to maintain their status, but that there remains the possibility of struggle and even of renewal. It is true that at the close of the trilogy the "ruined words" appear to be irrecoverable. The advertising man Dick Savage is playing court to Myra Bingham, one of the heirs to Doc Bingham's patent-medicine empire, and is thereby uniting the false word and the false thing. The party apparatus is in control of the radical Left. And Sacco and Vanzetti are dead and the Harlan miners are crushed. "We stand defeated America" is an apt response to these conditions. Nevertheless, Wesley Everest and Joe Hill were willing to die for truth in the past, and Veblen and Frank Lloyd Wright erected monuments of truth for the future. "We have only words against," but words can be as potent a weapon for truth as for falsehood. Out of the conscious ambivalence of this vision Dos Passos has created the vast tragic structure which is *U.S.A.*

*–Twentieth-Century American Literary Naturalism: An Interpretation* (Carbondale: Southern Illinois University Press, 1982), pp. 39–64

### Notes

1. The principal works by Dos Passos which provide information about his life and ideas are *The Best Times: An Informal Memoir* (New York: New American Library, 1966); *Occasions and Protests* (Chicago: Regnery, 1964), a collection of essays; and *The Fourteenth Chronicle: Letters and Diaries of John Dos Passos,* ed. Townsend Ludington (Boston: Gambit, 1973).

2. Some influential early studies which stress these themes in Dos Passos's work are: Maxwell Geismar, *Writers in Crisis: The American Novel, 1925–1940* (Boston: Houghton Mifflin, 1942), pp. 87–139; Alfred Kazin, *On Native Grounds* (New York: Reynal & Hitchcock, 1942), pp. 341–359; and Malcolm Cowley, "The Poet and the World," *New Republic,* 70 (27 April 1932): 303–305. (The essays by Kazin and Cowley are reprinted in *Dos Passos, the Critics, and the Writer's Intention,* ed. Allen Belkind [Carbondale: Southern Illinois University Press, 1971].) The themes appear in Dos Passos's essays as early as "A Humble Pro-

test," *Harvard Monthly,* 62 (June 1916): 115–120, and "America and the Pursuit of Happiness," *Nation,* 160 (29 December 1920): 777–778.

3. *The Fourteenth Chronicle,* p. 193.

4. The fullest study of Dos Passos's debt to his father's ideas occurs in Melvin Landsberg's *Dos Passos' Path to U.S.A.: A Political Biography, 1912–1936* (Boulder: Colorado Associated University Press, 1972), pp. 1–19. See also Dos Passos's own account in *The Best Times,* pp. 1–40.

5. See Landsberg, *Dos Passos' Path to U.S.A.,* for a number of other such borrowings by Dos Passos.

6. "Looking Back on U.S.A.," *New York Times,* 25 October 1959, sec. 2, p. 5.

7. "Statement of Belief," *Bookman,* 68 (September 1928): 26.

8. Introduction, *Three Soldiers* (New York: Modern Library, 1932), p. vii.

9. *U.S.A.* (New York: Modern Library, 1937), p. vii. Citations will hereafter appear in the text. Since the three novels of *U.S.A.* are paginated separately in this edition, I will cite both the novel and the page numbers, using the following abbreviations: FP–*The 42nd Parallel;* NN–*Nineteen Nineteen;* and BM–*The Big Money.*

10. Joseph Warren Beach offers some shrewd early comments on Dos Passos's verbal irony in his *American Fiction, 1920–1940* (New York: Macmillan, 1941), p. 66. A more recent discussion is by David L. Vanderwerken, "*U.S.A.:* Dos Passos and the 'Old Words,'" *Twentieth Century Literature,* 23 (May 1977): 195–228.

11. Landsberg, *Dos Passos' Path to U.S.A.,* p. 254 n. 41. A number of critics have commented in passing on the relationship between Dos Passos's narrative prose style in *U.S.A.* and Joycean stream of consciousness. These include John Lydenberg, "Dos Passos' *U.S.A.:* The Words of the Hollow Men," in *Essays on Determinism in American Literature,* ed. Sydney J. Krause (Kent, Ohio: Kent State University Press, 1964), pp. 97–107; Herbert M. McLuhan, "John Dos Passos: Technique vs. Sensibility," in *Dos Passos: A Collection of Critical Essays,* ed. Andrew Hook (Englewood Cliffs, N.J.: Prentice-Hall, 1974), pp. 148–161; George J. Becker, *John Dos Passos* (New York: Ungar, 1974), p. 48. One of the earliest comments about stream of consciousness in Dos Passos's fiction occurs in Jean-Paul Sartre's "John Dos Passos and *1919*" (1947), in *Dos Passos,* ed. Hook, pp. 61–69.

12. *U.S.A.,* p. vii.

13. "The Search for Identity in the Novels of John Dos Passos," *PMLA,* 76 (March 1961): 133–149; quoted from *Dos Passos,* ed. Belkind, p. 187.

14. Frank Gado, "An Interview with John Dos Passos," *Idol: The Literary Quarterly of Union College,* 45 (1969): 23.

15. A brief discussion of this aspect of the Camera Eye occurs in Townsend Ludington's "The Ordering of the Camera Eye in *U.S.A.*," *American Literature,* 49 (November 1977): 443–446.

16. *Writers on the Left* (New York, 1961), p. 348. Landsberg, in his *Dos Passos' Path to U.S.A.,* has a full account of Dos Passos's political ideas of the 1920s and 1930s. He and others have noted the important role which Dos Passos's dismay over the Communist involvement in the Harlan mine workers' strike played in his growing antagonism to the party.

*Christopher Holdridge, Dos Passos, Lucy Dos Passos, Rumsey Marvin, and Betty Holdridge Dos Passos at the Dos Passos home in Virginia, Easter 1966 (from Townsend Ludington, ed.,* The Fourteenth Chronicle: Letters and Diaries of John Dos Passos, *1973)*

## Reading John Dos Passos Reading Mass Culture in *U.S.A.*

Thomas F. Strychacz

*Thomas F. Strychacz teaches at Mills College.*

Early in *The 42nd Parallel* Mac's Uncle Tim, a printer, purchases a new linotype machine, an event that causes a temporary stoppage of work, speeds up the work of printing, and then indirectly leads to the eventual closure of Uncle Tim's business. The new press possesses an undeniable power. "For a whole day there was no work done," the narrator remarks. "Everyone stood around looking at the tall black intricate machine that stood there like an organ in a church. When the machine was working and the printshop filled with the hot smell of molten metal, everybody's eyes followed the quivering inquisitive arm that darted and flexed above the keyboard" ([1938] 1978, 31).[1] The linotype seems to focus the accumulated values of more than a century of a revolutionary democracy built on the constitutional guarantee of free speech, rational inquiry into the nature and abuses of political systems, and the free dissemination of printed knowledge. It allows Uncle Tim to articulate his beliefs and distribute them in the shape of a handbill entitled "An Ernest Protest" and signed "A Citizen." It seems the apogee of the Enlightenment. Yet the small printing press, even as the workers stare at it in awe, has already become an anachronism, more suitable for some museum charting the transformations of American industry—as the workers' first awestruck response perhaps suggests. For during a strike in the printing trades the master printers of Chicago buy out Uncle Tim's outstanding paper and force him into bankruptcy. And that silencing is foreshadowed by Mac's failure to distribute Uncle Tim's handbills when a cop asks to see the permit Mac does not possess. By the end of the trilogy that printing press seems as ancient as a Gothic cathedral, its intricacy supplanted by massive electronic systems of communication and the even more intricate systems of corporate capital that support them.

Taken as a whole, the *U.S.A.* trilogy documents in unprecedented detail the formation of interlocking structures of power at the turn of the century. As the preface (added after Dos Passos completed the trilogy) suggests, U.S.A. is "a group of holding companies, some aggregations of trade unions, a set of laws bound in calf, a radio network, a chain of moving picture theatres, a column of stockquotations." No one person masterminds this process of progressive agglomeration; no one person is truly responsible for locating and defining centers of power, arranging relays, and overseeing the entire system. In this respect Dos Passos's understanding of power is structuralist and close to Michel Foucault's sense of power as invisible, pervasive, secret, and autonomous. The consecutive biographies of Thomas Edison ("The Electrical Wizard") and Charles Proteus Steinmetz ("Proteus") in *The 42nd Parallel* are crucial to this vision. In "Proteus," Steinmetz's mathematical equations make possible "all the transformers that crouch in little boxes and gableroofed houses in all the hightension lines all over everywhere. The mathematical symbols of Steinmetz's law are the patterns of all transformers everywhere." Presumably, those electrical transformers also represent the human transformers of American society. Steinmetz, as his middle name and Dos Passos's title for the biography suggests, is one such transformer, imbued with the power to change the face of America "all over everywhere." Thomas Edison, who brings invention to bear on Steinmetz's formulas in order to produce "systems of generation, distribution, regulation and measurement of electric current, sockets, switches, insulators," is described as another such magician in "The Electrical Wizard." His seminal work on the movie camera sets up the Hollywood dream merchants, who would within a few years work their own protean transformations on the American imagination.

By the end of *The Big Money,* abstract systems of mathematical representation transformed into material systems for generating and distributing power are transformed back into the abstract systems of capital. In "Power Superpower," Samuel Insull's equally intricate and equally baffling regulation of capital operates by similarly delicate mechanisms. "It has been figured out," the narrator tells us, "that one dollar in Middle West Utilities controlled seventeen hundred and fifty dollars invested by the public in the subsidiary companies that actually did the work of producing electricity. With the delicate lever of a voting trust controlling the stock of the two top holdingcompanies he controlled a twelfth of the power output of America." As Dos Passos puts it nicely in the biography of "The House of Morgan," this architecture of power operates on "the cantilever principle, through interlocking directorates."

Insull called it "superpower"; yet "superpower," Insull's biography makes abundantly clear, controls him. At one point Insull panics for fear of losing his delicate leverage; after the stock market crash he becomes a "tottering czar," his power dissolving into the confusion of his business affairs. "Insull's companies," despite his vaunted sense of control, "were intertwined in a tangle that no bookkeeper has ever been able to unravel." The invisible structures that make possible his extravagant thieving, however, outlast him. Samuel Insull, far from being the great villain of "Power Superpower," seems its last great human architect; he seems the last human sign of the presence of power. In its protracted and comic account of Insull's attempts to escape justice, the biography hovers between satirizing Insull and presenting him as larger than life; it traces a trajectory from "superpower" to the tale of a rascally but charismatic "deposed monarch." As if in tacit recognition of the all-pervading invisibility of "superpower," the biography's colorful finale silences it. Superpower is not removed with the person of Insull; it continues on to invest the vacancy his removal creates.

But if the biography depicts an architect progressively overwhelmed by the cantilever structures he has never quite controlled, it is perhaps surprising that Insull masterfully interacts with the news media. This is nowhere more apparent than during his trial which, as the narrator remarks with a touch of dry Hemingwayesque humor, "was very beautiful." Unlike the grim story of Sacco and Vanzetti's trials and executions, partially played out in the accompanying Camera Eye sections, the Insulls "stole the show." They "smiled at reporters, they posed for photographers" and are eulogized by the newspapers; in a final lugubrious analogy to the Sacco-Vanzetti case, thousands of ruined investors supposedly sit "crying over the home editions at the thought of how Mr. Insull had suffered." Interestingly, Insull's career change from manipulator to "deposed monarch" is accomplished without direct manipulation on his part. "When the handouts stopped" directly after Insull's resignation, the narrator tells us, the "newspapers and politicians turned on him." But the newspapers, it seems, are not bound in any conspiracy at the trial. They offer aid gratis; they participate in the creation of a grand pseudoevent—all the more dramatic after the odyssey of Insull's Mediterranean escape from justice was played out before the news media; and they do so out of consent rather than coercion. Like William Randolph Hearst, whose biography precedes Insull's, Insull understands how to cash in on "geewhizz emotion" (1112). The narrator portrays his Horatio Alger tale of his "struggle to make good, his love for his home and the kiddies," the fiction of his "honest errors," his strategy of becoming just

*Dos Passos (© Bettman/CORBIS)*

"folks," as more than just lying of Odyssean proportions. The newspapers' unwitting complicity with ideologies that underpin American middle-class consciousness–father, big man, poor boy made good, the underdog–plays a major role in Insull's show. Dos Passos's rather Gramscian insight is that consent of such a wide-ranging and spectacular nature cannot be merely bought or engineered; it must in some fashion already exist, woven inextricably into the nation's psychosocial fabric.

Mass communication in America does not simply function by way of conspiracy; the conspirators themselves participate in an interlocked system of power "all over everywhere" that is not only too complex to be grasped by any individual but is fundamentally structural: Any individual seeking to understand it is always in the position of having been constituted and embedded within it. Dos Passos's trilogy thus concerns the largely silent functioning of the unconscious "transparent" domain of ideology, to which the mass of Americans consent as inalienably true and real. For every hired newspaper editor there is one (such as the one who fires Mary French) who just dislikes foreign-born strikers; for all the power of Hearst's empire of print, there are movie actresses and political careers (his own) he cannot launch and wars he cannot initiate (1116). Unexpected resistances arise out of a mass mind whose dynamic its would-be manipulators do not clearly understand. Nevertheless, Dos Passos is acutely aware that technicians of mass consciousness work most powerfully and completely at the unconscious level. The biography of Steinmetz provides an early analysis of

this issue. The biography appraises Steinmetz's role in the formation of vast industrial systems depending on a ubiquitous power grid; but it is General Electric that at once makes his discoveries significant and makes significance of his discoveries. "General Electric humored him, let him be a Socialist . . . and the publicity department talked up the wizard, the medicine man who knew the symbols that opened up the doors of Ali Baba's cave . . . the publicity department poured oily stories into the ears of the American public every Sunday and Steinmetz became the little parlor magician." He "became" the little parlor magician, that is, to the serpent-tongued PR men and to the deceived public. "Became" attributes to him a presence and solidity he does not possess (for he does not really become a magician) but also, oddly enough, underplays his far-reaching significance to General Electric as "the most valuable piece of apparatus" they had. Among varied representations of him (little parlor magician, Socialist, wizard, medicine man), Steinmetz disappears as a human being to emerge as the linking apparatus between the power grid and structures of ideological manipulation. It is with some irony, then, that the "mathematical symbols of Steinmetz's law are the patterns of all transformers everywhere," for the publicity department transforms his abstract mathematical symbols into a world of symbolic representations, and the wizardry of technology into a magical hocus-pocus.

This leads to a double consequence. Neither Steinmetz nor (presumably) the publicity department's public recognizes this radical disembodying of significance, this gradual warping of incalculable technological changes into a weightless rhetoric suitable for fairy tales. The PR man's "open sesame" to Ali Baba's cave of riches depends on foreclosing precisely that relationship between Steinmetz's abstract symbols and the power grab it occasioned. To extend Dos Passos's own figure of speech, talking up Steinmetz as magician is also to "talk around" him. And it has the further advantage, no doubt, of disguising the whereabouts of the forty (or more) thieves, who hide now behind "oily stories" rather than in empty jars of oil. But though the PR rhetoric masks from the public all knowledge of a crystallizing structure of power, that rhetoric, we should note, also creates a rich, dense, symbolic language to which *The Thousand and One Nights* may after all be an appropriate analogy. The publicity department, like Scheherazade, spins out stories to stave off the moment of death (or discovery); more importantly, their stories possess the kind of imaginative power most readers do associate with literature. In this sense, Dos Passos grants mass communication the kind of totalizing power we saw in Dreiser's *An American Tragedy* while posing the possibility that its idiom might be dramatic and entertaining rather than banal. Although the primary goal of the PR department is to work by way of a series of disengagements to pry apart language and its underlying formation of power, it captures Steinmetz in a free play of signifiers that is all the more dazzling for an ostensible plenitude of meaning. Steinmetz's menagerie of gila monsters and alligators plays off his physical deformity and oddly intensifies his charisma, while his "greenhouseful of cactuses lit up by mercury lights" pays homage to his own power of genesis and (electrical) generation; at the same time, the very extravagance of these hobbies suggests their essential triviality. The publicity department engineers him and language alike. Its signifiers lead to hidden signifieds: wizard (protean transformations, authority); gila monsters (an alien power, yet also perhaps dangerous, needing to be leashed); talking crows (Steinmetz was a Socialist who made "speeches that nobody understood"). The PR men brilliantly dramatize him as wizard yet diminish him as a little parlor magician firmly under the company's control.

In *U.S.A.*, the fictional J. Ward Moorehouse, counterpart to real-life publicity departments and Hearstian appropriations of the press, and based on the real PR man Ivy Lee, is the arbiter of this world of sliding, disembodied, yet powerful images and meanings. Class orator and essayist, book distributor, reporter and erstwhile songwriter, Moorehouse is responsible for the "molding of the public mind" (1145) and for nothing less than a new poetics of history, politics, and technology. Early in his career, for instance, we find Moorehouse puzzling "over what kind of literature from a factory would be appealing to him." He

> would see long processions of andirons, grates, furnaces, fittings, pumps, sausage-grinders, drills, calipers, vises, casters, drawerpulls pass between his face and the mirror and wonder how they could be made attractive to the retail trade. He was shaving himself with a Gillette; why was he shaving with a Gillette instead of some other kind of razor? 'Bessemer' was a good name, smelt of money and mighty rolling mills and great executives stepping out of limousines. (214)

Moorehouse neatly characterizes a number of advertising strategies. Not surprisingly, he associates products with concepts, seizing on archetypal images from the mass psychology of capitalism to spark a relationship made and apprehended, on the whole, unconsciously. Thus Moorehouse "smells" the value of Bessemer as a good name rather than intellectually defining its appeal. Images of the status to which Americans aspire, or should aspire, invest Moorehouse's lively dramas: tools in celebratory procession, almost as if cast in a Disney cartoon, and great executives stepping out of limousines. Moorehouse's colorfully spliced fragments of action–name, money, mills, executives, cars–sug-

---

*Davis Lee Clark, a University of Texas English professor, brought to Dos Passos's attention the unauthorized circulation of excerpts from* U.S.A. *by those wishing to halt the teaching of the novel at the university.*

The University of Texas
Austin 12
Department of English
December 29, 1944

John Dos Passos
c/o Houghton Mifflin Company
Boston, Mass.

My Dear Mr. Dos Passos:

No doubt you have heard something about the turmoil at the University of Texas. You may not know that one of the charges brought against the fired president and a number of the faculty about to be dismissed was the use of one of your novels, *The Big Money*, by certain members of the English staff in a sophomore course in modern literature. The governing board of the University, the Board of Regents, have declared the book to be filthy, etc. Some six thousand words have been excerpted by a lawyer for the Galveston Chamber of Commerce and by the Lieutenant Governor of the State and is being circulated. This seems to me to be a clear violation of copyright.

Sincerely,
Davis Lee Clark
Professor of English

Please be so kind as not to divulge my name for reasons you can readily surmise. I enclose a copy of part of the testimony before an investigating committee.

---

gests his intuitive grasp of a covert and interior relationship to power. And the very crudity of his imagination points, paradoxically, to a formal sophistication he does not know he possesses. One thinks of Dada, cubist collage, surrealism: arts of disruption, eschewing traditional logics of perspective, connectivity, and narrative for the immediacy of upwelling fantasies and the vibrant interval between juxtaposed images. One thinks of that modernist predilection for the primitive and of the Poundian "vortex," functioning, like Moorehouse's hard, concrete images, to create whirlpools of associative imagery. And one thinks of Dos Passos's own writing strategies, to which Moorehouse's intuitive mythmaking bears a curious affinity. Moorehouse carries other poetic credentials, too. A little later, on a train bound for Chicago, he eulogizes American industry like some latter-day Whitman or Shelley, his words coming in a spontaneous eruption as though he were more medium than orator:

> The rumble of the train made the cords of his voice vibrate. He forgot everything in his own words . . . American industry like a steamengine, like a highpower locomotive on a great express train charging through the night of the old individualistic methods . . . What does a steamengine require? Co-operation, co-ordination of the inventor's brain, the promoter's brain that made the development of these highpower products possible . . . Co-ordination of capital, the storedup energy of the race in the form of credit intelligently directed. (227; Dos Passos's ellipses)

These passages, the first in which Moorehouse meditates seriously on his PR work, initiates an increasing uncertainty about just how nonliterary his "literature from a factory" really is, and just how much to scorn his secretary, Janey, who admires the office's "literature about bathsalts and chemicals and the employees' baseball team" (279). Dos Passos defines much more clearly than James or Dreiser a new visionary company whose tactics really do draw on the stock of imaginings, images, and formal strategies thought to be the preserve of literary work. That debased sense of literature as "written material" quickly becomes subject to revision as we see Moorehouse's tactics colliding with and overlapping Dos Passos's at every step. Dos Passos's concern is U.S.A., "the speech of the people" (7); Moorehouse's is to use words as a form of capital, vast systems mediating the "storedup energy of the race" (227) and tapping energy from the main conduits of the American psyche. Moorehouse also imaginatively invests language with powerful symbolic meanings; indeed, those meanings must already and always have invested him. Moorehouse puts us in mind of William Randolph Hearst at Manila Bay, who "brandishing a sixshooter went in with the longboat through the surf and captured twentysix unarmed halfdrowned Spanish sailors on the beach and forced them to kneel and kiss the American flag/in front of the camera" (1113). The point is not that Hearst's cowboy heroics and the resulting dramatic tableau before the recording camera are false, for powerful collective emotions like patriotism and a desire for military power here find appropriate expression.

That process of capitalizing on language works, not because of the manipulations necessary to disguise the appropriation of language and the usurping of its true functions, but because of what is genuine and (as George Flack put it in *The Reverberator*) "straight from the tap." At the level at which images and words flow unbidden from a reservoir of largely unconscious impulses, desires, and beliefs, public relations and Flack's journalism become commanding idioms. Thus Manila Bay is not a "pseudo-event" in Daniel Boorstin's sense of the term as a spectacle staged for the benefit of the media, and therefore incomplete, false, empty. The staging does not invalidate the spectacle; like Moorehouse's fantasies of mighty rolling mills and limousines, these formal strategies of association, juxtaposition, and dramatic "retailing" of images (to use the pun Dos Passos often employs on retail/retell) are evocative and powerful. To call Manila Bay a pseudo-event is to ignore a new poetics that does not record history but imaginatively refashions it. Indeed, this form of historiography, whereby the recording eye is not viewed as trans- or ahistorical but itself part of the onrush of events has become increasingly common in the twentieth century, Dos Passos's own Camera Eye sections being the obvious analogy. This is not to say that Moorehouse and Hearst cannot be attacked, but that the hollowness we attribute to them should not be confused with the dramatic power of their fiction making. Put simply, the problem we face in uncovering the hollowness of Hearst at Manila Bay is not that the event is banal but *that it is dramatic*.

—*Modernism, Mass Culture, and Professionalism* (New York: Cambridge University Press, 1993), pp. 122–128

**Note**

1. Dos Passos's trilogy was published as *The 42nd Parallel* (1930); *1919* (1932); *The Big Money* (1936); and in one edition in 1938.

## The Banning of *U.S.A.* at the University of Texas
Virginia Spencer Carr

*Virginia Spencer Carr describes an effort in 1944 to have* U.S.A. *banned at the University of Texas.*

Sales of *U.S.A.* increased significantly during the summer and fall of 1944 when a member of the Board of Regents of the University of Texas called *U.S.A.* the "dirtiest, most obscene, most perverted book ever written in the English language" and demanded the firing of the professor who recommended it to his sophomore English class. The attack stemmed from an academic freedom and tenure controversy raging in Austin with political ramifications reverberating across the state when the nine-member Board of Regents led a Red witch-hunt against its liberal president, Homer Price Rainey (members reportedly branded anyone who had voted for Roosevelt an "undesirable" or a "radical"). Rainey was fired November 1, 1944, but could not be removed as a professor of the university because he was tenured. A Texas State Senate investigating committee heard testimony of the offended regent who asserted that "about 1400 or 1500 pages of *U.S.A.* are filled with filth and obscenity. No teacher who would put that book on a list for a sophomore to read is fit to teach in a penitentiary—let alone at the University. As long as I'm regent, I'm going to repress that book and put out any teacher who teaches it." A spokesman for the Southern Association of Colleges and Secondary Schools of Texas sided with the regent. Strident protests were registered by prominent teachers, administrators, and the university itself, whereupon a Committee of Correspondence of the Student Union of the University of Texas released the following statement:

> In reality, *U.S.A.* is a deeply moral book, protesting against materialism and public and private immorality of the Harding-Coolidge-Hoover era. In the novel, sin is depicted in repulsive forms, and the characters who engage in it are neither happy nor prosperous. There are passages in which wrongdoing

is depicted in strong language, but to elucidate the ancient text: "The Wages of Sin Is Death." These passages, when taken out of context, can be made to give a completely erroneous impression of the book. Shakespeare, Chaucer, Swift and other great masters of the past can be similarly abused. There is in the book a strong undercurrent of faith in the American way of life.

The controversy was still unresolved during the winter of 1944–45 when an English professor at the University of Texas—who asked Dos Passos not to divulge his name—wrote to apprise him that some six thousand words had been excerpted from his book by a lawyer for the Galveston Chamber of Commerce and by the lieutenant governor of the state and were being circulated. "This seems to me to be a clear violation of copyright," he added. Dos Passos chose not to act upon the infringement, however. He was more interested in knowing that his book was being read than in seeking redress as the injured party. A few months later, the Student Council for Academic Freedom at the University of Texas polled eighty-four leading universities and colleges across the country and learned that sixty-eight of them used *U.S.A.* in their English classes.

—*Dos Passos: A Life* (Garden City, N.Y.: Doubleday, 1984), pp. 428–429

*Dos Passos and Betty Holdridge Dos Passos (his second wife), late 1960s*
*(Collection of Lucy Dos Passos Coggin)*

421

## The Permanence of *U.S.A.*
Donald Pizer

I was in my teens, in the 1940s, when I first read *U.S.A.* I was living in a Brooklyn neighborhood, almost a village in its thin connection with the "outside" world. One sign of its insularity was that it lacked a public library, and thus one of the rituals of my boyhood was a weekly bicycle journey to a fairly distant (or so it seemed then) adjoining neighborhood, where I would draw out a supply of books from a tiny store-front library.

Like many of my generation, I was vaguely aware of *U.S.A.* as a book to read, and being young and a fast reader, I was not deterred by the immense size of the Modern Library edition with its thin, semi-transparent paper. I read the work slowly at first, and then more and more rapidly, until I was fully immersed in it. I had somehow stepped out of my narrow segment of life into a universe of people and events that was America. I didn't know then why and how the book held me captive, but I was indeed its prisoner. Today, as a student of the complex achitectonics of *U.S.A.*, I know a great deal more about how it achieves its effects and what these effects are, but I have never duplicated, in reading it again and again, the excitement, the rushing compulsion to read and to continue reading, of that first encounter.

When, some forty years later, I told my teenage daughter the story of my weekly trip to the library on my bicycle, through rain and snow, she asked, "Did you realize the Lincoln parallel then or did it come to you later?" But when she herself then read *U.S.A.* out of curiosity because I was working on Dos Passos, she too disappeared from human intercourse for the few weeks it took her to encompass it. And so it will always be, I think, whatever the means by which we are led to it, for this great work of the imagination.

–"John Dos Passos: A Centennial Celebration,"
in *Dictionary of Literary Biography Yearbook:
1996* (Detroit: Gale/Bruccoli Clark
Layman, 1997), p. 177

# Checklist of Further Reading

## Dos Passos's Publications

**Books:**

*One Man's Initiation—1917*. London: Allen & Unwin, 1920; New York: Doran, 1920. Republished as *First Encounter*. New York: Philosophical Library, 1945. Republished as *One Man's Initiation—1917*, unexpurgated edition. Ithaca, N.Y.: Cornell University Press, 1969. Novel.

*Three Soldiers*. New York: Doran, 1921; London: Hurst & Blackett, 1922. Novel.

*Rosinante to the Road Again*. New York: Doran, 1922. Travel essays.

*A Pushcart to the Curb*. New York: Doran, 1922. Poetry.

*Streets of Night*. New York: Doran, 1923; London: Secker, 1923. Republished, edited by Michael Clark. Selinsgrove, Pa.: Susquehanna University Press, 1990. Novel.

*Manhattan Transfer*. New York: Harper, 1925; London: Constable, 1927. Novel.

*The Garbage Man*. New York: Harper, 1926; London: Constable, 1927. Play.

*Orient Express*. New York: Harper, 1927. London: Cape, 1928. Travel essays.

*Facing the Chair: Story of the Americanization of Two Foreignborn Workmen*. Boston: Sacco-Vanzetti Defense Fund, 1927. Polemic.

*Airways, Inc.* New York: Macaulay, 1928. Play.

*The 42nd Parallel*. New York: Harper, 1930; London: Constable, 1930. Novel.

*1919*. New York: Harcourt, Brace, 1932; London: Constable, 1932. Novel.

*In All Countries*. New York: Harcourt, Brace, 1934; London: Constable, 1934. Travel essays.

*Three Plays: The Garbage Man, Airways, Inc., Fortune Heights*. New York: Harcourt, Brace, 1934.

*The Big Money*. New York: Harcourt, Brace, 1936; London: Constable, 1936. Novel.

*U.S.A.* New York: Harcourt, Brace, 1938; London: Constable, 1938. Comprises *The 42nd Parallel, 1919,* and *The Big Money*.

*Journeys Between Wars*. New York: Harcourt, Brace, 1938; London: Constable, 1938. Travel essays.

*The Villages Are the Heart of Spain*. Chicago: Esquire-Coronet, 1938. Polemic.

*Adventures of a Young Man*. New York: Harcourt, Brace, 1939; London: Constable, 1939. Novel.

*The Ground We Stand On*. New York: Harcourt, Brace, 1941; London: Routledge, 1942. History essays.

*Number One*. Boston: Houghton Mifflin, 1943; London: Constable, 1944. Novel.

*State of the Nation.* Boston: Houghton Mifflin, 1944; London: Routledge, 1945. Travel and polemical essays.

*Tour of Duty.* Boston: Houghton Mifflin, 1946. Travel.

*The Grand Design.* Boston: Houghton Mifflin, 1949; London: Lehmann, 1949. Novel.

*The Prospect Before Us.* Boston: Houghton Mifflin, 1950; London: Lehmann, 1951. Polemic.

*Chosen Country.* Boston: Houghton Mifflin, 1951; London: Lehmann, 1952. Novel.

*District of Columbia.* Boston: Houghton Mifflin, 1952. Comprises *Adventures of a Young Man, Number One,* and *The Grand Design.*

*The Head and Heart of Thomas Jefferson.* Garden City, N.Y.: Doubleday, 1954; London: Hale, 1955. Biography.

*Most Likely to Succeed.* New York: Prentice-Hall, 1954; London: Hale, 1955. Novel.

*The Theme Is Freedom.* New York: Dodd, Mead, 1956. Essays.

*The Men Who Made the Nation.* Garden City, N.Y.: Doubleday, 1957. History.

*The Great Days.* New York: Sagamore, 1958; London: Hale, 1959. Novel.

*Prospects of a Golden Age.* Englewood Cliffs, N.J.: Prentice-Hall, 1959. History.

*Midcentury.* Boston: Houghton Mifflin, 1961; London: Deutsch, 1961. Novel.

*Mr. Wilson's War.* Garden City, N.Y.: Doubleday, 1962; London: Hamilton, 1963. History.

*Brazil on the Move.* Garden City, N.Y.: Doubleday, 1963; London: Sidgwick & Jackson, 1964. Travel essays.

*U.S.A.: A Dramatic Revue,* by Dos Passos and Paul Shyre. New York: S. French, 1963. Play.

*Thomas Jefferson: The Making of a President.* Boston: Houghton Mifflin, 1964. History.

*Occasions and Protests.* New York: Regnery, 1964. Polemic essays.

*The Shackles of Power: Three Jeffersonian Decades.* Garden City, N.Y.: Doubleday, 1966. Biography.

*The Best Times: An Informal Memoir.* New York: New American Library, 1966. Memoir.

*The Portugal Story: Three Decades of Exploration and Discovery.* Garden City, N.Y.: Doubleday, 1969; London: Hale, 1970. History.

*Easter Island: Island of Enigmas.* Garden City, N.Y.: Doubleday, 1971. Travel.

*Century's Ebb: The Thirteenth Chronicle.* Boston: Gambit, 1975. Novel.

*John Dos Passos: The Major Nonfictional Prose,* edited by Donald Pizer. Detroit: Wayne State University Press, 1988.

*Afterglow and Other Undergraduate Writings,* edited by Richard Layman. Detroit: Omnigraphics, 1990.

**Selected Contributions to Books and Periodicals:**
"A Humble Protest." *Harvard Monthly,* 62 (June 1916): 115–120.

"Against American Literature." *New Republic,* 8 (14 October 1916): 269–271.

*Eight Harvard Poets*. New York: Lawrence J. Gomme, 1917, pp. 29–41.

"300 N.Y. Agitators Reach Passaic." *New Masses*, 1 ( June 1926): 8.

"The Pit and the Pendulum." *New Masses*, 1 (August 1926): 10–11, 30.

"An Open Letter to President Lowell." *Nation*, 127 (4 August 1927): 176.

"Statement of Belief." *Bookman*, 68 (September 1928): 26.

*Harlan Miners Speak*. New York: Harcourt, Brace, 1932. Passim.

"Whither the American Writer?" *Modern Quarterly*, 6 (Summer 1932): 11–12.

"Four Nights in a Garden: A Campaign Yarn." *Common Sense*, 1 (5 December 1932): 20–22.

"The Writer as Technician." In *American Writers Congress*, edited by Henry Hart. New York: International Publishers, 1935.

"Grosz Comes to America." *Esquire*, 6 (September 1936): 105, 128, 131.

"Farewell to Europe." *Common Sense*, 6 ( July 1937): 9–11.

"The Communist Party and the War Spirit." *Common Sense*, 6 (December 1937): 11–14.

"Presenting Tom Paine." In Thomas Paine, *The Living Thoughts of Tom Paine*. New York: Longmans, 1940.

"Looking Back on *U.S.A.*" *New York Times*, 25 October 1959, sec. 2, p. 5.

"What Makes a Novelist?" *National Review*, 20 (16 January 1968): 29–32.

## Publications about Dos Passos and *U.S.A.*

**Bibliographies:**
Potter, Jack. *A Bibliography of John Dos Passos*. Chicago: Normandie House, 1950.

Rohrkemper, John. *John Dos Passos: A Reference Guide*. Boston: G. K. Hall, 1980.

Sanders, David. *John Dos Passos: A Comprehensive Bibliography*. New York: Garland, 1987.


**Letters:**
Landsberg, Melvin, ed. *John Dos Passos' Correspondence with Arthur K. McComb; or, "Learn to Sing the Carmagnole."* Niwot: University Press of Colorado, 1991.

Ludington, Townsend, ed. *The Fourteenth Chronicle: Letters and Diaries of John Dos Passos*. Boston: Gambit, 1973.


**Biographies:**
Carr, Virginia Spencer. *Dos Passos: A Life*. Garden City, N.Y.: Doubleday, 1984.

Landsberg, Melvin. *Dos Passos' Path to U.S.A.: A Political Biography, 1912–1936*. Boulder: Colorado Associated University Press, 1972.

Ludington, Townsend. *John Dos Passos: A Twentieth Century Odyssey*. New York: Dutton, 1980.

**Essay Collections:**

Belkind, Allen, ed. *Dos Passos, the Critics, and the Writer's Intention*. Carbondale: Southern Illinois University Press, 1971.

Hook, Andrew, ed. *Dos Passos: A Collection of Critical Essays*. Englewood Cliffs, N.J.: Prentice-Hall, 1974.

Maine, Barry, ed. *Dos Passos: The Critical Heritage*. London: Routledge, 1988.

Sanders, David, ed. *The Merrill Studies in U.S.A.* Columbus, Ohio: Merrill, 1972.

**Book-Length Critical Studies:**

Becker, George J. *John Dos Passos*. New York: Ungar, 1974.

Brantley, John. *The Fiction of John Dos Passos*. The Hague: Mouton, 1968.

Casey, Janet G. *Dos Passos and the Ideology of the Feminine*. Cambridge: Cambridge University Press, 1998.

Clark, Michael. *Dos Passos's Early Fiction, 1912–1938*. Selinsgrove, Pa.: Susquehanna University Press, 1987.

Colley, Iain. *Dos Passos and the Fiction of Despair*. Totowa, N.J.: Rowman & Littlefield, 1978.

Nanney, Lisa. *John Dos Passos*. New York: Twayne, 1998.

Pizer, Donald. *Dos Passos' U.S.A.: A Critical Study*. Charlottesville: University Press of Virginia, 1988.

Rosen, Robert C. *John Dos Passos: Politics and the Writer*. Lincoln: University of Nebraska Press, 1981.

Wagner, Linda W. *Dos Passos: Artist as American*. Austin: University of Texas Press, 1979.

Wrenn, John H. *John Dos Passos*. New York: Twayne, 1961.

**Critical Studies–Parts of Books:**

Aaron, Daniel. "The Adventures of John Dos Passos." In his *Writers on the Left: Episodes in American Literary Communism*. New York: Harcourt, Brace & World, 1961.

Aldridge, John W. "Dos Passos: The Energy of Despair." In his *After the Lost Generation: A Critical Study of the Writers of Two Wars*. New York: McGraw-Hill, 1951.

Conder, John. *Naturalism in America: The Classic Phase*. Lexington: University Press of Kentucky, 1984.

Cowley, Malcolm. *Exile's Return: A Narrative of Ideas*. New York: Norton, 1934.

Diggins, John P. *Up from Communism: Conservative Odysseys in American Intellectual History*. New York: Harper & Row, 1975.

Fishkin, Shelley Fisher. *From Fact to Fiction: Journalism and Imaginative Writing in America*. Baltimore: Johns Hopkins University Press, 1985.

Frohock, Wilbur M. "John Dos Passos: Of Time and Violence." In his *The Novel of Violence in America, 1920–1950*. Dallas: Southern Methodist University Press, 1950.

Geismar, Maxwell. "John Dos Passos: Conversion of a Hero." In his *Writers in Crisis: The American Novel Between Two Wars*. Boston: Hougton Mifflin, 1942.

Gelfant, Blanche H. "John Dos Passos: Synoptic Novelist." In her *The American City Novel*. Norman: University of Oklahoma Press, 1954.

Gurko, Leo. "John Dos Passos' *U.S.A.:* A 1930s Spectacular." In *Proletarian Writers of the Thirties,* edited by David Madden. Carbondale: Southern Illinois University Press, 1968.

Kazin, Alfred. *On Native Grounds: An Interpretation of Modern American Prose Literature*. New York: Harcourt, Brace, 1942.

Lydenberg, John. "Dos Passos' *U.S.A.:* The Words of the Hollow Men." In *Essays on Determinism in American Literature,* edited by Sydney J. Krause. Kent, Ohio: Kent State University Press, 1964.

Magny, Claude-Edmonde. *The Age of the American Novel: The Film Aesthetic of Fiction Between the Two Wars,* translated by Eleanor Hochman. New York: Ungar, 1972.

McLuhan, Herbert M. "Dos Passos: Technique vs. Sensibility." In *Fifty Years of the American Novel: A Christian Appraisal,* edited by H. C. Gardner. New York: Scribners, 1951.

Millgate, Michael. *American Social Fiction: James to Cozzens*. New York: Barnes & Noble, 1964.

Pizer, Donald. "John Dos Passos: *Nineteen-Nineteen.*" In his *American Expatriate Writing and the Paris Moment: Modernism and Place*. Baton Rouge: Louisiana State University Press, 1996.

Pizer. "John Dos Passos: *U.S.A.*" In his *Twentieth Century American Literary Naturalism: An Interpretation*. Carbondale: Southern Illinois University Press, 1982.

Price, Kenneth M. "Whitman, Dos Passos, and 'Our Storybook Democracy.'" In *Walt Whitman: The Centennial Essays,* edited by Ed Folsom. Iowa City: University of Iowa Press, 1994.

Sartre, Jean-Paul. "Dos Passos and His '1919.'" In his *Literary and Philosophical Essays,* translated by Annette Michelson. New York: Philosophical Library, 1955.

Strychacz, Thomas F. *Modernism, Mass Culture, and Professionalism*. Cambridge: Cambridge University Press, 1993.

Wickes, George. "The Education of John Dos Passos." In his *Americans in Paris, 1903–1939*. Garden City, N.Y.: Doubleday, 1969.

Widmer, Eleanor. "The Lost Girls of *U.S.A.:* Dos Passos' Thirties Movie." In *The Thirties: Fiction, Poetry, Drama,* edited by Warren French. Deland, Fla.: Edwards, 1967.


**Critical Studies in Periodicals:**
Aaron, Daniel. "*U.S.A.*" *American Heritage,* 47 (July–August 1996): 63–72.

Butler, Robert. "The American Quest for Pure Movement in Dos Passos' *U.S.A.*" *Twentieth Century Literature,* 30 (Spring 1984): 80–99.

Cowley, Malcolm. "The Poet and the World." *New Republic,* 70 (27 April 1932): 303–305.

Edwards, Justin. "The Man with a Camera Eye: Cinematic Form and Hollywood Malediction in John Dos Passos's *The Big Money.*" *Literature Film Quarterly,* 27 (1999): 245–254.

Foley, Barbara. "History, Fiction, and Satirical Form: The Example of Dos Passos' *1919.*" *Genre,* 12 (Fall 1979): 357–378.

Foley. "The Treatment of Time in *The Big Money:* An Examination of Ideology and Literary Form." *Modern Fiction Studies,* 26 (Autumn 1980): 447–467.

Gelfant, Blanche H. "The Search for Identity in the Novels of John Dos Passos." *PMLA*, 76 (March 1961): 133–149.

Goldman, Arnold. "Dos Passos and His *U.S.A.*" *New Literary History*, 1 (Spring 1970): 471–483.

Hughson, Lois. "In Search of the True America: Dos Passos' Debt to Whitman in *U.S.A.*" *Modern Fiction Studies*, 19 (Summer 1973): 179–192.

Juncker, Clara. "Dos Passos' Movie Star: Hollywood Success and American Failure." *American Studies in Scandinavia*, 22 (1990): 1–14.

Juncker. "Romancing the Revolution: Dos Passos' Radical Heroine." *Works and Days*, 8 (Spring 1990): 51–66.

Knox, George. "Voice in the *U.S.A.* Biographies." *Texas Studies in Literature and Language*, 4 (Spring 1962): 109–116.

Landsberg, Melvin. "An Elegy for the Unknown Soldier." *John Dos Passos Newsletter*, no. 2 (June 1998): 1–4.

Levin, Harry. "Revisiting Dos Passos' *U.S.A.*" *Massachusetts Review*, 20 (Winter 1979): 401–415.

Maine, Barry. "Representative Men in Dos Passos's *The 42nd Parallel*." *CLIO*, 12 (Fall 1982): 31–43.

Maine. "Steinbeck's Debt to Dos Passos." *Steinbeck Quarterly*, 23 (Winter–Spring 1990): 17–26.

Maine. "*U.S.A.:* Dos Passos and the Rhetoric of History." *South Atlantic Review*, 50 (January 1985): 75–86.

Marz, Charles. "Dos Passos's Newsreels: The Noise of History." *Studies in the Novel*, 11 (Summer 1979): 194–200.

Marz. "*U.S.A.:* Chronicle and Performance." *Modern Fiction Studies*, 26 (Autumn 1980): 398–415.

Masteller, Richard N. "Caricatures in Crisis: The Satiric Vision of Reginald Marsh and John Dos Passos." *Smithsonian Studies in American Art*, 3 (Spring 1989): 23–45.

McHale, Brian. "Talking *U.S.A.:* Interpreting Free Indirect Discourse in Dos Passos' *U.S.A.* Trilogy." *Degrés* (Brussels), 16 (Winter 1978): c1–c7; 17 (1979): d1–d20.

Morse, Jonathan. "Dos Passos' *U.S.A.* and the Illusions of Memory." *Modern Fiction Studies*, 23 (Winter 1997–1998): 543–555.

Pizer, Donald. "The Camera Eye in *U.S.A.:* The Sexual Center." *Modern Fiction Studies*, 26 (Autumn 1980): 417–430.

Pizer. "The 'Only Words Against Power Superpower' Passage in John Dos Passos' *The Big Money*." *Papers of the Bibliographical Society of America*, 79, no. 3 (1985): 427–434.

Seed, David. "Media and Newsreels in Dos Passos' *U.S.A.*" *Journal of Narrative Technique*, 14 (Fall 1984): 182–192.

Suárez, Juan A. "John Dos Passos's *U.S.A.* and Left Documentary Film in the 1930s: The Cultural Politics of 'Newsreel' and 'The Camera Eye.'" *American Studies in Scandinavia*, 31, no. 1 (1999): 43–67.

Trombold, John. "Popular Songs as Revolutionary Culture in John Dos Passos' *U.S.A.* and Other Works." *Journal of Modern Literature*, 19 (Fall 1995): 289–316.

Vanderwerken, David L. "Dos Passos' Civil Religion." *Research Studies*, 48 (December 1980): 218–228.

Vanderwerken. "*U.S.A.:* Dos Passos and the 'Old Words.'" *Twentieth Century Literature*, 23 (May 1977): 195–228.

Weeks, Robert P. "The Novel as Poem: Whitman's Legacy to Dos Passos." *Modern Fiction Studies*, 26 (Autumn 1980): 431–446.

Westerhoven, James N. "Autobiographical Elements in the Camera Eye." *American Literature*, 48 (November 1976): 340–364.

**Newsletter:**

*John Dos Passos Newsletter,* edited by Melvin Landsberg. Lawrence: Department of English, University of Kansas, 1998–  . Quarterly.

# Cumulative Index

*Dictionary of Literary Biography,* Volumes 1-274
*Dictionary of Literary Biography Yearbook,* 1980-2001
*Dictionary of Literary Biography Documentary Series,* Volumes 1-19
*Concise Dictionary of American Literary Biography,* Volumes 1-7
*Concise Dictionary of British Literary Biography,* Volumes 1-8
*Concise Dictionary of World Literary Biography,* Volumes 1-4

# Cumulative Index

**DLB** before number: *Dictionary of Literary Biography,* Volumes 1-274
**Y** before number: *Dictionary of Literary Biography Yearbook,* 1980-2001
**DS** before number: *Dictionary of Literary Biography Documentary Series,* Volumes 1-19
**CDALB** before number: *Concise Dictionary of American Literary Biography,* Volumes 1-7
**CDBLB** before number: *Concise Dictionary of British Literary Biography,* Volumes 1-8
**CDWLB** before number: *Concise Dictionary of World Literary Biography,* Volumes 1-4

# W

Cumulative Index

ISBN 0-7876-6018-3